ANDREW JOHNSON

A BIOGRAPHY

OTHER BOOKS BY
HANS L. TREFOUSSE

Germany and American Neutrality, 1939–1941

Ben Butler: The South Called Him Beast

Benjamin Franklin Wade: Radical Republican from Ohio

The Radical Republicans: Lincoln's Vanguard for Racial Justice

Impeachment of a President:
Andrew Johnson, the Blacks, and Reconstruction

Carl Schurz: A Biography

ANDREW JOHNSON

A BIOGRAPHY

HANS L. TREFOUSSE

W·W·NORTON & COMPANY

NEW YORK   LONDON

Printed in the United States of America.
The text of this book is composed in
11/13 CRT Goudy Old Style,
with display type set in ITC Caslon No. 224 Bold.
Composition and manufacturing by the Haddon Craftsmen, Inc.
Book and ornament design by Margaret M. Wagner.

First published as a Norton paperback 1991; reissued 1997

LIBRARY OF CONGRESS
CATALOGING-IN-PUBLICATION DATA

Trefousse, Hans Louis.
Andrew Johnson : A Biography / by Hans L. Trefousse. — 1st ed.
p. cm.
Bibliography: p.
Includes index.
1. Johnson, Andrew, 1808–1875. 2. Presidents—United States—
Biography. 3. Reconstruction. 4. United States—Politics and
government—1865–1877. I. Title.
E667.T74 1989
973.8′1′0924—dc19
[B]

ISBN 0-393-31742-0

W. W. Norton & Company, Inc.
500 Fifth Avenue, New York, N.Y. 10110
www.wwnorton.com

W. W. Norton & Company Ltd.
Castle House, 75/76 Wells Street, London W1T 3QT

4 5 6 7 8 9 0

To
LaWanda Cox

CONTENTS

ILLUSTRATIONS

PREFACE

OF ALL the presidents of the United States, Andrew Johnson stands out as unique—unique in having been the only one to be impeached, unique in not having attended school for a single day, unique in originating in such poverty that even those who doubt the "log cabin myth" in the history of the presidency accord him a place of exception, and unique in returning to the Senate six years after leaving the White House. There is, however, an enigma about the tailor-president that has never been fully solved, a mystery that makes any final assessment of his accomplishments difficult. How was it that a statesman who experienced a spectacular rise from homeless newcomer to governor and senator, a political leader who succeeded in routing not only the powerful organizers of the opposing party but also the numerous antagonists in his own, a general who ruled with an iron hand as military governor in Tennessee, could be so seemingly inept in carrying out the functions of the office of president of the United States? What was it that made Andrew Johnson in 1861 first defy Southern opinion by staying loyal to the Union and then in 1865 and 1866 challenge a Northern majority in Congress to break with the party that had elected him vice president?

The answers to these questions have long troubled his biographers. From early adulation to speedy castigation, from renewed rehabilitation to resurgent accusation, the reputation of the seventeenth president has fluctuated with the passing of time. His most astute biographers have been satisfied with brief treatments, while all of the full-length *Lives* tend to be favorable to their subject. The meticulous editors of the Papers of Andrew Johnson at the University of Tennessee have recently made available a mass of material, so that a reassessment of the life of Lincoln's successor is now possible. To accomplish this task in the light of all the newly accessible documentation is the purpose of this book.

Mᴢ ACKNOWLEDGMENTS are due in the first place to Michael Les Benedict, LaWanda Cox, and W. John Niven, who read the manuscript in its entirety and offered most valuable suggestions. I should also like to express my gratitude to LeRoy P. Graf and Patricia P. Clark of the Andrew Johnson Papers Project at the University of Tennessee, without whose unfailing support this book would not have been possible. The American Council of Learned Societies awarded me a grant in 1984, which was greatly appreciated, and my special thanks are due to Mr. George Stevenson of the North Carolina State Archives in Raleigh, whose researches and careful essays about the youth of the seventeenth president were of immeasurable help. Mr. Richard Harrison Doughty, the knowledgeable historian of Greeneville, was most generous with his time and hospitality, while Mr. Hugh B. Johnson of Wilson, North Carolina, graciously shared his material on Andrew Johnson's ancestry. Robert V. Bruce, William S. McFeely, Betty Caroli, and James E. Sefton also assisted me with documents and advice, and my student aides, David Osborne, Michael Sappol, Andrew Gyory, and David Weinraub, were untiring in their efforts. The librarians at the various depositories I visited were unfailingly cooperative. This is especially true of the staff at the Manuscript Division of the Library of Congress, the North Carolina and Tennessee State Archives, Duke University, the Huntington Library, and the Universities of North Carolina and Tennessee. The librarians here in New York were equally cooperative, particularly those at the New-York Historical Society, Wagner College, the College of Staten Island, and my own institutions, Brooklyn College and the Graduate Center of the City University of New York, where Mrs. Helga Feder put up with all my requests for interlibrary loans without complaint. My editor, Steven Forman, and Mr. George P. Brockway were most encouraging, and last but not least I owe an immeasurable debt to my wife, Rashelle F. Trefousse, whose steady support, literary criticism, and good sense were indispensable.

ANDREW
JOHNSON

A BIOGRAPHY

I

RALEIGH POOR WHITE

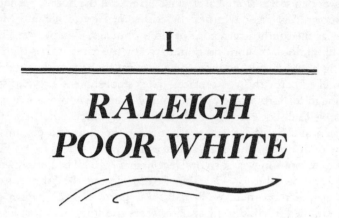

Wʜᴇɴ Andrew Johnson, the seventeenth president of the United States, was born, on December 29, 1808, his native Raleigh was still a raw settlement. Built on land acquired as late as 1792, it remained for a long time a "town of 'magnificent distances.' " Unsightly bramble bushes and briars, hills and morasses, grand old oaks, and a sparse populace who cast "an 'onwelcome look' to strangers" characterized this fledgling capital of North Carolina. Although the state assembly had decreed that state officials reside there, the governors, unwilling to live in the woods, evaded the law. By 1807 some of these problems had been overcome, but the number of inhabitants was still only 726 whites and 303 blacks, of whom 270 were slaves.[1]

Laid out according to well-considered plans, Raleigh consisted of rectangular blocks extending from Union Square in the center. The city was situated on a plot measuring some 4,500 feet from north to south, and about 4,000 feet from east to west. The regular streets were methodically named, first for the state's judicial districts, then for the original nine commissioners, and finally for other well-known personalities. To allow for recreation, the commissioners had wisely provided not only for the six-acre-large Union Square, but also for four smaller plazas of four acres each. On Union Square the state house, its exterior as "plain as a gigantic dog kennel," dominated the little city, which was so small that the capitol was also used for religious services, balls, theater performances, and Fourth of July celebrations.[2] Otherwise, Raleigh could boast only of a court building made of wood, an academy, two hotels, and some wooden stores along Fayetteville Street. Of the hotels, perhaps the best known was Casso's Inn at the corner of Fayetteville and Morgan streets, at the southeastern edge of Union Square. Comprising a collection of buildings, the inn was dominated by the three-stories-high main dwelling house, furnished with some twenty-five beds and containing a well-stocked bar with five fireplaces. The establishment also had stables big enough for forty horses, grain houses, a smoke house, and a garden with a well, all enclosed by a planked fence. Three times a week the Northern and Southern stages stopped at the tavern, a circumstance that made it one of the liveliest places in town.[3]

Andrew Johnson was born on December 29, 1808, in a little two-and-a-half-story log cabin on Carrabus Street. He was the Johnsons' third child; an older brother, William P., was born in 1804, and a sister, Elizabeth, died in childhood. In later years the story of Andrew's birth in a small building in the back of Casso's Inn became traditional. The story goes that his father, Jacob Johnson, and his mother, Mary, generally called Polly, worked at the hotel. On that December day a wedding party was in progress at the tavern—according to some, the wedding of Peter Casso's daughter Hannah to John Stewart, a prominent merchant. The festivities were interrupted by news of the birth of a baby to the Johnsons, and, according to the same tradition, the bride went to the cabin in back of the inn to see the baby. In a more imaginative version, Hannah named the infant Andrew in honor of Andrew Jackson. The alleged birthplace has been preserved as a historical relic.[4]

Unfortunately, this fanciful tale of Johnson's birth cannot be substantiated. None of the president's early biographers mention it; nor, even, did the speaker at the ceremonies on the occasion of Johnson's visit to Raleigh in 1867 to dedicate a tombstone for his father allude to it in any way. The story did not crop up until the twentieth century and can be definitely contradicted by reliable evidence, particularly the description of the real birthplace by Dr. Abraham Jobe, a U.S. Post Office agent who lived in Raleigh in the 1860s. Jobe often showed the log cabin to visitors, who unfortunately dismantled it for souvenirs.[5]

Both Jacob Johnson and his wife were average working people. Descended from Silvanus Johnson, a yeoman farmer who owned 934 acres of land in Amelia County, Virginia, and his wife, Elizabeth, Jacob's family moved to Johnston City, North Carolina, in 1754. Silvanus' son Richard, who farmed along the Neuse River, acquired enough land and money to buy two slaves. One of Richard's sons, William, was Jacob's grandfather, a farmer who in 1779 was granted 700 acres near Wake City. But his son William, Jr., ran into financial difficulties. Sold out at a sheriff's sale, he was unable to provide well for his children, and as a result Jacob, the president's father, was landless and illiterate; he made a living by engaging in various odd jobs, including milling. Yet Jacob enjoyed the respect of the community. In 1811 Colonel William Polk, a Revolutionary War hero and one of the most prominent citizens of the town—indeed he served as president of the State Bank of North Carolina—hired Jacob as a porter at the bank. He was later appointed constable and became a captain of the town watch as well as the city bell ringer.[6]

Mary McDonough, Jacob's wife, was known as "Polly the Weaver." She worked as a seamstress and laundress at Mrs. Thompson's millinery shop on Fayetteville Street. In 1801, when Polly was twenty years old, she met and married Jacob Johnson. Her father, Andrew McDonough, a Revolutionary War veteran, was born in Beaufort City, North Carolina, lived for a while in Plymouth, and then settled in Raleigh. In 1806 he moved to Bledsoe County, Tennessee, and later to Marion in the same state, but was buried in Pikeville, the county seat of Bledsoe. Of Scots-Irish descent, the McDonoughs continued in later years to play a role in the Chattanooga area.[7]

When Andrew Johnson became a prominent public figure, rumors circulated in Raleigh that Jacob Johnson was not really Andrew's natural father. One legend attributed paternity to Justice John Haywood of Tennessee, to whom Andrew bore some likeness and in whose house Polly had once been a laundress. A well-known lawyer in Raleigh before going west, Haywood later became a member of the Supreme Court of Tennessee. A different rumor had it that the relationship was with William Ruffin, another Raleigh lawyer. And while these stories surfaced frequently during Johnson's later campaigns and during his presidency, it is unlikely that they were heard at the time he actually lived in Raleigh. There was then no need for rumors, because he had not yet reached any position important enough to call for the invention of upper-class forebears. No proof was ever found for the Haywood story, and the Ruffin legend soon died of its own accord.[8]

Polly Johnson did not have an easy life. When Andrew, her youngest, was barely three years old, her husband died. A short time before, upon seeing a boat capsize on Hunter's Mill Pond, Jacob had jumped without hesitation into the water to save the passengers. One of these was Thomas Henderson, the publisher of the Raleigh *Star*, who had taken the fishing party out for a skim in the canoe in the first place. The other two were Henderson's friend William Peace and a Scottish visitor named Callum. When he was just above the pier head of the mill, Henderson accidentally rocked the boat and bore so heavily on the end where he was sitting that he tilted it and turned it over. All three fell into the water; Callum seized hold of Henderson, and both sank to the bottom of the pond. Jacob Johnson, who had been standing at the pier, leaped into the water, grabbed Henderson, and brought him up to the surface. Johnson managed to save all three, but some time afterward, while ringing the town bell, Johnson dropped dead, allegedly weakened by the incident.[9]

Henderson acknowledged his debt to the deceased. On January 12, 1812, an article appeared in the Raleigh *Star*:

> Died, in this city on Saturday last, Jacob Johnson, who for many years occupied a humble but useful station. He was the city constable, sexton and porter to the State Bank. In his last illness he was visited by the principal inhabitants of the city, by all of whom he was esteemed for his honesty, sobriety, industry, and his humane, friendly disposition. Among all among whom he was known and esteemed, none lament him, except perhaps his own relatives, more than the publisher of this newspaper, for he owes his life on a particular occasion to the kindness and humanity of Johnson.[10]

Left with the children and a scanty income earned by taking in washing, the widow, possibly because of her inability to write, relinquished her right to administer her deceased husband's estate. She soon married again, this time another poor white, named Turner Doughtry. William, the older son, was first apprenticed to Colonel Henderson, who seemed to continue to take an interest in the family of the man who had saved his life. Then William became an apprentice at J. Selby's tailor shop. On November 8, 1818, Polly made known her intention that Andrew, too, be apprenticed to Selby to learn the tailor's trade. The contract called for him to remain with Selby until he was twenty-one, although the actual apprenticeship deed was not recorded until 1822.[11]

Thus Andrew's early environment was not promising. As a poor white boy in a small Southern town, he could not help but realize his lowly position. The city boasted an elite, an aristocratic clique, among whom the most prominent were known as the "five Williams": William Polk, William Peck, William Peace, William Boylan, and William Hill. These and others, such as Chief Justice John Louis Taylor, Judge Henry Seawell, Judge Robert Potter, Joseph Gales, Beverly Daniel, John Sherwood, and the Haywoods, formed a closed society. They rode to the hounds, staged shooting matches and tea parties, crowned May queens, and presided at Fourth of July dinners. Colonel Polk was the president of the State Bank of North Carolina, where Johnson's father had worked as a porter. The family's lowly position undoubtedly made a deep impression on Andrew.[12]

Andrew could hardly miss feeling the striking contrast between himself and the elite. Unlike the children of the rich, he never had a day's schooling in his life; his mother was too poor to afford it, and there were no public schools in Raleigh. And the aristocrats' contempt was scarcely hidden. When Andrew and his cousins once ran across the path between the house of John Devereaux and that of his son, Devereaux sent his coachman to whip the boys back to their shanty—they were running naked, according to Devereaux's granddaughter. (In another version of the story, Devereaux gave Johnson a whipping for trying to steal some fruit from one of his daughters.)[13] Whatever the truth of this particular incident, the whip was habitually used on those the Devereaux called "poor white trash."

Growing up in Raleigh at that time meant growing up with the city. By 1817 the first church was built, and five years later there were three. The first brick inn, Charles Parish's Eagle Hotel, replete with a bath and ice house, was opened north of the state house, and in 1819, to disguise its plain exterior, the capitol was finished in stucco imitation granite.[14] Then Antonio Canova's magnificent statue of George Washington was placed in the middle of the state house, right underneath the new dome. Pulled by some twenty mules, it was escorted into the city by the Raleigh Blues, with their color bearer—enthusiastically waving his flag— perched on top of the monument. It was a great occasion, which young people like Andrew could really enjoy.[15]

Yet, poor though he was, Andrew must also have realized that he was not at the very bottom of the social scale. After all, he was white, a fact that gave him a standing immeasurably higher than that of Raleigh's numerous blacks. Although he freely played with mulatto children, he certainly could not escape the ingrained racism so prevalent in Southern society. Poor whites looked down on blacks, slave and free. Moreover, they disliked non-whites—fears of social and economic competition could hardly have occasioned friendly feelings.[16] Exposed to these attitudes at an early age, Johnson was never able to shake them off.

Like other poor boys, Andrew Johnson probably heard the praises sung of Andrew Jackson, whose victory at New Orleans in 1815 made him a national hero. Here was another Carolinian who had started at the bottom and not only had made it but had become the idol of the nation. Old Hickory's career seemed the very incarnation of the American dream; it was to be an inspiration for Johnson for years to come.

Young Johnson was a swarthy complexioned, black-haired boy with deep, dark eyes. Described as a "wild and harum scarum" youngster, he was a member of a gang formed by his cousins, known as "Jesse Johnson's boys." For a while he seems to have boarded with his Uncle Jesse, who occupied a shanty on the estate of Colonel Polk, his father's employer and the father of General Bishop Leonidas Polk. Like other boys, he played ball, went swimming and fishing in Hunter's Mill Pond, and enjoyed youthful sports.[17]

But Andrew was no ordinary boy. Though deprived of schooling and books, he had a zest for learning. On discovering that at Selby's tailor shop, where his brother was apprenticed, public-spirited citizens came to read to the tailors, he often came to listen. Then, when he himself was apprenticed to Selby, he became known to his fellow workers for his interest in obtaining an education. Not only did he listen attentively to the frequent political debates by citizens who visited the shop, he was delighted to hear a local intellectual, Dr. William Hill, read to the workers while they were busy with needle and thread. The book from which Hill read was called *The American Speaker* (the title was sometimes cited as *United States Speaker* or *Columbian Orator*), and Johnson liked it so much that Hill finally gave it to him. The book contained speeches of famous statesmen, both English and American, and Johnson never forgot them. In fact, to the end of his life he kept the volume as a memento.[18] Selby's foreman, James Litchford, believed that he was the one who taught Johnson to read, a reminiscence that may be true because employers had the obligation to teach the alphabet to apprentices, and Selby may have charged Litchford with this duty.[19]

North Carolina law placed apprentices in a position little better than that of slaves. To be sure, apprentices were freed after a stated period of time, usually at the age of twenty-one, but while serving their term they were entirely at their masters' beck and call. The master was supposed to prepare them for a trade, teach them to read and write, and feed and house them. In return apprentices owed him complete obedience, and if they ran away, they were liable to recapture. No other employer was permitted to give them work. This system, inherited from England, was liable to abuse because it did not take a master seven years to teach the mysteries of a trade to a youngster who would nevertheless have to work without pay for the full term.[20]

Unlike other apprentices, at least for a time, Andrew Johnson did not live at Selby's. Because of his mother's needs, a special arrangement was made allowing him to board at home and to receive cash in lieu of board.[21] But Selby does not seem to have been an indulgent master, at least not for an apprentice as restless as young Johnson. Andrew climbed so many fences and tore his clothes so often that Mrs. Selby once made a coarse undergarment that she forced him to wear for a short time. And the twelve hours of labor must have been oppressive.

One Saturday night when he was fifteen, Andrew and some companions pelted the house of a neighbor, Mrs. Wells, with pieces of wood,
either because he disliked her or possibly because he wanted to impress
her daughters. When she threatened to sue, Andrew, his brother, and
two boys employed in another shop fled Raleigh.[22] Selby posted a reward
for them in the paper, in which he offered ten dollars for their recapture,
but erroneously mixed them up in his description:

> TEN DOLLARS REWARD. Ran away from the Subscriber, on the night of the
> 15th instant, two apprentice boys, legally bound, named WILLIAM AND AN-
> DREW JOHNSON. The former is of dark complexion, black hair, eyes, and
> habits. They are much of a height, about 5 feet 4 or 5 inches. The latter is
> very fleshy, freckled face, light hair, and fair complexion. They went off with
> two other apprentices advertised by Messrs. Wm. & Chas. Fowler. When
> they went away, they were well clad—blue cloth coats, light colored home-
> spun coats, and new hats, the maker's name in the crown of the hats, is
> Theodore Clark. I will pay the above reward to any person who will deliver
> said apprentices to me in Raleigh, or I will give the above reward for Andrew
> Johnson alone.
>
> All persons are cautioned against harboring or employing said appren-
> tices, on pain of being prosecuted.
>
> JAMES J. SELBY, *Tailor*
>
> *Raleigh, N.C. June 24, 1824*[23]

It is obvious that even then Andrew was considered the ringleader. And
it is equally obvious that he was determined to make his own way.

After leaving their employer, the two Johnson brothers headed south-
west. They walked some fifty miles to Carthage, the county seat of
Moore County, where Andrew found employment as a journeyman
tailor. A small village built around the simple courthouse, which was a
rude wooden structure nailed together with homemade nails, Carthage
could not keep him for long, especially as he was always in danger of
apprehension as long as he remained in North Carolina.[24] So after a few
months he walked on. This time he crossed the state line to settle in
Laurens, South Carolina, where he found employment in a local tailor
shop, and stayed for almost two years. Laurens was a small Piedmont
town located between the Saluda and Enwee rivers, so hilly that good
ground for a ball field was hard to find. A bit larger than Carthage, the
village had an imposing brick, brown-plastered courthouse with a long,
broad piazza. When the court was not in session, judges and lawyers
would sit around a pine table there and play whist.[25]

Although Andrew was kept busy with his work, he was still thirsty
for further education. The host at the Laurens hotel, a Mr. Simons, later

recalled that he had boarded with Johnson at the same house and that the young man's nose was always buried in a book. Andrew's work seems to have been very satisfactory; he was even commissioned to make the wedding coat for the local schoolteacher. But he soon had interests other than the mere drudgery of everyday labor. He fell in love with a local girl named Mary Wood, whom he decided to woo. First he made a quilt for her; then he mustered enough courage to ask for her hand. But he was turned down. Her mother could see no advantage in tying her daughter's fate to a penniless tailor. Deeply disappointed, Andrew left Laurens. The Wood family preserved the quilt and his tailor's goose, a pressing iron with a long curved handle.[26]

Anxious to clear his name, Johnson now returned to Raleigh. His old friend James Litchford, Selby's former foreman, had opened a tailor shop of his own but could not employ his erstwhile companion because of Andrew's unfulfilled indenture. Selby was no longer in Raleigh; he had moved some twenty miles out into the country. Andrew paid a visit to his old master in the hope of coming to an agreement, but Selby was unreasonable. He would not allow his former apprentice to pay for his time without security, a sum of money Andrew could not obtain, and accordingly the dejected young man decided to leave North Carolina for good.[27]

It was a moonlit night when Andrew left. As his friend Tom Lomsdon remembered it, he was wearing a little cap and carried a bundle of shirts and socks thrown over his shoulder. For about two miles Lomsdon walked out of town with him, Johnson talking all the time about the great things he was going to accomplish in the West. Then it was time to say good-bye. There were tears in his eyes, but he was determined to strike out on his own, across the mountains in Tennessee.[28]

TENNESSEE TAILOR

THE LURE of the West, which enticed so many young Americans, now drew Andrew toward the lofty mountain ranges dividing North Carolina from Tennessee, where imagined opportunities beckoned. Footsore and hungry, he reached Chapel Hill, the seat of the University of North Carolina, some thirty miles from Raleigh, at around sunset. Not knowing where to get supper and a place to sleep, he trudged along wearily to the house of David L. Swain, later the president of the university, and asked where he could find food and lodgings. He was told that a kind and hospitable citizen, James Craig, was living just beyond the town, so Johnson sought him out.

Craig proved as good as his reputation. Warmly welcoming the poor journeyman, Craig invited him to a hearty supper and a good night's rest. The next morning, he also gave his guest breakfast and provisions to take along on the road to Tennessee.[1]

At the same time Johnson was trying to reach the West, a well-to-do Carolinian named Brown was moving to Tennessee with a train of covered wagons, slaves, and household goods. After Brown had crossed the mountains into the Volunteer State, he saw a boy sitting on the side of the road. The youngster was poorly clothed and was resting with his pack beside him. Brown, feeling sorry for the wanderer, gave him a ride.[2] In this way the future president reached Knoxville. Boarding a flatboat to sail down the Tennessee River, Johnson got off at Decatur, Alabama, and took a job in a tailor shop in the small town of Mooresville on the other side of the river. There, under the tutelage of Joseph Sloss, he learned the art of cutting out and making frock suits.[3] But he was still restless, and after a short time he left again, this time turning north to walk about seventy miles to Columbia, Tennessee, the home of James K. Polk, later president of the United States. There another tailor, James Shelton, gave Johnson a job, while Mrs. Shelton took a motherly interest in the lonely journeyman, for whom she sought to provide a good home. Later, she even claimed that she had taught him how to read and write, an assertion he correctly branded as untrue, although he fully acknowledged and remembered her kindness to him.[4]

Columbia was one of the most flourishing towns in Middle Tennessee. The county seat of Maury County, it comprised about 1,500 inhabitants, a college, an academy, three churches, twenty stores, taverns, groceries, craftsmen of all types, and a branch of the Union Bank of Tennessee. Johnson might easily have settled there; as it was, however, in 1826, after only six months, obligations to his family called him back to Raleigh.[5]

But of course he could not stay in his native city. His problems with Selby still had not been settled, and he decided to return to Tennessee for good. This time, accompanied by another tailor named A. D. February, he took his mother and his stepfather, Turner Doughtry, along. The family's meager belongings were piled into a two-wheeled cart and pulled, according to legend, by a blind pony.[6]

Originally, Andrew and the Doughtrys were anxious to join Polly's relatives, especially her brother, Andrew McDonough, who was living in the Sequatchie Valley of eastern Tennessee; Andrew's brother William had already preceded them.[7] But the trip was more difficult than anticipated. While camping one night, as February later described it, a "panther," probably a mountain lion, came out of the woods and knocked the skillet off the fire on which the small party was preparing supper. On another occasion, on top of the Blue Ridge Mountains, a bear was the unwelcome intruder. The travelers must have been delighted in September 1826 to reach human habitations again. They had come to Greeneville, the county seat of Greene County, an East Tennessee village pleasantly situated in a valley surrounded by hills, home of several colleges as well as of an active citizenry that prided itself on residing in one of the oldest towns of the state.[8]

Tired and worn out by the long journey, Johnson went into the village in search of fodder for the horse. After obtaining some from Joseph Brown, a prominent citizen who had been a schoolteacher and justice of the peace, Andrew asked whether there was a good camping site nearby. Brown directed him to the old Farnsworth Mill, abundantly fed by a nearby spring, where Johnson and the family spent the night. (So attached did he become to this site that he later bought it and planted a willow tree there, said to have been cut from a sprig on Napoleon's grave at St. Helena. The tree still stands today.)[9]

The next morning, a Sunday, Johnson walked to the village to find out if there were employment opportunities and rooms available. As his son-in-law, according to family tradition, later described the scene to Oliver P. Temple, author, jurist, and Johnson's future adversary,

> The peaceful stillness of a Sabbath in a Presbyterian Scots-Irish village reigned over Greeneville. Scarcely a sound was heard save the singing of the birds in the neighboring groves, and the noise of the water falling from the little mill that stood at the foot of a great hill south of the town—for though the mill rested on the Sabbath day, the water flowed incessantly. The scene was full of beauty and loveliness. The atmosphere was laden with the perfume of honeysuckles and wild roses. From the neat gardens cultivated flowers shed their fragrance on the soft air. Greeneville, at all times lovely, was never more so than on that . . . bright morning, as it lay in solemn stillness flooded with light, nestling serenely among the green hills. From the top of these hills, which so charmingly encircle the town, was seen off a few miles southward the great Smoky Mountains, more than six thousand feet in height, stretching far away forty or fifty miles southward and eastward in surpassing grandeur. The mountains, their lofty summits and wide graceful sweep of outline lifted up sharply against the deep blue sky, presented a view of restful majesty rarely to be found.[10]

The scene pleased Johnson. At the post office, where he went to get information, he met John A. Brown, another son of his new benefactor. When Brown told him that the village tailor, Robert Maloney, was getting old, Johnson determined to stay, a decision made easier when Brown ordered a suit of broadcloth from him. He went to work in George Boyle's tailor shop and rented quarters for himself and the family in the back room of the Russell House.[11]

When he was not busily engaged in stitching and sewing, the young tailor was able to meet some of the people of the village. Among these was Eliza McCardle, the daughter of a local shoemaker, who, after her father's death, assisted her mother in making quilts. According to the story commonly accepted in Greeneville, Eliza and a few girlfriends saw Johnson when he first arrived in town, and Eliza said to her mother, "There goes the man I am going to marry." According to a different version, she told her friends, "There goes my beau, girls, mark it." Although both of these stories are probably spurious, there is no question that the two young people soon fell deeply in love. Eliza, an attractive brunette, had a better than average education. Modest and retiring in her habits, she was generally esteemed and "regarded as a model woman by all who knew her."[12]

But Johnson had not originally come to Greeneville to stay. After a short time he pushed on, this time to Rutledge, the county seat of Grainger County. Situated on Richmond Creek just east of the Clinch Mountains, Rutledge was only a small village of 150 inhabitants. But a school, a church, three stores, and two taverns made it the focal point of the surrounding countryside. The village also had a tailor shop where Johnson found work as a journeyman.[13]

Although conditions in Rutledge were to his liking, Johnson could not forget Greeneville and the girl he had left behind. He wrote to her frequently to keep in touch, and by the spring of 1827, he had made up his mind. Returning to the little East Tennessee county seat, this time for good, he proposed to Eliza and shortly thereafter married her. The ceremony took place on May 17, 1827, in nearby Warrensburg, a post town on the Little Chuncky in the western angle of Greene County, where Eliza's deceased father, a shoemaker, had briefly run an inn. The justice of the peace who performed the wedding was Mordecai Lincoln, a first cousin of Thomas Lincoln, the father of the Great Emancipator. The groom was eighteen, the bride, sixteen and a half.[14]

Although Andrew and Eliza were married for nearly fifty years and had five children, it is difficult to say very much about their relationship. For much of her life Eliza was an invalid, suffering from consumption, while her husband was frequently away from home. Yet people who knew them, like George Washington Jones, whom Johnson later met in the Tennessee state legislature, and William H. Crook, the White House guard, were convinced that the relationship was an extremely happy one. "Their temperaments were unlike," wrote Jones, "he, fervid and aggressive; she, calm and retiring—but their union was fortunate, and, by her aid, he was better prepared for the long encounter which fate held in reserve."[15] Crook not only agreed with Jones about the couple's differences in temperament, but he even thought he saw in them the perfectly married couple—"two souls and minds merged in one." He admired Johnson's tender and anxious consideration for his wife, feelings she more than returned. Solicitous for her husband's comfort, Eliza always saw to it that his room was in order, and delighted him with an occasional new gown, always in excellent taste.

But these accounts probably do not tell the whole story. During much of her husband's career, which frequently called him to the state or national capital, Eliza stayed at home. These long periods of separation must have been taxing. Then, when the couple moved into the White

House, the First Lady rarely appeared in public—only a few times during the entire period of her husband's administration, in fact. Her eldest daughter took over the duty of presiding over the mansion's social functions. That Eliza helped her husband along when he was a struggling tailor is certain. Although she did not teach him how to read—he was already literate—she did assist him with his further education. And in spite of her poor health and retiring nature—Oliver P. Temple, who also lived in Greeneville, had no recollection of ever seeing her until he was twenty-eight—she sustained her husband loyally throughout his stormy career. Supporting him during the trying days of the Civil War, she and her children, marked as the family of the man considered an arch-traitor by the Confederates, for a time stayed behind in enemy territory. Later on, she again faithfully stood by his side during the ordeal of the impeachment. In many ways, however, because of the absence of papers and letters from her, Eliza remains an elusive person, hidden from publicity and thorough historical inquiry.[16]

Greeneville, though small—in 1833 there were only five hundred inhabitants—was an agreeable place in which to live and work. Largely settled by Scots-Irish pioneers, it had been the capital of the short-lived state of Franklin. Greeneville College, with a library of three thousand volumes, was located there, as were Washington and Tusculum colleges in the immediate vicinity, and the Rhea Academy for younger students. Two churches, one Presbyterian and one Methodist, dominated the skyline, and the town also boasted the large brick Greene County Court House, two taverns, four stores, and a stone jail. Three doctors practiced medicine, four lawyers constituted the local bar, and the mansions of the town's elite were substantial. At the east end of town there was a large spring that, about a quarter of a mile from its source, turned an overshot gristmill. The contemporary gazetteer commented upon the fact that the village and the surrounding countryside were very healthy.[17]

Of the 14,410 inhabitants of Greene County, only 1,070 were slaves, so that the "peculiar institution," so important elsewhere in the South, was not so significant here. In fact, it was in Greeneville that Elihu Embree had for a few years, beginning in 1819, edited his abolitionist newspaper *The Emancipator,* and not long afterward Benjamin Lundy published his even more outspoken *Genius of Universal Emancipation.* Friendly neighbors with their Masonic lodges and debating societies made Johnson feel at home. The natural setting was stunning, the main range of the Great Smokys in the distance and the nearby hills making the little town a beautiful place to settle.[18]

At the time of his marriage, Johnson rented a house on Main Street. He established living quarters for the family in the rear and converted the front into a tailor shop, which he conducted together with Hentle W. Adkinson, his partner. It was his first venture into business on his own. At first he was somewhat anxious about getting a commission. Then John A. Brown, who had become very fond of the young man, gave him an order for a coat. Johnson took Brown's measure in person and made him a well-fitting coat of steel-mixed cloth with steel buttons. The workmanship was excellent, so excellent that another customer, Hugh Douglas, promptly ordered a full suit. Johnson's reputation spread, and soon he was widely known for the handsome clothes he made.[19]

Some of the account books Johnson kept during those early years have survived. He charged $3.50 for a coat, $1.50 for pants, $3.50 for vests, and $10.00 for a suit. More fancy clothes cost a little more. Sometimes accounts were paid in cash, and sometimes in wood or produce. After a while he employed journeymen who boarded with him, and he was able to acquire some property.

Business flourished, for Johnson knew how to make money, with thriving investments in real estate as well as in business. He did so well that the editors of the Johnson Papers have called him an "artisan-businessman, perhaps even a petty capitalist."[20] In 1830 and 1831 he bought two town lots with two dwellings and a smith's shop at College and Depot streets, where the Andrew Johnson National Historic Site is now located. Then, when his first employer, George Boyle, moved to South Carolina, he acquired Boyle's shop and, according to tradition, moved it to the site he had purchased. Whether the smithy or Boyle's establishment eventually became the present tailor shop is difficult to determine. Whatever its origins, the structure has been carefully preserved and affords an excellent insight into early nineteenth-century working conditions.[21]

Not only his business but Johnson's private affairs were also moving along very well. In 1828, while still living on Main Street at the rear of the tailor shop, his wife gave birth to their first daughter, Martha. Two years later, in 1830, the first son, Charles, followed. Another daughter, Mary, was born in 1832, and another son, Robert, in 1834. Eighteen years later, in 1852, the Johnsons had still another boy, Andrew, Jr., whom everybody called Frank. For a while Johnson's brother William also lived in Greeneville. A table he made with his name on it is still preserved in the shop.[22]

Johnson was working hard at his trade, but he did not neglect his education. Reading every book he could find, generally works on politics and oratory, he acquired a knowledge of some of the famous legends of antiquity, stories he tended to use over and over again. With the help of his wife, he attempted to improve his writing, but not too successfully; his style remained turgid and his spelling extremely faulty. But as he soon discovered, he did know how to make speeches and get people to listen.[23]

As Johnson was becoming well known in the village, one of the visitors to his tailor shop, the town plasterer, Blackston McDannel, provided him with the chance to gain greater recognition. McDannel and Johnson often disagreed on matters they discussed—the then point of difference was a dispute concerning that portion of the Cherokees' territory lying within the state. The state legislature had just extended its criminal jurisdiction over the area and the population was divided about the wisdom of the measure. Johnson opposed it, while McDannel favored it. Finally the plasterer challenged the tailor to a public debate. Neither of the two had ever spoken in public before; both were diffident, but Johnson asked his opponent to name the time and place, a matter that was quickly settled.

When the time for the debate arrived, at first the contestants could not decide who should open the discussion. The judge of the contest solved the problem by pointing out that the affirmative always had the right to open a debate. Thus McDannel, greatly embarrassed and referring to a written text, delivered the first speech. Another contestant followed, and then it was Johnson's turn. Holding in hand a paper with three propositions, he began to speak, not as fluently as he would do later in his career, but well enough for the twenty minutes he was on the stump. "He hit the nail on the top every pop," said McDannel, who wanted to reply immediately. But it was midnight and the beginning of the Sabbath, so the judge stopped the encounter. The discussion was renewed at a later time, and the two antagonists became fast friends and made a habit of debating, even to the point of organizing a debating society, an organization which, according to Alexis de Tocqueville, was a common American substitute for theatrical entertainments.[24]

Having discovered that he was a persuasive public speaker, Johnson sought to cultivate his talent. He joined a debating society that was flourishing at Greeneville College and that included such other members as Mordecai Lincoln, who had officiated at his wedding, Major James Britton, John Jones, Augustus Russell, and John Park. Appreciating his efforts, these men soon sought his friendship. So much did Johnson enjoy debating that he habitually walked to Tusculum College, some four miles distant, and back again, to take part in its debating society's activities.[25]

The year 1829 was a banner year for the American democracy. Its hero, Andrew Jackson, was inaugurated on March 4, an event that was hailed with pride by Jackson's fellow citizens in his home state of Tennessee. In that same year, Workingmen's parties appeared in various cities. They professed to represent the workers and "mechanics" of the country, as the artisans and craftsmen were called at that time.

Greeneville, isolated and distant though it was, was not immune to the new winds sweeping the nation. The village, too, held an election; a mechanics' ticket made its appearance, and Andrew Johnson was one of the winners in the contest for alderman on this ticket, together with his friends Blackston McDannel and Mordecai Lincoln. True, he only received 18 to their 26 votes each, but his friends had put his name on the top of the ballot. According to the story told many years later by one of the participants, Alexander Hawthorne, his friends had met in secret in Hawthorne's house to prepare the ballot on the Saturday prior to the election. On the following Monday Hawthorne and his co-workers went to the polls and campaigned for their ticket until it was successful. The town's elite, men like Dr. William Alexander, who rode to the hounds, John Dickson, who owned dozens of slaves, and Valentine Sevier, the town clerk, were obviously surprised at the sudden success of the upstart tailor. But Johnson was flattered. Glorying in his position as the people's representative, he did so well as an alderman that he was reelected in 1830, and from that time on he never ceased seeking public office.[26]

If the new alderman was the mechanics' candidate, he nevertheless did not break with the town's elite. No matter how faulty his spelling, in 1832 he was still on good enough terms with Sevier to write to him confidentially,

> Dear Sir in my usual State of health through mercy[.] I hope this will find you and yours all well—my good friend I want you to Cum and See me if possible in 10 day[s] from the date of this[.] I have Sumthing that Conserns me to Communicate to Mr. Earnes and you when I git you together and a little for Mr Sevier by our Selves before I unbosom my Self to you boath[.] keep this to your Self to [till?] I See you—I conclude with my best compliments to my lady to you and the Doctor and all your famileys[.] farewell—

What the "Sumthing" was is not known, but Mr. Earnest was a prominent merchant and the doctor presumably Dr. Alexander Williams, about to become one of the leading Whigs in Greeneville. The rapidly rising tailor obviously knew the people who counted in the community.[27]

For some curious reason, nearly every biographer of Johnson prior to the 1980s has maintained that he was elected mayor in 1830. In reality, he did in fact succeed in becoming mayor, but not until 1834, when his colleagues on the Board of Aldermen chose him. The Mayor's Book of Greeneville is perfectly clear on this point, recording as it does the activities of the corporation from year to year as well as the mayors who presided. How this error crept into the biographical account is not quite certain, except that it occurred as early as 1866, when the first published biographies of Johnson appeared.[28]

The record of the Greeneville Mayor's Book is very interesting. The various entries indicate the type of business conducted, the presiding officers, and the problems facing the aldermen. On November 21, 1831, for example, the corporation met at the courthouse, Mayor R. M. Woods presiding. Andrew Johnson was present, but definitely as an alderman, not as mayor. On December 26 it appropriated $3 to enable Johnson to take care of improving Cross Street near the jail. Then, on the last Monday of December, an election was held at the courthouse for the purpose of voting for aldermen for the ensuing year, and Johnson was reelected. On the thirty-first the aldermen met at Johnson's tailor shop to be duly qualified according to law before John S. Reed, one of the acting justices of the peace for Greene County. Mordecai Lincoln was elected mayor.

One year later, Johnson was again among those chosen for the Board of Aldermen, and on January 5, 1833, the newly elected members were sworn in at the courthouse, elected Alfred Russell mayor, and then adjourned to Johnson's shop, where they continued their deliberations.

The corporation met frequently at the tailor shop, deliberated on such matters as came before it, including the necessity of appointing some lawyer, until on December 2, Alfred Russell resigned as mayor. William Carter took his place by election, and the board adjourned to meet again at the shop on December 16. On the thirtieth Johnson was reelected alderman, and on January 4, 1834, at a meeting at the courthouse, he was finally elected mayor, a position he was to hold, off and on, for the next four years.

Johnson's term of office brought few new concerns to the village government. On January 20 the board considered the problem of local taxes; on February 18, again at the tailor shop, it continued to consider the tax situation as well as the regulation of liquor sales and street repairs. As the entry in the Mayor's Book read, "The Mayor and aldermen then proceded to lay a tax for the presant year all White Pole over the age of twenty-one & under fifty Thirty seven and one half cents each all Black Pole over the age of 12 & under fifty seventy-five cents each and six cents on each $100 worth of Real Estate within the Corporation."[29]

Office holding in a small Tennessee town was not always easy. On August 29, 1834, Johnson was charged with assault and battery upon one Thomas McLay. What the cause of the fracas was is not known, but the mayor had to pledge to pay $100 by the first Tuesday after the first Monday in October. Fortunately, the complainant did not appear at the appointed time, and the debt was declared discharged.[30]

The corporation held further meetings throughout the year. Streets had to be fixed, liquor licences granted, and outhouses regulated, especially if they were located near streams. By July the mayor had decided to run for the state legislature and tried to resign. However, according to the record, "The resignation of Andrew Johnson was laid before the board but there not being a quorum to act on the same it is therefore ordered that the said Johnson hold his office until a further consideration." During the fall Johnson was still mayor; in December he was reelected alderman, and on January 3, 1835, George Jones was chosen to take his place as mayor. But by 1837 Johnson was again listed as mayor, and only in August 1838 did he finally disappear from the list of officers of the corporation.[31]

The penniless journeyman tailor had done well. Having moved his shop to its present location on College and Depot streets, he was one of the esteemed citizens of the village. College students liked to stop by at the shop, though it contained nothing but a bed, two or three stools, and a tailor's platform. Johnson knew how to make them welcome, as one of them remembered it, "with his social good nature, taking more than ordinary interest" in catering to their pleasures.[32] He joined the Tennessee militia, the Ninetieth Regiment—a court-martial in 1831 fined him for some trivial offense—and in 1834 was chosen a trustee of Rhea Academy, a signal honor for a man who had never been to school.[33] Five feet nine inches tall, swarthy, with dark, piercing eyes, always impeccably dressed, the young tailor looked impressive. He might have been the mechanics' candidate, but his appearance was always stylish. With his tailor shop a fashionable establishment, with his growing family, and with his succession of small political offices, it was obvious that young Johnson was making his way in the world.[34]

III

GREENEVILLE POLITICIAN

JOHNSON relished his newly found position of importance. It was satisfying to play a distinguished role in the village to which he had come as a poor journeymen not too many years earlier. And he enjoyed office holding. If he had been elected alderman and mayor, why might he not pursue his political career further and seek higher honors? The thought appealed to him, and once having decided upon his goal, he continued to pursue it with singular devotion.

The political situation in Greeneville was still a bit vague. Neither the Democratic nor the newly organized Whig party was as well defined in 1834 as it would be later on. As he enjoyed excellent relations with the mechanics as well as with the well-to-do, Johnson could afford to wait and see before he definitely cast his lot with either of the emerging parties.

Johnson's first opportunity to move beyond the political confines of the village arose in 1834, after he was first elected mayor. Long governed under its original constitution of 1796, Tennessee was beginning to feel the changes brought about by Jacksonian democracy. The result was the convocation of a convention to write a new constitution. This new charter eliminated many property qualifications for office holding and the right to vote and contained provisions for rates of taxation based on the value of the property to be taxed instead of keeping the rates equal as before. In addition, like many similar documents, the constitution disfranchised free blacks and encouraged internal improvements.

After the convention adopted the basic law, the document was submitted to the voters for their approval.

The struggle for the ratification of the new constitution was ready-made for Johnson. It was obvious that the document would succeed; it appealed to the same people with whom he liked to identify, at least while seeking votes, and its antiblack provisions corresponded to his own convictions—his background and his surroundings had made him a firm believer in the superiority of the white race, a prejudice he would never be able to overcome. Accordingly, he began to campaign for the constitution. His efforts were successful: the charter was adopted, and Johnson had the satisfaction of being on the winning side in both county and state, which registered a more than 70 percent majority for the new basic law.[1]

The victorious campaign for the adoption of the constitution was merely the first step in Johnson's quest for further honors. He wanted to go to the state legislature, and although Jacob M. Bewley, an artful politician, already represented Greene County, Greene and neighboring Washington counties were entitled to an additional representative between them, called a floater. It was this position that Johnson was seeking. One Saturday night in the spring of 1835, at George Jones' store, Major Matthew Stephenson and Major James Britton were announced as candidates for the floater seat. After the announcement, according to tradition, Johnson declared, "I, too, am in the fight." Britton was friendly with the tailor, with whom he had been active in the village debating society; Stephenson, a recent member of the constitutional convention, had distinguished himself by voting and actively protesting against the proslavery provisions of the new charter. But Johnson was ambitious and determined to bid for the seat.

The first debate between the candidates took place in Jonesboro in Washington County. To everyone's surprise, Johnson completely demolished his antagonists. His peculiar style—slashing, sharp, and ad hominem—was in evidence even then. It worked; Britton soon dropped out of the race, and although Stephenson continued to oppose the twenty-seven-year-old newcomer, Johnson finally defeated him by 1,413 to 800. When, according to custom, the votes were counted at a point on the dividing line between Greene and Washington counties, the victor was present. Johnson then returned to Greeneville, where he was met by a number of fellow citizens who had ridden out two or three miles to welcome him.[2] He leased out his tailor shop and soon set out for Nashville. The legislature was about to meet there.[3]

It must have been agreeable for Johnson to travel to the seat of government as an assemblyman-elect. When taking long trips before, he had generally either been on the run or unsure of his final destination. Now he was an established citizen with property, a tailor shop, a farm, houses, and other goods. He had earned the trust of his neighbors, who had elected him to the village Board of Aldermen, to the mayoralty, and now to the assembly. Although he would never be able to forget his humble beginnings, which left him with a sense of insecurity manifesting itself in frequent boasts about his popular origin, he would make the most of his new opportunity.

Nashville, though not yet the permanent capital of Tennessee, was a pleasant city. Still small with but five to six thousand inhabitants, it was largely confined to a single bluff on the left bank of the Cumberland River. The city was located at the apex of a long curve in the river and was dotted with a row of gently rising and continuous hills, their summits crowned with dense cedar groves. In the center of the city rose one central and higher hill, which would later become the site of the state capitol.[4] Although for political reasons he would later frequently vote to move the capital elsewhere, Johnson could not fail to be impressed by Nashville's many public buildings. The courthouse on the Public Square with its handsome front over one hundred feet long and its depth of over sixty feet, the university on an elevation at the end of College Street, the Masonic Hall, the several banks, the prominent churches, the female academy, the waterworks, the factories, the lunatic asylum, and the jail all attested to the city's importance. Vauxhall Gardens, one of the main attractions on Nashville's southern limit near the Franklin Turnpike, boasted of a circular railway 262 yards in circumference with specially equipped carriages. As the *Tennessee Gazetteer* described them, "The cars are so constructed that persons are enabled to propel themselves at a most rapid rate, simply by turning of a crank with the hands." The establishment contained large assembly rooms, a promenade, many walks, and places of amusement. Elegant stores, some forty lawyers, twenty-five doctors, and many academics gave the city a cosmopolitan tone.[5]

The legislature of Tennessee met in the courthouse, a building spacious enough to accommodate public offices in the basement, the state and federal courts on the second floor, and the senate and House of Representatives on the third. No register of debates was kept; the lawmakers' actions were recorded officially only in a printed journal.

Johnson arrived in Nashville early in October 1835 and took rooms with John Netherland, the representative from Sullivan County, who would later make a name for himself as a distinguished lawyer and Whig Unionist.[6]

The new representative took his seat on October 6, but just what party he called his own was not too clear. Party lines were then still somewhat fluid, although the newly organized Whig party was rapidly making progress. No doubt Johnson revered the Democratic president, Tennessee's Old Hero Andrew Jackson, but almost immediately after taking his seat he joined with his fellow legislators (who then chose federal senators) to elect Hugh Lawson White to the U.S. Senate, although White was not the Democratic candidate. He would also support White against Martin Van Buren in 1836.[7]

There were other indications that at that time Johnson was either independent or leaning toward the Whigs. His attitude toward a resolution commending the administration was an example. The resolution read, "That we approve generally of the principles and policy, both foreign and domestic, of the administration of the Federal Government during the term of service of our present Chief Magistrate, General Andrew Jackson." When loyal Democrats moved an amendment to strike the word "generally" on the grounds that it amounted to a censure, Johnson voted with the majority to defeat it. And, after some hesitation, he failed to support a motion to instruct the state's senators to support the Expunging Resolutions advocated by the Democrats to erase from the Senate Journal Henry Clay's censure of the president.[8] Moreover, he was happy to be able to inform Dr. Williams, one of Greeneville's most prominent Whigs, that the doctor's brother, Thomas, had been elected chancellor of the eastern division of Tennessee. He had been one of Williams' supporters.[9]

But there were other issues upon which the new legislator did not see eye to eye with the Whigs. A tendency to branch out beyond the desires of his immediate constituents, perhaps in the belief that he understood their requirements better than they did, or perhaps to secure support elsewhere, became a characteristic of Johnson's political behavior from the time he took office in the Tennessee House of Representatives. East Tennessee was badly in need of transportation; railroads seemed the answer, and Brookins Campbell, the representative from Washington County, introduced a motion calling for a committee to look into the expediency of extending the Charleston and Hamburg Railroad into Tennessee. Johnson, however, was no friend of railroads. He delivered speeches deploring their tendency to put inns and drovers out of business, and he generally voted against measures for their benefit. He even opposed the incorporation of the East Tennessee Railroad Company. His constituents did not appreciate his apostasy; Campbell's position was more to their liking.[10]

Laws the young representative did support were sundry measures calling for economy in government—he opposed the printing of a school bill, compensation for state solicitors, additional expenditures for the lunatic asylum, and even the payment of money to defray the expenses of the legislative session, a stance in which only one other colleague joined him. Johnson supported a bill for the firm control of the state's free black population, although, together with other representatives from East Tennessee, he opposed a stringent anti-abolitionist law. And he had a great interest in abolishing special privilege, which he showed by his effort to put an end to the exemption of justices of the peace from working on the roads.[11]

On Washington's Birthday, after 141 days in session, the legislature, having passed 85 public and 141 private bills, finally adjourned. The solons celebrated at Gowdy's with a dinner given to them by the citizens of Nashville and with a public ball that night to which citizens were invited. Whether Johnson was among the two hundred persons present is not recorded. Most likely he hurried home. He never had much time for "frivolity."[12]

Johnson had used his time well to make new acquaintances in Nashville and in the state at large. Among these was George Washington Jones, the Fayetteville tanner, who represented Lincoln County and was a convinced Democrat. Others were his roommate, John Netherland, an equally convinced Whig, and the numerous political leaders of the state—Democrats like Joseph C. Guild and Alfred O. P. Nicholson, and Whigs like Ephraim Foster and Gustavus A. Henry, to mention but a few. Soon he was also to draw close to his fellow townsman the grave, sedate Sam Milligan, who had taught at Greeneville College, later pursued a legal career, and was destined to become a lifelong comrade and mentor. Considering Johnson's ambition, it is to be assumed that he made good use of many of these acquaintances.[13]

Upon his return to Greeneville, Johnson's welcome could not have been very cordial. Had he not voted against various railroad projects dear to the people of East Tennessee? To be sure, the legislation passed, but his constituents did not forget his defection. And Johnson compounded his failing when he returned briefly to Nashville in October for a special session of the legislature, and again voted against the interests of the railroads. If at the same time he signified his devotion to education by moving an amendment to use the funds due to the state under the federal Distribution Act for the support of common schools, this hardly made up for his shortcomings. The session adjourned after twenty-three days, and Johnson came back home very uncertain whether he would run again. It was at this time that he voted for Hugh Lawson White, who was running for president against Martin Van Buren.[14]

Back home, Johnson resumed his tailoring enterprise and engaged in various other business deals. His rapidly growing family—Martha was now eight, Charles six, Mary four, and Robert two—required him to pay more attention to his livelihood, a task he always carried out successfully. In fact, he now became the employer of several tailors and eventually leased out the shop to devote himself completely to politics. By 1837 he was serving again as mayor; and, although he was hesitant to do so, he was much too ambitious not to seek reelection to the Tennessee House of Representatives.[15]

But as Johnson had surmised, his effort to return to the legislature encountered serious obstacles. Although Dr. Williams, one of Greeneville's wealthiest citizens, does not seem to have held Johnson's election in 1829 as the mechanics' candidate for alderman against him, now that the upstart tailor had reached out to elements beyond East Tennessee to vote against railroads and other internal improvements, the doctor sought to displace him. At a public dinner in honor of Brookins Campbell, who had so strongly supported such measures, Williams and his friends induced Campbell to run against Johnson. This turn of events greatly angered Johnson, and in a towering rage, just after the dinner, he ran into young Oliver P. Temple in the street and told the lad in no uncertain terms what he thought of the proceedings. The subsequent campaign was acerbic; Johnson attacked Campbell so fiercely for his support of legislation for the employment of a state geologist and other matters that his opponent never forgave him. It was all in vain, however. The tailor was defeated, the only time he was to lose an election until after the Civil War.[16]

The defeat undoubtedly rankled, but Johnson was soon preparing for a comeback. Presumably he was confident, as he was many times subsequently, that future events would justify him. The people, in whom he increasingly professed to trust, would vindicate him in the end. His chances for a comeback improved when the panic of 1837 set in. In 1838 the state legislature, in response to the depression, established the Bank of Tennessee to relieve debtors left in dire straits. Johnson was elected to a committee to determine the location of the various branches of the new bank, a position that again enabled him to establish contact with leading men in other counties of the state.[17]

Finally, in 1839, Johnson had his revenge. According to Oliver P. Temple, who was bitterly prejudiced against him, Johnson sought to make a deal with the Whigs of Washington County to allow him to run as a Whig against Campbell provided no other candidate appeared. However, another Whig contender, Robert Sevier, did come forward, and Johnson decided to declare himself a Democrat. As Campbell was also a Democrat, Johnson, in a speech at Jacob Boyle's in Greene

County, announced his adherence to John C. Calhoun, who had rejoined the Democratic party, and his state rights democracy. That stratagem, plus the fact that the panic did not help the incumbent, led to Campbell's defeat—Johnson was reelected to the legislature. Within one year the representative from Washington and Greene counties, who had long admired Andrew Jackson, became a regular Democrat and one of the electors for Martin Van Buren. And from that time on, he never wavered in his allegiance.[18]

Johnson's votes in the new legislature clearly indicated his newly found party regularity. Voting for all measures designed to show support for the Van Buren administration, he opposed resolutions calling for the reestablishment of the Bank of the United States and condemning the Independent Treasury scheme. He introduced a resolution calling on the Bank of Tennessee to suspend specie payments and was generally hostile to legislation favorable to the state's banks and corporations. So good a Democrat was Johnson that he worked hard for the establishment of a new county to be made up of parts of Greene, Washington, and Hawkins. To be called Powell, this new county was a device to create a safe Democratic constituency. His penchant for economy was still in evidence; he opposed sundry measures that would have cost money and pleaded for the saving of his constituents' tax dollars. Strongly appealing for retrenchment, Johnson denounced a proposal to appoint a Board of Bank Commissioners, "with salaries for the people to pay," as he put it. And, of course, he was active in the effort to endorse the renomination of Van Buren for the presidency.[19]

As soon as Johnson arrived at Nashville, he was placed on a ceremonial committee to welcome the Democratic governor, James K. Polk. The Maury County statesman had already served as speaker of the federal House of Representatives and was destined to become president. His manner and origin, even his policies, eventually separated him from Johnson, but for the time being, the two men trusted each other. The governor shared confidences with the representative from Washington and Greene counties, and Johnson strongly supported the administration.[20]

Soon Johnson also became identified with issues that would become peculiarly his own. To the horror of the fundamentalists, who must already have deplored his refusal to join any church, he successfully moved to postpone a resolution calling for daily prayers to open legislative proceedings. Service on the Joint Committee on the Common School Fund enabled him to demonstrate his interest in education. And last but not least, he backed a resolution concerning the public domain. "This General Assembly do believe," it read, that the public domain of the United States should not be treated by the General Government as a mere source for the acquisition of money at the public Treasury, but by reducing the price to reasonable and moderate rates, should rather be regarded as the great and extensive means of encouragement to the augmentation of our population, and the rewards of the laborer, the husbandman . . . who in time of peril, will be a powerful bulwark to the frontier, and the right arm of the safety and defense against the hostile invasion of a foreign foe.

It was one of the earliest recorded instances of interest in the public lands by the man who was to become the virtual father of the Homestead Act.[21]

Johnson's actions in Nashville paralleled his activities at home. Having definitely cast his lot with Jacksonian democracy, the tailor-politician proceeded to build up a strong Democratic machine in Greene County. His future opponent Oliver P. Temple described the method Johnson used to get his message across. First he called a meeting and sent out runners all over the county to summon the faithful. Because his gift of public speaking was already well known, people came on foot or wagon from all parts of the county to hear him. When Johnson appeared, between ten and eleven o'clock, the clerk of the county court, George W. Foute, came forward and read resolutions prepared by the speaker. These reaffirmed the correctness of Andrew Jackson's policies, especially his struggle against the Bank of the United States, and heaped abuse on the Whigs as successors of the Federalists. Allusions to the conflict between Alexander Hamilton and Thomas Jefferson, the War of 1812, and the blue lights the Federalists had allegedly hung out to guide the invading British fleet alternated with condemnations of Henry Clay and his "corrupt bargain" with John Quincy Adams.

Then Johnson began to speak. Starting in a low, soft tone, his voice grew louder as he went on. For two or three hours he held forth on the subject of the resolutions, and even Temple had to admit that after an hour or so, his speech "rang out on the air in loud, not unmusical tones. . . . There was no hurried utterance, yet no hesitation, no dragging, no effort after words. . . . Altogether . . . he was forcible and powerful, without being eloquent. He held his crowd spellbound. There was always in his speeches more or less wit, humor, and anecdote, which relieved them from tedium and heaviness."

The first such meeting became a model for many others. Johnson was always the sole speaker, while the high sheriff of Greene County, Richard M. Woods, gave the appropriate signs when to shout and when to laugh. As the speaker declared that eternal vigilance was the price of liberty and that power always meant stealing from the many to give to the few, the enthusiasm of the crowd knew no bounds. With his devoted group of supporters built up by such methods, Johnson soon so dominated the county democracy that it followed him unquestionably, no matter where he might lead it.[22]

Rewards came fast. In February 1840 the Democratic State Convention at Nashville appointed Johnson one of the two presidential electors at large for the state.[23] This honor gave him the opportunity to campaign throughout Tennessee and to become known in the other grand divisions of the state, an exposure essential to his rise to power in the statewide Democratic party. He did not disappoint his backers. On March 11 a great meeting attended by 1,500 to 2,000 people was held in Greeneville with Johnson as the featured speaker. A fifty-foot hickory pole with the Stars and Stripes attached to it served as the assembly's centerpiece, while three divisions of horsemen, 630 mounted troops in all, soon joined by 300 more, assisted in the festivities. Johnson spoke with his usual gusto.

Within a short time he traveled from his own county to confront such Whig orators as the famous Nashville lawyer and former U.S. senator Ephraim Foster, the ex-legislator from Athens Spencer Jarnagan, and Thomas A. R. Nelson, the Jonesboro attorney whose career would intersect many times with his. Because Foster and Jarnagan refused to appear in joint debates with the tailor he had to follow them. And although Temple maintained that Johnson "never appeared to a more sorry disadvantage, than when . . . trailing after the magnificent Foster," the Democratic Nashville *Union* thought Johnson had much the better of his opponent, and Governor Polk was sure that the Democrat was greatly the Whig's superior in debate. He was doing excellent work in East Tennessee, "our only man here," Polk learned.[24] Even the Whig William Campbell was warned that Johnson was "a strongminded man who cuts when he does cut not with a razor but with a case knife."[25]

In 1840 it became evident that the Democrats needed forceful speakers. The contest between President Van Buren and General William Henry Harrison was marked by such incessant hullabaloo that the Jacksonians soon found themselves on the defensive. It was difficult to compete with hard cider and log cabins, derisive songs and folksy touches, and above all with a party that had been out of power when the panic of 1837 devastated the country.

Against such odds, Johnson was at a great disadvantage. But he was so formidable that even the Whigs recognized his potential. The log cabin campaign, as it came to be known because of the Whigs' use of log cabins and hard cider to attract voters, marked the first instance of the lifelong clash between the redoubtable parson William G. Brownlow of nearby Jonesboro and the Greeneville politician, when the parson sought to demolish Johnson by labeling him a toady.

Brownlow was a vitriolic newspaper editor whose dislikes included Democrats, abolitionists, Protestant sects other than his own—he was a Methodist—and various personal enemies. Among the latter, Johnson soon became the parson's main target.[26] On October 28, 1840, readers of the Jonesboro Whig found an editorial entitled "TOADY ALIAS ANDREW JOHNSON." Mercilessly castigating his opponent in his peculiar fashion, Brownlow wrote: "This man is obtaining for himself quite an unenviable notoriety. He is justly considered the blackguard orator of the Loco-Foco party." Then followed an indictment of Johnson for having attacked General Thomas D. Arnold, who had run for Congress from Greeneville in 1835. Had not Johnson supported him at that time only to oppose him now that Arnold was a Whig elector and Johnson a Democratic one? The former tailor, charged Brownlow, was evidently on both sides of every question. How could such a man be trusted? He would refer to him as "Toady Johnson" for years to come.[27]

Although Harrison's Whig party won the campaign of 1840, in Tennessee as well as in the nation, Greene County remained Democratic, albeit by a smaller majority, and its principal speaker had become known throughout the state.[28]

Johnson's newly found fame stood him in good stead in 1841: he ran for the state senate from Hawkins and Greene, two safely Democratic counties, and won easily by a 2,000-vote majority. But his style of campaigning, his vituperative personal attacks, and his new popularity offended other aspirants for office. John Balch, the outgoing senator from Johnson's new district, had boasted that he would run against the interloper, only to be met with opposition from the party. Johnson could beat Balch and a Whig combined, Governor Polk was told by a Knoxville Democrat. So Balch was cast aside, a fact that hardly reconciled him to his successor. Opposition within his own party, often followed by personal success in the end, was a situation Johnson would encounter many times in his political career.[29]

When it came to political maneuvering, the legislator from Greeneville was very astute. When asked to run for Congress, he refused. He knew very well that he had absolutely no chance in a district dominated by the Whigs, and he had no desire to suffer defeat. Seeing considerable dissension in the Whig party, he suggested to the governor that the Democrats nominate no one and let the Whigs fight it out among themselves. His political skill was to become more and more evident as he rose to higher positions in Tennessee.[30]

Johnson had now become the wealthy proprietor of a business, real estate, a beautiful house opposite the tailor shop, and a farm on which he settled his mother and stepfather. Commonly referred to as Colonel Johnson—he had obtained field rank in the militia—he was a respected citizen of the town, which had grown to a community of some five hundred people, with one hundred dwellings and stores. Within a short time, Johnson would sell his tailoring business, although the shop remained his property, and devote himself to politics and various real estate deals. His material success was evident.[31]

As was customary for well-to-do people in antebellum Tennessee, Johnson also acquired a few slaves. Well-situated citizens had house servants, and the state senator was no exception. The first slave he bought was a young girl named Dolly. According to her son, she was being sold at auction and was looking around in a crowd of prospective buyers to find a good master. Liking Johnson's looks, she went up to him and asked him to buy her. He spent $500 for her, and shortly afterward also acquired her half brother, Sam, who survived Johnson. Well remembered as a dignified old man dressed in his Sunday best every Sabbath in a high hat and a black silk coat, Sam always took great pride in his relationship to Johnson. The same was true of Dolly's son, William Johnson, as he called himself, who recalled that as a child he was fondled by the master while sitting on one of Johnson's knees, with his sister on the other. The future president would rub their heads together and laugh.[32]

As time went on, Johnson bought additional slaves, some eight or nine altogether. In 1860 he owned one adult couple and three children, one boy and two girls. According to tradition, he never sold any, although David W. Bowen has shown that in 1851 he did dispose of a thirteen-year-old boy named Henry. Whether or not he sold slaves, he certainly had no compunctions about owning them. His attitude toward blacks was no different from that of his white neighbors, who considered them members of an inferior race whose natural lot was one of dependency.[33]

A man of Johnson's importance also had to have his picture taken. When a daguerreotypist came to town in 1842, he took a likeness of the aspiring state senator. The resulting daguerreotype is so unlike other portraits of its subject that its authenticity may be questioned; yet the dark mien and piercing eyes are unmistakable. With a face much less fleshy than in later reproductions, the picture shows a young man of pensive expression, prominent nose, and carefully groomed black hair. It is probably in fact the first likeness of the seventeenth president of the United States.[34]

If the statewide contest of 1840 had provided Johnson with the first opportunity to become known beyond the confines of Greene County, the 1841–42 session of the state legislature provided the second. Almost immediately upon meeting, it was faced with the question of electing two U.S. senators. Felix Grundy, the longtime Democratic leader who had held one of the state's seats in the upper house at Washington, had died, and Governor Polk appointed as his successor until 1841 Alfred O. P. Nicholson, who, like Johnson, had only recently become a regular Democrat. The other senator, Alexander Anderson, also a Democrat, had likewise reached the end of his term. Consequently, two Senate seats would have to be filled. Because the Democrats controlled the state senate by a majority of only one, and the Whigs the other house by a majority of three, and the new governor, James C. Jones, was also a Whig, the Whigs would be able to elect both of their candidates in a joint session.

To prevent this contingency, the Democrats, partly led by Johnson, simply refused to attend a joint session. Such a session was unconstitutional, the Jacksonians maintained, despite all precedents to the contrary. At most, they were willing to compromise by splitting the two seats between the two parties, at least for a time. But this scheme failed because ex-governor Polk, who had just been defeated for reelection, would not consent to any compromise by which his hated rival, John Bell, one of the Whig candidates, would ever be elevated to a Senate seat. Moreover, the Democrats themselves were not too sure who their candidate should be, especially since Polk did not trust one of the leading contenders, Alfred O. P. Nicholson, who, he thought, might eventually desert to the Whigs.[35]

Johnson took a lead in the ensuing struggle. In long speeches he castigated the most prominent Whig candidate, Ephraim Foster, for not having answered interrogatories put to him. The vagueness of the Whig program—the party had entered the campaign of 1840 without a platform—and the recent split between the administration of John Tyler and the regular Whigs afforded ample opportunity to torment the opposition. "Will the Senator on the other side of the chamber press the election of dumb candidates upon the country?" Johnson asked in reply to John R. Nelson, the senator from Knox County. "Are we, who are seeking information in good faith, to be blind folded, and compelled to vote for the dumb idols of the whig party?"

Recounting the several inconsistencies of various leading Whigs in recent elections, Johnson took decided objection to their calling the Democrats "Tories." Tories were supporters of monarchy, he rejoined. "Does the word Democrat mean one who is in favor of royalty? A

Democrat is one who is in favor of a Government by the people. From the time that Thomas Jefferson succeeded in putting down the Federal dynasty of the elder Adams to the present time, the sole and constant aim of the Democratic party has been to preserve our Government in its original purity." Then Johnson called the roll of Democratic heroes— President Van Buren, Governor William Carroll, Vice President Robert M. Johnson, and Old Hickory, Andrew Jackson himself—and asked if they were all royalists. "If this constellation of talent, of patriotism, and of genius constitute the tory party . . . we are proud of the association," he continued. He then launched into a turgid defense of the Democratic interpretation of the Constitution to justify the refusal of the "Immortal Thirteen," as the obstreperous Democratic senators were being called by their friends, to participate in a joint session. The word "legislature" did not mean a convention, but each of the two houses in its separate capacity, he maintained.[36]

The struggle continued all winter. On one occasion Speaker Samuel Turney, a Democrat anxious to see his brother Hopkins elected by the Whigs, deserted his party associates to join the members of the House in a joint session. But the other twelve Democrats remained in their seats in the senate chamber, thus preventing a quorum and an election. The result was the failure to elect either senator, and Tennessee remained unrepresented in the Senate of the United States.[37]

It is surprising that the Democrats would have committed so seemingly great a blunder. In the long run, the Whigs made the most of their opponents' responsibility for leaving Tennessee's seats in Washington unfilled and won control of both of the state's houses in 1843.[38] For Johnson, however, his party's miscalculation was not a disaster. He had merely been given another opportunity to prove his faithfulness to the organization and to make a name for himself in the state. That he was considered one of the principal leaders of the "Thirteen" was generally admitted by friends and foes alike. The Democratic Nashville *Union* forcefully emphasized this fact: "Col. Johnson, of Greene, made one of the most eloquent, powerful, and convincing arguments which we ever heard from the lips of man," it commented. "We consider him, in point of talent, as decidedly among the first men of the State. He is just the *man* for a crisis. Bold, prompt, and energetic, no responsibility can intimidate, and no obstacles discourage him. The Democracy of East Tennessee owe him much, and they will energetically seek to repay the debt of gratitude." And James K. Polk was even thinking of him as a possible candidate for one of Tennessee's two unfilled seats in the Senate.[39]

The Whigs also considered Johnson one of the ringleaders of the

"Thirteen." Although it stigmatized his speech in defense of his actions as "one of the weakest things we have ever seen," the Jonesboro *Whig*, Brownlow's paper, referred to him as "the adversary" among the opposition. John R. Nelson, the Whig senator from Knox County, also thought of him as one of the principal Democrats, as he wrote to his brother Thomas, the Jonesboro lawyer who was to collaborate with Johnson during the secession crisis and defend him during the impeachment trial.[40]

The senatorial crisis was not resolved during the winter of 1841. When Governor James C. Jones called an extra session in October 1842 to redistrict the state, neither the Democrats nor the Whigs were in a mood to compromise. The issue of Tennessee's two empty seats was not settled until 1843.[41]

But the senatorial question was not the only problem facing the lawmakers. For example, the problem of the location of the permanent capital came up frequently, and Johnson persistently voted against Nashville. Knoxville was his preferred location, as that city was situated in East Tennessee. Even then Johnson favored the creation of a new state to be called Frankland. He actually moved to ask the governor to confer with neighboring chief executives to carve a new mountain commonwealth out of eastern Tennessee, western North Carolina, and parts of Georgia and Virginia. But he opposed amendments to allow the people of the Ocoee and Hiwassee districts to vote on the proposition. Eventually, disagreements between the senate and the House caused the scheme to fail. However, it was a good example of Johnson's interest in the peculiar needs of the eastern mountain region, which, because of the three-fifths clause for counting slaves for purposes of representation in both the state and national constitutions, had long considered itself discriminated against.[42]

In economic matters Johnson voted as a Jacksonian Democrat of the strictest school. He resisted measures for government intervention in business, constantly advocated economy in government, and opposed the interests of the state banks. Repenting his momentary lapse from hard money orthodoxy in 1839, he offered resolutions requiring financial institutions to resume specie payment and threatened them with forfeiture of their charters unless they complied by July 1. He generally supported legislation furthering education, and, like other Jacksonians, did not favor bills to ameliorate the lot of free blacks. Upon leaving Nashville in February 1843, he signed a spirited defense of the "Immortal Thirteen" that accused the Whigs of refusing to be bound by instructions.[43] And when, following the adjournment of the legislature, four Whig senators asked the thirteen Democrats to resign and permit new elections, after some hesitation, he joined his colleagues in a scornful rejection of the suggestion.[44]

In the called session the following fall, Johnson was again a Democrat of the most radical sort. The session had ostensibly been called because of the necessity for redistricting the state, but, unwilling to concede this need, the senator from Greene and Hawkins challenged the Whigs at every turn. In an angry speech calling the governor's message an indication that Jones had fallen into a state of "mental hallucination," Johnson denied the necessity for a special session in the first place and discoursed extensively upon such national issues as the veto power and the Bank of the United States. On these questions, he passionately defended Andrew Jackson's administration and declared that "modern whiggery was a disease that preyed upon the understanding." Continuing his attack with another speech questioning the usefulness of the called session, he posed as the watchdog of the taxpayers' money and again opposed the interests of the banks.[45]

There were some issues, however, upon which Johnson still diverged from the mainstream of his party. To the surprise of many and the delight of his opponents, he not only continued to oppose daily prayers—Brownlow called him an "avowed infidel"—but even proposed the abolition of the three-fifths provision for the representation of slaves in laying out congressional districts. "Resolved by the General Assembly," his motion read, "that the basis to be observed in laying the State off into Congressional Districts shall be the voting population, without any regard to the three fifths of negro population." Proposing further that the 120,083 voters of the state be divided by eleven, he suggested that one-eleventh of that number be entitled to one member of Congress each. His friend Sam Milligan, who had been elected to the state's lower house, introduced similar resolutions there.[46]

The proposals caused a sensation. "Senator J—An Abolitionist!" headlined the delighted Brownlow in his papers. "This is news to us!" he continued after quoting the Nashville *Republican Banner* to the effect that Johnson was "an abolitionist in disguise." As he put it, "Little as we have been accustomed to think of *Andy*, we had not supposed him to be so great a friend to the 'voters of color.' " Had he not made much in 1840 of General Harrison's alleged abolitionism? And now the *Republican Banner* declared that the resolutions were merely "an entering wedge by which southern men with northern principles, or northern men with abolitionist principles, might the more successfully sever from the South a large portion of her political strength or forever sunder the Union itself." Of course the resolutions were resoundingly defeated, but Johnson's opponents never let him forget them.[47] In point of fact, they were totally wrong about his principles. As "sound" on the institution of slavery as any Southerner, he had merely sought to increase the political leverage for his largely white section.[48]

The other startling proposal Johnson made was for the election of representatives of each district by the people in the state at large—a proposition that also did not find great favor with the solons. But his interest in districting was rewarded with an appointment as chairman of the Joint Select Committee on Laying Out the State of Tennessee in Congressional Districts.[49] As chairman of the Joint Committee, he reported bills to readjust the boundaries of congressional districts, including the First, his own home. Although he voted against the final measure that was adopted, it resulted in a district in which the Democratic vote would be greatly increased, and in the end he became the principal beneficiary of the measure. After entering a vigorous protest against the alleged underrepresentation of Greene and Hawkins counties, whose representative he was, in the legislative apportionment decided upon, he returned home.[50]

In the few short years that the Greeneville tailor had been active in the state's politics, he had done well. Having rapidly become known as an effective speaker, he was the recognized leader of the East Tennessee Democrats. His personal affairs were prospering, his family was growing, and, confident of the future, he was able to look ahead to further political triumphs.

IV

FLEDGLING CONGRESSMAN

~~~~~~~

WHEN Johnson returned from Nashville in 1843, his thoughts turned toward a congressional career. Election to the U.S. House of Representatives was the next natural step for an aspiring politician who had served in both houses of the state legislature, and Johnson was determined to make a mark in politics. Comfortable enough financially, he had no desire to return to the tailor shop. Moreover, while the redistricting of Tennessee had brought about a favorable situation in the state legislature for the upper East Tennessee Whigs, in Congress it had resulted in an equally advantageous arrangement for the Democrats. Some said this was by prearrangement, and that Johnson had had a hand in it.[1] Whether or not this was true, he would make the most of it, and for the next ten years he proved unbeatable in the First Congressional District of Tennessee.

Johnson's first step in his quest for local political dominance was a petition signed by himself and four others for the removal of the local postmaster, William Dickson. A member of the village Whig elite, Dickson had long held his office, which, to Johnson's disgust, he had used to facilitate the distribution of Brownlow's Jonesboro *Whig*. Charging that Dickson was too old to prevent abuses in the conduct of the post office, to say nothing of the postmaster's enmity to John Tyler's administration, the petitioners asked Congressman Aaron V. Brown, a well-known Tennessee Democrat, to have him removed and to have Johnson's longtime local friend William M. Lowry appointed instead. Soon afterward, Dickson died, and Lowry was appointed. Johnson and the Democrats had won the first round.[2]

Johnson's second step was the displacement of the sitting Jacksonian congressman from Blountville, Abraham McClellan. As McClellan's home county of Sullivan had now been attached to the First District, Johnson would have to sidetrack him. Nothing daunted, he wrote to former governor Polk explaining the situation. Asserting that he was a candidate subject to selection by the district convention, he conceded that McClellan wanted to run, but he assured Polk that "our democratic friends" wanted the incumbent to "yeald the field without a Convention and thereby Save his feelings." Perhaps the former governor would be good enough to write McClellan a letter to that effect.[3] Johnson's maneuvers were successful. He was nominated for congressman from the First District, although his opponents united behind John A. Aiken, a Jonesboro Democrat, lawyer, and former state representative who favored banks and other conservative causes.[4]

This situation delighted the irrepressible Brownlow. Attacking Johnson for his assault upon the postmaster, an old man who had done his work well until he became ill, the parson reported that "Toady Johnson" had declared himself a candidate for Congress. As an uncompromising opponent of distribution, a tariff, and the national bank, "Toady" had surmised that Providence had taken President Harrison to preserve peace! "An avowed *Infidel* . . . attribute[s] this or that to Providence!" he wrote, once more raising the question of Johnson's opposition to paying chaplains in legislative bodies.[5]

The parson was now in his element. "TOADY JOHNSON AT BLOUNTVILLE," he wrote, reporting on the progress of the campaign.

This *distinguished* demagogue, unprincipled ingrate, and convicted liar and slanderer, now a candidate on the *ultra* Loco-Foco ticket in this district, addressed the citizens of Sullivan county, at Blountville, on Wednesday last. We are informed the villainous blackguard, and low bred scoundrel, with his characteristic baseness, malice, and coarse language, attended to our case in the course of his remarks! . . . He sprang from as mean a family as any rake who ever came from North Carolina. Tradition says his old father was once indicted in that State for *stealing chickens;* and we were at the Circuit Court in Raleigh, in 1841, when a *first cousin* of his, Madison Johnson, was condemned to be hung, for stealing and murder, and did, actually, in the spring of that year, in the vicinity of the city, *"pull hemp without foothold."*[6]

Brownlow's ways of campaigning were peculiar. On July 5, 1843, the *Whig* published a public letter signed "ARISTIDES," possibly written by the editor himself, declaring that Johnson was unfit for any office because he had been one of the Democrats who had refused to vote for a senator from Tennessee. The parson had, however, long decided that the tailor was a preferable candidate for Congress because his party hated him. Calling him a "brigand," Brownlow characterized him as "mean, corrupt, selfish, and notoriously reckless," but concluded that he was so low a reprobate that he would therefore serve the Whig cause better than other Democrats.[7]

Of course, Johnson did not allow his enemies to have the last word. In a spirited campaign, he denied most of the parson's charges, and, according to the Nashville *Union*, a Democratic paper, was most effective. "Colonel Andrew Johnson is fighting the battle with the apostate John A. Aiken with the arm of a giant," its correspondent reported, "and will beat him from 1500 to 2000 votes in this Congressional District." While the reporter's figures proved exaggerated, he was not entirely wrong. After a hard-fought campaign against the Jonesboro politician, with particular emphasis on banking questions, Johnson won by a majority of 547 votes. Governor Polk, however, was again defeated in his second try to regain his office.[8]

It was during the years of Johnson's service in the House of Representatives that he tended to be identified with the peculiar policies and attitudes for which he became best known. These included an unremitting advocacy of the rights of the poor, the laboring people, the mechanics, as they were called, against what he considered an overbearing aristocracy; extreme economy in government, and opposition to protective tariffs. Because he was a Southerner, his uncompromising patriotism included a spirited defense of slavery and white supremacy, but, as an American and agrarian, he insisted on free land for the landless. His devotion to many of these ideas had been evident earlier, but once he was in Washington, it became more fully defined.

All the precepts Johnson favored, and all the doctrines he opposed, fitted in neatly with his view of an agrarian universe. Kenneth M. Stampp has called him the "Last Jacksonian"; he shared many ideas with the radical left wing of the party represented by William Leggett, William Cullen Bryant, and other foes of privilege.[9] It might be equally correct and perhaps even more descriptive to refer to him as an Old Republican. The physiocratic agrarian view of the world—the nobility of the husbandman, the evil of the cities, the notion that that government is best which governs least—all these ideas were associated with the school founded by Thomas Jefferson. And an absolute conviction of the inferiority of blacks coupled with a belief in democracy confined to whites was equally typical of the precepts of Jeffersonian democracy. Of course, the great Virginian's thoughts developed and changed; Johnson's, on the other hand, remained constant.[10] The limited environment of his early life and the primitive circumstances of newly founded Raleigh and even more of rural, isolated Greeneville were to influence his outlook and beliefs and govern his actions long after the conditions that had given rise to them had disappeared. A pronounced streak of stubbornness was characteristic of Johnson in politics as well as in personal relations.

As long as the tailor-politician was able to appeal to people of similar background—and in eastern Tennessee he could always do that—his ideas found wide acceptance, and his political campaigns were eminently successful. The state at large was also sufficiently rural and agrarian-minded to give him a respectful hearing, so that prior to the Civil War he did not fail to achieve political triumphs. It was only when his field of action extended beyond his adopted state, to the great cities of the North and East and a different United States, that he would find himself in trouble. But in 1843 that time was still far in the future.

Johnson's stubborn adherence to certain principles did not mean that he would not compromise in order to achieve political advancement. Just as in the 1830s, before he definitively joined the Democratic party, he had often voted with the anti-Jacksonians, just as in 1839 he had sought an alliance and deal with the Whigs of the district, so in 1847 he apparently again made certain arrangements with the opposition party.[11] He would not abandon the underlying ideas; to gratify his ambition, however, very often he must have felt that the end justified the means.

Although Johnson's political skills enabled him to accomplish what he wanted, continual election to office and the rout of his opponents, his peculiar positions also created bitter resentment toward him. In many ways opponents within his own Democratic party were as hostile to him as the Whigs. But the organization needed him. Unable to dispense with the proved vote-getting ability of the Greeneville representative, it was forced to overlook his idiosyncrasies, even though at times, with his agrarian notions, he did not at all hew to the party line.

After the election Johnson lost no time in underscoring the issues he would make his own in Washington. In a letter to the Democratic Committee of Maury County, Polk's home, he made his intentions clear. As a good Democrat, he would ever be watchful against Whig intrigues. Neither the Bank of the United States nor the distribution of proceeds from the sale of public lands would find favor with him; he would steadfastly oppose all increases in public expenditures, excepting only the refusal of Congress to pay the fine levied upon Andrew Jackson in 1815 for contempt of a federal judge at New Orleans. Although the

Whigs had temporarily prevailed in Tennessee, he thought that the loss could be retrieved. "I am just getting ready to fight," he wrote, vowing eternal hostility to the principles of Henry Clay. So important had he become as a Democrat that in November the state convention elected him an alternate delegate to the national convention in Baltimore the following spring.[12]

Before setting out for Washington, Johnson took a parting shot at his arch-enemy, Parson Brownlow, by publishing a vindication of himself in the local Democratic newspaper. As he should have known, the result was merely a renewed attack by the ever more vitriolic Brownlow, who now called him "a living mass of *undulating* filth, a political *Skunk* . . . whose heart is covered with the blackness and darkness of crime." Again the parson raked up the effort to displace the postmaster, Johnson's attack upon Campbell and the subsequent censure of the senator in the legislature, and the fate of his unfortunate cousin.[13] Johnson, however, flourished under these onslaughts. He knew how to counter them.

When the new congressman arrived in Washington in 1843, he left Eliza at home.[14] Most members of Congress came alone during that time; Washington was not always a pleasant place for ladies. A "City of Magnificent Intentions," Charles Dickens called it, because he found that the scattered buildings were separated by barren tracts and swampy marshes. Planned on a grandiose scale by Major Pierre Charles L'Enfant, the city had grown slowly and was still raw and semirural. Some of the public buildings marked it as the capital of a nation; the Capitol impressed visitors favorably with its two wings for the two houses and its splendid rotunda topped by a dome in the middle. Other structures of importance were the president's house, about a mile from the Capitol, which reminded many of an English country mansion, the colonnaded Treasury at 15th Street and Pennsylvania Avenue, an imposing post office, and a patent building on F Street. These edifices gave the city whatever attraction it possessed. But other departments were housed in nondescript buildings; the climate, especially in the hot, humid summers, was terrible; the wide avenues were often so muddy as to impede traffic, and a smelly canal fed by the grandiloquently named Tiber Creek flowed between the Capitol and the White House.

In these uncouth surroundings, congressmen tended to live in various rooming houses and take their meals together in common messes. Society was distinctly Southern—the city was a big transfer point for the slave trade—and there was a college as well as a Union Literary and Debating Society. Washington also boasted a theater, and in nearby Georgetown the justly renowned Jesuit college was a popular educational institution for Protestants and Catholics alike.[15]

Johnson did not fit very well into this environment. Eventually, he took lodgings at Mrs. Russell's on North Capitol Street, where he could enjoy the company of his daughter Martha, who attended the Georgetown Female Seminary.[16] But he was not fond of social gatherings, did not like the theater, and at first had few friends in the city.[17] The result was that he spent much of his time in the Congressional Library. His early lack of schooling was not going to be in his way if he could help it. Studying classical works, he soon became wholly entranced with Joseph Addison's *Cato*, a play renowned more for its republican sentiments than its dramatic value, which he quoted continually throughout his career. And if his speeches were still repetitious, florid, and trite, he did not differ too much from many of his colleagues. Their flowery orations made a singularly poor impression upon foreign visitors, even though some in Congress were famous for the power and wit of their speeches.[18]

The Twenty-eighth Congress, which Johnson now joined, was paralyzed by the struggle between the leaders of the Whig party and the president. John Tyler, the strict constructionist from Virginia who had succeeded William Henry Harrison in the spring of 1841, had so alienated his fellow Whigs by vetoing Henry Clay's bank bills that he was read out of the party. In the midterm elections of 1842 the Democrats had recaptured the House, so that Johnson found himself a member of the majority.

Among his colleagues in the House, there were several who would play important roles in his career. Future vice president Hannibal Hamlin, a swarthy, olive-complexioned politician of considerable ability, was then a Democrat from Maine; ex-president John Quincy Adams, the courageous "Old Man Eloquent," represented the Plymouth District in Massachusetts, and the conservative Whig Robert Winthrop, whom Johnson would later particularly dislike, also represented a district in the Bay State. Hamilton Fish, the aristocratic New Yorker, and his colleague, the emotional Preston King, too, were to have some bearing on Johnson's future fate. John A. McClernand and Stephen A. Douglas represented parts of Illinois, while such Southerners as Jacob Thompson of Mississippi, Thomas L. Clingman of North Carolina, Thomas H. Bayly of Virginia, and Robert Barnwell Rhett of South Carolina spoke for the slave interest. Within a short time they would be joined by Jefferson Davis of Mississippi, William Lowndes Yancey of Alabama, Kenneth Rayner, Johnson's future biographer, of North Carolina, and later by such distinguished politicians as Alexander H. Stephens, the diminutive Georgian and future vice president of the Confederacy, and the Floridan David Yulee. In addition, Johnson for the first time encountered such Northern foes of slavery as John P. Hale of New Hampshire and Joshua R. Giddings of Ohio. His Tennessee friend George W. Jones was also present, having been elected in his home district.

While Johnson was in Washington, the Senate also counted a number of prominent, or soon to be prominent, men among its members. The famous Thomas Hart Benton of Missouri was still upholding the Jacksonian hard money cause; future president James Buchanan represented Pennsylvania, and before long, the three best-known senators of them all, Daniel Webster, John C. Calhoun, and Henry Clay, would return to the upper chamber, though Johnson was not intimate with any of them.

Johnson was sworn in as a regular Democrat. Fortunately for one who so admired the Old Hero, he delivered his first speech in the Committee of the Whole in favor of repayment of the $1,000 fine that had been levied on General Jackson in New Orleans.[19] Taking much more literally than others such Jeffersonian-Jacksonian concepts as opposition to internal improvements, tariffs, and unnecessary public expenditures, he voted in his first session against proposed improvements in the Ohio River, a general rivers and harbors bill, and all manner of public expenditures.[20] He introduced resolutions to reduce the number of clerks employed by the government, while denouncing naval appropriations, protective tariffs, and what he believed to be their concomitant, the system of distributing the proceeds of the sale of public lands.[21] Even when disaster struck and a gun exploded on the USS *Princeton*, maiming or killing several passengers, including the secretaries of state and the navy, he voted against compensation for the victims.[22] At the end of the session he once more emphasized his opposition to protection.[23]

Of course, Johnson was also superpatriotic. At a time when the annexation of Texas was one of the most controversial questions facing the nation, he was certain that the Lone Star State must be acquired and join the Union—"our glorious sisterhood of States," as he phrased it.[24]

On the slavery issue, too, Johnson was very much in tune with his Democratic, and especially Southern Democratic, colleagues. Should the Gag Rule automatically tabling antislavery petitions be included in the regulations for the Twenty-eighth Congress? Rising to speak on the problem, he flatly denied the authority, not merely of the federal government, but even of the states, to abolish slavery. The right to hold private property was guaranteed by the Constitution, he said; slaves were property and had been considered as such for thousands of years. As for antislavery petitions, they merely incited to bloodshed and were destructive of the Union. As he explained, the "black race of Africa were inferior to the white man in point of intellect—better calculated in physical structure to undergo drudgery and hardship—standing, as they do, many degrees lower in the scale of gradation that expressed the relative relation between God and all that he had created than the white man." That John Quincy Adams, the great champion of the repeal of the gag, had actually voted to strike the word "white" from the voting requirements in Alexandria was a scandal. It meant that "if the bill passed with the amendment, it would place every splay-footed, bandy-shanked, hump-backed, thick-lipped, flat-nosed, woolly headed, ebon-colored negro in the country upon an equality with the poor white man." That Johnson was a good Southerner was never in much doubt.[25]

But not all his votes pleased his party associates. There was a certain independence in his voting pattern, a rigid adherence to Jeffersonian and Jacksonian agrarian ideals that he would never abandon. His opposition to most tariffs, for example, did not endear him to those Democrats who were less unyielding; nor could they have been particularly delighted by his apparent lack of feeling for the victims of the *Princeton* disaster. And when he voted to allow Joshua R. Giddings the floor to respond to an insult he had received as the result of an antislavery speech, the more extreme Southerners were unforgiving.[26] But he was merely following the Jeffersonian precept of freedom of speech.

While he was in Washington, Johnson was extremely busy taking care of the various requests of his constituents. As a member of the Committee on Claims, he spent much of his time following through on sundry cases for compensation. It was a laborious task, but he fulfilled it faithfully.[27]

After the adjournment of Congress in the summer of 1844, Johnson decided to go to Raleigh to clear his father's name. Unfortunately, he discovered that one of Brownlow's charges turned out to be true. Johnson's cousin Madison, the son of his father's brother Aaron, had killed a man named Henry Beasly in a barroom brawl, was indicted for murder, found guilty, and, despite the jury's plea for clemency, was hanged on June 1, 1841. Johnson had at first tried to deny the story, but finally he had to admit its truth.[28] Another accusation, that his father was a chicken thief, not to mention intimations that he himself was illegitimate, was not true and infuriated him. After assuring himself of his father's good reputation, he delivered an angry speech in Raleigh attacking Governor John Motley Morehead and the editor of the Raleigh *Register* for conspiring with Brownlow to defame him. He was not going to sit idly by while his father's name was being besmirched. Before he left Raleigh, Johnson asked his old friend James Litchford to show him Jacob Johnson's grave, which consisted of a gray stone slab bearing the initials "JJ," nearly hidden by the overgrowth of weeds and brambles.[29]

The trip was very typical of Johnson. Always conscious of his humble background and his lack of formal education, he became ever more aggressively proud of his origins and rarely failed to assert the superiority of the common people from whom he had sprung. His impeccable clothing was part of this defensive mentality, as was his insistence upon giving his children the best possible education available. Andrew Johnson, plebeian, did not think he had to live like a pauper. If aristocrats, as he called them, could afford good clothes, good houses, and good schools for their children, so could he.

Johnson was now a politician of importance in Tennessee. With a presidential campaign against Henry Clay about to begin, he corresponded with many Democratic leaders and friends about the nomination of their own party. As he saw it, the Democrats could never regain control of the state with Van Buren as their candidate; the former president had made too many enemies for that. But ex-governor Polk was not much better. A twice-defeated politician could hardly hope to redeem Tennessee. As Johnson put it, "Polk's ristless ambition has very much operated against us." Lewis Cass of Michigan was preferable by far; Johnson thought he might be the ideal candidate and strongly urged the nomination of the senator from Michigan.[30]

Of course, things turned out differently. When Johnson came to Baltimore for the Democratic National Convention, to which he had been elected as an alternate delegate, he found that his advice was not being heeded. Far from jettisoning Polk, the Democrats brought him forward, not as a candidate for vice president, as had been rumored, but as their nominee for first place, on a platform calling for the "reannexation of Texas" and the "re-occupation of Oregon." The ensuing campaign against Henry Clay required the party to close ranks, and in spite of Johnson's earlier strictures against his fellow Tennesseean, he now actively stumped the state for his party's candidate. Joining forces with his friend Nicholson, he delivered fiery campaign speeches, and, according to the Nashville Union, effectively demolished his opponents. "Our Col. Johnson . . . is too much for the whole pack," the paper asserted. Its conclusion was somewhat premature, for though Polk won the election, he failed to carry his home state. The First District, however, remained safely Democratic.[31]

In the short session of the Twenty-eighth Congress in the winter of 1844–45, Johnson again tended to vote with his party, though he still maintained his independence. The most pressing issue facing the lawmakers was the annexation of Texas, and in his views on the question Johnson vied with the most extreme expansionists. In an hour-long speech justifying the annexation of the Lone Star State, he called Joshua R. Giddings a monomaniac on the question of slavery, asserted that Texas had been part of the Louisiana Purchase and should never have been alienated, and held forth on the military and economic advantages of adding the state to the Union. He attacked not only the Northern Democrat David Brinckerhoff of Ohio, whose antislavery stand irked him, but also the Southern Whig Thomas L. Clingman of North Carolina. Clingman, he maintained, had insulted the entire South. Had he not said the South would submit to the present tariff if it received enough offices from President Polk? Launching into a paean of praise for the president-elect, Johnson may have sought to compensate for his hostile attitude prior to the election. And in spite of his habitual defense of slavery, he even considered the possibility that the "sable sons of Africa" might pass from bondage to freedom, presumably in Mexico, where there were no distinctions based on color.[32]

Internal improvements continued to arouse Johnson's opposition. He might seek to attach amendments to general bills for post roads in Tennessee and add $500,000 to a rivers and harbors bill for the improvement of the Tennessee River, but he otherwise fiercely contended against all measures of this type. This Jeffersonian-Jacksonian commitment to laissez-faire extended to his persistent insistence on economy. Whether the subject was money for refurbishing the White House or books for congressmen, Johnson refused to countenance unnecessary expenditures. They did not tally with his agrarian ideas of governmental simplicity.[33]

In spite of these orthodox views on party issues, the tailor-statesman continued to show his independence. Startled readers at home found a headline in the Jonesboro Whig about a "Contest in the House Between Christianity and Infidelity," with a report about Johnson's support for a proposition to have congressional chaplains paid out of a fund established by contributions from members.[34] And not only Whigs were critical. Doubtless the Greeneville congressman's insistence upon economy in furnishing the White House when the next incumbent was to be a Democrat did not please many members of his own party.[35] Johnson had peculiar ideas from which nobody could dissuade him. But as many of these were shared by his constituents, they did him no real harm.

When in the spring of 1845 Johnson returned home, he again demonstrated his political finesse. His old Democratic antagonist Brookins Campbell, far from being discouraged by previous defeats, tried to challenge him once more for renomination to a second term. Furiously attacking his opponent, Johnson promised to abide by the decision of the local convention and finally succeeded in winning renomination. At first Campbell refused to withdraw from the race, and Brownlow was already crowing about the dissension in Democratic ranks; but in the end, the challenger abandoned his quest, and a superficial reconciliation was arranged between the two Democrats.[36]

But the irrepressible parson would not give up that easily. Finding himself nominated by Johnson's Whig enemies in Greeneville, he agreed to run against the tailor for the House seat, although his chances for success in the carefully laid out Democratic district were minimal. Brownlow poured out all his vitriol against his opponent and promised to show up the "malice and low pothouse meanness of . . . Andy Johnson." There were certain faces, he said, that could not possibly belong to honest men, and Johnson had one of these. A perjurer, an infidel, a swindler—these were some of the epithets he hurled at his enemy, and with great gusto he announced that he had discovered still another relative of the Democratic candidate who had been indicted for murder in Raleigh. Although refusing to debate Johnson personally because the result would be a "personal difficulty," the parson asserted that he was known all over the United States, and if Johnson wanted to find him, it would be easy enough to do so.[37]

The incumbent did not let these attacks go unanswered. It was in this campaign that Johnson really developed his pose as a defender of the poor against the aristocracy, saving his special venom for Dr. Williams, in whose house, he charged, Brownlow had first been nominated. His earlier friendship with the doctor had evaporated; for some time, he had been referring to Williams disparagingly as "Alexander the Great," and now he maintained that the doctor, like Daniel Webster and all other Whigs, thought the government ought to take care of the rich and let the rich take care of the poor. "The aristocracy in this district know that I am for the *people*," he wrote. "They know that I love and desire the approbation of the freemen of this State. . . . The fact of a farmer or mechanic stepping out of the field or shop into an office of distinction and profit, is particularly offensive to an upstart, swelled headed, iron heeled, bobtailed aristocracy, who infest all our little towns and villages, who are too lazy and proud to work for a livlihood [sic], and are afraid to steal." He himself was looking forward to the day when offices were held by mechanics like himself, admittedly descended from poor people, some of whom had committed offenses for which they had been punished. He thundered against the employment of prisoners in competition with free labor and again expressed his outrage at the injustice of Brownlow's accusations against his father, whose simple headstone had greatly affected him.

Johnson's refutations of Brownlow appeared in a postelection pamphlet entitled *To the Freemen of the First Congressional District of Tennessee.* The publication bore the date of October 15, 1845, but seems to have been circulated only in the following winter. Point by point it sought to contradict Brownlow's charges, especially those of infidelity and abolitionism, and it culminated in an attack on the aristocracy and the evocation of Johnson's humble beginnings. If the pamphlet reflected the candidate's campaign tactics, it showed how successful they were. When the August election returns were in, he had won by a majority of 1,343 votes, more than doubling his margin of two years before. But Brownlow would never speak to his opponent again until the Civil War temporarily brought the two antagonists together in a common defense of the Union.[38]

Whether because of Brownlow's campaign or because of an innate stubbornness, in Johnson's second term in Congress, which began in December 1845, he pursued an even more peculiar course of Democratic regularity alternating with defiance of his party. Fully supporting the war with Mexico, he was equally in complete sympathy with the administration on the protection of slavery and such other party questions as the tariff, internal improvements, and economy in government.[39] His Jeffersonian agrarianism and independence, however, again interfered with his party regularity on many other issues.

Following the annexation of Texas and Polk's dispatch of troops to the Rio Grande, Congress next had to deal with the outbreak of the Mexican War. Because of its likelihood to spread the "peculiar institution," many Whigs, especially those with antislavery leanings, bitterly opposed American expansion and the war. Johnson, on the other hand, entirely approved of both. For critics of the conflict, such as Columbus Delano of Ohio, he had nothing but contempt. "Had not the Mexican army crossed the Rio Grande, invaded American soil and shed American blood?" he asked. Mexico had started the fighting, and the United States might well have been chosen by Providence to relieve the Mexicans from the oppression of their own government. He voted for the admission of Texas as a matter of course, just as he had voted for its annexation, and he sternly opposed the Wilmot Proviso, with its outlawry of slavery in the conquered territories. In addition, he sought to obtain commissions for his friends back home and to facilitate the organization of regiments from Tennessee.[40]

Yet Johnson remained a maverick. Hardly had the session started than he renewed the proposition to support congressional chaplains by voluntary contributions—"Andrew Johnson Still an Infidel," headlined Brownlow's paper—and he refused to support a motion to rent the representatives' hall to a temperance society.[41] Totally committed to rotation in office for government employees, Johnson introduced a measure mandating a turnover of offices every eight years, a motion that greatly frightened Washington's civil servants.[42] Moreover, his passion for economy was so extreme that he voted against increasing soldiers' pay from $8 to $10 per month and thundered against the acceptance of funds for the Smithsonian Institution, which the British mineralogist James Smithson had deeded to the United States. He was worried that taxpayers would have to make good on moneys unwisely invested, he said, and he became a determined foe of the institution.

To emphasize his devotion to the working man, Johnson introduced a resolution against convict labor, going so far as to contemplate abolition of the federal penitentiary system altogether. For the same reason, he opposed a tax on coffee and tea, although his party had included such a tax in the Walker tariff of 1846. It would hurt the poor, he maintained. In addition, always adamant against special privilege, in the midst of the Mexican War, he seemed to belittle West Point by questioning its importance as a training school for good generals, while opposing any undue increase in the number of army officers.

Last but not least, on March 27, 1846, he introduced his Homestead Bill: "A Bill to authorize every poor man in the United States who is the head of a family, to enter one hundred and sixty acres of the public domain, 'without money and without price.' "[43] Many Southerners disliked the proposition, which was not only of limited use for slaveholders but might reduce the national revenue from land sales, necessitating renewed protective tariffs for raising needed government funds. The bill fell on deaf ears that spring, but Johnson would not rest until it was finally passed many years later.[44]

The Tennesseean's continued independence brought him into conflict with several party associates. Many of his Southern compatriots were less interested in the acquisition of all of Oregon than in the annexation of Texas; after all, no slaves were likely to be taken into the far Northwest. But although Johnson always defended the "peculiar institution" with vigor, he saw no difference between the two issues. "While he was a southern man," he said, "he was an American." He would stand by the administration and see it honor its pledge to take all of Oregon.

In making these remarks, Johnson referred in passing to Representative Thomas Henry Bayly of Virginia, a states' rights Democrat, who had differed with the administration on terminating the agreement with Great Britain for joint occupation of the Oregon Territory. When Johnson accused him of abandoning the government, the Virginian replied that he was not the man to follow any administration if he disagreed with it and that Johnson was misquoting him. The latter rejoined, "I am stating the gentleman's position correctly, and the documents will sustain it. The gentleman's scowls or threats have no terrors for me. He may go and show his slaves how choleric he is, and make his bondsmen tremble." Bayly was outraged, and although Johnson disclaimed any intention of personal insult, he did not mollify the Virginian when he insisted on the accuracy of his previous statements. This sort of encounter caused him to be viewed as a prickly outsider with whom it was difficult to maintain social relations.[45]

More serious was Johnson's altercation with the newly elected representative from Mississippi, Jefferson Davis. The future president of the Confederacy, then serving his first term in Congress, was proud of his military training at West Point. Seizing upon the occasion of a discussion of a resolution of thanks to General Zachary Taylor, Davis defended the academy against its traducers. Let its critics consider the utility and construction of the bastioned fieldwork opposite Matamoras, he said. Let them compare the few men who held it with the army that assailed it, and then say whether they believed "a blacksmith or a tailor could have secured the same results."

This allusion was too much for Johnson. Rising on the next day for some remarks on the conduct of the war, he replied to Davis. "The gentleman from Mississippi," he recalled, "in the course of his remarks yesterday, . . . had seen fit to make an invidious distinction, and to strike an unwarrantable and unauthorized blow upon a certain portion of the community. Mr. J. belonged to the class that was alluded to, and here, in the face of an American Congress, he was not ashamed to avow that he was a mechanic, and of that class to which the gentleman alluded yesterday." Davis immediately sought to explain that he had meant no offense, but Johnson continued on his course, extolling the laboring classes. As he put it, he knew we had an "illegitimate, swaggering, bastard, scrub aristocracy, who assumed to know a good deal," but who possessed neither talents nor any worthwhile information. Then he went on with observations about Adam, whom he called a tailor, Jesus Christ, the son of a carpenter, Ben Franklin, a printer, and others. The contretemps with Davis continued, and, according to the reporter, "the debate in all its stages not being of an entirely pleasant nature," neither Davis nor Johnson would ever forget it.[46]

Although Johnson fully supported the president and the administration, especially in connection with the war in Mexico, strains soon developed in the relations between the two Tennesseeans. True, Polk was very kind to Martha because Johnson had asked Mrs. Polk to look after his daughter during her stay at Miss S. L. English's Female Seminary in Georgetown. He invited her to the White House and took an active interest in her, but he could not have failed to hear about her father's opposition to his nomination at the national convention in Baltimore. Although at first he honored some of Johnson's patronage requests, providing jobs for the congressman's constituents, he increasingly turned a deaf ear to them.[47] Johnson was piqued.

In order to settle the matter, on July 21, 1846, Johnson came to the White House. Visibly agitated, he told the president that he had not been at the mansion in weeks. The postmaster general and Tennessee politician Cave Johnson had told him that the administration was aware of his opposition, he said. Because he was a Democrat, however, and had supported Polk with time and money, especially in 1844, he was irked about the fact that his policies should now be suspect.

The president was candid. While he had thought Johnson would continue to support him, he pointed out that he had heard that his visitor and George W. Jones were dissatisfied and finding fault with the administration. Not at all apologetic, Johnson recounted several patronage difficulties. If he was going to be the victim of Polk's anger, he said, he wanted to know about it. The interview, which lasted for an hour, ended on a sour note, and Johnson wrote home that East Tennessee was "not much known in these parts when favors and offices worth having are to be bestowed."[48]

To his friend Blackston McDannel Johnson unburdened himself more fully. "The democracy in my district and Geo——W. Jones' seem to have fallen under the peculiar displeasure of the administration," he wrote. After mentioning his failure to get what he wanted, he gave vent to his dissatisfaction with the president. "Take Polk's appointments all and all and they are the most *damnable* set that were ever made by any president since the government was organized. . . . There is one thing I will say," he continued, "that is, I never betrayed a *friend or* [was] *guilty of the black sin of ingratitude*—I fear Mr. Polk cannot say as much." Maintaining that the president was no leader, he asserted that the party was getting along in Congress without one, so that there was more dissension than ever before.[49]

The president likewise gave vent to his feelings. In recording the interview with the Tennessee representative in his diary, Polk wrote that Johnson wished to play the demagogue at home by having the administration make a victim of him. "The truth is," he mused, "that neither Johnson nor Jones have [sic] been my personal friends since 1839. They were in the Baltimore Convention in 1844, and were not my friends then. I doubt whether any two members in that convention were at heart more dissatisfied with my nomination for the Presidency than they were." He thought he could have destroyed them in their districts had he wanted to do so, but he had not. Nevertheless, the president concluded, "I would almost prefer to have two Whigs here in their stead, unless they act better than they have done at the present session of Congress."[50]

The hostility between the two Democrats from Tennessee was not difficult to explain. According to Polk's biographer, much of it was due to Johnson's opposition to professional men, slaveholders, and upper classes generally.[51] While these reasons undoubtedly form part of the explanation (although Johnson, a slaveholder himself, did not dislike owners of bondsmen per se), they do not tell the whole story. Long having represented different elements of the party in Tennessee, the two men could not be close. Johnson naturally opposed Polk's candidacy for the nomination; failing to prevent it, he even seemed to favor some of the policies of the president's Northern opponents, the Barnburners, though as a Southerner he could not make common cause with them. Thus he should not have been surprised at Polk's subsequent refusal to give him the patronage he thought his due. But his pride was hurt, and once crossed, he rarely forgave an opponent. To be sure, Johnson still spoke in favor of the administration's war policies and still assailed the president's Whig critics—Polk had merely defended the United States against a Mexican invasion, he said—but relations between him and the president did not improve.[52]

When, after the customary summer and fall at home, Johnson returned to Washington in December 1846 for the short session of Congress, he was not happy. To be sure, he still vigorously defended the administration and the Mexican War in his speeches, but his strained relations with the president, to say nothing of his agrarian extremism, his continued opposition to the coffee and tea tax, the Smithsonian Institution, and the appointment of additional general officers, were giving him trouble, even at home. Brownlow had already attacked him for voting against improvements in the Holston River, and he knew that opponents within his own party were scheming to displace him.[53] While he was sitting in his room one Sunday in January as a winter storm was brewing, his mood matching the weather, he wrote dejectedly to McDannel: "My dear friend," he began, "if there is one lefte that I dare call my friend." He was lonely; his wife was still at home, and only Martha, at Georgetown, could give him occasional comfort. He was in poor health—his legs, arms, and heart all gave him trouble—and the government seemed to be pushing to destruction. Moreover, Johnson feared his rivals in the party would not forgive him; even Sam Milligan, temporarily at odds with him, was apparently drawing closer to his opponents. At the same time, some real estate speculations in Greeneville had gone awry. "I never want to own another foot of dirt in the *damned* town while I live," he asserted. It was obvious that he would have trouble seeking reelection. While he eventually succeeded in obtaining commissions for both McDannel and Milligan, who in the end remained his friend, his difficulties at home were only beginning.[54]

It was at this point that Johnson's dislike of the administration led him to commit a blunder. Believing that his Democratic opponents at home would unite against him in an attempt to deny him reelection, and the Whigs would probably support the dissident candidate so that he would have to contend only with another Democrat, he denounced the administration in no uncertain terms. On February 2, 1847, rising to attack a proposed tax on tea and coffee, he asserted that various Democratic leaders, including the president, had in years past opposed such a levy on the necessities of the poor. If the whole American people could be assembled in some amphitheater in Washington and the veil that now concealed the various abuses in the capital could be drawn aside so that the public could view the intrigues "of officers in authority, from the highest to the lowest," it would "rip up and tear off some of those funguses that have been fixing and fixed themselves upon the vitals of this Government for years gone by" and "turn some mighty stream through the Augean stable until it was thoroughly cleansed from the abominable filth that has been preying upon the lifeblood of the republic too long." It was an ill-considered attack, which could only benefit the Whigs.[55]

In fact, Johnson's speech handed his opponents a convenient issue, and his troubles began as soon as he reached home. Landon C. Haynes, who was to be his lifelong adversary, was indeed anxious to obtain the Democratic nomination. Haynes even sought to make Johnson run for governor to get him out of the way. Johnson, however, traveling up and down the district and delivering hard-hitting speeches, managed to parry the thrust so that Haynes withdrew. And as most Whigs were convinced that they could not win, Johnson confidently expected to run unopposed.[56]

He was to be disappointed. Fully aware of the enmity Johnson had aroused in many Democratic circles, the Whigs sought to make the most of the situation. Their candidate for governor, Neill S. Brown, joined Brownlow in persuading young Oliver P. Temple, a Greeneville lawyer who had only been a member of the bar for one year, to challenge the incumbent. Knowing that Johnson would never have made his speech against the administration had he not expected to face Haynes, a fellow

Democrat, and not a Whig, Temple took full advantage of his opportunity. As he explained to Brownlow, "The true policy between me and Johnson is, to conduct it in such a way as not to *alarm* or *excite* the democrats. If they become alarmed or excited they will rally to the support of Johnson. If on the contrary they think there is no danger and they are not made *mad,* they will suffer him to fight for himself, and won't care much whether he is elected or not." The true strategy, therefore, was not to abuse Johnson too much, not to call him an infidel, and not to boast that he would be defeated.[57]

Temple acted accordingly. Appealing artfully to Johnson's Democratic enemies—the Blairs, the McClellans, and the Hayneses, all of whom the congressman had been denouncing as bloated aristocrats—Temple wooed their votes. In joint campaigns from village to village, the young lawyer pointed out Johnson's inconsistencies, his votes against higher salaries for soldiers, and his unpatriotic support of a resolution of censure against General Taylor. By correcting his opponent's historical legends in the presence of professors at Washington College, Temple made Johnson look foolish. Above all, he kept reminded listeners of the attack on Polk.

His tactics almost succeeded. On the evening of election day, in August 1847, for a while it appeared that Johnson had lost, and according to Temple, the incumbent was so mortified that he shed tears. But Johnson was a seasoned politician. Having made deals with the Whigs in Hawkins County to support their candidates for the state legislature if they would vote for him for Congress or abstain, he managed to defeat his challenger, even though his majority had declined to 314 votes.[58] Johnson returned to Congress somewhat chastened, although he was probably convinced once again that in the end, the people could be relied upon to support him.

Johnson's first two terms in Congress established his reputation as a shrewd politician, unbeatable at home, but not easily fitted into any general mold. A fanatical Jeffersonian-Jacksonian, he firmly clung to ideas to which many other Democrats often paid only lip service. Although this alienated many of his associates and marked him as an outsider, he was nevertheless determined to continue on his course.

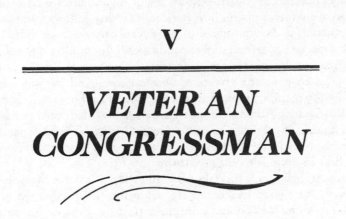

V

VETERAN
CONGRESSMAN

ALTHOUGH the years that followed Johnson's first two terms in Congress
were increasingly dominated by the sectional struggle, at first he did not
seem to take the matter too seriously. Still mainly concerned with his
Jeffersonian-Jacksonian proposals, the Tennessee congressman continued his campaigns for economy in government, devoted himself
wholeheartedly to the Homestead Bill, and took an interest in constitutional reform. Other party issues had his full support, but because of his
radicalism, he continued to alienate Democrats as well as Whigs. Thus
he had to be constantly on his guard. His opponents at home in both
parties left him no peace.

When in the fall of 1847 Johnson returned to Washington for his
third term, his performance was, if anything, even more unequivocal
than before. Economy had now become a veritable obsession. In part,
it accounted for his ever more pronounced vendetta against the Smithsonian Institution, which he attacked at every opportunity. After advocating the establishment of a committee of supervision for the institution, he so severely criticized one of its regents, his fellow congressman
Henry W. Hilliard of Alabama, that members of the House were appalled. Disgusted by Johnson's "real demagogical speech," David Outlaw of North Carolina characterized him as "an ugly customer before
the people . . . entirely destitute of any elevated or enlarged views." He
thought the former tailor's election to Congress had caused him to be
"quite inflated with his own importance."[1]

Other moves for economy followed. Whether it was the aggregate number of clerks in government offices, or their salaries, or the compensation of chargés d'affaires in American legations, Johnson, still favoring the rotation in federal offices of employees chosen from different districts, opposed governmental expenditures. Maintaining that such matters had best be left to local authorities, he even denied the power of Congress to pave the streets of Washington. And he was naturally opposed to spending money for the erection of a monument at the grave of John Quincy Adams, the purchase of James Madison's papers, and the granting of subsidies to mail steamers.[2] When federal expenditures were concerned, the congressman from the First District in Tennessee was deaf to appeals to his generosity.

In other matters, especially in connection with the Mexican War, Johnson was a good Democrat. He was against instructing the army to withdraw from Mexico and continued to defend the administration's war policy. He reaffirmed his belief in Mexico's responsibility for the conflict, while blaming the Whigs for the warlike resolution of the quarrel with the neighboring republic. Both Milligan and McDannel, who were serving with the army, kept him well informed about affairs in Mexico, and, rejoicing in the triumph of American arms, the tailor-statesman fully supported the peace treaty confirming the U.S. victory.

The president's right to veto bills, always under Whig attack, also met with Johnson's approval. Tracing the privilege all the way back to plebeian influence in ancient Rome, he defended it vigorously in a long and convoluted speech in support of the Military Appropriations Bill for 1849.[3]

In the increasingly acrimonious discussions of slavery, Johnson was also in full accord with the majority of his party in the South. Anything pertaining to the "peculiar institution" or the blacks found him as ready to tilt lances with Northern opponents as any of his colleagues. When John Gorham Palfrey, the Unitarian clergyman and historian from Massachusetts, praised the achievements of some Negroes, who, he said, were the equals of white men and of his own son, Johnson asked him whether he would allow his daughter to marry such a black man. His opposition to the Wilmot Proviso was a matter of record—he refused even to consider an applicant for the editorship of the Greeneville Spy who was reputed to be a supporter of the measure. No one could question his orthodoxy on this issue.[4]

The sectional conflict soon became more intractable than ever. Eighteen forty-eight was a presidential election year, and the struggle between slavery and freedom was bound to affect the two major parties.

Exactly what was the position of slavery in the federal territories, where Northerners maintained the government could abolish bondage while Calhoun's followers, citing the Constitution's protection of private property, denied it? In a letter to Nicholson, Johnson's candidate for president, Lewis Cass, tried to solve the problem by advocating "popular sovereignty," the right of the actual settlers to decide. Johnson himself did everything he could to make Polk's renomination impossible, and as a member of the Democratic Convention that year in Baltimore, he had the satisfaction of seeing Cass walk away with the prize.[5] The Whigs put their hopes in Zachary Taylor, whose victories in Mexico had made him famous, and sought to dodge the slavery issue by not adopting any platform. The opponents of slavery, not satisfied with either candidate, fielded a Free Soil ticket of their own, headed by Martin Van Buren and Charles Francis Adams.

Johnson did not have to worry about the Free Soilers in Tennessee, but Taylor proved a formidable antagonist. Actively campaigning for Cass in his home district, Johnson engaged in a series of debates with Thomas A. R. Nelson. But even though Parson Brownlow himself referred to his old opponent as "the Napoleon of his party," his efforts barely enabled him to hold his own district.[6] The victorious general was too popular; he carried Tennessee, won the election, and became Polk's successor.

As long as the Mexican War was going on, Johnson's quarrel with Polk was still somewhat muted. After all, he was exceedingly patriotic, believed in supporting the administration against the foreign foe, and needed patronage. In fact, he did what he could to procure commissions for his constituents and personal friends: Milligan and McDannel went off to Mexico, and Johnson was ever ready to press Tennessee's claims for more regiments.[7] But with the end of the war and Polk's defeat, the break became complete. When Johnson came to the White House on New Year's Day of 1849, the president was piqued. "Among the visitors whom I observed in the crowd today," he wrote in his diary,

was Hon. Andrew Johnson of the Ho. Repts. Though he represents a Democratic District in Tennessee (my own State) this is the first time I have seen him during the present session of Congress. Professing to be a Democrat, he has been politically, if not personally hostile to me during my whole term. He is very vindictive and perverse in his temper and conduct. If he had the manliness or independence to manifest his opposition openly, he knows he could not be elected by his constituents. I am not aware that I have ever given him cause for offense.[8]

As time went on and Johnson became more accustomed to Washington, he became a bit less unbending. The winter session of 1848–49 not only saw him at the White House, but also at other functions. Once he even joined a few friends for a trip to Baltimore. It was a pleasant diversion from his duties at the War Department, where he was busily processing all kinds of citizens' claims, and he made the most of the trip. "We all got on a *Kinder* of a '*bust,*' not a big 'drunk,' " as he put it. After a good supper he and his friends went to the Front Street Theater to see the "Danseuses Viennoises," whom he found charming. Who could resist forty-eight little girls dressed in the "richest and most gaudy manner, performing every imaginable evolution, and arranging themselves in every circle and figure . . . singing with a voice so sweet, and dancing with a foot so light, that *Job* in the midst of all his afflictions would have rejoiced at the scenes before him?" Hungry again after the performance, the revelers enjoyed a fine oyster supper before going to bed. Upon rising at six in the morning, they took another little drink, felt like *"giants refreshed with new wine,"* and then boarded the train back to Washington.[9]

The new congressional session was again marked by increased tension on the slavery issue. Northern congressmen asked leave to introduce several bills to end either slavery or the slave trade in the District of Columbia, and Joshua Giddings, with whom Johnson had had several arguments before, demanded a plebiscite to decide the question. Johnson naturally opposed all of these propositions, including an amendment by Abraham Lincoln, then serving his single term in Congress, to prohibit the introduction of new slaves into the district. It was in this Congress that Johnson met Lincoln for the first time. Considering the Illinoisan's opposition to the Mexican War, it is not likely that the Tennesseean was favorably impressed with him, though he felt friendly enough to tell Lincoln something about his relatives in Tennessee. Johnson's loyalty to slavery was undoubted, even if, along with other members from the slave states, he did not sign Calhoun's Southern address, an attempt to rally Southerners behind a common policy.[10]

Otherwise, Johnson still pursued his dream of agrarian democracy. He reintroduced his Homestead Bill and was determined not to rest until it passed. He again insisted on economy in government by continuing his vendetta against the Smithsonian Institution and seeking to reduce funds for presidential portraits in the White House. Keenly aware of his reputation as a demagogue, he confronted his critics head on. Abraham Venable of North Carolina had characterized a demagogue as "the filthy, slimy being, who, like the snail, always left his mark in the track where he moved." Johnson offered his own sarcastic definition: a demagogue, he said in reply, "was a man who dared come forward here and oppose appropriations of money for objects which the people themselves, if they understood them, would put down as being against their notions of right, economy and justice."[11]

There was one issue, however, upon which Johnson showed more flexibility. Railroad building had become a veritable mania, and Johnson could not afford to oppose it. Consequently he now favored state help for the construction of the East Tennessee and Virginia Railroad Company.[12] His constituents needed better transportation.

The congressman from Tennessee was now becoming better known, not only in his own state, but throughout the country. In May 1849 a biographical sketch of him appeared in the New York *Sunday Times.* After relating the story of his lowly origins and events in his political career, the reporter described the man: "Our subject . . . wears on his figure and countenance a something I cannot describe, though it looks all over like the self-made man. He is of medium size and height; has a dark complexion, with black eyes and hair. His head is decidedly intellectual in shape, while from his eyes there flashes the fierce radicalism that burns in his soul." The article emphasized his able debating and his fearless thrusts against his opponents. He might mispronounce polysyllabic words or those of foreign derivation, but his arguments were always well prepared and "well conned." His frequent remarks, though rarely on a subject other than party questions and the rights of the masses, were known for their disregard of their probable effect on his career. Although the last point was exaggerated—the article appeared two days after its subject had been renominated for Congress and was reprinted in the Nashville *Union*—Johnson was still pictured as a valuable member of the House, an excellent investigator, hardworking, and conscientious in committee work. He had every reason to be proud of this assessment.[13]

In the meantime, his children were growing up. Martha, a young lady of twenty, had returned from Georgetown and, with her energy and intelligence, seemed to resemble her father. For Charles, Johnson had asked his friend Nicholson to look into the performance of a newly established manual labor school at Nashville. He wanted to send the boy "from home to *chool Som wheare,*" as he put it. Apparently he was satisfied with what he heard, for Charles did go to Nashville. By 1849 he had come home to become one of the editors of the Greeneville *Spy,* a paper established by his father. Robert eventually attended the Nashville school as well, and Mary was to attend the Rogersville Female Academy, where she received long letters from her father admonishing her to study and to develop her character. Of one thing he was certain:

his children would have a good education, even if he had never had the advantage of one.[14]

In 1849 Johnson was again up for reelection to his seat in Congress. In preparation for the campaign, he contacted many of his supporters, submitted his name to the nominating convention in Greeneville, and managed to carry off the prize. Nevertheless, there was trouble, as usual. His chief rival for the nomination, Brookins Campbell, refused to withdraw, and Johnson had to face both his old Democratic opponent and the Whig candidate, Nathaniel G. Taylor of Carter County. Coordinating his campaign with the general election in the state, he advised the editor of the Nashville *Union* to concentrate on three issues: slavery, homesteads, and the election of judges, a scheme he had long favored. Such tactics, he believed, would enable the party to carry Tennessee and make it easy for him to defeat his opponents.[15]

Johnson had already made his position clear by taking, as he put it, "the high ground on the slavery question." On May 26 he delivered a long speech on the subject at Evans Crossroads. Even in East Tennessee with its few slaves, thousands of dollars were invested in this type of property, he argued; furthermore, slavery was indissolubly linked with the institutions of the country, and all attacks on it were unpatriotic. At the same time, he sought to show that Zachary Taylor and Vice President Millard Fillmore were friendly to antislavery advocates and contrasted this attitude with the firmly proslavery positions of Cass and William O. Butler, the defeated Democratic candidate for vice president. Johnson also maintained that, because of their investment in labor and their desire to obtain the highest prices for it, slaveholders were the most reliable supporters of high prices for labor. The defense of the "peculiar institution" was important to him and his constituents.[16]

His tactics were successful. Even though the Taylor administration actively aided his antagonists, Johnson not only won, but managed to roll up an increased majority over his two opponents, 719 as compared with his much more modest victory over Temple two years earlier. Moreover, William Trousdale, the Democratic candidate for governor, also won. The party seemed to be in good shape.[17]

When Johnson returned to take his seat in the fall of 1849, Congress was in an uproar. With the newly formed Free Soil party holding the balance of power, it proved impossible to obtain a majority for the election of a speaker of the House of Representatives. Day after day members of the House balloted, but no winner could be announced. Early in the process Johnson moved that a plurality be sufficient, a proposition that finally solved the problem when adopted by others a few weeks later. Much to Brownlow's amusement, Johnson even offered a resolution for prayer in Congress to help speed the termination of the contest. Attacking the record of such Southern members as Isaac Edward Holmes of South Carolina, Edward Stanly and Thomas Clingman of North Carolina, and Charles M. Conrad of Louisiana, the Tennessee lawmaker charged that the Southern Whigs had been voting for former speaker Robert C. Winthrop, even though Winthrop had favored the Wilmot Proviso and opposed the South. Let Southern members wake up and stand together, he urged—then they could not be defeated. Slavery was an important institution and must be defended at all costs. The struggle finally ended with the election of the Democrat Howell Cobb after the adoption of a plurality rule.[18]

The election of the speaker was only the beginning of one of the most controversial congressional sessions ever held. California had applied for admission to the Union; because her constitution forbade slavery, compliance with her request would permanently upset the equal balance between free and slave states, and many Southerners were threatening secession if Congress agreed to unsettle this equilibrium. The existence of the Union was at stake, and in order to save it, Henry Clay introduced in the Senate his famous compromise resolutions on January 29, 1850. Let both sides give a little, he pleaded, hoping to settle a whole series of controversial questions. California would be admitted as a free state, but in return, the South would get a new and stronger fugitive slave act. Slavery would continue to exist in the District of Columbia, but the slave trade there would be abolished. Utah and New Mexico, both acquired from Mexico, might organize as either slave or free territories according to the will of their inhabitants, and Texas, which had been claiming all of eastern New Mexico, would give up its claim in return for federal assumption of its debts. In addition, Congress ought to pass a resolution denying its right to abolish the interstate slave trade.

Clay's proposals ushered in a long series of debates. While the Senate listened to the famous speeches of Daniel Webster, John C. Calhoun, William H. Seward, Jefferson Davis, and Salmon P. Chase on opposite sides of the question, in the House Johnson offered his own proposal for a speedy solution to the problem. Believing strongly both in slavery and in the Union, on March 12 he submitted a resolution calling for a committee to report measures embracing the immediate admission of California "upon an equal footing with the other States composing the Confederacy," the legalization of the provisional governments in Utah and New Mexico, a stronger fugitive slave law, and the retrocession of the District of Columbia to Maryland.[19]

The proposal was typical of Johnson. Involving compromises for both the South and the North—a free California and a new fugitive slave law as well as a noncommittal attitude toward Utah and New Mexico—it would have solved the controversy over slavery in the District of Columbia by divesting the federal government of the problem, in effect protecting both slavery and the slave trade in Washington by putting the city under the jurisdiction of Maryland, where slavery was legal. His reasoning was simple. As he explained in a speech on June 5, "I trust and hope that Whigs and Democrats . . . will be brought to feel that the preservation of this Union ought to be the object which is paramount to all other considerations. I believe . . . that slavery itself has its foundation, and will find its perpetuity in the Union, and the Union its continuance by a non-interference with the institution of slavery." Having already severely attacked former speaker Winthrop for his antislavery stance and his aristocratic background, Johnson now reiterated his defense of slavery by repeating the principal portion of his speech at Evans Crossroads of the previous year.[20]

This position of coupling the defense of slavery with the preservation of the Union placed him in a posture of sharp antagonism to Southern extremists. Taking no interest whatever in the Nashville Convention called to consider separate Southern action, he remained what he had always been, a Southern Democrat and a patriotic American.

On July 9 President Taylor, who had fallen ill during the Independence Day celebrations, died. Vice President Fillmore, his successor, was much more amenable to the compromise measures. To be sure, he informed Congress of his intention to call out the militia to prevent Texas from taking over territory in dispute with New Mexico, a communication Johnson, as a good Southerner and believer in local authority, savagely attacked, but this harsh step proved unnecessary. In September Congress finally passed what has come to be known as the Compromise of 1850, in accordance with Clay's suggestions. Johnson voted for all its provisions except the one for the abolition of the slave trade in the District of Columbia.[21] As he had made perfectly clear, he wanted the district retroceded to Maryland.

While Johnson considered the question of the Union of paramount importance, at the time of the Compromise debates he was again wholly involved in promoting his Homestead Bill. He first attempted to have the legislation considered once more on February 21, then sought to introduce it in his capacity as chairman of the Committee on Public Expenditures, only to be ruled out of order. The measure belonged properly to the Committee on Public Lands, the speaker decided. Nothing daunted, Johnson tried again a few days later, this time with more success, and the bill was referred to the Committee on Public Lands.

Encouraged by news from home that his course was popular, he continued to agitate the question, and on July 25 made a strong appeal in a well-thought-out speech. Quoting passages from Leviticus, Vattel, and Andrew Jackson about the nobility of agriculture, he said the government existed for the people, and to effect the greatest good for the greatest number was the purpose of every body politic. Why, therefore, should the United States keep land that so many wanted to cultivate? The horrors of Ireland following the great potato famine showed the ill effects of landlessness for the masses and large estates for the aristocracy. The government might withhold the use of fire, water, and air from its citizens with the same propriety as it did the use of their own soil. Pass this bill, he pleaded,

> and you will make many a poor man's heart rejoice. Pass this bill and their wives and children will invoke blessings on your heads. Pass this bill, and millions now unborn will look back with wonder and admiration upon the age in which it was done. Pass this bill, and you will strengthen the basis of Christianity. . . . Pass this bill, and as regarded his humble self, he would feel that he had filled the full object of his mission here, and he could return home to his constituents in quiet and in peace.

In spite of his fervent pleas, Congress failed to act.[22] But he would try again.

Of course, Johnson also continued his campaign for economy. Having become chairman of the Committee on Public Expenditures, he had many opportunities to express his opposition to what he considered unnecessary spending. He opposed the acquisition of George Washington's Farewell Address, resisted additional appropriations for the completion of the Patent Office and for the salary of the chief clerk of the Department of the Interior, and begrudged even federal assistance for the search for the vanished Franklin expedition to the Arctic. He not only favored the reduction of salaries of government employees, but made an effort to reduce all federal salaries over $1,000 by one-fifth. Needless to say, his amendment for this purpose was defeated; nor did his popularity with his colleagues gain by the attempt.[23]

Johnson continued his crusade for economy in the winter session of 1850–51. Now seeking to make sure that all federal employees actually worked the required eight hours a day, he again advocated the reduction of federal salaries.[24] He still opposed rivers and harbors bills, but was again more circumspect in the matter of railroads, continuing to favor aid to the Virginia and East Tennessee line. In general, however, his devotion to Jeffersonian simplicity was clear.[25]

But it was the Homestead Bill that was still uppermost in his mind.

So important was it to him that he even sought to enlist Daniel Webster's aid, with some success.[26] Then, after failing to have the House consider the bill and seeing it again referred to the Committee of the Whole, at the very end of the session he tried once more to have the vote of referral reconsidered. He did not succeed, but he knew that sooner or later Congress would have to take up the ever more popular measure.[27] Its author was now so prominent among the Democrats of Tennessee that the Nashville *Union* reprinted many of his speeches in full and published another laudatory biography.[28]

It was in this congressional session that Johnson returned to one of his old ideas, the direct election of public officials. Instead of being chosen by the electoral college or the state legislatures, presidents and senators ought to be elected by the people, he thought, and judges should serve for no more than twelve years. After introducing an amendment for this purpose in February 1851, he was chagrined to see it defeated with the help of his colleague Isham G. Harris, the able Memphis lawyer and future secessionist governor, who had been elected to represent a West Tennessee district in the House. The two men were eventually to become bitter enemies.[29]

Because of the ascendancy of the Whigs in the executive branch, Johnson's skills as a politician were to be severely tested. Much to Thomas A. R. Nelson's and Brownlow's disgust, he succeeded in retaining government printing contracts for the Greeneville *Spy*. He fought bitterly with Senator John Bell about the retention of his friend William M. Lowry in the Greeneville post office, but he was only able to delay the postmaster's dismissal for some eighteen months. Considering the difficulties involved, even these limited successes showed that he was an extraordinary politician.[30]

It was hardly surprising that Johnson's radical notions did not increase his popularity with the conservative wing of his party. Even though in 1852 he pledged support for the construction of railroads, his rivals did not forget his former opposition to such internal improvements, and when it was time to run for Congress again, he found that his Democratic enemies had concentrated their forces and nominated Landon C. Haynes to run against him. An able lawyer and former Methodist minister from Jonesboro, Haynes was a powerful speaker who had long been active in East Tennessee politics. He resented Johnson's policies and coveted his job.[31]

The campaign that followed was fierce. All over the district the two rivals debated each other and sought to win support. So pleased were the Whigs with the spectacle of the two battling Democrats that they did not even nominate a candidate of their own. Johnson made the

Homestead Bill his main campaign issue; even before the race had started, he asked his friend Nicholson to write an article endorsing the measure for the Nashville *Union*. He also assured Governor William Trousdale of the bill's popularity in Tennessee and advised him to take a firm stand on the question.

But Haynes confronted the issue without hesitation. Homesteading was disadvantageous for the South, he charged; it was an abolition measure, and Johnson was its author. He also brought up the question of the railroads. Had not Johnson always been opposed to them even though he now professed to have changed his mind? Employing the congressman's own methods against him, Haynes delivered speeches full of personal vituperation, innuendo, and ad hominem attacks. To underline his opponent's former fondness for certain Whigs, he asked whom Johnson had voted for in 1836, even though his own course during the 1839 campaign for governor had been equally dubious, as Johnson promptly pointed out. And when Haynes once again raised the old charges of infidelity against the incumbent, Johnson could reply with a criticism of his opponent's religious record. Had he not been expelled from the Methodist ministry?

Calling each other liars, both men traveled throughout the entire district and attracted large crowds. In the end Johnson won again, this time by a majority of 1,653, partially procured, according to Brownlow's son, by a deal with the Hawkins County Whigs that facilitated the election of John Netherland to the state legislature. The campaign of 1851 was the fiercest congressional race Johnson had to run before the Civil War, and his triumph was sweet.[32] It proved to be the last time he was elected to the House, however, because the following year the opposition gerrymandered him out of his district.

Johnson's political successes and his business acumen enabled him to live well in Greeneville. His property had long been contested by the former owners, but by 1851 the dispute was settled, and he finally obtained a clear title to the house and the tailor shop. After selling some of this real estate, he bought a large home on Main Street, the core of the present Johnson House.[33] According to archeological evidence, it consisted of a two-story brick building with one story well extending toward the rear. There were six rooms above ground and two in the semibasement. Situated directly upon the street like most early Greeneville residences, it had a central hall with a stairway. Both on the first and second floors, there was a room at either side with chimneys at each end. The ell was two steps lower than the first floor and extended to a depth of two rooms toward the rear, with a porch on its northeastern side. An outside stair connected the kitchen with the dining room.[34]

Johnson needed a larger house, for in August of 1852 Eliza gave birth to another son, Andrew, Jr., whose nickname was Frank. In addition, his stepfather died and his mother moved in with the family. For the time being, the residence on Main Street was adequate. But as the years went on, it was to be greatly enlarged until it assumed its present shape.[35]

The older children were doing well. Martha, back from Georgetown, was still living at home. Robert had left Nashville and was about to become a lawyer in Greeneville, while Charles was for a while editor of his father's paper, the Spy. Then, in April 1852, Mary married Daniel Stover, a Watauga Valley farmer in Carter County. Johnson was proud of his family.[36]

Another source of special pride was his invitation to join the Masons. On May 5, 1851, he was received into Greeneville Lodge No. 3, and for the rest of his life he remained a devoted member of the fraternity.[37]

He was also kept busy with his newspaper, the Greeneville Spy. For a while, after Charles had devoted time to it, Johnson's friend Sam Milligan edited the sheet; but there was always a problem finding a suitable permanent editor.[38]

In the new session of Congress, December 1852, Johnson finally realized his dream of passing the Homestead Bill, at least in the House. Demands for some legislation giving free land to the landless were becoming ever more insistent, and the Tennesseean was widely considered the leader of the homestead forces in the House. He corresponded with agrarian reformers in various parts of the country, including Horace Greeley, the editor of the New York Tribune, whose antislavery convictions did not prevent cooperation on this measure. Johnson was indefatigable in promoting the bill: he raised the issue at every opportunity, making impassioned and carefully prepared appeals, opposed the imposition of property qualifications for prospective beneficiaries, and argued at length about the constitutionality of giving lands away. Would not the settlement of vacant lands create more revenue for the Treasury than land sales had ever produced? In the final vote on May 12, Johnson, who had the reputation of being "a little cracked on the subject," had the satisfaction of seeing the bill passed by a vote of 108–57, even Southerners favoring it, 33–30. The entire Tennessee delegation with the exception of Isham G. Harris voted for the bill, and Brownlow himself endorsed it. Although a long struggle in the Senate still lay ahead, Johnson had every reason to be proud of his accomplishment.[39]

After the bill had been passed, a group of New York land reformers led by George Henry Evans, who had been active in the homestead cause for decades, invited Johnson to come to the metropolis to address a meeting. The congressman was only too happy to accept, and on May

27, in company with Greeley, he delivered a speech to a crowd of sympathizers. The meeting began in the park under lowering clouds; then speakers and audience had to move to City Hall to escape a downpour. What Johnson said was similar to his previous remarks in Congress. As a well-received speaker in general—the *Tribune* made a special point of acknowledging his "ability, energy, and charm"—he knew exactly how to deal with hissing hecklers. When someone hissed, he tartly replied that only two creatures hissed in nature, one a viper from the malignity of its own venom, and the other a goose because of its stupidity. The crowd loved it.[40]

On other matters that came before the Congress, Johnson was true to his accustomed positions. Again pleading for economy in government, he opposed appropriations for the army and navy, lambasted such "aristocratic" institutions as West Point and Annapolis, and voted against subsidies for the Collins line of steamships. When a general increase in salaries for government employees was suggested, however, he insisted that laborers share in the benefits. Johnson reintroduced his direct election amendments and again tangled with Congressman Bayly, this time about the latter's attack on Duff Green, the Southern stalwart who had attempted to obtain the contract for the transfer of funds to Mexico authorized by the Treaty of Guadalupe Hidalgo. And to underline his devotion to Southern causes, he was less than enthusiastic in welcoming Louis Kossuth, the Hungarian freedom fighter whom Washington was then feting with great excitement. Southerners distrusted European "freedom shriekers."[41]

Eighteen fifty-two was another presidential year, and as usual, the Tennessee congressman was not pleased with his party's choice, the dark horse New Hampshire lawyer Franklin Pierce. Johnson had been advocating the nomination of Sam Houston, the Texas hero, because he believed, correctly as it turned out, that the Whigs would nominate Winfield Scott, the conqueror of Mexico, who was unpopular in the South. Under these circumstances, he thought the Democrats might carry Tennessee, provided they nominated a strong candidate. He would also have been satisfied with his old favorite, Lewis Cass, but the rapidly rising senator from Illinois, Stephen A. Douglas, did not suit him. Even though the senator favored the Homestead Bill, all the cormorants in the party, Johnson maintained, favored Douglas. In the end, of course, he campaigned for Pierce. But he regretted references in the platform to the Kentucky and Virginia Resolutions, which favored the Southern ultras, who, he believed, were determined to crush the Union men. And Pierce seemed friendly to this element.[42]

Not only was Pierce elected, the Whigs were so severely weakened in the election that they never recovered. But Johnson was not enthusiastic about the new administration. In December he was invited to a victory dinner at the United States Hotel in Washington to make a speech. But, as he wrote to McDannel, he would "just as soon have been caught in company with a gang of cormorants or carrion crows." As usual, he thought his own party was corrupt, and he was dissatisfied. And as Tennessee was one of the few states the Democrats had lost, the outlook for patronage was not good.

Johnson's attitude toward the new administration was not unrealistic. Now that the Whigs had been fatally weakened, there was no real reason for the various Democratic factions to hold together. Accordingly, he saw grave troubles ahead. He had no confidence in the Yankee nation, he wrote, and Pierce was from New Hampshire. Moreover, he thought that the party's factionalism might wreck it. As it turned out, on this last issue, he was not far from right.[43]

Johnson's last session in the House was not eventful. Much of his time was taken up with the investigation of the Gardiner claim, a scandal arising out of a false claim made by Dr. George A. Gardiner in connection with the Mexican indebtedness to the United States. As chairman of a committee that was looking into the matter, he conducted hearings even while Congress was not in session, and roundly condemned Secretary of the Treasury Thomas Corwin for having represented Gardiner while a senator. So great was Johnson's sense of personal propriety that for a time he refused to collect the full amount of per diem due to him for service on the committee after the adjournment of Congress. He had no right to reimbursement for travel, he maintained.[44]

And the Tennesseean was a good Jacksonian to the last. Thundering against any contemplated demonetization of silver, he delighted the bullionists. And at the very end of the session, he reintroduced seven resolutions for rotation in appointive offices, which he had favored for years.[45]

While Johnson was carrying out his usual activities in Washington, his enemies in the Tennessee legislature finally made an end of his career in the House. In control of the General Assembly in 1852, the Whigs, under the leadership of Gustavus A. Henry, enlarged the First District in such a way as to make it safe for their party. A new word was being added to the language, wrote the Nashville Union: "gerrymander" ought to be updated to "Henry-mander." Johnson himself was stunned. "I have no political future—my political garments have been divided and upon my vesture do they intend to cast lots," he complained.[46] But his depression did not last long. The Union seemed safe for the time being, and the crushing defeat of the Whigs in the election of 1852 gave the Democrats a new chance in Tennessee. If the Whigs had succeeded in districting him out of Congress, he would challenge them elsewhere. A battle for the governorship was looming.

VI

GOVERNOR OF TENNESSEE

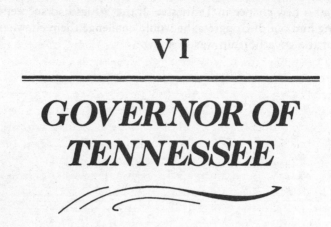

EVER since Johnson first began his climb to political power, he had given evidence of great ambition—ambition to be someone, to compete on even terms with self-styled aristocrats, to make a mark in politics. Therefore, when his opponents gerrymandered his district in the hope of making it safely Whig, it was hardly surprising that his reaction was not wholly passive. He was certainly not willing to retire without a murmur.

It is true that at first Johnson was not certain what his course should be. Should he really bow out and wind up his political career? Or should he seek further honors? "I will not deny it," he wrote in December 1852 to David T. Patterson, the Greeneville lawyer and later judge, soon to become his son-in-law, "for I have my ambition: but while I freely make the admission, I have always been determined not to let it run me into excessive error." Musing on the difficulties he had faced in the past and the successes he had achieved, he thought he might well retire. After all, in any try for governor or congressman he would have to overcome the Whig majority in the state and the district. In addition, the influence of former governor Aaron V. Brown and his friends was also against him. Naturally, he would prefer another term in Congress, but the governorship was not to be despised. Following two successive Whig victories, election to that office would constitute a vindication for him. Thus, if the consent of the other two grand divisions of the state could be secured for the nomination of an East Tennesseean, if the right platform was adopted, or, better yet, if no convention at all was held, he might be induced to make the race, even though he was worried about his health and the strain to which a statewide campaign would subject him.[1]

Actually, Johnson's candidacy had already been launched. His friend George W. Jones, the Fayetteville congressman, had put his name forward at a meeting of the state Democratic Committee in the fall of 1852. While the would-be candidate was still toying with the idea, a number of newspapers began to pick it up, and when in April the Democratic State Convention met in Nashville, the caucus that had assembled before the official opening found that he was the favorite of the majority. Although the caucus still sought to nominate Andrew Ewing, a distinguished Nashville lawyer, early in the convention Ewing and all other candidates withdrew so that Johnson was unanimously nominated. According to Oliver P. Temple, Ewing was induced to withdraw because Johnson maintained that Ewing had promised to support him.[2] Whether the story is true or not, the party settled on Johnson because it wanted a winner, and Johnson was its strongest man, as Nicholson informed President Pierce. Therefore, although the leading elements of the party, especially a conservative clique in Nashville, disliked the tailor because of his principles, personality, and origins, they acquiesced in his choice. They wanted to defeat the Whigs.[3]

The Democratic press was pleased. "We believe—feel it instinctively—that this nomination is the prelude to an overwhelming victory," commented the Nashville *Union*. "No man within the borders of our State had more in his character and history to challenge the wonder and respect of its citizens. A self-made man—a man for the people and of the people—strong in intellect—pure in patriotism, and unsullied in honor, we are free to state that his superior could not be found. . . . If we have not utterly misapprehended his character, he is, emphatically, *one of nature's noblemen.*" Not to be outdone, the Memphis *Appeal*, emphasizing that Johnson, a self-made man, was a splendid model for poor youths to emulate, concluded that a better nomination could not have been made. In neighboring Virginia the Richmond *Enquirer* expressed similar opinions.

If the Democrats stressed Johnson's strengths, the opposition concentrated on his weaknesses. Conceding that his old opponent was an able man, Brownlow nevertheless thought that Johnson, with the load of his longtime opposition to internal improvements to carry, would be vulnerable and could be defeated. The Nashville *Republican Banner*, reporting on the dissension within Democratic ranks, also predicted that Johnson would be beaten even more decisively than any other Democratic candidate.[4] To make doubly sure of victory, the Whigs, almost as if to deliberately challenge the Democratic nominee, selected Gustavus

A. Henry, the alleged author of the "Henry-mander," to oppose him. An able speaker and distinguished legislator of fine personal appearance, Henry had made a name for himself as the "Eagle Orator."[5] The campaign that followed was to test the Greeneville contender's skills to the utmost.

The Whigs' predictions proved wrong. Johnson's great ability on the stump, his populist appeals, his personal attacks, and his witty replies made it possible for him to carry the state against opposition not only from the rival party but also from an important segment of his own. A master of campaign technique perfectly adapted to a largely rural state like Tennessee, he was able to meet the electorate's highest expectations.

The schedule of campaigning in antebellum Tennessee was grueling: from late May until the end of July, braving the heat and the crowds, candidates were expected to debate one another in county seats from one end of the state to the other. But Johnson was physically and mentally attuned to this custom. Setting out from Greeneville in May 1853, he first met his opponent at Sparta on June 1. Henry spoke first. Attacking the Democrats in general and the Pierce administration in particular, he accused the latter of appointing fire-eaters and abolitionists to office, attacked his opponent's voting record, and sought to take credit for the Homestead Bill by asserting that a Whig, Daniel Webster, had originated it.

Johnson made a spirited rejoinder. Drawing a parallel that was to earn him the scorn of his critics, he asserted that progressive democracy pursued the perfection of man's mental faculties just as religion sought to improve his moral nature, two agents of renovation traveling not in diverging, but in converging lines. Denying imputations that his amendments for more democratic elections could hurt the South, Johnson pointed out that fifteen slave states could easily block any unwanted change. He defended himself against insinuations that he had voted against a proposal to increase the pay of volunteer soldiers and attacked his opponent for the gerrymander that had caused him to seek the governorship. Finally, he again stressed his interest in the Homestead Bill. Every poor man ought to have a home, he declared.

It was not clear who came out ahead in the first debate. Confident of winning, the Eagle Orator thought that he had done very well. He conceded that his opponent was "a smart fellow," but thought the tailor had no chance because of his opposition to the distribution of public lands for internal improvements and common schools, as well as his insistence on constitutional amendments allowing direct elections.[6] As the future would show, however, Johnson had not been unsuccessful. His populist appeal was very effective.

A series of debates followed, usually along similar lines. Johnson continued to stress the importance of amending the Constitution. Frequently referring to his belief in homesteads for the common people, Johnson denied charges that he had always been opposed to internal improvements. And was not the "Henry-mander" as unnecessary as it was unfair?[7]

Henry and the Whigs attacked Johnson by taking issue with him on all these points. Making the most of his opponent's estrangement from the leaders of his own party, the Eagle Orator said that while the tailor statesman might not campaign as a good Democrat, he, Henry, was a true Whig. As for the "Henry-mander," did Johnson think he owned the First District? And he loved to bring up Johnson's proposal to change the ratio of representation, the three-fifths principle, in the state constitution. "Democrats," he pleaded, "don't you see that your nominee . . . is daily avowing and advocating principles, which, if fully carried out, must involve the subversion of our present form of government, the dismantling of the Union, and ultimately . . . both civil and servile war?" Always believing that he was ahead, Henry was more worried about his health and the heat than about the Democrats. "This canvass is enough to kill anybody," he complained to his wife.[8]

Brownlow gave whatever assistance he could. "Keep it Before the People," his paper warned in a detailed analysis of all Johnson's alleged misdeeds. The "Immortal Thirteen," the efforts to amend the Constitution, a reputed vote against aid for the "starving Irish," and the supposed opposition to increases of soldiers' pay during the Mexican War all showed, the parson admonished, that the public life of the Democratic candidate contained nothing but objectionable passages.[9]

The spirited campaign created tremendous excitement. People came from all parts of the state to listen to the contenders, take part in the rallies, and marvel at the amazing rise of the Greeneville tailor, "a man of fine sense, an able man," whose wife had taught him to read and write, as a Jackson citizen recorded in his diary. Johnson often reinforced this popular image by mentioning the story of Eliza's efforts to educate him.[10]

Billed as the "Mechanic Statesman," and rarely failing to express pride in his plebeian origins, the Democratic candidate made a special appeal to the laboring people of the state. His warmest sympathies were with them, he said. But they must have land. Were not those who had a home to defend the best patriots?[11]

Although the two candidates kept slashing at each other day after day, Henry thought Johnson behaved very well during the electioneering. They had agreed to treat each other as gentlemen and generally lived up to this promise. To be sure, at Memphis, toward the end of the campaign, when Johnson remarked that the Eagle Orator's talons had never yet been fleshed in him, Henry shot back with the reply that the national bird never touched carrion. But when, after two months of grueling debates, Henry asked to end the contest because his family was sick, the two candidates made a joint announcement that they would close the canvass at Knoxville on July 30.[12]

Less than two weeks later the Democrats were able to announce a "Great Victory." By a majority of 2,250, Johnson carried the state, significantly obtaining a majority only in Democratic Middle Tennessee. The unexpected Democratic success was due almost entirely to the tailor statesman's political finesse. His populist appeals, his wheeling and dealing, and his knowledge of his home section had succeeded in sufficiently increasing the Democratic vote in East Tennessee to capture the state. Apparently he made arrangements with the Whigs in Johnson City near Greeneville to vote for him in return for his support of Nathaniel G. Taylor, the local Whig candidate for Congress. The victory was even more remarkable in view of the fact that a large segment of the Democratic party remained opposed to the populist candidate, who, according to Samuel R. Anderson, the postmaster of Nashville, lost at least 4,000 votes because of this antagonism. "Johnson has gained a great triumph in Tennessee," Anderson explained to Nicholson. "He has beat Henry, the whig party as well as a large part of the leaders of the democratic party. The masses have done the work, the mechanic, the day laborer, have in this election, come to the rescue. You have no idea how cold and indif[f]erent *many* of the *big* men of our party, were towards Johnson."[13]

The Whigs' disappointment was acute. Hoping to the last that Henry would prevail—the first reports after the election seemed to confirm this expectation—they sought all kinds of explanations for their sudden defeat. Absolving Henry from all blame, Brownlow pointed out that his candidate had run ahead of other Whigs in seven out of ten districts, while Johnson trailed a large number of Democrats. Democratic gains in East Tennessee were responsible, he thought. Many Whigs there were distressed at their party's failure to recognize the section's claim to office. The parson also believed that there were some abolitionists in the area who had been alienated by Henry's attack on the proposal to scrap the three-fifths ratio of representation, an idea that also occurred to ex-governor William B. Campbell. "Johnson the arch demagogue has succeeded over Henry with a considerable majority," he wrote. "East Ten. has done the work, and Johnson's abolition notions, or his opinions on subjects connected with slavery have operated with the white population who have no slaves."[14]

Of course both Brownlow and Campbell were wrong about Johnson's stand on slavery. Johnson was glad that his victory had redeemed Tennessee from an unnatural alliance with such antislavery states as Massachusetts and Vermont, both generally Whig. Not until 1863 did he ever falter in his defense and support of the "peculiar institution," and if some nonslaveholders had voted for him because of their jealousy of their neighbors, they had mistaken their man. A slaveholder himself, the governor-elect was a firm defender of slavery.

Johnson was in no hurry to come to Nashville to assume his new duties but remained in Greeneville until after the legislature had assembled. There he consulted about what course of action to take with his friend Nicholson in Washington, to whom he admitted that he did not know exactly how to proceed. The failure of certain party leaders to support him had rankled; yet he was determined to write a thoroughly Democratic inaugural address. He arrived at the state capital just in time to be sworn in, on October 17, 1853.[15]

The inaugural was a remarkable affair. The governor-elect, described as a man "of about the middle height, well made, with a bright, intelligent eye, and a face in which firmness and sagacity are strongly combined," was in the prime of life, his jet-black hair untouched by any premature gray. He was staying at the Nashville Inn, where the Governor's Guard ceremoniously called for him. True to his Jeffersonian heritage, he refused outgoing governor Campbell's invitation to ride with him in his carriage and walked to McKendree Church, while the procession wound slowly through the streets. After Campbell had finished his short valedictory, Johnson was sworn in; then he delivered a speech that was long to be remembered, especially by his enemies.[16]

True to his decision to utilize the new office to give publicity to his Democratic Jeffersonian-Jacksonian opinions, he called upon the party to return to first principles, to "primitive republican simplicity and economy . . . within the ancient landmarks laid down by Jefferson and his patriotic associates." Stressing that he himself belonged to the progressive wing of the party, he insisted that man was capable of amending the Constitution to conform to modern conditions. As he had already elaborated in the campaign, he declared again that democracy was based on man's capacity for self-government. Democracy in the political sphere and Christianity in the moral proceeded in converging lines. Notwithstanding his earlier anti-clerical proposals, he was not irreligious. As he put it, "Democracy is a ladder, corresponding in politics, to the one spiritual which Jacob saw in his vision: one up which all, in proportion to their merit, may ascend."

Then he turned to more mundane matters. Condemning internal improvements at federal expense, Johnson counseled careful funding for improvements undertaken by the state. He restated his enthusiastic support of the Homestead Bill and public education, urged economy in keeping up the army and navy, and concluded by expressing his gratitude to the people. "They have so far never deserted me," he said, "and *God* being willing, I will never desert them."[17]

This "Jacob's Ladder" speech with its defiant assertion of radical democratic equality confirmed Johnson's opponents' low opinion of him. "I did not expect much from Gov. Johnson," wrote former governor David Campbell of Virginia to his nephew in Tennessee, "but his inauguration is below my expectations. It is the most contemptible public address I have ever read. I do not know how the religious community of his own party will receive it but no atheist could go farther in advocating man's perfectibility than he has done. It has more·the appearance of a French demagogue than an American citizen. The only difference is that a Frenchman who pretended to say anything at all, would express himself much better as to style." The Nashville *True Whig* called it a "melange of politico-theological speculation which . . . would confound all the wisdom and learning of all the commentators in Christendom." Even the London *Times* took notice of the speech: everyone knew that America "flogged" all creation, it sneered, while in Great Britain, "this benighted country, there is no such variety of methods of scaling the skies." Of course Democratic papers defended the governor, but the inaugural showed that he was not going to please the conservatives, be they Democrats or Whigs.[18]

The city that was to be Johnson's home for the next few years had changed considerably since he first arrived there in 1835. Pleasantly situated in the Cumberland Valley, it had become a busy capital of nearly thirty-two thousand inhabitants, spread out all over the hills and valleys for miles around. The steep elevation in the middle of the valley was now crowned by the new capitol, designed by William Strickland in Greek classical style, with an eighty-foot-high tower above the roof in the center. Boasting sixteen churches, three railroads, and some one hundred steamboats plying under the two great bridges spanning the Cumberland River, Nashville was an important trading center. If it was still a bit raw—the capitol would not be finished for several years—it nevertheless offered many amenities.[19]

From the very beginning of his term, Johnson knew that his power would be limited. The governors of Tennessee could not veto any laws, could do very little to enforce them, and had few prerogatives of appointment. With the exception of the chief military officers and a few selected civil servants, most top governmental officials were elected by the legislature. All the governor could do was to send in a biennial message outlining desirable legislation, pardon prisoners, and administer certain public institutions such as the penitentiary and the Bank of Tennessee. In addition, the Whigs had captured a majority of the legislature. They firmly controlled the House, and the senate was made up of thirteen Democrats and twelve Whigs.[20] But the office had one advantage. Its occupant was the first citizen of the state, a position that gave him considerable exposure and could be used as a springboard for higher honors. Governor Polk had gone on to become president of the United States, Governor Jones was even then in the Senate, and Governor Neill S. Brown had become minister to Russia. The lesson of their examples could not have been lost on Johnson.

The new governor immediately made use of his limited powers of appointment. The military staff caused few problems; Sam Milligan became inspector general, and three other supporters from different parts of the state were made adjutant, quartermaster general, and aide-de-camp.[21] The directors of the Bank of Tennessee were a different matter. Encountering difficulties in the confirmation of his choices, among them Cave Johnson, President Polk's postmaster general, he used his influence to induce the Whigs to endorse his appointees by withholding Democratic support from John Bell, the former Whig speaker of the federal House of Representatives and secretary of war who was then making a bid for reelection to the Senate. Because of factionalism among the Whigs, torn between the rival claims of not only Bell but also Thomas A. R. Nelson and the disappointed Gustavus A. Henry, the Democrats could delay the senatorial election until a deal had been struck. This was especially true of those in West Tennessee who, hoping for a rail terminal at Memphis, were inclined to support Bell anyway. In the end, Bell was reelected and Johnson's candidates confirmed.[22]

The third group of appointments, that of the prison inspectors, caused even more trouble. The administration of the penitentiary was important to Johnson, who had long inveighed against the practice of employing convicts in trades where they were competing with honest mechanics. He was especially anxious to control the appointment of the warden, an officer chosen by the Board of Inspectors. When in December he named three Nashville mechanics to the board, he hoped that they would select Richard White, a Democrat from Lincoln County with strong political backing, as warden. To his surprise, however, the inspectors chose Jesse Page of Davidson. After a stormy interview with Johnson—according to the Whig press, the governor said, "If Nashville and Davidson County don't like it they may go to Hell and be damned"—he asked the senate to reconsider its confirmation. Although the Whigs complained bitterly about "executive usurpation," the upper house complied, and Johnson appointed a new board, which, after some legal delay, duly chose White.[23]

On December 18, 1853, the governor, who had been delaying it, finally delivered his first biennial message. This time there were no philosophical flights. Presenting a sober, unpretentious view of the condition of the state, its indebtedness, its internal improvements, and its educational system, he made a number of recommendations for reform. Among these were several for which he had long been known, such as the endorsement of the federal Homestead Bill and amendments to the Constitution. He also proposed a simplification of the state's judicial system, the abolition of the Bank of Tennessee, and the establishment of an agency to safeguard the keeping of weights and measures.

Knowing that he had little power to influence the legislators, Johnson left specific measures up to them. For example, he expressed concern about the existing status of Tennessee's common school system, which, he maintained with some exaggeration, was the second worst in the country. To correct this evil, he suggested that taxes be raised either on a statewide basis or county by county. Both of these methods had their advocates; when a mixture of the two was finally enacted, the governor was able to take credit for it.

In the same way, Johnson skirted the controversial issue of internal improvements. Noting that the state constitution enjoined the General Assembly to encourage public works, he said that the type of projects to be undertaken must be determined by the legislature, which ought to see to it that the three grand divisions of the state were woven into a coherent whole. It was a formula leaving much leeway for the Jeffersonian chief executive. More specific recommendations included the condemnation of the existing system of mandatory work on the highways and a suggestion that taxes be levied instead. Finally, criticizing the penitentiary system, Johnson expressed the hope that laws would be passed to protect mechanics from competition with convicts. The message was well received, at least by the Democrats, and the Whigs were unable to renew their attacks on his philosophical vagaries.[24]

The governor, who had left his family in Greeneville, was alone in the capital. Living at the Nashville Inn, he soon made the acquaintance of some of the city's leading citizens, among them Mrs. Lizinka Campbell Brown, the daughter of the American minister to Russia during Monroe's administration. Lizinka, one of the most accomplished hostesses in Nashville, and Johnson became close friends until their relationship was interrupted during the Civil War, when she married Con-

federate general Richard S. Ewell. An old acquaintance from Greeneville, Hugh Douglas, also lived in Nashville, where he carried on a
prosperous business and frequently saw the governor. But even while he
hobnobbed with the rich, Johnson never forgot his populist principles.
In a gesture typical of the "Mechanic Statesman," he turned down
several sought-after invitations in order to take his first meal of the new
year with a party of rivermen at the house of a roustabout.[25]

Although the legislature failed to act on most of the governor's
proposals during his first term, it did give him some reasons for satisfaction. One was the passage, in February, of a school bill. Called by the
state's historian the "most important act for common schools . . . in
Tennessee before the Civil War," the bill levied taxes, both locally and
generally, that doubled the funds available for public schools. For Johnson, with his lifelong dedication to education, possibly because of his
own lack of formal schooling, the measure was particularly welcome.
Moreover, it was very popular in East Tennessee, while the other two
divisions were either cool or opposed to it. Another success was the
passage of a bill establishing the office of superintendent of weights and
measures. Johnson had recommended it and promptly appointed John
Heriges, sealer of weights and measures for Nashville, to the position.
Finally, the lawmakers set up an Agricultural Bureau, of which the
governor was a member and to which he could appoint eight other
members. The institution could hardly have been unwelcome to an
executive who had always favored farmers.[26]

During much of the time, Johnson was kept busy by the routines of
his office. Petitions for pardons had to be acted upon, extradition requests signed or answered, and various proclamations issued. In pardoning many more felons than his predecessor, Johnson revealed a tendency
to show mercy, a characteristic that was to become a great issue during
his presidency. The governor was also required to make certain payments to railroads upon the completion of particular lines, a duty that
was not always uncontroversial. For example, he disbursed certain
bonds to the Georgia and East Tennessee Railroad that his predecessor
had refused to issue. Because he was sick at the beginning of the new
year, it was not until three weeks later that he was able to send a message
to the legislature explaining his action. As he pointed out, the laws of
the state obliged him to make the payment upon completion of every
fifty miles of road—the attorney general, whom he had consulted, had
so ruled. The Whigs raised technical objections, but the governor had
his way.[27]

While carrying on these activities, Johnson never forgot the main
advantage of the governorship, the opportunity to advertise himself and

his opinions. How firmly he held these opinions and how gladly he seized occasions to voice them was made clear when he received a shovel made by hand by Judge William W. Pepper, a Springfield Whig who had once been a blacksmith and prided himself on his origins. Instead of answering Pepper at once, Johnson busied himself with sewing a broadcloth coat for his fellow mechanic, which he sent him during the summer. In the accompanying letter the governor stressed once again that he held "in utter disregard the sickly and false notion . . . that all persons who follow any of the industrial pursuits in life are thereby degraded and are not, for want of respectability, entitled . . . to fill any of the posts of honor and profit in the State and General Government." Insisting as always that the farmers and mechanics had aided "substantially to support all the other business pursuits of life," he concluded that agriculture and "mechanism" were in fact the foundation upon which all other interests must depend for support. It was Johnsonism pure and simple.[28]

When in March 1854 the legislative session ended, the governor, who had not seen his family since the previous fall, was anxious to go home to Greeneville. Delayed by the Georgia and East Tennessee Railroad's application for one quarter of its bonds, which had to be signed by the comptroller, who was temporarily out of town, he did not set out until late in April. He found the family in good health, dabbled in real estate, but had to return soon to the capital to attend to his official duties. Remaining in Nashville until September 2, he came back home again, this time to stay until the end of October, an absence for which he was criticized by the Whig press. The Democrats explained that he had gone home not to have a good time, but to plant some wheat, and that a member of his family was unwell, so he had to stay longer than anticipated. That this explanation satisfied his opponents is doubtful; the president of the Memphis and Charleston Railroad Company, who wanted more money from the state, was already complaining that the absent governor had not answered his last letter.[29]

Greeneville affairs were very much on Johnson's mind. His former seat in Congress had been filled by his old Democratic antagonist Brookins Campbell, because the Whigs had at first been so divided that they were unable to take advantage of the "Henry-mander." Then Campbell died and another contest took place, this time resulting in the election of Johnson's opponent Nathaniel G. Taylor, who defeated the governor's friend Sam Milligan. If these developments were of great interest to him, he was even more concerned about the efforts of his son-in-law to be, David T. Patterson, to obtain a judgeship in East Tennessee. Encouraged by Johnson's help, Patterson won the post in May. And even though Sam Milligan had lost his bid to succeed Campbell, the governor was able to secure for him the profitable agency for the Bank of Tennessee for the district. In addition, anxious to improve the educational system in his hometown, he urged Patterson to see that two female teachers from New England were hired for the schools.[30]

In the meantime, the question of the 1855 gubernatorial election was becoming acute. For the Democrats, the outlook did not seem too auspicious. As Johnson had foreseen, the Pierce administration had not proved a source of strength to the party. Its support of Senator Stephen A. Douglas in repealing the Missouri Compromise had aggravated the sectional struggle, but the breakup of the Whigs, which followed the passage of the Kansas-Nebraska Act, had not really destroyed the opposition in Tennessee. The rise of the Know Nothing order, with its intolerant attitude toward immigrants and Catholics, had become a convenient vehicle for the party of Henry Clay to use to renew the struggle under a different name. And the prohibition question had also made things difficult for the Democrats, who were generally opposed to sumptuary legislation.

These developments merely convinced the Democrats that their safest bet was to renominate Johnson, the strongest vote getter in the state, for governor. Calling for a second term for Johnson, the Nashville *Union and American* in January 1855 characterized him as a politician "that we may see only now and then, untarnished by vice and unswayed by personal prejudice." Other Democrats agreed.[31] But Johnson was not at all certain that he wanted to run. For one thing, he dreaded another campaign during the hot summer and thought conditions were anything but propitious. In addition, he was opposed to a convention, although he could not prevent the party from holding one. The situation became even more complicated when in February Meredith P. Gentry, a well-known Whig congressman and renowned orator, became the opposition candidate without a party convention, although a secret Know Nothing meeting did nominate him later on. A well-respected figure with many years of distinguished service in Nashville and Washington, Gentry was bound to become a powerful antagonist. True, he had deserted the party by refusing to support Winfield Scott, but so had many Southerners.[32]

In the end, Johnson allowed himself to be drafted. When the Democratic Convention met in March, it passed a number of resolutions endorsing the national administration and denouncing the Know Nothings. Renominating the governor for another term, the convention failed specifically to endorse his stewardship of the past two years. The conservative members of the party, especially the Nashville clique, who did not like his egalitarian notions, simply could not bring themselves to praise the tailor statesman, whom they disliked intensely. In his pointed acceptance, Johnson made it clear that he was especially pleased that his nomination emanated "from the true source of all political power, the people."[33]

Why, in view of the uncertain outlook for the party and the hostility of some Democratic leaders to him personally, Johnson chose to make the race is not certain. It is most likely that he sensed the publicity value of a second campaign and possible term of office. Still ambitious for higher office, he must have realized that at that time the only way to reach it was to seek reelection. As it turned out, the successful campaign and subsequent second term provided exactly the springboard he required.

Even before Johnson was nominated, the state's Temperance Convention appointed a committee to solicit the rival candidates' views on prohibition. In the previous campaign the issue had been excluded by mutual consent, but it could not be totally disregarded a second time. Gentry, who did not favor temperance, prevaricated by endorsing a local option plan; Johnson replied that he did not favor a law mandating temperance. As a good Jeffersonian, he could do no less.

In announcing the beginning of the campaign, Parson Brownlow predicted that "such a contest for interest, and excitement, has never come off in Tennessee." Whatever may be thought of his methods, in this particular he was correct. The campaign became memorable for the crowds it drew, the furious debates it engendered, and the astonishing victory of the Greeneville tailor, who was generally expected to lose.[34]

The first debate took place on May 1, 1855, at Murfreesboro. Before a crowd of between four and five thousand who had assembled in the Public Square, among them six hundred who had arrived in fifteen railroad cars from Nashville, Johnson delivered a slashing attack on his opponent. Gentry, he said, was true to Federalist and Whig doctrine. Had he not favored the federal assumption of state debts, had he not voted for a tax on tea and coffee, and had he not wanted to raise the salaries of federal officials? Then, turning to the election of 1852, he brought up Gentry's desertion of the Whig party and his promise to retire to his farm. Why was he now seeking office again? Reserving his most acerbic attacks for an assault on the Know Nothings, Johnson lambasted the bigoted order in no uncertain terms. Foreigners had helped win the War for Independence and contributed to the country's greatness. In any case, their right to vote was purely a state question with which the federal government had nothing to do. Above all, anti-Catholicism was contrary to the principles of religious freedom guaranteed by the Constitution. How could any sane man believe that the 1,400

Catholics in Tennessee could possibly menace over 756,000 Protestants? And was not San Marino, the world's oldest republic, a Catholic state? "The Devil, his Satanic Majesty," presided over a secret conclave held in "Pandemonium" to make war on all Christian churches, he said. By making war against one of them, the Know Nothings had become the allies of the Prince of Darkness.

Gentry's reply was a defense of his record and an attack on Johnson's unorthodox opinions. The governor was not even sustained by his own party, he pointed out. Denying that he was opposed to worthy foreigners, Gentry maintained that he merely did not want them to take over the government. But he was on the defensive, and the crowd sensed it. "Gov. Johnson opened in a masterly speech of two hours length. Col. Gentry commenced well but gagged and finally gave out. I was much disappointed in the Col.'s speech. He did not sustain his high reputation for talent and eloquence," commented the socially prominent Nashville lawyer Randal McGavock.[35]

The Murfreesboro debate set the stage for dozens to follow. At Pulaski, at Shelbyville, at Petersburg, at Clarksville, at Nashville, at Franklin, at Knoxville, from east to west, from north to south, the two candidates kept attacking each other. It was an exhausting experience for the participants, who again and again debated such issues as Know Nothingism, slavery, the Kansas-Nebraska Act, and each other's performance in office.

It was the question of intolerance that brought about the most merciless arguments, the governor becoming ever more violent in his denunciations. "Show me the dimensions of a Know Nothing and I will show you a huge reptile, upon whose neck the foot of every honest man ought to be placed," he declared at Manchester, and further characterized the order as an organization replete with secret oaths requiring its members "to carry a lie in their mouths."[36] The cause was a good one; the language, shocking to many citizens. But it was effective, especially in rural Tennessee.

The slavery issue became important early in the campaign. Once more citing Johnson's advocacy of the repeal of the three-fifths clause in the Tennessee constitution, the ever persistent Brownlow charged that the governor would be more fit to run in a Northern than a Southern state. Had he not defended his proposition by asking whether it was fair that the honest working men of East Tennessee were borne down by the slaveholders of the other two grand divisions so that their fair daughters and virtuous wives were weighed in the balance against the "Negro wenches" of the proud slaveholder? Johnson countered with allegations that Gentry had favored a free constitution for California, had not taken a clear stand on the Kansas-Nebraska Act, had opposed the veto power protecting the South, and would not have vetoed the Wilmot Proviso had he been president. While Gentry had voted together with abolitionists to keep New Mexico temporarily closed to slavery, he, Johnson, as he reminded his listeners at Clarksville, had "never cast a single vote upon any Southern question not up to the extremest standard of Southern rights."

When it came to his own record, Johnson vigorously defended his actions. When Gentry, who called him a "curse" on the soil of Tennessee, attacked him for using unappropriated funds to repair the penitentiary after a fire, especially since he had declared his opposition to the institution, he replied that he had no power to pass bills to improve the prison and had merely repaired it from funds available rather than call the legislature for an expensive special session. When Gentry accused him of abusing the pardoning power, the Democratic press denied the allegations, as it also refuted charges that the governor had his buggy repaired at the penitentiary or his horse shod and fed there. The party might not have endorsed the governor's administration, but it steadfastly defended his actions.[37]

By the end of July, when the campaign had shifted to East Tennessee, the strain of the incessant traveling and speaking was beginning to tell. Johnson was able to stand it better than his competitor, but he was no doubt relieved when Gentry, because of illness, asked him to end the campaign. Visiting the opposition candidate in his Knoxville hotel, the governor found him prostrated and acceded to his wishes. Although Nelson came from Jonesboro to take Gentry's place, and both he and Johnson continued to make a few addresses, the campaign was really over.[38]

When the election returns came in, it became obvious that the governor had achieved what many had believed to be impossible. Despite the bitter opposition within his own party, despite Gentry's undoubted ability, despite widespread anti-Catholic prejudice, he had once again carried off the victory, albeit by a diminished majority. And it was again Middle Tennessee that gave him a majority, the other divisions, including his own East Tennessee, favoring Gentry. The Know Nothing issue had probably caused some Whigs either to stay home or else to support Johnson. And notwithstanding charges that the foreign vote had elected the governor, it was easy to show that in fact the cities, where the small number of immigrants to Tennessee were concentrated, had generally gone for Gentry, while Johnson had carried many of the rural, wholly Protestant counties. He remained the farmers' and mechanics' candidate.[39]

The campaign had provided Johnson with an excellent opportunity again to advertise his opinions, and he continued to give expression to his philosophy during the victory celebrations that followed his success. Stopping off at Dalton, Georgia, while waiting for a connecting train to Nashville, Johnson delivered a speech in which he once more attacked the Know Nothings and traced their origins back to the Federalists who had passed the Alien and Sedition Acts. When he arrived in the state capital, friends escorted him to the Nashville Inn, where, before a crowd of two thousand hailing him as the next presidential candidate, he gave a repeat performance of the Dalton address. This speech almost led to a duel. When at one point Johnson said that the American party, as the Know Nothings called themselves, took secret oaths to support each other in political as well as social relations, Thomas T. Smiley, a prominent Whig lawyer, touched him on the arm and said in a low voice that it was not true. More belligerent than ever, Johnson replied, "If you deny the word *Social* you are a *Counterfit-Know Nothing* [sic] which is worse than a real one and I am responsible for what I say *privately* and *publicly.*" Smiley wrote him a note indicating that he resented the implication and was ready to fight. Fortunately, a duel was prevented by the intervention of Washington Barrow, another Whig politician, and Benjamin Cheatham, the future Confederate general whom Johnson would confront in the election of 1872.[40]

The victory celebrations continued. Johnson was feted at Gallatin, at Lincoln, at the State Fair in Nashville, and responded with his usual remarks. Brownlow was so incensed at the governor's victory speech in Knoxville that in front of the capitol he declared, "I . . . pronounce your Governor, here upon his own dunghill, an UNMITIGATED LIAR and CALUMNIATOR, and a VILLAINOUS COWARD." The parson's rage was understandable; his arch-enemy, as the Kentucky *Herald* reported, had not only "made a brilliant canvass," but, with heavy odds against him, had achieved reelection, "a thing which has been shown to be almost impossible" in Tennessee.[41] The only problem that marred the victory was the fact that the opposition had again carried the legislature. Thus Johnson's second term would largely be a repetition of the first, with the governor unable to accomplish much in the way of legislation, although he could still keep his name and opinions before the public.

Johnson's second biennial message on October 6 illustrated the similarity between the two terms and the use he made of his office. It hardly differed from the first; whole paragraphs, especially those dealing with a proposed tax on merchants, the upkeep of public highways, the reform of the judiciary and the penitentiary, the endorsement of constitutional amendments, and the Homestead Bill, were identical. The governor also suggested once again that the state dismantle the Bank of Tennessee, establish a uniform system of weights and measures, and further encourage the Bureau of Agriculture.

The second inauguration was not as sensational as the first. In a brief ceremony on October 22, the speakers of the two houses waited upon the governor at eleven o'clock and escorted him to the House of Representatives. After a prayer, Johnson delivered a short address, another invocation of the virtues of democracy contrasted with the evils of an enemy that came "as a thief in the night," and ended with his accustomed conclusion that the people had never deserted him and he would never·desert them. The whole proceeding took barely fifteen minutes.[42]

The lengthy session of the legislature that followed, however, was as unfavorable for the governor as the previous one had been. Blithely ignoring or voting down most of his suggestions, the lawmakers made few concessions to his wishes. They did pass a measure incorporating his long-standing proposals for a uniform system of weights and measures and pleased him by authorizing the acquisition of the Hermitage, Andrew Jackson's home, which was to be offered to the federal government as a branch of West Point. Otherwise they engaged in running controversies with Johnson, clashes made more heated by the resentment of many Know Nothing members who could not forget his denunciations of the order.[43]

The most bitter struggle again concerned the penitentiary. Two of the inspectors on the board had changed their party affiliation; Johnson, still anxious to protect his warden of choice, keeper Richard White, wanted to appoint successors more to his liking. But the senate turned down the three inspectors he proposed, whereupon he submitted another trio, which was also rejected, as was a third group of nominees. In the meantime, one of the previous inspectors resigned; the two remaining members appointed another keeper, whom Johnson refused to recognize. The result was that White retained his office, although he was sued by his competitor. The outraged senate appointed a select committee to investigate and summoned the governor to testify. He complied; in the end, however, the courts upheld Johnson's actions, although his victory did not lessen the Know Nothings' antagonism toward the man they now called the "tyrant" governor.[44]

Another controversy arose because of Johnson's failure in 1855 to issue a Thanksgiving Proclamation in time. Although he finally did proclaim the holiday, Parson Brownlow, as could be expected, once more accused him of atheism and suggested that, because the day had been set aside by a governor who did not really believe in the Christian religion, the proclamation ought to contain a prayer asking

God not to turn a deaf ear to the people's supplications.[45]

His duties kept Johnson in Nashville during the entire winter. The secretary of state, whose presence was required for all sorts of certifications, was frequently out of town, so the governor could not even come home for Christmas.

His enforced stay in the capital was especially annoying because his favorite daughter, Martha, was about to be married. The groom was none other than Johnson's good friend and political supporter Judge David T. Patterson, who had formally asked for her hand during the fall. Johnson gladly gave his blessings. "This is a question which has been left for her own determination," he wrote. "You have known each other long and well and now that the union has been agreed upon between you and her let it be consummated. It is not necessary for me to state to you the deep interest I feel in regard to the future of my little family and especially my oldest and favorite child—I do most devoutly hope that your union will be attended with all that will make you prosperous and happy." The wedding took place in Greeneville on December 13 without the father of the bride, who must have been especially vexed because he had also become a grandfather and undoubtedly wanted to see his new granddaughter, Lillie Stover, who was born in 1855.[46]

The routine tasks of his office—requests for extradition and pardons and the appointment of commissioners for various purposes—were still taking up much of the governor's time. One of the most troublesome of these duties was resolving a controversy with Georgia about the jurisdiction of the courts of Tennessee in cases affecting Georgia's state-owned railroad, which extended into the Volunteer State. After much correspondence Johnson duly appointed, first, ex-governor Aaron V. Brown and then James A. Whiteside, the "father of the railroad system in Tennessee," commissioners, and the controversy was finally settled.[47]

Another duty incumbent upon the governor was the execution of the 1854 law for the removal of emancipated slaves to Africa. Passed because of the increased fear of free blacks as the sectional controversy became ever more serious, the measure made the governor responsible for the transportation of freedmen. Accordingly, Johnson entered into negotiations with William McLain, the secretary of the American Colonization Society. A newly freed slave named Hector was to be sent to Liberia with his wife and children. McLain wrote that a ship would be ready to sail from Savannah in June, but Johnson, anxious for the freedman to earn some money to pay for the passage, asked if the matter could not be delayed for a while. In the end he made arrangements for the emancipated family to sail in December from Baltimore. He appointed his son Robert to take them as well as two other blacks to the port, and the younger Johnson succeeded in arranging for embarkation at Norfolk, which was much nearer. This unsavory business did not faze the governor. He was interested in the welfare of whites, not freed blacks.[48]

When the legislature finally adjourned, Johnson was anxious to go home for a visit to his family. But again he was delayed in the capital, and almost lost his life as well, when on April 13, 1856, a fire broke out at the Nashville Inn. Shortly before, in preparation for his trip home, he had withdrawn $1,200 from the bank and put the money under his pillow for safekeeping. Aroused by the commotion, Johnson left his room to see where the fire was, only to meet a lady who appealed to him for help. He escorted her to safety, but this gallant act made it impossible for him to return to his room to pick up his bank notes, all of which were burned.[49]

After the fire the governor, who had not been in Greeneville since the previous year, finally went home, eager to see his grandchild and his newly married daughter, to say nothing of his wife and small son. But in Greeneville he did not find everything to his liking. In February his mother had died. Moreover, son Charles had long been a source of worry—while preparing to become a pharmacist, he had developed a strong taste for alcohol, a matter of great concern to his father. Charles did possess a great deal of musical talent but failed to stick to any one profession and never married. His younger brother Robert also upset the family. He was pursuing a legal career but suffered from frequent pulmonary attacks, and Johnson was wondering whether the disease would not cut his career short. True, the Pattersons were doing well, and little Andrew, commonly called Frank, delighted his father, who loved to buy toys and boots for him to "keep him from burning his feet on the stove when his curiosity [sic] [took] him too far into things where he ha[d] no business." The family's difficulties did not make it any easier for the governor to be absent so often.

And the opposition immediately publicized the governor's absence from his office. "Where is Governor Johnson?" queried Brownlow, complaining that the chief executive was not at the capital and had not been there for weeks. Ironically, the article appeared when Johnson was already back in Nashville, where he arrived on May 24.[50]

There was one important difference between Johnson's first and second terms: the political outlook was more promising. 1856 was a presidential election year, and the governor was determined to make the most of it. Johnson at this time harbored a vague hope of the presidency, and in order to press his own claims at the forthcoming Democratic Convention in Cincinnati, he intended to use his influence to prevent the selection of delegates pledged to President Pierce. When in January the Tennessee Democrats met in Nashville, he made a brief speech once more defining his view of democracy and stressing its compatibility with slavery. However, while expressing the party's gratitude to him, the convention failed to endorse him. Nicholson and his friends were too firmly committed to the president.[51]

But the governor and his supporters did not give up. Local and county conventions continued to name him as a favorite son, and the Nashville *Union and American,* in an obvious bid for his nomination, published a favorable biographical sketch. His friends thought his chances were pretty good.

Although the reality turned out to be different, Johnson could still look forward to a more promising future. To be sure, he was hurt at Nicholson's failure to help him; nor did he hide his disappointment when the party finally nominated James Buchanan and John C. Breckinridge. Buchanan's record as a trimmer was hard to defend. It was also true that in spite of the fact that the Republican candidate, John C. Frémont, could hardly count on any support in Tennessee and that the opposition now supporting ex-president Fillmore was broken up by the collapse of the Whigs and the failure of the Know Nothings, Johnson thought the Democratic ticket would have a hard time in the state.[52] But if the party could finally carry Tennessee in a presidential election and he could have a part in the victory, it would greatly redound to his favor.

In need of new accommodations in the capital, Johnson moved into the Verandah Inn. His work was cut out for him: the presidential campaign was about to get under way, and if he wanted to utilize it to secure higher office, he would have to take an active part. But he was less than enthusiastic about doing so.

Buchanan, he thought, was the "slowest man" of all possible nominees; Breckinridge did not impress him much more favorably, and he was not well. Plagued by arthritis, he had temporarily lost the use of his forefinger. And that same season another fire swept the city. Although this time he did not lose any money, the conflagration threatened to engulf the offices of the newspaper most supportive of him, the *Union and American.* After the danger was over, an old man said to him, "The Union is saved and we will elect Buchanan next fall." Johnson himself was less confident.[53]

Nevertheless, the governor did not hesitate to take part in the campaign. In a three-hour speech at Nashville on July 15, he asserted that Millard Fillmore was a worse abolitionist than Frémont. Had he not answered an 1838 abolitionist query in the affirmative? In view of the approaching storm, the South must stand together. Fillmore had no chance; therefore it was incumbent upon Southerners to vote for Buchanan. Insisting that Southern institutions depended on the continuance of the Union, he counseled unity and the defeat of the bigoted Know Nothing candidate. According to the Democratic press, a greater speech had never been delivered in the state.[54]

Johnson spoke elsewhere as well—at Yellow Creek, at Christiana, at Chattanooga. Although he refused to attend a conference of Southern governors called by Governor Henry A. Wise of Virginia to meet in Raleigh, he even made a side trip to Huntsville, Alabama, and he combined campaigning with a visit to the family at Greeneville. In the end, his efforts paid off: he was able to take pride in a Democratic triumph, not only in the country at large, but also in Tennessee. It was a tremendous victory, for not since 1832 had the state voted for a Democratic president.[55]

But Johnson could see clouds on the horizon. As he understood only too well, the slavery issue had not really been solved; he feared that if Buchanan did not succeed in taking a firm hold, the election of a Republican candidate—he called the Northern party abolitionist—would result in the breakup of the Union. He himself had already declared his readiness to send arms to citizens threatened by slave insurrections, which were widely feared during the winter of 1856, and proved as good as his word by forwarding weapons to the citizens of Springfield. As before, he was firmly committed to the "peculiar institution."[56] Moreover, Johnson was not certain about his influence in Washington. After pleading with Nicholson to procure a diplomatic appointment for his friend Milligan, he finally had to go to the national capital himself to see what could be done—without much success, as it turned out.

Johnson was also uncertain about his own future. Was he going to seek a third term? Or had the time come to try for higher office? With the sweeping Democratic victory in 1856, it might be possible to elect a Democratic legislature and thus a Democratic senator the following year, and the governor did indeed want to try for the Senate. Explaining that the very fact of giving up a secure position increased the chances for another one, he finally decided not to seek reelection. "I would prefer changing positions and now is the time to do it," he wrote, suggesting that Isham G. Harris, his most likely successor, be induced to reconsider his negative attitude toward the Homestead Bill. Above all, the governor sought to influence the choice of candidates for the legislature, which would elect the next U.S. senator.

Johnson's family problems, however, were such that he wondered whether he should really try for political advancement. He was deeply concerned about his sons, about Robert's health and Charles' drinking.

Although in the following February he did receive more cheering news from home—Martha had given birth to a son, Andrew Johnson Patterson—the new grandfather's worries about his family did not cease.[57]

In the meantime, the governor continued to perform his official duties. In December 1856 he presided over the meeting of Tennessee's Democratic electors, who cast their votes for Buchanan and Breckinridge. Shortly afterward he received the gift of a bay gelding in recognition of his part in demolishing the Know Nothing party. Sent by a Williamson County farmer, a self-styled old Jacksonian, the present gave the governor not only pleasure but also another opportunity to avow his agrarian principles. Coming as it did from one of the community who "constituted the salt of society," he gladly accepted the horse, as he wrote to the donor. It was an agreeable interlude in an otherwise worrisome period.[58]

Johnson's indecision about the future did not last long. Determined to remain politically active, he set out for Washington early in 1857, where he not only hoped to obtain the long-coveted job for Milligan but also to carry out the Tennessee legislature's mandate to turn over the Hermitage to the federal government. In addition, he made up his mind to seek the return of the $552 still due to him as a congressman from the Gardiner investigation. Because all the other members of the congressional committee had accepted compensation, Johnson had come to the conclusion that it was morally right to do the same. In this endeavor he was successful; otherwise, the trip was a disappointment. Nothing came of the offer to put the Hermitage to use as a military academy, and Milligan did not obtain a diplomatic post. The governor was also dismayed to learn that the new president's cabinet included his Democratic opponent from Tennessee, former governor Aaron V. Brown, who became postmaster general.[59]

But if Johnson's stay in Washington was unsuccessful, his trip home was even worse. Traveling by way of Georgia, he was badly injured when his train ran off the track between Augusta and Atlanta. The cars fell down an embankment of sixty feet and were wrecked. Johnson's right arm was crushed near the elbow, an injury serious enough to force him to stop at Atlanta for treatment. He did not arrive in Nashville till February 3, greatly troubled by the slowly healing arm, which was to give him cause for concern for years to come.[60]

In the meantime, the gubernatorial campaign had begun. On January 1 Johnson had made clear his desire to retire, although his quest for a Senate seat was no secret. When the Democratic Convention met in April, it nominated Isham G. Harris for governor, while the opposition chose Robert Hatton, a Whig lawyer from Lebanon. The issue was not merely the election of a chief executive; as former governor Campbell explained to his uncle, "The great anxiety of the Whigs is to elect a majority of the Legislature so as to defeat Andrew Johnson for senator. Should the Democrats have the majority, he will certainly be their choice, and there is no man living to whom the Americans and Whigs have so much antipathy as Johnson." Some former Whigs did indeed enter the race for the legislature chiefly to defeat the governor's senatorial ambitions. They considered him a dire danger.[61]

Because of the importance of this campaign for his future, Johnson took great interest in it. Not that he was fond of Harris—he had never forgotten the candidate's opposition to his favorite measures in Congress. But Harris did not seem to engender much enthusiasm. As a result, the election of the legislature was put in doubt, and, as Johnson pointed out, "if we elect the Governor without the legislature it will be a barren victory and the last three battles fought in the state thrown away." In view of the fact that he had so important a stake in the outcome of the contest, Johnson consented to deliver a number of speeches. Active campaigning on his part might assist in the election of legislators friendly to himself.[62]

To underline his willingness to campaign in person, first the governor traveled to East Tennessee. "Democracy is making a more undying & unfair struggle here now than ever before," wrote a Greeneville opponent. "We attribute it to *Johnson's great* anxiety to go to the Senate of the US." Next the governor took advantage of an invitation to Shelby County to deliver a speech in Raleigh, near Memphis, in which he once again stressed his orthodox opinion about slavery. Asserting that the Negro slave in America was better off than he had been as a free man in Africa, he insisted that contact with the white race elevated the black, whom he characterized as "an inferior type of man, incapable of advancement in his native country." Thus, all charges against him arising from his proposals for representation based solely on the white electorate were false. Had he not always stood up to abolitionists and defended the interests of the state? Concluding with a renewed attack upon the Know Nothings, he connected that party with the abolitionists in the free states. No wonder his opponents took offense at his words. According to the Nashville *Union and American,* they were "writhing under his just exposures."[63]

Johnson's speeches once again proved effective. Undaunted by the ever-mounting attacks on himself, Johnson moved on to deliver another speech in Bolivar, where he fell ill. The contest was almost over, however, and the work had been done. When the election results were in, it became apparent that Harris had not only carried the state by a record majority but that the legislature, too, had been taken by the Democrats. Even East Tennessee had supported the victorious party.[64]

The victory was satisfying, but to win the Senate seat the governor still had to overcome the opposition of the conservatives within the party. To be sure, he had worked hard to secure a legislature favorable to him, going so far as to contribute to some members' campaign expenses, but the conservative Nashville clique would not give up. Instead of trying to appease his opponents, however, Johnson simply went about his business, apparently seeking to overwhelm them with his usual populist appeal. The opportunity for doing so offered itself when his third biennial message to the legislature fell due.[65]

This document, delivered on October 6, 1857, was a recapitulation pure and simple of Johnson's populist philosophy. First turning to the need for economy, he gave an account of the indebtedness of the state, while suggesting that the debt be reduced to the lowest limit consistent with the credit of Tennessee. More radical proposals followed. Not only did he once again recommend the abolition of the Bank of Tennessee, but he went so far as to advocate the end of all banks in the state, a currency based strictly on gold and silver, and the end of all paper money of less than $5. Again calling for a tax rather than labor service for the upkeep of public roads because this obligation fell mainly upon the poor, he praised the state Agricultural Bureau, suggested legal reform, and pleaded for funds for the Mechanics' Institute. The governor concluded with a patriotic reference to Andrew Jackson, proposing that the Hermitage, if rejected by the federal government, be used as a mansion for Tennessee's governors. He pleaded for a speedy completion of the new capitol as well. According to the Nashville *Union and American*, the message was one "of unprecedented importance."[66]

Two days later Johnson reaped his reward. Senator Jones' term having expired, the legislature elected the outgoing governor United States senator from Tennessee.[67] For Johnson, it was a tremendous victory. The penniless runaway of 1826 was now a member of the nation's upper house.

The opposition was appalled. Professing horror at seeing the tailor occupy the seat formerly held by prominent Tennesseeans, Brownlow cited the Richmond *Whig*, which characterized the senator-elect as "the vilest radical and most unscrupulous demagogue in the Union." Ex-governor Campbell complained bitterly that with the election of such men as Johnson, the state had fallen on strange times. The Nashville *Republican Banner* called him a "mobocrat." But there was no denying that the Greeneville tailor, by relying on his populist tactics, had overcome all opposition and won the confidence of the people.

And this was exactly what the Democratic press pointed out. The Nashville *Union and American* emphasized that the "Man of the People" was now recognized "as such alike by the masses . . . and by their representatives in the State Capitol." As he had "sowed the seeds" of the new Democratic majority in the state, he now justly reaped "the first fruits of that ascendency." His triumph could be compared with that of Andrew Jackson.

Johnson himself took the victory in stride. After responding briefly to a serenade on the evening of his election—a "Jacobinical harangue," according to the Whigs—he again managed to thank his constituents, first on October 12, in an impromptu speech at the opening of the Nashville Agricultural Fair, and then on November 3 in his valedictory at the inauguration of his successor. At the same time, he played an important role in the Democrats' selection of Nicholson as a second senator to take the place of Whig John Bell, whose term would not expire until 1859, but whose resignation the Democrats hoped to force. Then the former governor went home to Greeneville.[68]

How are we to evaluate Johnson's performance as governor? Although he is usually given credit for improving the state's educational system, he played only an indirect role in the reform. He did succeed in the establishment of a system of uniform weights and measures according to federal standards and conscientiously attended to the details of his office.[69] His greatest achievement, however, was the successful use of his position to advertise himself and his ideas, so that he was able to wrest control of the party from his conservative enemies while prostrating the opposition. It was a record of which he could be proud. A national career would be the result.

VII

UNITED STATES SENATOR

DURING Andrew Johnson's first years in the Senate, he was still anxious
to further the same causes he had advocated for so long: first, the passage
of a homestead law to secure land for the landless, and second, economy
in government, no matter what the cost. Both of these principles fitted
in well with his agrarian ideology, and their advocacy also helped him
to become nationally known. Given his ambition, it was not surprising
that he would attempt to translate this wider exposure into a quest for
the presidency. But his dream of higher office ran afoul of the all-
pervasive issue of slavery and sectionalism. As a Southerner espousing
homestead legislation, Johnson would soon find himself in a difficult
position. Senators from the slave-holding states were becoming almost
solidly opposed to the idea of free or virtually free land.

After his departure from the state capital, Johnson did not stay long
in Greeneville. Congress was to assemble on the first Monday in December, and the new senator was ready when Jesse D. Bright of Indiana, the
senior member present, administered the oath to the newcomers. Asa
Biggs of North Carolina presented Johnson's credentials; the Tennesseean took the oath and was assigned his seat.

The Senate still met in its old chamber, where open fires with four
grates beneath mantel shelves and two Franklin stoves near the main
entrance lent some comfort and homeyness. Each senator had his own
desk, equipped with a sandbox for blotting. Arranged in semicircles,
these desks were important to their frock-coated occupants, who had no

secretaries. The nearest telegraph office was blocks away at Pennsylvania Avenue and 6th Street, and the Capitol contained neither bathrooms nor a barbershop.[1]

Washington had changed since Johnson's first stay there in 1843. The city, now comprising some fifty thousand inhabitants, boasted a new patent office occupying two whole blocks, a post office extension in palatial style, and the neo-Gothic castle of the Smithsonian Institution, which Johnson had attacked so persistently. But the greatest change was taking place right at the Capitol, where two wings had been added, one for the Senate and the other for the House, both with spacious galleries for hundreds of spectators. The new additions were ready for occupancy in 1859, although the dome was yet unfinished, its enormous size and firm construction a veritable symbol of the developing country.[2]

Congress, too, had changed since Johnson first came to Washington. A number of committed antislavery leaders represented the new Republican party. Charles Sumner of Massachusetts, it is true, was temporarily absent because of health problems arising from Preston Brooks' attack upon him the previous year, but before Johnson's term was up, Sumner would return to employ his oratorical skills in attacks upon the institution he hated. His colleague Henry Wilson, a former cobbler, represented the Bay State, and such other antislavery stalwarts as "Bluff" Ben Wade of Ohio, a fearless radical, the wordy but earnest John P. Hale of New Hampshire, the famous William H. Seward of New York, and harsh Zachariah Chandler of Michigan frequently clashed with their Southern opponents. Lyman Trumbull of Illinois, William P. Fessenden of Maine, and James Harlan of Iowa had also joined the new Republican party, which found able antagonists in Jefferson Davis, the forceful statesman Robert Toombs of Georgia, Calhoun's disciples R. M. T. Hunter and James M. Mason of Virginia, and the outspoken James H. Hammond of South Carolina. These lawmakers were to be joined in 1859 by Republican James W. Grimes of Iowa and the fire-eating Louis T. Wigfall of Texas.

The House also contained a number of members who were to play important roles in the controversies surrounding Johnson. Thaddeus Stevens of Pennsylvania, club-footed, wig-bedecked, and sarcastic, even then had a reputation for radicalism and great parliamentary skill. Owen Lovejoy of Illinois had joined Joshua R. Giddings as one of the most outspoken foes of slavery; Galusha Grow of Pennsylvania was the main advocate of homesteads in the lower house, and in 1859 James M. Ashley of Ohio, fanatic and determined, entered the chamber to lend strength to the antislavery cause. In that same year, the Southern contingent was supplemented by such passionate speakers as the South

Carolinians Lawrence M. Keitt and Porcher Miles, as well as the eloquent Roger Pryor of Virginia. Johnson's friend George W. Jones still
represented his Tennessee district, while the senator's relations with his
colleague Nicholson, who was sworn in in 1859, remained outwardly
correct.[3]

The new senator took quarters in the small St. Charles Hotel at the
corner of Pennsylvania Avenue and 3d Street. Still alone, he was visited
by his wife only once, in 1860. He soon acquired the reputation of a hard
worker and student, whose opinions, once made up, were not easily
changed, and who did not associate intimately with his colleagues. Now
nearly fifty years old, with dark, piercing eyes, erect carriage, and fault-
lessly tailored clothes, he cut an impressive figure. And while his opponents tended to stress his lack of literary interests, in his years in Washington he even tried his hand at poetry.[4]

Johnson lost no time in pressing for his Homestead Bill. Rising in the
Senate on December 22, 1857, he asked and obtained leave to introduce
legislation granting to every head of a family a homestead of 160 acres
on condition of residence and cultivation for a specific period of time.
Characteristically, he was not satisfied with this simple parliamentary
announcement; he explained that the measure had been introduced as
early as 1846 in the House, which passed it in 1852, and expressed the
hope that the Senate would act upon it in a shorter period of time. But
although Johnson had considerable support for his proposition, especially in the North and West, he had great difficulty in inducing the
Senate to take it up.[5]

The main problem with Johnson's bill was its unpopularity in his own
South. Although the Dred Scott Decision in 1857 had given the sanction of the Supreme Court to the legality of slavery in the territories,
the rise of antislavery sentiment in the North and the outbreak of virtual
civil war in Kansas had created a climate of ever-deepening antagonism
between the sections. This clash was aggravated when in 1857 and 1858
President Buchanan endorsed the Lecompton Constitution, framed by
the proslavery settlers in Kansas. Because this document did not provide
for a free vote on slavery, Senator Stephen A. Douglas of Illinois, the
author of the Kansas-Nebraska Act, broke with the administration.
Southerners, more than ever convinced of the advantages of their "peculiar institution," became more and more agitated, and Senator Hammond of South Carolina went so far as to declare that cotton was king
and to assert that all society rested on a foundation of "mud-sills"
necessary to do the menial work. Consequently, homestead proposals,
fully supported by most Republicans, frightened many of Johnson's
fellow Southerners. They were still worried about the unsuitability of

160 acres of land for cultivation by slave labor, to say nothing of the measure's depleting effect on the Treasury, with consequent needs to raise the tariff. Senators Mason and Hunter of Virginia, Thomas L. Clingman of North Carolina, Wigfall of Texas, and Clement C. Clay of Alabama became the chief antagonists of Johnson's pet scheme.[6]

But the senator from Tennessee refused to give up. Attempting to mollify his Southern critics, on May 20 he delivered a long speech seeking to demonstrate the compatibility of his ideas with the existence of slavery. He had prepared thoroughly for this effort by borrowing, for example, Barthold Niebuhr's *Lectures on the History of Rome* from the library. Citing Moses, Vattel, Jefferson, Washington, and Jackson as progenitors of the homestead law, Johnson reiterated his conviction that the middle class, and especially the agricultural middle class, was the keystone of society. Referring to Niebuhr, he argued that Rome fell because of the decline of the middle class and insisted that those who believed the protection of private property was the main purpose of government ought to be his firmest supporters. Would not the donation of homesteads make property holders of the great masses of people, who would then have a real interest in the stability of the government? He also believed that the measure would reconcile North and South so that the North would finally recognize the usefulness of slavery. Again recurring to his old theme of the advantage of slavery for free labor, the Tennesseean stressed his interest in the welfare of the working classes. Moreover, he reminded the Senate that the Homestead Bill had been introduced and passed by the House long before the slavery question had become acute. Thus it had nothing to do with the Compromise of 1850, the Kansas-Nebraska Act, or the troubles in Kansas.

The speech failed to persuade Johnson's colleagues. By a vote of 30 to 22, the Tennesseean voting in the affirmative in order to be able to move for a reconsideration, they decided to postpone the subject until the next session. Subsequent efforts to reconsider were also unsuccessful. No matter how earnestly he sought to explain his role in originating the bill, no matter how convincingly he rejected the notion that William H. Seward, the famous antislavery senator from New York, had had anything to do with it, he would have to wait until a later day to try again.[7]

Local affairs took up much of the former governor's time during his first session in the Senate. Uneasy about the fact that his old opponent Aaron V. Brown was Buchanan's postmaster general, he was anxious to keep the Nashville clique from controlling the leading Democratic newspaper in the state capital, the Nashville *Union and American*. As its owner had sold part of his interests in the paper, Johnson sought to induce Milligan to take it over. The plan did not succeed, but although the sheet remained in friendly hands, the senator's fear of Brown's influence was justified. His Democratic enemies in Nashville continued to agitate against him. Unlike the populist senator, who headed the party's radical faction, they represented its opposing group of well-placed planters and their allies.[8]

The other Tennessee problem that took up some of his time was the effort to discredit his colleague John Bell. Bell, Tennessee's leading Whig, stood for everything Johnson disliked: government aid to industry, the growth of banks, and opposition to Andrew Jackson. Nicholson had already been chosen as his successor, although Bell's term was not yet up. When the state legislature passed resolutions instructing Tennessee's representatives in Congress to vote for the Lecompton Constitution, which Bell disliked, and deplored his failure to resign after opposing the Kansas-Nebraska Act, allegedly favored by the voters of the state, Bell was furious. An outspoken Southern moderate who had opposed both the Kansas-Nebraska Act and the Lecompton Constitution because of his interest in sectional harmony, he declared that he considered resolutions instructing him on how he should have voted four years earlier to be insulting. Denying that he had ever disregarded the will of the people of the state, he asserted that none of the elections since 1854 had turned upon the Kansas-Nebraska Act.

Anxious once more to establish his orthodoxy concerning slavery, Johnson immediately sought to contradict his colleague. Apparently, said Johnson, Bell had not always opposed popular sovereignty, the principle underlying the Kansas-Nebraska Act. Had he not voted for the repeal of the Missouri Compromise when he consented to the Compromise of 1850? Part of New Mexico lay north of 36°30', the line established in 1820 to divide slave from free territory. Consequently, Bell could hardly object to the same idea in Kansas. In any event, the principle of allowing the people of a territory to make decisions about their own institutions was just. It was the same doctrine the colonists had upheld in their struggle against the British crown.

Then Johnson turned to Bell's refusal to resign. Had not the senior senator said he would not stay in the Senate a single day if the people of Tennessee disapproved of his course? Well, they did, and he ought to quit. Recalling how, in election after election, Johnson himself had debated the Kansas-Nebraska Act from one end of the state to the other, he insisted that it was not true that the measure had not played a part in the several campaigns Bell mentioned. Though living in a part of the state that had few slaves, he for one had always supported the "peculiar institution." Bell could hardly say the same.

But Bell was not willing to be pilloried in this manner. Accusing his traducer of carrying "the torch of domestic discord from Johnson county in the east to Shelby county in the west," he pointed out that Johnson, who had introduced the reapportionment question as early as the early forties, had a devious record, while his own efforts at conservative adjustment were a matter of pride for him.

Of course, Johnson insisted on another rebuttal. Contrasting his constant defense of slavery with what he called the senior senator's equivocations, he professed pity for his colleague, who, he said, was now out of power. Although Bell was able to finish his term, Johnson had once more reached out to establish his credentials as a faithful spokesman, not only for the principle of popular instruction, but also for Southern rights.[9]

Matters of economy and other Jeffersonian notions took up the remainder of Johnson's time during his first Senate session. Opposing the enlistment of more regular troops to quelch Mormon resistance to federal authority in Utah, he pleaded for restraint in spending money for the armed forces. Temporary volunteers would be much better, he said, and argued that the genius of American government was inimical to standing armies. Although this stance was not unusual for a Southern senator, in the course of the debate he clashed with Senator Alfred Iverson of Georgia and took issue with the recommendations of Jefferson Davis, who had become chairman of the Armed Services Committee. Neither Iverson nor Davis forgot it. In addition, Johnson, declaring that the Mormons were not the only group practicing polygamy, pleaded for religious tolerance. Did not Congress spend money to receive representatives of the sultan of Turkey?

There were other typical pleas for economy. Johnson voted against a rivers and harbors bill, sought to deny funds for the entertainment of a visiting Turkish admiral, and even attempted to refuse to pay the clerk of the Committee on Claims for services rendered during a trip to Maine. He wanted the citizens of the District of Columbia to contribute at least one-half of the expenses of their police force and public schools, opposed the building of an aqueduct and other public works in Washington, and again suggested that the entire federal district be retroceded to Maryland.

Johnson's attitude toward expenditures for the District of Columbia was rooted in his firm belief in states' rights. Explaining that he viewed the question as a matter of state sovereignty, a concept he always defended, the senator denied the federal government's right to spend money raised in the states for the benefit of the people of the federal district. But he was consistent: having voted for the admission of Kansas under the proslavery Lecompton Constitution, he equally favored the entry of free Minnesota under its basic law. He also denied vigorously the right of the federal government to determine the suffrage requirements of the individual states. His Jeffersonianism was as pronounced in the Senate as it had been in the House, and if such committee chairmen as Davis, Brown, Iverson, Mason, and Hunter resented it, he did not care. No matter how firmly he believed in Southern solidarity, he considered basic principles more important.[10]

When the session ended in June 1858, Johnson did not go home directly. As his arm had never healed properly—it even had had to be broken again unsuccessfully—he traveled first to Philadelphia to see Dr. Samuel Gross, a renowned surgeon. But in spite of the doctor's efforts, the arm continued to give trouble.[11]

The trip home was much easier this time. In May the East Tennessee and Virginia Railroad had finally reached Greeneville, which celebrated the event with a fitting civic festival. Johnson was now able to take the train all the way home; en route, he could even stop at Carter's Station to visit Mary and her family, which now included her newly born second daughter, Sarah. In spite of his early opposition to railroads, he must have enjoyed the comfort they were bringing to formerly isolated East Tennessee.[12]

But even at home, political and financial questions were much on the senator's mind. Because of the Panic of 1857, financial problems had once more become of the utmost importance, and a meeting to define Democratic attitudes toward financial institutions was called to convene in September at Nashville, which Johnson attended. Bullionist and enemy of state banks as he was, he was only too glad to join his colleagues in declaring against the rechartering of existing banks, while favoring reforms mandating the conversion of bank funds into gold and silver and the eventual liquidation of the Bank of Tennessee. In addition, he expressed worries about the Democratic party's future. What should be the course of Tennessee Democrats in case of the nomination of Stephen A. Douglas for the presidency? After having castigated Bell for opposing the Lecompton Constitution, how in good conscience could they lend their aid to the Little Giant?[13]

In December Johnson, in hopes of promoting the Homestead Bill, returned to Washington. In the St. Charles Hotel, where he stayed once again, he made a favorable impression on one of his fellow boarders, the Republican senator from Maine, Hannibal Hamlin, whom years later the former tailor was to replace as vice president. "Andrew Johnson, the Senator from Ten. boards with us," Hamlin wrote home. "He is the man whom his wife taught to read and write. There is a wife for you." The inaccurate old story of Eliza's efforts was becoming legendary.[14]

As time went on, it became doubtful whether anything could really be done in Congress during the short session. The senator found Washington dull, more so than ever before, and believed nothing would happen because both parties were waiting to see what 1860 would bring. Busying himself with the concerns of his constituents, he was in no hurry to visit the White House, though he did see his old friend Lewis Cass, the secretary of state.[15]

Johnson's efforts in behalf of the Homestead Bill during the 1859 short session were to be in vain. After presenting more petitions in favor of the legislation, he gave notice that he would call it up at the proper time. Then, on February 1, the House passed its Homestead Bill, which the senator reported without amendments. Three weeks later, when Benjamin F. Wade of Ohio, an ardent radical Republican, moved to take the bill up, Johnson said he was willing to accept it, though he preferred the Senate version. Against strenuous Southern opposition, the motion passed. In the end, however, after some parliamentary maneuvering, Senator Hunter of Virginia again moved to postpone, this time with the result of a tie. Vice President Breckinridge thereupon used his casting vote to sustain the Virginian.

One week later Johnson's cause suffered another serious embarrassment. When, during a debate on a bill to buy Cuba, Republican James R. Doolittle of Wisconsin moved to lay aside the pending measure in order to take up the Homestead Bill, Robert Toombs of Georgia, furiously attacking the Republicans, charged them with cowardice. They were shivering in their boots at the mention of Cuba's name, he insisted, and accused them of promising land for the landless, mere lacklanders. But he received a stinging retort from Wade. "We are shivering in the wind, are we, sir, over your Cuba question?" he shouted. "You may have occasion to shiver on that question before we are through with it. . . . The question will be, shall we give niggers to the niggerless or land to the landless?" With such support, it was not surprising that Johnson could not make much progress during the short session. However, he was determined to try again under more favorable circumstances.[16]

In other respects, Johnson continued to pursue his Jeffersonian crusade for economy. Early in January, just after ceremonies marking the solemn transfer of the Senate from the old to the new chamber, an extravagance of which he no doubt disapproved, he took advantage of a recommendation for retrenchment in the president's annual message to declare that he had been trying to bring about such a reduction of expenditures ever since he had first entered Congress. He had never been successful, but now that the president himself was on his side, he thought a committee, and more particularly the Committee on Finance, ought to undertake a study of how to bring it about. R. M. T. Hunter, the committee's chairman, insisted that the task would overwhelm his group. Johnson, however, convinced that Hunter's committee was exactly the right one to undertake the study, insisted. Eventually, the Senate appointed a special committee and offered Johnson the chairmanship, which he refused. He was still convinced that only the Committee on Finance could accomplish anything.[17]

The failure of his effort did not deter the senator from continuing his advocacy of retrenchment and other Jeffersonian principles. When a bill to build a transcontinental railroad was under consideration, he attacked it as unconstitutional as well as wasteful, much to the annoyance of Jefferson Davis, one of the measure's proponents. It would create a permanent debt, Johnson asserted, the very burden against which Thomas Jefferson had warned long ago. At the same time, once more differing with Davis, he again emphasized his preference for the direct election of presidents. Whether appropriations concerned the army, the navy, or waterways, Johnson questioned them all. He even favored the abolition of the congressional franking privilege and sought to reduce the sums appropriated for the furnishing of the committee rooms of the new wings of the Capitol. On this subject, he clashed again with Jefferson Davis, who told him he would not like Johnson to select the furniture to be bought. The Tennesseean had a reputation for being aloof; as Davis later reminisced, because of his "intense, almost morbidly sensitive" pride, the Tennesseean's "position with his Southern associates had never been pleasant." He considered them much too aristocratic. They were probably not surprised when in the last days of the session he renewed his demand for a committee to investigate expenditures.[18]

Anxious to get away from Washington and to go home, after attending the special session of the Senate in March, he did come back as one of the official representatives of Congress to accompany the body of the recently deceased postmaster general. Worried about Charles' mounting drinking problems and Robert's intention to run for the state legislature, he apparently left the train at Greeneville instead of going on to Nashville with the rest of the group.[19]

When he reached home, he found the family well. Martha was expecting another child; Robert was contending for a seat in the legislature as the representative of Greene, Hawkins, Jefferson, and Hancock counties, and even Charles had temporarily stopped drinking. Johnson's enemies were trying hard to defeat his son, but they met their match in the father, who seems to have spared no effort to elect Robert.[20]

At the same time, the senator himself was called upon to assist the Democrats in their congressional struggle. Although he had tried to sidetrack his old opponent Landon C. Haynes—"Delenda est Carthago," he commented about Haynes' candidacy—his adversary was nominated, and Johnson had to deliver a speech at Greeneville supporting him. He had fought Haynes in the past, he said, but he was now ready to campaign for him. Repeating the effort at Bristol, he reiterated the firmness of his devotion to the cause of the South and to the protection of slavery. In the end, although Haynes lost to Thomas A. R. Nelson, Robert was elected. Brownlow was convinced that this result was the outcome of a deal between Johnson and Nelson, a distinct possibility in view of the senator's dislike for the Democratic candidate. Johnson rarely forgave his opponents; although Governor Harris was seeking reelection, the senator did not campaign for him.[21]

During a great part of the 1859 recess, Johnson remained at home, enjoying his position as Tennessee's elder statesman. He took great care that prints with his likeness were made available to the general public. While still in Washington, he had furnished several photos to Charles H. Brainard, a well-known publisher, from which to make a suitable print. Although the result earned a favorable review in the Boston *Transcript,* which commented that the senator's "frank and open countenance" bespoke "an honesty of purpose somewhat rare amongst the politicians of the present day," he did not like the result. Thinking the face too smooth and youthful, he protested against the placement of his right hand, which, he said, was "extended some distance from the body and resting on nothing." But he obviously did not mind the publicity.[22]

Johnson continued to buy and sell property, especially real estate, and in doing so managed to acquire a considerable fortune. "There is no use in buying property unless there is a bargain [in] it," he wrote to Robert, who, along with his brother Charles, did much of the buying and selling for him. Whatever he might say about the common people, he was a firm believer in the profit system and always resented being called an agrarian. But then he had in mind the older definition of the word, implying a redistribution of land.[23]

Even at home, Johnson continued to be deeply involved in his other great expertise, politics. First he helped Robert in his quest for office; then when his son was elected to the state legislature, he gave him advice. Citing Jefferson as an example, he urged Robert to favor hard money and low interest rates, and to oppose the recharter of banks. Finally, as the conclusive sign of his political ambition, he let it be known that he was a candidate for the forthcoming presidential election.[24]

When Johnson arrived back in Washington in December, the city was in an uproar. John Brown's raid upon Harpers Ferry had given a boost to Southern extremists who charged that the old abolitionist represented the sentiment of the Northern people and of the Republican party.[25] Anxious to put himself right with his Southern colleagues, Johnson, who needed support for his Homestead Bill, to say nothing of his quest for the presidency, decided to deliver a strong speech on the subject of Harpers Ferry and the "peculiar institution."

The occasion for the address was James M. Mason's resolution to appoint a committee to investigate the incident. Taking issue with Lyman Trumbull of Illinois, who had introduced a parallel resolution for the investigation of an 1855 raid upon a federal arsenal in Missouri, the senator from Tennessee asserted that the famous phrase in the Declaration of Independence proclaiming that all men were created equal could not apply to Negroes. Was not Thomas Jefferson himself a slaveholder? And did not the constitution of Illinois, which contained the same phrase, deny the vote to blacks? Stressing his conviction that God himself had created the differences between the races, Johnson bitterly denounced Northern attempts to outlaw an institution vital to the well-being of the South. As for himself, he stood by the Union; if anyone endangered it, it was the North, which had been attacking it ever since the days of John Adams. All the South wanted was the Constitution as it was, with all its guarantees intact. Johnson cited statistics substantiating his familiar assertion that slavery, far from being hostile to free labor, tended to boost white workers' wages. And as for John Brown, who had just been executed, he was a sanguinary assassin, red with blood, who had butchered proslavery settlers at Pottawatomie without mercy. The speech was well received; some of his constituents thought it the best ever delivered on the subject of slavery and urged its wide distribution.[26]

Johnson's real purpose during the first session of the Thirty-sixth Congress, however, was to persuade his colleagues finally to pass the Homestead Bill. As the measure was becoming increasingly politicized, most Southerners opposing and most Republicans ardently championing it, he could sense trouble ahead unless he established his Southern credentials to appease Southern senators. To some extent, the Harpers Ferry speech may be considered such an attempt. But he would have to make much greater efforts to induce his fellow Southern senators to support him.

Johnson introduced his bill on December 20, 1859. Although disappointed in the makeup of the Committee on Public Lands, which he believed was stacked against the measure (especially since his namesake Robert W. Johnson of Arkansas, a lukewarm supporter, was the chairman), he persisted in his efforts at persuasion. When the House again passed homestead legislation of its own, on March 22, Johnson reported the House bill to the Senate with the recommendation that his own Senate version be substituted. Ben Wade, however, insisted on the House measure, though Johnson warned him that it could not pass. The House bill was too liberal, and Johnson was pragmatic enough to seek maximum support for the reform he had championed for so long. He regretted the way the issue had become politicized since he had first introduced it in the House, and he expressed his continued hope for passage of the Senate bill. He was viciously attacked by Louis T. Wigfall of Texas, a fire-eater who denied the right of the federal government to give away public lands he insisted belonged to the states. But despite the fact that it was finally postponed again, the measure continued to enjoy wide support.[27]

In the weeks that followed, Johnson, although he always asserted that he did not believe in compromises, proved once more his mettle as a politician. Compromise was necessary because Southerners had been attacking ever more forcibly the whole idea of free land for the landless. James S. Green of Missouri asserted that the Homestead Bill would discourage industry, enterprise, and energy, notions Johnson vigorously attempted to refute. Wigfall continued his assaults, and Thomas M. Clingman insisted upon an amendment authorizing land warrants to benefit settlers in the older states. All these objections, the obvious Republican eagerness to pass the bill, and intimations that the president might veto it alerted Johnson to the necessity of compromise, and on April 11, 1860, he reported a series of amendments for the consideration of the Senate. The amendments provided that only heads of families could apply for homesteads and required settlers to pay twelve cents per acre. In case of irregularity, the land was to revert to the government, and preemptors were to have two additional years to pay the fees for the land they occupied. Substantially a sugarcoating, these changes included many of the demands of Southern critics.

Johnson defended the new version of the bill in an impassioned speech. Again deploring the sectional nature of the controversy, he said that if the Ten Commandments were to come up for consideration, somebody would find a Negro in them somewhere and the slavery question would be raised. In any case, he pointed out, Southerners had supported homestead legislation from the earliest days of the republic.[28]

But his concessions were not far-reaching enough to ensure passage, and on April 17 the senator came up with an entirely different set of amendments, in effect a new bill, which had been perfected in the Committee on Public Lands in lieu of both previous House and Senate versions. Again the bill provided that only heads of families were eligible, was applicable only to lands subject to private, not public, entry, and required homesteaders to pay twenty-five cents per acre for their land. At the end of a period of years, if the lands were still unsold, they would be given to the states. In addition, aliens who had taken out their first papers were to be eligible for ownership.[29]

In the ensuing debates Johnson stuck to his bill, defending it against efforts by John J. Crittenden of Kentucky to deny its privileges to future immigrants, whom Johnson called one of the great assets of the country's rising strength. He also countered Republican accusations that it was no longer a real homestead measure. Far from offering worthless lands, he insisted, the measure gave settlers the right to enter choice bottoms, applied equally to all, and ought to be passed. His pleading and compromising proved effective. Overcoming most open opposition, on May 10 the Tennesseean had the satisfaction of seeing the Senate accept the bill by a vote of 44 to 8. For the man who had been striving for a homestead bill ever since 1846, it was a great victory.[30]

But the struggle was not over. Because the House repeatedly disagreed with the bill's provisions, it took three conference committees finally to iron out all remaining differences. Anxious to retain provisions necessary to reconcile the South to the measure, Johnson himself was responsible for various renewed compromises. He saw to it that only heads of families, not all males over twenty-one, remained eligible. In return, he permitted the House to make the bill applicable to one-half of the lands not yet surveyed. The representatives had demanded the inclusion of all of these lands, while the Senate had favored a restriction to surveyed lands only. In return for retention of the final section concerning the eventual reversion of land to the states, the senator assented to a House request to drop a provision for marketability within two years. Finally, on June 19, the Senate accepted the compromises with only two votes in opposition. All that remained was the president's assent, and Johnson hoped that the compromises might win it.[31]

Buchanan, however, was not to be swayed. Convinced of the necessity of appeasing the South, he vetoed the measure on June 22. He argued that the bill illegally gave away public property, was unfair to previous settlers as well as to the older states, and discriminated in favor of one class, the farmers. In vain did Johnson urge the Senate to override, in vain did he point out that the president was obviously opposed to any sort of homestead bill, in vain did he defend the provisions concerning foreigners, which Buchanan had also criticized. The Senate was able to muster only 28 of 36 votes to override, 3 short of the necessary two-thirds; Johnson also voted nay so that he could call for a reconsideration. In spite of his pleas to senators to stand firm, virtually all Southerners voted in the negative. For the Southern father of the Homestead Bill, it was an embarrassing situation.[32]

His preoccupation with the Homestead Bill did not keep Johnson from pursuing other causes, however. Still considering himself the people's tribune against unnecessary spending, he voted against the granting of various pensions, the erection of a statue to George Washington, the improvement of the St. Clair Flats, and appropriations for the observation of an eclipse of the sun. But he did favor improvements in the Tennessee River and money for furnishing the new wings of the Capitol, all concessions to political and practical realities, which, when necessary, he was perfectly capable of making.[33]

And Johnson was anxious not to be separated from his Southern associates. In March 1860 he saw a report of a speech Senator Daniel Clark of New Hampshire had made at Dover, in which Clark compared the lack of "energy" of slave Tennessee with the enterprise of free New England. In addition, he asserted that the South could not dissolve the Union. Johnson, he said, had told him that during the disturbances of 1856 the planters were ready to join with others to drive all slaves out of the state. Outraged, Johnson rose to give a spirited reply. Defending Tennessee against what he considered an unwarranted onslaught and comparing his adopted state favorably with New Hampshire, he denied ever having made the remarks concerning slavery. All he had said, he insisted, was that in 1856 he had observed that if an effort was ever made to abolish slavery, the nonslaveholders would unite with the planters to "reduce the negro to subjection," and, if necessary, "join the master in extirpating . . . this race from existence, rather than see them liberated and turned loose upon the country."[34]

Johnson's efforts to build bridges were imperative. Other than the Homestead Bill, his chief problem during the winter of 1859–60 was the coming presidential election and the sectional question so closely connected with it. His ambition left him no peace; he had had his eyes on the presidency ever since 1852 and thought that in 1860 he might really have a chance. After all, he was a moderate Southerner, firm on slavery, and known for his advocacy of the Homestead Bill. Thus he could count on both Northern and Southern support. True, the front-runner for the Democratic nomination was Douglas, but his stand on popular sovereignty had made him unpopular in the South. Therefore, when Harvey Phillips, the editor of the Chattanooga *Advertiser*, asked Johnson about his intentions, the senator replied that he was not seeking higher office but intimated that he was not averse to its seeking him. The *Advertiser* took the hint and boosted Johnson.[35] Other papers followed suit, and although there was also some talk of a vice presidential candidacy, the senator kept his sights high. As the Greeneville *Democrat* pointed out, Johnson's chances for the nomination seemed at least as good as those of Douglas.[36]

The first step in securing the nomination was the endorsement of the Democratic Convention in Tennessee. When his son Robert asked him if it was true that he had told Nicholson that he was not a candidate, Johnson wrote a furious denial of the rumor. Knowing full well that a powerful faction of the party was opposed to him, the senator needed influential support to counter his antagonists. Robert, well posted because of his service in the legislature, kept his father informed about goings on in Nashville; Milligan and Lowry took care of things in Greeneville, and Harvey M. Watterson and Washington C. Whitthorne, a Columbia politician, became active on Johnson's behalf at the convention. Their efforts proved successful: when the convention met in January 1860, it endorsed the senator as its favorite son. Neither Governor Harris nor the conservative Nashville clique were pleased with this development, but they were unable to prevent it.[37]

Johnson was serious about his candidacy, although he was beset by doubts about its feasibility and the future of the party. Knowing that the Democrats would face serious trouble that year, he deplored the resolutions for the passage of a federal slave code for the territories introduced in Congress by Jefferson Davis and Albert G. Brown of Mississippi. "For my own part I can see no good that is to Come out of them at this time, except divission and distruction of the democratice party," he wrote in his peculiar spelling to his friend George W. Jones, and he was right. The Republicans would be the beneficiaries of their opponents' troubles, and as a Southerner, he could not contemplate this development with equanimity.[38]

But Johnson continued to seek support. Though at times despairing of his chances and even considering the acceptance of the vice presidency on a Douglas ticket, he doubted that the Little Giant could ever be nominated or elected. Once this inability became evident, Douglas' delegates might switch to him as a compromise candidate. Sam Milligan, who believed this strategy to be feasible, began to prepare a collection of the senator's speeches, and newspaper after newspaper in various parts of the country came out for the Tennesseean. A medium even announced that she had contacted John Brown in hell, and he had prophesied that Johnson would be nominated. Nevertheless, friends warned him that the Tennessee delegation to Charleston, where the Democratic National Convention was to be held, was not reliable.[39] And as Johnson was too busy with the Homestead Bill in Washington to direct his own campaign, his chances at Charleston were greatly diminished.

The senator's interests at the convention were in the hands of Robert, Milligan, and Whitthorne, who tried to keep the Tennessee delegation firm. This was no easy matter, for Harris had been opposed to the senator, while others were also not to be trusted. Nor did Johnson know exactly what to do. Before the convention even met, he had become convinced that Douglas would be nominated, and wrote to tell his son to try for second place. "If Tenn is not now first She can be Second and first next time without doubt," he predicted. Perhaps he might win the prize in 1864.

The convention met amid great excitement. Would the Democratic party hold together? And would the Union survive a split in the last remaining major nationwide institution? The crowds, influenced by Charleston's rabble-rousing element, favored the extremists, a situation boding ill for the convention, the party, and the country.

Determining to adopt a platform first, the delegates opted for a minority plank that favored Douglas' version of popular sovereignty instead of following the majority's call for a federal slave code for the territories. Thereupon the Gulf states, urged on by the fire-eater William L. Yancey, walked out. The remaining Southern states then saw to it that two-thirds of the whole convention would be necessary for a nomination, so that, when the balloting started, Douglas, though receiving a majority, could not secure the prize. His delegation, embittered and determined, voted for him fifty-five times and refused to switch.

Thus Johnson's plans of emerging as a compromise candidate, or of joining a successful Douglas ticket, were thwarted. To be sure, the Tennessee delegation, all but two of whom were opposed to the Little Giant, voted thirty-five times for its favorite son. Then it was alienated by rumors, some planted by the Douglas faction, that the senator might accept second place on the Little Giant's ticket. After voting for Johnson one more time, they abandoned the cause. "We have withdrawn you," former Memphis postmaster William H. Carroll, who favored Douglas, telegraphed to the senator. "Douglas has majority ought we support him[?]" Johnson refused to commit himself, and almost the entire delegation cast its votes for James Guthrie of Kentucky, another possible compromise candidate, although Milligan still hoped to renew the Tennesseean's claims at a later time. Unable to make a choice, the convention finally adjourned to meet again in June in Baltimore, where there would still be a chance of change of fortune.[40]

During all this time Johnson, busy with his Homestead Bill, remained in Washington. Uneasy as he was about the situation, he was cheered by the arrival of his wife and little Frank, together with Robert, who came from Charleston to report to his father in person.[41] Johnson's family had been very much on his mind. He was proud of Robert, to whom he gave advice about events in the state legislature, and could take pleasure in the fact that his son was building a good reputation in Nashville. Upon the completion of the Louisville and Nashville Railroad, Robert took part in a legislative junket to the Kentucky metropolis and from there traveled to Ohio, where he delivered speeches and seemed well liked. He was even contemplating marriage, although in the long run nothing came of his nuptial plans. The family was growing: Martha had given birth to another baby, this time a daughter, whom she called Mary Bell, and Mary was also expecting again. Only Charles was still a problem because of his alcoholism. But he was not incapable. The co-proprietor of a drugstore in Greeneville, he bought and sold stocks and property for his father and helped his brother take care of the senator's financial interests.[42]

But the presidential question continued to occupy Johnson. Various correspondents, among them Milligan, still thought the senator had a chance. Yet there were also suggestions that Douglas, with Johnson as his running mate, was the only man who could possibly defeat Abraham Lincoln, who had been nominated by the Republicans at Chicago. The aspirant from Tennessee was perplexed.[43]

When the Democratic Convention reassembled in Baltimore in June, it became evident that the split that had rent it in Charleston could not be healed. Divided again, this time about the problem of seating Douglas or anti-Douglas delegates, the rival factions met in separate halls. Johnson, finally discouraged, instructed Milligan to withdraw his name. In the end, the moderates nominated Douglas, while the seceders, supported by the administration and calling themselves National Democrats, chose Vice President Breckinridge and Joseph Lane of Oregon. The two platforms mirrored the original division at Charleston, Douglas favoring his brand of popular sovereignty and Breckinridge, a federal slave code for the territories.[44]

Johnson was very perturbed about these developments. Coinciding as they did with the veto of the Homestead Bill, they left him in a quandary. At first there were rumors that he was going to support Douglas—in view of Buchanan's veto, not an unreasonable assumption. In the end, however, he threw in his lot with the seceders and backed Breckinridge. Mainly concerned with the preservation of the party and the Union, he was still hoping for a last-minute coalition of the feuding Democratic factions. But since the great majority of the Tennessee delegation at Baltimore had joined the Breckinridge movement, and Douglas had no chance of carrying the state against Johnson's old enemy John Bell, who was running on an independent Constitutional Union ticket, the senator thought he had no choice but to support the vice president, albeit without much enthusiasm. Feeling unwell both physically and emotionally, he returned home dispirited and with gloomy forebodings about the future. Nevertheless, on July 31 he was one of the speakers at the Greeneville Breckinridge and Lane ratification meeting.[45]

The senator's depression was easy to explain. He believed he had missed his chance for higher office because of the precipitate action of William L. Yancey's followers in walking out of the convention at Charleston, and he was sure that the split in the party at Baltimore was even worse. After all, in the latter convention the initial cause of the division had not even been a principle but merely the question of whether to seat Douglas or anti-Douglas delegates. All this seemed to prove to him his long-held conviction that conventions had outlived their usefulness. As for the doctrinal differences between Breckinridge and Douglas, he tended to minimize them. In his vocabulary, "popular sovereignty" meant the right of the people in a territory to write their own constitution after the territorial stage, in preparation for statehood. The Northern version of popular sovereignty, the right of the inhabitants of a territory to outlaw slavery, he called "squatter sovereignty" and believed unconstitutional. Because both Douglas and Breckinridge had made it clear that they were going to abide by the Constitution and particularly the Dred Scott Decision, however, the senator saw no reason why they could not cooperate. Anxious to save the Union by defeating Lincoln, he was equally intent on saving the Democratic party in Tennessee as well as in the country by beating Bell.[46]

The campaign was no pleasure for Johnson. Like his friend Jones, who predicted Lincoln's election and the coming of disunion and civil war, he doubtless would have liked to sit out the contest. However, as party leaders implored him to take part in the struggle, he delivered a number of speeches for Breckinridge in Nashville, Winchester, Springville, Fayetteville, Memphis, and elsewhere, although he also encouraged a movement of union with the Douglas party as proposed by his Greeneville acquaintance James Britton. In all his addresses the senator stressed his dislike of the convention system, which had now proved its failure, the necessity of fighting the opposition rather than other Democrats, and the importance of saving the party and country. He was annoyed at Yancey's appearance in Knoxville, where the fire-eater from Alabama made slurring remarks about working women. He was briefly encouraged by a renewed movement for his nomination, but in the long run, he did not have much confidence in the outcome of the election.[47]

His forebodings proved correct. Tennessee went for Bell, Lincoln won the election, and although secession had not been an election issue, in Tennessee or elsewhere, the crisis of the Union was at hand.[48] Johnson would have to make the most difficult choice of his life.

VIII

UNCONDITIONAL UNIONIST

THE ELECTION of 1860 and the success of the Republican ticket was a disaster for Southern Unionists. With South Carolina preparing to secede and other states ready to follow suit, upholders of the government were faced with the collapse of all they held dear—the Union, their ideals, and often their livelihood. Hoping against hope, they naturally sought to avert the drift toward disaster and continued to work for a last-minute compromise.

What was true for Southern Unionists in general was even more true for Andrew Johnson. The ordeal of the Union was a real crisis for him, not merely because he was genuinely devoted to its preservation—Andrew Jackson was his model—but also because his position at home was becoming increasingly difficult. Like other states in the upper South, Tennessee was still hoping for an adjustment. The majority of the population favored the Union, but as in other slave states, this loyalty was often conditional. Only in the eastern part of the state was there a large number of unconditional Unionists; in the other two divisions, the states' rights element had considerable strength. In addition, the Unionists, especially the unconditional ones, tended to be former Whigs, while their opponents were generally Democrats.[1] For the leading Democrat in Tennessee, this situation created a critical challenge.

The senator's best hope was to attempt to stay the secession movement. Together with like-minded leaders of all parties, on November 24, 1860, he joined in a convention at Greeneville, where he took a distinctly moderate position, shared a platform with his erstwhile Whig antagonist Thomas A. R. Nelson, and pleaded for the adoption of conservative resolutions declaring secession unconstitutional. While asserting the importance of maintaining the Union, the resolutions reaffirmed the legality of slavery in the territories, emphasized the harm done to the South by antislavery agitation, and deplored the purely sectional nature of the election of the new president. Johnson helped to defeat a motion for a plank conceding that the election of Lincoln and Hamlin was not a sufficient cause for secession.[2]

Congress convened on December 3, and on the fourth Johnson arrived in Washington to take his seat.[3] On the same day, President Buchanan delivered a message holding secession unconstitutional while asserting the executive's inability to do anything about it. To work out some sort of solution, Congress soon appointed two committees of compromise. But it was evident that Southern ultras wanted no part of any adjustment. Determined on secession, they rejoiced at every manifestation of Southern hostility toward the Union.

Johnson, like other Unionists, was appalled by these developments. Attending a Southern caucus on the evening of December 8, he found his colleagues divided.[4] South Carolina was going ahead with her preparations for secession, and something had to be done. But what? Sam Milligan, as disturbed as his friend, proposed the formation of a central confederacy about which the Union might be rebuilt, if necessary without South Carolina and some New England states. Johnson, however, decided to propose once again his amendments to the Constitution, changed somewhat to take care of the sectional crisis. On December 13 he introduced suggestions for the direct election of the president and vice president and the appointment of justices of the Supreme Court for twelve years instead of for life, with the proviso that these officers alternate between citizens of slave-holding and free states. He also renewed his proposition for the popular election of senators and proposed that the Senate Committee of Thirteen, about to be established to reach a compromise, be instructed to report amendments dividing the remaining territories between the slave and free states. States responsible for the nonenforcement of the Fugitive Slave Law would have to pay for any lost servants; slavery in federal naval yards and the District of Columbia would be protected; and tampering with the interstate slave trade as well as with the three-fifths ratio of representation would be prohibited. These changes were to be forever unamendable. In part, they paralleled the Crittenden Compromise, shortly to be considered by the committee.[5]

Up to this point the senator had still been striving to maintain an even course. But now the time had come to make a decision. It might have been possible to prevaricate; it might have been possible to do nothing—but that was not Johnson's way. On the day he made his proposals for amendments, Congress adjourned for the weekend. The air was ripe with rumors; South Carolina was about to secede, and Senator Crittenden was quoted as saying he could perceive no move toward compromise by the Republicans. Ben Wade was getting ready to make a radical speech. Johnson now decided to commit himself.[6]

He launched his great effort on December 18, shortly after Wade had defiantly challenged the South. Technically speaking on behalf of his amendments, the senator from Tennessee maintained that if these had been adopted years ago, there would have been no crisis. "I believe it is the imperative duty of Congress to make some effort to save the country from impending dissolution, and he that is unwilling to make an effort to preserve the Union . . . is unworthy of public confidence," he insisted. In most of what he was going to say, continued Johnson, he was not going to differ much from his Southern friends. It was the mode and manner "by which this great end is to be accomplished" that was different. Firmly opposed to secession, he believed it was no remedy for Southern complaints. "I am unwilling, of my own volition, to walk outside of the Union which has been the result of a Constitution made by the patriots of the Revolution. . . . So far as I am concerned, and I believe I may speak with some degree of confidence for the people of my State, we intend to fight that battle inside and not outside of the Union, and if anybody must go out of the Union, it must be those who violate it." The Union, he asserted, was perpetual. Then the senator came to the crux of his argument.

> They say here is a State that, perhaps by this time, has seceded . . . that if the State secedes . . . you must talk very delicately upon the subject of coercion. . . . I do not believe the Federal Government has the power to coerce a State . . . but . . . this Government can, by the Constitution of the country and the laws enacted in conformity with the Constitution, operate upon individuals, and has the right and the power . . . to enforce and execute the law upon individuals within the limits of a State.

A brief exchange between Jacob Collamer, Johnson, and Judah P. Benjamin followed; then the Senate adjourned.

On the following day Johnson resumed his oration. Relying on precedents set by previous presidents, he denounced the doctrine of secession as unwarranted. South Carolina had put herself "in an attitude of levying war against the United States," an action defined by the Constitution as treason. "It is treason," he declared, "nothing but treason, and if one State, upon its own volition, can go out of this Confederacy without regard to the effect it is to have upon the remaining parties to the compact, what is your Government worth? . . . It is no Government at all upon such a construction." Pointing out that the continuance of slavery depended upon the preservation of the Union, he adduced additional arguments against secession, a step supposedly designed to protect the institution. Florida, Texas, California, and Louisiana had been acquired by the common effort of all the states. Could they now simply take leave of the confederacy? Moreover, Lincoln had been constitutionally elected. Johnson himself had fought against the Republicans in this election; nor did he like its sectional character. But it had been conducted according to the forms of law. Thus it furnished no reason to sever constitutional bonds, especially as the president-elect would be hemmed in by a Democratic majority in Congress.

The old Jacksonian could not forgo a final summation of his philosophy:

> I have an abiding faith, I have an unshaken confidence in man's capability to govern himself. I will not give up this Government that is now called an experiment. . . . No; I intend to stand by it, and I entreat every man throughout the nation who is a patriot . . . to come forward . . . and rally around the altar of our common country, and lay the Constitution upon it as our last libation, and swear by our God, and all that is sacred and holy, that the Constitution shall be saved, and the Union preserved. Yes, in the language of the departed Jackson, let us exclaim that the Union, "the Federal Union, it must be preserved."[7]

The address caused a sensation. "Great Speech of Senator Johnson, of Tennessee," headlined the *New York Times*, while the Chicago *Tribune* granted Johnson the "honor of striking the first really stunning blow at the treason of the seceding States." In the Senate, where Jefferson Davis and Louis Wigfall briefly tried unsuccessfully to contradict him, he was immediately called to task by Joseph Lane of Oregon, who insisted that Northern Democrats would lend no aid to efforts to coerce "gallant" Southern states. A great number of letters arrived from all over the country. Hailed as "a genuine patriot," "the 'Old Hickory' of this age," "independent & unselfish," the senator was lionized and his words circulated by the thousands. Many of these tributes were from the North, but the border and Southern states were by no means unrepresented. "Keep on in your Noble endeavours & all will yet be Well!" wrote "A Southerner and Lover of his Country" from Baltimore, while letters of approval arrived from Virginia and Mississippi as well.[8]

Other Southern opinion, however, was anything but friendly. Commenting that the speech was "the theme of universal praise among the abolitionists," the Richmond *Dispatch* professed to "see how certainly agrarianism leads a man to take sides with the abolitionists against his own people." The Charleston *Daily Courier* accused Johnson of advocating coercion; Governor John W. Ellis of North Carolina stated that "the world has ever known Johnson to be a demagogue, and now he has advertised himself as a traitor to his section," and a businessman in Mobile expressed the opinion that "no man having a drop of southern blood in his veins would openly proclaim such doctrines." One Mississippi secessionist threatened to send his "impudent" mulatto slave to Washington to horsewhip the senator, because, as he wrote, "coming in contact with you will so effectively disgrace him . . . that he will make a good obedient slave." As if to underline the South's disapproval, there was even a rumor that Johnson had shot Jefferson Davis.

Some Southerners were still conditional Unionists willing to wait and see whether some compromise might yet be worked out. The Greeneville statesman, however, had made it clear that he would stand by the Union at all costs. He had declared himself an unconditional Unionist. It was obvious that there was no turning back.[9]

Tennessee's reaction was of special interest. Johnson's strong stand for the Union divided the state, and to some extent worked a veritable political revolution. Lifelong supporters now turned against him; old opponents rallied to his side. Most dramatically, Parson Brownlow forgot his longtime aversion to the man he had once called "Toady Johnson" and declared that the senator deserved support. The parson admitted that he had never been one of Johnson's admirers, but now that the Democratic leader stood for the Union and Constitution, he must be sustained. Other Whigs felt the same way, and the senator found himself in the peculiar position of being upheld by former implacable antagonists.[10]

The Democrats' reaction was generally different. Often sympathizing with secession, they were outraged at Johnson's forceful defense of the Union. In Memphis, after hanging him in effigy, secessionists burned the remains "as a rebuke to his reported speech in the Senate . . . in favor of making 'conquered provinces' of the seceding Southern States." Other demonstrations followed, although an effort to repeat the Memphis performance in Knoxville was prevented. On December 29 a meeting in Nashville declared that the senator "wholly misrepresents his constituents"; another one in Madison County passed resolutions stating, "We repel, with indignation, the doctrines and opinion . . . of

Andrew Johnson." Johnson's friend Hu Douglas explained that the leading elements of the party, who had never liked him, now saw a chance of getting even. In the Tennessee legislature there was even a movement to instruct him out of the Senate; Johnson was told that Governor Harris was planning to supplant him. His friends in Greeneville, however, remained steadfast. Although Lowry eventually sided with the South, Milligan and McDannel approved of their fellow citizen's course; his family fully supported him, and Robert fought the secessionists in the legislature. If Johnson had taken a fateful step, it might cause trouble for a time; in the long run, however, it would redound to his credit.[11]

That the senator fully believed in the Union and that his famous speech represented his innermost convictions is beyond doubt. After all, as a radical Democrat he had always followed the example of Andrew Jackson. Nevertheless, he had also taken a politically expedient course. The leaders of the secession movement in Tennessee tended to be the very Democrats whom he had battled all his life within the party. Governor Harris was anxious to lead the state out of the Union; Landon C. Haynes declared for secession, and the Nashville clique largely did likewise. "The fact is there are a great many old Sores to be cured that you have caused," Hu Douglas correctly pointed out.

> You have been in the way of many of our would be great men for a long time. At heart many of us never wanted you to be Governor only none of the rest of us Could have been elected at the time and we only wanted you to use you. Then we did not want you to go to the Senate but the *people would send you.* Then Some of us wanted a *very distinguished man* to be President and wanted to Commit our delegates in favor of him [Harris], but instead of this (the people again interfered) they *expressed* a wish that you should have the nomination for President.

Johnson fully realized the significance of his stand. If the Southern leaders were to set up a separate government, as they eventually did in February 1861, what future would there be for a statesman of Johnson's views? During his long career in both houses had he not made enemies of most of the leaders of the secession movement, particularly of Jefferson Davis? During the homestead debates he had clashed with C. C. Clay, James H. Hammond, Thomas L. Clingman, and others. Obviously, in a government dominated by these men, his Homestead Bill would have no chance. Most of the territories would be gone, to say nothing of the incompatibility of homesteads with the speculative land policies of the large slaveholders. Moreover, under such circumstances, what was the likelihood of the adoption of his proposed amendments and other measures looking toward further democratization of the political structure? Finally, what personal opportunities for preferment would there be for a senator advocating such measures? Whether at this early time Johnson was able to foresee the great popularity he would gain in the North and the political clout this fame would give him is a moot point. But it must have been evident to him that, if he went with the South, he had no chance for higher office, while considerable opportunities remained if he stayed loyal.[12]

Johnson's break with the secessionists did not mean that he abandoned Southern interests. Convinced that the South had been wronged and that slavery needed protection, he still hoped for a compromise that would provide the necessary safeguards to satisfy Southern demands. When Jefferson Davis attacked him as an ally of Ben Wade, he forcefully reminded the future president of the Confederacy that if Southern states remained in the Union, Democrats would be in control of Congress after Lincoln's inauguration so that they would be able to protect the South.

Johnson also actively supported the Crittenden Compromise, which, among other guarantees to Southern slaveholders, would have restored the Missouri Compromise line, and, when it came up for a vote, was sickened by Southern extremists' refusal to sustain the settlement. Seated behind Senator Judah P. Benjamin of Louisiana, he asked his colleague, "Mr. Benjamin, why do you not vote? Why not save this proposition and see if we cannot bring the country to it?" The senator's negative reply convinced Johnson that Southern extremists, the aristocrats he had so long denounced, did not want a compromise. In fact, he accused them of scheming to suppress the nonslaveholders at home. "It is not guara[n]tees in reference to slavery they want," he complained to Milligan, "it is a go[vern]ment South so that they Can have the absolute Control of it in their own hands—And would erect today a monarchy if they had it in their power. . . . It is not the free men of the north they are fearing most: but the free men South and now desire to have a goment so organized as to put the institution of Slavery beyond the reach or vote of the nonslave holder at the ballot box." He was sure his own way for safeguarding the South was much better.[13] The small landholder could flourish in a slave state, but he needed allies, even Northern ones against the large planters.

In Tennessee matters were swiftly reaching a climax. As early as December 7 Governor Harris had called the legislature to meet in special session one month later. News of the secession of South Carolina on December 20 and that of other states early in January strengthened the

Tennessee secessionists, and when the special session met, Harris asked the legislators to call a state convention. The lawmakers, however, failed to comply in full. They finally passed a measure calling for an election on February 9 to test whether the people wanted a convention and to choose delegates for it. In the debates leading to this result, Robert Johnson firmly defended the Unionist cause and kept his father fully posted.[14]

Johnson was vitally interested in the election. If the secession movement could be squelched, if Harris could be set back, all might yet be well. So, in order to strengthen the Unionists, he determined to deliver another speech in the Senate.

His opportunity arose on February 5, 1861, shortly after Judah P. Benjamin delivered his parting address, replete with implied attacks on the Tennesseean. Rising to reply, Johnson said he had been the butt of attacks ever since his last speech against secession, although he had merely followed the doctrines of Washington, Jefferson, Madison, Monroe, and Jackson. How could Benjamin claim Louisiana had been oppressed by the United States? Had she not been bought with American money and defended with American lives? Violently opposed to the doctrine of secession, Johnson had made war upon it—"a war for the Constitution and the Union"—and he intended to "sink or swim upon it." Not that he had ever advocated coercing a state, as charged by his enemies; all he had said was that the government had power to enforce its laws upon individual citizens. Secession was treason, a crime the Constitution properly defined. As for South Carolina, its citizens had contemplated rejoining the British Empire during the revolution, had attempted to nullify the tariff of 1832, and for decades had been planning to disrupt the federal Union.

Then he turned to Joseph Lane. If now the senator from Oregon attacked him, he was showing rank ingratitude. Had not Johnson campaigned for him "through dust and heat, through the mud and rain?" Had it been known that Lane was a disunionist, he would not have been able to get 10,000 votes in Tennessee.

Lane and Louis Wigfall wanted to interrupt, but a motion to adjourn intervened, and it was not until the next day that Johnson resumed. Continuing his attack on the doctrine of secession, he insisted that if a line between the states had to be drawn, he preferred one between Tennessee and the Gulf states to any other, for, he emphasized again, slavery could not survive the breakup of the Union. To link him with Ben Wade, as Jefferson Davis had done, was an outrage; had he not for years stood for orthodox proslavery doctrines? If, however, he was called Wade's ally in upholding the Union and Constitution, he was proud of

it. The Southern members of the Committee of Thirteen had themselves rejected the Crittenden propositions; interested in nothing but
their own aggrandizement, they were as destructive as the abolitionists
who also wanted to break up the country. And if Tennessee were to be
forced out of the Union, he assured the Senate that there were many
whose "dead bodies would have to be trampled over" before such an
act could be consummated. As for himself, he intended to stand by the
flag, and when it should be trailed in the dust and the Union buried,
he wanted "no more honorable winding sheet than that brave old flag,
and no more glorious grave than to be interred in the tomb of the
Union." In conclusion, pleading once more for national unity, Johnson
declared: "I have an abiding confidence in the intelligence, the patriotism, and the integrity of the people, and I feel in my own heart that, if
this subject could be got before them, they would settle the question and
the Union of these States would be preserved."15

This speech, too, caused a sensation. As Johnson spoke, the galleries
frequently broke into applause, and Republican members of the House
came over to hear him. Southerners, on the other hand, were outraged.
In a furious reply on February 7, Wigfall lashed out at the man he called
a "Red Republican," pandering to the lowest elements of the North. He
would find himself totally repudiated in Tennessee, the Texan prophesied, and there were rumors of a duel between the two men. The
Nashville Union and American called Johnson's address "another war
speech," while the Richmond Dispatch labeled its author a traitor. Senator Bragg of North Carolina, however, was more perceptive. "Johnson
has all along entertained the opinion that he was one day to be President," he wrote in his diary. "Most of the seceders in Congress have
treated him with little or no respect—he knows that in a Southern
Confederacy he would be nowhere—Hence he rather sides with the
North, and is extremely bitter towards the secession leaders."16

Northern opinion, of course, was favorable. Praised by newspapers in
the East and West, the address was hailed by the New York Tribune as
the "strongest anti-secession speech" delivered in the Senate, and by the
Chicago Tribune as "the heaviest blow yet struck by a Southern member
against secession." The senator from Tennessee was rapidly becoming
a hero in the free states.17

The most important result of the speech, however, was its effect on
the Tennessee election. Turning decisively against secession, the voters
defeated the call for a convention by 68,282 to 59,449, while giving the
Unionist delegates a majority of 91,803 to 24,749. Many observers gave
Johnson credit for the victory. As one of the Unionist candidates in
Rogersville explained, but for the senator's speech, Unionists would

have had trouble, even in East Tennessee. Joseph Armstrong, a Hawkins County justice of the peace, agreed. "Your late speech has made hundreds of votes for the union ticket," he informed Johnson, who also heard from Bradley County that his speech had "had a powerful effect on traitors here," beaten by about 1,400 votes. And although these assessments were probably exaggerated—in some localities, no copies of the address were available until after the election—Johnson's determined stand certainly strengthened the Union cause.[18]

The outcome of the plebiscite greatly encouraged the senator. "Gov. Harris, & Landon C. Haynes, are nowhere," McDannel exulted, and Johnson's future looked bright. There was talk of his inclusion in the new cabinet, of his running for governor with the endorsement of the Whigs, and of his becoming president in 1864. He could feel secure enough to welcome Lincoln to the Senate when the president-elect visited the chamber in late February, the only Southerner to do so, although he maintained his Democratic record by voting against the Morrill Tariff and a Pacific railroad. While he also supported the proposed amendment permanently protecting slavery in the United States, he was still singled out for attack by extreme Democrats.[19]

Among these was the retiring senator from Oregon, Joseph Lane. Trying to clear himself of Johnson's charges, on March 2 Lane resumed his argument with the Tennesseean. Everyone understood Johnson to have advocated coercion, he said; as for himself, he would never join the Republicans in coercing sovereign states. And he was no traitor. Unlike Johnson, he had fought in the Mexican War, as had Jefferson Davis, "a pure patriot." If Northerners called Johnson noble, what was he noble for? His abandonment of the rights of the states? of his section? All Johnson had ever done in the Senate was to attempt to give away public lands, and he had not even succeeded in accomplishing that.

The senator from Tennessee immediately replied. It was his last speech for the session, now rapidly drawing to a close. When the excited galleries cheered him on, so much so that the presiding officer threatened to have the spectators removed, Johnson temporarily calmed the audience by vouching for its future good behavior. As for Lane, he castigated him as well as all similar traitors. If he were president, he continued, he would have such traitors arrested, and if convicted, executed. Proudly flaunting the results of the vote in Tennessee, Johnson contrasted the election with the inability of voters in the seceding states to register their wishes. Northerners who were more Southern than natives could not be trusted. He appealed once more to patriotism, quoted the "Star-Spangled Banner," and concluded with an emotional statement: "Will Tennessee ever desert the grave of him who bore it in triumph, or desert the flag that he waved with success? No; we were in the Union before some of these States were spoken into existence; and we intend to remain in, and insist upon—as we have the confident belief we shall get—all our constitutional rights and protection in the Union, and under the Constitution of the country." A faint cheer in the ladies' gallery was the beginning of an enormous round of applause, "the most vociferous and unrepressed that has ever taken place in either House of Congress," according to the press.[20]

When, two days later, Abraham Lincoln took the oath of office, it must have occurred to some that there was a superficial resemblance between the lanky lawyer from Illinois and the determined tailor from Tennessee. Both had been born poor, both had risen by their own efforts, both believed in the common people, and both were ardent Unionists. But the comparison could be carried too far. Lincoln always hated slavery; Johnson profited from the institution and defended it. Lincoln had long been an ardent Whig who believed in aid to railroads and other industries; Johnson was a Democrat who was just as strongly opposed to such measures. In addition, Lincoln's views were infinitely more flexible than Johnson's. Capable of steady growth, the president had a splendid sense of timing and knew how to adjust to changing conditions, important skills that Johnson definitely lacked. From the very beginning, however, the new president was favorably impressed with the senator.[21]

That Johnson appealed to Lincoln is not surprising. As the only Southern senator from a state that finally seceded to remain loyal, the Tennesseean was becoming ever more popular in the North. With no Republicans to speak of in Tennessee, Lincoln might have been expected to turn over the state's patronage to old Whigs like John Bell, Thomas A. R. Nelson, Horace Maynard, and the West Tennessee Unionist Emerson Etheridge. But after the president had appointed the old Jacksonian Montgomery Blair postmaster general instead of the Whig Henry Winter Davis, he decided to rely on Johnson instead. Blair favored the Democrat, who might attract additional support for the Union. Johnson became the virtual arbiter of federal patronage in the Volunteer State.

The senator's disposal of positions required finesse. He could throw all his weight behind the doubtlessly firm Whig Unionists; if he did so, however, he would cut off all connection with his own party and in the end be left without support. On the other hand, he could turn to the Democrats, a course that might alienate former Whigs from the cause of the Union. Johnson, however, was always a convinced Jacksonian. He decided to favor Democrats, a decision that may well have hastened the desertion of many Whigs. John Bell, for example, was deeply disappointed and, after Fort Sumter, joined the secessionists. McDannel became U.S. marshal, Milligan was appointed associate justice of the Nebraska territory, and other Johnson supporters received lucrative jobs in various parts of the state. The senator's correspondence was bulging with applications.[22]

In the meantime Johnson, who remained in Washington for the special session of the Senate, was becoming ever more popular. Three days after the inauguration serenaders appeared in front of his hotel to cheer him, and he replied with a few remarks about his favorite ideas. He had rather be a subject of the Russian tsar than a citizen of the Southern Confederacy, he told them. Tennessee would remain true to the Union and her rights would be secured to her by the North. At Frederick, Maryland, where he had been invited to speak, he made similar remarks; when he defended his report on contingent expenses against certain aspersions by John Hale of New Hampshire, his critic disclaimed any intention of impeaching Johnson's integrity. "I look upon him as the Aristides of Athens in this community and in this country," Hale said, "and if his constituents ever get tired of him they will get tired of him . . . because they were tired of hearing him called 'the just.' "[23]

In the last analysis, whether Tennessee would really remain loyal depended upon national events. Granting concessions to protect slavery was a course Johnson always counseled, especially as in letter after letter from home he received warnings that the Union victory was not definitive. The secessionists might try to recoup their chances. Under the circumstances, it was evident that Lincoln's actions concerning beleaguered Fort Sumter in Charleston harbor, one of the few forts still in federal hands and under siege by the Confederates, would have a great effect on the fortunes of the state, and the president was advised that Fort Sumter ought to be evacuated, while Fort Pickens in far off Florida ought to be held.[24] Lincoln himself toyed with the idea for a time, but in the end decided to force the issue by sending supplies to Sumter after giving the governor of South Carolina due warning. The outbreak of Civil War was the result. Lincoln called for troops to suppress the rebellion, and the border states were faced with the dreaded issue of coercion.

The situation in Tennessee now became critical. The moment news of Fort Sumter reached Nashville, the secessionists called a public meeting. When it convened on April 21, speakers excoriated "the traitorous conduct of Andrew Johnson," and mention of a Unionist telegram from the senator allegedly intercepted by the governor of Virginia brought forth shouts of "Hang the traitor." Even in Greeneville secession meetings cursed the village's most prominent citizen. Governor Harris, haughtily refusing Lincoln's call for troops, summoned another special meeting of the legislature, and it was clear that the secessionists had the upper hand.[25]

Although he had long been urged to come home to strengthen the state's Unionists, Johnson lingered in Washington after the adjournment of the special session, concerning himself with patronage matters. But after Fort Sumter, he finally set out on the dangerous trip home. His voice was needed in defense of the Union.[26]

He almost did not make it. When the train reached Lynchburg, an infuriated crowd, egged on by a Tennessee secessionist, invaded the car in which he was sitting, and one ruffian pulled his nose. He drew his pistol to defend himself, but the railroad officials calmed the mob so that he was permitted to ride on.[27] His troubles were not over, however. At Bristol on the Virginia-Tennessee line, another mob gathered. He might well have been lynched there, but apparently Jefferson Davis, now president of the newly formed Confederate States of America, intervened. Anxious not to make a martyr of Tennessee's best-known Unionist, he was reported to have given orders to move the train along. Promptly speeded ahead to Jonesboro, it reached Greeneville without further incident. Yet the senator could hardly have been reassured by a Confederate flag flying in his hometown.[28]

As in past days, Johnson was able to find renewed strength in the company of his family. Eliza, who had been ill, presumably with the "consumption" that was to plague her for the rest of her life, was getting somewhat better, and Robert, then in Nashville to attend the special session of the legislature, still kept his father posted about the secessionists' plans and actions. Although Robert held out little hope of saving the state, he thought that East Tennessee might be held. "I am for East Tennessee holding on, and never enter the Southern Confederacy," he wrote to his father. "I never will, so help me God, be bound down by Jeff Davis & Co." Charles and Judge Patterson, too, were true to the Union, as was his other son-in-law, Daniel Stover. Even his brother William, now in Texas, wrote Johnson antisecessionist letters.[29]

Johnson lost no time in entering the fray. Speaking in Knoxville on April 27 from an empty box on Main Street because the crowd was too large for a hall, he castigated secession, invoked the spirit of Andrew Jackson, and paid compliments to the former Whigs who were now cooperating with him. While a noisy group of Confederate soldiers, marching down Cumberland Street, threatened to interrupt the meeting, Thomas A. R. Nelson arrived, and the speaker announced that he and Nelson, though former opponents, were now standing "shoulder to shoulder" in battling for their common country. The Confederates left for their camp, and a clash was narrowly averted.[30]

Cooperation with the opposition in East Tennessee now became the norm. On the day after the Knoxville meeting, Johnson, together with Nelson, Horace Maynard, Oliver P. Temple, and C. F. Trigg, all former Whigs, sent a telegram to Unionists in the state legislature. "By firmness and deliberation the State may be saved. With reasonable time for a canvass, East Tennessee will give twenty thousand majority against secession."[31] The legislature soon took action. Governor Harris, who was about to enter into a league with the Confederacy, counseled secession, and it was evident that he would have his way. Continuing to resist, Unionist members met in Robert Johnson's room on April 28 and decided to stand firm by voting against all secessionist propositions. But on May 7, against Robert's and other Unionists' continued opposition, the legislature ratified Harris' league with the Confederates, passed a declaration of independence, and voted to join the Confederacy. The electorate was to pass on these measures on June 8.[32]

The following weeks witnessed an unprecedented campaign in the state, particularly in East Tennessee. Johnson, who believed he could not get a hearing in the middle and western divisions, left these areas to others. In his own East Tennessee, disregarding the danger to his life, he embarked on a joint speaking tour with Nelson and addressed crowds in county after county. At Elizabethton, he likened secession to such biblical precedents as the expulsion from the Garden of Eden, where Adam and Eve, after eating the forbidden fruit, "seceded and retired from the enjoyments that had been placed before them in Paradise," and Judas' betrayal of his master after which "he also seceded to put an end to his existence." Reaffirming his conviction that no state had the right to break up the general government, the senator sought to appeal to the patriotism of his audiences.[33]

The infuriated secessionists tried hard to stop these assaults. When Johnson started speaking in Jonesboro, Nelson's hometown, the crowd began to boo, called him "a damned traitor," and forced him to sit down. Until a shower broke the meeting up, Nelson was permitted to continue. Then the assembly was adjourned to the basement of the courthouse, where the senator was finally allowed to deliver his remarks. From time to time, secession flags were thrust through the windows, and he was jeered on the way to Nelson's house. At Athens, an infuriated mob also called him a traitor, and at Blountsville, a meeting at the courthouse passed a resolution asking the pair not to speak in Sullivan County. Avoiding Blountsville, they went on to Kingsport, where another large crowd awaited them, although secessionists bent on causing a disturbance first had to be ejected from the hall.[34] And on June 7, the day before the election, when Johnson spoke at Kingston, he received another warning. Parson Brownlow, hearing that a regiment of soldiers might kill the senator on the train to Knoxville, sent his son with a buggy to rescue his old opponent. Johnson protested, but he finally allowed young Brownlow to drive him back to town. On the next day, taking back roads to foil his enemies, he left for Greeneville by private conveyance.[35]

In the last days of May a Union Convention meeting in Knoxville passed resolutions asserting the illegality of secession and affirming its loyalty to the Union. Johnson spoke for three hours, after which Nelson, acting as president, issued a call to reassemble in Greeneville. Knoxville was rapidly becoming too dangerous.[36]

As expected, the election of June 8 showed that the voters approved of secession, at least in the middle and western divisions. In East Tennessee, however, the secessionists lost by a vote of 32,923 to 14,780. Observers agreed that Johnson and Nelson had had much to do with this result. Even Oliver P. Temple, despite his animus, gave Johnson sole credit for carrying with him the Democratic voters of Greene County. "Nothing in the whole history of Andrew Johnson shows so strikingly as this canvass the dominating power he held over the minds of his party in the section where he lived," Temple admitted. "Perhaps no such example of devotion and confidence can be found in our political annals."[37]

The results of the election made it impossible for the senator to stay in Tennessee any longer. Even before the vote, his friend Jephtha Fowlkes, the editor of the Memphis *Avalanche,* had warned him that as the state was surely going to secede, further resistance was useless; it would be dangerous for him to travel in Middle and West Tennessee, and he had better cease all his activities. Johnson's enemies were not content with smearing his name; when they intercepted a letter to him from Amos Lawrence, the Boston industrialist, offering monetary aid, they tried to get the funds for the Confederacy by forging a series of letters to Lawrence.[38]

Because Johnson was told that it was dangerous to take the direct route to Washington, he decided to go by way of Cumberland Gap, and on Wednesday evening, June 12, after bidding good-bye to his family, he left Greeneville in a covered buggy belonging to the Reverend John P. Holtsinger of the Cumberland Presbyterian Church, who, together with a few mounted men, accompanied him. After narrowly escaping arrest at Bean's Station, the travelers spent the first night in what is now

Hamblin County. On the next day they reached Cumberland Gap, where bushwackers fired on them. Johnson then parted from the minister and made his way to safety through Kentucky. He was not to see Greeneville again for the next eight years.[39]

The senator had left just in time. To be sure, on June 17 the reconvened Union Convention met in Greeneville and passed resolutions again declaring secession illegal and petitioning for a separate state for East Tennessee, but the entire region was soon occupied by Confederate troops. Unionists were persecuted, and bitter civil war devastated the mountain counties. For a time, Johnson's family members stayed behind; harassed by the Confederates, they led a precarious existence until permitted to pass through the lines to join their husband and father.[40]

But Johnson's spirit was unbroken. In Lexington he delivered a fiery speech damning the secessionists. From there he went to Covington, where the Kenton Guards conducted him by ferry across the river to Cincinnati. Years later John Law, an Indiana congressman, remembered how the fugitive appeared at the Burnet House, the leading local hotel. A troop of weary horses rode up, and a civilian, in very dusty citizen's clothes, came forward and dismounted. Enthusiastically welcomed by the crowd, he delivered an impromptu patriotic address. That afternoon, he made another speech from the hotel's balcony and was fervently greeted and feted by a large number of admirers.[41]

Johnson traveled on to Washington, which he reached on June 21, and was hailed as a hero wherever he went. Well-wishers assisted by the Twenty-fifth Pennsylvania Regimental Band serenaded him at his old hotel, Democrats spoke of him as the next president, and Republicans sought his support. As the only senator from a seceding state to have remained loyal, he enjoyed a unique position, so that Lincoln listened attentively to his pleas for aid for his persecuted fellow citizens in East Tennessee.[42]

When on July 4 Congress met in special session, Johnson was in his seat. Ever the agrarian Jeffersonian-Jacksonian Democrat, he now emphasized his Unionist conviction that the government had a solemn obligation to guarantee his constituents a republican form of government. On July 13 he presented the credentials of John S. Carlile and Waitman Willey of Virginia; they were to take the places of Hunter and Mason, who had resigned when the state seceded. But he refused to vote for the expulsion of secessionists. Their seats were merely vacant, he insisted. And although he naturally supported the retroactive approval of emergency measures taken by the president, he made sure that his Jacksonian views about the crisis were adopted by Congress. It was he who introduced in the Senate a resolution similar to one Crittenden had already presented to the House:

> Resolved, that the present deplorable civil war has been forced upon the country by the disunionists of the southern States now in revolt against the constitutional Government and in arms around the capital; that in this national emergency Congress, banishing all feeling of mere passion or resentment, will recollect only its duty to the whole country; that this war is not prosecuted upon our part in any spirit of oppression, nor for any purpose of conquest or subjugation, nor for the purpose of overthrowing or interfering with the rights or established institutions of those States, but to defend and maintain the supremacy of the Constitution and all laws made in pursuance thereof, and to preserve the Union, with all the dignity, equality, and rights of the several States unimpaired; that as soon as these objects are accomplished the war ought to cease.[43]

This resolution, which was adopted by the Senate with only five dissenting votes, precisely reflected Johnson's Jacksonian concept of states' rights supported by federal authority, and remained the lodestar of his policy for years to come.

In the meantime, Washington, which had been virtually cut off from the North in April, was again threatened by Confederate forces when, on July 21, the federal army suffered a serious reverse at Bull Run. With Confederate troops encamped almost within sight of the capital and with several border states still on the brink of secession—Kentucky going so far as to declare her neutrality—the outlook for the Union did not seem bright. But Johnson did not lose faith.

It was on July 27, when the situation appeared most desperate, that he made a three-hour address in the Senate in support of special war powers for the president. Border state senators like Breckinridge and Trusten Polk of Missouri condemned the proposals as violations of the Constitution, and Johnson felt called upon to reply. The war was a test of the government's ability to maintain itself against internal foes and traitors, he said. The president was merely trying to defend the Constitution, and if he had made summary arrests, he had only done what Washington and Jackson had also done. It was the secessionists, not Lincoln, who had started the war, who had refused compromises and had long plotted to erect a new government based not on popular sovereignty but on slave holding only.

The South had lost none of its rights, Johnson continued; its institutions were secure. The whole struggle was a contest for popular rights and democracy, notions Confederate leaders, thwarted in their ambition for power, were opposing. He asserted that there was open talk of monarchy in the South; Isham Harris had been spoken of as king, though he, Johnson, would not own the governor as a slave, much less bend the knee to him as king. It was democracy itself that was on trial, the type of democracy the senator as a Democrat had always upheld. "The people whom I represent appeal to the Government and to the nation to give us that constitutional protection that we need," he concluded. "The time has arrived when we should show to the nations of the earth that we are a nation capable of preserving our existence, and to give them evidence that we will do it."[44]

After this speech Johnson's popularity, which had been steadily rising, reached a new peak. Invitations to lecture poured in, while patriotic citizens deluged him with letters expressing their gratification. Francis Lieber, the famous German-American political scientist, summed up the Unionists' feeling when he wrote: "May God prosper you and all who struggle, by word or sword, to save the *integrity* of our *Country*." And Alexander H. Stephens, vice president of the Confederacy, believed the address to have been the "most notable, as it was certainly the most effective, ever delivered by any man on any occasion," because "the Resolutions referred to, and the speech especially, gave the war a vigor and *real* life it had not before, and never would have had without them on the Northern side."[45] Under ordinary circumstances, the senator could have been most pleased.

But circumstances were not ordinary. Johnson was a fugitive, a refugee, and letters and news from East Tennessee confirmed the troubles of those he had left behind. Hounded, harassed, imprisoned, their relatives sometimes killed, the Unionists demanded relief. Johnson and Horace Maynard now became their chief advocates in Washington.

Peculiarly enough, the first request for aid to beleaguered East Tennessee came as a result of the forged letters from Johnson's enemies to Amos Lawrence. A committee of citizens in Boston, headed by Edward Everett, hearing about the need for assistance from Lawrence, wired Lincoln that they had received word of it from Johnson. Lincoln was sympathetic, and when Johnson himself arrived in Washington and asked for relief, Secretary of the Treasury Salmon P. Chase was able to reassure him. "Our great and good friend the President . . . expressed the strongest wish to gratify you," he wrote, holding out promise of military support. Perhaps there was hope for succor to the suffering Unionists of East Tennessee.[46]

Harsh realities, however, frustrated Johnson's efforts. Much as Lincoln favored a movement into East Tennessee, both for military and political reasons, the proposal encountered great difficulties. Communications through the mountains were abominable, and the troops were ill trained. In the end, other priorities interfered.

Johnson was outraged. Indefatigably seeking to further the projected advance, he pointed out the need for speed. If no help was forthcoming, the people of his section might well despair. Young East Tennesseeans were being taken by the Confederate army; the time to strike was at hand. He pleaded, cajoled, and wrote letters, but all in vain. Federal troops did not come.[47]

In the meantime, the special session was rapidly drawing to a close. In its last days Congress passed the first Confiscation Act freeing slaves used in support of the rebellion, a war measure Johnson supported. But when Congress adjourned, he could not go home. "Andrew Johnson is reported to have said very *naively* that he would not return to Tennessee, unless . . . accompanied by a Union army," taunted the Nashville *Union and American.* "Therein the said ANDREW has displayed singular discretion, and 'discretion is the better part of valor,' especially when a man is in the peculiar situation of the Tennessee renegade. This will be something novel . . . to see a man professing to represent a State in the Senate, coming home with an army to subdue his constituents."[48]

But his constituents, at least in East Tennessee, did not agree. They believed the advance of the Union army would soon relieve them. Many fled to Kentucky, where they tried to assemble troops to liberate their homes. And although the senator received invitations from various parts of the country, including one from Indiana to regard himself a guest of the state until he could go home, he refused them all. Believing that his mission was to liberate his home and to help his constituents, he traveled to Kentucky and Ohio to urge on laggard generals, strengthen the Unionists, and deliver speeches in support of the longed-for military movement.[49]

East Tennessee was indeed in trouble. After the August elections, when Harris was reelected along with Unionist congressmen such as Maynard in the Second (Knoxville) and Nelson in the First (Jonesboro) District, repression increased. Although Maynard succeeded in reaching Washington, where he aided Johnson in seeking support for his home area, Nelson was captured and forced to submit to the secessionists. Brownlow, who continued his attacks on the Confederates in his newspaper, was eventually silenced and jailed before being sent north, and members of Johnson's family, now "alien enemies," were considered a threat to the Southern government. Sequestration proceedings were started against the senator's property; Judge Patterson was arrested, Robert had to go into hiding, and Dan Stover took part in guerrilla operations, one of which was the bridge burning organized by William

Blount Carter, a Carter County minister. This action infuriated the Confederates, who retaliated with great brutality.[50]

Johnson's tour of Kentucky and Ohio took up his time between sessions of Congress. Anxious to spur the army on even before he left Washington, he explained his plans to William T. Sherman at Willard's Hotel. An invasion of East Tennessee was to be carried out by men recruited from the border states, and he had high hopes of its success. Then, armed with special authority from Secretary of War Simon Cameron to approve all disbursements sanctioned by Congress for the protection of loyal citizens in states in rebellion, the senator sought to stiffen Kentucky Unionists' resolve and aid in the organization of refugees for the invasion of East Tennessee. Recruits from Kentucky had gathered at Camp Dick Robinson near Lexington, and he spent time with them to raise morale. In speeches delivered in various parts of the state as well as in Ohio, he stressed the Confederate leaders' responsibility for the war, the need to stand by the Union, and his own unshakable conviction of ultimate victory.

Wherever Johnson spoke he was received with enthusiasm. The generals might resent his speech-making, but the Unionists were delighted. In Cincinnati a huge concourse of people called him to the balcony of the Burnet House, where he was staying; at Newport a procession greeted him at Court House Square, and at Columbus the audience completely filled the hall in the state house, where rain had made it necessary to meet, and where the senator harangued his listeners for three hours.[51]

But his efforts to induce the generals to undertake a movement into East Tennessee did not succeed. Worried about their lack of action, even after, in September, Kentucky abandoned her neutrality and stayed loyal, Johnson vainly attempted to supersede General George H. Thomas with Ormsby Mitchel, an astronomer turned general whom he had met in Washington. At the beginning of October Lincoln himself drew up a plan for an operation that included a descent through Cumberland Gap to seize the East Tennessee–Virginia Railroad; Johnson repeatedly conferred with Sherman and Thomas and had high hopes for the success of this mission. But Thomas resented his interference—at one time he was reported ready to arrest the visiting statesman—although he, too, agreed that the idea was feasible. Yet obstacles continued to interfere, and Sherman finally ordered a withdrawal behind the Kentucky River. Although Thomas managed to have the order revoked, the Tennessee troops threatened to mutiny and advance on their own. Then Sherman was replaced by Don Carlos Buell, who, in spite of Johnson's pleas, in the end proved totally unsympathetic.[52]

It was in an angry mood that Johnson returned to Washington for the second session of the Thirty-seventh Congress. Worried about his family and friends, disappointed at the generals' hesitation, he was determined to do his utmost to bring about the liberation of East Tennessee and the speedy suppression of the rebellion. He was truly an exile: "I have not the means of writing to my own family and do not expect to have any means of doing so until this nefarious rebellion is put down," he wrote. Reading the constant attacks on him by Tennessee newspapers with their denunciation of the "evil counsels of those arch-traitors, Johnson and Maynard," the senator became ever more set in his defense of democracy as he understood it: the maintenance of the Union, popular government, and resistance to aristocratic usurpers.

Before a week had passed in the session, Johnson joined with Maynard in calling on Lincoln and the new commanding general, George B. McClellan, both of whom seemed to agree with them. "We have just had interviews with the President & Gen'l McLellan [sic] & find they concur fully with us in respect to the East Tennessee Expedition," the two Union members wired Buell. "Our people are oppressed & pursued as beasts of the forest[.] the government must come to their relief[.] we are looking to you with anxious solicitude to move in that direction[.]" Though he responded favorably, in the long run Buell would favor a movement toward Nashville instead.[53]

Johnson did not give up. He vigorously pushed for the construction of a railroad to East Tennessee as advocated by Lincoln in his annual message, continued his attempts to induce the administration to move upon the occupied region, and became a member of the Joint Committee on the Conduct of the War, the radical engine for goading on laggard generals.

This committee was established following a resolution to investigate the disaster of Ball's Bluff, where Lincoln's friend Senator Edward Baker of Oregon was killed. Ben Wade was made chairman, and under his guidance the committee became an agency for radical propaganda, the removal of sluggish generals, and the unconditional waging of war. Johnson joined the Republicans Zachariah Chandler and Wade to represent the Senate, while the House contingent included the Republicans George W. Julian of Indiana, John Covode of Pennsylvania, and Daniel Gooch of Massachusetts, as well as the Democrat Moses Odell of New York. Accused of unconventional, star-chamber proceedings, the committee actually had less power than generally believed. While it was largely dominated by its chairman, during the short time he served on it, Johnson was by no means inactive.[54]

Johnson's questions in committee meetings showed his impatience with the generals in Kentucky. Was it not better for an army to move than to stay in winter quarters? Was not a long period of inactivity bad for morale? And was not strategy designed to penetrate East Tennessee the best way of winning the war? These and similar queries were his chief contributions to the committee, and the answers merely confirmed his suspicions.

The most important of the committee's early investigations concerned McClellan's operations. Dashing, young, and a brilliant organizer, the "Young Napoleon" had succeeded in whipping the army back into shape after the disaster at Bull Run. But he was cautious to a fault, consistently overestimated the strength of the enemy, and for months after his appointment refused to move forward. The radical Republicans thoroughly distrusted him, particularly because he was a Democrat. Johnson, who might have felt a certain political kinship with the general, at that time disliked him because of the failure to move into East Tennessee and possibly because of a putative rivalry for the 1864 presidential nomination. When the committee first summoned McClellan, he answered that he was too ill to appear. But the investigators called several of his subordinates, whose testimony convinced them that the general already had enough troops to go forward, and on New Year's Eve 1861 committee members went to see the president.

It was a stormy interview. "Mr. President," fumed Wade, "you are murdering your country by inches in consequence of the inactivity of the military and the want of a distinct policy in regard to slavery." Lincoln said nothing in reply, and as far as is known, Johnson did not protest about the reference to emancipation. On the next day the president sought to reassure the general, but within a week the committee returned, this time to meet with the entire cabinet. Again demanding information about McClellan's plans, the members were surprised to learn that Lincoln did not know any details and asked the president for the general's dismissal. McClellan, however, recovered. He testified before the committee and eventually produced a plan to attack Richmond from the sea.[55] ·

At the same time, the members also investigated the reverse at Ball's Bluff. Summoning Charles P. Stone, the unlucky commander in charge of that river crossing, as well as his subordinates, the committee heard tales of incompetence and accusations of disloyalty, which it considered warranted. Johnson himself found that Stone had received letters from Confederates and soldiers disloyal to the government. After hearing testimony from the general again, the committee submitted its dubious evidence to the newly appointed secretary of war, Edwin M. Stanton.

Stone's totally unwarranted incarceration at Fort Lafayette was the result.[56]

John C. Frémont was another general the committee examined in detail. Lincoln had dismissed "the Pathfinder" after his unauthorized emancipation of slaves in his department, an incident that had endeared Frémont to the radicals. Although at this time his commitment to slavery was still strong, Johnson fully cooperated. Accompanied by Daniel Gooch, he went to see the president to plead for the general. Frémont was eventually given another command.[57]

The new secretary of war collaborated closely with the investigators. Johnson and Wade, who had visited McClellan and, much to Wade's disgust, found him busy constructing pontoon bridges, now complained to Stanton. When they saw him on February 19, 1862, the secretary called the general in. McClellan made his usual excuses: he did not have enough troops, he said, and he had to protect his rear. With 150,000 of the most effective soldiers in the world upon the other side of the Potomac, there was no need of a bridge, Wade promptly replied. They could beat any force the enemy could bring against them, "and if any of them come back let them come back in their coffins." In his report about the interview, Johnson stated that it "had been a very satisfactory one; that the Secretary listened attentively to everything the chairman said, and although the chairman sometimes made his statements in pretty strong language, the Secretary endorsed every sentiment he uttered." So, presumably, did Johnson.[58]

The senator's service was to be cut short by his appointment as military governor of Tennessee. He did have the satisfaction, however, of rejoicing in the victories at Mill Springs, where General Thomas defeated Felix K. Zollicoffer, who was killed, and the even more important capture of Forts Henry and Donelson, successes that were to be followed by the invasion of Middle and West Tennessee and the capture of Nashville. But East Tennessee remained under Confederate occupation.

Conditions at home were becoming worse and worse. From direct reports from Robert, who had finally managed to escape through the lines, the senator learned that Unionists were being hounded, his property confiscated, his slaves taken away, and his two sons-in-law harassed. Patterson, it is true, had come to an arrangement with the Confederate authorities; after a brief imprisonment he was permitted to resume his judicial position, though in constant danger of arrest. Daniel Stover was in hiding. Charles, after temporarily making his peace with the occupying power, became the subject of sequestration proceedings when the Confederates refused to accept his father's transfer of debts due to him to the son. Eliza and eleven-year-old Frank were staying with Mary, while the Greeneville homestead was eventually taken over for use as a military hospital. The senator had reason to worry.[59]

Before he left the Senate to take up his new position as military governor, Johnson seized a fitting opportunity to explain his position once again. Jesse Bright, an Indiana Democrat, had written to Jefferson Davis recommending a friend for a job; a resolution for his expulsion was under consideration, and on January 31, 1862, the Tennesseean rose to comment on the subject. But Johnson, not Bright, became the main topic of the address. "I am a Democrat now," he said. "I have been one all my life; I expect to live and die one, and the corner-stone of my Democracy rests upon the enduring basis of the Union." Reiterating his conviction that the Union had to be preserved, he reminded his audience of the nation's duty to guarantee a republican form of government to all states, an obligation his constituents expected to be carried out. His property had been confiscated, his family hounded, he was an exile, but he had the right to ask for protection. As for Bright, he had written traitorous letters and therefore ought to be expelled. Let the war be brought to a successful conclusion and all would yet be well.[60]

In line with his strong Union feelings, Johnson introduced a resolution for the reading of George Washington's Farewell Address on February 22.[61] It was a fitting conclusion to his final service in a body that he was now leaving for a new assignment. He had proved his loyalty to the Union. His reward would follow.

IX

MILITARY GOVERNOR

BY FEBRUARY 1862 Union forces had recaptured enough Confederate territory to give some thought to its administration. But this problem raised the question of Reconstruction, which had already caused several debates in Congress. Who was to be in charge of the process? Congress? The president? And regardless of who was in charge, how was it to be managed? If secession was illegal, as good Unionists asserted, were not the rebellious states still part of the Union? This seemed to be the meaning of the Johnson-Crittenden Resolutions, but several members of Congress, among them Charles Sumner, disagreed. Arguing that the states had become territories, Sumner insisted that they had committed suicide. Others had still different ideas.

The president finally determined to take the matter into his own hands. He decided to appoint military governors for the reconquered states, and the first of these was Andrew Johnson, easily the most famous Southern loyalist, whom on March 4 he appointed military governor of Tennessee.[1]

Lincoln's decision was controversial, and he had to be careful to select someone acceptable to Congress. But he possessed an uncanny political finesse, which he showed by picking Johnson. The popular Tennesseean, the only senator to have remained loyal while his state seceded, a Democrat who had served on the Committee on the Conduct of the War and enjoyed excellent relations with several different factions of the Republican party, could hardly be rejected by his colleagues. It has even been suggested, though without compelling proof, that by sending him to Tennessee, Lincoln might rid himself of a dangerous rival in 1864.[2] Whatever the reason, the maneuver succeeded. Approving of the choice without opposition, the Senate unanimously confirmed Johnson's simultaneous appointment as brigadier general.[3]

From Lincoln's point of view, the nomination may have been politically astute, but in Tennessee it did not meet with universal approbation. General William Nelson, who entered Nashville with Buell's army, wrote to Salmon P. Chase that Reconstruction ought to be fostered there by the support of men who could elect their own leaders. But, he cautioned, "do not send Andy Johnson here in any official capacity. He represents a party! Let him come as Senator if he wants to. He is too much embittered to entrust with a mission as delicate as the direction of a people under the present circumstances."[4]

Assistant Secretary of War Thomas A. Scott, also in Nashville, agreed. Suggesting to Stanton that a military governor ought to be appointed, some "wise and prudent man," he proposed General William B. Campbell. When Scott learned that Johnson was being considered, he protested. "While I know of no man personally I would rather see in that position than Mr. Johnson, yet I believe that it would not be a prudent appointment at this time." Johnson had been opposed to the Confederates for so long, said Scott, that he would have trouble reconciling former rebels to their proper allegiance. They would fear that he might be vindictive and would organize a party to oppose anything he might attempt. Many of his former supporters were now secessionists; in fact, Scott concluded, "it has been intimated to me that the feeling against Mr. Johnson—if he were in power—is so bitter that attempts might be made to destroy his life, for the purpose of creating fresh troubles and gratifying revenge against him for his past course in opposition to the Southern Confederacy." General Buell naturally could not have relished civilian interference, and some of these assessments were not totally wrong.[5]

In the country at large, however, the news of Johnson's new job was generally greeted with great satisfaction. The New York Herald called the appointment "eminently proper," an opinion with which the Philadelphia Press and the Democratic New York World fully agreed. The Chicago Tribune prominently featured the announcement, and the New York Times also expressed its approval: "Gov. Johnson undoubtedly has a most difficult task before him," the paper commented, ". . . and it will require discretion as well as nerve and courage to lead the State safely through this period of transition. But the appointee has experience and character of the very kind required." Tennesseeans in Washington were delighted, while friends elsewhere in the country sent their congratulations. Johnson's new career seemed to have an auspicious beginning.[6]

Johnson himself had some misgivings. Though his new position could be justified either by the constitutional provision guaranteeing the states a republican government, or by the president's power as commander in chief of the army and navy, he worried about its dubious constitutionality.[7] But he accepted it; considering his own career, he hardly had another choice. His term in the Senate would be up within another year, and there was no legislature to reelect him. In addition, the appointment would enable him to help the Unionists in Tennessee, and might well become a springboard for higher office.

The wording of his commission was vague. "You are hereby appointed Military Governor of the State of Tennessee," it read, "with authority to exercise and perform, *within the limits of that state,* all and singular, the powers, duties and functions pertaining to the office of Military Governor (including the *power* to *establish all necessary offices and tribunals,* and *suspend* the *writ of Habeas Corpus*) during the pleasure of the President, or until the loyal inhabitants of that state shall organize a civil government in conformity with the Constitution of the United States." Yet it was generally expected, as the Chicago *Tribune* commented, that Johnson was "commissioned to form a provisional Government, call a state convention to depose Governor Harris, and form a new government." To facilitate this task, he was authorized to draw on a fund to aid in the organization of a home guard. If his lack of great administrative skill made his success doubtful, his Northern admirers tended to overlook this drawback.[8]

The new military governor left Washington without delay, in the company of Horace Maynard, Emerson Etheridge, William A. Browning, his private secretary, and his son Robert. After taking a train to Pittsburgh and Cincinnati, he continued by boat to Louisville. From there he caught a rickety train rigged up from the debris the retreating Confederates had left behind. Pulled by an engine without headlights, cowcatcher, or cab, the train looked like a "snorting wreck on wheels," and every time it hit an upgrade, everybody but Johnson, who was sitting in a boxcar, got out and walked while the engine made running jumps to reach the top. The group reached Nashville on March 11, no doubt apprehensive about the changes that had taken place in the city since he had last seen it.[9]

Nashville had been evacuated by the Confederates soon after the fall of Fort Donelson. Governor Harris and the legislature fled to Memphis; the Southerners had blown up two bridges over the Cumberland River, and many citizens took to flight. "You must not expect to be received

with enthusiasm," General Buell warned Johnson, "but rather the reverse and I suggest you arrive without any display." Whatever Union
feeling there was in the city had been thoroughly cowed, and secessionists were in a majority. With many of the stores closed, the attitude of
sullen submission of the population, and the hastily constructed pontoon bridge over the river, the city, though still showing signs of its
former prosperity, was very different from the one Johnson had left not
so many years earlier. The uncertainty of the military situation—Confederate troops were still operating in many parts of the state, and East
Tennessee was to remain under enemy occupation for some time—made
it difficult for the Unionists to reassert themselves.[10]

Johnson was undaunted. Firmly taking control from the beginning,
on March 13 he delivered his first address to the crowd assembled in
front of the St. Cloud Hotel, where he had established his residence. "I
return to you with no hostile purpose," he said. "I come with the olive
branch in one hand and the Constitution in the other to render you
whatever aid may be in my power in re-erecting . . . the Star Spangled
Banner." He blamed the Civil War on secession occasioned by ambitious men wanting to safeguard slavery, and reaffirmed his conviction
that the "peculiar institution's" only protection was the Constitution
of the United States. In line with a deeply ingrained habit of personaliz-
ing public issues, the governor followed up this analysis with a frighten-
ing description of the suffering of his family, friends, and neighbors in
East Tennessee, and though he maintained that he was not animated
by hatred, he stressed the motto that was to become his trademark in
the years to come: Traitors must be punished and treason crushed.
Etheridge and Maynard then delivered similar speeches. The military
governorship had begun.[11]

What Johnson told the crowd represented his own idea of the situation. He had not changed; he merely tried to hold in abeyance some of
his Jeffersonian-Jacksonian ideas for the sake of the first imperative, the
preservation of the Union. This point of view carried him through the
difficult years in Nashville, and it was going to remain his lodestar in
the even more difficult period that followed.

The war against "traitors" began immediately. On March 17 the
governor issued orders to the provost marshal of Nashville to seize the
Bank of Tennessee and the court records left behind by the Confederates. Justifying his actions in an "Appeal to the People of Tennessee,"
he cited the administration's duty to safeguard republican government.
Then in a Union meeting at the capitol he further explained his view
of the aristocratic nature of secession.[12] A few days later Johnson pe-
remptorily demanded that the city fathers take an oath of allegiance to

the United States. When they refused, he dismissed them and appointed new ones in their place. The mayor, Richard B. Cheatham, found himself in jail, where he stayed a few weeks before submitting. Other Confederates, including ex-governor Neill S. Brown, followed suit.[13]

Johnson continued his campaign of rigor. He shut down hostile newspapers, encouraged the establishment of loyal ones, and appointed well-known Unionists to prominent positions. Edward H. East, a distinguished Nashville lawyer, became secretary of state, Horace Maynard, attorney general, and Joseph S. Fowler, the Gallatin professor of mathematics and future U.S. senator, comptroller. In June the governor summoned several eminent ministers to the capitol and also asked them to take the oath. When they refused, they, too, were imprisoned.

Secessionists were appalled. "Where is your boasted liberty, your boasted *Religious* freedom, when a man cannot even pray as he wishes," commented Amy Devereaux Edmondston, Johnson's old neighbor from Raleigh. The former mayor of Nashville, then a federal prisoner, agreed. "When such men [as Johnson] are permitted to retake the reigns of government in Tennessee, I have but little hope for the restoration of . . . peace," he commented. He would soon call the governor's rule a "reign of terror."[14]

But Johnson stuck to his course. In August he levied an assessment against wealthy secessionists for the support of "wives and helpless children, who have been reduced to poverty and wretchedness in consequence of their husbands and fathers having been forced into the armies of this unholy and nefarious rebellion." On October 1 he appointed more aldermen and councilmen, and he continued to arrest prominent rebel sympathizers, including his former colleague Nicholson. It was his way of attempting to punish traitors and make treason odious.[15]

How successful these policies were is questionable. According to one well-placed observer, Buell's lenient policy had softened the people and made them turn once more to the old flag. Johnson's tactics, however, undid all that the general had accomplished and made the public ever more ardent secessionists. General Nelson agreed. "Since you left here the hostility to the United States Government and the troops has increased 1000 per cent. It seems settled into a fierce hatred to Governor Johnson . . . ," he wrote to Buell. "Their resentment is fierce and vindictive, and this country, from being neutral at least, when you left it, is now hostile and in arms." Assistant Secretary of War Scott's predictions may not have been entirely mistaken.[16]

Johnson himself, though under constant threat of assassination, thought he was making progress. "The Union sentiment here . . . is much stronger than I anticipated," he wrote to Stanton three days after his edict to the city government requiring an oath of allegiance. "I feel satisfied that whenever the Confederate armed forces are driven beyond our limits, the people of the State will be for the Union by an over-whelming majority." He asked Secretary of the Treasury Chase not to abrogate the permit system for trade with enemy-held territory, adding, "The requiring of all persons to take an oath to the U.S. is having the finest effect." To Lincoln, too, he sent word assuring the president that "reaction was rapidly going on" and that "much good has been done in preparing the public mind in being reconciled to the Government." Some later historians might not agree, but the governor was convinced that he was the right man for the job.[17]

In the midst of these controversial actions, Johnson had the peculiar experience of a reunion with his old enemy and present supporter, Parson Brownlow. After having been expelled from the Confederacy, the Knoxville firebrand arrived in Nashville in no mood to be gentle to rebels. According to Oliver P. Temple, the two men "rushed into each other's arms and wept like women." Their collaboration would last throughout the war, only to turn to hatred again after Johnson became president.[18]

As Johnson had written to Stanton, much depended on the military situation. The large portion of the population that was undecided would obviously favor the winning side, and as long as there was a constant danger of the Confederates' return, efforts to revive Unionism in Middle and West Tennessee were seriously compromised. And in 1862 the military situation was often not favorable. In April, as U. S. Grant was pushing up the Tennessee River, he was surprised at Shiloh by a South-ern force under Albert Sidney Johnston. Buell, hurrying to Grant's aid, naturally denuded the defenses of Nashville. Even before the emergency, Johnson had wired in dismay to Stanton that the city had been left almost defenseless by Buell, whom he distrusted. Promising "immediate measures to correct the evil," the secretary of war promptly instructed Henry W. Halleck, the field commander, to send reinforcements. "You can appreciate the consequence of any disaster to Nashville," Stanton pointed out, "and are requested to secure it immediately against all danger."[19]

The immediate peril was thus averted; Johnston was killed, and Shi-loh was a success. The simultaneous victory at Island No. 10 also encour-aged the Unionists. But the long-term danger was not over. While Buell was pursuing the enemy toward Corinth, Nashville was exposed to constant hostile raids. "This place is almost defenceless now and tends to keep alive the rebellious spirit," Johnson wired Lincoln on April 12, at the same time begging the president to appoint a new commander at

Cumberland Gap. His great concern for East Tennessee was now reinforced by his desire to relieve the pressure on the state capital. In
addition, on April 25, he complained to Buell that Louis D. Campbell's
Sixty-ninth Ohio, which had been raised in his name under the command of his friend, a former congressman from Ohio, had been ordered
away, a matter he also brought to the president's attention. But he could
not really reverse the situation in central Tennessee.[20]

The weakness of the federal forces in and around Nashville, about
which Johnson had been correctly complaining, was a standing invitation for raiders to do their work in the vicinity. And during almost the
entire period of Johnson's stay in the city, two of the Confederacy's most
talented cavalry leaders, Nathan Bedford Forrest and John Hunt Morgan, made the most of their opportunity. Raiding, cutting rail lines,
blowing up bridges and railroad tunnels, and at times approaching to
within a few miles of the city, they terrorized the Unionists and made
havoc of federal communications. No wonder Johnson was dissatisfied.

The situation became critical in July. On the thirteenth Forrest
swooped down upon Murfreesboro, causing untold damage as he went,
while at the same time Morgan was engaged in a raid in Kentucky.
Nashville became apprehensive; Johnson, however, confident of holding
the city, conferred with his military advisers on how to defend it. All
expressed optimism, only to be upset a few days later, when Lebanon
and Hartville were captured and three Unionists were hanged within
twenty-five miles of the capital. By July 23 Forrest was at Antioch, only
six miles away, and soon the enemy approached to within a mile and
a half of the city.

In this crisis, Johnson remained calm. Threatening to level the houses
of secessionists if Nashville was fired upon, he spent endless hours in the
capitol, even sleeping there at night while awaiting an attack. Finally, on
July 29, the enemy withdrew. Samuel Glenn, a New York *Herald* reporter who shared the governor's sleeping accommodations at the capitol, thought the Confederates did so largely because of Johnson's
threats.[21]

Of course the governor did his best to obtain reinforcements. As soon
as he heard of Morgan's movements, even before the Murfreesboro
disaster, he demanded more troops from Lincoln. The raid in Kentucky
was aimed at the Louisville and Nashville Railroad, "which should be
protected by all means necessary for the safety of this place and all
middle Tennessee," he insisted. He also requested that the president
remove Buell's assistant adjutant general, Captain O. D. Greene, who
refused to order the necessary troops to defend the city. Lincoln tactfully
replied that what Johnson was asking was to put him in command of

the West—"I do not suppose you desire this," the president added— and suggested that the governor communicate with Henry Halleck.[22]

This advice fell on willing ears, but Halleck, just then about to travel to Washington to assume his duties as general in chief, could do but little. Lincoln told him to help the governor, whom he called a "true and valuable man, indispensable to us in Tennessee" Halleck, however, never did meet with Johnson; thus the governor had to continue direct- ing the defense of the city himself.[23]

Even after Forrest's withdrawal, the danger was not over. In August Morgan appeared at Gallatin, where he cut the railroad and blew up a tunnel north of the town, thus interrupting Nashville's tenuous rail connections with the North. And this incursion was merely the prelude to the much more serious invasion of Kentucky that Braxton Bragg launched later that month. To be sure, the Confederates were eventually contained and they retreated into East Tennessee, but for a while, Nashville's situation was very perilous.[24]

Not only the fate of the capital but, as always, that of his home and family was constantly on Johnson's mind. He pleaded, he begged, he tried to raise new troops, but as long as Buell continued his dilatory tactics, the governor had little hope of success. In desperation, Johnson wrote to General Thomas expressing his hope that Thomas might be put in command of an expedition to free East Tennessee, but the general was noncommittal. Trying to reassure the governor, he maintained that Buell would eventually free the entire state. Johnson remained uncon- vinced.[25]

In order to counter Braxton Bragg's moves, Buell finally marched through Nashville. Again he clashed with the governor. Believing that the city did not have real military importance, he gave Johnson to understand that he might have to evacuate it. Three times Johnson urged him to reconsider, and finally Buell did leave Thomas behind in command of the capital. When Buell later faced a court of inquiry, he denied that he had ever thought of giving up the city, or that Johnson was responsible for changing his mind, but it is undoubtedly true that in the crisis during the late summer and early fall of 1862, the governor was a rock of firmness.

From about the middle of September until Rosecrans' arrival early in November, Nashville was totally isolated. As reporter Samuel Glenn recorded it, "Days, weeks, nay months roll around and there seems to be no change for the better." Seeking to take the city, Forrest and other raiders maintained that even its destruction would be a cheap price to pay if they could catch Andy Johnson. "The coolness and calmness of the Governor amid these trying scenes are beyond all praise," Glenn continued. Doing all he could to preserve order, the governor spent most of his time at the capitol, where he set an example for all by his seeming confidence. "Andy Johnson says if the rebels retake Nashville, they will find his remains under the ruin of the Capitol," reported the Nashville *Dispatch,* and there was little doubt that the governor was serious. He was determined to set fire to the city rather than surrender it.[26]

Because of his utter disgust with Buell, Johnson tried hard to have him removed. The general, he wrote Lincoln in September, "would never enter and redeem the Eastern portion of this State"; he was pursuing wholly defensive tactics and ruining Unionism in Tennessee. "General Buell is very popular with the Rebels," he continued, "and the impression is that he favors the establishment of a Southern Confederacy." Though the governor himself thought this last charge exaggerated, he nevertheless believed that if Buell had deliberately set out to do so, he could not have pursued a policy that would have been more successful in establishing the Confederacy and surrendering Tennessee to the rebels. In October Johnson wrote again, this time suggesting that General George W. Morgan's entire command be sent to Tennessee in order to liberate his home section. But by this time, as Lincoln intimated, the governor had already been partially successful. Buell had been relieved by William S. Rosecrans, and Johnson could hope for some relief.[27]

How tremendous the strain was during this difficult period is illustrated by a story Lincoln told the painter Frank Carpenter. During the time Johnson believed that Buell had decided to evacuate Nashville, Granville Moody, a Methodist chaplain, one day found the governor rapidly pacing the floor. To quote Carpenter,

Johnson, manifesting intense feeling . . . said, "Moody, we are sold out. Buell is a traitor! He is going to evacuate the city, and in forty-eight hours we shall be in the hands of the Rebels!" Then he commenced pacing the floor again, twisting his hands, and chafing like a caged tiger, utterly insensible to his friend's entreaties to become calm. Suddenly he turned and said, "Moody, can you pray?" "That is my business, sir, as a minister of the Gospel," returned the Colonel. "Well, Moody, I wish you would pray," said Johnson; and instantly both went down on their knees, at opposite sides of the room. As the prayer waxed fervent, Johnson began to respond in true Methodist style. Presently he crawled over on his hands and knees to Moody's side, and put his arm over him, manifesting the deepest emotion. Closing the prayer with a hearty "Amen" from each, they arose. Johnson took a long breath, and said, with emphasis, "Moody, I feel better!" Shortly afterwards he asked, "Will you stand by me?" "Certainly I will," was the answer. "Well, Moody, I can depend upon you; you are one in a hundred thousand!" He then commenced pacing the floor again. Suddenly he wheeled, the current of his thought having changed, and said, "Oh! Moody, I don't want you to think I have become a religious man because I asked you to pray. I am sorry to say it, but I am not, and have never pretended to be, religious. No one knows this better than you; but, Moody, there is one thing about it—I DO believe in ALMIGHTY GOD! And I believe also in the Bible, and I say 'd——n' me, if Nashville shall be surrendered!"

As the painter added, *"And Nashville was not surrendered."*[28]

Finally, Nashville's ordeal came to an end. Rosecrans' troops lifted the siege in November 1862, and when, at the turn of the year, the general checked Bragg at Murfreesboro, Johnson was greatly heartened. "The Battle of Murfreesboro has inspired much confidence with Union men of the ultimate success of the Govt & has greatly discouraged Rebels but increased their bitterness," he wired to the president. If the Confederate army could be expelled from Tennessee altogether, and especially from East Tennessee, he believed that the restoration of the state by a decided majority could not be far off.[29]

But, of course, East Tennessee was not to be liberated until the late summer and fall of 1863, and parts of it not till even later. While the immediate threat to the capital had been lifted, the state had still not been completely redeemed. In view of the perilous situation of East Tennessee Unionists, it was not surprising that the fate of his home section continued to occupy the governor's thoughts. He heard horror stories not only from Brownlow and other refugees, but also from his own family; for Eliza finally made it through the lines to Nashville.

As the wife of the Tennessee Unionist Southerners hated most, Eliza had not had an easy time. Expelled by the occupying authorities, she was at first too unwell to travel and during the summer of 1862 stayed with her daughter Mary Stover in Carter County. Then, in October, the Confederates made her leave again. Accompanied by Frank, Charles, and the Stovers, she arrived at Murfreesboro at nine in the evening. It was raining, there was no place to stay, and she finally had to sleep on the floor of an unheated house. At six in the morning, she was summoned before the raider Forrest, who declared that not even Jesus Christ would be allowed to cross his lines and ordered her back on the seven o'clock train. But apparently Governor Harris, much as he loathed the man he called "that infamous wretch, Andrew Johnson," interfered to allow Eliza and her party to cross the next morning. Joyously welcomed by her husband, she moved in with him at his quarters, the former house of Neill S. Brown.[30] Her experiences merely hardened Johnson's resolve to relieve his home region. He cajoled, he combined with Maynard, he urged Lincoln and Stanton to act, but he had to wait until Rosecrans and Burnside freed the region in August and September 1863.[31]

Johnson's great concern about military security led him to seek to raise as many troops in Tennessee as possible. Authority to do so was granted to him when he first arrived in Nashville; and after he was given the right to draw on the treasury at Cincinnati for $10,000 to organize a home guard, he pursued that object with untiring vigor. By April 23, 1862, he reported that two regiments were ready and four others nearly, but the necessary equipment was in short supply. In June, responding to his request for more troops, Stanton permitted him to raise two additional regiments. During the military crisis in July, he asked for and received authority to recruit more cavalry, and on August 1 he was given permission to enlist troops for three years, primarily for the liberation of East Tennessee. On March 28, 1863, Stanton empowered him to recruit ten regiments of infantry and a like number of artillery and cavalry units. Soon thereafter Johnson was authorized to raise troops in other states as well.

Of course, these activities caused conflicts with other generals, and the end result was disappointing. While it has been estimated that Johnson raised twenty-five regiments and while he succeeded in detaching troops from Rosecrans to organize his Governor's Guard, he was always short of horses and equipment. His friend and protégé Brigadier General Alvan C. Gillem was to have a brief moment of triumph when he caused the death of John Hunt Morgan at Greeneville, but Gillem was to be driven back again shortly afterward. Johnson's political skills were not sufficient to overcome military obstacles.[32]

His recruiting was not the only cause of trouble between the governor and many of the Western commanders. He remained independent, always a maverick, and distrustful of professional soldiers, qualities that caused him to clash with Buell, Rosecrans, James S. Negley, Stanley Matthews, and others. True, he had favorites. Gillem, a Tennessee Unionist, enjoyed his special confidence. He saw to it that Gillem was promoted and obtained a suitable command, and generally furthered his career. General Thomas, too, now impressed him, and Johnson persistently sought to keep the brilliant general in commands where he could liberate East Tennessee and protect Nashville. But on the whole, the governor encountered severe difficulties with the military.[33]

It was Buell who aroused Johnson's special ire. Considering the slow, methodical manner in which the general liked to conduct his operations, to say nothing of his failure to follow up demands for the invasion of East Tennessee, the quarrel between the two men is not surprising. Special irritants, such as the refusal of Buell's assistant adjutant general, Oliver B. Greene, to cooperate with the governor, heightened the controversy, particularly when Greene arrested Johnson's friend Lewis D. Campbell, whom he had appointed provost marshal of Nashville. In the end Greene was dismissed—Johnson had enough influence in Washington to have his way—but the problem with Buell remained until he was relieved by Rosecrans.[34]

Rosecrans, a tall, strongly built West Pointer who was quick to anger but equally quick to forgive, maintained better relations with the governor. The timing of his arrival to relieve Nashville and his success at the Battle of Murfreesboro soon afterward made a good impression on the beleaguered governor. But he, too, had his problems with Johnson. The main point of contention was Colonel William Truesdail, Rosecrans' chief of detectives in Nashville, who soon crossed swords with Johnson. Not only did Truesdail seem to feather his own nest, but he definitely considered Rosecrans, not Johnson, his superior. Johnson demanded that Rosecrans establish a commission to investigate the detective; the general appointed an investigating officer instead, and the latter did not recommend any action. On the surface, relations between Rosecrans and Johnson were patched up and Truesdail's powers curbed, but underlying tensions remained.[35]

Stanley Matthews, Campbell's predecessor as provost marshal, also clashed with the governor. A prewar federal prosecutor in Cincinnati, Matthews had gained much unpopularity for his enforcement of the Fugitive Slave Law; now a colonel in the Fifty-first Ohio, he seemed much too friendly to the secessionists, at least to Johnson. Complaining about him to Henry Halleck, the governor succeeded in having him removed from his post. When Matthews came up for promotion, Johnson wrote to Sherman recommending that Matthews be denied his star, and as a result he remained a colonel. Yet Matthews' career was not finished: in 1864 he served as an elector on the Lincoln-Johnson ticket, and Rutherford B. Hayes later appointed him to the Supreme Court.[36]

Another military opponent was General James Scott Negley, affable, urbane, but independent. Left in charge of the post of Nashville, Negley feuded with Johnson about their overlapping commands, and the governor asked Lincoln that the general be removed. When Negley was routed at Chickamauga, his military career came to an end, and the controversy ended as well. Yet it highlighted Johnson's consistent inability to get along with most of the army commanders with whom he came in contact.[37]

In the meantime Johnson continued to administer the affairs of the civilian government as well as he could. He also delivered fiery speeches to encourage the troops and rally the Unionists. The content of these orations was generally pure Johnson: the wickedness of the aristocratic rebels, their enmity to popular government, and the supremacy of the Union guaranteed by the Constitution. He detailed these truths to the Third Minnesota Regiment at Nashville, and he repeated them at Columbia and Shelbyville, only to sum them up once again on the Fourth of July before a cheering crowd in the courtyard of the state capitol. "The time has arrived when treason must be made odious and traitors impoverished," he declared on that occasion, once more invoking his (slightly changed) slogan.[38]

Like other commanders in occupied cities, Johnson found it more difficult to handle the women than the men. Passionately devoted to the Confederacy, Southern belles showed their hatred of the invaders by heaping indignities upon them and spilling slop upon Union soldiers. Ben Butler, then in command of New Orleans, stopped this behavior by threatening to treat each one of the perpetrators as "a woman of the town plying her avocation," an order Johnson preserved among his papers. He himself was less inflexible. When his hotel keeper's daughter, Laura Carter, was arrested for spitting at a federal officer, he was told that she had refused to listen to pleas that she ought to behave while the governor was her father's guest. One day she would dance on Johnson's grave, she had boasted defiantly. "Oh, you mustn't mind these little rebels . . . ," he said. "There is no harm in Laura. Dance on my grave, will she? She will plant flowers instead." Although he could at times lecture sternly to them, he was generally polite even to secessionist ladies—he simply did not believe in making war on what was then called the "weaker sex." And while he was unable to win over many of the Southerners, he did manage to keep them under control.[39]

And Johnson's policy toward all secessionists, not just female, was much more conciliatory, even lenient, than his uncompromising language might indicate. Once having asserted his authority, he saw no occasion for further severity. Thus he permitted William G. Harding, the prominent secessionist owner of the Belle Meade plantation, whom he had arrested in April, to return on parole, eventually freed the obstreperous non-juring ministers, and offered protection to various prominent rebels. After sending a commission to Ohio to induce Tennessee prisoners of war to take an oath of allegiance, he sought and obtained from Lincoln control over their release, which he generally granted. Moreover, he tended to respond favorably to requests from condemned soldiers for a commutation of their death sentences.

Whether the Confederates realized it or not, his harsh words often cloaked an attitude of forgiveness.[40]

Johnson worked very hard while in Nashville. Seeking to provision the city and to keep the hostile secessionists in check, he supervised the building of a railroad from the capital to the Tennessee River. In his office in the capitol—which was furnished with heavy oak chairs, two sofas, and two portraits, characteristically one of Andrew Jackson and the other of himself as governor during his two previous terms—he received a constant stream of visitors. They found a man of medium height, strongly built, with black hair, very black piercing eyes, a prominent nose, and almost a scowl, impeccably dressed in black broadcloth, frock coat, and waistcoat, with black doeskin trousers and a silk hat. Some Unionists appreciated him, but secessionists regarded him with ever-increasing loathing.[41]

One of the gravest problems facing the governor was the question of slavery. His long-standing defense of the "peculiar institution" had done him little good; yet when the war began he insisted and continued to insist that the only security for slavery was the preservation of the Union. The war was being fought for the Union, not for the abolition of slavery, he declared, and when General John M. Palmer told him Northern antislavery forces opposed the institution because it was unjust, Johnson answered, "D——n the negroes; I am fighting these traitorous aristocrats, their masters." Convinced that blacks were inferior to whites and ought to be treated that way, he stated, "I believe slaves should be in subordination and I will live and die so believing." As time went on, however, the governor moderated his tone. "I believe indeed that the Union is the only protection of slavery—its sole guarantee," he said in the summer of 1862. "But if you persist in forcing the issue of slavery against the Government, I say in the face of Heaven, 'Give me my Government and let the negroes go!' "[42]

Because of the agitation of the radicals and the pressure of foreign events, Lincoln, himself not averse to ending slavery, was steadily moving toward a policy of at least partial emancipation. To be sure, as late as May 1862, much to Johnson's satisfaction, the president still saw fit to countermand General David Hunter's order freeing the slaves in the Department of the South.[43] But only a few weeks later, he drew up the Emancipation Proclamation for the liberation of all slaves held in areas still in rebellion. And although the preliminary proclamation was not issued until September 22, to go into effect on January 1, 1863, its appearance represented a strong challenge to the Unionists of Tennessee.

Always a clever politician, Johnson sensed which way the country was moving. Nevertheless, convinced that Tennessee was still part of the Union, he could not allow Lincoln's proclamation to apply to his state. Consequently, on December 4, 1862, he signed a petition that ex-governor Campbell was circulating on executive stationery asking the president to exempt Tennessee from the proclamation. According to James G. Blaine, Lincoln was largely influenced by the governor to grant the petition, and Tennessee was consequently not listed as one of the states in rebellion. "Your proclamation of the 1st excepting Tennessee has disappointed & disarmed many who were complaining & denouncing it as unjust & unwise. I think the Exception in favor of Tennessee will be worth much to us," Johnson telegraphed the president on January 11.[44] It would not be long before he himself declared for emancipation.

Johnson had now reached a dividing line in his governorship. Should he go along with the conservative proslavery Unionists and continue to oppose Lincoln's emancipation policy, or should he join the other side, ingratiate himself with the radicals, and support the administration? His entire future was at stake, and when in February 1863 he decided to travel to Washington, by way of several Northern states, the trip helped him to make up his mind.

The main reason for Johnson's visit to the capital was probably his desire to clarify the extent of his powers and to plead once more for the liberation of East Tennessee, although he must have been fully aware of the political possibilities of the trip. As it turned out, his journey became a speech-making tour in the course of which he was enthusiastically welcomed by crowds from Indiana to New York, and from Philadelphia to Washington. Accompanied by his friend former governor Joseph A. Wright of Indiana, the governor first stopped off at Indianapolis, where he addressed a large Union meeting and delivered a speech lasting three hours. The gist of his remarks, and he would say the same thing over and over again, was that the South was to blame for the war, that Southern aristocrats had always wanted to secede, and that there could be no compromise with rebels. As for the blacks, he reiterated the position he had taken at Nashville a year earlier.

I have lived among negroes, all my life, and I am for this Government with slavery under the Constitution as it is, if the Government can be saved. . . . I am for the Government of my fathers with negroes, I am for it without negroes. Before I would see this Government destroyed, I would send every negro back to Africa, disintegrated and blotted out of space. . . . If the institution of slavery denies the Government the right of agitation, and seeks to overthrow it, then the Government has a clear right to destroy it.

As in the past, he declared himself ever a Democrat, invoked the spirit of Old Hickory, and reiterated his belief in democracy and religion as parallel lines of human progress.

At Cincinnati Johnson delivered a similar address, which he repeated in slightly altered form to the Ohio legislature a few days later. On March 6, after a cordial invitation from the Pennsylvania senate had set off a furious debate with local Peace Democrats, the group opposing the war, the citizens of Harrisburg heard an analogous speech at the courthouse; on March 11 the governor spoke to a huge audience at Philadelphia's Music Fund Hall, on March 15 at Cooper Union in New York, and a few days later at the Maryland Institute in Baltimore, where Secretary of the Treasury Salmon P. Chase, Postmaster General Montgomery Blair, Horace Maynard, and General Burnside were in the audience. And, of course, Johnson continued speaking after he arrived in Washington. This time it was an address on March 30, in the Capitol itself, with the president and cabinet in attendance.[45]

While in Washington, Johnson achieved much of what he had hoped to accomplish. He received more specific authority to recruit troops and more ample powers as military governor. He urged the promotion of his protégé Alvan C. Gillem, who eventually won his general's star. Conferring steadily with the president, Secretary of War Stanton, and other members of the cabinet, he was able to look forward to a campaign for the liberation of his home section. Apparently he also assisted his former colleagues on the Joint Committee on the Conduct of the War in writing their report. And Lincoln, taking advantage of the opportunity, shrewdly planted a seed in Johnson's mind. "I am told you have at least *thought* of raising a negro military force," he wrote to the governor on March 26. "In my opinion the country now needs no specific thing so much as some man of your ability, and position, to go to this work. . . . If you *have* been thinking of it please don't dismiss the thought." And if Johnson had believed before that the Emancipation Proclamation was a mistake, he was beginning to make the necessary adjustments, particularly because Lincoln's antislavery opinions made it difficult to pursue a contrary course in Tennessee. The trip had been an eye-opener.[46]

Just exactly when and why the governor turned so openly toward emancipation in the summer of 1863 is still not entirely clear. But the trip through the North and the enthusiastic welcome he received must have made him aware of the political opportunities awaiting him. Except for timing, Lincoln and the radicals were as one on the question of ending slavery. By coming out for unconditional emancipation, Johnson would earn the gratitude of both.[47]

His personal problems may also have helped him to make up his mind. Eliza was unwell when she arrived in Nashville; in order to speed her recovery, the Stovers took her north shortly after the siege of Nashville was lifted. In early December 1862 she moved to Vevay, Indiana, a small town overlooking the Ohio River, to seek a cure. But her health remained feeble, and Johnson, in great agitation, wrote to her from Washington. Was she getting better? It was hard for him to write—his elbow still caused him trouble, and the constant speaking had affected his throat. Worry about Martha, still in Greeneville, and about Robert and Charles, both of them now addicted to drink, depressed him. "I feel sometimes like giv[in]g al up in dispare," he complained, and sent Eliza his love, "the best wishes of a devoted husband's heart."[48]

Worse was to follow. Charles, who had entered the army as a surgeon, suffered an accident in a fall from a horse and died in April 1863. The bereaved father, away in Washington, could not even come to the funeral. And Robert, a colonel attempting to equip a regiment with horses, was in steady difficulties with his superiors and given more and more to drinking. The governor, who had helped Robert in his efforts to raise a cavalry regiment, in the end decided it would be better to have his son close by and recalled him to Nashville. Dan Stover, also in the army, was in poor health, and only little Frank, now in school at Louisville, seemed to be doing well. In this unhappy situation, a radical break with the past may not have seemed so consequential to Johnson. He might as well stake all on the future.[49]

His trip back to Nashville took longer than anticipated. He was delayed at Louisville to give testimony to Buell's Court of Inquiry and stayed in the North for a while longer because of Eliza's continued illness, so that he did not reach Nashville until May 30. Eliza, Mary, and her children were with him; he was welcomed by a large crowd at the station and ceremoniously taken home to Lizinka Brown's house, where he had taken up residence. His successes in Washington could be expected to encourage the Unionists.[50]

Johnson's enhanced military powers resulted in more severe policies toward the Confederates. Even before he left for the North, in accordance with the Confiscation Act of the previous summer, he had issued a proclamation warning tenants renting from persons now behind enemy lines to suspend payments. Now he went further. Encouraged by the victories at Gettysburg and Vicksburg, on August 22 he delivered a speech at Franklin in which he reiterated more forcefully his long-held opinions. Defending the Confiscation Act on the ground that "treason must be made odious and traitors . . . punished and impoverished," he again declared: "I am for my Government with or without slavery, but if either the Government or slavery must perish, I say give me the Government and let the negroes go." Then, a week later in Nashville, he finally came out unequivocally for emancipation. Slavery was a "cancer on our society," he asserted, and the time had come for its total eradication. Having at last opted for freedom for slaves, he was greatly encouraged by Lincoln's approbation, upon which his future might depend. Burnside's recapture of Knoxville early in September and the temporary liberation of Greeneville soon afterward made his position more secure. The long struggle for East Tennessee had finally ended in success, and the governor could afford to disregard the conservatives, the proslavery Unionists whose support had long been essential.[51]

Johnson's endorsement of full emancipation finally gave him an opportunity also to cooperate with Lincoln in raising black troops. At first hesitant to embark on so controversial a program and unwilling to use the blacks for anything other than labor, he clashed with Major George L. Stearns, the Boston abolitionist sent by Stanton to facilitate black recruitment. After observing the freedmen's performance, however, and receiving assurances that he was in command, the governor composed his differences with Stearns. He succeeded in securing an extra $300 to be paid to loyal slaveholders for every soldier furnished, and in the long run established excellent relations with Stearns' successors, who eventually raised more than twenty thousand black troops for the federal service.[52]

Yet, because Unionists now split into two factions differing in their attitude toward emancipation, Johnson's new position on slavery greatly complicated his efforts to reestablish a civilian state government. His original mission had been to reconstruct the state as quickly as possible; because of the continued presence of enemy raiders and the Confederate occupation of East Tennessee, for a long time this task proved unattainable. To be sure, on May 12, 1862, shortly after Johnson had taken over, a large Union meeting assembled at the capitol. Former governor Campbell, assisted by Edmund Cooper, Johnson's private secretary, chaired the gathering. Despite the sneers of Southerners, who denigrated the participants, the number of Unionists was impressive and many were well known. However, they were unable to do much more than pass resolutions declaring it essential for Tennessee to return to the Union and endorsing the administration.[53]

The first elections after the establishment of Johnson's regime took place in Nashville late in May 1862. In a contest for a circuit judge, the secessionist Turner S. Foster won by a vote of 706 to 550. Johnson gave Foster his commission; then he arrested him for disloyalty and appointed his rival instead. It was not a hopeful beginning.

That Lincoln was not pleased with these results was not surprising. Anxious to speed up the Reconstruction process in order to weaken the Confederacy, on July 3 he made his position clear. "If we could, somehow, get a vote of the people of Tennessee and have it result properly it would be worth more to us than a battle gained," he admonished. "How long before we can get such a vote?"[54]

The governor was unable to oblige. Besieged by the enemy's armies, plagued by marauders and secessionst sympathizers, he could not call for elections, at least not until Unionist East Tennessee was freed. In October Lincoln, still hoping for a speedy vote, sent a special commissioner to help restore the state; perhaps the preliminary Emancipation Proclamation, with its hundred-day period of grace for rebels to return to their allegiance to save their property in slaves, might encourage the doubtful. But it was not until December that Johnson was finally able to order at least limited elections confined to the Ninth and Tenth congressional districts in West Tennessee, and even this effort proved unavailing because Forrest invaded the districts concerned. New elections were scheduled for January, but General Grant postponed them still further.[55]

The Emancipation Proclamation, far from encouraging Reconstruction, created additional difficulties. The Unionists now split; those that continued to oppose emancipation, largely led by Emerson Etheridge, Balie Peyton, and ex-governor Campbell, could no longer make common cause with those who favored it, led by Brownlow and Johnson, who was rapidly moving toward endorsement of freedom. It is true that in July 1863 a group of Johnson's friends at a convention in Nashville passed resolutions supporting him and calling upon him to issue writs of election, but he hesitated. East Tennessee was not yet freed, and without its strong Unionist support, an election would be doubtful. Nothing daunted, his Unionist opponents, even before he had fully come out for emancipation, took advantage of the regular August elections to nominate ex-governor Campbell for governor. Although only a few votes were cast for him or anyone else, the conservative Unionists declared Campbell the winner. Johnson, supported by Lincoln, refused to recognize either the election or the governor-elect, but the time was rapidly approaching when he would have to do something about the restoration of the state government.[56]

This was especially true after the federal successes in East Tennessee. Fully aware of his responsibility, Johnson told visiting Assistant Secretary of War Charles A. Dana that he would hold elections in October, but he did not follow through on his promise. Lincoln continued to pressure him. Now that all Tennessee was cleared of enemy troops, he wrote, the time had come to hold elections, although he warned that they must not be allowed to result in a secessionist victory. "I see that you have declared in favor of emancipation," he concluded, "for which, may God bless you." Suggesting that emancipation be enshrined in the new state constitution, the president urged that black troops be raised in support of Reconstruction.

But Johnson was still delaying. Unsure of the outcome of any vote and anxious to maintain Unionist supremacy, he was not eager to take the risk. After assuring Lincoln that he was wholly committed to immediate emancipation, he asked that his instructions from the president include a reference to Article IV of the Constitution, obligating the federal Union to guarantee a republican form of government to the states. Lincoln sent him the desired modification; yet Johnson continued to procrastinate.[57]

Johnson's hesitation soon gave rise to rumors that he was loath to give up power. The Louisville *Journal* even charged that he had made a bargain with the radicals not to restore Tennessee until it was a free state. The governor naturally denied all such gossip, but his position was becoming more and more awkward.[58] Briefly relieved of the necessity of action in September because of Rosecrans' defeat at Chickamauga, he had to do something after Grant's subsequent victory at Chattanooga and James Longstreet's failure shortly afterward to recapture Knoxville.

The problem of Reconstruction became even more urgent when on December 8, 1863, Lincoln issued his Amnesty Proclamation, which authorized the reestablishment of governments when 10 percent of the voters had taken a simple amnesty oath. The proclamation had great appeal to many Tennesseans. It was clear to Johnson that citizens would want to take advantage of the president's offer, but it was less clear that the program would operate in favor of unconditional Unionists endorsing emancipation, especially because upper East Tennessee was not to be completely cleared of the enemy for another year.

The governor would have to take some measures to deal with this problem. Summoned to Washington in the middle of December, presumably to discuss the situation, he returned prepared to inaugurate his own plan of restoration. Johnson proceeded with deliberation. On New Year's Day a premature meeting of Unionists in the representatives' hall in the capitol declared that Tennessee had committed suicide as a state, a contention both the newspapers and the governor himself categorically denied. Other gatherings in various parts of the state asked for restoration in accordance with Lincoln's scheme, and on January 8, 1864, Johnson took advantage of the anniversary of the Battle of New Orleans to deliver another speech in which he called once more for emancipation. He had owned slaves, he said; they had been confiscated, but two of them had run away and come to him to work for wages, an arrangement much better than the previous one. He denied that any state could commit suicide, invoked the spirit of Andrew Jackson in pleading for the maintenance of the Union, and as yet said little about the process of Reconstruction. Nevertheless, on the same day, the Nashville *Dispatch* announced that he would soon make known his plan for speedy restoration.[59]

Two weeks later Johnson did in fact announce his program. On January 21 a large meeting assembled in the House of Representatives, passed resolutions condemning slavery, and asked President Lincoln to restore Tennessee to the Union. When Johnson appeared in a corner of the hall, the audience loudly called for him, and he complied by delivering a two-hour speech. Under Article IV of the Constitution, he said, the state was guaranteed a republican government; Tennessee was still part of the Union, and it was necessary to begin restoring its proper relationship to the United States. This process could be initiated by first electing county officials. Then a convention ought to be called to end slavery. Johnson pointed out once again that he considered blacks inferior and that they would occupy a subordinate place in society. Perhaps they might even be sent to Mexico. He expressed his hope that the restoration question be settled quickly, but said there was a problem about the electorate; surely his listeners agreed that none but loyal men should have the right to vote. In order to see that this was done, he proposed that prospective voters be required to take an oath not merely to support the government, but also to affirm their desire for the timely overthrow of the rebellion. This would make it possible for secessionists to repent; at any rate, only the leaders of the rebellion ought to be punished, and they ought to be hanged. The audience applauded loudly and passed the requisite resolutions.[60]

But no matter how carefully Johnson sought to justify this oath of allegiance, it could not be denied that his plan to secure a safe majority was much more stringent than the president's, and his scheme was still somewhat vague. People had been hoping to learn how the actual process of restoration would work, the Nashville *Daily Press* pointed out. The governor knew how to use weapons against his adversaries, the paper continued, but he lacked administrative talent. This fact had been apparent when he had been elected governor, and it was even more true now. That this criticism was not entirely wrong would be shown by later developments.[61]

A few days later, on January 26, Johnson finally issued his long-awaited proclamation. Calling on the legal voters to elect justices of the peace, sheriffs, constables, trustees, circuit and county court clerks, registrars, and tax collectors on the first Saturday in March, he demanded that the prospective voters take an oath. "I solemnly swear," the oath read, "that I will henceforth support the Constitution of the United States and defend it against the assaults of all enemies." But this was not all. The applicant also had to swear

> that I ardently desire the suppression of the present insurrection and rebellion against the Government of the United States, the success of its armies, and the defeat of all those who oppose them, and that the Constitution of the United States, and all laws and proclamations, made in pursuance thereof, may be speedily and permanently established and enforced over all the people, States and Territories thereof; and further, that I will hereafter heartily aid and assist all loyal people in the accomplishment of these results. So help me God.[62]

Conservative Unionists were outraged. Asserting that Lincoln was already offering amnesty, the Nashville *Daily Press* accused Johnson of knowing better and fearing that the state would be restored following the president's principles. Exhorting Tennesseeans to take Lincoln's oath rather than Johnson's, the paper advised them to challenge the latter's legality. It accused the governor of having totally ruined the state's prospects for Reconstruction. "No man in Tennessee—not even Isham G. Harris," the Nashville *Daily Press* complained, "has done more than Andrew Johnson to create, to perpetuate and embitter in the minds of the Southern people, that feeling of jealousy and hostility against the free States, which has at length culminated in rebellion and civil war. Up to 1860, he had been for 20 years among the most bigoted and intolerant of the advocates of slavery and Southernism, and the most unsparing denouncer of everything and everybody north of Mason's and Dixon's line." At present, he wanted higher office, and for that reason changed his mind to delude the Southern people. Had he not interfered there would have been a reasonable prospect of a respectable vote in the election, but now everything was ruined, all because of his ambition, for he seemed "to have but one aim, the Vice Presidency of the United States, on any rabid ticket . . . likely to be successful." Former congressman Edwin H. Ewing expressed his opposition more politely. "If the oath prescribed by you is necessary to be taken," he queried, "I would respectfully ask by what authority is it founded?"

Other Unionists also objected. "Why require us Union men, who never sinned against the Government, to be classed with rebels, to take the same oath?" protested a Bedford County Unionist. "The phraseology . . . 'that I shall *hereafter* aid and assist all loyal persons in putting down the rebellion,' implies that heretofore we have been against these things." Evidently this was not the case, and loyalists resented being classed with their enemies.[63]

Johnson refused to budge. In February, he went to Washington once more to confer with the president. Lincoln said there was no difference between his own proclamation and the governor's—evidently he, too, was anxious for a favorable pro-emancipation vote in Tennessee. But as few citizens went to the polls, the March elections were disappointing.[64]

The governor was undeterred. At his suggestion, the Greeneville Convention of 1861 was reassembled in Knoxville, and Johnson himself traveled to East Tennessee to attend the meeting. Delayed on the way by a railroad accident at Athens, he did not arrive in Knoxville until three in the morning. But he addressed the gathering on schedule. Blaming slavery for the evils that had befallen the state, he insisted that the institution must be eradicated. At the same time, he sought to scotch a renewed movement for separate statehood for East Tennessee—now he needed the section's Unionists for his plans for the Reconstruction of the entire state.

The convention did not turn out as he had expected. Conservatives like Thomas A. R. Nelson, William B. Carter, and John Baxter clashed with unconditional Unionists, led by Brownlow and Daniel C. Trewhitt. Johnson's policies were the main cause of the controversy, and after four days Sam Milligan, attempting to prevent embarrassment for his friend, moved that the body adjourn. It did so without passing any resolutions.

Johnson was furious. At a mass meeting in Knoxville on April 16, he explained why he had wanted to call a state convention. Slavery had brought the war upon the country, he said, and it had to go. It was for this reason that a convention was needed; those who opposed him were merely trying to save slavery. Was it not true that, in accordance with the constitution of Tennessee, the legislature had no right to emancipate without the consent of the slave owners? The new government must pass into the hands of loyal men; it was for that reason that he had devised the special oath, and it was sheer effrontery on the part of pardoned rebels to protest against it. At the same meeting, Oliver P. Temple, though he did not approve of his old antagonist's plans, consented to present resolutions written by William A. Browning, Johnson's private secretary, endorsing the military governor. But because the reorganization of the state became enmeshed with the governor's nomination and campaign for the vice presidency, Johnson was unable to complete the restoration until after the election.[65]

Thus by 1864 Johnson's military governorship had failed to achieve the main object of his appointment. To be sure, he finally would create a new free state organization, but only in early 1865, after many delays. His vigorous measures had kept Nashville firmly in Union hands, though they had often embittered Confederates more than necessary, especially as his predilection for reconciliation frequently went unrecognized. Unfortunately, Johnson's ambition for higher office eventually made him careless. He achieved his personal goal, but his administration of the state suffered. For a time, however, his great popularity in the North caused admirers to overlook his shortcomings. These would not become evident until later.

X

VICE PRESIDENT

JOHNSON had always been ambitious, and his ambition grew with each of his successes. He had harbored presidential hopes at least since 1852, expectations that even his failed bid for the presidency in 1860 could not dispel. Then, after his Union speech in December 1860, when he became a popular hero in the North, the thought of future honors never left him. His friends flattered his aspirations, and it was not surprising that in 1864 he should emerge as a strong contender for higher office.[1]

Some people thought that the governor was a natural candidate for the presidency. Lincoln was being challenged by Salmon P. Chase as well as by various generals; why should not one of the nation's leading War Democrats be in the running as well? In the fall and winter of 1863–64, various newspapers endorsed the governor, and in February the Fairfield, Illinois, *War Democrat* advocated a joint ticket of Johnson and John Logan, the Illinois Democrat turned general. Lincoln and Vice President Hannibal Hamlin had done well, the paper conceded, but Johnson was the man who could safely bring the ship of state into harbor.[2]

In view of Lincoln's political skill, neither Johnson nor anyone else had much of a chance of displacing him. The second office, however, was another matter. Vice President Hamlin, a radical from Maine, was a gifted politician, but he was unable to add much strength to the ticket. And because the Republicans were anxious to attract as many War Democrats as possible—they would soon rename their organization the

Union party—a Democratic running mate for the president was a distinct possibility.

Exactly how Johnson's nomination came about, and more particularly, what role Lincoln played, later became a matter of heated controversy. In July 1891, a few days after Hamlin's death, Alexander K. McClure, the Pennsylvania newspaper editor who in 1860 had had a hand in securing the nomination for Abraham Lincoln, declared that the president had engineered the coup. But John J. Nicolay, Lincoln's former secretary, who had already presented a different account in his great biography coauthored with John Hay, promptly refuted him. Nicolay referred to a telegram sent to him on June 6, 1864, by Hay, stating that the president had deliberately adopted a hands-off attitude. McClure later incorporated his own version of Johnson's nomination in his book *Abraham Lincoln and the Men of War-Times*, while Hamlin's grandson in his biography of his grandfather tended to follow Nicolay and Hay.[3]

What few contemporary pieces of evidence can be found seem to indicate that Lincoln was indeed interested in strengthening the ticket by the addition of a War Democrat. Early in 1864 he sent Simon Cameron to Fort Monroe to sound out Ben Butler for a possible position on the ticket. Butler, corpulent, partially bald, and afflicted with a drooping eyelid that gave him the appearance of being cross-eyed, was a prewar Democrat who, following his wartime experiences in New Orleans and elsewhere, had turned radical. He was also a shrewd politician, popular despite his inability to dispel rumors about his involvement in all manner of unsavory deals. In later years Butler maintained that he had told Cameron he would not quit the military to be vice president unless Lincoln gave him bond "that within three months after his inauguration he would die unresigned." While this reply is probably the product of an imagination helped by later events, the general did say no, and Lincoln had to turn somewhere else.[4] In May 1864 the president sent General Daniel Sickles, another ex-Democrat who had shot and killed his wife's lover and lost his leg as well as much of his military reputation at Gettysburg, to Nashville on a fact-finding trip. While Sickles denied that he was there to sound out or assess Johnson, it is most likely that that was precisely part of his mission. At any rate, the president apparently mentioned his preference for the governor not only to McClure and Cameron, but also to others: Abram J. Dittenhoefer, a New York Lincoln supporter of Southern antecedents, the president's old friends Ward Lamon and Leonard Swett of Illinois, and S. Newton Pettis, the western Pennsylvania attorney whom he had appointed a judge in the Colorado Territory, all knew about his wishes, as did William O. Stoddard, his former secretary who was now a U.S. marshal in Arkansas. If firm contemporary substantiation is lacking, circumstantial evidence would generally seem to bear out McClure's account.[5]

An extraneous factor also aided Johnson in his bid for the vice presidency. Secretary of State Seward was extremely anxious to prevent the nomination of his fellow New Yorker Daniel S. Dickinson, another War Democrat very much in the running. Should Dickinson become vice president, Seward would probably have to relinquish his position, two New Yorkers in such high posts being inappropriate. In addition, Charles Sumner, eager to have his opponent, the New England politician William Pitt Fessenden, replaced as senator from Maine and knowing of Hamlin's desire to return to the Senate, was also interested in finding a new vice presidential candidate. Nor can it be denied that Johnson's prominence in 1864 and his popularity in the North helped to make him a most available choice.[6]

There was one other consideration that must have occurred to Lincoln and most definitely played a role in Johnson's thinking. By choosing a candidate from Tennessee, the state's status within the Union would be emphasized; Johnson had always insisted that secession was impossible and that the Southern states were still part of the Union. And Lincoln might need the vote of the reconstructed Southern states in order to make sure of the outcome of the election. But the president was anxious to keep his decision a secret; he had been warned that abandoning Hamlin would cause a row in New England.[7]

Of course, Johnson was not passive in the weeks before the convention. Alerted by the journalist Benjamin Truman that Sickles had come to check up on him, he sent the newspaperman to Washington to enlist the help of his fellow editor and secretary of the Senate, John Forney, in his cause. Various meetings in Tennessee endorsed his candidacy, and newspapers reported that his nomination was generally expected.[8]

But the governor was almost sidetracked. On the day before the Baltimore Convention met, Daniel Dickinson's candidacy seemed to catch fire. Seward and his friend Thurlow Weed, now thoroughly frightened, began to lean toward Hamlin. Late at night, however, they learned that Massachusetts favored a War Democrat. It was then that the secretary of state definitely turned to Johnson to ward off the danger of Dickinson's being nominated.[9]

On the next day, June 7, 1864, when the convention opened, the Johnson movement received an additional boost. Skillfully pleading for the right of Tennessee's delegates to be seated with full powers, Horace Maynard, seconded by Brownlow, succeeded in obtaining general sup-

port. Suggesting that Johnson might well be the vice presidential candidate, Brownlow grandiloquently declared: "We have a man down there
whom it has been my good luck and bad fortune to fight untiringly and
perseveringly for the last twenty-five years—Andrew Johnson. [Ap-
plause] For the first time, in the Providence of God, three years ago, we
got together on the same platform and we are fighting the devil Tom
Walker and Jeff Davis side by side." His plea was effective.

In the following session on June 8, the delegates renominated Abraham Lincoln. Cameron's motion to endorse Hamlin as well—the Penn-
sylvanian knew how to dissimulate—was defeated. When the convention proceeded to the consideration of the vice presidency, C. M. Allen,
a delegate from Indiana, nominated Johnson, who was quickly seconded
by an Iowa member. In support of the nomination, Maynard recalled
the governor's loyal course since December 1860, his narrow escape at
Lynchburg, and his return "to invoke the aid of the Government for
his people." On the first roll call the Tennesseean received 200 votes to
Hamlin's 150 and Dickinson's 108. Then Kentucky switched, initiating
a stampede for the governor, who ended up with 494 to Hamlin's 17
and Dickinson's 9 votes before the nomination was made unanimous.
The ticket of Lincoln and Johnson represented the choice of the Union
party.[10]

In general, the result was well received. "The nomination of Andrew
Johnson, of Tennessee, for Vice President will be responded to everywhere with the expression of hearty satisfaction by the loyal people of
the country," commented the Louisville *Press*. "No man has labored
more earnestly in the cause of the Government than he has. His name
is inseparably connected with the history of this mighty struggle for the
maintenance of the Union and free government." The *New York Times*
agreed. Calling the nomination "eminently fit to be made," the paper
emphasized the importance of the War Democrats for the Union party,
as the combination of Republicans and War Democrats now called itself.
Lincoln himself was satisfied—"Andy Johnson, I think, is a good man,"
he commented—and word came that even in New York, the home of
Daniel S. Dickinson, Johnson's candidacy was popular. It was generally
conceded that he would add strength to the ticket.[11]

Yet there was also discontent. The Democratic New York *World*
delighted in pointing out the maneuvering that had led to the selection
of a new candidate for vice president; the New York *Herald* doubted the
constitutionality of the nomination of a Tennesseean; and even some
leading Republicans were unhappy. Dr. Robert Breckinridge, the presiding officer of the Baltimore Convention, opposed Johnson throughout;
the German immigrant leader Gustave Koerner, then in Madrid as

minister to Spain, also had no use for the governor—"I am afraid we have caught a tartar," he said—and Thaddeus Stevens, the radical leader of the House, had never held a good opinion of the Tennessee loyalist. "Can't you find a candidate for Vice President in the United States, without going down to one of those damned rebel provinces to pick one up?" he protested to McClure. Believing that the seceded states were in fact conquered "provinces," he could not have been pleased with the implication that Johnson was still a citizen of a state in the Union. Earlier he had reportedly told Lincoln, "Mr. President, Andrew Johnson is a rank demagogue, and I suspect at heart a damn scoundrel."

Johnson was unconcerned about these comments. When word of his nomination reached Nashville, a cannon boomed, the St. Cloud Hotel was brilliantly illuminated, and an enthusiastic crowd demanded that the governor make an appearance. His speech of thanks stressed his pride in representing a Southern state. "That convention," he said in reference to the Baltimore meeting, "announced and confirmed a principle not to be disregarded. It was that the right of secession, and the power of a State to place itself out of the Union are not recognized." By taking a nominee from one of the rebellious states, he continued, "the Union party declared its belief that the rebellious States are still in the Union, that their loyal citizens are still citizens of the United States." The principle was of prime importance to him, and he never forsook it. Accordingly, representing the War Democrats who held identical views, he endorsed Lincoln's message explaining his pocket veto of the Wade-Davis Bill, the congressional scheme of Reconstruction, with its implied suggestion that the Southern state governments were invalid.[12]

On July 2 Johnson wrote a formal letter of acceptance in which he stressed once again his devotion to the Union and to democracy as he understood it, his Jacksonian past, and Old Hickory's conviction that the agitation about the tariff in 1832–33 had been a mere pretext for the defense of slavery. Emancipation by constitutional amendment had been one of the planks adopted at Baltimore; Johnson endorsed it, he said, and called for an unqualified assertion of federal supremacy.

The Nashville *Daily Press* severely criticized the governor's stand. Accusing him of belonging to a "class of political vaulters and contortionists," the paper charged that he had betrayed the cause of his associates for the sake of political preferment. Johnson himself, however, was convinced that he had been perfectly consistent. As he saw it, he had never changed his principles. He was merely defending the government to which he had always been devoted; slavery had gotten in its way, and therefore the institution must disappear.[13]

It was hardly surprising that Johnson's nomination complicated the process of restoring the civilian government of Tennessee. Determined to reconstruct the state in accordance with Lincoln's Amnesty Proclamation, conservatives accused the governor of being the principal obstacle to their plans. And to some degree, they were not wrong. Not willing to entrust his future to the conservative Unionists of Tennessee, Johnson had indeed delayed and complicated the Reconstruction process. But now that he had been selected for higher office, he permitted the state executive committee to call a convention of loyal men to discuss the problem. Over fifty counties were represented when the delegates met in September 1864 at Nashville; by careful preparation, Johnson had seen to it that the radicals were in control and that his friend Milligan was elected president. But the convention soon split on the question of endorsing the Lincoln-Johnson ticket; conservatives demanded that delegates confine their discussion to the means of restoring the state, and strongly resisted efforts to turn the meeting into a Union party convention.

But that is in fact what the meeting became. The convention, ably run by Milligan, not only endorsed the national ticket but called for the participation of the state in the presidential election. To ensure the Union party's success, it prescribed an even more restrictive oath than the one Johnson had instituted in the spring. Prospective voters had to swear not only that they sincerely rejoiced in all triumphs of the armies of the United States but that they opposed "all armistices or negotiations for peace with rebels in arms."[14] In view of the fact that the Democrats had nominated General McClellan on a peace platform implicitly calling for negotiations, the conservative Unionists, who supported the Democratic ticket, were outraged. A "Bedlamite" convention, they called the meeting, while accusing their opponents of being afraid of the constitution of Tennessee.[15]

In spite of the conservatives' outcry, on the day the convention met, Johnson promptly issued a call for the restoration of civil government. He announced that he would continue to appoint officers willing to take his amnesty oath, and when the delegates adjourned, he followed their recommendations. On September 30 he issued a proclamation requiring voters in the presidential election to take the new oath rather than the one he had earlier established for the restoration of the state and thus in effect disfranchised the Democrats. Sure of the president's support, he could risk this radical expedient.[16]

Why Johnson, the committed believer in the principles of democratic government, took so uncharacteristic a step remains to be explained. His enemies tended to ascribe his action to his personal ambition, but there were other factors at work as well. Having staked his all on the defeat of the rebellion and being convinced that a McClellan victory would put this goal in doubt, he was willing to utilize any means to defeat McClellan. "Our Union: *It must be preserved,*" Andrew Jackson had said, and his disciple took his words to heart.[17] In addition, Johnson was now so thoroughly committed to the proposition that the state had never seceded, at least not legally, that he felt bound to prove it by his election. His lapse from democratic principles did not mean that he had abandoned them; on the contrary, he was certain that his method was the only way to save them.

Johnson's conviction of the rectitude of his course and the necessity of emancipation dominated his entire campaign for the vice presidency. In a speech on July 19, 1864, at a camp near Gallatin, the governor announced he was still a Democrat. He believed in the government established by Thomas Jefferson and upheld by Andrew Jackson but he had nothing in common with the Peace Democrats, who were nothing more than sympathizers with rebellion. Not Lincoln, but the secessionists, by firing on Fort Sumter, had freed the slaves, and the clamor about Negro equality was ridiculous. It was in the South, not in the North, that equality was flourishing. Had not "the blood of the South, once pure . . . become contaminated by negro . . . blood?" Let the blacks have a chance to rise by their own labor, that was all he asked.[18]

Radical Republicans loved his stance. So impressed were they with the governor that they urged John C. Frémont, who had been nominated for president by an extreme faction, to withdraw. "Something tells me that Lincoln will never fill a second term," one of Frémont's supporters wrote to him. "If I am right, Johnson will be the President, a man who I have loved since sixty-one. I have no doubt he will do you and your friends justice."[19]

Although it was not customary for candidates to campaign actively, Johnson violated the rule, not only in Tennessee, but also elsewhere. In October he delivered a number of speeches in Indiana, in which he stressed once again his conviction that his nomination proved Tennessee's status within the Union. "Fellow citizens, and I trust I shall be permitted to call you such, notwithstanding I reside in a state that was said to have rebelled and separated itself from the United States, for I hold to the doctrine that a State cannot secede," was the way he began a speech at Logansport. This was followed by his usual discourse on the superiority of democratic government and a declaration that the old parties were dead. There was only one issue left, the maintenance of the Union, he insisted, while professing great pride in the fact that a "boorish tailor," as the opposition referred to him, had been nominated for the second highest office in the land. Turning to the race question, Johnson maintained that the end of slavery emancipated more white men than blacks, reiterated his belief that the Negro should be given a chance to work out his own destiny, and emphasized once more that he believed in a "white man's government." Decrying all talk of compromise, he called those who advocated it traitors. After speaking in Indianapolis and Louisville, he returned home. When Indiana finally voted, the governor could take some credit for the victory the Union ticket won there.[20]

As time went on, Johnson became ever more uncompromising. In September he initiated a call-up of the militia that included blacks, a most radical measure, not only because of his disregard of the old color bar but also because it was now impossible for fence sitters to remain neutral. On October 21, a body of troops interfered with a McClellan meeting in Nashville.[21] In part, his radicalism may have been due to his fear that the Democrats might still carry Tennessee—there was every indication that this would happen were it not for his stringent oath.[22]

Under these circumstances, it was not surprising that attacks upon him mounted. Conservatives constantly criticized him, reminded him of his former stand, recalled the Johnson-Crittenden Resolutions, and branded him a "usurper and oppressor." "Whoever thinks a nigger as good as a poor white man" ought to vote for Lincoln and Johnson, mocked the Nashville *Daily Press*.[23]

These attacks prompted the governor to reply in kind. The opportunity presented itself on October 24, when a torchlight parade of freedmen reached the steps of the capitol and loudly called for him. Johnson began to speak. "Looking at this vast crowd of colored people," he said, "and reflecting through what a storm of persecution and obloquy they are compelled to pass, I am almost induced to wish that, as in the days of old, a Moses might arise who should lead them safely to their promised land of freedom and happiness." "You are our Moses," shouted the crowd, and Johnson replied: "God no doubt has prepared somewhere an instrument for the great work He designs to perform in behalf of the outraged people, and in due time your leader will come forth, your Moses will be revealed to you."

"We want no Moses but you!" shouted the crowd again.

"Well, then," replied the speaker, "humble and unworthy as I am, if no other better shall be found, I will indeed be your Moses, and lead you through the Red Sea of war and bondage to a fairer future of liberty and peace."[24]

Whether the governor meant to lead the blacks out of the country altogether or whether he merely spoke in the excitement of the moment is not recorded. At any rate, his speech caused a sensation. The Nashville *Dispatch* reported that he was not well, while the *Daily Press* demanded to know whether, after this performance, there was anyone left in Tennessee who still had one particle of faith in the honesty of Andrew Johnson. The son-in-law of the Northern abolitionist Lucretia Mott, Edward M. Davis, on the other hand, wrote him an enthusiastic letter of congratulations. But whatever his motives, his remarks did not mean that Johnson had overcome his ingrained prejudices.[25]

The conservative Unionists who favored McClellan did not propose to retire quietly from the field. Drawing up a stinging protest against Johnson's oath and methods, they sent John Lellyett, the former postmaster of Nashville, to Washington to ask Lincoln to interfere. The president, however, was unwilling to comply with their wishes. "I expect to let the friends of George B. McClellan manage their side of this contest in their own way and I will manage my side of it in *my* way," Lincoln said to Lellyett. In a more formal written reply, he reiterated his stand. Explaining that it was not the duty of the executive to conduct political campaigns in any state, he denied having had anything to do with Johnson's plans. "Except it be to give protection against violence," he concluded, "I decline to interfere in any way with any presidential election." Opposition newspapers railed at this "disfranchisement of loyal men in Tennessee" and called the president hypocritical, but Johnson had his way, and on October 29 Lellyett, William B. Campbell, and Balie Peyton withdrew the McClellan ticket in Tennessee.[26]

In the meantime, prospects for the Union party ticket had improved. During the summer the outlook for the ticket had been so bleak that Lincoln despaired of success, while several radicals started making plans to displace him. But then a series of Union military victories at Mobile Bay, Atlanta, and in the Shenandoah Valley made a mockery of the Democrats' assertion that the war was a failure. In Tennessee, too, Unionist hopes were bolstered by federal successes. Strengthened by Johnson's constant appeal for troops, Alvan C. Gillem succeeded not only in liberating Greeneville, at least temporarily, but also in bringing about the death of John Hunt Morgan within a few blocks of Johnson's house. With great exultation, the governor announced the victory to Lincoln; unfortunately, Breckinridge soon drove Gillem out again, and the general and the governor became engaged in a renewed squabble with local commanders. But the military situation in the rest of the country continued to be favorable.[27]

When the election was finally held, Lincoln and Johnson won a majority of both the popular and electoral vote. Carrying every loyal state except Kentucky, Delaware, and a few electors in New Jersey, the two men succeeded in vindicating the policy of the government. In Tennessee, though the Union ticket won by a majority of 25,000, participation was slight, as the McClellan forces largely boycotted the elections, and Confederate military operations in various parts of the state interfered with the ballot. It was obvious that the election in the Volunteer State was not a fair expression of the popular will, and in the end Congress refused to count the result toward the completion of the ballot.[28]

Assured of higher office, Johnson was now eager to end the military government in Tennessee, and he began to prepare in earnest for the reorganization of the state. On November 12 the Executive Committee of East Tennessee issued a call for a convention in Nashville on December 19, but military reverses interfered. In East Tennessee General Breckinridge continued to drive back Gillem's forces, and in the central part of the state, John B. Hood, with a useless arm and only one leg, led the invasion that was to culminate in the Battle of Nashville. In addition, the weather was so cold and the roads so full of snow that delegates found it impossible to travel, so that the convention had to be postponed once again.[29]

This time the delay was only temporary. On December 15–16 General Thomas so thoroughly defeated the invading Confederates at Nashville that they practically ceased to exist as an army. It was the most decisive victory of the entire Civil War, and Johnson, who had personally observed the battle, was ecstatic. "This is the most crushing blow which has been given since the inauguration of the rebellion," he wrote to Brownlow. "Thomas has immortalized himself and stands equal, if not superior, to any military chieftain of the times." The convention was postponed until January 8, and this time there would be no further interruption.[30]

If, up to the election, Johnson had procrastinated, he was now becoming increasingly anxious to complete the restoration of Tennessee prior to his departure for Washington. On December 30 Thomas wrote him, "As the enemy is now Entirely driven out [of] the state of Tennessee, I would Respectfully request that immediate measures be taken for the reorganization of the Civil Government of the state." Johnson was able to answer that steps had already been taken; the convention would assemble on the ninth.[31] When the delegates met the next month, Milligan took the chair and, in spite of conservative opposition, converted the assembly into a constitutional convention that passed amendments abolishing slavery, annulled the state's declaration of independence and the league with the Confederacy, and called for popular ratification of these measures on February 22. In addition, the delegates provided for elections for a legislature and governor on March 4 and nominated Brownlow to head the ticket.[32]

Vitally interested in the success of this convention, the governor took no chances. In an address to the delegates on January 12, 1865, when they were still procrastinating, he told them that when it was a matter of saving the republic, some irregularity was a virtue. It was essential to abolish slavery, and the way to do it was to draft amendments for submission to the people. The secession ordinance must be declared null and void. To hold another convention was not necessary, nor did he think it wise to fix voting requirements—that was a subject best left to the legislature. Declaring that he had wanted to restore the state from the first, Johnson reminded his audience that the enemy had always interfered with his efforts. However, now was the time to proceed. "I shall be with you but a short time longer," he said in conclusion, "till transferred to another place of action, but my warmest wishes will be directed toward you. You took me by the hand when a poor and friendless boy, and led me to honor, and by God's blessing, in the close of my little political career, I shall try to be your friend still and protect your interests. I thank you gentlemen kindly." The speech had the desired effect, and the convention acted in accordance with his wishes.

Johnson was delighted. "The Convention composed of more than five hundred delegates from all parts of the State have unanimously adopted an amendment to the Constitution forever abolishing Slavery in this State and denying the power of the Legislature passing any law creating property in man," he wired to Lincoln. "Thank God that the tyrants [sic] rod has been broken." He asked that Tennessee be exempted from the renewed version of the Wade-Davis Bill then pending in Congress, and expressed his belief that if left alone his home state would soon "resume all the functions of a State according to the genius and theory of the Government." Before the delegates adjourned, he congratulated them on the successful conclusion of their labors—"the greatest work of the age," as he called it—and expressed his delight that the abolition of slavery could be openly discussed and finally accomplished in a city like Nashville.[33]

But the governor still had one wish before leaving the state—to preside over the inauguration of the civil government and his successor in person. He therefore wired to Washington asking for permission to delay his arrival until after the inauguration of the president, only to be told that this would hardly be feasible. Lincoln, who had consulted his cabinet on the matter, replied that it would be unsafe for Johnson to stay away and asked him to be present at the inauguration. Loath to abandon his quest, the governor asked his friend John Forney to research precedents for vice presidents arriving later than inauguration day. Forney sent him the required material, but he also cautioned Johnson to come early so that he could represent the War Democrats. Enough of Lincoln's Republican partisans would be on hand in any case.[34]

Forney's concern about the War Democrats raised a very real issue. Shortly after the election, he had already sent Johnson a long letter of congratulations in which he rejoiced in the governor's nomination, especially because his Democratic antecedents had been the main objection to it. Now Forney regarded it as Johnson's duty to see to it "that the Union Democrats . . . shall be considered and recognized in every possible way by Mr. Lincoln." Unless this was done, they would return to their own organization, and in less than a year the Johnsonites might find themselves a defeated party. No man in the country, he continued, was more concerned about this than the governor. Evidently expecting Johnson to run for the presidency in 1868, he added, "and you know what I mean when I say this."[35]

The specific question at issue between the War Democrats and the Republicans, or at least the more radical Republicans, was precisely the problem of continued statehood of the seceded states, a principle Johnson sought to emphasize by his candidacy. During the winter of 1864–65, radical members of Congress sought to exclude the newly elected senators and representatives from Louisiana, whose position was similar to that of any potential claimants from Tennessee. In addition, the controversy over black suffrage, advocated by the radicals not merely for ideological but also for political reasons, complicated the issue. On December 30, 1864, Johnson wrote a letter (now lost) on this subject to Forney, who promptly replied that he was delighted with the governor's stand. He believed that no party would be able to resist the demand for peace should the Southern states return and accept the emancipation amendment. Negro suffrage was a question for the states to decide, he stated, and expressed the hope that Johnson would soon arrive in Washington. "Your presence and counsel are needed," he insisted.

Forney was not the only War Democrat anxious for Johnson's assistance. Francis Blair, Sr., a former member of Jackson's Kitchen Cabinet, also put his faith in the vice president–elect. Congratulating Johnson on his election, Blair expressed the opinion that on the question of emancipation, he and Johnson were one. If the governor wanted to be the blacks' Moses, Blair thought that to separate the races, he ought to lead them out of the South, to some region in Texas or along the Rio Grande. Such a policy would disarm the radicals with their program of not admitting states until they recognized black suffrage. Equating Johnson's reconstruction policy with Lincoln's, Blair put his trust in the vice president's influence. The War Democratic State Committee of New York did the same. In a memorial to the president castigating the radicals' plans for Reconstruction, it called on him to grant more influence than usual to the vice president.[36]

Johnson himself was circumspect. Aside from his insistence that the seceded states were still in the Union and his letter to Forney, he did not commit himself publicly. So shrewdly did he conduct himself that in spite of his differences with them he did not lose the confidence of his former radical associates on the Joint Committee on the Conduct of the War.

There were a few instances, however, when Johnson revealed his true position. On his way to Washington, at the Burnet House in Cincinnati, he met Stanley Matthews. Apparently choosing to overlook his wartime differences with the Ohio politician, the vice president–elect remarked to his visitor, "You and I were old democrats. . . . I will tell you what it is, if the country is ever to be saved it is to be done through the old democratic party." And in coming out against black suffrage in Tennessee, at least in the form of an amendment, he also gave a clear indication of his preferences.[37]

Shortly before the governor left for Washington, he had the satisfaction of completing the process of emancipation and restoration in Tennessee. After the blacks of Nashville presented him with a beautiful gold watch in recognition of his "untiring energy in the cause of Freedom" on February 25, Johnson issued a proclamation certifying the ratification of the amendments to the state constitution and calling for elections of a governor and a legislature. Emancipation was now a fact; he could honestly rejoice in it, although he certainly had no great interest in the future of the freedmen.[38]

The vice president–elect's trip to Washington was not as pleasant as he might have expected. Reluctant to leave Tennessee prior to the inauguration of the civilian government, he entered on his journey in poor health, which did not improve for weeks. He tendered his resignation as military governor and brigadier general to Secretary of War Stanton, who responded by expressing his deep gratitude and admiration for the services rendered. Then, after making a few speeches on the way, Johnson arrived in Washington still not well. A new formal black frock coat, a silk vest, and doeskin pants were to be his clothes for the occasion, and on the night before the inauguration, he celebrated with his friend Forney, with whom he shared many glasses of whiskey. Eliza, as usual, had not accompanied him; neither had his daughters or grandchildren—they had all stayed behind in Tennessee.[39]

Inauguration day dawned rainy and dark. Johnson, in poor health and not particularly steadied by the previous night's activities, stopped in the vice president's office in the Capitol prior to going to the official ceremony. Hamlin and his son Charles were already waiting for him, and a cordial conversation ensued. The governor, still feeling unwell, asked for some whiskey. It was sent for; he filled his glass and drank it straight. Then he had another, and on the way to the Senate chamber, he ran back to have a third.[40] In his weakened condition, these drinks affected him severely, and it is possible that had Hamlin not been hurt by his treatment at the Baltimore Convention, he might have prevented Johnson from going to the ceremony in a state of inebriation.

The Senate chamber was packed. Senators had been massed on one side of the hall to leave room for members of the House and notables on the other. Senator Solomon Foot of Vermont was in the chair; the president and members of his cabinet had taken their places to his left, Abraham Lincoln, tall and lanky, dominating the front row. "A gorgeous array of foreign ministers in full court costume" was seated at the right of the chair behind the justices of the Supreme Court. Mary Lincoln, accompanied by Senator Ira Harris, was in the diplomatic gallery, and military and naval officers in full uniform completed the picture, General Joseph Hooker and Admiral David G. Farragut being especially conspicuous.

Precisely at noon the vice president–elect entered arm in arm with Hamlin and took his seat on the dais with the presiding officer. Hamlin made a few remarks, and then Johnson, unsteady because of his condition, began his speech. The noise in the visitors' gallery made his remarks barely audible, but as he proceeded, it became evident that he was drunk. Glorying in his rise from the masses, he pointed out that all who were sitting before him owed their positions to the people. He turned toward the cabinet. "I will say to you, Mr. Secretary Seward, and to you, Mr. Secretary Stanton, and to you, Mr. Secretary—(to a gentleman near by [Forney], sotto voice, Who is the Secretary of the Navy? the person addressed replied in a whisper, Mr. Welles)—and to you, Mr. Secretary Welles, I would say, you all derive your power from the people." Before he ended his harangue, he stressed the fact that Tennessee was a state in the Union and had never been out. Hamlin finally nudged him to stop, and the ordeal was over.

The audience was horrified. According to Noah Brooks, the Washington correspondent of the Sacramento Union, Johnson did not even address the members of the cabinet by their titles, and their reactions can be imagined. Seward and Welles seemed bland, Stanton appeared to be petrified, Attorney General James Speed sat with his eyes closed, and Postmaster General William Dennison was red and white by turns. Senator Henry Wilson's face was flushed, Sumner "wore a saturnine and sarcastic smile," and Justice Samuel Nelson's lower jaw dropped down in sheer horror. Matters were not helped by Johnson's performance when taking the oath. His hand on the Bible, he turned and held the book up, saying in a loud and theatrical voice, "I kiss this Book in the face of my nation of the United States."[41]

The contrast with what followed was startling. Assembled outside the Capitol, a rapt audience listened to Lincoln deliver his impressive Second Inaugural Address, which elicited praise even from so critical an observer as Zachariah Chandler. "The inauguration went off very well except that the Vice President Elect was to [sic] drunk to perform his duties & disgraced himself & the Senate by making a drunken foolish speech," Chandler wrote to his wife. "I was never so mortified in my life, had I been able to find a hole I would have dropped through it out of sight. The President's inauguration was bright and good." The French chargé d'affaires agreed. "The account of the ceremony of the fourth . . . conveys well the mixture of grandeur and baseness of this democracy," he reported to Paris, comparing the "drunk Vice President" with the "immobile, serious, and grotesque" president.[42]

Still another observer took note of a more serious problem. Frederick Douglass recalled that when Lincoln pointed him out to Johnson prior to the ceremonies, the vice president responded at first with a bitter expression of contempt before trying to assume a more friendly attitude. Douglass concluded right then and there that the Tennesseean was no friend of the black race.[43]

Following the inauguration the opposition press had a field day. "The pity of it, the pity of it," wrote the New York *World*, "that the life of [the] Chief Magistrate should be made precious to us by the thought that he at least excludes from the most august station in the land the person who defiled our chief council-chamber on Saturday with the spewings of a drunken boor." On the next day the Democratic paper went further. In comparison with Johnson, it asserted, "even Caligula's horse was respectable." The New York *Herald* deplored the "disgraceful" speech and noted that Republican senators had hung their heads in shame. The Confederate Richmond *Sentinel* gleefully commented that the people of the United States were already thoroughly disgusted with the "low sot whom they have elected as their Vice-President," and Democratic senators were seen to be chuckling at the undignified sight of an inebriated vice president.[44]

Directly after the ceremony Johnson sought solace with the Blairs in nearby Silver Spring, Maryland. He presided over the Senate on March

6, but then went into seclusion. Still unwell, he did not reappear in the Senate until adjournment day, and his long absence gave rise to rumors that he was continuing his drunken binge. He was able to edit the official record of his speech, so that a sanitized version appeared in the *Congressional Globe,* while some friendly newspapers omitted it altogether.[45] In the Senate Henry Wilson and Charles Sumner sought to push through a resolution calling for the vice president's resignation, but Ben Wade and Preston King prevented any such move. Apparently they agreed with Lincoln, who professed to be unconcerned. When his new secretary of the Treasury, Hugh McCulloch, remarked that after the disgraceful affair on March 4 the country had an even deeper stake in his life than ever, the president replied: "I have known Andy Johnson for many years; he made a bad slip the other day, but you need not be scared; Andy ain't a drunkard."[46]

Lincoln was right. Johnson often drank, but he was not an alcoholic. Benjamin Truman, who knew him well and during the war shared his table at Nashville for at least eighteen months, never saw him take wine or liquor with any meal. To be sure, on some days he would consume two to four glasses of whiskey, but on others, no liquor at all. Former Assistant Secretary of War Charles Dana saw him imbibe heavily throughout his governorship, but never saw him drunk; even Brownlow, when still a bitter enemy, did not accuse him of overindulgence. Judge David Davis, too, remembered that Johnson never drank when in the Senate. So although his sons suffered from alcoholism, and he himself was constantly accused of it after his inauguration, it seems evident that, unlike a true alcoholic, Johnson could take or leave his liquor at will and was inebriated in public only once, on March 4, 1865, when he was debilitated by disease.[47]

Within two weeks of inauguration day Johnson recovered. He appeared in the company of his friend Preston King in the vice president's room at the Capitol and received a number of senators who wished him well. Anxious to see his son-in-law David Patterson elected to the U.S. Senate, he was making plans to return to Tennessee, where, after the ratification of the antislavery amendments and the election of a radical legislature, Brownlow was about to be inaugurated as his successor. Horace Maynard was already in Nashville, and he prepared to follow suit.[48]

But then Richmond fell to the Union forces, and Johnson stayed in Washington to make public appearances again. Speaking to a huge throng gathered to celebrate at Willard's Hotel, he called the rebellion more odious than that of Catiline. Yet, he insisted, it had been defeated because the government rested on the consent of the people. Careful not to engage in controversy, he refrained from mentioning Reconstruction, although he demanded that traitors, at least the leading ones, be executed and made to pay for the damage they had inflicted. The audience cheered wildly.[49] Following this speech the vice president traveled to City Point, where the president was conferring with his generals. Apparently he was unable to see Lincoln, but on April 6, in company of Preston King and his secretary, William A. Browning, he did go to Richmond to inspect the ruins of the fallen enemy capital, after which he returned to Washington.[50]

Johnson was serious about punishing the leading rebels. He made a point of it in conversation with Charles Dana, and on Good Friday, April 14, he even paid a special visit to the White House to induce Lincoln not to be too lenient with traitors. Naturally, the impression spread that he was a radical of radicals, but those who were close to him knew better.[51]

Just how the vice president was planning to implement his plans to represent the War Democrats during his tenure of office was not certain. But his visit to the White House on April 14 proved to be his last significant action as the nation's second officer. That night's terrible events would change everything.

X I

UNIONIST PRESIDENT

GOOD FRIDAY of 1865 has always been considered a day of bad omen in American history; how ominous it was, however, no one realized at the time. The assassination of the president was serious enough; the accession of his successor had more fateful consequences than anyone could have foretold.

Johnson had gone to bed early that night. Shortly after 10:15 he was awakened by a loud knock at the door. When he did not respond immediately, his fellow boarder at the Kirkwood House, former governor Leonard J. Farwell of Wisconsin, called in a loud voice, "Governor Johnson, if you are in this room I must see you." The vice president sprang out of bed. "Farwell, is that you?" he replied. "Yes, let me in," was the answer. The door opened, and Farwell, who had just come from Ford's Theater, excitedly told Johnson the news. The president had been shot. The vice president, stunned, grasped Farwell's hands, and the two men fell upon each other, holding on for mutual support. Soon there were guards outside to prevent any attempt to murder Johnson. Secretary of State Seward already lay seriously wounded in his home, and no one knew how widespread the assassination plot was.

Johnson quickly regained his composure, and calmly, without exhibiting any signs of fear, considered what was to be done. In order to get some firsthand information about the condition of the president and the secretary of state, he sent Farwell to the scene of the crime, where the Wisconsin politician found that the dying president had been carried to the Peterson house across the street from the theater. Returning to the Kirkwood House, Farwell told this to Johnson, who now resolved to hurry to Lincoln's bedside. His friends thought it was too dangerous for him to leave the hotel; Major James R. O'Beirne, the provost marshal of the District of Columbia, offered troops to protect him, but the vice president determined to go without them. Buttoning up his coat and pulling his hat well down, he left for the Peterson house with no one but Farwell and O'Beirne to accompany him.[1]

The sad scene in the room where the president lay dying was overwhelming. Lincoln was resting diagonally on a bed too small for him, breathing heavily, his respiration lifting his clothing with each breath he took. The room was crowded with doctors, members of the cabinet who came and went, and various onlookers, while the grief-stricken Mrs. Lincoln, in an adjoining room, was completely beside herself. Charles Sumner was holding the unconscious chief executive's hand. Johnson did not stay long—his presence might have been misinterpreted—and he returned to his hotel, where he paced the floor of his room while wringing his hands, and saying, "They shall suffer for this. They shall suffer for this."[2]

Lincoln died at 7:22 in the morning of April 15. The cabinet immediately decided to notify Johnson. Asked when and where he wished to be inaugurated, he designated his hotel at the earliest convenient time. Accordingly, Chief Justice Salmon P. Chase administered the oath of office between ten and eleven at the Kirkwood House. The ceremony was brief. Chase was accompanied by Secretary of the Treasury Hugh McCulloch, Attorney General James Speed, Frank Blair and his son Montgomery, Senators Solomon Foot, Alexander Ramsey, Richard Yates, William M. Stewart, and John Hale, and Representative John F. Farnsworth of Illinois. All were deeply moved by the great tragedy and watched the proceedings with sad faces. Johnson repeated the oath after Chase "very distinctly and impressively." At its close, he kissed the Bible. When he handed the book back to the chief justice, Chase said to him, "You are President. May God support, guide, and bless you in your arduous duties." The other guests also offered their congratulations, though under the circumstances, it was difficult for them to find the right words. Johnson replied with a short, dignified address. He was overwhelmed by the sad events that had just occurred, he said, and felt incompetent to perform the duties of an office as important as that which had so suddenly been thrust upon him. The only assurance he could give for the future was by reference to the past. His course in connection with the rebellion could be regarded as a guarantee for events to come. According to the newspapers, he appeared to be in remarkably good health and "his manner was solemn and dignified." His whole bearing produced "a most gratifying impression upon those who participated in the ceremonies."[3]

At noon Johnson went to Secretary McCulloch's office in the Treasury Department to preside over his first cabinet meeting. After asking all present to remain at their posts, he referred to the appropriate heads of departments the problem of arranging for a proper funeral for the fallen chief executive and appointed William Hunter, the chief clerk of the State Department, acting secretary of state. All in all, he had done whatever could be done under the trying circumstances of his accession.[4]

In later years, when Johnson's break with Congress had embittered many contemporaries, all kinds of rumors surfaced concerning his actions on the night of the assassination and the first day of his presidency. Senator Stewart of Nevada, whose prejudices were so deep that he characterized the Tennesseean as "the most untruthful, treacherous, and cruel person who had ever held [a] place of power in the United States," told a fantastic story. Maintaining that he himself together with the chief justice and Senator Foot were the first persons to bring Johnson news of the tragedy, he alleged that the visitors found the vice president half dressed, dirty, shabby, with matted hair as though from mud in the gutter, apparently trying to overcome a hangover. According to Stewart, the chief justice informed Johnson that the president had been shot and between seven and eight in the morning administered the oath of office. After the callers informed Secretary of War Stanton, they returned, only to find Johnson asleep again. Dressing him, they took him to the White House, where they sent for a tailor, doctor, and barber, bathed him, and put new clothes on him. But, still according to the senator, Johnson did not recover sufficiently until late in the afternoon, when a few persons were permitted to satisfy themselves that there was a president in the White House.[5]

The falsity of these assertions is evident. Stewart's account of the swearing in is contradicted by most other contemporary sources, including a memorandum in the chief justice's papers prepared the next day. The fact that the president took his oath at a later time than eight in the morning is well attested by various newspapermen, who failed to see any sign of drunkenness or a hangover. Moreover, the cabinet meeting at noon, which Welles recorded in his diary as well as in other memoranda, is proof positive of Johnson's condition and whereabouts on the fifteenth. In order to give the distraught Mrs. Lincoln a chance to move out, he did not even occupy the White House for several weeks after his inauguration.[6]

Other detractors have made much of the card that John Wilkes Booth, Lincoln's assassin, left at the Kirkwood House on the day of the crime. "Don't wish to disturb you. Are you at home? J. Wilkes Booth," it read. In view of the fact that George Atzerodt, the conspirator who was supposed to murder the vice president, also had a room at the hotel, the whole incident seemed bizarre. But it is evident that Booth, justly distrusting his associate, merely sought to cast suspicion on Johnson, an objective he realized long after he was dead. The fantastic stories of plots and counterplots that surfaced after the assassination naturally involved the vice president, too, but they are also devoid of substance. As William Hanchett has shown so conclusively, John Wilkes Booth assassinated Abraham Lincoln because of pro-Confederate sympathies, and no one other than his known collaborators had anything to do with the conspiracy.[7]

Johnson's accession to the presidency was to have fateful consequences—for the freedmen, for their former masters, and for the country. It has often been asserted that the new president was merely following in the footsteps of the old, that Johnson's program of Reconstruction was similar to Lincoln's, and that, had the Emancipator lived, he would have had as much trouble with Congress, and particularly with the radicals, as the tailor from Tennessee.[8] Nothing could be further from the truth. Lincoln's 10 percent plan of amnesty and Reconstruction was a wartime measure, designed to further the war effort as much as to effect a restoration of the seceded states; when Johnson became president, however, the war was virtually over, and what Lincoln might have done in times of peace is a largely unanswered question. That his approach to Reconstruction would have been different from what it had been before, however, is clear. He gave proof of it when, after Lee's surrender at Appomattox, he revoked the invitation to the Confederate legislature of Virginia to reassemble and take the state out of the Confederacy; he gave additional proof when in his last public address he openly advocated limited black suffrage in Louisiana.[9]

In addition, the two men's views on freedmen's rights were radically different. To be sure, Johnson had belatedly endorsed emancipation—he had even promised to be the black man's Moses—but his deep-seated racial antipathies never faded away. Lincoln, on the other hand, had gradually come to realize the possibility of black development in the United States, a change of outlook he made so abundantly clear in his last speech. That he would have allowed the freedmen to be left to the mercies of their former owners is unlikely. Johnson had no such inhibitions. Consequently, his Reconstruction program was very different from anything Lincoln might have designed in the postwar period.

Moreover, Lincoln with his sense of timing was a supreme pragmatist. While adhering firmly to certain fundamental principles, he knew how to yield when it was necessary to do so. Johnson, too, was capable of making political compromises, but his manner of dealing with adversaries was much less subtle than his predecessor's. And Lincoln, a former Whig, always conceded some concurrent powers to Congress. Johnson, a good Jacksonian, firmly believed in the power of the executive to direct Reconstruction policies. Consequently, his "restoration" program was very different from anything Lincoln might have designed in the postwar period.[10]

Johnson's "restoration" policy, however, still lay in the future. For several weeks after his inauguration, the new president took particular care not to commit himself to any specific program. His constant repetition of his determination to punish leading rebels and his unremitting insistence on the recollection of his wartime record were comparatively inoffensive and won general approval; nobody could have predicted what his real course would be. In fact, both radicals and their opponents could feel reassured by his utterances.

Johnson was circumspect from the very beginning. When he assumed his high office on April 15, 1865, he took care not to repeat his performance of over a decade earlier when he was inaugurated governor of Tennessee. This time there was no Jacob's Ladder speech, no controversial airing of his views. Stressing only his proved record, he sought to reassure his audience and the nation that he would carry on the government as before. One of his most important actions in this respect was his invitation to the members of the cabinet to retain their offices, a decision to which he adhered despite attempts of various factions to place their favorites into places of prominence.[11]

Johnson demonstrated how diplomatic he could be almost immediately. On April 15 a caucus of radicals had met and decided to seek an interview with him. The participants wanted him to appoint a new set of advisers: Ben Butler was to be secretary of state, Henry George Stebbins of New York, secretary of the navy, and Congressman John Covode of Pennsylvania, postmaster general. When the president saw the group led by Ben Wade as chairman of the Committee on the Conduct of the War, he received his visitors cordially. "Johnson, we have faith in you," Wade said to him. "By the gods, there will be no trouble now in running the government." Johnson, deliberately noncommittal, replied: "I am very much obliged to you gentlemen, and I can only say you can judge of my policy by the past. Everybody knows what that is. I hold this: Robbery is a crime; rape is a crime; *treason* is a crime; and *crime* must be punished. The law provides for it; the courts are open. Treason must be made infamous and traitors punished." The committee applauded his declaration and departed.

When the radicals returned a second time to discuss matters with the president, he managed to impress them even more strongly. While not obliging them in instituting cabinet charges, he did answer their request for specifics about the punishment of leading rebels. According to James G. Blaine, he asked Wade what the senator would do if he were in the president's place, and Wade told him he would force into exile or hang about ten or twelve of the worst offenders, perhaps by way of good measure, "thirteen, just a baker's dozen." Johnson reportedly protested that it would be difficult to pick out so small a number, and Wade, worried that the president might be too extreme, warned that it would never do to execute too many Confederates.[12]

It is difficult to determine just how accurate this story is, but it is certain that Johnson continued to meet with the radicals' approval. Sumner, who also saw him on the evening of April 15, found him very careful in what he said but very determined. Several weeks later the senator still thought there was no difference between him and the president, as Johnson had distinctly told him so. And Ben Wade later remembered that the president had assured him that he would take no step that did not meet with the sanction of the Union party.[13]

The radicals were not the only group Johnson managed to satisfy. The conservatives, who were actually much closer to him, were also reassured. Much to the disgust of George W. Julian, one of the most extreme of the members of the Joint Committee, Johnson was in close contact with such opponents of radicalism as the Blairs, Henry W. Halleck, and Winfield Scott. And very soon he selected as his most intimate adviser ex-senator Preston King of New York, who came to Washington to live with him. A close friend of the Blairs, King had Jacksonian antecedents that appealed to Johnson.[14]

While Johnson's emphasis on stern retribution for individual rebels probably represented his firm conviction at this time, it also continued to be a convenient way of avoiding any definite commitment to a specific policy of Reconstruction, as he showed in his replies to various delegations that came to visit him. Sixty Washington ministers met with the president on April 17, a group of citizens from Illinois and a deputation headed by John Mercer Langston, the president of the National Rights League, on the eighteenth, and one from Massachusetts on the twentieth. Delegations from Ohio, Indiana, Virginia, and elsewhere followed, and all were told essentially the same thing. The president's policy could be explained by reference to his past record; treason was a crime and must be punished, and he would deal with traitors with a strong hand.

Senator Andrew Johnson, ca. 1857. Courtesy of the National Archives, Smithsonian Institution, Washington, D.C.

"Locket
pictures" of
Andrew and Eliza McCardle
Johnson, presumably in the 1840s.
Courtesy of the Andrew
Johnson Papers Project,
Knoxville, Tennessee.

Eliza Johnson in later years.
Courtesy of the National Archives.

Silhouette of Andrew, Martha, Mary, and Eliza
Johnson, 1853. Courtesy of the Tennessee State
Museum, Nashville.

President Andrew Johnson.
Courtesy of the Forbes Magazine
Collection, New York.

Andrew Johnson's tailor shop, Greeneville, Tennessee. Courtesy of
the National Archives.
State capitol, Nashville, Tennessee, during the Civil War. Courtesy
of the National Archives.

Grand Review, Washington, D.C., May 22–23, 1865, showing the president and cabinet. Courtesy of the National Archives.
Managers of the House of Representatives of the impeachment of Andrew Johnson. Courtesy of the Forbes Magazine Collection.

FROM LEFT TO RIGHT, SEATED: *Benjamin P. Butler, Thaddeus Stevens, Thomas Williams, John A. Bingham;* STANDING: *James F. Wilson, George S. Boutwell, John A. Logan.*

CLOCKWISE BEGINNING TOP LEFT:
Edwin M. Stanton. Benjamin F. Butler. Thaddeus Stevens. Hannibal Hamlin. Courtesy of the Library of Congress.

Cartoon lampooning the National Union Convention,
Harper's Weekly, September 29, 1866.

According to George Templeton Strong, the New York lawyer who was the treasurer of the Sanitary Commission, "he seemed dignified, urbane, and self-possessed." The visitors left well satisfied with the chief executive.[15]

The other example of Johnson's desire to reassure the nation, his retention of Lincoln's cabinet, was a decision that left him with an odd collection of representatives of various factions of the Union party. William H. Seward, the secretary of state, was an old acquaintance. Politically astute, intensely disliked by the radicals, and determined to pursue an expansionist foreign policy without engaging the country in another war, Seward had been seriously injured by Lewis Paine, Booth's brutish accomplice, who had also wounded the secretary's son. It was not until May that he returned to duty, but thereafter his influence upon Johnson was considerable.[16]

Because Lincoln had only just appointed a new secretary of the Treasury, the Indiana banker Hugh McCulloch, who had been comptroller of the Treasury under Chase, the secretary's power was at first somewhat limited. But he soon established considerable rapport with his chief, who initially shared his contractionist hard money views. In the long run McCulloch was to become a center of controversy, and Johnson's financial opinions changed as time went on. But as a good Jacksonian, in 1865 the president could hardly oppose the secretary's policies.[17]

The most controversial member of the cabinet was Edwin M. Stanton, the secretary of war. In view of the later break between him and the president, it is often forgotten that in 1865 the two men had enjoyed excellent relations. As an able subordinate, the governor of Tennessee had earned Stanton's respect, and both were determined to root out every last vestige of the rebellion. The new president left the stern secretary, who had taken charge in the hours immediately following Lincoln's assassination, a free hand to proceed vigorously against the perpetrators of the crime, a task Stanton carried out with enthusiasm. That he was devious, imperious, and eventually disloyal to his chief did not lessen Johnson's trust in him, at least in the early months.[18]

Stanton's colleague in the Navy Department, Gideon Welles, sympathized with Johnson almost from the beginning. A Connecticut politician of Democratic antecedents, he shared the president's conviction that suffrage was a matter for the states to decide and was favorably impressed with the new president, who, he wrote in his voluminous diary, "deported himself admirably" on his first day in office. Although Welles believed that early in the administration Johnson did not yet "sufficiently generalize," he was certain that with a little experience the chief executive would correct this shortcoming. His diary became one of the chief sources for the history of the administration, its sympathetic slant serving the president well.[19]

John P. Usher, the secretary of the interior, had already been slated for removal when Johnson took office, and Lincoln had picked James Harlan, the senator from Iowa, as his successor. So anxious was Johnson not to initiate any changes that he refused to accept Harlan's declination, which, because of pressure from Usher's friends, the senator offered to him. The president told Harlan he wanted him, and the Iowan joined the cabinet in the middle of May. In the long run Johnson was not favorably impressed with the secretary, who, he complained, could not look him in the eye, but in keeping with his policy of continuity in the cabinet, he tolerated him.[20]

Attorney General James Speed also did not win Johnson's favor. The president considered him a person of no great consequence—Speed's wife was the better man of the two, he told his private secretary. Moreover, the Kentucky Unionist did not see eye to eye with Johnson on Reconstruction, so that conflict between the two was bound to develop. Nevertheless, the president kept him in the cabinet.[21]

Postmaster General William Dennison, a determined Ohio radical, was a friend of the chief justice. Excessively reserved, he had few intimates, and his political opinions precluded close relations with the new president. But he, too, stayed on, at least for a while, so that the illusion of continuity was preserved.[22]

Because of Mrs. Lincoln's total prostration, Johnson waited some weeks before taking up residence in the White House. Congressman Samuel Hooper, a wealthy Boston merchant, made his house on 15th and H streets available to the president and his friend King, although, since the food and the servants had to be paid for and the horses fed, Johnson found the arrangement very expensive. Hooper even returned to stay on in his own house as the president's guest. It was not until late in May that Mrs. Lincoln vacated the White House so that Johnson could move in. His patience in spite of the inconvenience could not have failed to make a good impression upon the country.[23]

These temporary arrangements made it necessary for the country's executive business to be transacted in the Treasury Department, where during the early weeks of Johnson's presidency all cabinet meetings took place. According to Secretary of the Navy Gideon Welles, these sessions were better attended than they had been under Lincoln, and various measures were more generally discussed, circumstances allegedly making for a better administration. Welles, however, was a prejudiced observer.[24]

In the meantime, Johnson had been assembling a staff. Eventually, he would employ twice as many secretaries as Lincoln. Chief among them was William A. Browning, the son of a Washington tailor who had been with him ever since 1861. Browning was assisted by the Tennesseean Robert Morrow and Lieutenant Andrew K. Long, a member of General Gillem's staff, though in the end the president's son Robert was summoned from Tennessee to take Long's place. The War Department provided the services of Major (later Colonel) William G. Moore, whose meticulous diary has provided a wealth of information for historians, and, among others, Reuben D. Mussey, another acquaintance of Nashville days, who had superseded George Stearns on black affairs. Johnson also retained William Crook, Lincoln's bodyguard. Although changes in the staff were frequent, the president seems to have been well served.[25]

Continuity in administration, a competent staff, great forbearance in not moving into the White House for weeks—all these created a favorable image of the new administration. The president also realized that he could not leave his family in Tennessee as he had done when serving in the House and Senate. The public would never understand it, and in any case, he now wanted his family with him. Upon hearing of Lincoln's assassination, Martha had written to him, in great alarm, "Are you safe, and do you feel *secure?*" She did not have to wait long for the answer. The next day Johnson wired her husband, Judge Patterson, that the whole family, including Mary, who was in East Tennessee, should prepare to move to Washington. But for some unknown reason, arrangements were not completed till June, when Eliza and Martha arrived in Washington to stay at the White House.[26]

The president, who liked to refer visitors to his actions in the past, could now point with pride to developments in Tennessee. Sam Milligan, as before, was looking out for Johnson's interests there and kept him well informed about events. "Johnson," he wrote, "I forgot—Mr. President!" and went on to express the hope that Patterson would be elected U.S. senator, which he was. Brownlow's government had been inaugurated, and although Johnson was missed at the ceremony, his influence was extremely powerful in his home state.[27]

The president had a busy schedule during his first weeks in office. On April 19 the funeral ceremonies for the departed chief executive took place in the somberly decorated Capitol draped in black. Two days earlier Lincoln's casket had been placed in the East Room of the White House, where it rested upon a catafalque some fifteen feet high. This consisted of an elevated platform on a dais covered with a domed canopy of black cloth supported by four pillars. The room was bedecked with black crepe relieved by tastefully arranged flowers. It was a solemn occasion when Johnson quietly stepped up to the coffin to gaze sadly upon the still face of his predecessor. On the day of the funeral the president, accompanied by Hannibal Hamlin and Preston King, took his place opposite the main entrance of the East Room. Behind him stood the members of the Supreme Court and the cabinet, with their wives; throughout the crowded room were the diplomatic corps, senators, congressmen, governors, military officers, and other dignitaries. The pallbearers were at the north end of the room, while the family and friends were seated in a little semicircle of chairs at the foot of the catafalque. At the casket's head, visibly affected, General Grant stood watch throughout the impressive services. At the conclusion of the ceremonies, the body was taken in solemn procession to the rotunda of the Capitol, the president's carriage following that of the family. After lying in state in the Capitol for two days, Lincoln's remains were transported by train to their final resting place in Springfield, Illinois.[28]

The funeral obsequies were hardly over before Johnson was faced with his first major crisis, a contretemps he again handled diplomatically. In a special cabinet meeting on April 21, he learned that General William T. Sherman had concluded an armistice with General Joseph E. Johnston that not only ended all armed resistance but contained various political provisions, including the recognition of existing Confederate state governments, guarantees of property rights, and a universal amnesty. Nothing in the document confirmed the emancipation of the slaves or the rights of the freedmen. In keeping with his wish to maintain existing policies, particularly the military surrender of General Lee at Appomattox, the president, with the unanimous support of the cabinet, asked Grant to inform Sherman that the agreement was not acceptable to the government. Grant then went to North Carolina; Sherman met once again with Johnston, and the Southern general agreed to a new convention omitting the political terms. Stanton, however, not only published his disapproval in the newspapers but gave reasons for it, an action that insulted Sherman, who was further infuriated when Henry W. Halleck ordered troops in North Carolina to disregard the original arrangement. Sherman was so angry at Stanton that he refused normal social intercourse with him. "I was hurt, outraged, and insulted at Mr. Stanton's public arraignment of my motives and actions, at his endorsing General Halleck's insulting & offensive dispatch, and his studied silence when the press accused me of all sorts of base motives," he wrote to Grant a few weeks later.[29]

In spite of this serious rift, Johnson succeeded in his policy of conciliation. His prompt action in disapproving of the initial armistice satisfied radicals as well as moderates; even Milligan thought that Sherman had merely confirmed the bad opinion the president had originally formed of the general. In reality, however, Johnson, though at first outraged at the truce, was beginning to change his mind about the impulsive commander, to whom he would draw closer and closer. He succeeded in convincing Sherman of his goodwill, and the general, admitting that the president had been more than kind to him, reciprocated. Johnson had once again managed to retain the support of men of diametrically opposed views.[30]

The president also pleased a large portion of the public by taking stern action against the Confederates, although the virtual end of the war brought with it new difficulties. Jefferson Davis, who had fled south after the capture of Richmond, was somehow believed to be implicated in Lincoln's assassination, and public feeling was especially bitter against Confederate agents who had operated from Canadian soil. In a cabinet meeting on May 2, Stanton produced a memorandum signed by Judge Advocate General Joseph Holt, charging that Davis and various Confederates in Canada, such as Jacob Thompson, William C. Cleary, George N. Sanders, Clement C. Clay, Beverly Tucker, and others, had instigated the crime; Johnson issued a proclamation offering a reward of $100,000 for the apprehension of Davis and lesser sums for the others. Many well-informed observers, including Thaddeus Stevens, doubted Davis' guilt from the beginning, but in view of the excited atmosphere, Johnson's action reflected popular demands.[31]

The president continued to satisfy the clamor for punishment of the Confederates when on May 10 Davis was captured. He was promptly confined at Fortress Monroe, even briefly shackled by a zealous subordinate, and held for trial. Whether judgment should be rendered by a military commission or a civil court was not clear, and Johnson carefully sought the opinion of leading politicians and lawyers upon the question. But he refused to make a definitive decision.[32]

Johnson was quick to decide, however, upon a procedure in the trial of the main conspirators involved in Lincoln's assassination. Booth was killed on April 26, but his associates, David Herold, George Atzerodt, Lewis Paine, and their alleged collaborators, Mrs. Mary Surratt, Samuel Arnold, Michael O'Laughlin, Edward Spangler, and Dr. Samuel Mudd, were all apprehended. Attorney General James Speed suggested that they be tried by a military commission, and although there were warnings against such a procedure, the president, with the consent of the cabinet, decided to follow his advice. On May 1 he issued the appropriate orders, and for the next six weeks, the country was fascinated by the proceedings of the commission in Washington. The trial ended in the conviction of the conspirators, with Herold, Atzerodt, Paine, and Mrs. Surratt receiving the death sentence, and the others, lesser terms. In spite of the frantic pleas of Mrs. Surratt's daughter, Johnson approved the sentences, and the condemned defendants were hanged.[33]

The high point of Johnson's first few months in office was the giant victory parade and military review that took place in Washington on May 22 and 23. Arriving in Congressman Samuel Hooper's carriage, the president took his place in the middle of a box on a reviewing stand that had been erected near the White House, from which the Stars and Stripes, for the first time since the assassination no longer at half staff, was fluttering proudly. Stanton, Grant, and Speed were sitting on Johnson's right; General George G. Meade, other members of the cabinet, and various generals were on his left and behind him. On a higher platform farther behind, the members of the diplomatic corps in full costume had taken their places, and military notables by the dozens occupied other stands. It was a splendid day; the sun was shining brightly. As each army corps passed the president's stand, he and his guests rose, the commander saluted him with lowered sword while flags were dipped, and then walked up to shake hands with the distinguished reviewers. When it was Sherman's turn, the general refused Stanton's outstretched hand and barely managed a cool bow. But even this embarrassment could not spoil the splendid occasion. To make the celebration complete, the last Confederate troops in Texas also surrendered at that time, so that the war was truly over.[34]

The victory parade was a fitting climax to Johnson's regained popularity. The press had been favorably impressed with the new president from the beginning; the Washington *National Intelligencer* became his official organ, and even the New York *World*, so hostile only a few weeks earlier, now praised his Democratic roots and expressed confidence in his future course. Long biographies appeared in various newspapers, while the New York *Herald* began to run the reminiscences of its reporter Samuel Glenn, who had been present when Johnson defended Nashville. Of the other New York papers, the *Sun* compared the president with Andrew Jackson, the *Tribune* praised his executive abilities, while the *Times* called him a man "of courage, of sound moral judgment, and of patriotism" which had "stood the test of the . . . most terrible trials."[35] Johnson's refusal to accept the gift of a splendid carriage offered to him by a group of New York merchants—he believed that it would be unseemly for officials occupying high public positions of trust to accept such tenders—gained him additional praise, the *Times* calling it an act "of inestimable value as a monition and an example." But the acid test was still to come. As the Chicago *Tribune* pointed out, "Lincoln gained immortality of fame by emancipating the negro—let President Johnson deserve eternal honor by using his power and influence in assuring the national salvation through enfranchisement."[36] The president evidently had the support of the country. What he would do with it, particularly in connection with the freedmen, was the question.

XII

PRESIDENTIAL RECONSTRUCTIONIST

SOONER or later the president, who had procrastinated and prevaricated in making firm decisions about his future course, would have to make up his mind. The problem that would determine the failure or success of the administration was Reconstruction: How were the states' relations to the federal government to be normalized? What was their condition in law and in fact? If they had never left the Union, as Johnson asserted, what was to be done to secure their rights within it? If, however, notwithstanding any law, they had seceded in fact, as some members of Congress insisted, how were they to be brought back? And above all, what was to be done with the freedmen whose status was still so insecure? Should they be given the rights of ordinary citizens, including suffrage, and be fully integrated into society, or should they continue to occupy some sort of inferior position, at least until they were ready to assume the full burdens of citizenship?

It was clear that these questions could not be decided in a vacuum; speedy restoration of the Southern states to their former rights in Congress would eventually result in the supremacy of the Democratic party, a contingency the victorious Republicans could hardly view with equanimity. Moreover, the lapse of the three-fifths compromise, which had based representation on all free persons and three-fifths of all slaves, would result in an increase of Southern representation now that all slaves were free. Northerners could hardly be expected to be ready so lavishly to reward their recent foes.

It so happened that some of these problems had been discussed at the last cabinet session over which Lincoln presided, on April 14. Stanton had proposed a plan to administer North Carolina and Virginia with military governors and provost marshals; the subject of suffrage, however, had not been taken up. Upon Welles' objection that Virginia, where the government had already recognized the authority of Governor Francis Pierpont, the father of West Virginia, ought to be treated separately from North Carolina, it was decided to refer the plan back to Stanton. He was to modify it in accordance with this suggestion, with which Lincoln agreed.[1]

The assassination intervened, and by the time the cabinet met again with Johnson presiding, everything had changed. Stunned by their defeat and its possible consequences, Southerners were ready for almost anything. As the editor of the Raleigh *Press* told the newspaperman Whitelaw Reid in the summer of 1865, they were "willing to acquiesce in whatever basis of reorganization the President would prescribe." Even black suffrage "would be preferable to remaining unorganized and would be accepted by the people."[2]

Johnson missed this opportunity to inaugurate a policy that would at least have protected the minimum rights of the freedmen. Not that he was not warned. Blacks in Alexandria, Unionists in Maryland and Virginia, officials in Louisiana, among others, sent him letters and petitions cautioning him not to abandon the Unionists and blacks to the tender mercies of returning rebels.[3] After repeated pleas from Charles Sumner for justice to the blacks, the president, unwilling to tip his hand, put the senator at ease. "There is no difference between us," he said, and warned against haste in initiating Reconstruction. Chief Justice Chase, too, suggested a plan of Reconstruction, including full citizenship for freedmen. He warned Johnson not to start the process in North Carolina but instead to introduce universal suffrage in Florida and Louisiana. After a visit with the president in company with Charles Sumner, Chase professed to be as pleased with Johnson's forthcoming attitude as the senator.[4] Even Ben Wade, who cautioned Johnson against the dangers that had beset other vice presidents after succeeding to the presidency, was certain that the president was on his side; Johnson assured him that he was neither a Tyler nor a Fillmore.[5]

But in reality the president did not take heed of these admonitions from his advisers. From the very first, he was disinclined to interfere with suffrage requirements. The Constitution clearly left voting qualifications to the states, and, convinced that the seceded commonwealths were still part of the Union, he considered interference on his part a violation of his firmly held beliefs in states' rights. Stanch friends encouraged John-

son in his views, particularly the Blairs, who had taken care of him after
the March 4 fiasco, and they were in close contact with Democratic
leaders who sought to make the most of his disinclination to tamper with
the ballot in the states. His old acquaintance Lewis D. Campbell, who
came to Washington after having been summoned from Ohio, also
urged him not to pay any attention to the suffrage question, while
Secretary of State Seward, still in bed because of his injuries, was equally
opposed to radical measures.[6]

The remainder of the cabinet was divided. When the suffrage issue
came up on May 8 and 9, Stanton presented his revised plan splitting
off North Carolina from Virginia. Along with the secretary of war,
postmaster general Dennison and Attorney General Speed favored
black suffrage, while Welles, Harlan, and McCulloch were opposed. It
was decided to postpone the matter. But on May 9 Johnson issued a
proclamation recognizing the Pierpont government in Virginia. On the
problem of the suffrage, the document said nothing.[7]

The proclamation alarmed Thaddeus Stevens. "I see the President is
precipitating things," he wrote to Charles Sumner. "Virginia is recognized! I fear before Congress meets he will have so bedevilled matters
as to render them incurable. It would be well if he would call an extra
session of Congress. But I almost despair of resisting Executive influence!" Yet at a radical caucus on May 12 at the National Hotel, held
to consider the necessity of taking measures for saving the administration from conservative control, Wade and Sumner still insisted that
Johnson was in no danger. The president believed in Negro suffrage,
they said, and no action was taken. Other radicals, however, were
becoming uneasy.[8]

They had every reason for their anxiety. The president had at last
made up his mind to act. He decided to restore the Southern states as
quickly as possible, under his own authority, and without calling Congress into special session. Thus the task would be completed by December, when the lawmakers would meet. And because he was convinced
that he had no authority to interfere with the suffrage requirements of
the states, he decided to leave the subject alone. Accordingly, relying on
the advice of Attorney General Speed, Johnson drew up a proclamation
offering amnesty to all insurgents except certain exempted classes, including Confederates with taxable property of more than $20,000. In
addition, he was ready to appoint a provisional governor for North
Carolina, whose duty it would be to call upon all loyal legal voters to
restore the state to its constitutional relations with the federal government.[9] These voting provisions would, of course, exclude the freedmen.

Before he published the two proclamations, Johnson invited an old

North Carolina acquaintance, William W. Holden, to come to Washington. Like himself a former Democrat and Unionist, though he had wavered back and forth between Whigs and Democrats, Unionists and secessionists, Holden came from the white yeomanry of North Carolina, and he seemed a good choice for restoring the president's native state. At the same time, three former governors—D. L. Swain, president of the University of North Carolina, Bartholomew F. Moore, and William Eaton, Jr.—men of much more conservative persuasion, also came to see him. When Johnson showed them the proclamations, they objected on constitutional grounds, but the president claimed authority under Article IV, Section 4, of the Constitution, which guaranteed every state in the Union a republican government. They returned on the following day; Holden and Swain then left, and the remaining visitors inserted Holden's name in the space Johnson had left blank for the appointment of the governor of North Carolina. Then, on May 29 the president published the two proclamations.[10]

The promulgation of these proclamations and subsequent parallel actions appointing governors for South Carolina, Georgia, Alabama, Mississippi, Florida, and Texas inaugurated what has become known as presidential Reconstruction. Its effect on the country was predictable. Conservatives and Democrats hailed it. Lincoln's conservative former attorney general, Edward Bates, expressed his full satisfaction; the Washington *National Intelligencer* praised the proclamations' "wise, just and humane sentiments," and the New York *Sun* expressed its admiration for the "magnanimity" of Johnson's sentiments.[11] Democratic party associates urged Jeremiah S. Black, Buchanan's secretary of state, to return to Washington; Johnson, they thought, was ready "to return to the true fold." No wonder the Petersburg, Virginia, *Daily News* could write with satisfaction that the president had proved he was not "likely to stand idle, while black stars were substituted for white in the banner of the Union."[12]

Radicals, of course, were appalled. "Is it possible to devise any plan to arrest the government in its ruinous career?" Thaddeus Stevens queried Sumner on June 3. "When will you be in Washington? Can't we collect bold men enough to lay the foundation for a party to take the helm of this government, and keep it off the rocks?" A few days later he wrote again: "Is there no way to arrest the insane course of the President in Washington?" If something was not done, he thought the president would be "crowned king" before Congress met. Sumner fully agreed. "We must speak and act," he replied, asking Stevens to go and see Johnson in person. "The North was ready for the true doctrine & practice. It is hard—very hard to be driven to another contest."[13]

Sumner wrote in a similar vein to Wade, and General Carl Schurz, the influential German-American immigrant leader; addressing the president directly, implored him to modify the proclamations when dealing with South Carolina. Why not take advantage of the fact that that state had always had unrepublican voting restrictions for whites? These could be set aside and the blacks enfranchised, and Johnson would still be acting according to the theory that the states had never seceded. Robert Dale Owen, son of the famous socialist Robert Owen, who had served in Congress with Johnson, wrote him a nineteen-page letter imploring him to counteract the lapse of the three-fifths compromise with black suffrage, which could be asked as a condition of pardon, even though he, too, professed to agree that the states were still in the Union.[14]

At the end of June a number of radicals came to Washington to persuade Johnson to call Congress into special session to take care of the problem of Reconstruction. Among them were Wade, Thaddeus Stevens, and Henry Winter Davis. Wade was most reluctant to admit that he and the president were parting company. In several interviews with Johnson, the senator sought to win his cooperation. But his efforts were in vain. As he wrote disgustedly to Sumner after returning home, the president was determined to carry on a policy bound to surrender the party to the "tender mercies of the rebels." Stevens also attempted to induce Johnson to delay his Reconstruction scheme, but by August the "Commoner," too, had given up hope.[15] For a while, some tried to console themselves with the expectation that the president was merely carrying on an experiment, although he soon made it perfectly clear that they were mistaken. Gradually, congressional leaders came to see that Johnson was determined to go through with his plans, and they prepared to oppose him. "I am glad you are laboring to arrest the President's fatal policy," Stevens wrote to Sumner on August 26. "I wish the prospects for success were better."[16]

In the meantime, Johnson, encouraged by his friends, had carried his policy further. As soon as he issued his North Carolina proclamation, delegations from other states began to arrive in Washington to plead for similar treatment. On June 8 Judge William L. Sharkey and William Yerger arrived from Mississippi, where the last Confederate governor had appointed them commissioners. Asked whether the North Carolina proclamation would suit them, they immediately answered in the affirmative, and on June 13 Johnson appointed Judge Sharkey provisional governor. That the judge had been a lifelong Whig made no difference; he was a Unionist and that was what the president wanted. It must have pleased him that Sharkey had been born in East Tennessee and had gone to school in Greeneville. His cordial manner impressed the judge, who was delighted that the president required so little of him. Johnson merely told the Mississippians that slavery was gone and that he expected them to ratify the Thirteenth Amendment.[17]

The president followed the same procedure with other states. On June 17 he issued proclamations for Texas and Georgia. Andrew Jackson Hamilton, a Democratic Unionist who had always been loyal and had been Lincoln's choice, was appointed governor of Texas. James Johnson, a Unionist Whig and Know Nothing lawyer from Columbus, who had nevertheless sided with his state, was to head Georgia. Alabama came next, on June 21, when Johnson appointed Lewis E. Parsons, another Know Nothing Unionist, provisional governor. Bitterly opposed to black suffrage, Parsons may have appealed to the president because in 1860 he had been a Democrat, although he supported Douglas at Baltimore. At any rate, he was Johnson's choice, much to the disgust of Northern radicals.[18]

The most difficult appointment was yet to be made. South Carolina, the cradle of secession, was still without government, and a meeting of citizens in Charleston sent a delegation to the White House to ask for a provisional governor. William W. Boyce, ex-governor William Aiken, and James L. Orr met with the president; notwithstanding the state's unpopularity, they, too, received a warm welcome, and Johnson asked them to submit a list of possible appointees. From this panel he selected the name of Benjamin F. Perry, a Greenville lawyer long known for his Unionist conservative views, although he had held office under the Confederate government. Perry, who heard that Johnson professed to know him, thought they had probably met when young Andrew was in Laurens. When he met with Johnson in Washington, the president told him that South Carolina ought to ratify the Thirteenth Amendment and suggested that the state change its constitution in such a way as to make the white population the basis for representation and to provide for the popular election of governors as well as presidential electors.[19]

For Florida, the last remaining state to be restored, Johnson picked another Unionist, William Marvin, to serve as provisional governor. Marvin had held federal judicial office ever since Andrew Jackson had appointed him district attorney; he lived in Key West, which had remained within Union lines. According to his lights, Johnson had thus put all the states back on the road to restoration, apparently demanding nothing of them but their ratification of the emancipation amendment, and even that not unconditionally, although later he also suggested nullification of the secession ordinances and repudiation of the Confederate debt.[20]

Why Johnson, a consistent Jeffersonian-Jacksonian Democrat and foe of the old Southern aristocracy, picked provisional governors without regard to their previous political affiliation, including some who did not fit his preconception of a popular Democrat at all, is not quite clear. It is certain, however, that the president was now so firmly committed to his long-held view that the states had never seceded that he was anxious to test his theories by restoring them as quickly as possible. In addition, he had always been able to make alliances with forces originally opposed to him: with the opposition during his campaigns in his home district, with Brownlow and his Know Nothing supporters during the secession crisis, and with sundry former Whigs throughout Tennessee during the war. This gambit had always worked to his advantage. He might have alienated some of his old party associates, in the long run, however, he had not only succeeded, but during the conflict gained such great popularity in the North that he eventually had been able to satisfy his fondest ambitions. Why should he not now repeat this maneuver and seek to forge new alliances with the South? Given the undoubted popularity of his policy in the former Confederacy, where he could count on the backing of former secessionists, it was not impossible for him to imagine that he would be able once again to build up a large following in his home section. These supporters, combined with conservatives in the North, might well give him the coveted nomination for a second term.

It is true that Johnson could have reached this objective more easily by cooperating with the radicals or even the moderates; but he could not really ally himself with them. Their views on the position of the states were foreign to him, to say nothing of their ideas of racial uplift, opinions shared by radicals and the majority of moderates alike. Thus it made sense to seek a new power base. If these were his calculations, he obviously underestimated the storm any premature alliance with the old Southern leaders would cause in the North; nor could he know that the Southern states would be kept out of Congress and the electoral college as long as they eventually were. For the time being, the president could see only the favorable reaction to his policy.

In the South that reaction was favorable indeed. Benjamin F. Hill, the prewar Georgia Unionist and later Confederate senator, then a prisoner at Fort Lafayette, addressed Johnson from his cell. "By this wise and noble statesmanship you have become the benefactor of the Southern people in the hour of their direst extremity and entitled yourself to the gratitude of those living and those yet to live," Hill asserted. Duff Green, a former member of Jackson's Kitchen Cabinet and later advocate of Southern rights, insisted that the Democrats were relying on the South to restore them to power and that, if Johnson treated the section correctly, he could win their support in 1868. Thomas E. Bramlette, the

Democratic governor of Kentucky, assuring him of widespread support, wrote flatteringly: "The heart and mind of the true men throughout our whole country yield to you homage and applause for the noble stand you have taken in your administration of the Government." From New Orleans the Louisiana conservative Thomas Cottman reported that the entire conservative element of the country would enter actively upon the support of the government, and J. B. Bingham wrote from Memphis that because of Johnson's policies his most bitter enemies were now avowing "their determination to see you and your administration through in spite of all opposition."[21]

Even more encouraging, probably, was Richard Taylor's advice. Taylor, a Confederate general and son of President Zachary Taylor, contemplated emigration after the defeat of the Confederacy, but was greatly affected by Johnson's actions. He told Democratic friends that Southerners were universally pleased with the president's course; the new governors were the very best men in the South for their positions, and had the choice been given to him, one acquainted with the prominent citizens of South Carolina and Mississippi, he would have selected Perry and Sharkey himself. Taylor secured a personal interview with Johnson, who talked him out of his idea of emigrating and persuaded him to apply for a pardon. Taylor in turn urged Johnson to secure the affections of the Southern people by "not perpetuating a dead idea by giving it the sanctity of martyrdom."[22]

The president took Taylor's advice, and as time went on, the gratitude of the South became even more pronounced. "Our *Southern* brothers are beginning to know that you are their friend, their protector, and to *feel* that 'in thy hands a nation's fate lies circled,' " wrote an admirer from Pulaski, Tennessee. General Gideon Pillow assured him that he would be sustained by the entire Southern people. A doctor from South Carolina let Johnson know that his policy of forgiveness would spur the whole South to rally to his support for president in 1868, while Sharkey reportedly stated that Johnson was making treason odious in the eyes of the rebels themselves. According to the superintendent of the Virginia and Tennessee Railroad, who had checked the mob that had tried to molest Johnson at Lynchburg in 1861, the president's official course "in our estimation has been just, independent, statesmanlike and highly satisfactory to us, and we hope and pray that God may permit you to remain at the head of our government." The South Carolina legislature unanimously resolved to endorse the administration, asserted its cordial approval of the mode of pacification proposed by the president, and pledged its cooperation with him "in the wise measures he has inaugurated for securing the peace and prosperity of the whole Union." As

Johnson's old friend and later Confederate critic Nicholson, whom he had pardoned, summed it up, "My hope and that of our people has been centered on you, and I think I can safely say, that at no time of your life have you enjoyed so much of the confidence of our people as since your policy as President has been developed."[23]

If Southerners were pleased with the president, Democrats were also encouraged. Three days after Johnson's inauguration Montgomery Blair had urged S. M. L. Barlow, an influential New York Democratic leader, to support the new president, whose ideas on Reconstruction, he insisted, were sound. The North Carolina proclamation seemed to support this assertion, and in its wake Johnson's old friend former governor Joseph A. Wright of Indiana, whom he appointed minister to Prussia, assured him that the Democrats would sustain the administration. The president was reputed to be listening mainly to Republicans of Democratic antecedents, and by June 15 Barlow promised Blair that the Democrats would cooperate. Although Barlow was worried about Seward's and Stanton's continued influence and habitually decried the use of military commissions to try conspirators, he was willing to reserve his judgment of the new president. Jeremiah S. Black, Buchanan's last secretary of state, learned that Johnson was moving toward the Democratic party and that the anteroom to his White House office looked as if the Democrats were in power. Black promptly wrote Blair that it had been the "sincere desire of the democracy" of Pennsylvania "to make up a perfect reconciliation with President Johnson," although Pennsylvanians, too, were upset about the continuing military trials and the execution of the conspirators.[24]

The New Yorkers were soon prepared to establish contact with the administration. Barlow, Dean Richmond, and Samuel J. Tilden, all prominent Empire State Democrats, stood ready to inform the president of their approval, and later they saw to it that the Democratic State Convention actually endorsed Johnson, although they realized that the president intended to use their help to create a new conservative organization. As Barlow commented, "Johnson is insane enough to imagine that he can build up a . . . party in the South as well as in the North which shall embrace the conservative elements of all the old factions and that thus he can rid himself of an alliance with the democratic party proper." The New Yorker was sure that this scheme would fail and that the president would either become the head of the Democrats, or he would have no party at all in Congress, and at the end of his term would be totally powerless. But this suspicion did not prevent temporary cooperation.[25]

It is true that Johnson for his part distrusted the regular Democratic organization. To win him over, Blair appealed to his racial prejudices by explaining that the rebellion was crushed, but that it had given rise to new troubles—Negro suffrage and social equality of the races. "What can come of the adulteration of our Anglo-Saxon Government by Africanization," Blair asked, "but the degradation of the free spirit & lofty aspirations which our race inherited from their ancestry and brought to this continent, and then turn that whole portion of it engaged in manual operations into that class of mongrels which cannot but spring from the unnatural blending of the blacks and whites in one common class of laborers. . . . The result will inevitably be to make a distinction in caste and put a brand on all our race associated in employment with people of color & crimped hair." To prevent this development of a caste system and aristocracy, Blair argued, Johnson must cooperate with the Democrats. It was an argument well calculated to appeal to the president's strongly held predilections for the laboring classes and his deepest prejudices against the blacks. Combined with the praise coming from the South, it could not fail to influence his thinking.[26]

For the time being, however, Johnson was not yet prepared to break completely with the Union party, or even with its more extreme adherents. When early in July the military commission trying the Lincoln conspirators rendered its verdict, it attached to the documents submitted to Johnson for his signature a recommendation for mercy for Mrs. Surratt, chiefly because she was a woman and because the evidence against her was merely circumstantial. On July 5 Judge Advocate General Joseph Holt saw the president alone; he brought the papers with him, and Johnson signed the execution orders. According to Holt, the president saw the recommendation for mercy, a contention Johnson later vehemently denied. Whether or not he really laid eyes on it is difficult to determine; the matter was to cause controversy for years to come. In reality, he was so ill at the time that it is possible he did not even realize what he had seen. At any rate, he refused all pleas for mercy, and on July 7 the conspirators who had been sentenced to death were duly executed.[27] The man who had vowed to punish traitors was carrying out his promises. Those seeking vengeance could only approve of his action.

Johnson also sought to disarm his critics by inducing Southerners to enfranchise a few blacks. Although he believed neither in universal suffrage nor in the right of the federal government to dictate voting requirements to the states, when the Mississippi State Convention assembled, he sent an often-quoted telegram to Governor Sharkey:

If you could extend the elective franchise to all persons of color who can read the Constitution of the United States in English and write their names, and to all persons of color who own real estate valued at not less than two hundred and fifty dollars, and pay taxes thereon, you would completely disarm the adversary and set an example the other States will follow. This you can do with perfect safety, and you thus place the southern States, in reference to free persons of color, upon the same basis with the free States. I hope and trust your convention will do this, and, as a consequence, the radicals, who are wild upon negro franchise, will be completely foiled in their attempt to keep the southern States from renewing their relations to the Union by not accepting their senators and representatives.[28]

The telegram was indicative of his attitude, even of his understanding of political realities. But in a perverse insistence on his principle of no federal interference, he failed to apply any pressure on Sharkey to translate his suggestion into action. Thus in the end neither Mississippi nor any other Southern state enfranchised a single freedman.

Johnson continued to seek to mollify his critics. Late in August he met with a number of Republicans and succeeded in satisfying them, at least for the time being. On September 7 he asked a Louisiana newspaperman why Southerners could not solve the suffrage question without bothering him. Let them do as Massachusetts does, he advised: enfranchise those who could read the Constitution. Not five hundred would be affected, but their right to vote would still the clamor in the North. Some four weeks later George Stearns, his old Massachusetts acquaintance from Nashville days, came to see him. Stearns, who later reported that the president's manner and conversation was as free as it had been in Tennessee, and his appearance even healthier, asked Johnson about his relations with the Democrats. "Major," the president replied laughingly, "have you never known a man who for many years had differed from your views because you were in advance of him, claim them as his own when he came up to your standpoint?" This was the case with the Democrats, said the president, and as for Negro suffrage, he himself did not oppose it. But, he insisted, the suffrage was a matter for the states to decide. Were he in Tennessee, he would try to introduce black voting gradually, first enfranchising those who had been in the army, those who could read and write, and perhaps those who owned property worth $200 or $250. Universal suffrage at that time would be dangerous; the blacks would vote with their former masters rather than with the poor whites whom they hated, and a war of races would result. Stearns went away greatly encouraged.[29]

Another example of Johnson's efforts to maintain his standing in the

Union party was an interview he granted to a regiment of black soldiers who had returned from the South and paid their respects at the White House. Thanking them sincerely for their service to the Union, he assured them that in his opinion the United States was their country as well as that of their white comrades. Their future was here, he said, advising them to try to make something of themselves through hard labor and a morally impeccable life. "This country is founded upon the principle of equality," he reminded them, while maintaining that the standard by which persons were to be estimated was according to their merit and worth. Whether the two races could live peacefully side by side Providence alone could show, but he thought the experiment should be tried. Widely reported in the press, the speech seemed to belie Democratic assertions that Johnson had joined the opposition. He had given the lie to Copperhead claims that he regarded the United States a white man's country, boasted the Chicago *Tribune*. [30]

Unfortunately for the future of the country and of Reconstruction, however, Johnson's remarks to the blacks were somewhat disingenuous. He had never changed his conviction of the inferiority of blacks, nor would he ever do so. When he heard that his house in Greeneville had been used by black troops, he sent a furious wire to General Thomas:

> I have information of the most reliable character that the negro troops stationed at Greeneville Tenn. . . . are committing depredations throughout the country, domineering over, and in fact running the white people out of the neighborhood. . . . The negro soldiery take possession of and occupy property in the town at discretion, and have even gone so far as to have taken my own house and converted it into a rendez vous for male and female negroes, who have been congregated there, in fact making it a common negro brothel. It was bad enough to be taken by traitors and converted into a rebel hospital but a negro whore house is infinitely worse.

After all their sufferings, the people of East Tennessee in particular, he pointed out, should be freed from the burden of having black troops in their midst, and he ordered the soldiers to be sent away. In addition, he promised Governor Sharkey of Mississippi, who had requested the removal of black troops from his state, that he would remove the objectionable soldiers as soon as possible. Andrew Johnson's prejudices had not vanished with his conversion to emancipation; his policies clearly reflected his views.[31]

The president not only agreed to Sharkey's request to remove black troops, he also supported the governor's effort to raise a white militia. This policy brought about a break with Carl Schurz, whom Johnson had first met in Nashville when he tried to induce Lincoln to give the German-American a new active command. After the war the president had sent Schurz on a trip through the Southern states, but the German's reports did not please him. Radical and wholly antagonistic toward the president's policies, Schurz found that the Confederates had not changed their attitude, that Johnson's program encouraged them to offer resistance, and that they treated the freedmen with cruelty and callousness. He arrived in Mississippi just after the commanding general, Henry W. Slocum, had countermanded the governor's order to raise a local militia. Schurz sent Johnson a telegram strongly supportive of the general's action. Once federal troops were withdrawn, he pointed out, no Northerner would be safe in Mississippi. But Sharkey, too, contacted the president, and reminded him that at their last interview Johnson had promised to sustain him. The president promptly countermanded Slocum's orders and wired Schurz that the main objective of his mission to the South was "to aid as far as practicable in carrying out the policy adopted by the Government for restoring the States to their former relations with the Federal Government." Indeed, he asserted, one great aim of his policy was to induce the people of the South to come forward in the defense of the state and federal governments. When Schurz went on to Louisiana, where Johnson was also supporting a conservative faction, the break became complete, and the German-American returned to Washington to a most chilly reception. The result was that he prepared a scathing report, which could later be used against the president.[32]

According to Johnson's theories, the end of the war required as speedy a normalization and as near a return to prewar conditions as possible. He sought to emphasize this idea by publishing a series of proclamations restoring commercial intercourse with the South, lifting the blockade, and ending wartime regulations. But his lack of sympathy for the blacks and his anxiety to restore many of the features of the old order led him to sanction the return of property to its former owners even if it was already in the hands of freedmen. On July 28, 1865, General Oliver O. Howard, the head of the newly created Freedmen's Bureau, issued a circular regularizing the return of lands to previous owners but specifically exempting such abandoned lands as were already being cultivated by freedmen. Some months before, in January, General Sherman had set aside a coastal strip in South Carolina, Georgia, and Florida for the exclusive use of former slaves. Johnson, however, nullified both of these arrangements. In September 1865 he ordered Howard to issue orders rescinding his former exemption so that pardoned owners could reclaim their property, and in October he nullified Sherman's orders by decreeing that arrangements be made between the original proprietors and the blacks. It was a decision with fateful consequences for the freedmen.[33]

The president's restoration of rebel property was part of his larger policy of granting special pardons whenever possible. His amnesty proclamation exempted fourteen classes, including high military, civil, and judicial officers of the Confederacy, officers who had surrendered their commissions in the armed forces of the United States, war criminals, commerce raiders, and those with taxable property of more than $20,-000. It also provided that special applications for pardons by the exempted classes might be made to the president and promised that clemency would be "liberally extended."[34]

Johnson did in fact liberally extend clemency. As he explained to Orville H. Browning, the conservative Republican from Illinois, he "was anxious to pursue a policy which would heal the wounds and repair the ravages of war, and bring those who had been in rebellion against the government back to their allegiance, and convert them into peaceable, law abiding citizens." Although Johnson also thought that he would hold the principal Confederate leaders in suspense for some time, he was perfectly ready to begin a broad policy of forgiveness.[35]

The president was as good as his word. After several months of caution, during which he even seems to have considered briefly the possibility of trying General Lee for treason, he initiated an ever more noticeable program of pardoning prominent, wealthy insurgents.[36] The result was a steadily mounting flood of applications for special consideration from all manner of Confederate leaders. Generals, cabinet members, diplomats, all asked and generally received either a pardon or a parole. And Johnson did not forget his old friends. Lizinka Brown Ewell fared well; he granted her an interview, during which, though he chided her for marrying "a wooden-legged traitor," he proved generally friendly so that she eventually procured her husband's freedom and the return of her property. He also pardoned his old Tennessee associate W. C. Whitthorne, to say nothing of his friend George W. Jones, with whom he soon resumed confidential relations. By October leading members of the Confederate cabinet had been paroled, and the number of successful applicants was still growing—even Confederate Vice President Stephens was among their number.[37]

Whether Johnson really took great pleasure in responding favorably to pleas of haughty Southerners who had formerly despised him is debatable. It is true that he bantered with various applicants whom he had known. He asked Thomas Avery, a Memphis Democrat, if he remembered the sign A. Johnson, Tailor, in the Greeneville shop and chatted with him for some time; but Avery, unlike Stearns, thought he no longer looked as robust and carefree as formerly. On the contrary, he seemed careworn. It might have afforded him some satisfaction to exercise authority over people who had formerly despised him, but his policy was due to different considerations. He believed that the authority to grant pardons was one of the few rights a president could fully exercise in dealing with Reconstruction without infringing on the rights of the states he so firmly considered to be still in the Union.[38]

As was to be expected, the pardoning policy greatly upset many Northerners. Finding the anterooms to the White House crowded with Southern pardon seekers, they were repelled, and the fact that pardon brokers seemed to make a profit by selling the requisite documents did not mollify their anger. "With the President I could not talk at all," Francis Lieber complained to Sumner. "He received me very kindly (and with perfect manners) but there were 11 women sitting in the room, and 3 men, all I dare say for pardons. All I could do was to urge strongly upon him to break up this thing. The nation does not set up the presidency for this abominable thing. The ground floor of the White House was crowded."[39]

The most notorious of the pardon brokers was Mrs. Lucy Cobb, a Washington citizen of dubious reputation, who managed to secure access to the White House. Rumors soon circulated that she was exerting undue influence upon the president, even that she was having an affair with him, and Lafayette C. Baker, the chief of the Secret Service, tried to lay a trap for her. He did indeed catch her selling documents required for pardons, but, according to his own testimony, was roundly abused by the president for his efforts. When he tried to incriminate her on another occasion, he was dismissed. In view of the fact that Baker's reputation for veracity was not high, and that he gave his testimony and wrote his memoirs after he had lost his office, when the president was about to be impeached, it is difficult to say how much credence he may be given. Nevertheless, his tales hurt Johnson's reputation.[40]

Above all, the pardoning policies did not contribute to the success of the president's own plan of Reconstruction. Even with Governor William Holden's advice and help, he was seemingly unable to use his powers to bring about election results favorable to him in North Carolina. Somehow his political finesse, so evident in Nashville, now deserted him in Washington.[41]

Not merely politically, but personally, too, the president was a troubled man that summer and fall. To be sure, his family arrived in June to assist him, but Eliza was too much of an invalid to serve as a hostess and First Lady. That job devolved upon Martha, who carried it out most satisfactorily and made an excellent impression upon all who observed her.[42] Early in July and well into August, Johnson was ill. Pale and languid, he was burdened by overwork and a taxing routine. He habitually rose at six o'clock, read papers, breakfasted at eight, and at nine went to the executive office, where he took care of business until four in the afternoon. At five he dined; then he took a walk or a carriage ride, only to receive visitors again from nine to eleven before retiring. Worried about his health, Gideon Welles invited him for a short boat trip down the Potomac and into Chesapeake Bay, which helped him a bit, though he was not able to recover completely until the middle of August.[43]

In addition, his worries about Robert were increasing. The young man came to Washington to become his father's private secretary, but he unfortunately began to drink heavily again and gave the family a bad name. In October the president learned that his brother William, recently appointed surveyor in Velasco, Texas, had accidentally shot himself while hunting, and died. And then, in November, Preston King suffered a severe depression and drowned himself in the Hudson River. It was a serious blow for Johnson.[44]

In the meantime, the provisional governors appointed by the president were putting the process of presidential Reconstruction into operation. They called conventions which generally followed the president's directive and abolished slavery, nullified or repealed the secession ordinances, and repudiated wartime Confederate debts. It might have been expected that the governors would have no trouble meeting such lenient requirements, but in some cases they did not even fulfill these minimum terms.

Why Johnson did not see to it that his own program was carried out fully is difficult to understand. However, in keeping with his theories of state sovereignty, he refused to intervene decisively. To be sure, he cautioned the governors to appoint Unionists to office, but as he explained to Governor Holden, his intention "was merely . . . to call your attention to the impression being made by those who are opposed to the southern States resuming their former relations to the federal government." He wanted to deprive his critics of all excuse for opposing the restoration of state government.[45]

The president's attitude made it possible for some states to defy his wishes. He insisted that South Carolina repudiate her debt incurred during the war, but he applied no real pressure and the state refused. It is true that in a similar situation in North Carolina, he was more successful. Wiring to Governor Holden that "every dollar of the debt created to aid the rebellion should be repudiated, finally and forever," he added that the "great mass of the people should not be taxed to pay a debt to aid in carrying on a rebellion, which they, in fact, if left to themselves, were opposed to." It was a typical Johnsonian reaffirmation of his belief in the innocence of the common people led into secession by intriguing aristocrats. Holden saw to it that the president's wishes were carried out, but his wire hardly constituted real pressure.[46]

After the conventions had done their work, elections were held for state officers, new legislatures, and members of Congress. Again, true to his principles of noninterference, Johnson, instead of using his influence to obtain a desirable result, merely suggested that it would be unwise to elect such prominent Confederates as Alexander H. Stephens. Then, after Holden's defeat in North Carolina, he publicly deplored the outcome.

The result was a disaster. The legislatures elected by the enfranchised voters tended to be dominated by arch-conservatives and secessionists. Imbued with reverence for the lost cause, they became notorious for passing black codes so stringent as to constitute a virtual reestablishment of slavery under a different name. Freedmen quitting work in violation of their contracts could be forcibly carried back to their employers; they could be auctioned off for "vagrancy," and their children, if not properly provided for, could be apprenticed to suitable employers. The president again refused to interfere.[47]

If there was one action Johnson wanted these legislatures to take, it was the ratification of the antislavery amendment. Yet he was almost as undemanding about this requirement as about others. Instead of telling his governors what to do, he almost pleaded with them to see to it that their legislatures ratified. "There is a deep interest felt as to what course the legislatures will take in regard to the adoption of the amendment . . . ," he wired to South Carolina governor Benjamin Perry. "I trust in God that restoration of the Union will not now be defeated, and all that has so far been well done thrown away. I still have faith that all will come out right yet." Pointing out that he thought the opportunity "ought to be understood by the people of the southern States," he made it clear that his earnest desire was "to restore the blessings of the Union, and tie up and heal every bleeding wound which had been caused by this fratricidal war." South Carolina did ratify the amendment, but similar entreaties to Mississippi were in vain.[48] For so experienced a politician, it was a strange way of handling matters. But by the fall the president had so convinced himself of the illegality of real interference and the importance of speedy restoration that he failed to make use of the most elementary weapons at his disposal. His obsession with states' rights now made him blind to political necessities.

Nor did the election of governors and congressional delegations by the various Southern states give him much cause for satisfaction. Such conservative figures as Jonathan Worth in North Carolina and Confederate general Benjamin Humphreys in Mississippi became governors, while four Confederate generals, five colonels, and Alexander H. Stephens were elected to Congress. Some had not even been pardoned; however, Johnson granted them clemency in order to enable them to take office, a procedure that was neither to make things easier with Congress nor to further his own designs. But he was so anxious to complete the process of restoration that he abandoned all political prudence.[49]

In view of these developments, it was not surprising that the radicals were becoming more and more alarmed. On September 15 Joseph Medill of the Chicago *Tribune*, warning the president not to judge the political opinions of the North by the columns of Democratic newspapers, admonished him that the people would never again be ruled by Southern oligarchs. "You may affect to despise the Radicals," he wrote, "but their votes made you President." Cautioning him not to "Tylerize" the Union party, he expressed the conviction that the "great doctrine of *equal rights*" was bound to prevail. Let Johnson "lead the column" of progress! And although in October James M. Ashley, the Ohio extremist, still assured an audience in San Francisco that the president was sound on black suffrage, others were rapidly despairing of him. By November Wade was so depressed that he temporarily lost faith in democratic government itself. The president's course, he thought, had done more to jeopardize the liberties of the country than the war with all its rebel leaders combined.[50]

Nevertheless, Johnson was not yet prepared to make common cause with the Democrats. To be sure, Barlow, with considerable success, tried to commit the party to the administration's program, particularly in New York, but with an election coming and the Republicans also professing support for the president, the problem of patronage loomed large. Still anxious to steer a middle way in the North, Johnson, influenced by Seward and Thurlow Weed, appointed his friend the former New York senator Preston King collector of the Port of New York. This important post gave the state's Republicans, especially the conservative ones, a great advantage, and the Democrats complained that because of the hostile influence of the customs house and the post office, they were compelled to fight at the same time both the president and his opponents. The result was a Republican success, hardly a surprise under the circumstances, as Barlow was quick to explain to Blair.[51] In the long run the president would have to determine how to marshal the disparate forces sympathizing with him. For the time being, however, he could be satisfied. All the Southern states except Texas had been reorganized under either Lincoln's plan or his own.

For the country, Johnson's policies were less desirable. The trouble with his course was that it amounted to throwing away a splendid opportunity to initiate a promising racial policy. His attitude, in effect, caused the South to reassess its relations with the victorious government. Apparently there was to be no large-scale retribution, no imposition of outside rule, no requirement of black suffrage; so Southern moods changed. While in the spring of 1865 he might have imposed almost any conditions upon the South, news of his magnanimity brought about a profound reaction. When Whitelaw Reid arrived in Mobile, he noticed a marked difference in attitude from what he had observed on the Atlantic Coast. "There they were just as vehement in their protestations against negro suffrage," he wrote,

> but they ended in entreaties that the conquerors would spare the infliction of such disgrace. Here came threats. Everywhere else it was manifest that if the restoration of civil authority depended on negro suffrage, it would be accepted. Here, for the first time, we were told the people would not stand it. The explanation is simple. They were just beginning to get a knowledge of the North Carolina proclamation, and to imagine that the President was willing to concede to them more power than they had dared hope.

His colleague J. T. Trowbridge heard the same sentiments. When traveling in the South during the fall, a radical Union supporter told him that immediately after the war, the Southern leaders had been thoroughly subdued. Expecting no mercy from the government, they were prepared to submit to anything, even Negro suffrage, they thought would be required of them. "But the more lenient the government, the more arrogant they became."[52]

This reversal of the initial feeling of resignation was widespread. When he first arrived in Richmond, Unionist John A. Anderson recalled that everybody greeted him kindly and was glad to see him. As soon as the people "found out the policy of the President of the United States," however, they changed, and he was proscribed. Another adherent of the federal government, Watkins James, remembered similar experiences in the Shenandoah Valley. Shortly after the surrender, he found the inhabitants "quiet and peaceable, disposed to submit to almost anything." Matters became very different afterward, however, and he believed the cause was the leniency of the government.

From New Orleans, testimony about similar conditions came from

Justice Rufus K. Howell, who said that "at one time, immediately after the surrender," there would have been a pretty close vote between Unionists and secessionists, but that "after the policy of the President began to be understood . . . the old feeling of hatred returned." In Florida, too, Johnson heard that the great majority of the people were determined to return directly and quickly to the fold in any form he might prescribe, at least in May 1865. General Custer observed the same reaction in Texas; Bingham reported an immediate surge of conservatism in Memphis following the news of the amnesty proclamation, and General John W. Sprague wrote at the same time from Little Rock: "For some time after the surrender those who had returned from the Rebel armies were the most quiet and orderly, it is not so now."[53]

That Johnson had made any effective Reconstruction impossible was recognized at the time. As his assistant General Mussey expressed it in October of 1865, "It seems to me that we had the opportunity when Lee surrendered and more than that when Lincoln was assassinated to make our own terms." It was a conclusion Carl Schurz emphasized in his report: "When news of Lee's and Johnston's surrenders burst upon the Southern country, the general consternation was extreme. . . . The public mind was so despondent that if readmission at some future time under whatever conditions had been promised, it would have been looked upon as a favor." But, he continued, "the worst apprehensions were gradually relieved as day after day went by without bringing the disasters and inflictions which had been vaguely anticipated, until at last the appearance of the North Carolina proclamation substituted new hopes for them." Thereafter the attitude of Southerners changed.[54] And in 1871 Christopher Memminger, the former Confederate secretary of the Treasury summed it up in a letter to Schurz: "I think you are right in saying that if we had originally adopted a different course as to the negroes, we would have escaped present difficulties. But if you will consider a moment, you will see that it was as impossible, as for us to have emancipated them before the war. The then President held up before us the hope of a 'white man's government,' and this led us to set aside negro suffrage."[55]

These observations were accurate. Johnson put into operation policies that were in accordance with his deeply felt views on states' rights. At the same time, however, he reanimated Southern resistance and fatally undermined efforts to integrate the freedmen into society. What action Congress would take remained to be seen.

XIII

PUGNACIOUS PRESIDENT

PERHAPS the most crucial period in the administration of Andrew Johnson was the time span between December 1865 and July of the following year. It was during that interval of seven short months that Johnson broke with Congress and charted the stubborn course he was to follow ever after. His motives for the break—his reasons for not going along at least halfway with the Union party—are therefore a problem of great importance, and no biographer of the seventeenth president can avoid coming to grips with it.

At first sight, Johnson's policy with respect to Congress during the winter and spring of 1865 and 1866 seems well-nigh inexplicable. After all, the radicals, whose ideas were furthest removed from his, constituted merely a minority of the Republican party. The largest Republican contingent by far consisted of moderates, men like Lyman Trumbull, the able chairman of the Senate's Judiciary Committee, William Pitt Fessenden, the equally talented head of the Finance Committee, the president's Iowa friend James W. Grimes, and John Sherman, the senator from Ohio and the general's brother. These men and their counterparts in the House had almost as little liking for the small minority of radicals like Sumner, Stevens, and Wade as Johnson; they were anxious to cooperate with the administration, and cooperation with them would have given the president control of the Thirty-ninth and Fortieth Congresses.[1] Yet he refused to collaborate with them, so that in the end, much to his discomfort, they often made common cause with the radicals. The question of why he rebuffed them has puzzled observers ever since.

To find the explanation for this riddle, Johnson's personality and ideology must be kept in mind. Firmly believing in the states as entities that could never secede, he was now so unequivocally wedded to his own plan of Reconstruction that any deviation from it was unthinkable to him. According to Gideon Welles, the president was a "Unionist, a states rights man—a strict constructionist," while his opponents were "centralists, consolidationists, loose constructionists."[2] Johnson would have agreed with these characterizations. Because for the president secession was impossible, he was certain that the states had never been out of the Union. The authority of the government had merely been temporarily displaced by a hostile force, and as all the insurgent commonwealths had been reconquered, the Constitution and the laws applied to them at once, "without waiting for further legislation to restore them to their relations with the Union." So strong was Johnson's conviction on this point that he thought it would have been better to have let the rebel states secede without firing a gun than to treat them as conquered territories to be governed by military authority. Positive that without the states there was no general government, he insisted that all states must stand on a footing of absolute equality. It was for this principle that East Tennessee had endured all its privations, he said, and he was determined to hold to this theory no matter what the consequences.[3]

It might be objected that a man of the president's political experience must have realized what the effect of such a policy would be—the possible loss of the Union party's control of Congress and the abandonment of the blacks to the mercy of their former masters. Neither of these considerations, however, could sway him. Never having declared himself a Republican, even though he said he wanted to fight out his battle within the Union party, Johnson was now ready for the organization of a new conservative grouping, so that the congressional Republicans' probable loss of power was of no great moment to him. As early as August 17, 1865, the New York Herald pointed out that the president fully realized the importance of making a full sweep of the Republicans plotting to defeat his policies and that he intended to rally around himself conservative men of both parties.[4] In a conference with Thomas G. Pratt, the former governor of Maryland, Johnson himself indicated that the Herald was right, as the Democrats fully realized. S. M. L. Barlow may have believed that the president would fail in this endeavor, but others were certain that he had a chance. Henry Watterson, whose father he had sent on a fact-finding tour in the South, expressed the hope that he would succeed "in the construction of that National

Administration party, on which reposes the sole hope of the country."
Montgomery Blair was sure that Johnson would prevail, and so were
others. At the end of the year, the New York *Sun* repeated the *Herald*'s
observation that the president's policy was to maintain the approval of
the conservatives of both sections; both papers were correct.[5]

If the well-being of the Republican party was not an issue to Johnson,
the imperiled blacks caused him even less worry. Although he had
promised to be their Moses, he really had no objection to their renewed
subordination to the whites. He felt strongly that the freedmen should
not lord it over the dominant race; undoubtedly believing that the
South was a "white man's country," he fully intended to keep it that
way. As Senator Joseph Fowler put it, full political and legal freedom for
blacks "was too rapid a movement for Mr. Johnson. He was not a
reformer; he belonged to the conservative element, and looked upon
great changes in social and political relations as dangerous to the safety
of government." Doubting the Negroes' "capacity to exercise with safety
the highest rights of the Anglo-Saxon," he did not believe that the
South could endure the rule of the African. According to the Cincinnati
Enquirer, Johnson wrote to Governor Thomas C. Fletcher of Missouri,
"This is a country for white men, and by God, as long as I am President,
it shall be a government for white men." Whether the paper quoted him
correctly cannot be determined with certainty, but he did make his racial
views perfectly clear to Benjamin B. French, the commissioner of public
buildings. "Everyone would, and *must* admit," he explained to French
in the fall of 1865, "that the white race was superior to the black, and
that while we ought to do our best to bring them . . . up to our present
level, that, in doing so, we should, at the same time raise our own
intellectual status so that the relative position of the two races would be
the same." Accordingly, far from worrying too much about the effect on
the blacks of his policies, he must have rejoiced at their probable consequences. They would indeed keep the South "a white man's country."[6]

Still, it might be objected, Johnson could have secured his renomination to the presidency much more reasonably by working with the
moderates. It must be remembered, however, that the moderates failed
to recognize the one principle most important to him, the states' un-
changeable status as members of the Union, to say nothing of their
principles of black uplift, even if only partial uplift. In fact, the president
said that if the states could be restored according to his plan, he would
not even seek a renomination. Although his true intentions may be
doubted, he was now so determined to reconstruct, or rather to restore,
in line with his own policies, which he believed to be consistent with

the Johnson-Crittenden Resolutions, that he may really have judged all other considerations secondary.[7]

But the president was facing serious opposition. His most determined opponents, the radicals, though in a minority, were ably led by such men as Thaddeus Stevens in the House and Charles Sumner, Benjamin Wade, and Zachariah Chandler in the Senate. Stevens was at that time over seventy years old; cadaverous, stern, and single-minded, he was a master of parliamentary tricks, which he used unsparingly for the radicals' benefit. Though he was sometimes accused of harshness and vindictive feelings, Stevens was more interested in the elevation of the blacks than in the punishment of Southern whites, and his basic philosophy probably had much more to do with his extreme views on racial equality than with any losses he might have incurred during the war at Gettysburg or his putative relationship with his mulatto housekeeper. Sumner was very different: fanatical, totally devoted to racial justice, and not very effective at parliamentary give-and-take, he delighted in delivering lengthy speeches punctuated by classical allusions that set the Republican party's moral tone. Wade and Chandler, the two Western radicals, were generally direct, sometimes brutally frank, and, though themselves not above racial prejudices, equally devoted to the cause. In December 1865 the radicals were ready for a showdown.[8]

It was difficult for these men to comprehend the frame of mind of their former associate on the Joint Committee. Sumner, for example, sought to impress on Johnson that the key to the entire problem of Reconstruction was black suffrage. He came to see the president two nights before Congress met, on December 2, 1865, and though the two saw eye to eye on foreign policy, Sumner found that on the Southern question, he could not come to an agreement with Johnson. The president began the interview warmly if antagonistically, and at its close, thanked the senator for his visit, but Sumner felt that Johnson did not understand the case. "Much that he said was painful, from its prejudice, ignorance & perversity," he wrote. Lewis D. Campbell, who was present that Saturday evening, thought the senator's conversation arrogant. Sumner had been overbearing and offensive, Campbell remembered, and his entire complaint was that the Negroes had not been enfranchised. The audience had hardly been a success. Sumner left in a huff, determined to attack the administration. That Johnson, in the excitement, used the senator's hat as a spittoon did not improve matters.[9]

It must have been clear to the president from the beginning that things would not be easy when Congress convened. The newspapers had long intimated that the clerk of the House, Edward McPherson, would refuse to call the names of the Southern delegates, a procedure he actually followed. Not even Horace Maynard's name was read, though the East Tennessee Unionist certainly had an unimpeachable record for loyalty. By arrangement, the entire subject of Reconstruction was referred to a Joint Committee of Fifteen; Johnson had lost the first round.[10]

But in all probability the president won the second, when he submitted his annual message on the state of the Union. An ably written document prepared by George Bancroft, the famous historian who had been Polk's secretary of the navy, the speech asserted unequivocally what the president had always believed, that "all pretended acts of secession were, from the beginning, null and void." The Southern states' vitality had been impaired but not extinguished. Consequently, it was incumbent upon the general government to resume the exercise of all its functions as soon as possible. Taking the Constitution as his guide, Johnson had acted on this principle and sought to restore the rightful energy of the federal government and the states. He had appointed provisional governors, restored the courts and post offices, and even invited the states to participate in amending the Constitution, for he was convinced that the ratification of the antislavery amendment was vital for the future safety of the United States. As the states had chosen representatives and senators, he continued, it was now up to Congress to judge the qualifications of its members.

Then the president turned to the question of black suffrage. Asserting that the problem of the government's relations with the freedmen had engaged his most serious consideration, he emphasized that the Constitution left the matter of voting qualifications to the individual states, so that he had been unable to extend the franchise to blacks. Nevertheless, he expressed the hope that the reform would be accomplished gradually and insisted that it would be realized sooner by the states than in any other way.[11]

In general, the message was favorably received, and before long Congress asked that the president submit a report on the actual state of affairs in the South. Complying with the request on December 19, Johnson declared that as a result of his policies, peaceful conditions had been restored in all the Southern states except Texas. Moreover, he took pride in the fact that all of these except Mississippi had ratified the antislavery amendment, which Seward had declared to be in force on the previous day. A brief report describing peaceful conditions in the South, written by General Grant, accompanied the message.[12]

The Grant report was merely an answer to the unfavorable one that Carl Schurz had prepared and that Congress now demanded. Too long to be read in its entirety, the Schurz report was printed as a separate document and widely circulated. Because the German-American had pointed out all the shortcomings of the Reconstruction process Johnson had initiated, his conclusions did not help to bolster the president's position. Apparently the South was neither peaceful nor loyal.[13]

On the day before Johnson sent in his report, December 18, Thaddeus Stevens launched a bitter attack on the president's principles. In a powerful speech, Stevens held that it was nonsense to maintain that the states had not seceded; they were out and could come back only after the adoption of an amendment abrogating the three-fifths compromise. Denying that the United States supported a white man's government, he demanded land for the freedmen and other radical reforms—propositions that could not but further distance him from the president. And on the nineteenth Charles Sumner, in an equally aggressive mood, compared Johnson's report with Franklin Pierce's whitewash of atrocities in Kansas, a charge he sought to subtantiate the next day by detailing outrages against blacks in the South.[14]

Shortly after this bout with the president, both Houses adjourned for the holidays, and Johnson enjoyed a respite with his daughters and his grandchildren, who were staying at the White House. Martha had become his mainstay. With her plain ways and efficient management, she quickly gained the admiration of Washington observers. "We are plain people from the mountains of Tennessee, called here for a short time by a calamity," she said. "I trust too much will not be expected of us." Rising early in the morning and donning a calico dress, she would go downstairs to skim the milk and attend to the dairy before breakfast. She energetically set to work to recondition the war-ravaged mansion, covering old carpets with pure linen and freshening up the rooms with newly cut flowers. Martha remained at her task throughout the summer until the job was done. People were already comparing her favorably with Mary Lincoln.[15]

The result of her labors was apparent when on New Year's Day 1866 the first White House reception was held. Although snow and drizzle somewhat dampened the customary good spirits, the mansion looked surprisingly inviting, and the formalities in the blue drawing room—the East Room was still closed—went off very well. The redecorated walls—scarlet, blue, and green with gilt panels—were much admired. At eleven in the morning the president, accompanied by his daughters, Commissioner French, and a marshal, came down from his private quarters and took his place to receive the diplomatic corps, the members of the Supreme Court, the cabinet, senators, congressmen, and other distinguished guests and their ladies. It was an agreeable occasion, and observers remarked favorably on the simplicity of the president's daughters' attire: Mrs. Patterson wore a dress of heavy silk velvet, trimmed with black lace and a white point collar, with a pure white japonica her only ornament, while Mrs. Stover was still in black in mourning for her husband, who had died of consumption in December 1864. Eliza remained in her room because of her ill health.[16]

The New Year's reception was only one of the splendid affairs hosted at the White House. Diplomatic receptions, levees, and dinners honoring foreign visitors alternated with such official occasions elsewhere as the commemoration of the anniversary of Lincoln's birthday, when George Bancroft, in the presence of the president and other notables, delivered an oration at the Capitol. At all of these affairs, Johnson appeared immaculately dressed, observed the proprieties, and looked dignified and fully in command of the situation. He knew how to entertain.[17]

The president could take pride in his family, except that Robert, succumbing completely to his alcoholism, was once again causing him trouble. "There is too much whiskey in the White House, and harlots go into the Private Secretary's office unannounced in broad daylight," Norman Judd, the former envoy to Berlin, complained to Lyman Trumbull. "Mrs. C. [presumably Mrs. Cobb] did that . . . while a friend of mine was waiting for an audience—and she came out leaning on the arm of a half-drunken son of the President. There were a large number of gentlemen awaiting an audience and saw it all." The president was deeply embarrassed; Secretary Welles suggested a sea voyage for the young man, and it was decided to send him on a mission to Asia and Africa to look into the abuses of the slave and coolie trade. Robert's papers to facilitate his mission were duly made out, but in the end he refused to go. His alcoholism could not be cured.[18]

If there was a time when Johnson could have come to an agreement with the moderates of the Republican party, it was the period following the return of Congress in January 1866. During the clashes in December, many moderates were still criticizing radicals like Sumner and George Boutwell for trying to cause a rupture between Congress and the president; John Sherman had long been known to be friendly toward Johnson; state chairmen expressed the hope that moderation might prevail between the White House and the Capitol, and Horace Greeley warned Speaker Schuyler Colfax not to drive the president into the arms of "our adversaries."[19] Above all, both William Pitt Fessenden, the Maine senator who headed the Joint Committee on Reconstruction, and his good friend James W. Grimes, leading moderates, were eager to come to some agreement with the president, as was Lyman Trumbull, the head of the Senate Judiciary Committee. The president did indeed grant several interviews to Fessenden, who, after seeing him on January 28, believed that the Tennesseean would collaborate with the moderate leadership in Congress. On the next day, however, the newspapers published an interview with "a distinguished Senator" during which the president had deplored the idea of passing any further amendments. Fessenden was disappointed—Johnson had never said anything like that to him—and in fact, it turned out that the "distinguished Senator" was James Dixon of Connecticut, who, along with James Doolittle of Wisconsin and Edgar Cowan of Pennsylvania, was one of the few Republicans who stood by the president unconditionally.[20]

The key to an understanding with the moderates lay in two bills Trumbull was preparing, one to extend and expand the functions of the Freedmen's Bureau, and the other a civil rights measure designed to grant blacks citizenship and to counteract the black codes. Like Fessenden, Trumbull conferred with the president and thought he had obtained Johnson's approval, but of course he was wrong.

The president had no more idea of signing the two bills than he had of yielding to Sumner and Stevens, and in a number of instances, made his lack of sympathy for the freedmen very clear.

First, he refused to countenance a measure providing for black suffrage in the District of Columbia. It was merely an entering wedge for the agitation of the question in the states, he said, "ill-timed, uncalled for, and calculated to do great harm," which would engender enmity and strife between the two races and end in the extermination of the blacks.[21]

Second, Johnson brusquely rebuffed a delegation of freedmen, including Frederick Douglass, who had come to petition for impartial suffrage. After listening to their address, the president replied that, having risked everything in the cause of the Union, he was a great friend of the race. Yet the blacks looked down upon the poor whites and preferred their former masters. Thus an enmity had developed between the blacks and the nonslaveholders. Because of the war, the Negroes had gained a great deal; the poor whites, on the other hand, had lost even more. Therefore, would any change in blacks' condition be justified? The suffrage question was one for the people of each state to decide for themselves. Although Douglass tried to argue the case, Johnson insisted on his point of view. "The President sends us to the people, and we go to the people," the great abolitionist remarked when parting, and Johnson interjected, "Yes sir, I have great faith in the people. I believe they will do what is right." It was not surprising that in a reply published the same day in the *National Chronicle,* the delegates labeled the president's opinion "entirely unsound and prejudicial to the highest interests of our race as well as to our country at large."[22]

His visitors may have been miffed, but Johnson was furious. "The President no more expected that darkey delegation yesterday than he did the cholera," his private secretary told Philip Ripley of the New York *World*. As Ripley, speaking of Johnson, described the incident, "He saw their little game & when they tried to withdraw, he told them to 'hold on.' When they went out after *his* speech, he turned to his Secretary . . . and uttered the following terse Saxon: 'Those d——d sons of b——s thought they had me in a trap. I know that d——d Douglass; he's just like any nigger, & he would sooner cut a white man's throat than not.' " It was obvious he had not changed his mind about blacks' supposed racial inferiority.[23]

In addition, Johnson made clear his strong conviction about a states' rights interpretation of the Constitution in one interview after another. He emphasized it in his annual message, made a point of it to Orville H. Browning on January 2, and stressed it again on February 10 in a meeting with a committee of the Virginia legislature:

> My efforts have been to preserve the Union of these States. I never, for a single moment, entertained the opinion that a State could withdraw from the Union of its own will. . . . Dissolution has been attempted; it has failed; and now I cannot take the position that a State which attempted to secede is out of the Union, when I contended all the time that it could not go out, and that it never has been out. I cannot be forced into that position. Hence, when the States and their people shall have complied with the requirements of the Government, I shall be in favor of their resuming their former relations to this Government in all respects.[24]

With convictions like these, Johnson felt he could not sign the Freedmen's Bureau Bill. In spite of efforts to win his agreement in return for the admission of Tennessee, in spite of misgivings on the part of members of the cabinet, on February 19 he sent a strong veto message to the Senate. Using drafts prepared by Seward, Welles, James Doolittle, Edgar Cowan, and others, but deliberately rejecting Seward's more conciliatory formulations, the president strongly put his own stamp on the final draft.[25] He objected to the legislation because it substituted military jurisdiction for civilian law in the South; he doubted its very necessity in time of peace. And as an old Jeffersonian, he could not countenance the idea of governmental largess to support a portion of the population. "The Government," he declared, "has never felt itself authorized to expend the public money for the thousands, not to say millions, of the white race who are honestly toiling from day to day for their subsistence." The former slaves ought to become self-supporting and not to rely on the bounty of the Treasury.

After stating certain other objections, Johnson finally came to what seemed to him the crux of the matter: signing the bill would put into effect important legislation affecting the South when the Southern states were unrepresented. The Constitution provided for representation; loyal representatives of the states in question were ready to take their seats, and Congress had no authority to "shut out, in time of peace, any State from the representation to which it is entitled by the Constitution." Because the president was elected by all the people, he believed it incumbent upon himself to represent them, and so, he said, he had decided to veto the bill.[26]

The great majority of the members of Congress were outraged. That the radicals vehemently denied the president's arguments was not surprising—Wade went so far as to introduce a one-term amendment to affect future presidents—but moderates were equally disappointed. Trumbull believed himself to have been misled; Fessenden, Grimes, and Sherman voted to override the president's veto.[27] Although Democratic newspapers featured headlines proclaiming, "ALL HAIL! GREAT AND GLORIOUS! GREAT VICTORY FOR THE WHITE MAN," their Republican counterparts were sharply critical. Since the assassination of Lincoln, no event had created such a profound sensation "as the formal act by which the President has severed himself from the loyal party and united with its enemies, North and South," commented the Chicago Tribune. Pointing out that Johnson could have confined himself to vetoing only certain items, the Boston Advertiser deplored the fact that he objected to the law in general terms, thus placing himself, "unfortunately for himself and the country, in his present position of antagonism with the majority of both houses of Congress." The veto was barely sustained, but Trumbull, castigating the president's action, delivered a regretful speech that foretold grave difficulties for the administration.[28]

Johnson, however, was undeterred by the furor he had aroused—he was used to attacks. Forgetting that what was feasible in Tennessee was not always so in Washington, he decided to appeal directly to the people. Popular support against political enemies had long been his salvation, and throughout his presidency he retained his faith in ultimate popular approval. Now, when he was being reproved in and out of Congress, he felt heartened when on Washington's Birthday a crowd appeared at the White House to serenade him. Secretary McCulloch, who had read in the papers that a large number of well-wishers would be present, had warned his chief not to make a speech, and he promised merely to make a brief reply.[29] But the crowd presented resolutions of appreciation, and Johnson was carried away.

Expressing his heartfelt gratitude for their support, he reminded the audience of the importance of the day. Then he recurred to one of his favorite themes, his Jacksonian heritage. The sentiment "which was enunciated by the immortal and the illustrious Jackson—'the Federal Union, it must be preserved,' " was an injunction, he said, he had been trying to carry out and was still trying to carry out. Recounting, as was his wont, the sufferings he had experienced during the war—according to Eric McKitrick, he mentioned the words "I," "mine," and other forms of the first-person pronoun 210 times—he vowed to continue the struggle. "I am opposed to the Davises, the Toombses, the Slidells, and the long list of such," he shouted. "But when I perceive on the other hand men . . . —I care not by what name you call them—still opposed to the Union, I am free to say to you I am still with the people. I am still for the preservation of these States, for the preservation of this Union, and in favor of this great Government accomplishing its destiny."

There were calls from the audience for names, and, much as he had responded in Greeneville, Johnson continued: "The gentleman asks for three names. I am talking to my friends and fellow-citizens here. Suppose I should name to you those I look upon as being opposed to the fundamental principles of this Government, and as now laboring to destroy them. I say Thaddeus Stevens, of Pennsylvania; I say Charles Sumner of Massachusetts; I say Wendell Phillips of Massachusetts." (A voice, "Forney!") Because John W. Forney had broken with him, Johnson replied, "I do not waste my fire on dead ducks. I stand for the country; and though my enemies may traduce, slander, and vituperate, I may say that has no force." He went on about his activities as a tailor, when he had always sewn a close fit, announced that he was ready to shed his blood for the Union, and, after citing Lincoln in support of his stand against further amendments, reaffirmed his unshakable belief in the indestructibility of the states.[30]

This tactless harangue horrified even the most moderate Republicans. "The speech of the President is very unacceptable to our people," commented John H. Geiger, an Ohio moderate who had long supported the administration. "It has no defenders. A great many who stand by the veto . . . are saddened by the language of the Executive. It is unworthy of his position and his manhood." The Ohioan's misgivings—he even wondered whether Johnson had been drunk—expressed the general opinion, and, except for the Democrats, the president found few defenders.[31]

The radicals, of course, had expected nothing less. Two weeks later in the House, Thaddeus Stevens stated sarcastically that the speech was merely an invention of the Copperhead party, which had been persecuting the president ever since March 4, 1865. He gave a copy of the New York *World* of March 7 to the clerk to be read, and the House was treated to a public recitation of the assertion that in comparison with Johnson, Caligula's horse would have been respectable. "If these slanderers can make the people believe that the President ever uttered that speech, then they have made out their case," Stevens continued. "But we all know he never did utter it." He ironically concluded that now, having proved the whole speech to be fallacious, he hoped that his friends would permit him to occupy the same friendly position with the president he did before. It was difficult to counter this thrust.[32]

Yet despite the general condemnation of his actions, it was not yet too late for Johnson to mend fences with Congress. Loath to break irrevocably with the chief executive, Fessenden for one was still anxious to patch up the quarrel; Sherman agreed, and any number of Republicans were fearful that a break would fatally weaken the party. Among these was Chief Justice Chase, who counseled moderation, while *Harper's Weekly*, conceding the president's sincerity, also expressed hopes for an adjustment. Many others held similar views.[33]

The way to reestablish cordial relations was reaching some sort of agreement on the Civil Rights Bill, Trumbull's second measure, which moderates believed the president might still countenance. "It is essential that you sign the Civil Rights Bill," urged Henry Ward Beecher. "The thing, itself is desirable. But, aside from that, I am persuaded that it would go far to harmonize the feelings of men who should never have differed, or permitted a difference." Oliver P. Morton, the former governor of Indiana, who had been close to Johnson and who had just returned from a mission to France, concurred in a long interview at the White House. Even Jacob D. Cox, Johnson's firm supporter, warning him that the Democrats were not really his friends, pleaded with him to approve of the measure. It would reassure the public.[34]

But, of course, the president had no intention of signing. He was convinced that no measure concerning the South ought to be tolerated as long as the affected states remained unrepresented, nor was he particularly upset about the break with Congress because of his hope for a new political alignment. And his resolve must have been strengthened when Welles told him that the bill was totally subversive of the principles of the American government, even more objectionable than the Alien and Sedition Acts because it broke down all barriers protecting the rights of the states. On March 27 Johnson vetoed the bill.[35]

The veto message was again based upon the drafts of friendly advisers like Seward, Welles, and Henry Stanbery, a well-known Ohio attorney then in Washington to argue the famous *ex parte* Milligan case. Once more rejecting Seward's more moderate version in favor of his own racist views, the president took no precautions to mollify Congress. He objected to the attempt to confer citizenship on all persons born or naturalized within the United States because the subject had always been left to the states, and the effort to make citizens of members of races previously excluded constituted an invasion of states' rights. Moreover, he believed it to be frivolous to confer immediate citizenship upon men who had just emerged from slavery while withholding it for five years from worthy foreigners seeking naturalization. In addition, he repeated his objection to legislation affecting states that were still unrepresented in Congress and stressed that he completely disapproved, again on the basis of states' rights, of the judicial provisions of the bill, namely the transfer of civil rights cases to federal courts. Finally, good Jeffersonian that he was, Johnson insisted that the measure was an infringement of the laws of economics, constituting as it did an attempt of the government to intervene in the normal relations between capital and labor, a policy he considered totally wrong. And lest anybody doubt his position, the president again emphasized his disapproval of establishing safeguards for the security of the colored race that "go infinitely beyond any that the General Government has ever provided for the white race." While professing his readiness to cooperate in the protection of the freedmen, he nevertheless refused to sign this particular legislation.[36]

Naturally, the veto of the Civil Rights Bill infuriated Johnson's opponents. Congress had acted in the interest of the blacks, the president had acted in the interests of their oppressors, commented the Washington *Daily Chronicle*. A Hartford clergyman went so far as to pray that the Lord "speedily telegraph for President Johnson to come up to Heaven," and even so friendly a journal as the New York *Atlas* had to admit that the "differences between the President and the ruling element in the republican party" were irreconcilable. The Chicago *Tribune* thought it was fortunate that the veto was so sweeping as it showed the president would not approve of any measure at all for the protection of the freedmen. The veto was not surprising, continued the paper—it had been expected ever since Johnson, "in company with Saulsbury, Cox, Voorhees and Wirz's lawyers [three Democrats and counsel for the commandant of the Andersonville prison], gave . . . his adhesion to the Southern Confederacy." When Orville Browning and Edgar Cowan visited Johnson on March 30, however, they found him in good spirits, not in the least worried by these attacks. He was certain that in the long run, the people would sustain him.[37]

But his support in the Senate was dwindling. Democratic senator John P. Stockton of New Jersey, whose title to a seat had been questioned before on a technicality, was now ousted after Senator Lot M. Morrill of Maine broke a pair (an arrangement not to vote), and Trumbull bitterly charged the president with inconsistency because he had been kept informed about the bill all along. So when on April 6 the measure came to a vote in the Senate, this time his veto was overridden by 33 to 15, only four Republicans standing by the administration. Even such moderates as Edwin D. Morgan of New York and Waitman T. Willey of West Virginia, who had voted to uphold the Freedmen's Bureau Bill veto, now turned against Johnson.[38]

The president, though sorry about the failure of his veto, was undaunted by threats. Deep in thought, pacing the floor in his bedchamber, he turned to his private secretary and said, "Sir, I am right. I know I am right and I am damned if I do not adhere to it." He had already underlined his unshaken conviction on April 2 by publishing a proclamation announcing the end of the rebellion in all states except Texas.[39]

This proclamation, while conforming to his theories of "restoration," also formed part of the virtual war he was waging against the Freedmen's Bureau. Appearing as it did at almost the same time as the Supreme Court's decision ex parte Milligan, declaring military tribunals unconstitutional when the civil courts were open, it cast doubt on the bureau's jurisdiction in certain cases. And although in an interview with General Oliver O. Howard on April 9 he was still hedging, on April 27 Johnson issued an order denying commanders the right to convene military commissions. General Grant and Secretary of War Stanton, working in concert, might try to ameliorate the effect of these orders, but the president's intentions were clear. He collaborated with conservative commissioners like General Joseph S. Fullerton, who, in company with Johnson's friend General Steedman, was sent on a tour to investigate the bureau's alleged shortcomings; he sought to remove officers who did not sympathize with him, and in general he attempted to hamper the agency whenever he could. At any rate, considering the bureau graft-ridden, he believed its functionaries merely exploited the blacks, prejudices Steedman and Fullerton tried hard to confirm.[40]

During the same period, in a sensational interview on April 16 with the representative of the London Times, the president once again expressed his controversial views in public. Because they were afraid that a restored South would again ally itself with the Democratic party, his opponents were merely using the Negro issue to shore up their political

power, he said. He specifically attacked Trumbull for his alleged ignorance of racial conditions in the defeated section; he labeled the Freedmen's Bureau a cheap way of obtaining low-paid Negro labor allegedly
being transported back from the North "by the very men who were
asserting that the lives of the freedmen were not safe in the South"; he
maintained that the blacks would be treated better in the South than
in the North, and predicted that the radicals' policies would lead to a
race war with foreknown results for the blacks. Once more calling
himself a tribune of the people, he disavowed any further political
ambitions, an assertion as dubious as his statement that though he had
bought and owned slaves, he had always opposed slavery. And the
British reporter, too, was told that in the end the people would sustain
the president.[41]

How peculiar the administration's party position had become was
illustrated by the spring elections in Connecticut. The Republican candidate for governor, Joseph R. Hawley, was a friend of Gideon Welles,
the secretary of the navy, and the Republican platform endorsed both
Johnson and Congress, while the Democrats, whose candidate for governor, James E. English, had supported the war, were unequivocally behind the president. The administration attempted to adopt a hands-off
attitude, Johnson simply declaring that he would stand behind the
candidate who was "for the general policy and the specific measures
promulgated, by my administration in my regular message, speech on
22d of February, and the veto message sent in this day [of the Civil
Rights Bill]." The outcome was a narrow victory for Hawley by a reduced
majority, a result that cheered neither the Republicans, who felt deserted by the president, nor the administration, which was now weakened in an important state.[42]

To strengthen his position, Johnson sought to use patronage to the
best advantage. The most important example of this policy was his
search for a successor to Preston King as collector of New York, a
position he attempted to use in his effort to form a new political organization. Seward and Thurlow Weed at first favored a War Democrat like
Henry Stebbins, a former congressman, then suggested a conservative
Republican like naval officer Abram Wakeman; Senator Edwin Morgan
preferred a Republican of the type of Assistant Treasurer H. H. Van
Wyck; Barlow and Blair wanted a Democrat, either Sandford E. Church,
a New York regular, or Barlow's friend William D. Shipman of Connecticut, and McCulloch, pursuing an independent policy, was pushing for
Treasury agent J. F. Bailey or the New York judge Henry E. Davies. Some
Republicans also suggested Chauncey Depew, the New York secretary
of state and future railroad magnate.

For a long time Johnson hesitated. Unable to satisfy all the various factions—War Democrats, regular Democrats, and conservative Republicans, all of whom might have supported him—in the end he settled upon the banker Henry A. Smythe, a lukewarm Republican who was Mrs. Barlow's cousin and acceptable to her husband. He had seen Smythe some months earlier, but pressure from Weed, the Blairs, and sundry Democrats for their candidates, as well as the uncertainty of confirmation, kept him from making up his mind. In March, anxious to reach a conclusion, he met with Seward, Henry J. Raymond, and Morgan, who, because of the ill feeling in the Senate as a result of the Civil Rights Bill veto, counseled further delay. Smythe, however, promising complete loyalty to the president's policies, finally wrote to David T. Patterson, Martha's husband, to protest against the continued uncertainty, and Johnson appointed him shortly afterward. How much strength a businessman so little versed in politics could provide was problematical.[43]

As he had said over and over again in defying the party in Congress, Johnson was certain that in the long run, the people would support his policies. This conviction was his ultimate consolation, and he never lost faith in it.

His actions, however, were based on the assumption that the South was now truly loyal and willing to abide by the verdict of the war, a premise that was unfortunately far from the truth. The president's own correspondents bore ample witness to this fact. In January he heard from William E. Chandler, the assistant secretary of the Treasury, then in Georgia, that the South was peaceful but not friendly. Northerners and Treasury agents were not safe from annoyance, and even though the former insurgents liked the president, they would never vote for him as a Republican if there was a Democrat in the field. From Texas, where Johnson had specifically warned the governor that the state's constitutional convention should act in such a way as to buttress the administration's position, he learned that two-thirds of that body consisted of secessionists lacking all semblance of loyalty to the United States. To make matters worse, in Louisiana, which had been organized while Lincoln was still alive, the most conservative secessionists won local elections, so that even Johnson's supporters were embarrassed by the result: nine-tenths of the state legislature were reported to be unrepentant rebels who admitted Mrs. Jefferson Davis to the honors of the House.[44]

If Johnson's own news from the South was discouraging, his opponents received even more distressing reports. Thaddeus Stevens' mail was full of lament; he heard that in Virginia, avowed rebels were customarily chosen in preference to Union candidates and that the state was no more fit now for Union legislation than in 1863. As one of his correspondents wrote from the Old Dominion, "The old secession pro-slavery oligarchy intend to ruin every man at the South who opposed the rebellion. . . . No justice is to be meted out to us unless the Federal Government comes to our aid." From Arkansas, Stevens learned that twenty-four Negroes had been hanged and their cabins burned; from North Carolina, that the state was thoroughly rebellious and oppressive to its Union citizens, and his information was amply borne out by the correspondence of other Republicans.[45]

One of these was the chief justice. The grand jury that had brought in a true bill against Jefferson Davis in Richmond was being hounded, Chase wrote to his daughter, and all agreed that "sympathy with the Union cause was now regarded as a disgrace & offence." The tales of distress suffered by the Union men, black and white, in the rebel states made his heart ache every day, he said.

Similar information came from other states. Trumbull heard complaints about the president's emissary in Florida, Benjamin Truman, who, according to the local Republican Daniel Richards, much to the detriment of Union men, had been listening only to rebels who were keeping him drunk and supplied with women.[46] Unionist Joshua Hill wrote to John Sherman from Georgia, where the senatorial elections had resulted in a victory for Alexander H. Stephens and Herschel V. Johnson, that he and others had been beaten because of their loyalty. The news from Alabama was no more encouraging—there was no loyalty there, merely a submission to necessity, Sherman's confidant wrote. Even Johnson's firm supporter Senator Doolittle received a plaintive letter from Elizabeth Van Lew, the Unionist wartime spy in Richmond, who detailed the sufferings of the adherents of the federal government in the city. Justin Morrill, too, obtained information that in North Carolina, loyal candidates were being defeated and the disloyal elected. Oppression of Negroes throughout the South was proverbial, and even Sam Milligan was unhappy about the attitude of secessionists in West Tennessee.[47]

In fact, it was in Johnson's home state where the situation came to a boil. On May 1 in Memphis an altercation took place between black troops, which had been resented throughout the South from the beginning, and the police, and a massacre of defenseless blacks—men, women, and children—was the result. Congress was so agitated that it set up a committee to investigate the affair, and the hearing during the spring produced new evidence of atrocities.[48]

Many of the outrages perpetrated against blacks and Unionists had already been aired before the Joint Committee on Reconstruction, which began extensive hearings in January of 1866. Blacks, Southern conservatives, Southern Unionists, and Northern observers all testified exhaustively before the committee, and the collected evidence seemed to indicate that life for Unionists in the South, especially if they were black, was anything but easy.[49] It was evident that something would have to be done to remedy this situation, and eventually, the committee, after much struggling, reported a constitutional amendment designed to protect blacks' civil rights. In addition, it sought to disfranchise certain leading Confederates, outlaw the Confederate debt, and reduce the representation of the defeated section whenever any state denied the right to vote to any of its male citizens over twenty-one. In the end, after many changes, the measure became the Fourteenth Amendment.[50]

Under normal circumstances the amendment would have offered a perfectly reasonable compromise to the administration. Congress had rejected the most radical suggestions and most radicals were anything but happy with its moderate nature: black suffrage did not form part of the proposal. But conditions were not normal. Johnson was totally unwilling to cooperate with Congress, an attitude confirmed by the fact that on May 15 he successfully vetoed a bill to admit Colorado as a state. He had long been making it clear that he was opposed to any constitutional change as long as the Southern states remained unrepresented. The proposed amendment contained some of the provisions of the Civil Rights Bill, to which he had so forcibly objected, and although he was not able to veto any proposal to amend the Constitution—a two-thirds vote in both Houses, enough to override any veto, was necessary to pass it—he was not going to endorse it in any way. In fact, he decided to use all his influence to prevent its ratification.[51]

The president's opposition to the amendment was to have serious consequences. Any number of Republicans were sanguine that it would serve as a final solution to the Reconstruction problem, and Chief Justice Chase agreed with their expectations. Senator Morgan, a confirmed moderate, pleaded with Gideon Welles for its acceptance. There was really very little difference between the president and Congress, he said, pointing out that the Senate version of the amendment, which was finally accepted and substituted a mild disfranchisement of leading insurgents for a harsher provision, was a great improvement over the House rendition. Secretary of War Stanton heard similar pleas; after all, his correspondent pointed out, the amendment was much more reasonable than earlier demands for black suffrage. If Johnson would only acquiesce, unity between the two branches of government could be restored. Even Jacob D. Cox apparently found the proposal acceptable—he informed the president that the Union party's Ohio platform had endorsed the amendment. Had Johnson yielded, the history of Reconstruction would have taken a much less dramatic course.[52]

But the president would not yield. His repugnance for the Fourteenth Amendment, which he considered an expression of congressional opposition to his program, was such that he not only expressed himself in the "most decided terms of hostility to it," but on June 11 told a group of supporters that he was willing to spend $20,000 of his own funds if necessary to defeat the plans of the opposition. His only ambition was to bring all the states back to their proper relations to the general government, he said, and restore unity, tranquillity, and prosperity to the country. Then he was ready to retire. But as long as Congress was in the hands of the radicals, he thought this could not be done. Considering the majority's measures revolutionary, he believed that if persisted in they would subvert the government and ruin the country. It was to avert this calamity that he was ready to use all the capital he possessed, including federal patronage and even the presidency for the next term. His visitors, who included Senators Cowan, Doolittle, and Orville Browning, agreed with him that the time had come for a convention of "all the friends of the country," the president's new conservative party. It was evident that no reconciliation with Congress was in sight.[53]

The amendment received the necessary two-thirds vote of both houses on June 8 and 13, 1866; on the eighteenth, the Joint Committee published a report in which it took issue with the president's assertion that the Southern states were ready for representation. Johnson had no choice but to inform Congress that the secretary of state had transmitted the amendment to the states, which he did on June 22. But the president protested that the action had been merely ministerial. Amendments, he declared, must be regarded as of paramount importance even in ordinary times; in this case, the customary joint resolution concerning the proposal had not been forwarded to him (the two houses had preferred to pass a concurrent resolution that did not require presidential approval), and in addition, eleven of the thirty-six states were still unrepresented. He also thought that the people should have been consulted, although there really was no precedent for such a course. "Mr. Johnson rode his hobby into Congress yesterday," commented the New York *Tribune*. "Nobody wanted him, nobody expected him, nobody felt he had any business there. His message was about as appropriate as though it had contained the bill of fare for his breakfast, his latest tailor's account, or his opinions upon the cause of thunder." His opinions were rapidly becoming irrelevant; unless he was careful, he would be left without any Republican support in Congress at all.[54]

How weakened the president had become was revealed the next month. After passing another version of the Freedmen's Bureau Bill, Congress sent it to the White House, where Johnson vetoed it again. But this time his objections were overridden on the same day he sent them in, all the moderates voting against him.[55]

Perhaps the most painful episode of this stormy session, at least for Johnson, was the readmission of Tennessee. Naturally anxious to have his home state fully represented and his son-in-law seated in the Senate, he was nevertheless very unhappy about the way in which it was accomplished. Simultaneously with the proposed amendment, a bill providing for the readmission of states that ratified it had been introduced, and in Tennessee the president's opponents carried the day. Parson Brownlow, now governor, had gradually once again turned against his old antagonist. To be sure, as late as the end of November 1865, the parson's son had still been praising Johnson as a "steadfast friend" of the "simon-pure men of East Tennessee," but by January Brownlow himself was changing his mind. That his conservative opponents in the legislature were supporting the president was more than the parson could stand, and he declared himself a radical. Then the president used his patronage to help the conservatives, and by March Brownlow had become completely hostile. "I announce to you that if Andy Johnson is to lead the way in reconstruction, with the Democratic party at his back, I go the other way," he declared at Knoxville. "I go with the Congress of the United States, the so-called radicals."[56]

When the Fourteenth Amendment passed, the parson recalled the legislature to ratify it. It soon became evident that Johnson was working hard to prevent the presence of a quorum; Brownlow, not to be outdone, saw to it that the House ordered the arrest of absent members, who were forcibly kept in the chamber while the vote to ratify was taken. In triumph, the governor sent to the clerk of the Senate his often-quoted telegram, "We have fought the battle and won it. We have ratified the Constitutional Amendment in the House. . . . Give my respects to the dead dog of the White House." The resolution readmitting Tennessee followed in short order.[57]

This action placed Johnson in an embarrassing position. He certainly did not wish to keep his home state out any longer, but he wholly disapproved of the preamble to the readmission bill, which declared that the state could only be restored to its former political relations to the Union by "the law-making power of the United States." Senators Doolittle, Cowan, and some other friends told him to accept the measure and send in a message denouncing the preamble; he followed their advice, and on July 24 Tennessee resumed her place in Congress. Some radicals still tried to keep David Patterson out when he presented his credentials—he had briefly served as a judge during the Confederate occupation of East Tennessee, though his loyalty had never been in doubt. In the end he was admitted, as was his colleague Joseph S. Fowler and the entire congressional delegation. At least the president was now once again a citizen of a state fully restored to the Union.[58]

Thus by the summer of 1866 it had become evident that Johnson's efforts to restore the Southern states by executive fiat, without any significant conditions or safeguards for the Union party and the blacks, was in deep trouble. Whether or not he could salvage his position by a realignment of the party structure, the ensuing political campaign would tell.

XIV

BELEAGUERED PRESIDENT

P<small>ARTY</small> regularity in the usual sense of the term had never been Johnson's strong point; although a Jacksonian Democrat from 1839 to the Civil War, he had often engaged in bitter struggles with ruling elements of his party, including its presidents. It is therefore not surprising that when, because of his stand on Reconstruction, he found himself in difficulties, he again tried to wrest control of his party from the opposing faction, and, failing in this endeavor, to found a new political organization. After all, he had prevailed against the conservative Nashville clique before the war and later against the leaders of the secessionist democracy, and the situation now seemed to require a similar attempt.

The quarrels in which he was engaged during the early months of 1866 intensified Johnson's interest in reorganizing the political structure. "I care not by what name the party administering the Government may be denominated—the Union party, the Republican party, the Democratic party, or what not—no party can administer the Government successfully unless it is administered upon the great principles laid down [in the first annual message]," he said early in February to a visiting delegation from Montana, and he believed that people were already uniting behind his program. On March 23, in an interview with the Connecticut politicians Alfred E. Burr and Colin M. Ingersoll, he again emphasized that he considered the Union party to be the party of those who supported his policy of restoring the Union, "whoever they may be, and no others." Just as he had formerly considered himself the true heir of the Democratic tradition of Jefferson and Jackson, so he now believed himself to be the faithful preserver of the Unionist ideal.[1]

Many of his political friends supported these notions. Lewis D. Campbell suggested to David Patterson that Johnson should realize that the traditional Union party was gone and that he organize a new one based on his own principles. James Gordon Bennett of the New York *Herald* offered similar advice. The radicals had declared war on the president, Bennett wrote to Johnson; yet they were in a minority, and the executive could unite all conservatives in Congress upon his own platform. As General Dix put it in a letter to Blair, while the Democrats could never be resuscitated under their old leaders, there was a good prospect of organizing a new party in support of the administration.[2]

William H. Seward and Thurlow Weed, upon whose advice Johnson had come to depend, urged a similar course. Weed sought to put himself in communication with various Democrats to pave the way, and the secretary of state, as usual, supported his collaborator. "Some of our Union friends were preparing a bridge upon which they may expect to see the southern states and their old Democratic allies come together once more into political ascendency," Seward explained. Though loath to break the political ties that had bound him for so many years to the Republican party, by June the secretary of state must have seen that his colleagues Welles and McCulloch were right: with Johnson's general concurrence, the secretaries agreed that because the radicals were using the organization to injure the president, it was not possible to go with the party much longer. The Democrats in Congress were more in harmony with the administration; why should they be repelled?[3]

How to proceed was the next question. One June 11 the president met with Orville H. Browning, Edgar Cowan, James Doolittle, and others; it was then that he declared he was willing to spend $20,000 of his own money as well as to use all his influence to accomplish his aims of bringing "all the states back to their proper relations with the general government." On the fifteenth, Doolittle and Welles, convinced that the administration had to take a stand, came to the conclusion that a call for a convention ought to be issued; the president agreed, and within a few days, Doolittle began to prepare it, with Philadelphia as the place for the meeting. The problem of the Fourteenth Amendment, however, as well as the relations between Seward and the Democrats, caused trouble. Seward insisted that all condemnation of the amendment be omitted, and Johnson yielded the point, but Blair and others demanded again that the president reorganize his cabinet. It was clear that it would be difficult to obtain Democratic cooperation as long as

Seward and Weed retained their influence, and the party cared even less for Stanton.[4]

In order to solve this problem, Doolittle addressed a letter to the members of the cabinet asking them to collaborate in the call for a convention. Because three of the secretaries did not approve of it, the result was a thorough shake-up of the cabinet: James Harlan, William Dennison, and James Speed resigned; Orville H. Browning was appointed secretary of the interior, ex-governor Alexander W. Randall of Wisconsin became postmaster general, and the eloquent Ohio lawyer Henry Stanbery was made attorney general. Despite all rumors to the contrary, however, Seward and Stanton remained in their posts.[5]

Johnson liked his secretary of state. As LaWanda and John Cox have shown, he never forgot the role Seward had played in securing him the vice presidential nomination, and he retained the New Yorker's services to the end of his administration.[6]

Why he did not remove Stanton is more difficult to explain. He received repeated warnings that the secretary was not true to him; Stanton himself did not even pretend to disapprove of the pending amendment, and it was clear that he did not support the president's program. Nor was this all. Unlike the other members of the cabinet who disapproved of the call for a Union convention, Stanton did not resign. In answer to Doolittle's inquiry, he prepared an acid reply: "The within letter is returned to the person by whom it is addressed to me," he declared, "because I do not choose to recognize him as an organ of communication between the public and myself on any subject." Stating that he approved of the Fourteenth Amendment, he severely criticized the call. "Understanding the object of the so-called Philadelphia Convention to be the organization of a party consisting mainly of those who carried on the rebellion against the Government, and undertook to destroy the national life, by war, in the rebel States, and those in the northern States who sympathized with them, I do not approve the call of that Convention," he wrote.

The secretary of war finally decided against sending the letter, but on August 7, in a cabinet session, he admitted his opposition. He informed Welles that application had been made to him for bunting for the convention, and that as he had none, he was therefore turning the matter over to the Navy Department. His bunting had always been promptly shown, Welles replied, and it would be well were Stanton now letting the cabinet have sight of his. Taken aback, Stanton remarked again that he had no bunting. "Show your flag," said Welles. "You mean the convention," was the answer. "I am against it." In response to a charge that he had not answered the inquiry to the cabinet, Stanton merely stated that he did not chose to have Doolittle "or any other little fellow" draw an answer from him.[7]

Yet Johnson was reluctant to remove Stanton. Whether it was his desire to remain on good terms with Grant, or his fear that Congress would not confirm a successor, he retained the refractory secretary of war, who continued to act as the Republicans' representative in the president's official family. In spite of his firm views, in spite of his ringing vetoes, in spite of his call for a convention, Johnson was not ready to break completely with the Union party. It was the party that had won the war, that had saved the country and that had nominated him for the vice presidency. And, however mistaken, Johnson was convinced that he was carrying out Lincoln's policies and had inherited Lincoln's enemies. Thus he could not bring himself to jettison Lincoln's organization.[8]

The preparations for the convention were soon under way. Conservatives and Democrats throughout the country elected delegates from both groups to meet in Philadelphia on August 14. As was to be expected, congressional radicals reacted angrily. In a caucus on July 12, sentiment was for continuing the session all summer to prevent Johnson from making obnoxious appointments, and while nothing came of this notion, the intent was clear. Johnson would not have a free hand in making removals.[9]

At this very period, the president's policy received another serious blow. Conditions in Louisiana had long been chaotic; conservatives dominated the state government but were opposed by an active radical faction and the governor, J. Madison Wells, was a trimmer who was unreliable. Two days after Congress adjourned, on July 30, the radicals sought to reconvene the convention of 1864 in New Orleans. The conservatives, determined to prevent this meeting called to enfranchise the blacks, used force. Aided by the police, rioters wantonly shot down their antagonists; some 40 radicals of both races were killed and over 140 wounded, among them Dr. Anthony P. Dostie, a prominent leader of the radical faction. Johnson's assertion that he had peacefully restored the South and that law and order reigned in the former Confederacy was shown to be a gross exaggeration.[10]

The president had also played a role in this drama. After being informed on July 27 by Louisiana lieutenant governor Albert Voorhees that the radicals were planning to reconvene the convention, on the twenty-eighth Johnson wired back that the military would be expected to sustain and not to obstruct the proceedings of the courts. At the same time, he demanded to know from Governor Wells by what authority he had issued the proclamation calling the assembly into session. On July 30, the day of the riot, the president instructed the state attorney general, Andrew S. Herron, to call on the commanding general to sustain the civilian government "in suppressing all illegal or unlawful assemblies, who usurp or assume to exercise any power or authority without first having obtained the consent of the State. If there is to be a convention," he added, "let it be composed of delegates chosen first from the people of the whole state."[11]

Johnson added to his troubles after the New Orleans riot was over. Instead of expressing sympathy for the victims, he blamed the radical Congress for having instigated the melee. In addition, he censured Stanton for having withheld from him a telegram from Absalom Baird, the local commander, who had asked for instructions prior to the affray. Then, when General Sheridan finally sent in his report of the riot, in which he did not excuse the actions of some of the radicals but severely criticized the police, the president published the first half of the report but suppressed the second. The general had called the riot "an absolute massacre by the police not excelled in murderous cruelty by that at Fort Pillow," an apt description too strong for Johnson, whose sympathies could hardly be in doubt.[12]

Johnson's actions made a very bad impression in the North. "The President must be held directly responsible for all that has been done in New Orleans," commented the Chicago *Tribune*, which would soon refer to "the criminality of the President." The New York *Independent* pointed out that the disaster showed the difference between the radicals and the conservatives; the latter had authorized "a rebel mayor . . . to disperse, by an organized force under the rebel flag, the delegates of the people of the state," a task executed "by the cold blooded butchery of at least 100 loyal men." *Harper's Weekly* emphasized the contradiction between the president's assertion that the Southern states were as calm as New York and his message to the governor of Louisiana in which he demanded to know by what authority Governor Wells allowed the convention to meet. Private comments were even harsher, and it was evident that Johnson's cause had been severely damaged.[13]

Yet in spite of his difficulties, the president kept his composure. Perhaps it was his stubborn nature that strengthened him; perhaps it was his faith in his ultimate vindication by the public. Thus he calmly bore the continuing burden of Robert's drinking habits, as well as the blow of the suicide, early in July, of his friend Senator James H. Lane of Kansas—even though it was said that Lane had been despondent about his friends' turning from him after he had upheld the Civil Rights Bill veto.[14] Johnson buried himself in work; his bodyguard, William H.

Crook, called him the hardest-working occupant of the White House during the latter half of the nineteenth century, next to Grover Cleveland. Though plagued by what he called "the gravel," probably kidney stones, and though rarely seen to smile, he greatly impressed his visitors. "I never saw him look better or appear better," wrote Benjamin French after seeing him on July 6. "I believe him to be as honest, as true a patriot as this country has within its vast boundaries, and so thinking, I sustain him with all my might." And Governor Perry, on his way to the Philadelphia Convention, visited him also. "The President was looking remarkably well," he wrote, "and seemed in good spirits. I thought he had improved in every regard since I last saw him—his appearance giving the lie to all the slanders about his drinking. He is indeed a very wonderful man."[15]

As he kept his composure, so Johnson held on to his Jeffersonian-Jacksonian principles. When in June Congress passed a bill enabling the New York and Montana Mining and Manufacturing Company to acquire valuable mining lands at the minimum price, the president promptly vetoed the measure. The "public domain," he wrote, "is a national trust, set apart and held for the general welfare upon principles of equal justice, and not to be bestowed as a special privilege upon a favored class." And in August he told members of a Workingmen's Delegation in Baltimore that he had struggled for years for labor, the country's "aristocracy," and though he would not directly commit himself in response to the demand for an eight-hour day, he insisted he favored the "shortest number of hours consistent with the interests of all."[16]

In the meantime, Johnson's troubles kept mounting. From the very beginning, the organization of the Philadelphia Convention was hampered by the rift between its Democratic and Republican supporters. Although more and more members of the Democratic party came to support him, they tended to alienate the Republicans. This was especially true of the most notorious Copperheads, men like Clement L. Vallandigham and Fernando Wood. Sustained by their Southern friends, the Peace Democrats, as they liked to call themselves, were kept away only with difficulty, and the country at large did not forget their entreaties.[17]

Then there was the problem of Jefferson Davis. The Confederate president was still a prisoner at Fort Monroe, and his wife and friends constantly complained about his condition. Johnson actually sent McCulloch to the fortress to make sure that Davis was not being mistreated, but it was difficult to know what to do with him. Attorney General Stanbery advised that he be tried by a civilian court, and he was indeed indicted in Virginia, but it was doubtful whether any jury could be found to convict him there. Moreover, Chief Justice Chase, in whose circuit Richmond was located, refused to preside over the trial as long as conditions were not normal. Not even Johnson's proclamation ending the rebellion satisfied him. The only way he could hold court in Virginia, Chase told the president, was for Johnson to issue a proclamation distinctly declaring that the habeas corpus was restored and martial law abrogated. To issue such orders, however, would only expose the president to more criticism, so in the end he did little more than to receive Mrs. Davis at the White House, where he treated her civilly. Nevertheless, he was blamed for his failure to punish the Confederate leader, and the House of Representatives actually passed a resolution demanding that the prisoner be tried. In spite of several debates on the issue in the cabinet, where Stanton held out for severity, the problem was not resolved until the following spring.[18]

Johnson faced other problems as well. One was the Fenian issue—the Irish, hoping to assist the freedom movement in their homeland, were attempting to invade British North American provinces. Usually firm supporters of the Democratic party, now they were alienated by the administration's dutiful effort to suppress Fenian raids into Canada. They could not understand that the neutrality laws as well as international comity obligated Johnson and Seward to try to stop them.[19] Another problem was the president's Mexican policy, which came under attack. Willing to yield to Seward's pleas for a patient course of watchful waiting to force the French to withdraw—in the fall of 1865 he had even sent General John M. Schofield on a mission to Paris to defuse the situation—Johnson drew upon himself the ire of more bellicose Republicans who wanted the French intruders expelled at once.[20]

In spite of these troubles, Johnson went ahead with his plans for the convention, and when the delegates gathered in Philadelphia, he avidly followed the proceedings. Called to order on Tuesday, August 14, by Postmaster General Alexander Randall, the convention assembled under the temporary chairmanship of General John A. Dix. Then, amid great cheering, the delegates from South Carolina and Massachusetts entered arm in arm. On the next day Doolittle was elected permanent president, and on the sixteenth resolutions endorsing the president's program were adopted. Then the meeting adjourned, and Doolittle, together with Welles and Browning, called on Johnson to give him a firsthand report.[21]

The public presentation of the results of the convention took place on the next day. Senator Reverdy Johnson of Maryland delivered the proceedings to Johnson, who replied with a fervent speech. Asserting that language was inadequate to express the emotion and feeling produced by the occasion, he confessed that when he had heard that the delegates of Massachusetts and South Carolina had entered arm in arm, his own feelings had overcome him so that he could not finish reading the dispatch to his companion. He said that the proceedings of the convention were more important than those of any that had met since 1787 and that its resolutions constituted a second Declaration of Independence. Again recalling his rise from alderman to president, Johnson disavowed any further ambition except that of occupying "that position which retains all power in the hands of the people." It was a scene that so disgusted Chief Justice Chase that he wrote to Sumner, "Have you read the two Johnsons, Reverdy and Andy? Arcades ambo!" (Blackguards both).[22]

The country's reaction to these proceedings was very dubious. To counteract Johnson's Philadelphia Convention, the radicals called a Southern Loyalists' meeting of their own in the City of Brotherly Love; and when the Johnson forces organized a Soldiers' and Sailors' Convention at Cleveland, the radicals countered with one of their own at Pittsburgh, where General Butler delivered an uncompromising speech and hinted at the impeachment of the president. Johnson's opponents were greatly encouraged.[23]

The president responded to the attacks in his accustomed manner. When he had campaigned in Tennessee, he had always been the main target of his opponents' assaults, which he had met by delivering stump speeches from one end of the state to the other. Consequently, when the opportunity arose to travel to Chicago to assist in the laying of a cornerstone to a monument to Stephen A. Douglas, Johnson seized it to inaugurate a campaign trip, a "swing around the circle," to the Windy City and back. No matter that stump speeches might not be as appropriate in New York, Cleveland, St. Louis, Pittsburgh, and Indianapolis as in the small towns of Tennessee; no matter that he was now president of the United States and in danger of being drawn into the muck by hecklers; no matter that it was not then customary for the chief executive to engage in active campaigning—Johnson had always campaigned in his own way, against Henry, Gentry, and others, and he had no intention of changing. Secretaries McCulloch and Browning warned him not to deliver any impromptu speeches on the trip, but he did not listen.[24]

Johnson set out from Washington on August 27, with an entourage that included General Grant and Admiral David Farragut as well as Seward and Welles. After stopping in Baltimore and Philadelphia, where the local authorities avoided him, he reached New York, which accorded him a tremendous welcome replete with a parade, review, and an official reception. Public displays of affection and respect were evident. The president then proceeded by river steamer to Albany, and from there to Auburn, Niagara Falls, and Buffalo, the home of ex-president Fillmore, who greeted him cordially. At every stop Johnson delivered speeches, or rather substantially the same speech, in which he thanked his audience for its welcome, paid homage to the army and navy, and declared that the humble individual standing before them had not changed. His views were the same he had held during the war, and he still favored the preservation of the Union of the states. Generally recounting his rise from the tailor's bench to the presidency, he compared himself to Jesus Christ and explained that like the Savior, he, too, liked to pardon repentent sinners. But Congress, and especially Stevens and the radicals, still wanted to break up the Union, an effort he was trying to prevent.[25]

These set statements were not always in the best of taste, but they were nothing compared with his impromptu replies to hecklers, who became ever more challenging as he traveled west. At Albany Governor Reuben E. Fenton deliberately snubbed his old antagonist, Secretary of State Seward, and Thurlow Weed in a brief interview tried to warn Johnson that glittering generalities would be better than attacks on Congress. But, as the famous lobbyist remembered afterward, "He was aggressive and belligerent to a degree that rendered him insensitive to considerations of prudence and those common sense qualities which, under other auspices, were marked traits of his character."[26]

The result was a series of confrontations that greatly hurt the president's cause. The first of these occurred at Cleveland, where he arrived on September 3. General Grant, who did not relish his role on the trip, had taken to drink and was too much under the influence to appear. When the crowd asked for him, Johnson said, "I know a large number of you desire to see General Grant, and to hear what he has to say. (A voice: 'Three cheers for General Grant.') But you cannot see him tonight. He is extremely ill. I repeat, I am not before you to make a speech, but simply to make your acquaintance, to say, 'How are you?' and bid you 'Good-by.' " Continuing with his usual account of his faithfulness to duty, he recalled that he had been placed on the Union ticket with Lincoln. "I know there are some who complain (a voice: 'Unfortunately'). Yes, unfortunate for some that God rules on high and deals in right. (Cheers.)" Then Johnson went on to make his claim that "notwithstanding the subsidized gang of hirelings and traducers," he had discharged all his duties, only to be interrupted by shouts of "Three cheers for the Congress of the United States." Attempting to continue in his accustomed vein, he was again interrupted with "How about New Orleans?" and "Hang Jefferson Davis." "Why don't you hang him?" The president replied, asserting that he was neither the chief justice nor the prosecuting attorney.

The confusion mounted. "I called upon your Congress that is trying to break up the Government," Johnson continued. "You be d——d!" someone yelled, and cheers mingled with hisses. "Don't get mad, Andy," others shouted, only to be told, "Well, I will tell you who is mad. 'Whom the Gods wish to destroy, they first make mad.' Did your Congress order any of them to be tried? ('Three cheers for Congress.')" And so it went. Replying to hecklers who brought up his Washington's Birthday speech, he avowed that "though the powers of hell and Thad. Stevens and his gang were by," they could not turn him from his purpose.[27]

The president's outbursts frightened his friends. A few days earlier Doolittle, announcing that he would join the party in Buffalo, had written to Johnson not to allow the excitement of the moment to draw from him any extemporaneous speeches. "*Our enemies—your enemies,*" he wrote, "have never been able to get any advantage from anything *you ever wrote.* But what you have said extemporaneously in answer to some questions of interpretations has given them a handle to use against us." And the Democrats agreed. "Is there no way of inducing the President to believe that *everybody* in America now knows that he has plied every station from Prest. down to tailor? Does Seward mean to kill him off by this tour?" one of his correspondents warned Samuel Tilden. "Depend upon it, this sort of thing cannot go on without hurting us more than it helps." Wrong as the Democrats were about Seward—they were never reconciled to his participation in the Johnson movement—they were not so wrong about the president's speeches.[28]

But Johnson continued on his ruinous course. In Chicago, where local authorities again refused to welcome him, he spoke to the people from his hotel balcony, and on the next morning he attended the cornerstone-laying ceremony at the Douglas Memorial. In a short speech, notwithstanding his former misgivings, he expressed his high esteem for the Democratic statesman, who, he said, perished in the public service. Johnson then went on to Springfield to visit Lincoln's tomb, much to Mrs. Lincoln's disgust. "The President encountered much that would humiliate any other than himself, possessing such inordinate vanity and presumption as he does," she commented, particularly offended by the presidential party's pilgrimage to her husband's resting place. Representative Washburne of Illinois heard that "Moses" was doing great work for the radicals by justifying the New Orleans riot "and playing the blackguard all over the country." The New York *Tribune* headed its account of Johnson's progress "The President's Trip. From Springfield to St. Louis. He Denies That He Is Judas Iscariot."[29]

What these accounts were referring to was the disastrous speech Johnson delivered in St. Louis. Addressing a crowd in his usual way on September 8, he said that with the end of the rebellion, the time had come when there should be peace, "when the bleeding arteries should be tied up." At that point he was interrupted by a shout, "New Orleans," and he lost control. "Go on," he said,

> perhaps if you had a word or two on the subject of New Orleans you might understand more about it than you do. (Laughter.) And if you will go back—if you will go back and ascertain the cause of the riot at New Orleans you would not be so prompt in calling out "New Orleans." If you will take up the riot at New Orleans and trace it back to its source or its immediate cause, you will find out who was responsible for the blood that was shed there. If you will take up the riot at New Orleans and trace it back to the radical Congress (cheers and cries of "Bully!"), you will find that the riot at New Orleans was substantially planned.

He went on to charge that the convention called by the radicals was intended to enfranchise the "colored population" which "had just been emancipated, and at the same time disfranchise white men," and concluded that the blood that was shed was traceable to the radical Congress.

Then Johnson became blasphemous.

> I know I have been . . . abused . . . . And I have been traduced, I have been slandered, I have been maligned, I have been called Judas Iscariot and all that. Now, my countrymen here to-night, it is very easy to call a man Judas, and cry out traitor, but when he is called upon to give arguments and facts he is often found wanting. Judas Iscariot—Judas. There was a Judas, and he was one of the twelve apostles. Oh! yes, the twelve apostles had a Christ. (A voice, "and a Moses, too;" laughter.) The twelve apostles had a Christ and he never would have had a Judas unless he had had twelve apostles. If I have played the Judas, who has been my Christ that I have played the Judas with? Was it Thad. Stevens? Was it Wendell Phillips? Was it Charles Sumner? (Hisses and cheers.) These are the men that stop and compare themselves to the Saviour; and everybody that differs with them in opinion, and to try and stay and arrest their diabolical and nefarious policy, is to be denounced as a Judas. ("Hurray for Andy!!" and cheers.)

According to the Chicago *Tribune*, this harangue was the "crowning disgrace of a disreputable series."[30]

The remainder of the trip, if anything, was even more unfortunate. The president continued on his course, even when, after leaving Louisville, Seward fell seriously ill and could not participate any further. When Johnson arrived in Indianapolis, the disorder and turbulence exceeded anything that had gone before. After a long introduction by General Sullivan Meredith, the president tried to speak, but the unruly crowd, shouting "Shut up," would not let him finish. Still, unwilling to abandon his efforts, he continued on to Cincinnati, where he repeated his biblical allusions, and to Columbus, only to be snubbed by the governor of Ohio just as he had been avoided by the Indiana authorities. By the time he reached Pittsburgh, the disorder was so great that he again could barely be heard. Yet, though constantly interrupted by cries of "Jefferson Davis" and "New Orleans," as well as by shouts for Grant, Johnson responded in his usual bellicose mood. What was "My policy," as his opponents derisively referred to his boasts? It was nothing but the restoration of the Union! By the end of his trip, the entire country had once more been treated to the spectacle of a president behaving like a common stump speaker. Although he was welcomed by an enthusiastic crowd when on September 15 he returned to Washington, his trip had not furthered his cause.[31]

The New York *Independent* summed up the prevalent feeling in the North. "For the first time in the history of our country," the paper commented, "the people have been witness to the mortifying spectacle of the President going about from town to town, accompanied by the prominent members of the Cabinet, on an electioneering raid, denouncing his opponents, bandying epithets with men in the crowd, and praising himself and his policies. Such a humiliating exhibition has never before been seen, nor anything even approaching to it."[32]

As Gregg Phifer has shown, the trouble with Johnson's speeches was that he never fully prepared any of them in detail. His tendency to make only general preparations led to blunders upon which his enemies could pounce. It is true that his voice was one of his most valuable assets, its penetrating reach making it audible in the furthest corners of the places where he spoke so that it carried conviction, but during the "swing around the circle," constant use wore it out and he became hoarse. While his sincerity could never be questioned, the type of stump speaking in which he excelled was really not effective in his current position, and neither his friends nor his enemies were wrong in condemning it.[33]

Johnson's own previous speeches now provided amunition for his opponents. "Mr. Andrew Johnson delivered a radical speech of the worst kind against President Andrew Johnson in the United States Senate on the 19th day of December 1860," charged the New York

Tribune. "There can be no doubt whatever that he then thought the Rebel States were no better than provinces." Quoting his assertion that according to the principles of the Ostend Manifesto, the United States would have the right to seize Louisiana, Florida, and even South Carolina and to hold them as provinces, the paper continued, "It is for something less than this that Mr. Johnson calls Thaddeus Stevens and Charles Sumner traitors." Even though Johnson had only referred to contingencies if the states in question were really out of the Union, a possibility he denied, the argument was difficult to refute.[34]

If he was relying on Northern racism to rally moderate Republicans to his standard, he failed to consider the fact that fear of renewed Southern power was still a far stronger emotion. Moreover, his invocation of the peril of unlimited black suffrage was blunted by the evident truth that the amendment did not call for it.

The first indication that the country no longer supported the president came early in September, when the Republicans carried Maine by overwhelming majorities. William Pitt Fessenden, who had parted with the administration without breaking off social relations, explained the causes of the defeat to McCulloch. First, in Maine, "contemptible politicians" had permitted Johnson to put offices up for sale. Second, the president's attacks on Congress and his speeches had destroyed confidence in him. Third, the senator believed that Seward had "destroyed the President as well as himself." Predicting results similar to those in his home state elsewhere, Fessenden professed to regret Johnson's discomfiture. "I mourn over Andy," he wrote. "He began by meaning well, but I fear that Seward's evil counsels have carried him beyond the reach of salvation." He was certain that Americans would rather wage war than permit Confederates to have an equal share in the government until some adequate security for Southerners' future conduct toward the freedmen had been obtained.[35]

Fessenden was not mistaken. The strains of the coalition of conservative Republicans and Democrats and the general dislike of the secretary of state, whom the Democrats loathed, to say nothing of the wartime feeling against unpardoned rebels, made Johnson's task almost impossible. That the Democrats urged the administration to cooperate with them was natural. As Welles' Connecticut friend, the printer and editor of the Democratic Hartford *Times,* Alfred E. Burr, had put it in spring, "It is plain enough, this question of supporting the President. The Democratic voters, to a man, are with him. The Republican voters, by a very large majority, are against him. Unite all the friends of the President, and he will carry all of the Northern States, or at least a majority of them. But if he depends on his friends in the Republican party, and on those only, he will certainly be defeated at every point." This advice was good as far as it went. The Democrats were with the president, but they wanted patronage, they wanted recognition, and they felt that he owed them something. And they wanted nothing to do with Seward or Weed. Because the only hope of victory was cooperation with the Democrats, the president might still have complied, at least in the matter of patronage.[36]

Somehow, however, Johnson was unable to do so unreservedly. He was committed to stick by the party that had won the war and he had been told that a policy of ruthless dismissal of Republicans in favor of the opposition only caused alienation in otherwise favorable districts. Nor had his liking for Seward diminished; he refused to part with his secretary of state. The result was that he settled on a compromise course and satisfied nobody. The Democrats, deprived of some important patronage, were miffed and despaired of success, while the Republicans, seeing their old antagonists appointed to office, used the issue to fight the president.[37]

The race question also caused problems. Much as the Democrats in their campaigns habitually indulged in the most vulgar form of Negro baiting, Johnson, notwithstanding his fundamental prejudices, sought to convey the impression that the radicals were merely using the freedmen for partisan purposes, while he was the black man's true friend. Thus on New Year's Day 1866 he welcomed black well-wishers to the White House, and on April 19, in a speech to Washington blacks celebrating the third anniversary of their emancipation, he made use of the occasion to elaborate his position. "I know how easy it is to cater to prejudices," he said, "and how easy it is to excite feelings of prejudice and unkindness." He was not engaged in the work of freedom as a hobby; nor did he "ride the colored man for the sake of gaining power." What he had accomplished in securing the amendment abolishing slavery—"as much, if not more . . . than . . . any other living man"—had been the establishment of the principles of freedom. The day would come when blacks would know who had in fact been their best friend. In July, anxious again to publicize his ideas, the president granted an interview to P. B. Randolph, a freedman who was trying to raise money for Negro schools in New Orleans. The Johnson press emphasized the fact that it was after Sumner had turned Randolph down that he was received with great friendliness at the White House, where the president told him that although he had owned slaves, he had always been fond of the black race and thought Randolph's project a worthy one. He even invited the visitor to stay for supper, which, however, Randolph was served in a room presumably all by himself.[38]

Whatever impression Johnson sought to convey by these actions, the Washington *National Intelligencer,* his official mouthpiece, was much more in tune with the Democrats, who sought to make capital of Frederick Douglass' reception at the Philadelphia Southern Loyalists' Convention. "APPEAL TO THE RADICAL LEADERS," read its headline on August 9. "We could remind these Radical leaders that there are millions of females, of the young and the old, who are innocent of any guilt of secession, but who might be sacrificed in the event of a general war of the races at the South." And in the following month the paper joined the Democrats in condemning the convention for welcoming Douglass. It was the first time a great party had practically carried out the theories of Negro equality, it commented, in spite of the fact that the white race had at all times held itself superior to the black. It was obvious that Johnson shared this sentiment, and presumably few blacks or their supporters were taken in by his efforts to appear as their friend.[39]

Nor did the president's effort to continue his restoration policy during the election campaign help his cause. In line with his April proclamation declaring the rebellion to be at an end everywhere but in Texas, on August 20 he specifically announced that the insurrection had also ceased in the Lone Star State, where the process of calling a convention, electing new officers, and ratifying the Thirteenth Amendment had finally been completed. The reaction of the radical press was not favorable. "Texas can be but little worse than Louisiana, whose terrible warning the President has let pass unheeded, blindly to follow the precipitate policy in which he has risked all, and will lose everything," commented the Chicago *Tribune.* The proclamation could not win any votes for its author.[40]

In fact, Johnson was rapidly losing more and more supporters. Late in August Hannibal Hamlin resigned from his post of collector of the Port of Boston. Charging that efforts were being made to organize a party "consisting almost exclusively of those actively engaged in the late rebellion, and their allies who sought by other means to cripple and embarrass the Government," Hamlin stated that he had no sympathy with such a party and could not acquiesce in its measures by his silence. His resignation delighted the radicals, who were soon to obtain other converts. After the "swing around the circle," even Henry J. Raymond, refusing to run for Congress again, deserted the president, and the mercurial James Gordon Bennett of the New York *Herald* followed suit. The loss of the *Herald* was a severe blow, because the paper had been one of Johnson's main supporters in the Northeast. Isaac N. Arnold, Lincoln's close Illinois confidant and biographer, resigned as auditor of the Treasury; his publicly stated reasons were that Johnson was betraying the Union party and persecuting his predecessor's friends. Wild rumors about the president began to circulate. Radical newspapers printed a purported series of questions Johnson had posed to Attorney General Stanbery, among them whether the Thirty-ninth Congress was a legal body. In addition, there were new innuendos about unsavory female pardon brokers. Orville H. Browning, in a widely published letter to Illinois friends sought to restate Johnson's well-known position, but the outlook continued to be dim.[41]

A final problem for the president was his foreign policy. The most pressing issue facing the country was still the French intervention in Mexico, a flagrant violation of the Monroe Doctrine. Although Johnson himself had long favored some sort of action to drive the French out—he seemed sympathetic to the Mexican minister, Mattias Romero—Seward had different ideas. Fearing war with France and convinced that a patient policy of persuasion would be effective, he continued to oppose more decisive measures proposed by the friends of the Mexican president, Benito Juarez, among whom General Grant was the most prominent. As time went on, Johnson began to rely more and more upon the secretary of state, and the radicals were able to make the most of his passive policy. In order to counter this attack, Johnson took Romero along on the swing around the circle. When the Mexican noticed the political nature of the trip, however, he left the party in Chicago.[42]

Johnson then tried to persuade Grant to accept a mission to Mexico, to accompany Campbell, the minister to Mexico, so that he would be in a position to render aid if necessary. It would also conveniently remove Grant from Washington so that Johnson could offer the War Department to General William T. Sherman, whom he had recently recalled to the capital. But Sherman was unwilling to accept, and Grant refused to go. He was a soldier, not a politician, he insisted, and finally the president sent Sherman in his stead. This gesture was not sufficient, however, to dispel the impression that he was less than active in defending the Monroe Doctrine.[43]

In October, when the final congressional elections drew closer, there was real apprehension of serious trouble, especially in Baltimore, where radical election commissioners were in conflict with those favored by the conservative governor. With talk of impeachment becoming more menacing, Johnson's friends were worried about his nonchalant attitude. They considered him totally unprepared to defend himself and were especially upset about Stanton's continuing tenure in the War Department. Even Grant, who was gradually distancing himself from the administration, seemed unreliable. Johnson, however, merely dispatched General Grant and some troops to Baltimore to keep the peace, and the election in Maryland resulted in a Democratic victory.[44]

In the rest of the country, the result was exactly the opposite. The Republicans swept state after state; their two-thirds majority in Congress was increased, and former supporters urged the president to give in and support the Fourteenth Amendment as a settlement of the country's problems.[45]

But Johnson remained adamant. As he had earlier said to Romero, he was too old to change his opinions, and no mere temporary defeat could budge him. Congressman Samuel S. Cox, who saw him in the beginning of October, found that when asked whether he would modify his views, "he got as ugly as the Devil. He was regularly mad . . . & couldn't talk like a reasonable being." Cox told him he "wouldn't darken his doors with his small shadow again" because the president could not talk in a reasonable way, whereupon Johnson calmed down and "grew sweet." His visitor concluded that there was "no bridge in him. . . . He did not care if three States had voted. It didn't change him. . . . He had done all to reorganize the States, they were in. If Congress kept them out . . . it was their business."[46]

The president's mood did not change in November after the election results were in. Although with Seward's aid he first drew up a comparatively conciliatory annual message, he then produced a more truculent one, which on November 30 he had read to the assembled cabinet. Without specifically mentioning the Fourteenth Amendment, he invoked the Johnson-Crittenden Resolutions and exhorted Congress to admit the Southern members still excluded. "I deem it a subject of profound regret that Congress has so far failed to admit to seats loyal Senators and Representatives from the other States whose inhabitants, with those of Tennessee, had engaged in rebellion," he stated. Asserting that he knew of "no measure more imperatively demanded by every consideration of national interest, sound policy, and equal justice, than the admission of loyal members" from the unrepresented states, Johnson pointed out that the Constitution, as it existed, was obligatory upon all. "Let there be no change by usurpation," he warned, quoting Washington, "for it is the customary weapon by which free Governments are destroyed." Stanton said he was sorry that the message did not endorse the amendment, but none of his colleagues agreed. It was obvious that the president had no intention of yielding. It was equally obvious that relations with Congress would not improve.[47]

XV

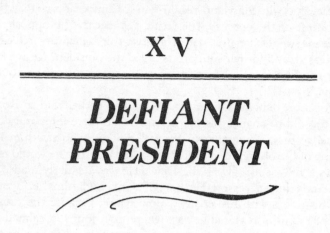

DEFIANT PRESIDENT

AFTER the elections of 1866, Johnson might well have retreated, tried to seek an arrangement with Congress, and restored confidence in his shattered administration. Under certain circumstances the old political professional was perfectly able and willing to compromise, but in November 1866 he did not think the time had come. Convinced that in the long run the people would sustain him, the president was determined to frustrate congressional Reconstruction in order to maintain the Union as he believed the Founding Fathers had designed it and to protect Southern whites from what he considered the horrors of complete racial equality. Thus he prepared his unyielding annual message, refused to endorse the Fourteenth Amendment, and defied his antagonists.

These opponents were in no mood to accommodate him. Thaddeus Stevens, widely considered the leader of the radicals in the House, returned to Washington convinced that the amendment needed only the assent of three-quarters of the loyal commonwealths to become part of the Constitution and that the reduction of the insurgent states to territories was the solution of the Southern problem. With his mail full of complaints of Southern Republicans about the lack of safety for Unionists and blacks, allegations borne out by the correspondence of his colleagues, Stevens was in a fighting mood. "He says he was rather Conservative last winter, but is now Radical, and expects to continue so the remainder of his days," reported the *National Intelligencer*. [1]

What the radicals had in mind was no secret. While it would take the Republicans until March 1867 to perfect their Reconstruction legislation, outlines of these proposals began to emerge by January. It was at that time also that Congress finally passed the long-debated measure for black suffrage in the District of Columbia.

Not even Johnson could deny that Congress possessed the power to legislate for the district "in all cases whatsoever," and he might well have signed the bill. Believing that the measure was merely a prelude to similar experiments in the states, however, he made up his mind to veto it, a decision with which all the members of the cabinet except Stanton agreed. Holding that "in legislating for the District of Columbia, under the Federal Constitution, the relation of Congress to its inhabitants is analogous to that of a Legislature to the people of a State," Johnson argued that the will of the voters ought to be considered. He reminded Congress that in a special election in December 1865 local residents had rejected black suffrage by an overwhelming margin and cautioned that a possible black majority might develop that would make "the white population a subordinate element in the body politic." Thus, though regretting the conflict between the two branches of government but calling to mind the Founding Fathers' warning against an unbalance between them, he felt he had to interpose. The veto was promptly overridden.[2]

Johnson also readily vetoed two other bills, legislation admitting Nebraska and Colorado into the Union. His previous opposition to the Colorado bill in the spring of 1866 had never been tested, and he had pocketed the Nebraska measure passed at the last moment of the previous session, but the radicals wanted four more votes and had hopes of obtaining them in the West. Ben Wade, the chairman of the Committee on Territories, introduced the necessary legislation, and after lengthy debates about the proposed states' failure to provide for black suffrage, the admission bills passed with the proviso that the new state constitutions be altered in the interests of universal enfranchisement. Determined not to allow his opponents to succeed and singling out the voting provisions for his special attention, the president immediately sent Congress his objections, in which he repeated his warning against the admission of states with populations too small to elect a single representative under the existing ratio. In the case of the Nebraska veto, which Wade tried to push aside without even allowing the clerk to read it, the Senate overrode Johnson's disapproval. Colorado, however, where there was a strong movement against statehood, was a different matter. In spite of Wade's strenuous efforts, the bill died with the session before the veto could be overridden. The president could congratulate himself on one small success.[3]

This victory was even more welcome because in December the Supreme Court had reached its final opinion in *ex parte* Milligan. The case concerned the death sentence of Lambdin P. Milligan, an Indiana Copperhead who had been convicted of seditious activity by a military tribunal. Lincoln had delayed carrying out the sentences, and when after the president's death the culprit was about to be executed, his lawyer intervened, and the Supreme Court took up the issue of the legality of trials by military commission when the civilian courts were open. Finding this procedure unconstitutional, the court seemed to confirm Johnson's objections to military jurisprudence in the South.[4]

The decision must have been especially gratifying because the president had long been trying to enlist the court on his side. But his effort to name Stanbery to the tribunal had been rejected by the Senate, and his opportunity to appoint another justice was taken from him by the simple device of the passage of an act reducing the number of justices. And now the court, diminished though it was, seemed to uphold the president, not only in the Milligan case, but also in two test oath cases in January, in which restrictions on lawyers in federal courts and clergymen in Missouri were held to be unconstitutional.[5]

Possibly encouraged by the Milligan decision and still trusting in the people to vindicate him in the end, Johnson actively interfered with the ratification of the Fourteenth Amendment. To be sure, many moderates urged him to accept the proposed constitutional change as the best settlement he could obtain. The New York *Herald* publicly admonished him to change his opinion and its representatives also sought to convince him in private; even General Grant advised him to take such a course.[6] But the president would not yield. He was certain, as Browning had put it in October, that the amendment would result in Congress claiming and exercising "new and enormous power" and the revolutionizing of the whole structure of the government. In a telegram sent on October 30 to Texas governor James W. Throckmorton, whose state legislature had rejected the amendment, Johnson stated, "I have nothing to suggest further than urging upon the Legislature to make all laws, involving civil rights, as complete as possible." Again expressing his faith in the ultimate wisdom of the American people, he reaffirmed his conviction that the states would soon be restored. He said nothing about the amendment.[7]

When in December Congress reassembled, there was still a chance that a number of Southern states might adopt the proposal. In spite of some objections, Ben Wade in the Senate reaffirmed his belief that once the amendment was ratified, the states would be admitted, and it is likely that this course would have led to a speedy resolution of the Reconstruction problem.[8] Johnson, however, disagreed. He was not at all certain that no further conditions might be imposed, as he said in a widely reported interview with Representative Benjamin Eggleston of Ohio. And at the end of December, in a meeting with state senator T. C. Weatherly of South Carolina, repeating his conviction that the amendment was "unconstitutional," he urged continued resistance.[9]

His most decisive action against the proposed change in the Constitution took place in Alabama, where Governor Robert M. Patton was already in favor of it. The president wired Alabama's ex-governor Parsons not to give up in the fight "to sustain the several co-ordinate departments of the Government." "What possible good can be attained by reconsidering the constitutional amendment?" he telegraphed.

> I know of none in the present posture of affairs. I do not believe that the people of the whole country will sustain any set of individuals in attempts to change the whole character of our Government. . . . I believe on the contrary that they will eventually uphold all who have patriotism and courage to stand by the Constitution, and who place their confidence in the people. There should be no faltering on the part of those who are honest in their determination to sustain the several co-ordinate departments of the Government, in accordance with its traditional design.

The result was that Alabama rejected the amendment, and Southern leaders elsewhere, equally aware of Johnson's feelings, persuaded every unreconstructed state that had not yet done so to follow suit.[10]

Yet Johnson was not as inflexible as he has often been pictured. Faced with the alternatives of military rule in the South and harsher conditions proposed by Stevens, at the end of January he was seriously considering new suggestions brought forward by Southerners themselves. After conferring at length with Edward Orr, William Marvin, Parsons, and two North Carolinians, Lewis Hanes and Nathaniel Boyden, he endorsed an amendment that would enfranchise all citizens who could read and write or owned $250 worth of property. The amendment, reaffirming the perpetual nature of the Union, would prohibit both the secession and exclusion of individual states and, with the exception of the restrictions on Southern whites, would include most of the provisions of the Fourteenth Amendment, as well as a grandfather clause exempting voters who had been previously enfranchised. Senator Dixon eventually introduced an amendment along these lines, but Congress was in no mood to consider it. Notwithstanding objections from the White House, the lawmakers were now determined to go ahead with their own plans.[11]

The Republican majority was in a strong position that winter. "The people expect a bold and independent course with regard to the President," Ben Wade observed. "They demand that his power be curtailed[;] to this end they have armed Congress with full power to carry out the mandates of the people independent of the President and now if we fail to do it, the fault is our own."[12] Certain of an increased majority in its next session, Congress prepared to hem in the executive, whom it correctly considered the main obstacle to the attainment of its objectives. The legislators' first step was to pass a bill repealing the president's pardoning powers under the second Confiscation Act of 1862. Although the effect of this measure was negligible because of the executive's remaining constitutional rights, its intent was to rebuke him for his liberal pardoning policy. Johnson took no notice—he neither signed nor vetoed the bill—so that it became law without his signature. But he continued his practice of pardoning individuals as before.

Congress next passed a bill calling the Fortieth Congress into session as soon as the Thirty-ninth had ended. Unwilling to allow the president the customary intervals between sessions of Congress in March and December, the lawmakers took advantage of a seldom-used clause in the Constitution to convene sooner. It was not the sort of law an executive felt called upon to veto, and the measure also became law, as did a companion piece of legislation for equal suffrage in the territories.[13] But the congressional proposal to restrict the president's power of removal was a different matter.

The use of patronage was unquestionably one of the weapons that the president still possessed, and he was determined to use it. Although some of his friends complained that he had not acted more ruthlessly, he had nevertheless removed 1,655 postmasters between July 28 and December 6, 1,283 of these for political reasons.[14] Louis J. Weichman, one of Judge Advocate Holt's chief witnesses at the assassination trial, wrote to the judge advocate general that he did not care about being the only Republican government clerk left. "I am hopeful for the future," he added, "and I am convinced that Congress, which meets very soon, will not be guilty of another adjournment without passing some bills to protect themselves, and their brave constituents, men who by hundreds are being 'kicked out of office.' " And George W. Blunt, a New York officeholder, warned Welles that unless the president supported his old friends and restored Union men to office, "Congress will ride a high horse and there will be no check on it."[15]

Congress did indeed act to perfect a Tenure of Office Bill. Designed to curtail the president's powers of removal, it made the consent of the Senate a condition for any dismissal of officers appointed with its concurrence. The question of the cabinet caused some problem; while the more radical members were particularly anxious to protect Stanton, others felt that the relations between an executive and his advisers were confidential so that no bar ought to be placed upon the power of removal in such cases. The outcome was a compromise: members of the cabinet should hold office "for and during the term of the President by whom they may have been appointed, and for one month thereafter, subject to removal by and with the advice and consent of the Senate." Whether Stanton, who had been appointed by Lincoln, was covered by this provision depended on individual interpretation.

When this measure reached the White House, in February 1867, it was fully discussed in the cabinet. Everybody present, including Stanton, expressed opposition to it, and Johnson asked Stanton to prepare the veto. The secretary said he was too busy and that he was suffering from rheumatism of the arm, so the task fell to Seward, who prepared an exemplary message. Citing various constitutional precedents, the veto declared the bill contrary to the usages of the country and admonished Congress to abide by the basic law. Of course, the veto was promptly overridden. John Bigelow, who watched the proceedings, was struck by the lack of respect paid to the message. "Nye called my attention to the utter contempt with which anything coming from the White House was treated. . . . He [Johnson] is of no account, he said. We pay no attention anymore to what he says," the diplomat recorded in his diary.[16]

Stanton, though opposed to the Tenure of Office Bill, had already seen to it that he was protected in other ways. Early in December, when George Boutwell, the radical ex-governor of Massachusetts and now a congressman, came to Washington, he received a letter asking him to visit the War Department. There Stanton took him into his private room, and without much of an introduction, told him that he was more concerned about the fate of the country than at any time during the Civil War. Johnson was issuing orders without taking Grant or himself into his confidence, and there was danger the general might be sent away from the capital. He requested that Congress do something, and Boutwell wrote out a measure requiring the president to issue orders through the general of the army, who had to be stationed in Washington. This peculiar and highly unusual piece of legislation was incorporated in the Military Appropriations Bill for 1867–68.[17]

Johnson was furious at this interference with his constitutional prerogatives as commander in chief of the army and navy. He was determined not to sign it, and the postmaster general prepared a veto. However, other members of the cabinet dissuaded him from this course.

Stanton said, when the president asked him point blank for his opinion, "I have already approved your taking whatever action you may think best." The result was that Johnson signed the bill. "I am compelled to defeat these necessary appropriations," he wrote, "if I withhold my signature from the act." Nevertheless, he protested against this interference with his proper constitutional powers. His message made little impression upon his opponents.[18]

The measure that met with the president's most strenuous opposition was the Reconstruction Act, which both radicals and moderates in Congress, exasperated by the South's refusal to ratify the Fourteenth Amendment and outraged by continuous reports of atrocities against blacks and Unionists, finally hammered into shape late in February 1867. After much parliamentary maneuver, during which the Democrats, in order to prevent a compromise, at times joined the extreme radicals, the House passed a bill providing for military government in the South. The Senate, for its part, agreed to a version that added the ratification of the amendment and the institution of impartial suffrage as requirements for the restoration of the affected states. After further maneuvering, the two versions were combined so as to embody in general the Senate provisions, including a clause characterizing the existing state governments in the South as merely provisional.[19]

Neither of these versions lessened the president's concern. As early as December 28 he requested the cabinet to consider the new proposals for congressional Reconstruction and asked for united action, meaning opposition to them. All agreed except Stanton, who held his head and said nothing. On January 8 Johnson again asked for consideration of bills reducing the Southern states to territories; as before, all his advisers except Stanton expressed their entire disapprobation, and Stanton merely said that whether Congress possessed the power to territorialize states or not, he had approved Lincoln's and Johnson's Reconstruction plans and considered the existing governments lawful.[20]

Johnson's dismay mounted as the measures were being perfected. After the House bill passed, on February 14, the *National Intelligencer*, no doubt voicing the president's opinions, declared, "THE BLACKEST RECORD ever made by an assembly of the representatives of a free people stained yesterday the proceedings of the House of Representatives." The measure recalled the days of the Long Parliament, trampled upon the prerogatives of the president, and made war on the Constitution and the Supreme Court. "It is treason enveloped in the forms of law," the newspaper continued. "It is usurpation assuming the sanctity of constitutional enactment."[21]

To Johnson, it was clear that he must oppose the bill with all his might. Charles Nordhoff, the managing editor of the New York *Evening Post*, saw him on February 1 and was astonished at the depth of the president's feelings. When the discussion turned to the legislation, Nordhoff wrote to William Cullen Bryant, the president

> grew much excited, & expressed the most bitter hatred of the measure in all its parts, declaring that it was nothing but anarchy and chaos, that the people of the South, poor, quiet, unoffending, harmless, were to be trodden under foot "to protect niggers," that the States were already in the Union, that in no part of the country were life and property so safe as in the Southern States, that whatever the local differences might be, the people ha[d] true allegiance to the General Government, that the military (U.S.) ought to be, & must be, under the strictest subordination to the local & State governments . . . & that all that was needed was for Congress to admit loyal representatives.

The editor replied that Congress would not admit the Southern representatives, that the Fortieth Congress would be more extreme, and that Johnson's refusal to sign would only give strength to extremists of the type of Thaddeus Stevens.

But the president refused to be convinced. The South was safe, he said. If a rape case in New York about which he had read in the papers had taken place in the South, and the victim had been black, there would have been a howl. "Yes, unless the criminal had been promptly arrested," Nordhoff answered, but Johnson insisted, "It's all damned prejudice." The impression the president made on his visitor was that he was "a pig headed man, with only one idea . . . a bitter opposition to universal suffrage & a determination to secure the political ascendancy of the old Southern leaders, who, he emphasized, must in the nature of things rule the South." The editor thought that this attitude was due to the fact that Johnson had never been opposed to slavery. As he had said in 1865 to Senator John Conness, the blacks were happiest in that condition or one near it, and whites alone must manage the South. Thus the Reconstruction bill, with its provisions for black suffrage, to say nothing of its denial of statehood to the seceded states, was anathema to him.[22]

How deeply Johnson felt about the measure he made clear to his confidential secretary, Colonel Moore. Rather than sign a bill "which deprived an American citizen of habeas corpus, which subordinate[d] the civil to the military, and which denie[d] the right of trial by jury," he said, he would sever his right arm from his body. Despite pleas by friends that he give the bill his approval or merely pocket it in order to end the Reconstruction controversy or at least gain some delay, he persisted in his determination.[23]

Under these circumstances, it was not surprising that when the bill passed, Johnson did his utmost to defeat it. With the help of Jeremiah Black and Stanbery and the concurrence of the entire cabinet with the exception of Stanton, he composed a resounding veto message: "I am unable to give [the bill] my assent for reasons so grave that I hope a statement of them may have some influence on the minds of the patriotic and enlightened men with whom the decision must ultimately rest," he wrote. Maintaining that the measure contradicted its own preamble, which asserted that the bill's purpose was the establishment of peace and good order in the ten states in question, he pointed out that the measure provided for their restoration after meeting certain conditions that had nothing to do with peace and order. But the most telling reason for his opposition was the establishment of military rule under despotic generals possessing powers that no king of England had wielded for five hundred years. "In all that time no people who speak the English language have borne such servitude," he asserted, while recalling that "the men of our race in every age have struggled to tie up the hands of their Governments and keep them within the law." The Constitution, Johnson continued, gave no powers to the general government to reduce the states to nullity, nor to interfere with the suffrage, particularly in times of peace. Quoting *ex parte* Milligan as well as the Johnson-Crittenden Resolutions to make his point, which was so important to him, the president questioned whether the purpose of providing for Negro suffrage justified such radical departure from constitutional practice. The war had been fought to vindicate the principles of the Constitution, and it did not behoove Congress to disregard them now that the rebellion was over, merely "to force the right of suffrage out of the hands of the white people and into the hands of negroes." Moreover, if no government existed in the Southern states, the ratification of the Thirteenth Amendment and the status of slavery was put into question. Reminding lawmakers once more that they were legislating for states that were not represented, he exhorted them to "pause in the course of legislation, which, looking solely to the attainment of political ends, fails to consider the rights it transgresses, the law which it violates, or the institutions which it imperils."[24]

Congress immediately repassed the bill over the president's veto, and Johnson was depressed. He was calm, but, according to Welles, "more dejected than I had almost ever seen him." As he said to Colonel Moore, "It is too bad, this law which practically breaks up Government to gratify bitter partisan feelings. If by leaving my right arm upon this little field and having it severed from my body with a cleaver I could settle this thing, it would soon be disposed of." At times he was downright angry. When in cabinet McCulloch urged the immediate appointment of the five military commanders to create a favorable impression and prevent impeachment, Johnson swore violently. "They might impeach and be d——m—d," he said. He was tired of being threatened and would not be influenced by any such considerations. On the contrary, he "would go forward in the conscientious discharge of his duty without reference to Congress, and meet all the consequences."[25]

But, of course, he soon did turn to the problem of appointing the generals. Too shrewd a politician not to take advantage of the fact that Grant, the most popular officer in the country, was not very well liked by some of the radicals, he consulted the general and largely accepted Grant's recommendations. He appointed John Schofield to the First District (Virginia), Daniel Sickles to the Second (the Carolinas), John Pope to the Third (Georgia, Alabama, and Florida), Edward Orr to the Fourth (Arkansas and Mississippi), and Philip Sheridan to the Fifth (Louisiana and Texas). Welles was appalled at the designation of such radicals as Sickles, whom he considered Stanton's friend. Johnson, however, wanted to please Grant, and he gave commands to Sickles, Sheridan, and Pope, who certainly did not sympathize with him. As time would show, he could always dismiss them later on.[26]

Because the Reconstruction Act, as hastily drawn in the waning days of the Thirty-ninth Congress, had not made any firm provisions for initiating the Reconstruction process, the Fortieth, which assembled on March 4, 1867, sought to remedy this difficulty. A second Reconstruction Act providing for the registration of prospective voters able to swear to past loyalty by registrars appointed by the military commanders, as well as for the calling of conventions and the ratification of their resolutions by a popular majority, passed on March 23. Naturally, the president no more approved of this supplementary measure than he did its predecessor. With Jeremiah S. Black's assistance, he again vetoed the bill, and his message reiterated his contention that what the bill required of the Southern states was "to impose upon themselves this fearful and untried experiment of complete negro enfranchisement and white disfranchisement." Pronouncing this requirement unconstitutional and unwarranted, he denounced it as destructive of American liberty. The veto was again promptly overridden.[27]

How perilous Johnson's position had become by this time could be seen by the accelerating movement to impeach him. There had been occasional talk of such a dramatic course as early as 1865, and the Chicago *Tribune* advocated it after the veto of the Civil Rights Bill.[28]

But it was not until the 1866 campaign that the movement gained momentum. At that time, Ben Butler became its foremost advocate.

Butler was one of the most colorful personalities in nineteenth-century America. A lawyer from Massachusetts, he had been a Democrat before the war and made a name for himself when in 1862 he became the commanding general in New Orleans. Ruling the city with an iron hand, he hanged one rebel who tore down the American flag and issued his famous "woman order" to stop harassment of his soldiers. Rumors of corruption pursued him wherever he went and, though never proved, gave him an aura of mystery. Because of the difficulties Butler encountered with foreign consuls and others, Lincoln finally removed him, but by 1864 he was back in command of the Army of the James, which failed to do its part in the capture of Petersburg and Richmond. Grant finally relieved him, and in his postwar report criticized the political general for his wartime failures. The furious Butler promptly sought to besmirch the victor of Appomattox with a devastating book, which, however, never saw the light of day. Butler was best known for his outrageous sallies, his courtroom theatrics, and his political agility. He soon changed his prewar proslavery attitude, raised one of the first black units for the federal army, and became a full-fledged radical who never again wavered in his support for black rights.

As a former Democrat, Butler might have been expected to sympathize with Johnson, as indeed he did when the president was inaugurated. But his failure to obtain a cabinet position and Johnson's break with the Union party caused a complete rift between the two men. As time went on, Butler insisted ever more firmly that the president be impeached.[29]

The other principal spokesman for impeachment was Representative James M. Ashley of Ohio, a Toledo radical who had been instrumental in the passage of the Thirteenth Amendment. Perfectly fanatical in his advocacy of extreme measures, Ashley had convinced himself that all presidents who died in office had somehow been done in by their successors, and Lincoln was no exception. It was he who finally brought in the first successful resolution looking toward impeachment.[30]

Other impeachers, or would-be impeachers, included radicals like George Boutwell of Massachusetts, Benjamin Loan of Missouri, Zachariah Chandler of Michigan, old abolitionists like Wendell Phillips and William Lloyd Garrison, and last but not least, Thaddeus Stevens. The Pennsylvania radical was convinced that no scheme of Reconstruction could be successful unless Johnson was ousted.[31]

On Saturday, January 5, 1867, a Republican caucus met in Washington. Representative Rufus P. Spalding of Ohio moved that no impeachment resolution should be offered without first having been considered in caucus. When this motion passed, Stevens, emphasizing his justifiable belief about the impossibility of reconstructing the South with Johnson in the White House and in control of the army, tried to table it, but he was outvoted. A debate ensued between him and the Ohio moderate John A. Bingham, and in the end the Republicans present agreed that no motion to impeach should be considered until after it had been referred to the Judiciary Committee. Ashley still insisted that he would introduce the appropriate resolutions, but the caucus had effectively decided not to entrust the matter to so erratic a member as the gentleman from Ohio.[32]

Still, Ashley was good as his word. On January 7, the Monday following Saturday's caucus, after Benjamin Loan and John R. Kelso had offered resolutions that Congress ought to impeach the president, the Ohioan introduced his own. Announcing that he was impeaching "Andrew Johnson, Vice President and Acting President of the United States," of high crimes and misdemeanors, Ashley charged Johnson with the usurpation of power and violation of law by corruptly using the appointing, pardoning, and veto powers, by disposing corruptly of the property of the United States, and by interfering in elections. In accordance with the caucus decision, the House referred the resolution to the Judiciary Committee.[33]

The Judiciary Committee, headed by James F. Wilson of Iowa, a respected lawyer of excellent reputation, was not a radical body. Its members included Frederick E. Woodbridge of Vermont, Daniel Morris of New York, and Francis Thomas of Maryland, all moderates. Thomas Williams of Pennsylvania, Burton C. Cook of Illinois, and William Lawrence of Ohio were the radicals on the panel, while Andrew J. Rogers of New Jersey represented the Democrats. The fact that Ashley's motion was referred to so balanced a committee indicated that many Republicans themselves were opposed to extreme measures.[34]

In fact, while the action of the House reflected widespread disappointment in Andrew Johnson, it also indicated a fear that so important a step as impeachment, if not successful, might backfire. "If the proposed impeachment should not be sustained," editorialized the Chicago *Tribune,* "the result would be disastrous."[35] The Constitution carefully specified that federal officers, including the president, could only be impeached for "treason, bribery, or other high crimes and misdemeanors." Impeachment required a majority vote of the House, but two-thirds of the Senate were needed to convict. It was obvious that it would be very difficult to prove that Johnson had actually committed any of the offenses outlined in the Constitution.

The Judiciary Committee promptly began its inquiries. Conducted in secret, they were monitored by Allan Pinkerton, the famous detective, who kept the White House informed.[36] The investigators tried hard to find damaging evidence. Some members, especially Ashley, sought to prove that Johnson had been engaged in improper correspondence with Jefferson Davis; others, that he had corruptly sold offices, had drawn money out of the Treasury without congressional approval, had illegally appointed provisional governors in the South, and had wrongfully disposed of railroads seized by the government during the war. To substantiate these far-fetched accusations, the committee summoned such dubious witnesses as Lafayette C. Baker, the slippery secret service chief, and Edward R. Phelps, a New York office seeker who had unsuccessfully employed the questionable power broker Jennie A. Perry to obtain a job. The inquisitors also called Judge Advocate General Holt, Secretary McCulloch, and Secretary Stanton. Baker did tell them that Booth had left a diary from which eighteen pages were missing, and Holt elaborated on this testimony. By the end of the session, however, the committee had found nothing substantial, and concluded that it was "inexpedient to submit any report beyond the statement that sufficient testimony had been brought to its notice to justify and demand a further prosecution of the investigation."[37]

The Fortieth Congress went along with this recommendation. Again Ashley introduced his resolution, and although Ben Butler was anxious to let a select committee take charge, a caucus decided against his proposal, so that the Judiciary Committee was again charged with the task of ferreting out information. The committee, whose members now included John C. Churchill, a New York Republican, and two Democrats, Charles A. Eldridge of Wisconsin and Samuel S. Marshall of Illinois, replacing Burton C. Cook, Morris, and Rogers, continued its search, this time even investigating Johnson's bank accounts. The committee questioned Jeremiah S. Black about his assistance with various vetoes, Howard and Rufus Saxton about the restoration of land to former Confederates, Confederate Secretary of the Treasury George A. Trenholm about his pardon, and various members of the cabinet about appointments, Booth's diary, the New Orleans riot, and pardons. This time, it spent a great deal of effort on the failure to try Jefferson Davis and even called Chief Justice Chase. But on June 3, by a split vote, the members decided to adjourn.[38]

Johnson was furious about the committee's actions. He tried to defend himself by seeking information on Butler and Ashley, and when he learned of the effort to examine his bank accounts, he burst out to Colonel Moore: "I have had a son killed, a son-in-law die during the last battle at Nashville, another son has thrown himself away, a second son-in-law is in no better condition, I think I have had sorrow enough without having my bank account examined by a Committee of Congress."[39]

His anger was probably aggravated by the fact that in the late winter and spring of 1867 he was again suffering from extremely painful kidney stones. John Bigelow, just back from Europe, was shocked by the president's appearance. "The President was alone when we entered," he wrote in his diary. "He arose and came forward, almost tot[t]ering & looking very feeble & wretched. I should say he was not 3 days off from typhoid fever. It will be a miracle if he lives a month in my opinion. . . . I found his only thought was how soon I would leave him." In Congress General Banks said Johnson's mind had been affected and maintained that Eliza was worried about her husband's ability to survive for two weeks longer under his burdens. By April, however, Johnson had recovered, and Commissioner French found that he had never looked better. "He was so cheerful and kind," French noted,

and listened to all I had to say so pleasantly and patiently, that had I not liked him so well before, I should have loved him for his kindness yesterday, and for the deep interest he manifested in the matters about which I went to see him. They may abuse Andrew Johnson as they will, I say he is a good man, a good President and a good patriot, and the time will come when he will receive the credit from the whole people to which he is entitled.[40]

In spite of his occasional indisposition, the president maintained a very busy social schedule. A glittering New Year's reception started the year, with the diplomatic corps and the usual dignitaries present. Ten days later Johnson hosted a dinner for a visiting East Tennessee delegation, an affair in which the cabinet participated. Then, after six more days, he gave another reception for the members of Congress, which all but the most radical Republicans attended; a similar event, a state dinner for members of Congress, was held on February 5; and two days later, at another evening reception, Eliza herself made an appearance, much to the delight of the guests. The president's wife was present again for a comparable occasion on Washington's Birthday, and Commissioner French thought her "a very amiable, unassuming woman," who "acts her part so modestly and so well as to win the affections of all who see her." On the next day Secretary of the Interior Browning presented various Indian delegations, while on April 18 a visiting Japanese mission was entertained at the White House. The president was a good host, and, contrary to the charges his enemies constantly repeated, he was never seen drunk, as at his vice presidential inauguration, again.[41]

One role Johnson enjoyed more than others was that of being a Freemason. As a proud brother he took part in the ceremonies of the Washington Templars. Late in November 1866 the fraternity met at the Holiday Street Theater, where brethren from all over the country had gathered for a long march to the Washington Monument and to their new temple. There on a platform they greeted "Brother Andrew Johnson," clothed in Masonic regalia. The brothers received the president again at a Masonic fair one month later, escorted him into the hall, and passed in review before him. One of the high points of Johnson's Masonic activities came on June 20, 1867, when he was inducted into the higher degrees of the order. After offering the Masonic officers lunch in the White House library, he took them upstairs to his private quarters, where they conferred upon him all the degrees between the fourth and the thirty-third. As one of the participants remembered, "Illustrious Brother Johnson expressed himself much gratified, and said that the doctrines indicated were such as he had been preaching and practicing all his life." On the following day he set out on a trip to New England to dedicate a new Masonic temple in Boston.[42]

The trip to New England was not the only one Johnson undertook that spring and early summer—earlier that June he had accepted invitations to attend the unveiling of a monument to his father in Raleigh and commencement exercises at the nearby University of North Carolina. In company of Seward, Postmaster General Randall, and his ever faithful private secretary, Colonel Moore, the president boarded a ship to Petersburg on June 1. From there he traveled by train to Richmond, where he stayed at the Spotswood House and attended services at St. Paul's. On the third he arrived in Raleigh, to be welcomed by the governor, General Sickles, the mayor, and a large crowd of well-wishers. Overcome by emotion, he quoted Sir Walter Scott's famous poem:

> Breathes there the man, with soul so dead,
> Who never to himself hath said,
> This is my own, my native land!

He also repeated his often-stated affirmation of loyalty to the Constitution, and, with himself as an example, exhorted young men to exert themselves to rise in the world. On the next day Johnson was present at the ceremony at his father's grave, where a single shaft of red limestone was dedicated. It bore the inscription "In memory of Jacob Johnson; an honest man, beloved and respected by all who knew him. Born—. Died January 1812, from a disease caused by an over-effort in saving the life of a friend." On the seventh, he took part in the university's commencement exercises. The difference between his reception then and his trek through Chapel Hill forty years earlier was striking, and he did not fail to remark upon it. Then he returned home by way of Richmond and Fredericksburg.[43]

The New England trip followed. Traveling north in slow stages and stopping off in New York and New Haven, Johnson was received everywhere with pomp and respect. At Yale he told students that his one regret was his failure to choose the right profession—he should have been a schoolmaster! In Boston he was present at the dedication of the Masonic temple at Tremont and Boylston streets and made a few appropriate remarks. Then he returned to Washington, and on the thirtieth, looking better and more robust than ever, he was back in the White House.[44]

When the Thirty-ninth Congress expired and on the same day the new Fortieth was sworn in, the Senate met with a new presiding officer. Because at that time, in the absence of a vice president, the president pro tem. of the Senate was the legal successor to the president, this change was significant, particularly for the leading impeachers. The choice of the upper house had fallen upon Ben Wade, the old Ohio radical whose ideas about female suffrage and the relationship between capital and labor were so advanced that his election has been called a turning point in the impeachment process. Chosen because of his radicalism, he nevertheless frightened less outspoken colleagues. There were many Republicans who preferred Johnson, with all his faults, to the reputed vagaries of Ben Wade.[45]

In the House the radicals had been strengthened by the election of Ben Butler, who soon stole the limelight by engaging in a furious debate with John A. Bingham. Anxious to press forward the impeachment process, probably because he hoped to prevent Grant's election to the presidency by sending Wade to the White House instead, Butler began to look into the details of the assassination of Lincoln and the facts surrounding the missing pages of Booth's diary. In the course of a controversy with Bingham, who had accused him of having voted fifty times for Jefferson Davis as his candidate for president, Butler declared that it ill became a man like the Ohioan to make such charges, for while Butler had been doing his part in the war, "the only victim of the gentleman's prowess . . . was an innocent woman hung upon the scaffold, one Mrs. Surratt." When Bingham demanded evidence, Butler insisted that there was proof. "Who spoliated that book," he shouted, "who suppressed that evidence? Who caused an innocent woman to be hung when he had in his pocket the diary which had stated at least what was the idea and the purpose of the main conspirators in the case?" The matter interested Johnson sufficiently to request Stanton to give him the copy of Booth's diary in his possession, and it turned out that the missing pages had never been in the hands of the government. At the very least, however, it shed considerable doubt on the guilt of Mrs. Surratt, a fact that was to be deeply troubling for the president who had signed her death warrant.[46]

The controversy about the diary became even more important because of the fact that Jefferson Davis was at that very time being delivered to a civil court in Richmond and admitted to bail. The diary certainly contained no substantiation of the charge that the Confederate president had been a party to the assassination plot, but as Davis refused to apply for a pardon—he said he had never committed any crime and therefore could not ask for forgiveness—Johnson refused to pardon him.[47]

In the meantime, the administration was able to achieve one definite success, the purchase of Russian America, which Sumner renamed Alaska. Anxious to rid themselves of a possession that was indefensible in case of difficulties with Great Britain and that was administered by a company facing bankruptcy, the Russians were eager to sell. Equally anxious to expand, Seward was more than willing to buy and secured Johnson's support. On March 15, the cabinet discussed the matter and agreed, while the president merely listened without taking part in the conversation. After further negotiations with Edouard de Stoeckl, the Russian envoy, Seward completed the treaty on the night of March 29, 1867, and on the next day Johnson sent it to the Senate. With the support of Charles Sumner, the treaty was ratified, though the newspapers ridiculed the new acquisition as "Johnson's Polar Bear Garden." The value of the transaction has hardly been questioned since.[48]

The Alaska Treaty was ratified in the special session of the Senate that met after the adjournment of Congress. That anything Johnson proposed at that time could be passed was surprising, for the entire session was marked by one long struggle between the Senate and the president about appointments. He would send in his own nominees; the Senate would refuse to confirm them, and the session ended on a sour note.[49]

Johnson's opportunity to undermine congressional Reconstruction arose after the lawmakers had gone home. In May and June, in two separate opinions, Attorney General Stanbery so interpreted the Reconstruction Acts that voting registrars retained considerable leeway in deciding whom to register. At the same time, Stanbery upheld the authority of the existing governments in the South as well as the supremacy of the civilian courts. In view of the fact that Generals Sickles and

Sheridan had issued orders to the contrary, this opinion created grave problems. Sheridan particularly had sought to enforce the congressional mandate by removing various state and local officers in Louisiana, including, in the end, the governor himself. In addition, he had set brief periods of registration because he knew that an opinion restricting his powers and those of the registrars was forthcoming; in fact, Grant had warned him and informed him that he and Stanton would try to protect him to the best of their ability. The president had ordered Sheridan to extend the time for registration, but when Stanbery's opinion appeared, other commanders were miffed. Sickles, considering himself slighted, sent in his resignation and asked for a court of inquiry.[50]

But Johnson, encouraged by a Democratic victory in Connecticut and more determined than ever to frustrate radical designs to remake the South, was delighted with the attorney general's opinion. On June 18 and 19 he submitted it to the cabinet and asked the members to agree point by point to its various propositions. All but Stanton did so, and after the secretary of war gained a concession to omit a preamble about the cabinet's unanimous approval, the opinion was published. The president again ordered Sheridan to extend further the time for registration, and Grant advised the general to comply with the order but to publish it only at the last moment. He knew that Congress might have a different view of the matter.[51]

Congress had in fact taken precautions. Before adjourning in spring, it had provided for a possible session in July. The presiding officers of each house were given the power to adjourn once again until December in case no quorum was present, an arrangement calculated to make sure that Congress met only if necessary, that is, if Johnson persisted in defying it. By endorsing Stanbery's opinion, that was exactly what he did, and the lawmakers determined to intervene. "The truth is that Mr. Johnson has continued to excite so much distrust that the public mind is easily played upon by those who are seeking only the accomplishment of their own purposes," wrote the moderate senator Fessenden to Edwin Morgan. "It is quite astonishing that he and his advisers could not see the necessity of letting well enough alone." Congress met; the members grumbled about the terrible heat, but within a short time they passed a third Reconstruction Act specifically overturning the opinions of the attorney general.[52]

The president's veto of the new bill was indicative of his deep resentment. First he deplored the imposition of absolute military government over ten states. "It is impossible to conceive any state of society more intolerable than this," he wrote. "Yet it is to this condition that 12,000,-000 American citizens are reduced by the Congress of the United

States." The supremacy of the military over civilian tribunals he considered equally objectionable, and he characterized the power to remove state officers, a right given to commanding generals, as one that "hitherto all departments of the Federal Government, acting in concert or separately, have not dared to exercise." Moreover, if the existing governments were merely provisional, how could they have ratified the Thirteenth or been asked to give their assent to the Fourteenth Amendment to the Constitution?

Then Johnson turned to a vigorous defense of his own prerogatives. "Within a period of less than a year," he pointed out, "the legislation of Congress has attempted to strip the executive department of the Government of some of its essential powers." As long as he was president, however, he would never willingly surrender the trust given to him to see that the laws were faithfully executed. "It is a great public wrong," he concluded, "to take from the President powers conferred upon him alone by the Constitution, but the wrong is more flagrant and more dangerous when the powers so taken from the President are conferred upon subordinate executive officers, and especially upon military officers." Asserting that the remedy must come from the people themselves through the ballot, Johnson said he was still confident that in the end "the rod of despotism" would be broken, "the armed heel of power lifted from the necks of the people, and the principles of a violated Constitution preserved." The veto, though well phrased, was overturned on the same day it was sent in. "The President can outreason Congress," commented the New York *World*, "but Congress can outvote him."[53]

The reassembled Congress also gave the impeachers a renewed opportunity to continue with their attempts to find something against the president. When early in June the Judiciary Committee had voted to adjourn because of insufficient evidence, it had been unable to do more than to pass a resolution censuring Johnson. But the impeachers did not give up. On June 26 the committee reassembled and resumed its examinations. This time it called various former and current members of the cabinet, Horace Greeley, and even General Grant. No matter how hard the committee tried, however, it could not find anything sufficiently damaging, and in the end it reported that it would not be ready with any resolution until the following session.[54]

Yet such determined impeachers as Butler and Ashley would not abandon their quest. Although Stevens realized that it would be impossible at that time to conduct a successful trial, as he admitted in an interview with the New York *Herald*, the principal impeachers were now intent upon proving that Johnson himself had been a party to the assassination. After forming a select committee in the House to investigate the crime, with Butler as chairman, they scoured records and various spurious leads to find some evidence against Johnson, but for obvious reasons they, too, were wholly unsuccessful.[55]

The investigation was merely what Johnson had expected for some time. When in November 1866 John Surratt, the executed widow's son, was arrested in Egypt, the president wanted the conspirator to be kept incommunicado so that the radicals would not be able to suborn him. That Johnson's fears were not entirely unjustified became clear when he found out that Butler and Ashley had made efforts to induce a convicted perjurer, Charles A. Dunham alias Sanford Conover, then in jail in Washington, to testify against the president in return for a pardon. Conover, however, attempted to gain his freedom by turning against the radicals and by directly asking for a pardon from Johnson himself. This sordid affair infuriated the president, who, stung to the quick by his enemies' tactics, now thought the time was finally ripe to rid himself of his secretary of war.[56]

Relations between Johnson and Stanton had been worsening steadily. As early as September 1866, during the "swing around the circle," the secretary had taken a position clearly undercutting his chief. "There is indeed 'danger ahead,'" he asserted in a letter to Ashley, "the most serious being that Johnson and Grant, as you put it, 'suck the same quill.'" Certain that the president was trying to win over the general, Stanton expressed apprehension that things were in such a state that "means should be found to end them." Then, in December, he approached Boutwell, and made it was obvious that he was wholly opposed to Johnson. Yet despite incessant pleading from friends, the president refused to dismiss Stanton.[57]

This peculiar behavior was in keeping with Johnson's political practice. Long unwilling to cut all ties with the party that had elected him and unable to forget Stanton's friendship during the war, he became incensed at his adviser only when it became difficult to dismiss him because of the Tenure of Office Act. By the summer of 1867, however, the president had had enough. Despite his reluctance to dismiss Stanton, he had long suspected the secretary of disloyalty, and when Stanton failed to oppose the Reconstruction Acts, which Johnson considered anathema, relations became more and more strained. Then in April 1867, when Mississippi and Georgia sued for an injunction to keep the president and the secretary of war from carrying out the new legislation, and the whole cabinet agreed that Johnson ought to resist the motion,

Stanton believed the administration should stay out of the case, though he deferred to Johnson's opinion.

The president was now thoroughly aroused. The secretary was playing the same old tricks, he said; had it not been for the influence of the War Department "with this damned extreme gang during the past session," all the administration's troubles would long since have been brought to a close. A few weeks later he accused Stanton of having criticized the Alaska purchase after voting for it in cabinet. "If Stanton had proved all right at the beginning of Congress," he asserted, "Senators and Representatives from the excluded States would have been admitted before that Congress adjourned."

Then, because of the secretary's failure to sustain the attorney general's interpretation of the Reconstruction Acts, Johnson's hesitation to dismiss his refractory adviser vanished completely. Taking direct issue with Stanbery, the secretary of war brought in a paper maintaining not only that the generals had absolute power in the South but also that they could remove state officials. That he had long collaborated with Grant to block the administration's policies could not have been entirely unknown to the president, and his disapproval of the veto of the third Reconstruction Act made the rift complete.[58]

After this clash events moved rapidly toward a climax. Sheridan removed the governor of Texas; despite Grant's opposition, Johnson determined to supersede Sheridan.[59] Then the Conover affair seemed to create the proper atmosphere for a decisive move, and the president stood ready to remove Stanton. How this could be accomplished was his next problem.

XVI

FIGHTING PRESIDENT

ONCE Johnson made up his mind, he could be stubborn, and now that he had decided finally to defy his opponents and get rid of Stanton and his radical subordinates, he moved with firm deliberation. In order to carry out his design, he believed he had to have the cooperation of the general commanding the army, and so he sought to enlist Grant, possibly to alienate him from the congressional majority, or at least to neutralize him. Although he was aware of the fact that he could not rely on the general and must have known how closely Grant had worked with Stanton, the president felt he could not disregard Grant's overwhelming popularity. As Colonel Moore, Johnson's private secretary, explained to a petitioner who had a grievance against the general, Johnson hated to cross Grant, and he had every reason not to do so.[1]

By the beginning of August the president judged the time right for his risky move. Congress had adjourned, so he could make an ad interim appointment without violating the Tenure of Office Act, and the revelations of Butler's and Ashley's dealings with Conover could create favorable publicity for the administration. Consequently, he spoke to Grant on August 1, told him he was going to suspend the secretary of war and remove Sheridan, and asked him whether he would take over Stanton's office.

The general was very hesitant. Arguing that to dismiss Stanton would be impolitic, he maintained that those who had been hostile to the secretary had generally been opposed to the war as well. Moreover,

Grant professed to be unfamiliar with many of the duties of the secretary of war. It could not be said that he had been opposed to the war, Johnson answered, pointing out that War Department matters with which Grant was unfamiliar, various claims, for instance, could be referred to Congress. Greatly disturbed, the general put his objections in writing. He spelled out his opposition not only to the dismissal of Stanton, who, he maintained, was protected by the Tenure of Office Act, and could not have been removed without the consent of the Senate while Congress was still in session, but also to the recall of Sheridan, whom he called one of the best-loved Union generals, with an excellent record of administration in his department.

But Johnson was determined. Remarking that Stanton must have realized for a long time that his resignation would be acceptable, he dictated a letter to Colonel Moore asking the secretary to vacate his office.[2] In a cabinet meeting on the next day, after Stanton had left the room, the president took up the pending questions, especially the advisability of Sheridan's removal, with the remaining members of the cabinet. Although Sheridan had not merely dismissed the governor of Louisiana but the Texas governor as well, McCulloch expressed his fear that any move at that time would only drive the more conservative Republicans into the arms of the radicals and bring about an impeachment. Browning agreed, but Welles said that neither Sheridan nor Sickles should have been appointed in the first place and the administration had suffered a loss of confidence because of its failure to act with determination. Randall thought Sheridan ought to be dismissed. The president, his eyes flashing because of Welles' remarks, declared that he had no faith in the conservative Republicans. If he were to be impeached for doing his duty, for ordering away an officer who he believed was doing wrong, he was prepared for it. For the time being, Sheridan's removal was postponed, but not even the intervention of Chief Justice Chase, who pleaded with Johnson not to antagonize Congress further, could change his mind.

On August 3 Welles met with Johnson again. This time, influenced by McCulloch, he said Sheridan's transfer might possibly be deferred, but the president remained firm. Again expressing his contempt for the "conservatives" and his indifference to an impeachment, he told Welles about his interview with Grant concerning his desire to remove Stanton. Welles replied that he should have rid himself of hostile cabinet members long ago, a remark to which the president assented "with some emotion," although he thought it would have been difficult to get rid of Stanton earlier. Now he was ready to go ahead, and Welles believed that the secretary might comply with the invitation to leave, though, considering Stanton's peculiarities, one could not be sure.[3]

Two days later, after details of the recommendation of mercy for Mrs. Surratt had appeared in the press, the president sent for the papers in the case. When he discovered the recommendation fastened to the papers containing the death sentence, he declared he had never seen it before. This cast suspicion upon Stanton and Holt, and was bound to create a favorable climate of opinion for him; he therefore asked Colonel Moore to deliver the letter of dismissal to Stanton. Now dated August 5, the letter was brief: "Sir: Public considerations of a high character constrain me to say, that your resignation as Secretary of War will be accepted." The president speculated on Stanton's probable course and agreed with Moore that he would most likely be unwilling to comply, although Johnson found it hard to believe that even a man like Stanton could refuse to vacate an office when asked.

He did not have to wait long. The next morning, at 11:45, the answer came. "Your note of this date has been received . . . ," Stanton wrote. "In reply I have the honor to state that public considerations of a high character, which alone have induced me to continue at the head of this Department, constrain me not to resign the office of Secretary of War before the next meeting of Congress."

Hardly surprised by the reply, the president thought Stanton's friends were pursuing a course they would not be able to sustain before the country. He determined to leave Stanton "hanging on the hooks of uncertainty for a few days," and then suspend him from office.[4] During the days that followed, Johnson conferred with the cabinet, listened to suggestions that either General Steedman or Frank Blair be appointed secretary ad interim, but did not change his mind. On August 11 the president informed General Grant that he definitely intended to remove the secretary of war. It would be better if Grant rather than a stranger took his place, he said, and the general replied that he would obey orders. Was there any substantial point of disagreement between them? the president asked. Nothing personal, answered Grant, though he alluded to a difference of opinion about the Fourteenth Amendment and the Reconstruction Acts. Then Johnson directed his secretary to deliver his letter of dismissal to Stanton.

The letter, dated August 12, was in strict conformity with the Tenure of Office Act. "By virtue of the power and authority vested in me, as President, by the Constitution and the laws of the United States," it read, "you are hereby suspended from the office as Secretary of War, and will cease to exercise any and all functions pertaining to the same. You will at once transfer to General U. S. Grant, who has this day been authorized and empowered to act as Secretary of War ad interim, all records, books, papers, and other public property in your custody and charge." Originally, he had intended to say "suspended and removed" but thought better of it and stayed within the letter of the law. After sending the letter, Johnson calmly joined Seward to go to church.[5]

Moore promptly delivered the letter to the War Department. "I will send an answer," said Stanton. Then the colonel went to army headquarters to hand Grant the document appointing him secretary of war ad interim. After a deliberate reading, the general folded it up and said, "Very well."

At 12:30 that same day, Inspector General Edmund Schriver brought Johnson Stanton's reply. The secretary denied the president's authority to suspend him without the consent of the Senate but maintained that, in view of Grant's appointment and acceptance, he had no alternative except to yield. After reading the letter, Johnson unburdened himself to Moore. "The turning point has come; the Rubicon is crossed," he said with an expression of great feeling. "Col. Moore, you do not know what Mr. Stanton has said and done against me." Recalling the secretary's actions during the past few months, he stressed Stanton's opposition to the Tenure of Office Act and his statement that no man of honor would remain in office if not wanted. Johnson was greatly relieved at the temporary solution of his problems.[6]

The conservative secretary of the navy was less satisfied. Welles considered Grant insincere and deplored the general's approval of the Reconstruction Acts. In addition, he thought Grant a "political ignoramus" playing up to the radicals in order to secure a presidential nomination.

Nevertheless, some radicals, upset by Grant's acceptance of the office, also distrusted him. Although the general had written a letter of appreciation to Stanton, the secretary had been miffed, and it was not surprising that the editor Horace White thought the general had made a mistake in consenting to serve; it would make people think he was tainted with "Johnsonism." Moreover, it would give new impetus to the impeachment movement, which White recognized as an anti-Grant undertaking to make Wade president. Judge Advocate Holt decided that the general was lost to the cause, and Zachariah Chandler thoroughly distrusted him. Although Johnson professed to have little faith in the moderates, for a moment it seemed as if he might succeed in driving a wedge between Grant and the majority Republicans.[7]

The ouster of the secretary of war constituted only one part of the president's offensive. He was now determined to get rid of all the radical district commanders, especially, in spite of objections, Sheridan, still in charge of Louisiana and Texas. Long distrustful of the general, Johnson had been outraged at Sheridan's June 22 letter to Grant seeking to evade the president's order to extend the registration period in Louisiana and calling Stanbery's interpretation of the Reconstruction Acts "a broad macademized road for perjury and fraud to travel on."[8] But at that time Congress was about to convene, Stanton was secretary of war, and Grant himself was protecting Sheridan. Now conditions had changed. Congress was in recess, Grant had been partially co-opted, and Johnson thought he could without too much trouble replace the commander of the Fifth District with George H. Thomas.

He was wrong; the removal did cause great difficulty. Grant had not changed his mind; when Johnson broached the subject to the general, he demurred. Sheridan was an excellent officer well beloved by the people, Grant said, and he forcefully advised against his replacement. Then, as usual, the general put his objections in writing. Asking that Johnson reconsider the order assigning Thomas to take Sheridan's place, he asserted that it was "unmistakably the expressed wish of the country that Gen. Sheridan should not be removed from his present command." The United States was a republic where the will of the people was the law of the land, he continued; Sheridan had performed his duties faithfully and intelligently. His removal would only be regarded as an attempt to defeat the laws of Congress and embolden the former rebels. At the same time, he sent a warning to Sheridan.

Johnson was not the man to yield to such objections. While he had asked Grant for suggestions before carrying the order into effect, he had not expected a written answer. Replying in a "forcible" letter, the president expressed his surprise at the general's written protest and pointed out that he was not aware that the question of changes in commanders had ever been submitted to the people for determination. Grant came to see the president; after a brief conversation, he acquiesced, though he was apprehensive about a rumor that the removal of Sheridan was merely the first step in the dismissal of other commanders, including himself. The president smiled and, reminding the general that he had long desired him to act as secretary of war, put Grant at ease. Grant finally even admitted that the dismissal of Stanton might not have been such a bad development after all.

But the problem had not yet been solved. Thomas, it turned out, was not well; his doctor thought New Orleans might not be healthy for him. Johnson, who had been anxious to send the more conservative Winfield Scott Hancock to the Fifth District anyway, seized the opportunity to do so, only to receive another protest from Grant. Thomas himself had not yet written, he argued. The immediate removal of Sheridan would leave the district without a commander, and Hancock's transfer would be considered an effort to defeat the Reconstruction Acts. Moreover, Grant believed he should have been consulted. Under the law, the Reconstruction Acts were his responsibility.

Johnson was furious. Pronouncing the letter insubordinate, he held that if it were published it would in the minds of all sensible persons condemn its author, and wondered whether it should be answered at all. He finally told the general in a peremptory reply to enforce his orders and in a personal interview, induced him to withdraw the offending communication. Sheridan was removed, to the great satisfaction of Southern sympathizers.[9]

Sickles' turn had also come. The irascible general had issued orders superseding the actions of the civil courts, especially in staying the collection of debts, and Johnson resented this subordination of civil government. On August 26, the same day he assigned Hancock to the Fifth District, he relieved Sickles of command and appointed Edmund R. S. Canby in his stead. Grant tried to defend Sickles in cabinet, but he was not successful.[10]

Although the president had handled Grant with great diplomacy, his relations with his subordinate remained strained. Grant, playing a double game, asked leave to retire when matters of no concern to his department were under discussion in cabinet, and eventually stayed away from routine meetings. Johnson was appalled. He characterized the general as one who was unable to apprehend matters of government and was controlled by prejudice and passion. Grant even seemed to think that the commanders of the five districts were autonomous.[11]

And Grant acted in such a way as to confirm the president's suspicions. He wrote an encouraging letter to Sheridan after the latter's dismissal, issued orders forbidding commanding generals to appoint any officers already removed by their predecessors, and opposed pardons for high-ranking Confederates. Afraid that the general was siding with the radicals, in October Johnson tried to replace him with General Sherman, whom he had called to Washington to influence Grant in his favor, but Sherman refused the post.[12]

In the meantime, the president continued his aggressive tactics. In a defiant mood, just before the fall elections, he again made his position clear by issuing a proclamation calling upon the army to sustain law and order as expounded by the civil courts in the Carolinas. A few days later he promulgated a general amnesty for all but the most prominent Confederates. Then he awaited the election results.[13]

The outcome of these contests gave Johnson a tremendous boost. Always convinced that in the long run the people would sustain him, he thought that the Democratic gains in state after state were the justification for which he had been waiting. In Ohio the results were especially gratifying: not only did the voters reject impartial suffrage, they elected a Democratic legislature that was certain to turn Ben Wade out of the Senate in 1869. Calling the outcome "the logic of events," Johnson told a group of well-wishers that he had always held the people would in good time teach their public servants the right way. "They often exhibit more wisdom . . . than Presidents, Congresses, or conventions," he added.

His trust in the ultimate wisdom of the electorate seemed confirmed by further successes in November, and the president again did not let the occasion pass without once more emphasizing his firm reliance on the wisdom of the people. "I am gratified, but not surprised at the result of the recent elections," he told a group of serenaders on the thirteenth. "I have always had undoubted confidence in the people. They may sometimes be misled . . . but never perverted, in the end they are always right. In the gloomiest hours through which I have passed—and many of them God knows have been dark enough—I had still an abiding confidence in the people and felt assured that they in their might would come to the rescue. They have come, and thank God! they have come, and . . . our Republic will be saved."[14]

In Johnson's mind saving the republic, one of his main goals, was increasingly becoming synonymous with rescuing the South from "Negro rule." Confidants from many states told him that in the elections, the race issue had been decisive; many radicals themselves were convinced that it had been the cause of their losses, and the president was confirmed in his long-standing conviction of the necessity for white supremacy. "Now I can but wish that you may personally enjoy the honor of restoration to the 'White Men' of the South, the Constitution, as it was," wrote a delighted supporter from Tennessee, and the president deliberately incorporated that sentiment in his annual message to Congress in December. "The subjugation of the States to negro domination would be worse than the military despotism under which they are now suffering," he wrote, while emphasizing the great difference between the races and asserting the inferiority of the blacks. His opposition to congressional Reconstruction was not merely based on constitutional scruples; it also reflected his deeply felt racial prejudices.[15]

Another result of the election was the emergence of Grant as the candidate not only of the conservatives and moderates, but of the radicals as well. They might not like him or trust him, but he was now the only contender who could win the next presidential election for them.[16]

Johnson, sensing this development, became more and more uneasy about the general. Concerned that Grant had gone over entirely to the radicals, he followed the advice of Gideon Welles, who urged him to have a frank talk with his subordinate. Grant assured him that all fears about his loyalty were unfounded; should he change his mind, he promised to inform the president. Nevertheless, a real question about the general's exact position remained unanswered, and Johnson considered various possible replacements for him, including J. D. Cox, Frank Blair, and the two Ewings, Thomas, Sr. and Jr.[17]

Finally, the elections slowed the continuing movement to impeach Johnson. Some observers believed the Democratic and conservative gains would end the idea of impeachment; others were not so sure. In any case, the chief impeachers continued to press forward. Some even thought the setback was due to their failure to put the president on trial in the first place, and they became more determined than ever to realize their goal.[18]

The drive toward impeachment had received a great boost during August and early September. Johnson's defiant removal of Stanton, Sheridan, and Sickles convinced many Republicans, even moderates, that he would have to be ousted. "With regard to political matters, I see that the D——l will be to pay when Congress meets," Fessenden warned McCulloch on September 2. "The sentiment of New England was decidedly, almost unanimously adverse to the operations of Wade, Butler & Co., when we last adjourned. Now, I meet no man who is not in favor of impeachment if any decent pretense for it can be found. It does seem as if Johnson was resolved upon destruction." Carl Schurz thought a trial was likely, and Burke Aaron Hinsdale, Congressman James A. Garfield's Ohio friend, wrote to Garfield in August that while he had hitherto been opposed to impeachment, he was now beginning to think that Johnson must be put out of the way.[19]

Then the elections took place, and some of the radicals became desperate. As soon as the first results were in, Speaker Schuyler Colfax wrote in alarm to Garfield: "Before July, the majority of our party was against it [impeachment] as a matter of policy. Now they are solidly for it. It must come. And the election returns & his wicked advisers have so excited 'the humble individual' that he is decidedly on the war path. I should not be surprised by *any* measure he might resort to. We must expect the most exciting scenes." While further unfavorable results frightened off some of the impeachers, others, and particularly the impeachment committee, persisted.[20]

There had long been rumors that the vote against a positive report might be changed, and late in November the Judiciary Committee resumed the examination of witnesses. Various newspaper reporters testified, as did Colonel Moore; Lafayette Baker appeared again; and finally Ashley himself took the stand. Pressed to explain why he had not presented certain evidence he allegedly possessed, Ashley answered that it was not the kind of proof that would satisfy the great mass of men, especially those who did not concur with his "theory about this matter." He believed that all previous presidents who had died in office had been poisoned; that efforts had been made to poison Buchanan at his inaugural; and that Lincoln's assassination was equally suspicious. But he was forced to make an admission. "From my stand-point," he conceded, "I could come to a conclusion which impartial men, holding different views, could not come. It would not amount to legal evidence." His testimony was not helpful; nevertheless, the committee proceeded to render a report recommending, by a majority of 5–4, that Johnson be impeached of high crimes and misdemeanors. Congressman Churchill, who had opposed impeachment in June, had changed his mind. James F. Wilson and Frederick R. Woodbridge dissented, as did the Democrats, who handed in a separate opinion.

The majority report, written by Thomas Williams, contained a hodgepodge of charges centering on Johnson's Reconstruction policies. It accused him of having illegally promulgated the North Carolina proclamation, pardoning "notorious traitors," profiting from the illegal disposal of railroads in Tennessee, being responsible for the New Orleans riot, and defying Congress. He had vetoed Congress' measures, denied its right to reconstruct the South, and tried to prevent the ratification of the Fourteenth Amendment. "Every great abuse, every flagrant departure from the well settled principles of the government, which has been brought home to its present administration . . . ," Williams maintained, "is referrable to the one great overshadowing purpose of reconstructing the shattered governments of the rebel States in accordance with his own will." Although generally agreeing with these conclusions, Wilson and Woodbridge found that they did not constitute a crime, the commission of which, unlike the majority, the two dissenters believed necessary for impeachment. In their separate opinion the Democrats disagreed totally with their colleagues and referred to the recent elections. The impeachers had just been "themselves impeached," they concluded. The committee report was not a strong indictment, and it was evident from the very beginning that it would not be easy to induce Congress to endorse it.[21]

Johnson heard of the report on the night before it was adopted. At 8:30 on November 21 Edmund Cooper, his confidential secretary, burst into the White House library and said he had heard the Judiciary Committee had decided upon impeachment because Churchill had changed his mind. "If it be so, let it be," said the president. Outwardly calm, he was nevertheless deeply agitated about this development.[22]

What was he to do in case Congress attempted to suspend him pending the trial? The problem bothered him, especially as the possible use of force had been under discussion for some time. For months he had received offers from Democrats and Confederate veterans to raise troops to help resist Congress, and rumors to that effect circulated from time to time, but, of course, he had not thought of doing anything of the kind. As Georges Clemenceau, then in the United States to learn, teach, and write for *Le Temps,* observed correctly, these reports were ridiculous. "Everybody knows . . . ," he wrote, "that Mr. Johnson expects his salvation to come from the people and the elections." The Frenchman was right, but Johnson did prepare to resist an unconstitutional attempt of premature suspension.[23]

On November 30, after discussing his forthcoming message, the president brought up the problem in cabinet. Setting forth the background of the impeachment proceedings and the possibility of the passage of Stevens' bill to suspend the executive pending a trial, he declared that he believed it to be his duty to resist such unconstitutional attempts. Then he asked the members of the cabinet to express their opinion on the matter. The answer must have been wholly satisfactory to him—the entire cabinet, including Grant, who believed such a law if passed now would constitute ex post facto legislation, voted to sustain Johnson's position. Fortunately, the matter did not have to be put to a test. Congress never passed Stevens' bill.

Johnson was in fact delighted with the cabinet's action. The day had produced great results, he told Moore. Did the colonel remember his statement that the Rubicon had been crossed? The time for defense had passed, and now he could stand and take the offensive on behalf of the Constitution and the country.[24]

The impeachment resolution, which Boutwell introduced on December 5, did not get very far. In the first place, the charges were flimsy. Obviously, Johnson had not committed an indictable crime, and many members of the House believed with Wilson that specific violations of the law were necessary for a successful prosecution. In addition, the principal impeachers, Butler, Stevens, and Wade, had become closely identified with a plan to pay off part of the national bonds in greenbacks, an inflationary scheme of great concern to the financial community. "All the great Northern capitalists are afraid of the consequences of impeachment," the conservative T. W. Egan wrote to Johnson. "To use the words of one of them—'the President might be crushed, but the finances of the country would go to ruin.' " This was also Senator Grimes' opinion. "The great question . . . today is the financial question," he admitted to Edward Atkinson, the Boston economist, "and must, ought to override the reconstruction and impeachment questions." If Stevens and Butler were in control of the government, "with their revolting repudiating whims in the ascendency," he did not think the government could last for twelve months. So when Johnson sent in his annual message containing his conservative financial opinions—he advocated speedy resumption of specie payments—the result was immediate. His views had won over of the capitalists of the country, he was told, and Boutwell's resolution would be tabled.[25]

Then there was the fear that even if the House could muster the votes to impeach, the Senate might not convict, and the resulting trial would be as expensive as it would be useless. Nor were the prospects of Wade's succession very cheering. As early as July James G. Blaine had been quoted as saying Congress would never vote impeachment because it did not want any of Ben Wade's "Shellywaggers" around the White House. Wade's elevation was viewed as an obstacle to Grant's chances for the presidential nomination, and this weakened the impeachment drive. As George G. Fogg, the New Hampshire lawyer, journalist, and diplomat warned Elihu B. Washburne, impeachment would constitute a great danger for the Republican party. "Force on us more 'extreme' measures, under repudiated extreme leaders, and the reaction is fated to be a 'revolution,'" he wrote. "Maintain things as they are and nothing can prevent Grant from being the next President."[26]

The result of these considerations was that the first effort to impeach the president failed. On December 5 Boutwell delivered an impassioned speech in favor of his resolution. On the following day Wilson replied equally forcefully and moved to table, but this stratagem was defeated. On the seventh, however, after further parliamentary sparring, Wilson, who was still attempting to table, withdrew his motion by arrangement, and the direct question of impeaching lost by a vote of 108 to 57. This victory confirmed Johnson in his determination to continue aggressively on his course.[27]

The president showed his mettle very quickly. Delighted with General Hancock's order declaring the supremacy of the civil power over the military, issued when he assumed command, the president prepared a message to Congress suggesting a vote of thanks to the conservative commander. After hesitating only a few days, he sent his message to the Capitol, not only to defy the radicals once again, but also to censure Grant, who he still believed was drifting into the radical camp. The lawmakers greeted the message with laughter; the Washington *Daily Chronicle* called it a "direct taunt in the face of Congress," while Sheridan considered it an attempt to secure the Democratic nomination for the presidency.[28]

·But Johnson was not yet finished. He was determined to protect the South by putting conservative generals in command, and Pope had tried to enforce radical Reconstruction measures in his district. Consequently the president decided that the general had to go, particularly as Southerners had been asking for his removal. Johnson was also anxious about his friend Alvan C. Gillem, and General Ord had long asked to be relieved, so that he, too, could be dismissed. Accordingly, late in December the president replaced Ord with Gillem and substituted George G. Meade for Pope. "The removal of the District Commanders must embarrass reconstruction very much, if it does not defeat it under the Congressional plan," the Republican editor Lyman W. Hall wrote to James Garfield, and this was indeed its purpose.[29]

The complaints of Southern Unionists and their friends brought home to Republican members of Congress the effectiveness of Johnson's opposition to the Reconstruction Acts. Before the publication of Attorney General Stanbery's opinion, wrote a captain from Huntsville, people in that part of Alabama had pretty much made up their minds to accept the terms offered by Congress. Since that time, however, a decided change had come over them. A Northern settler in Mississippi reported that planters were threatening blacks with the loss of their jobs if they attended political meetings. The removal of Stanton and Sheridan had further encouraged them, and only the impeachment of Johnson would render Reconstruction safe.

Governor Pierpont of Virginia agreed. "The late action of the President has very much unsettled the political situation in Virginia," he wrote to Sumner in September after the publication of the amnesty proclamation. "I fear there will be no peace in the country as long as Johnson is in the Presidential Chair." The mayor of Woodville, Mississippi, detailed similar news to Washburne, while a Texas Unionist deplored the effects on the "rebels" of the balloting in the fall. "The recent elections in the North embolden them . . . ," he complained, "and they cling to the hope that the President will yet be triumphant in his policy." In Georgia a member of the state constitutional convention expressed his dismay at the displacement of Pope. He was certain that the Reconstruction Acts would be a failure "because of the Persistent opposition of A. Johnson and the Encouragement of Rebels to oppose the Letter and the spirit of the Acts themselves." The Unionist Foster Blodgett, also in Georgia, wrote to his Northern friends that the "rebels" were rejoicing about the removal of Pope. They were bragging that Reconstruction was a failure; Unionists were being persecuted, and freedmen hardly had any rights at all. From his own point of view, Johnson's policies had indeed been fruitful. He was not inclined to abandon them.[30]

Despite the strain of being under constant threat of impeachment, the president maintained his composure. His family life was no happier: Eliza, still an invalid, generally stayed in her rooms, and Robert never recovered from his alcoholism. In fact, Robert's debts haunted his father; though often small amounts, they were constant reminders of the son's failure. To add to his troubles, Johnson received letters from the pardon broker Jennie A. Perry, who attempted to blackmail him with tales about an illegitimate son, though he apparently never took her threats seriously.

The president was, as he always had been, something of a loner, but he was buoyed up by the pleasant relations existing between him and his secretary Colonel Moore, as well as his other aide and secretary, Edmund Cooper, a congressman from Tennessee who had been defeated in the recent election and now worked for the president. Johnson also increasingly sought the advice of Jeremiah S. Black, Buchanan's last secretary of state, though the wily Pennsylvania lawyer was already deeply involved in an effort by some Baltimore investors who were his clients to have the government recover the guano deposits on the island of Alta Vela, granted by the Dominican Republic to another group of Americans. And the president continued to maintain an active social life; he visited Antietam on the fifth anniversary of the battle there, and he gave dinners for various dignitaries. Although viciously attacked by the radical press, public officials like Commissioner French never lost their admiration for him. In fact, he was so considerate that he made a point of frequently visiting Welles when the secretary was sick, sometimes as often as twice a day.[31]

Johnson's relations with his advisers generally remained correct. True, he did not have much confidence in Postmaster General Randall, but he was on excellent terms with Welles and Stanbery. Yet there were constant rumors of contemplated changes in the cabinet. The Blairs had long sought to influence him to dismiss Seward, and John Tyler, Jr., made suggestions for a new secretary of the Treasury and postmaster general. In fact, a regular campaign was started against McCulloch, who was accused of being under the influence of Johnson's enemies. The president himself distrusted him, but in the long run thought better of dismissing the Treasury head, whose conservative financial policies were useful in blunting the impeachment forces. Seward was not happy about the dismissals of Stanton and Sheridan and in August, constantly under attack, tried to hand in his resignation. Johnson, however, who appreciated the capable secretary of state, refused to accept it.[32]

Of course, the problem of the secretary of war remained. Suspecting that Grant was now on the side of his enemies, Johnson was nevertheless not prepared to let him go. At any rate, Stanton had only been suspended. The Tenure of Office Act required that the reasons for the suspension be communicated to the Senate within twenty days of the meeting of Congress, and upon the urging of Stanbery and Thomas Ewing, Johnson complied with the provision. Both the attorney general and the president prepared drafts, of which Stanbery's was the longer one. Stressing Stanton's own condemnation of the Tenure of Office Act as well as his failure to reply to Baird's telegram at the time of the New Orleans riot, Stanbery's message seemed to put Johnson's case in the best possible light; it was duly sent to the Senate, together with an additional section emphasizing Grant's able performance as secretary ad interim, which Welles had suggested.[33]

At first the message was well received. Even the Chicago *Tribune*, no friend of the administration, held that if it was true that Stanton was opposed to the Tenure of Office Act and had only refrained from writing a veto message because of ill health, it was not necessary to defend him now. No president could retain an adviser under such circumstances. Within a short time, however, opinions changed. When Stanton declared that he had stayed on at the Union party's behest and Johnson dismissed even more generals, the *Tribune* came to the conclusion that the secretary had done nothing wrong.

But Johnson was worried that he would not prevail in the Senate. Directing Colonel Moore to prepare a letter removing Stanton in case his suspension was not upheld, he tried to extract a promise from Grant that in case of need the general would simply withdraw from the department and leave it in the president's hands to dispose of as he wished. Grant's acquiescence would have left Johnson in an ideal position. If the Senate did reinstate Stanton, the president remarked, the war secretary could be at once removed and Grant could be dismissed as well. Grant, Johnson said, had served the purpose for which he had been selected, and it was desirable that he should be superseded in the War Office by another. But Grant never conceded that he had agreed to the president's request.[34]

Johnson's premonitions were correct. After long consideration, on January 13, 1868, the Senate voted not to concur with the president, and Stanton promptly returned to the War Department.

The circumstances surrounding these events became a subject of heated controversy between Johnson and Grant. General Adam Badeau, Grant's friend and biographer, stated that on Saturday, January

11, the president, wanting to test the constitutionality of the Tenure of Office Act, offered to pay the $10,000 fine that the act would impose on Grant if he stayed in office, but the general refused to disobey the law. Johnson said he had really suspended Stanton under the Constitution rather than the doubtful legislation, and as he remembered it, Grant promised to return the office to him or to inform him should he change his mind. But apparently, Grant never did let the president know of his intentions.

The general, somewhat perplexed, conferred with his friend Sherman, then in Washington to serve on an army board that met in the War Department in the room next to Grant's. Worried about the implications of the penalties imposed by the Tenure of Office Act, Grant was anxious to relinquish his post. Had he told Johnson? Sherman asked. Grant said that there was still time, and, not anxious to have Stanton resume office, the two generals decided to suggest the appointment of former governor Cox of Ohio as secretary of war. Sherman also enlisted the cooperation of Senator Reverdy Johnson, who saw the president on Sunday, January 12, on Cox's behalf. On Monday Sherman went to the White House himself on the same errand, while Grant met Johnson briefly at a levee that night. But the president, unwilling to have a cabinet choice dictated to him and still anxious for a court test, refused to appoint Cox. Firmly believing that Grant had in fact promised to cooperate, he did not consider the brief meeting on Monday night the agreed-upon interview.[35]

On Tuesday, January 14, Grant, informed of the action of the Senate, returned the War Office to Stanton. Then he sent his aide, General Cyrus B. Comstock, to inform the president of his actions.

Johnson was most unpleasantly surprised. Summoning Grant to a cabinet meeting that day, he asked for an explanation. The general said that after the Senate had informed him of its disapproval of Stanton's suspension, he had gone to the secretary's room at the War Department. There he had bolted one door inside, locked the other outside, and given the key to the adjutant general. Was there not an understanding, asked the president, that if Grant did not hold on to the office he would turn it over to Johnson? The general admitted as much, but said he had not examined closely the second and fifth sections of the Tenure of Office Act providing for five years' imprisonment and a $10,000 fine for noncompliance. To Johnson's reminder that he had been willing to pay the fine himself, Grant simply answered that he had tried to solve the problem by sending Sherman and Reverdy Johnson to the White House, who, the president admitted, had indeed come to see him. The general then left the meeting, seeming somewhat embarrassed.

Throughout this encounter Johnson, though manifestly excited and indignant, retained perfect control of himself. In private, he told Colonel Moore that if Stanton tried to enter the president's office, he would kick him out of the room.

On the next day, January 15, Grant came again, this time accompanied by Sherman. Complaining about an article detailing the affair in the *National Intelligencer*, he nevertheless offered once more to induce Stanton to resign. The president said that the article was substantially correct, and his visitor left in a downcast mood.

Grant and Sherman continued in their own attempts to get Stanton to step down, especially because Grant was annoyed at the secretary's brusque behavior at the time of his return to the War Department. However, their efforts were in vain. Stanton held on to his office.[36]

Events were now rapidly moving to a climax. On January 17 Johnson asked members of the cabinet to confirm his recollections of the events of the past few days which they unanimously did. On the nineteenth, he told Grant to disregard the orders of the secretary of war. Five days later he received a reply from the general, who requested a confirmation in writing. The president complied, but Grant still demurred. The message he had received, the general stated on the twenty-eighth, left him in doubt. "I am compelled to request these instructions in writing," he demanded, "in consequence of the many and gross misrepresentations affecting my personal honor, circulated through the press for the last fortnight, purporting to come from the President, of conversations which occurred." Then he detailed his own views of the events, in which he denied ever having made any firm promises to Johnson, and sought to justify his actions in surrendering the War Department.

The president now lost his patience. "I have tried to be decent," he said to Moore. "I know my nature and I will be damned if some things have not gone about as far as they are to go." Citing his favorite play, Addison's *Cato*, he compared himself with Sempronius, who, when asked by Cato whether to resist Caesar to the last, answered his voice was for war. "As for Grant," he continued, "he has been spoiled. I am tired of having his attention thrown upon me. . . . I really wanted to be his friend, for knowing some of the difficulties under which he labored, he had my sympathy." Then, on the following day, he once more sent the general firm written instructions "not to obey any order from the War Department, assumed to be issued by the direction of the President, unless such order is known by the General commanding the armies of the United States to have been authorized by the Executive."[37]

Grant, however, continued to resist. In reply to Johnson's communication, he stated: "I am informed by the Secretary of War that he has not received from the Executive any order or instructions limiting or impairing his authority to issue orders to the army as has heretofore been his practice under the law and customs of the department. While this authority to the War Department is not countermanded, it will be satisfactory evidence to me that any orders issued from the War Department, by direction of the President, are authorized by the Executive." It was obvious that an impasse had been reached; no president could function while neither on speaking terms with the secretary of war nor in accord with the general commanding the army.

Johnson acted with determination. In a firm letter to Grant he emphasized that his version of the story varied completely from the general's recollections and cited the cabinet as witnesses. He then sought out Sherman and asked him to take over the War Department, an offer the general declined. Johnson persisted in vain efforts to bring Sherman to Washington—he attempted to create a new Department of the Atlantic with the general as commander and even sought to promote Sherman to full general by brevet—but finally honored the general's wish to be left in St. Louis.

But the quarrel with Grant was not over. In the beginning of February the House demanded the publication of the acerbic correspondence between the general and Johnson, including an angry letter from Grant on February 3 reiterating his position and seeking to vindicate his reputation. "And now, Mr. President," the letter read, "when my honor as a soldier and integrity as a man have been so violently assailed, pardon me for saying, I can but regard this whole matter, from the beginning to the end, as an attempt to involve me in the resistance of law, for which you hesitated to assume the responsibility in orders, and thus to destroy my character before the country." Asserting that nothing less than a vindication of his personal honor could have induced him to engage in this correspondence, Grant in fact was appealing to the judgment of the general public. By the sixth, the letters had appeared in the press.

Johnson was outraged and determined to respond to the published letters, but not until he had once more secured written confirmation of his recollections from the entire cabinet. On February 10 he answered Grant in a letter strongly restating his case. Supporting his position with the cabinet's own replies, he concluded with a reminder to the general of his duty to obey the commander in chief of the army. A complete break between the two men was the result.[38]

Johnson's rift with Grant might be criticized on the grounds that it was politically unwise because of the general's tremendous popularity at the time. However, the president, by trying for months to separate Grant from the mainstream of the Republican party, even though he had been aware of the general's dubious attitude, had done all that was possible to keep Grant on his side. Now that it had become clear that the effort had been in vain, it cost Johnson little to break completely with the victor of Appomattox. Still intent on protecting the South from legislation he considered harmful, he could no longer cooperate with an officer who had long tried to frustrate this attempt. In addition, Johnson was angling for the Democratic nomination for the presidency, and that party had now completely repudiated the general.[39]

Congress had for some time resumed its warfare against the White House. Early in January a resolution condemning the dismissal of Sheridan and censuring the president had passed both houses; a fourth Reconstruction Act to enable Southern states to ratify their radical constitutions by a majority of those voting instead of those registered was being perfected, and some ultras even tried to interfere further with the president's authority as commander in chief of the army by vesting all power under the Reconstruction Acts in the commanding general. The lawmakers, worried by a legal challenge to their legislation by the Mississippi editor William H. McCardle, also sought to require the Supreme Court to decide cases by a two-thirds majority. Now, taking advantage of the break between Johnson and Grant, Thaddeus Stevens, ill and bitter, tried to renew the impeachment movement in his Committee on Reconstruction. Accusing the president of an attempt to violate the Tenure of Office Act, he induced the committee to examine a few witnesses, but in the end it voted 6 to 3 against taking action. The furious Stevens called the Republicans a party of cowards and vowed never to touch the impeachment question again.[40]

Johnson, though irate about the general and the committee, still maintained his outward calm. "I never saw him more cheerful or in better health or spirits," wrote Joseph B. McCullagh, the correspondent of the Cincinnati *Commercial*, who met him on February 9. The president told the journalist, known by his pen name of "Mack," that he had a perfect right to bypass Stanton, who was merely a clerk transmitting his orders. Laughing at the idea that his opponents wanted him disqualified because they were afraid of him, he expressed the hope that they would find a strong antagonist. As for the problem posed by the secretary of war, he was determined to solve it within a short time. If it led to a final showdown with Congress, he was prepared to deal with it.[41]

XVII

PRESIDENT IMPEACHED— PRESIDENT ACQUITTED

B Y THE middle of February 1868, Johnson had come to the conclusion that he must act. It was now or never; either he would rid himself of his unwanted secretary of war or he might as well resign. And, convinced that he was in the right, he was even willing to risk impeachment.[1]

Master politician that he had been in Tennessee, Johnson did not move without some semblance of political advantage. After all, the radicals had just received a severe setback in the fall elections; impeachment, as the December effort had shown, was not popular, and the widespread fear of Ben Wade's putative succession was no secret. Moreover, in view of the fact that the Republican nominating convention was to meet that spring, it was evident that many of Grant's friends were not anxious to complicate their candidate's problems by the temporary elevation of Wade to the White House, especially as Ben Butler, still Grant's inveterate foe, was one of the principal advocates of impeachment. All these issues could be turned to the president's advantage. If, on the other hand, he delayed, the expected admission of many radical Southern states would create new difficulties.

The remaining problem was whom to nominate for secretary of war in place of Stanton. Sherman proved wholly unwilling to enter into controversy with his old friend and commander, General Grant, so some other suitable candidate would have to be found. The president briefly thought of the chief clerk of the War Department, John Potts, but he was also averse to becoming involved. Stanton had appointed

Potts' son to a good position in the army, Potts said, and his relations with the secretary had always been friendly. Moreover, he claimed he was holding his job by Stanton's appointment.

The president, however, was not prepared to give up. Even before he approached Potts, one Sunday after returning from church he had asked Moore to read him his cherished play, Addison's *Cato*. The dramatist's description of the noble Roman's character deeply impressed him. Cato was a man, Johnson said, who would not compromise with wrong but, being right, went to his death rather than yield. Seeing himself in a similar situation, when Potts refused the office, the president turned to another candidate, General Lorenzo Thomas.[2]

Thomas was a garrulous old man who had been adjutant general early in the war until Stanton, who detested him, shifted him to another position. Because his successor, Edward D. Townsend, was beholden to Stanton, on February 11 Welles suggested that he be superseded. Johnson agreed and reappointed Thomas adjutant general. The president knew Thomas was right-minded and, after restoring the general to his former job, seriously contemplated appointing him secretary of war. Would such a nomination carry any weight, Moore asked? His chief conceded that it would not; nevertheless, he was determined to remove Stanton. As Johnson put it, his self-respect demanded it, and if the people did not entertain sufficient respect for their chief magistrate to uphold him in such a measure, he ought to resign.[3]

There were two additional appointments the president had in mind. One was the assignment of McClellan as envoy to Great Britain, evidently to mollify the Democrats, and the other, the promotion of George H. Thomas to brevet lieutenant and full general. Though warned by friends to be careful, on February 21 Johnson took the final step. He directed Moore to write out the appointment of Lorenzo Thomas, the removal of Stanton, and the promotion of George H. Thomas, to notify the secretary of war of his actions, and to ask Seward to bring the document proposing McClellan's nomination with him to a cabinet meeting. Then he sent for Adjutant General Thomas, to whom, after explaining the laws concerning the case, he handed a letter of appointment and the order removing Stanton. The president remarked that he wished to proceed according to the Constitution and the laws and advised him to have witnesses present when delivering the letter to Stanton. He took this decisive action without informing the cabinet beforehand; nor did he apprise the Democrats of his intentions.[4]

Thomas returned before one o'clock in the afternoon. He had delivered the letter to Stanton, he said. The secretary was sitting on a sofa, read the paper removing him, and asked, "Do you wish me to vacate at once, or am I to be permitted to stay long enough to remove my property?" "Certainly," replied Thomas, "act your pleasure." Then he showed Stanton his orders; the secretary asked for a copy, which was quickly made and certified by Thomas as secretary of war. When Stanton received it, he said he wanted some time for reflection. "I don't know whether I shall obey your orders or resist them," he added; he actually had no intention of obeying. On the contrary, he conferred with Grant, who supported him in his decision to resist.[5]

That same afternoon, Johnson met with his cabinet. After the routine business of the day had been disposed of, he informed his advisers of his actions. Perhaps he had delayed too long, he said, but at all events, he thought it was time the difficulty was resolved. A general discussion concerning Stanton's probable actions ensued, with the secretaries expressing their doubts that their colleague would yield peacefully.[6]

They were right. After Colonel Moore had delivered his messages to Congress, both houses reacted with great excitement. In the Senate Trumbull was just delivering a speech. His colleagues rushed to the desk to open Moore's package, and a group of Republicans immediately went to the War Department to advise Stanton to resist. With Grant's support, the secretary then made preparations to hold his office against all comers. Messages from senators began to pour in to Stanton, advising him to stay; Sumner sent his famous one-word telegram, "Stick," and members of Congress supported Stanton in his preparations. The Senate went into executive session, which lasted into the night and resulted in the resolution that the president had no right to suspend the secretary.[7]

In the House the reaction was even more impassioned. When the Speaker received notification from Stanton that the secretary had been ousted, he informed the House. Clusters of excited members formed. Stevens, leaning on Bingham's arm, moved around from group to group, constantly repeating, "Didn't I tell you so? What good did our moderation do you? If you don't kill the beast, it will kill you." John Covode of Pennsylvania offered a motion to impeach the president of high crimes and misdemeanors, and the proposal was referred to the Reconstruction Committee. Before decisive action could be taken, however, the House adjourned.[8]

Amid all this excitement, Johnson seemed to maintain his calm. That night he hosted a dinner for the diplomatic corps, an affair which was still in progress while the Senate was in executive session. Although John Bigelow thought he seemed preoccupied, said little, and looked fagged, even broken down, others marveled at his composure. His critics might call him "Sir Forcible Feeble," but no one could accuse him of lack of courage.[9]

General Thomas was socially active, too, that night. At a ball at Mannix's, he boasted that he would take the War Department the next morning. His vainglorious statements came to Johnson's attention. Alerting Moore, he suggested that on the following day the colonel keep an eye on the old man.

That next morning, Saturday, February 22, Thomas was arrested on Stanton's complaint. Thomas immediately went to see the president, who told him, "Very well, that is the place I want it in—the courts," and advised him to seek the attorney general's counsel. After conferring with Stanbery, Thomas obeyed the summons and posted a $5,000 bond for his appearance on the following Wednesday. Then he went to the War Department, where he found Stanton. After some argument as to who was secretary of war, Stanton ordered Thomas back to his old office. Thomas refused and went into the room opposite, until finally Stanton came to see him again. "The next time you have me arrested, please don't do it before I get something to eat," complained Thomas, who had had no breakfast. Putting his hand around the adjutant general's neck, Stanton turned to General Schriver and ordered him to get something to drink, whereupon the two men took some whiskey together. But Stanton continued to maintain his vigil at the department.[10]

Congress was in session again that Saturday. In the Senate, because it was Washington's Birthday, little was done. As was the custom, the Farewell Address was read and then the Senate adjourned. In the House, however, things were different. In his capacity as chairman of the House Committee on Reconstruction, Thaddeus Stevens reported John Covode's resolution of impeachment. A debate too lengthy to be concluded prior to adjournment followed, but it was certain that the resolution would pass on Monday, when Congress was to meet again.[11]

At the White House the day was also one of constant activity. Stanbery suggested that Thomas Ewing, Sr., be nominated secretary of war; the president agreed and sent Colonel Moore to the Senate with the necessary papers, but the aide found that the upper house had adjourned. According to Moore, Johnson did show some concern that day. Nevertheless, insisting that his actions were demanded by his self-respect, he remarked that if he could not be president in fact, he would not be president in name alone. "I have nothing to gain by a wrong step of this kind," he added. "But I am right and I intend to stand by. I do not want this Government relapse into a despotism. I have ever battled for the right of the people and their liberties and I am now endeavoring to defend them from arbitrary power." In the evening he conferred with Secretary of the Treasury McCulloch and Noah L. Jeffries, the register of the Treasury, who suggested sending a measure to Congress proposing to submit the entire contest to the courts and offering to resign if the Tenure of Office Act were held constitutional. But, as Welles correctly remarked, Congress was in no mood to let the courts decide. It had made up its mind to do so itself.[12]

There was one other officer whom Johnson called in that day, the military commander of the District of Columbia, William H. Emory. Johnson asked him about recent troop dispositions in Washington, and was told that no great changes had taken place, but that under the Military Appropriations Act, all orders to Emory had to come through General Grant. Johnson remarked that the law was not in conformity with the Constitution; Emory, however, said he felt bound by it.[13]

On Sunday the president again conferred with Stanbery, who helped him prepare a message in reply to the Senate's resolution denying his power to remove Stanton. Moore delivered the message to the Senate on the next day, but at that time all eyes were riveted on the House.[14]

Enormous crowds were milling about the Capitol, where that Monday the lucky holders of tickets to seats in the tightly packed galleries had a field day. After listening to speech after speech, they witnessed what they had come to see, the passage of Covode's resolution impeaching the president of high crimes and misdemeanors by a strict party vote of 128 to 47. Then the House appointed a committee to draw up specific charges.[15]

While these dramatic events kept the spectators at Capitol Hill spellbound, the president was quietly taking dinner with Colonel Moore. When news of the House vote was brought to the White House, he took it very calmly, simply remarking that he thought many of those who had voted for impeachment felt more uneasy over the position in which they had put themselves than he did in the one in which they had put him. As he had already told the reporter of the Washington *Express* earlier in the day, he was confident that "God and the American people would make all right and save our institutions." After all, he had merely wanted to bring the matter of the Tenure of Office Act before the Supreme Court. If this argument was somewhat disingenuous—he was really interested in deciding a political question as well—it made for good reading."[16]

When on Wednesday, February 27, Thomas was due to appear in court, the president hoped that he would submit to arrest and apply for a writ of habeas corpus, so that the judiciary could decide the question of the constitutionality of the Tenure of Office Act. But Stanton, sensing the danger, dropped the charges, and this opportunity to seek a legal resolution was lost.[17]

In the meantime, preparations were being made for the trial of the president. On the twenty-fifth, a cold and snowy day, Bingham and Stevens appeared at the bar of the Senate to give notice of the impeachment; on the twenty-ninth the House committee reported nine articles, all but the last concerned with the dismissal of Stanton and the appointment of Thomas, while the ninth charged the president with remarking to Emory that the command of the army provisions of the Military Appropriations Act were unconstitutional. After the House, on the second, adopted these charges, it added two more articles. One, written by Butler, accused the president of having brought Congress into disrepute in his various speeches. The other, drafted by Wilson and edited by Stevens, was a catchall enumeration of the previous charges; it also accused Johnson of having denied the validity of the laws of a Congress in which some of the states were not represented. On March 5 the court convened to swear in the senators; on March 13 the defense asked for a forty-day delay and obtained ten; on the twenty-third, the president sent in his replication, and on March 30 proceedings opened in full.[18]

All these steps were highly dramatic. The newspapers reported every incident with relish, and huge crowds sought admission to the Senate. The election of a board of managers was particularly arresting. Consisting of the radicals George S. Boutwell, Benjamin F. Butler, John A. Logan, Thaddeus Stevens, and Thomas Williams, as well as the moderates John A. Bingham and James F. Wilson, the board of managers could be expected to provide steady entertainment. Butler was well known for his courtroom antics, and Stevens, then already mortally ill and usually carried about in a chair by two strong young men, was fanatic in pursuit of his great antagonist.[19]

Though remaining outwardly unruffled during this period, Johnson was in fact very agitated. The family expected that he would soon have to leave the White House. "They have impeached me for a violation of the Constitution and the laws," he said. "Have I not been struggling, ever since I occupied this chair, to uphold the Constitution which they are trampling under foot?" By refusing Edmund Cooper's suggestion to make use of patronage to prevent a judgment against him, he thought he had angered his aide. But, he added, "I will do nothing of the kind. If acquitted, I will not owe it to bribery. I would rather be convicted than buy my acquittal." The Butler article of impeachment in particular annoyed him. "I hear Ben Butler wanted to add another article to the Articles of Impeachment in which to recite my speeches," was his comment. "I think he has never grasped one of them but I am much obliged to him for bringing them to public notice. There is even more truth in them than I thought they contained." Johnson asked Edgar Cowan to prepare a statement about the horrible end of the signers of Charles I's death certificate; he did not hide his contempt for his accusers and their charges. Jefferson Davis had not been brought to trial but he was, he complained, and "by people who took only a wordy part in the war." Moreover, he was more certain than ever that the secretary of war held office by sufferance of the president alone. But his trust in the people remained unshaken and sustained him.[20]

The conduct of his defense showed that the president had not lost some of the political skill that had enabled him to overcome his enemies in the past. After listening to the suggestions of the cabinet as well as prominent political advisers such as Reverdy Johnson and Thomas Ewing, he carefully picked both Republicans and Democrats to defend him. One was the former associate justice of the Supreme Court Benjamin Robbin Curtis, another, the distinguished member of the New York bar William M. Evarts, and still another, Attorney General Stanbery. The Ohio War Democrat William S. Groesbeck, as well as his old antagonist and later friend Thomas A. R. Nelson completed the team. Curtis was nationally known; one of the dissenters in the Dred Scott Decision, he had built up an enviable reputation as a trial lawyer in Boston, and his conservative Republican principles made him an ideal choice. Evarts, a future attorney general and secretary of state, was a prominent supporter of Grant for the presidency, with excellent connections; his later career attested to his ability. At the time he was a Republican in good standing who had attacked Johnson only a few months earlier. Attorney General Stanbery was a remarkably handsome and attractive six footer, whose erect carriage and rich, resonant voice lent force to his arguments. As well known as almost any lawyer in the country, he resigned from the cabinet in order to avoid a conflict of interests. Groesbeck, a slender figure with a massive head, a hooked nose, and a projecting chin, which gave him the look of a Cicero, was an attorney of great repute who had befriended Johnson during the war. Nelson was the president's own choice. Needing someone he knew well and trusted, he summoned the Tennessean to assist him when Jeremiah S. Black, whom he had also included in the defense, resigned because of his advocacy of the claimants to the guano island of Alta Vela, for which he had vainly solicited government protection.[21]

From the very start, Johnson's attorneys decided that he should not appear at the trial in person, and when, on March 13, the crier loudly summoned the president, the expectant crowd waited in vain. To the great amusement of onlookers, only Ben Butler walked in, looking up at the presiding officer in startled disbelief. Johnson was to speak only through counsel; his lawyers, and particularly Stanbery, told him that under no circumstances was he to give any further interviews to the press. And they were right. The president's careless pronouncements had caused him great trouble. Even Senator Doolittle during the 1866 campaign had bemoaned Johnson's extemporaneous speeches. "He falls into the great error of supposing it possible for him to lay aside his official character and speak as a private citizen about public affairs," the senator complained, and commented that this habit, more than anything else, had given the radicals an advantage. The defense was determined to prevent similar pitfalls.[22]

Nevertheless, it was difficult for the president to take this advice. Several times he criticized his lawyers for what he deemed an inadequate demurrer or reply to various charges, especially after Alexander H. Stephens on March 16 urged him to conduct his own defense. Drawing upon his experience with Johnson during ten years in Congress, the former vice president of the Confederacy maintained nobody could do it better, and Johnson was more convinced than ever of his own skill. He threatened to appear in person if his defense was not conducted according to his own ideas, and said if he were then convicted, nobody but himself could be blamed. A week later his patience was severely tested because of what he considered Evarts' weak answer to the eleventh article. His defense ought to be as strong as his own speeches, Johnson insisted. Nor did he think he would take back anything he had said on the "swing around the circle." In fact, he had already started to write a speech he intended to deliver in the Senate. In the long run, however, discretion prevailed, and he followed the advice of counsel.[23]

When proceedings opened on March 30, 1868, another large crowd had assembled on Capitol Hill. Ben Butler was to make the opening argument; his histrionics were notorious, and the audience undoubtedly was hoping to be well entertained. The newspapers remarked upon the brilliant appearance of the Senate galleries: ladies in their finery, foreign diplomats, distinguished guests—all were there. At 12:30 Chief Justice Chase took his chair. The defense entered. Then came the House of Representatives, led by Stevens and Bingham arm in arm. When Butler, with a pile of manuscripts before him, standing with his back to the chief justice and facing the Senate, began to speak, all were expectant.

At first they were disappointed. A long, dry legal argument against the contention that the high crimes and misdemeanors for which the president could be impeached had to be statutory crimes was not very interesting. Nor did the attempt to deny Johnson's right to test the constitutionality of a law or the theory that the Senate was not a real court of law bound by ordinary rules of evidence cause much excitement. Butler sought to prove not only that Stanton, though appointed by Lincoln, was covered by the Tenure of Office Act, but that the appointment of Thomas, as charged in the first eight articles, was a serious offense. Only toward the end of his plea, when he reached the tenth article, his own, did Butler live up to his reputation. "By murder most foul," he thundered in his attack upon the president, "did he succeed to the Presidency and is the elect of an assassin to that high office, and not of the people." It was not very dignified, but as expected, radical journals praised his performance, while the opposition thought it was below par.[24]

As for Johnson, the opening of the trial again tested his patience. Still strongly impelled to go to the Capitol in person, he impatiently awaited the appearance of his attorneys at the White House. If he could only defend himself in his own fashion! However, when his lawyers saw him, they apparently again argued against his personal participation. He had to remain at the mansion.

In the days that followed, nothing of great impact occurred. After all, the facts were hardly in dispute; the question was one of intent and legal interpretations. When one of Thomas' fellow citizens testified that he had encouraged the general by telling him, "The eyes of Delaware are upon you," there was general merriment. But the testimony of prosecution witness after witness added little that was not already known, and interest flagged until April 9, when the defense presented its case. Benjamin R. Curtis, in a masterful speech, demonstrated that Stanton, because he had been appointed by Lincoln and not by Johnson, was not covered by the Tenure of Office Act, that in any case, the president had a right to test a law's constitutionality, and that the last two articles involved a question of freedom of speech. Pointing out that a difference of opinion was no crime, he concluded with an appeal to simple American justice. Even Butler had to concede that after Curtis had presented the case of his client, "nothing more was said in his behalf, although . . . much else was said."[25]

Because the defense was anxious to prove Johnson's lawful intentions, his lawyers tried to summon witnesses to substantiate their contention. General Sherman, Quartermaster General Montgomery Meigs, and others were called and questioned, but the board of managers objected. It was not until April 13 that Senator Reverdy Johnson, in the face of constant objections, succeeded in directly questioning Sherman about the president's purpose in tendering the office of secretary of war to him on January 30. Sherman's testimony suggested that Johnson's intent had been to have the office administered in the interest of the army and the country and that he thought if Stanton's case could be brought before the courts it would not stand half an hour. It was striking testimony.

The next day the trial was delayed because Stanbery had fallen ill, but later that week questions put to members of the cabinet, and particularly to Gideon Welles, though constantly subject to objection, seemed to substantiate previous statements of the president's lawful intent. This was the point the defense wanted to make, and by the end of April the trial was virtually over, except for the final arguments of the defense and the board of managers.[26] Some of the closing speeches were peculiar; for example, Boutwell, in a speech Clemenceau characterized as "the longest, weakest, and dullest" since the opening of the trial, suggested Johnson be banished to the black hole in the Southern sky. Butler clashed violently with Evarts and Nelson, while Stevens, too weak to finish his summation, handed it to Butler to be read. Thus it was not until the first week in May that there was any possibility of a final vote.[27]

During this entire period Johnson still maintained his outward calm. On the day following the impeachment, Browning noted that he did not even make an allusion to it. Although the president suggested that Moore look for another job while there was still time, he kept up his social schedule replete with receptions, newspaper interviews until counsel stopped them, and public dinners. On February 28 he hosted a dinner party for forty people. Eliza, as usual, stayed in her room, but Martha and Mary efficiently took her place as hostesses. Their father appeared well and not at all troubled. On March 23 Johnson held a reception for members of Congress, some of whom attended to see how "Andy" was "taking it." If they had had any hopes of encountering an anxious president, they were disappointed. He was "taking it" with dignity and aplomb.[28]

Johnson even maintained his ordinary schedule of private visits, calls upon sick servants, and attendance at weddings and funerals. His steward, William Slade, was ill with dropsy and, as it turned out, already on his deathbed. On one of his many visits the president took Slade's hand and offered to do anything he could for him. The patient thanked him profusely for coming, but succumbed shortly afterward. On March 18 Johnson was present at the funeral. But he also continued to participate in gala celebrations, and on April 22 attended a notable Washington wedding.[29]

Privately, of course, he freely expressed his emotions. On Sundays he usually went with Moore to Dr. Phineas D. Gurley's Presbyterian Church on New York Avenue; on one Sunday he even attended a Catholic service where he heard a homily about the struggle between the poor and the aristocracy. The sermon stimulated him. As he said to

Moore afterward, the Gracchi impressed him; they wanted to divide the land among the people, only to run afoul of the Senate. "This American Senate is as corrupt as the Roman Senate," was his comment. He thought that when the interests of the people were concerned, no more dependence could be placed on it than on its classical predecessor.

On March 31, in the presence of counsel, Johnson discussed with his advisers the facts surrounding the veto of the Tenure of Office Act. All agreed with Seward that the cabinet had been unanimous in advising Johnson that it was unconstitutional, and that Stanton had made the main argument against it.

In the following week the president sought to analyze the nature of the opposition to him. As he saw it, there were those who desired his removal because he was an obstacle to their selfish designs, those who had failed to control him, and finally, those who had a grudge against him because of his part in the war. Annoyed at an article in the Cincin-nati *Commercial* that quoted him as charging Grant with drunkenness and Lorenzo Thomas with undue elation at his appointment to office, Johnson labeled both statements untrue. That Thomas had made a great mistake in not taking possession of the War Department at once was true, he admitted. Although regretting the general's indiscretions, he continued to maintain that Thomas was a gentleman. For Grant, on the other hand, he had no good words. He was infuriated by an article in the New York *Tribune* stating that Grant favored conviction and was giving advice to the Senate. Even though Moore thought the report false, Johnson believed that it pointed to military influence upon the radicals.

What irked the president most was his conviction that the proceed-ings against him were unfair. How could the same body that passed an unconstitutional law try him instead of waiting for the Supreme Court to decide? "Their intent is clearly to obtain control of the Union for political purposes," he argued, "never mind how much they may violate the Constitution or trample upon jurors." He had brought his favorite Bible, a fine London edition, from Tennessee, and cited 1 Samuel 12:3: "Behold, here I am: witness against me before the Lord, and before his annointed: whose ox have I taken? or whose ass have I taken? or whom have I defrauded? whom have I oppressed? or of whose hand have I received any bribe to blind mine eyes therewith? and I will restore it to you." He deeply resented the injustice to which he believed he was being subjected.[30]

In the middle of April the president became more nervous and ex-pressed greater interest in the proceedings. Unwell and gloomy, he was deeply moved when he received encouraging messages. The salutes of blacks celebrating the sixth anniversary of their emancipation in the District of Columbia buoyed him up a little, but he was still very disturbed about his counsel. "Look at Mr. Evarts' reply to Butler the other day when he loosed his tirade of abuse—when he opened his billingsgate upon me," he complained. "All Mr. Evarts had to say was that it was a harangue . . . and I believe he thinks he did a most smart and dreadful thing when he so termed Butler's references to me. Then was the chance to have administered a rebuke that would not only have told upon the Senate but upon the whole country." Particularly resenting the failure of counsel to reply to the managers' characterization of himself as a criminal, he thought he had a right to appeal to the Supreme Court should the verdict go against him.

Later in the month Johnson became more composed and hopeful. On the nineteenth he calculated that he had the necessary votes for acquittal, especially if Wade did not vote, as he thought likely. Though still furious at Butler, whom he would have liked to answer in person "in a manner that would make him feel his meanness all the days of his life," he was pleased with Groesbeck's final argument, to say nothing of Nelson's, which recounted his career and trials in Tennessee. By the beginning of May, though temporarily disappointed by the postponement of the vote on the twelfth, he was confident of success. As time would show, his optimism was well-founded.[31]

Johnson's counsel had been optimistic from the very beginning. As early as March 16 Stanbery told him not to worry. "Mr. President," he said, "you will come out all right. I feel it in my bones." His colleagues agreed with him. In the White House library not long afterward, they laughed at the idea of the managers' securing a conviction based on Johnson's speeches; nor did they have any doubt about his acquittal on the other charges. On April 24 Curtis informed Johnson that "during the last twenty-four hours impeachment had gone rapidly astern."

Other supporters were equally hopeful. "The feeling here *against* conviction is increasing *hourly,*" Collector Smythe reported from New York on April 8, and by the fourteenth, even the pessimistic Welles had to admit that impeachment had lost ground during the last few days. By May 5 Seward was confident enough to bet a basket of champagne on acquittal.[32]

As time went on, the opposition, so confident at first, also began to become more doubtful about the outcome. Butler admitted to Evarts that he wished he were on the other side, and by the end of March even the radical *Independent* expressed some reservations about the result. On May 3 the beleaguered Stanton, still at the War Department, heard that Evarts knew the president would be acquitted, and other radicals shared his apprehensions. "There is today a fearful impression that impeachment will fail," the worried George W. Julian, one of the most radical members of the House, wrote to his wife on the fifth. "It makes me awfully blue." "PROBABLE ACQUITTAL OF JOHNSON," headlined the radical Cincinnati *Gazette* on May 12. Even Stevens was reported to have given up. When the Senate met for the vote on May 16, Johnson could look forward to the result with some confidence.[33]

Of course, the president, in keeping with the political skills he had learned in Tennessee, had not left anything to chance. Despite his frequent disavowals of any deals to secure acquittal, he did in fact engage in various maneuvers to win over doubtful senators.

One of these senators was James Grimes of Iowa. Politically moderate, financially conservative, and appalled at the prospect of Wade's elevation to the presidency, Grimes was not anxious to oust Johnson. But he thought he needed some guarantees that the president would not continue to interfere with Reconstruction. On April 5 Grimes met with Gustavus V. Fox, the recent assistant secretary of the navy, a relation of Montgomery Blair who was well connected in Washington. Telling Fox of his apprehensions, the senator said it would be most helpful if the president appointed a secretary of war in whom the country had confidence. In addition, he wanted assurances that Johnson "would be guilty of no indiscretion, commit no rash act, and consult with his cabinet." In that case, Grimes said, he and his friends would have no trouble voting for acquittal.

The administration was ready to give the senator the desired guarantees, but Grimes insisted on a personal interview with the president. Intermediaries—according to John Francis Coyle of the *National Intelligencer*, Coyle himself, and according to Samuel S. Cox, Senator Reverdy Johnson and William Warden—arranged a private dinner party at which Johnson gave the senator from Iowa the required pledges. Convinced of his sincerity, Grimes assured his friends, particularly Senator Fessenden, that they could vote for acquittal without fear of the consequences.[34]

Johnson also followed up Grimes' suggestion about appointing a new secretary of war. On April 21 Evarts met with General John M. Schofield at three o'clock in the afternoon at Willard's Hotel. For the safety of the country, Evarts told Schofield, the president might send in the general's name for secretary of war. Schofield said he would have to ask Grant, whom he visited that evening. Though opposed to any deal with Johnson, Grant expressed his acquiescence.

That night Schofield saw Evarts again. The president could not be convicted on the evidence, the lawyer pointed out. If Johnson were to be found guilty, the verdict would merely be a political one, a judgment that would be bad for the Republican party. If Schofield accepted the nomination, the minds of several Republican senators would be set at ease so that they could vote for acquittal. Could he not oblige both party and country? Schofield answered that he would have to confer once more with Grant, and did so, only to find out that the general of the army did not believe in compromising with the president. Nevertheless, Grant said that if the facts were as represented, Schofield should not refuse.

The next morning Schofield called on Evarts once more. There was but one difficulty, he said. He needed guarantees about the president's future policies, as he thoroughly disapproved of recent administration measures; otherwise he could not accept. Because Evarts mentioned that it would not be politic to arrange for a personal meeting between the general and the president, Schofield stipulated that Johnson should signify his assent by sending the general's name to the Senate. The president complied.[35]

Senator Edmund G. Ross of Kansas also received assurances from the president. Anxious to see congressional Reconstruction put into effect, on May 4 the senator approached the White House through intermediaries and asked that Johnson transmit the radical constitutions of South Carolina and Arkansas without delay. The gesture would have a salutary effect, and he and others could then vote for acquittal. Johnson promptly complied. But despite considerable pressure, he refused to dismiss Secretary McCulloch. Although he distrusted him, the secretary had important backers in the financial community whom Johnson could not afford to affront.

Why did Johnson, who had never compromised with the moderates before, now begin to meet them halfway? The answer to this question would seem to be one of timing. While he had always believed that the gap between himself and the moderates, particularly on problems of Reconstruction and the future of the freedmen, was too large to be bridged, apparently he now felt the time was ripe for an accommodation. He had done all he could to frustrate congressional efforts at Reconstruction; his conviction would be of no help to the South, while an acquittal might well be the signal for the turning of the tide. Thus he agreed to the terms offered by Grimes, Schofield, and Ross, though he adamantly refused a putative invitation to threaten with exposure for alleged misdeeds the dubious senator Samuel C. Pomeroy of Kansas, who was said to have been ready to sell his vote in return for patronage.[36]

While the trial was in progress, the legislative business of the country was neglected, and only a few major measures were passed. One of these was a fourth Reconstruction Act. Designed to frustrate Southern efforts to defeat Reconstruction constitutions by abstaining from voting, as had happened in Alabama, the bill provided that a majority of those voting, rather than those registered, was sufficient to ratify. Passed late in February, the act became law without the president's signature on March 11. Congress also passed a bill denying the right of appeal in cases like the McCardle litigation then before the Supreme Court. Johnson vetoed it, only to have his objections overridden as usual. At the same time, in Connecticut, the Democratic governor was reelected, but the legislature, which would elect the next senator, became Republican. And in New Hampshire the Republicans won easily.[37]

By May 7 the last arguments were finished. Only a few technicalities remained, and then the vote could be taken on May 12. Excitement in the city rose to fever pitch; rumors about the probable votes of senators abounded, and political pressure on Republicans to vote for conviction increased steadily. But on the appointed day the illness of Senator Jacob Howard of Michigan occasioned another delay. The Senate voted to adjourn the court until Saturday, May 16.[38]

The president was disturbed about this latest postponement. As he had remarked to Moore two days earlier, "This thing has gone far enough! It is about time to stop it." While the majority of the cabinet was certain of acquittal, and his friends were already sending congratulations, he could not know for certain whether his opponents might not postpone the matter indefinitely. And so much depended on the verdict! In spite of his commitments to Grimes and Ross, in the final analysis his entire policy for the last three years, his efforts to maintain the South with many of its institutions intact, his desire to assure the survival of the Constitution as he understood it—all would hinge on the outcome. His acquittal would be such a blow to his antagonists that in the long run, their policies would be severely undermined. He had every reason to be apprehensive.[39]

At last the crucial day dawned. It was a beautiful spring morning; a sunny haze covered the capital. A great throng of people congregated on the terraces of the Capitol and in the streets; tickets to the Senate galleries had again been in great demand, and long before the senators drifted in, not a seat was to be had. At twelve noon Chief Justice Chase took his chair. Some fifteen minutes later the House of Representatives entered, the board of managers and the defense counsel took their accustomed places, and the proceedings began. After some preliminaries, Senator George H. Williams moved that the eleventh article be considered first, and the motion carried. During the vote Jacob Howard, wrapped in a shawl, tottering, and scarcely able to walk, was brought in, supported by Zachariah Chandler and Charles D. Drake. Shortly afterward Grimes, who had suffered a stroke, was also escorted in and helplessly sank into a chair at the chief justice's right. At last the Senate was ready. After warning the galleries that anyone violating the rules of silence would be arrested, Chase asked the clerk to read the article. When he had finished, the chief justice ordered him to call the roll. There was complete silence. The name of Senator Henry B. Anthony was called. Chase rose. "Mr. Senator Anthony," he intoned, "how say you? Is the respondent, Andrew Johnson, President of the United States, guilty or not guilty of a high misdemeanor, as charged in this article?" "Guilty," was the answer, and the same procedure was repeated as the clerk continued calling the senators in alphabetical order.

As the vote progressed, all the Democrats and conservatives, among them David Patterson, as expected, voted "not guilty." Most of the Republicans voted to convict, but, as it turned out, seven of them, William Pitt Fessenden, Joseph S. Fowler, James W. Grimes, John B. Henderson, Edmund G. Ross, Lyman Trumbull, and Peter G. Van Winkle, resisted the pressure upon them and furnished the necessary votes for acquittal. The final result was 35 to 19, exactly one vote short of the required two-thirds for conviction. After the doubtful Senator Ross had voted to acquit, only one hope remained for the managers, Van Winkle of West Virginia. But he also voted "not guilty." As there were no other doubtful senators further down the alphabet, Ross' vote seemingly became the decisive one. Wade, who had not taken part in any balloting until the very end, finally voted to convict, an action for which he, as the legal successor to the president, has been severely criticized. By the time the clerk had reached the letter "W," however, the result was already determined, and the Ohio senator's vote no longer made any difference. He had long held that his state was entitled to two votes and remained consistent to the end. When the last ballot had been cast, instead of proceeding with the other articles, the Senate adjourned until May 26.[40]

While this drama was unfolding in the Capitol, Johnson was anxiously waiting at the White House. An orderly was posted at Willard's Hotel to bring him the vote the moment it was known, and within minutes of the final ballot, he was informed of the outcome. Thus he knew the result even before William Crook breathlessly came racing into the mansion to bring him the news in person. He had run all the way from the Capitol, he said. After delivering his message to Johnson in the library, Crook went to Eliza's room to tell her, but she maintained that she had always known what the outcome would be. Nelson and Stanbery, having lashed their horses at top speed, also arrived to tell their client he had won. Then the White House was thrown open to crowds of well-wishers.[41]

Of course, the president was delighted with the result, even though he still had to face another vote on May 26, after the forthcoming Republican National Convention. He merely expressed his surprise at the votes of a few senators, particularly those of Anthony and Henry W. Corbett of Oregon. On Sunday he went to church as usual, and, on the next day, as if nothing had happened, received a delegation of Sunday School children.[42]

His opponents were crestfallen. Stevens, still carried by his attendants and yelling, "What was the verdict?" found himself in the middle of a crowd. Enraged and disappointed at the result, he brandished his arms in the air and shouted, "The country is going to the devil." Butler, certain that bribery had done its work, initiated an investigation of lobbyists and recusant senators, with special attention to Ross and Henderson. Of course, it yielded nothing, even though he did not hesitate to subpoena private telegrams and look closely into the most far-fetched rumors. "How does it happen," he wrote to the radical newspaperman John Russell Young, "that just enough & no more Senators are convinced of the President's innocence. Why have not these conscientious convictions on which the seven act struck any more of them? Is conscience only confided to just enough to acquit the President?" John Greenleaf Whittier consoled himself with the hope that Grant would still set everything right; Elihu B. Washburne felt humiliated and disgusted, and the *National Anti-Slavery Standard* bemoaned the probable fate of Southern loyalists, white and black, "with this Pasha of Assassins again let loose." There was little doubt that the cause of advancing the freedmen had received a serious blow, and its adherents knew it.[43]

The Democrats publicly hailed the result. Nevertheless, many of them would probably have preferred a different verdict in order to make use of the damaging effect a conviction would have had on the radicals. "What can we do with him? and yet if he isn't convicted now he will be saddled on us," was the comment of one of Manton Marble's correspondents. It was an attitude that was widespread; James B. Bingham wrote Johnson on May 23 how terrible the behavior of Memphis Democrats had been. But in spite of this intelligence the president still considered himself a good Jacksonian.[44]

During the next ten days the impeachment trial was in recess. The Republican National Convention met in Chicago, where, as expected, it nominated General Grant. Neither its platform, however, nor its vice presidential nominee was very radical. It did not endorse universal male suffrage; the issue was too dangerous. And instead of Wade, who might well have received second place on the ticket had the president been convicted, the Republicans nominated the speaker of the House, Schuyler Colfax. The impeachment vote had frightened the party.[45]

When the delegates returned, on May 26, attention was once more riveted on the Capitol, and the galleries again were completely filled. Motions to vote article by article were defeated, as were efforts at further postponement. Finally, the Senate decided to take up the second article. Again the roll was called. Again the chief justice asked his question. And again conviction failed by one vote, the same senators voting "not guilty." The third article was next, with the same result. Then the majority gave up. A motion to adjourn without day carried by a vote of 34 to 16, and the great trial was over.

As before, Johnson awaited the result in the White House. Surrounded by the cabinet, he was again kept informed of the balloting by an orderly at Willard's Hotel who was awaiting the telegraphic dispatches. As the results were brought in, no sudden outburst of boisterousness marred the solemnity of the occasion. Still, a quiet excitement showed in almost every face, only Seward maintaining his imperturbability to the end. As for the president, he remained calm, dignified, placid, and self-possessed, with no outward sign of agitation. As Browning noted, "He received the congratulations of his cabinet with the same serenity and self-possession" that had characterized him throughout his ordeal. The result turned out to be what he had always expected, he said; he had predicted it, his confidence in the people was undiminished, and he expected history to give him credit for "high patriotism in the discharge of his difficult duties at a time of great excitement." Congratulations from friends began to pour in, and within a short time General Townsend delivered a letter of resignation from Stanton. He asked for orders, but the president, wary of renewed difficulties, for the time being refused to give any.[46]

So Johnson had won; his gamble had paid off. To find the reasons for his victory, the political situation and the circumstances of the trial must be kept in mind. True, the Republicans enjoyed an overwhelming majority in both houses, the president had forfeited much of his popularity, and the country was anxious to proceed with Reconstruction, but it proved impossible to convict the executive on the charges presented. In the first place, they were dubious. From the very beginning, Thaddeus Stevens himself realized their weakness. "As the Committee are likely to present no articles having any real vigor in them," he wrote Butler on February 28, "I submit to you if it is not worth our while to attempt to add at least two other articles." The result was the addition of the last two charges, which even radical newspapers and editors criticized as a mere afterthought.

Considering the lack of substance of the original nine articles, these criticisms were to the point. To argue that Stanton was covered by the Tenure of Office Act, the Republicans had to disregard their own comments at the time the bill was being considered, for the secretary had been appointed by Lincoln, and not by Johnson, and the final version of the bill seemed to exclude cabinet members not appointed by an incumbent. Speaking of the president, Senator Timothy O. Howe wrote to his niece, "The Republican press will deny his authority to remove Mr. Stanton. If so, the Republican press will lie." Howe explained that he himself had struggled for weeks in the Senate to secure an amendment that would cover the secretary, but in the end a compromise was reported that by its terms did not protect Stanton.

The House should have waited a few days before acting, Representative Thomas A. Jenckes heard from his home in Rhode Island. "Johnson would then have been mad enough to commit some further misdemeanor upon which you could have prosecuted him with the certainty of convicting him." The charges added up to a "penny whistle affair," thought Benjamin B. French, and Senator John B. Henderson characterized them as counts of "narrow bounds in offense both in act and intent." The Emory article was generally admitted to amount to nothing, so that all that was left, in effect, as John Sherman pointed out, was the effort to appoint Thomas without the consent of the Senate. It remained for Senator Trumbull to sum the case up forcefully: he insisted that the president had violated no law, for "neither the removal of that faithful and efficient officer, Edwin M. Stanton . . . nor the ad interim designation of Lorenzo Thomas, were . . . forbidden by it."[47]

If the case was weak, the managers' conduct did not help. "The managers of the House of Representatives have been poor judges of human nature and poor readers of human motives," wrote the Chicago *Tribune* on May 9. One could hardly call Johnson a "great" criminal as they had done. Butler, who had vowed to try the case as he would a horse case, appeared aggressive and offensive. By trying to prevent the cabinet from testifying, he merely raised doubts in various senators' minds. Nor did Boutwell's violent abuse do much good. It disgusted even faithful Republicans. Because the managers had a poor case, they took refuge in various legal devices, a tactic seen as a confession of weakness. For example, their refusal to allow a vote on the first article, which they knew was offensive to Senators Sherman and Howe, could only increase the impression that the entire proceeding was nothing but a political maneuver.[48]

In addition, there was widespread apprehension about Ben Wade. His clearly expressed ideas on inflation, protection, women's rights, and justice for the workingman frightened many moderate and conservative Republicans, and he was viewed as an obstacle to Grant's presidential ambitions. Should Wade move into the White House, it was likely that he would receive the next vice presidential nomination, a prospect that alarmed many. "There are Republican papers that believe the President guilty of crime, and favor impeachment," commented the Cincinnati *Gazette*, "but they hate the idea of Mr. Wade becoming Acting President."

The journalist Horace White agreed. "I don't know how it may look to you," he wrote to E. B. Washburne, "but the gathering of evil birds around Wade (I refer to tariff robbers) leads me to think that a worse calamity might befall the Republican party than the acquittal of Johnson." Edward Atkinson, the Boston economist, thought that the only "irreparable injury" an executive could inflict was to tamper with the currency. "Upon this question," he complained to Sumner, "Johnson has been right and Mr. Wade is suspected of being wrong. Should such be the truth I would regard the removal of Mr. Johnson a great misfortune in its ultimate effects." Chief Justice Chase also disliked his fellow Ohioan, and throughout the trial he was believed to be favorably inclined toward the defense. James A. Garfield warned that conservative Republicans worried that conviction meant the transfer of the presidency to "a man of violent passions, extreme opinions and narrow views; a man who had never thought thoroughly or carefully on any subject except slavery . . . surrounded by the worst and most violent elements in the Republican party." Under these circumstances, Garfield admitted that he would not be particularly surprised if Johnson was acquitted. When his expectations were fulfilled, Republican newspapers freely cited the prospect of Wade's succession as one of the causes of the failure.[49]

Constitutional considerations also played a role in Johnson's acquittal. The genius of the American system was widely believed to be founded on the tripartite division of government. The legislative, executive, and judicial branches supposedly operated each in its proper sphere, and as the impeachment trial coincided with attacks on the Supreme Court, particularly in connection with the McCardle case, there was widespread fear of the danger of legislative supremacy. Assessing the case many years later, Edmund Ross came to the conclusion that "the impeachment of the President, was an assault upon the principle of coordination that underlies our political system and thus a menace to our established political forms, as, if successful, it would, logically, have been the practical destruction of the Executive Department." And Trumbull, in justifying his vote for acquittal, stated:

> Once set the example of impeaching the President for what, when the excitement of the hour shall have subsided, will be regarded as insufficient causes . . . no future President will be safe who happens to differ with a majority of the House and two-thirds of the Senate on any measure deemed by them important, particularly if of political character. . . . what then becomes of the checks and balances of the Constitution, so carefully devised and so vital to its perpetuity? They are all gone.[50]

The short time left of Johnson's term was also a factor. "To convict and depose a Chief Magistrate of a great country while his guilt was not made palpable by the record, and for insufficient cause, would be fraught with greater danger to the future of the country than can arise from leaving Mr. Johnson in office for the remaining months of his term," Trumbull wrote in his opinion. Conviction would not have benefited Grant, and the Republicans were now determined to elect him president. Thus Republicans failed to find Johnson guilty, as he had gambled they would.[51]

In view of all these difficulties, it may be asked why Congress ever started impeachment proceedings in the first place. After all, moderates had long been opposed to a trial; why did they now join with their radical colleagues in an all-out effort to oust the president?

The answer to these questions must be sought in the Republicans' concern about Reconstruction. As long as Johnson remained in the White House, Republican hopes for a reformed South with a modicum of rights for the freedmen seemed endangered, and his latest actions— the changes in commanding generals and the bestowal of patronage on Southern conservatives—heightened this apprehension. Then, by openly challenging the Tenure of Office Act, the president frightened moderates as well as radicals, and they became convinced of the necessity of removing him. There was also widespread concern that, by drawing a combination of Southern and Northern Democrats to his side, Johnson might endanger future Republican successes. Thus it is not surprising that the attempt to oust him was made. As he may have guessed at the time, it failed, but in the beginning most observers, even those friendly to Johnson, thought it would succeed.[52]

And what had the president accomplished by his victory? Above all, he had succeeded in preserving the Constitution that he admired so much. No other president would ever again be impeached for political differences with Congress; the separation of powers was preserved, and the United States retained its presidential form of government, which set it apart from the cabinet systems of European countries.[53]

In addition, Johnson had given renewed confidence to the South, where he enjoyed enthusiastic support. "You will perceive that we have hoisted your name at our masthead . . . ," wrote the editor of a Georgia newspaper in February. "We believe the true popular heart beats in accordance with your policy, and we shall not swerve an iota from defending to the best of our humble ability, the man who so fearlessly insists on southern equality, southern representation and a white man's government." Edward A. Pollard, the well-known Richmond editor, sent him a fulsome letter, and Augustus H. Garland, the Arkansas politician whom he had pardoned, in March 1868 wrote the president that he was now "the only barrier between us and destruction." Southern hopes were pinned upon acquittal, and Garland assured Johnson that he was the last bulwark of the friends of the Constitution. Convinced that all was lost if Johnson was defeated, former insurgents were praying for his success in the trial.[54]

If Southern conservatives believed Johnson's conviction would spell their doom, their Unionist antagonists were equally certain that for them it was a dire necessity. Whole delegations of Southern Republicans arrived in Washington to make it clear to senators that acquittal would mean the end of their existence; they would have to leave their homes and plantations if the president was allowed to remain in power. Brownlow declared that there was not a Union man, white or black, who did not feel that upon the impeachment of the "usurper" depended his most sacred interests; Senator Willey was warned that acquittal would mean the end of West Virginia as a state, and Alabama Unionists, pleading for a provisional government with an auxiliary military force to sustain it, were certain that only the deposition of the president and the enactment of radical measures would bring relief. A Union man could not live in the South if the president was not convicted, commented a Virginian; if he was, the result would be similar to the surrender of General Lee. From Florida, too, Unionists reported that conviction was absolutely necessary for their success; as long as Johnson was in the White House, their opponents held all the good jobs. And from Louisiana, Stephen B. Packard, the Republican chairman of the Board of Registration, sent warning that blacks were constantly being murdered there. "Can nothing be done to protect loyal people from assassination?" he wired to Grant on May 14. The implication was clear: Johnson must be removed.[55]

Under these circumstances, it was not surprising that the acquittal had an electrifying effect upon the South. Guns were fired off, fireworks illuminated the sky, and popular demonstrations marked the great event. "The news reached here last night and filled our little community with great joy & hopes as to the future," wired former governor Perry of South Carolina. Johnson's old supporter James B. Bingham wrote from Memphis that the mass of the people there and in neighboring Mississippi and West Tennessee were delighted with the result, while another Memphis acquaintance expressed the hope that universal amnesty would follow "to relieve us of the miserable Negro rule under which we groan in despair of any improvement in affairs." East Tennessee supporters were equally overjoyed. As his old collaborator A. A. Kyle put it, "We now feel that you, with the Constitution in your right hand (holding it aloft), has [sic] made a most complete & overwhelming triumph. We now have an abiding faith in the perpetuity of Republican institutions—& that 'Mongrel Radicalism' is dead! dead!" "THE TIDE TURNING," proclaimed a big headline in the Richmond *Whig*, which expressed the conviction that a conservative change was in progress in every direction.[56]

Southern Unionists were deeply depressed. "It is with sadness we learn that the greatest traitor of the century is acquitted," Daniel Richards wrote to E. B. Washburne from Florida. "News of the failure to convict Johnson will be like Greek fire throughout the entire south. May God save our country from the consuming conflagration. The eyes of the rebels sparkle like those of the firey serpent. They hope they have found their 'lost cause' and think they see it. I am not certain but they are right." And George E. Spencer, the Tuscaloosa Register in Bankruptcy, put it even more strongly. "It is impossible to paint in true colors the woeful condition of Union men in the South since the news of the failure of Impeachment," he stated. "Our best men both white & black are leaving us, & making haste to place them in a condition to be allowed to remain in the country." From South Carolina, Sumner heard that since the acquittal, Union men had been in deadly danger, and that one of the Republican members-elect of the state legislature had already been brutally murdered. "Our condition South since the acquittal of Andrew Johnson is a perilous one," a black Republican reported from Georgia. He himself had to be guarded nightly by fellow freedmen, and, because of a threat against his life, finally had to leave the county. In Mississippi, where in June the new constitution was defeated, the Whig Unionist James L. Alcorn blamed the failure of the impeachment for the setback. The cause of congressional Reconstruction had suffered a severe reverse in the South.[57]

Thaddeus Stevens sensed the dimensions of the defeat. His life had been a failure, he complained. "With all this great struggle of years in

Washington, and the fearful sacrifice of life and treasure," he declared, "I see little hope for the Republic." He was especially despondent about the future of the freedmen.[58] Johnson had evidently restored hope to the South, and probably he had so undermined the process of Reconstruction that it could not succeed afterward. To be sure, it was not until after the acquittal that the new constitutions of Southern states with their provisions for black enfranchisement went into effect, and after the election of General Grant, black suffrage was guaranteed by the Fifteenth Amendment. However, Republican rule in the South proved ephemeral. It could not be established on a permanent basis, no matter how many force acts sought to guarantee it. Johnson's adamant opposition at a time when radical measures might have succeeded may well have laid the foundation for this failure. From his own point of view, therefore, he had not been unsuccessful. He had preserved the South as a "white man's country."

XVIII

PRESIDENT IN LIMBO

JOHNSON could truly congratulate himself on his acquittal, but the remaining months of his administration were not such as to make him feel at ease. While the failure to convict him had given new hope to the South, congressional Reconstruction was only just beginning, and it was not yet evident that it would end in failure. While the president still had power to make appointments, the Senate could, and frequently did, reject them. While he was still commander in chief of the army and navy, he had pledged himself to abide by the will of Congress. And while he could still veto obnoxious legislation, his vetoes were routinely overridden. Nevertheless, having been upheld, he was more convinced than ever that he had been right all along. Continuing to believe that in the end the people would sustain him, he was determined to seek vindication.

Because of this fixed purpose, Johnson could and did take great pride in favorable election returns. Early in June the Democrats won in Oregon, and in elections in the District of Columbia they gained control of the Washington Common Council and four of the seven city wards. These results tended to underline the president's belief in final justice, and he continually sought new platforms to voice his convictions of the sacredness of the Constitution as he understood it, the supremacy of the white race, and the need for Jacksonian economics.[1]

But first he had to complete some of the arrangements made during the trial. Senator Edmund Ross asked him to appoint allies to office, and he promptly honored these requests. As for Schofield, the president duly nominated him, only to have the nomination run into difficulties in the Senate. Some of his friends even urged him to withdraw Schofield's name—he was too friendly with Grant, they asserted—but Johnson refused. Although he did not trust Schofield—the general would collaborate with whoever was successful, he said—he allowed Seward to make an arrangement with Schuyler Colfax, and the nomination was confirmed. Then, for once, the president was seen to laugh. Standing in the War Department, where he had come to install the new secretary in person, he remarked with a smile, "It is a long time since I have been in this room."[2]

Johnson also had to chose a new attorney general. Ever since Stanbery's resignation to serve as defense counsel, Browning had held that portfolio in addition to his own. After Stanbery's loyal service during the trial, Johnson naturally wanted to give him his old office back, but the Senate refused to confirm him. Then Johnson thought Benjamin R. Curtis would be a good substitute, only to find that the former justice declined to be considered. Finally he turned to Evarts. This time he was successful; Evarts accepted and was confirmed.[3]

The impeachment continued to rankle the president. He had been deeply hurt by the intemperate attacks on himself, and ever after, he judged people by their attitude during the trial. Outraged at having been put to the test while Jefferson Davis was allowed to escape, as late as March 1869 he reiterated biblical passages in support of his innocence. When Thaddeus Stevens and Thomas Williams sought to revive the impeachment by introducing new far-fetched charges, he reacted with indignation. Vindication he must have, and vindication he sought first by entering the contest for the Democratic presidential nomination. But this effort merely underlined his lack of real power.[4]

Johnson had always been ambitious, and it was no secret that he was anxious for a second term. To be sure, he had long been denying that he was a candidate, but as early as March 1865 supporters began to boost his candidacy. The movement gained strength, especially in the South after his Reconstruction policies became known. The whole South would rally to his support in 1868, a South Carolina physician assured him in September 1865, and his subsequent struggles with Congress made him even more popular there. "The President has completely won the Southern heart in his contest with radicalism," a Georgia editor wrote in January 1868, "and if the Southern states are admitted into the Union before the Presidential election, their votes would be cast solidly for him."

And the presidential boom was not confined to the South. From

Northern admirers, too, Johnson received evidence of support as visiting committees reinforced his self-confidence. By August 1867 Montgomery Blair discovered not only that Johnson was intensely ambitious, as had long been known, but also that all his thoughts were bent on nomination and reelection.[5]

During the first months of 1868, the Johnson boom gathered speed. The South was still in the forefront of the movement, and letters offering support kept pouring into the White House. In February, on the very day the House voted for impeachment, a group in New York formally nominated Johnson for president and Winfield Scott Hancock for his running mate. The acquittal, if anything, seemed to give him another boost. Various delegates to the Democratic National Convention scheduled to meet in New York at the beginning of July offered him their support, and he now began to take active steps to further his candidacy.[6]

To bolster his claims, Johnson prepared a new proclamation of amnesty to be issued on the Fourth of July. His intention was to make it so sweeping as to permit of no exceptions, not even of Jefferson Davis, but Browning, Welles, and Seward argued against such a course; Browning feared his chief might be impeached again. Johnson, however, was hard to convince. Exempting the Confederate president would only make him a martyr, he argued, although in the end he yielded and accepted a compromise that excluded all those under indictment, including, of course, Davis, whose case was still pending. The president published the proclamation on July 4, no doubt fully aware of the fact that it would be widely interpreted as a bid for the nomination.[7]

At the same time, Johnson also sent his own confidential agents to New York. Among these, his former secretary Edmund Cooper and William Warden were his most active boosters, buttonholing the Democratic delegates and seeking incessantly to further his chances. When a group of New Yorkers requested that the president publicly throw his hat into the ring, he complied. He had no further ambition for service, he declared in a letter to the group, "unless by a call so general and unequivocal that it would be an endorsement by the people of my endeavors to defend the Constitution and the reserved rights of the several commonwealths, comprising what was once, in fact, the Federal Union." Those who suggested he had no party were wrong. Seeing himself as the defender of the Republic, he added: "Caesar had a party, and Pompey and Crassus had a party, but . . . the commonwealth had none." The president went on to endorse a lowering of tariffs and concluded: "Whilst I know that the struggle for the rights of the people and for defense of the Constitution is not yet over, yet believing that with the failure to do violence to that great instrument and the Executive office, the worst that faction for the present can do has been accomplished," he expressed hope that the next candidate would defend and protect the Constitution.[8]

But Johnson really had no chance of obtaining the nomination. The Democrats had never forgiven him for becoming Lincoln's running mate in 1864, nor had they been satisfied with his patronage policy. True, for a short time during the campaign of 1866 he had sought to purge the civil service of some of his enemies; on the whole, however, the public offices remained in the hands of his opponents. He simply had never removed enough Republicans to please the opposition. "I feel sick at heart . . . ," wrote John Tapley, a Wisconsin supporter, to Senator Doolittle on June 5, "when I look over the state and see the patronage of the government in the hands of . . . your enemies and Mr. Johnson's." He thought nineteen of every twenty officeholders were "bitter radicals." While Tapley's estimate may have been exaggerated, Johnson, in hopes of attracting the moderates after all, had indeed refused to heed the advice of friends to make use of the most potent weapon at his disposal.[9]

Thus the Democrats were unwilling to take their chances with him. As James B. Bingham complained, Johnson was obviously the strongest candidate against Grant, but the Democratic leaders had been foolish during the last two years. "Instead of *aiding* you, they have stood aloof and given you a cold shoulder, and permitted you to fight the . . . enemies of the constitution solitary and alone," he wrote to the president. The most they were willing to do was to contemplate "administering on his estate," as Washington McLean of the Cincinnati *Enquirer* put it.[10]

But Johnson refused to give up. It did not matter that George H. Pendleton, the Ohio Democrat who had endorsed the payment of government bonds in greenbacks whenever possible, had won a clear majority of the delegates in the West or that Chief Justice Chase was also fishing for the Democratic nomination or that General Hancock and Horatio Seymour, the wartime governor of New York, were both strong candidates—the president wanted his vindication. As he saw it, during the last two years and more a great political contest had been waged for the government and the Union, a struggle involving their existence, but neither Seymour nor Chase had done anything to sustain those who were battling for the country. And although his friends and agents on the ground informed him that the outlook was bad, he continued to hope for success. On July 3, when Colonel Moore remarked to Johnson that he wished the Democrats would nominate him, the president answered: "Why should they not take me up. They profess to accept my measures; they say I have stood by the Constitution and made a noble struggle. It is true I am asked why don't I join the Democratic party. Why don't they join me . . . if I have administered the office of President so well?"[11]

The Democratic Convention opened on July 7. The platform was all Johnson could wish for. Specifically declaring "that the President of the United States, in exercising the powers of his high office and resisting the aggressions of Congress upon the Constitutional rights of the States and the people, is entitled to the gratitude of the whole American people," it tendered to him the party's thanks "for his patriotic efforts in that regard." But the balloting did not please him at all. Surprisingly, after Thomas A. R. Nelson nominated him, Johnson showed much greater strength than had been expected, running second with 65 votes to Pendleton's 105 on the first ballot; but he gradually lost his support, mainly to Pendleton and Hancock, until only a few delegates from Tennessee stood by him. Most of his votes came from the South, and when on the twenty-second ballot Seymour finally obtained the prize, Johnson's support had dwindled to four votes from his home state.[12]

Throughout the balloting, the president, more anxious than ever for vindication, remained hopeful. Even while losing delegates, he sent a defiant telegram to his agent, George H. Parker. "The will of the people, if truly reflected, would not be doubtful. I have experienced ingratitude so often, that any result will not surprise me. . . . You have no doubt read in this morning's paper Stevens' Articles of Impeachment together with his speech thereon, in which he states 'the block must be brought out and the axe sharpened;' [and that] 'the only recourse from intolerable tyranny is Brutus' dagger,' which he hopes may not be used." But how could one maintain "any position against a vindictive and powerful majority" if abandoned by those who professed to agree with the administration? "Such an abandonment . . . would seem an admission that the administration was wrong." Johnson was perfectly willing to have the dispatch published so that the question of the impeachment might be kept "before the public," and even during the final day of the convention, with all signs pointing to his defeat, he still appeared to harbor some hope that the delegates might finally compromise upon his name. Then, shortly after noon on July 9, he received word that Seymour had been nominated, and although he said little, Moore could see how deeply he felt the disappointment.[13]

The aftermath of the convention left Johnson in a bitter mood. It is true that during a cabinet meeting on the day following its adjournment, he seemed more composed, but he made no secret of his anger. Seymour was personally hostile to him, he told John Van Buren. The governor had even desired his removal, and the president threatened not to endorse the ticket. Friendly newspapers expressed their regrets, supporters suggested the formation of a third party, and many expressed their fury at the ingratitude of the Democrats.[14]

Yet Seymour needed Johnson's support, and his backers tried to secure it. J. W. Leftwich, alarmed at rumors that the president would not rally behind the Democratic ticket, warned that because of the great enthusiasm for it in Tennessee, such a course would be detrimental. Johnson must declare himself in favor of it. Sam Ward, the famous "King of the Lobby," went further. Explaining to Manton Marble that Johnson, whom he had seen on the last day of July, had been quite specific "upon the absurdity of a ticket and a party expecting his support while treating him with disregard—not to say uncommon indecency," he argued that the president had great power to aid or injure the cause and suggested that he be placated. Seymour then approached Johnson through John F. Coyle of the *National Intelligencer* and let him know how much he admired him. He would take the ex-president's counsel if elected, he promised. Sanford Church also came to see him on the party's behalf. While Johnson still remained silent, in the end he did endorse the Democratic ticket.[15]

In the meantime, there was little he could do about the progress of congressional Reconstruction. After all, he had made certain commitments to the moderates, and he had to keep them. There could be no further attorney general's interpretations of the Reconstruction Acts ameliorating their effects; there could be no additional efforts to test their constitutionality, and there could be no renewed attempts to win over the commanding general of the army. "Andy has behaved very well so far," Fessenden was able to report on June 12, "and I think he will hold on until after the convention."[16]

But Johnson could still voice his objections, and voice them he did. Refusing to forgo his negative in view of his strong convictions of his constitutional duty, he continued to reiterate his disapproval of the Reconstruction Acts. Thus on June 20 the president vetoed the measure to readmit Arkansas under its new constitution. His consent, he declared, would mean his admission that the acts were constitutional. "My opinion, however," he continued, "in reference to these acts has undergone no change, but on the contrary, has been strengthened by the results which have attended their execution. Even were this not the case, I could not consent to a bill which is based upon the assumption either that by an act of rebellion of a portion of its people the State of Arkansas seceded, or that Congress may at its pleasure expel or exclude a State from the Union."

Nor had Johnson forgotten his role as protector of the white race. In April Colonel Moore noted that "the President has at times exhibited morbid distress and feeling against the negroes." On one occasion, annoyed at the sight of some blacks working in the White House gardens, he asked peevishly whether all white men had been discharged. The evident discrimination against white people, he thought, "was sufficient to excite the disgust of all reflecting men." In his veto message to the Arkansas measure he recurred to the subject. The constitution of the state might enfranchise blacks, but, he asserted, "it is well known that a large portion of the electorate in all the States, if not a large majority of all of them, do not believe in or accept the political equality of Indians, Mongolians, or negroes with the race to which they belong." It was an argument with appeal, for, as the humorist Petroleum Nasby had written, "The Democrat may not always understand the finanshel question, or not havin any bonds to be paid, or greenbax to pay 'em with, he may possibly not care a continental cuss about it. But on the negro he is alluz alive, alluz active, alluz vigilant. Whenever he is brot face to face with a nigger, his proud Caucassian blood tu wanst rebels, and he instinktively strikes." But the Republicans were in control, and they overrode the veto on the same day it was received.[17]

Five days later Johnson also vetoed the Omnibus Bill to admit all the remaining states except Virginia, Texas, and Mississippi. The message was brief—he stated that it was not necessary to repeat all the grave constitutional questions about Reconstruction as he had already cited them in his Arkansas veto. The House repassed the bill within thirty minutes, and the Senate did not take much longer.

The admission of the Southern states made possible the ratification of the Fourteenth Amendment, and Congress, on June 25, made it the duty of the president to make known the action of the states within ten days of their receipt. Accordingly, on July 11 Johnson, still determined to signify his disapproval, reported that a document "purporting to be a resolution of the legislature" of Florida had been received at the Department of State on June 16, "prior to the passing of the Act," and one from North Carolina had arrived on July 4. Then he proclaimed that North Carolina had ratified the amendment. Because Florida had done so within fewer than the ten days stipulated by Congress, he left that state out of the proclamation, so that Republican papers, with considerable gusto, could delight in criticizing this "silliness." On the fourteenth, however, Johnson was constrained to transmit to the Senate the notification of the final ratification of the amendment, unpleasant as it was for him.[18]

One week later the president seized another opportunity to voice his objections to a bill he considered unconstitutional. In order to prevent any difficulty in the forthcoming presidential election, Congress had passed a measure excluding the electoral votes of states that had not yet been reorganized. Naturally, Johnson dissented. Ever since the adjournment of the New York Convention, Judge Nicholson of Tennessee had been staying with him at the White House, and he now put Nicholson to work drafting a veto. The finished message stated that the bill was based on the theory that the affected states were not entitled to representation, an idea that Johnson had been consistently denouncing. He not only asserted that Congress had no power to receive or reject electoral votes, but again argued that votes cast under the Reconstruction Acts were illegal. Moreover in the Southern states, as in many of their Northern counterparts, only a portion of the population had rebelled. Hence these commonwealths could no more be deprived of representation than New York, where many had been disloyal. This veto, too, was quickly overridden.[19]

As Johnson thus continued to reiterate his interpretation of the Constitution, he also persisted in his efforts to democratize elections— for the presidency, the Senate, and the judiciary. Ever since his service in the House of Representatives, he had favored constitutional amendments to bring about these changes, and now he renewed his efforts. With Nicholson's help, he drafted proposals recommending again that presidents be elected for one six-year term, directly rather than by the electoral college; that senators likewise be elected by the people rather than the state legislatures, and that justices of the Supreme Court be popularly chosen for terms of twelve years. The cabinet opposed these suggestions. Seward believed that a six-year presidential term was wrong; Johnson would have been convicted had it been in effect, he said. McCulloch and Welles agreed with Seward, and Schofield and Randall remained noncommittal. But the president insisted; he sent the message to Congress, where it was promptly buried. He had again proved his consistency.

Johnson also kept up his opposition to the Freedmen's Bureau. On July 25 he returned with his disapproval a measure prolonging the agency's life for another year. The bill interfered with the "appointing power conferred by the Constitution upon the Executive," he said. But this veto, too, was speedily overturned.[20]

In economic matters as well, Johnson kept to his old-fashioned Jeffersonian-Jacksonian views. While after considerable reflection he signed a bill taxing tobacco and distillers, late in July he pocketed a funding measure refinancing the outstanding government bonds. As a longtime believer in hard money and opponent of the new bonds' exemption from taxation, he could do nothing else. "The plundered laboring masses of the country will appreciate this act of the President, and thank him for his firmness," commented the *National Intelligencer*. In fact, he still conceived of himself as the protector of the common people.[21]

On July 27 Congress finally adjourned. As it had done a year before, however, it made provision to meet again in September should this seem necessary, putting Johnson on notice that he would be watched closely. So threatening did this maneuver seem to Thomas Ewing that he thought impeachment would be renewed in the coming session, but when the appointed day in September arrived, the legislators recessed once more, this time to October 16, when they met and adjourned again. No further action was taken in the matter of impeachment. Moreover, Johnson's most implacable foe, Thaddeus Stevens, had died on August 11.[22]

The presidential campaign was now going into high gear. Still miffed, Johnson broke his silence after the October elections, when it appeared that the Democratic ticket was in serious straits. In a telegram to Seymour, he expressed his pleasure that the candidate was about to take a personal part in the contest. "Let the living principles of a violated Constitution be proclaimed and restored," he wired, "that peace, prosperity and fraternal feeling may return to a divided and oppressed nation." Yet there was talk of Johnson's replacing Seymour as the Democrats' standard bearer, and he did not seem uninterested. The cabinet was reported split. Schofield's May 25 letter supporting Grant was republished in October. Shortly before the election Seward delivered a speech at Auburn seemingly endorsing the general, though never mentioning his name. Evarts, too, was counted in the Republican column, while McCulloch, Welles, Browning, and Randall favored Seymour. In general, however, the secretaries maintained a studied silence. When Grant finally won, Johnson was disappointed. "He seemed disheartened that the people of the country should have voted to continue Radical," Moore observed.[23]

Fortunately for the president, that fall he was able to achieve some successes, even though only temporary, with his Indian policy. Ever since he had assumed office, he had been plagued by Indian wars in the West, brought on by the advancing frontier's ever-increasing pressure upon the Native Americans. In the spring of 1865 Johnson had sent Senator Doolittle to the plains to try to make peace, but his efforts had been in vain. When the Indians massacred Captain William J. Futterman and his entire command on the Bozeman Trail in 1866, the War Department, in a belligerent mood, wanted to take over Indian affairs from Interior; all Johnson, who wanted peace, had been able do was to hope that the differences between the House and Senate on the issue would prevent the transfer from taking place. In accordance with a law of Congress, he appointed a peace commission, which succeeded in 1867 in concluding treaties with the Southern Indians at Medicine Lodge and in 1868 with the Sioux at Fort Laramie. For a moment it looked as if the army's main purpose, the clearing of Kansas and Nebraska of hostile Indians, had been achieved. The Arapahoe, Cheyenne, Apache, Comanche, and Kiowa were concentrated in the western part of the Indian Territory, and the Sioux, Crow, and others, in the western half of present-day South Dakota. In the long run, however, the Indian problem was not solved. Though the Sioux remained peaceful for a while, their Southern brethren soon went on the warpath again.[24]

In most other fields the president's lack of power was glaringly evident. He had been unable to win the presidential nomination; he had been incapable of influencing the outcome of the campaign; he was unable to stop the further progress of congressional Reconstruction, at least for the time being, and he could not even rid himself of subordinates he suspected of peculation. This problem became particularly glaring in connection with the Treasury.

Johnson had long distrusted Secretary McCulloch. Coyle, the editor of the *National Intelligencer*, was McCulloch's bitter enemy and undoubtedly influenced the president against him, so much so that during the impeachment trial Johnson suspected the secretary of secret opposition to him and seeking the favor of Congress. By July he even doubted McCulloch's loyalty to the Union. At any rate, the Treasury was staffed by many radicals, men like William E. Chandler, the assistant secretary, and Edward A. Rollins, the commissioner of internal revenue. Chandler quit in November 1867, but when in June Rollins sent Johnson a letter of resignation, he phrased the message in such a way as to make his resignation contingent upon confirmation of a successor. The president accepted the resignation on August 5; whether the office was really at his disposal during the congressional recess, however, was questionable.[25]

Nevertheless, Johnson was determined to get rid of Rollins, who was not only a radical but suspected of wrongdoing. Accordingly, he asked the solicitor of the Treasury, John M. Binckley, who had earlier supported the administration in the public prints, to go to Brooklyn to look into alleged whiskey frauds there. If charges against Rollins were warranted, Binckley was to bring them, which he promptly did. Appearing before the United States commissioner for the Southern District of New York, Binckley accused Rollins and others of bribery and conspiracy to evade payment of revenue upon distilled spirits. However, the local district attorney, Samuel J. Courtney, not only refused to cooperate but soon quarreled with Binckley, and the outcome was that the commissioner decided the charges were spurious. Obviously, the whiskey ring was too strong for the Treasury Department's solicitor.[26]

But Johnson was unwilling to give up. James Gordon Bennett, editor of the New York *Herald,* pointed out why the public at first supported the investigation only in a lukewarm fashion. It was thought that Johnson had expended his powers in fighting impeachment; now that he was showing his strength, he would be sustained. As the editor told an intermediary, "For the President, my compliments, and impress upon him the necessity of powerful action. This is his opportunity—his last chance before retiring from office—let him embrace it! If he is successful in his effort, he will have achieved much to perpetuate his name; and it will be a great and crowning glory to all else he has accomplished to popularize his name for future ages." Apparently, Johnson agreed. At any rate, he continued the investigation, only to be stymied once again, this time by a committee of Congress. He simply could not overcome his unpopularity, even when he was right.[27]

When Congress met again in December, the president used his last annual message to lay his views once more before the country. He minced no words. Maintaining that most, if not all, of the nation's troubles were due to violations of the organic law, he cited the Reconstruction Acts as an example. "After a fair trial they have substantially failed," he asserted, "and proved pernicious in their results. . . . States to which the Constitution guarantees a republican form of government have been reduced to military dependencies," and three of them were yet unrepresented in Congress. Then he turned to his well-known views on race relations. "The attempt to place the white population under the domination of persons of color in the South has impaired, if not destroyed, the friendly relations that had previously existed between them; and mutual distrust has engendered a feeling of animosity which, leading in some instances to collision and bloodshed, has prevented that cooperation between the two races so essential to the success of industrial enterprise in the Southern States." Again reviewing the history of Reconstruction, Johnson maintained that all would have been well had Congress admitted the Southern members in 1865. Once more excoriating the Tenure of Office Act, he also urged the repeal of the command of the army provisions of the Military Appropriations Act for 1868, and, reiterating all his previous arguments, he repeated his proposals for constitutional amendments. In addition, in keeping with Seward's expansionist views, he strongly endorsed the acquisition of certain Caribbean islands.

The most sensational part of the message, however, dealt with his financial proposals. After stating in good Jacksonian fashion that a permanent public debt would create a favored class of a few, dangerous to the government, the president asserted that the bondholders had already received more than enough to compensate them. Hence he advocated the application of 6 percent interest paid upon the debt to the reduction of the principal in semiannual installments, so that the entire debt would be extinguished in fewer than seventeen years. Also, still the orthodox Jacksonian, he called for a speedy resumption of specie payments and the return to specie currency. A strange combination of Jacksonian hard money views with the implied repudiation of national obligations, the message revealed the president's failure to come to grips with the country's main financial problems, and the newspapers were quick to call him to task for it.[28]

The message was Johnson's own idea; the cabinet was less than enthusiastic about it. Welles criticized the financial proposals, though he liked the parts dealing with Reconstruction; Browning was opposed to the reiteration of the president's proposed amendments; and Seward could only approve of the Caribbean suggestions, probably his own idea. It was not surprising that the message was not well received. The Senate, declaring that its members cherished and upheld the good faith of the United States, passed a resolution utterly disapproving of and condemning the president's sentiments, and the House followed suit. Joseph Medill of the Chicago *Tribune* called them "a mess of d——d trash," *Harper's Weekly*, "an insult to common honesty and common sense," and the Republican press in general fiercely denounced what it considered a scheme of repudiation. Johnson himself was disappointed; he had hoped some of the soft money radicals would rally to his defense. But his combination of hard money views and calls for repudiation was too unorthodox a program to fit into neat economic theories. To be sure, his friends tried to defend him: he was merely suggesting that agreement be reached with bondholders for a terminable annuity, a process that would maintain the nation's credit and yet pay off its debt, explained the *National Intelligencer*, and Francis Blair expressed his heartfelt concurrence. But the general reaction was negative. Johnson simply no longer had the ear of the nation.[29]

With his usual stubbornness, however, the president persisted in hewing to his course. In spite of all opposition, he had, during his term of office up to the beginning of 1869, issued 13,914 pardons, 13,350 for participation in rebellion and 564 for crimes, and he was certain that the general amnesty without exception that he had wanted to issue on July 4 was long overdue. Consequently, on December 25, 1868, he issued a Christmas proclamation extending amnesty to all former insurgents, presumably including even Jefferson Davis. The outraged Senate demanded that he explain by what authority he had acted, and he responded with a recital of the history of presidential amnesties from Washington to Lincoln. But Johnson did not stop there. He took advantage of the last months of his term to pardon such varied offenders as the remaining prisoners at the Dry Tortugas, Dr. Samuel A. Mudd, Edman Spangler, and Samuel B. Arnold, as well as the despicable Sanford Conover, alias Dunham. He also ordered the bodies of the executed assassins of Lincoln to be turned over to their families. However, no matter how much those affected pleaded with him, he refused to withdraw the proclamation of May 4, 1865, implicating Jefferson Davis and other Confederate leaders in the assassination conspiracy.[30]

On December 30 Johnson turned sixty. Still vigorous, he continued to make a striking impression upon visitors. "His appearance is remarkable," wrote a reporter a few months earlier. "The dark eyes are deep set and peer out like shining orbs under a massive brow, on each side of which fall a lock of raven hair; below, the nose is aquiline and the mouth firm set and vigorous, with an expression of determination bordering on obstinacy. In stature he is middle sized, well built, of strong physique and well balanced muscular development." The journalist was greatly taken with his "striking and impressive presence and his excellent manners at public receptions." Charles Dickens, who also met the president during his 1867–68 trip to America, agreed. "I was very much impressed with the President's face and manner," was his comment. "It is, in its way, one of the most remarkable faces I have ever seen. Not imaginative, but very powerful in its firmness (or perhaps obstinacy), strength of will, and steadiness of purpose." Dickens was also struck by Johnson's obviously composed manners as well as his excellently tailored clothes. Whatever people might say about the president, he was a dignified head of state.[31]

To celebrate his birthday, Johnson hosted a children's party at the White House for some two to three hundred youngsters. Carpeting was laid to receive the young guests; the private dining and anterooms were turned into girls' and boys' dressing rooms. The marine band played, the Green, Blue, and Red rooms were richly adorned with flowers, and a whole suite of apartments on the first floor was thrown open for the guests to meet the president's grandchildren. The gathering was nonpartisan, Welles was happy to record, except that General Grant did not permit his children to attend. Two days later, at the New Year's reception, another large crowd appeared, this time Washington dignitaries, including, of all people, General Butler, who said there was a difference between Johnson the man and the president, and he had nothing against the former. The general's unexpected appearance in the Blue Room to shake the president's hand caused a sensation.[32]

Johnson liked nothing better than to play with his grandchildren. He loved to take them to Rock Creek, where they could take off their shoes and go wading. The children's reception on the occasion of his birthday was another indication of his fondness for them, and even Eliza, who had not been well at all, made an appearance at the party. There were now five grandchildren altogether, two boys and three girls, the Pattersons' two children and the Stovers' three. The oldest of these was Lillie Stover, thirteen years old in 1868, followed by her sister Sarah, nine, Andrew Johnson Patterson, nine, Mary Belle Patterson, eight, and Andrew Johnson Stover, eight. Sixty years later one of Andrew Stover's friends remembered how he used to visit the boy at the White House, and how the president brimmed with humor and asked the children's views on various subjects. These were the rare occasions when he could relax and reveal a personality different from the one he presented to the public.[33]

Johnson was also still engaged in managing his private fortune. Always a good businessman, especially in matters of real estate, he now bought a 350-acre farm six miles east of Greeneville, with two flour mills, water power, and rail connections. With the grain he milled, he not only made money, but amused himself by feeding the mice in the White House.[34]

As time went on, Johnson became more and more impressed with his secretary of state. No matter how much Seward's enemies pressed for his dismissal, no matter how often he was attacked, Johnson retained the experienced New Yorker, and the diplomatic successes of the administration must be ascribed to Seward. Not only had he successfully maneuvered the French out of Mexico without war, but he had also completed the purchase of Alaska, even though the House of Representatives tried to hold up payments in the hope that Johnson might be removed. In the summer of 1868, however, the House finally appropriated the necessary sums, and the famous bargain was carried out. Seward also acquired Midway Island in the Pacific, although some of his other expansionist schemes, such as the purchase of bases in the Caribbean and of the Danish West Indies, failed. The latter attempt was embarrassing; the Danes were willing to sell, and the local population approved of the transfer in a plebiscite, but Congress refused to go through with the transaction. Seward did, however, succeed in signing a treaty with the Chinese embassy headed by Anson Burlingame, the former congressman from Massachusetts, now employed by the imperial government, and Johnson, who had carefully studied Chinese antiquities, had the pleasure of receiving the embassy and its colorful delegates in the White House.[35]

Just before the end of Johnson's term, the secretary was hopeful of settling long-standing disputes with Great Britain, particularly the debts arising from British complicity in the escape of the Confederate cruiser *Alabama*, which had inflicted tremendous losses on American shipping. In July the president appointed Reverdy Johnson minister to the Court of St. James. In keeping with senatorial courtesy, the senator was confirmed, but the treaties he negotiated were not popular. Seward ordered him to revise the treaties, and several changes were made in America's favor. But even with these, the protocol was roundly defeated after Johnson left the White House, partly because of antagonism to him, and partly because the text failed to include any sort of apology for the damage done. At any rate, Charles Sumner, the chairman of the Senate Committee on Foreign Relations, thought that the only way in which Great Britain could discharge her debt was to pay the entire cost of the war after Gettysburg, a sum of over $2 billion, which could only be satisfied by the cession of Canada. Thus Andrew Johnson could hardly be blamed for the failure of the Johnson-Clarendon Convention, as the abortive treaties were called, even though he might have foreseen its unpopularity.[36]

The time was now drawing near when Johnson would leave the White House. Speculation was rife about his future plans; it was generally assumed that he would seek office again, perhaps first as governor of Tennessee and then as United States senator. But there were also reports of a possible career as a railroad official. The president said nothing, although it was certain that he would attempt to seek vindication in one way or the other.[37]

Johnson did not propose to leave the office he had occupied for almost four years without a continued fight for his principles. He vetoed a tariff on copper on the grounds that it would diminish the federal revenue while enriching corporations and monopolies at the expense of the poor, who would be saddled with additional taxes. He sought to defend the right of the Department of the Interior to administer black schools in the District of Columbia by disapproving of a measure that would have put them under the control of the school boards of Washington and Georgetown. He pocketed still another funding bill. In addition, throughout the last year of his administration, Johnson took advantage of the reorganization of the Southern military districts, occasioned by the return of many of the reconstructed states, by appointing generals like Alvan C. Gillem in Mississippi, George G. Meade in

Georgia, and Lovell H. Rousseau in Louisiana. He continued to assist conservative Southerners wherever possible. Thus he refused to sustain Governors Henry Clay Warmouth in Louisiana and Rufus Bullock in Georgia in their requests for aid against terror, and both states were carried by the Democrats.

To explain his policies once more, in February 1869 the president delivered a short talk to a group of Georgetown College cadets who had come to wish him a happy retirement. Reiterating his conviction that he had tried to uphold the Constitution, he warned his young visitors against incompetent rulers who might lead the country toward a monarchical form of government. It was obvious that he was referring to his successor, for he was still the old Andrew Johnson, tenacious to the last.[38]

In effect, his administration had not been unsuccessful, at least not from his own point of view. His policies had so strengthened the Southern conservatives that he had greatly complicated the task of integrating the freedmen into society, if he had not made it impossible at that time. The very lives of Unionists and blacks were often in danger. "The decided & emphatic endorsement of Andrew Johnson of the cruel murders at New Orleans & his known sympathy with the perpetrators, is producing its daily fruits," a Southerner informed Stevens in April 1868. "A state of war is felt to be in existence still, by these deluded people, & under cover of the favorable countenance of the President, they justify themselves in the murder of Union men, as common enemies." In Mississippi, radicals were certain that the loss of the state constitution framed in accordance with the Reconstruction Acts was the administration's fault, and a local correspondent, writing to Sumner, ascribed to the president's influence the unspeakable terror unleashed against Union men and the horror of blacks murdered in cold blood. As the collector of customs at Natchez complained in January 1869, in his district General Gillem had long been "the willing tool of President Johnson in so executing the Reconstruction Acts of Congress as to defeat the will of the American people." In Georgia Joshua Hill in June 1868 warned E. B. Washburne that administration influence would throw the state into the Democratic camp, while in Florida radical Unionists asserted that their opponents were kept in power through the same agency. The president had evidently not labored in vain.[39]

The last problem of the administration was the transfer of power. Johnson was worried about the coming ceremonies on March 4, when Grant was to be inaugurated. In discussions with Welles, he considered the matter. After all, the general had refused to allow his children to attend the birthday party at the White House; he had gone to Philadelphia to avoid Johnson's New Year reception, and he had allegedly deceived the president. Johnson thought that perhaps, together with the cabinet, he ought to make an appearance at the Capitol and then leave again. Welles rejoined that it was not necessary to be present at all. Had not John Quincy Adams stayed away from Jackson's inauguration? Johnson thought it over, and after a few days, inclined toward Welles' opinion. Reflecting that he could not, with proper self-respect, witness the inauguration of a man whom he considered a deliberate deceiver, especially after finding Grant's letter to Sheridan of July 24, 1867, authorizing the latter to disregard the attorney general's opinion, he decided to stay away. The matter continued to be discussed in cabinet, but, despite Seward's and Evarts' advice to the contrary, the president did not change his mind.[40]

During the last weeks of the administration, interrupted only briefly by a scare when a crazed woman was found wandering in the executive mansion with the intention of killing him, Johnson continued to discharge his social functions, which culminated in a great public reception at the White House on the evening of March 3, 1869. On the fourth, inauguration day, the cabinet met at nine o'clock in the morning. A large number of bills had to be signed, though Johnson still pocketed a number of them. It was only right that Congress should forward the bills to the White House, he said. Some of the cabinet members were still hoping that he might attend the inauguration after all. Evarts did not even take off his overcoat, and when Seward walked in at last, smoking his cigar, he asked if all were ready. The president, however, kept writing. At last the secretary of state said, "Ought we not to start immediately?" only to hear Johnson reply that he was inclined to think he would finish at the White House. In view of the fact that Grant himself had refused to ride in the same carriage with him, and the congressional committee had arranged for two vehicles, the president's decision not to attend was understandable.

Shortly after noon, after shaking hands with each of them, Johnson took leave of his official advisers. Then, accompanied by Colonel Moore, he led them downstairs to the portico of the main entrance, where he stepped into his carriage and was driven away to the house of his friend Colby of the *National Intelligencer*. The inauguration went ahead without him.[41]

But Johnson managed to fire one last parting shot. In a Farewell Address to the American People, he once more sought to justify himself. Taking pride in his refusal to lend his aid to "purposes and plans 'outside of the Constitution,'" and to "become an instrument to schemes of confiscation and of general and oppressive disqualifications," he reminded the people that he had disbanded an army of nearly a million men and had preserved the peace. He again declared that his sole ambition had been "to restore the Union of the States, faithfully to execute the office of President, and, to the best of my ability, preserve, protect, and defend the Constitution." After once more attacking the Reconstruction policies of Congress, Johnson finished with one of his typical flourishes. "Forgetting the past," he wrote, "let us return to the first principles of the Government, and, unfurling the banner of our country, inscribe upon it, in ineffaceable characters, 'The Constitution and the Union, one and inseparable.' "[42]

The address was not well received. It was a display of "bad temper," commented the *New York Times.* But it was the New York *Herald* that made the most telling observation. "These parting words of the retiring President might have done very well at some political gathering in Tennessee . . .," it wrote. "But as they stand they smell of chagrin, distrust, ill nature and bad blood."[43] Of course, the paper was right. The president had never abandoned the style of politicking that he had so successfully employed in his home state. That it did not go over well in the country at large was not surprising. That it would still work in Tennessee, however, he was to prove in the years that were left to him.

Johnson's Farewell Address was his last effort at obtaining vindication while still in office, but he did not really have to justify himself. Considering the effect of his policies upon the South, he had achieved at least in the long run what he wanted, the continued existence of viable Southern state governments within the Union and the maintenance of white supremacy. His boost to Southern conservatives by undermining Reconstruction was his legacy to the nation, one that would trouble the country for generations to come.

XIX

EX-PRESIDENT

~~~

JOHNSON was now out of office for the first time since 1839. But his retirement from the presidency did not mean that he would withdraw from politics as well. He was much too ambitious and restless, to say nothing about his desire for vindication—vindication for his policies, for his contentions, and for his administration. And he did not wait long to prepare for his comeback.

The first opportunity arose when he was still in Washington with the Coyles, where he stayed for some two weeks. He had not come to the capital in a hurry, he said, and he was not going to leave quickly. After receiving an invitation from the Common Council of Baltimore, on March 11 he took off for the city on the special train his hosts had provided. He arrived at eleven in the morning, was greeted with great fanfare, and, accompanied by the mayor and governor, was driven to the Exchange in an open carriage. After a festive reception there, he went to Barnum's Hotel, where he was an honored guest at a dinner for two hundred people, including ex-secretaries Orville H. Browning and Alexander W. Randall, former governor Thomas Swann, and various members of Congress. In his reply to the toasts, Johnson complimented Maryland for having sustained him in his struggle for constitutional liberty and asserted that he felt more pride in being an American citizen than he would "in being inaugurated President on the ruins of a violated Constitution." Loud cheers greeted his talk.[1]

On March 18, accompanied by Eliza, Robert, the Pattersons, and

Mrs. Milligan, Johnson left for Greeneville. The trip was like a triumphant tour with grand receptions along the way. The city of Lynchburg, which had treated him so badly in 1861, gave him a splendid welcome, and, again responding to toasts, he expressed his gratification at the evident popular approval of his course. In Charlottesville, where he was also enthusiastically feted, he complied with a student's request for a speech. Admonishing the young people to study and stand by the Constitution, he again made use of the opportunity to stress his devotion to the basic law of the land.

These receptions were nothing compared with what followed when he reached Tennessee. From Bristol to Greeneville, one continuous procession made his homecoming memorable. In Greeneville itself, in the same spot where eight years before there had been displayed a banner reading "Traitor, Traitor," with a sketch of Johnson hanged in effigy, there was now a large flag with the inscription "Welcome Home" strung across the street. In spite of the steady drizzle, a large crowd had assembled at the depot. At the platform a delegation of young ladies led by Belle McGaughey, the granddaughter of the first customer of Johnson's tailor shop, greeted him with flowers, and then, together with his Knoxville friend Colonel John Williams, he rode to his house in a barouche. Thomas A. R. Nelson and others delivered welcoming speeches, to which the former president responded with appropriate remarks. After reviewing his career from alderman to president, Johnson said he was glad to be home and asserted he had no further ambitions. But judging by his later actions, this was merely a polite expression of unwonted modesty.[2]

Shortly after his return Johnson granted an interview to a Cincinnati *Commercial* reporter. As the two men sat in a room with portraits of Lincoln, Washington, and Jackson on the wall, the former president discoursed on the economic opportunities of East Tennessee. Capital ought to be invested in the region to develop it, he said. As for his policies, he insisted that he had always wanted peace. Johnson's "hair is now quite grey," his guest reported, "but otherwise there is nothing about him that would indicate his being over 45. His face is elegantly shaved, quite pale, as it always is, and in conversation he looks you straight in the face." It was obvious that the former president could not be considered an old man whose career was over.[3]

Late in March Johnson fell ill. His doctor said he was suffering from neuralgia with calculus, and in fact, he was again subject to another one of his frequent attacks of kidney stones. Alarming reports began to appear all over the country; one newspaper even reported that he had died. But, resilient as always, he quickly recovered and could soon again be seen walking through the village accompanied by a black youth whom he liked to take along on his lengthy strolls through the woods.[4]

The former president's recovery speeded his search for vindication. Hardly the type to sit still and accept a gracious retirement, he desperately wanted to return to Washington. Greeneville bored him, and he thought he might have a chance to obtain the Senate seat Joseph Fowler was about to vacate. To accomplish this goal, however, he would have to exercise all his political wiles. As he was hated by the die-hard secessionists for his Unionism and by the radicals for his abandonment of the Republican party, his only chance would be a split in either political organization.[5]

And such a division was about to take place. Governor Brownlow had resigned in order to become a U.S. senator; his successor was the speaker of the state senate, De Witt C. Senter, who was anxious to be reelected in his own right in August. But Senter was opposed by another Republican, the Middle Tennessee Unionist William B. Stokes, and he sought to beat Stokes by winning the votes of some of the conservatives, as the opposition, both former Whigs and Democrats, liked to call itself.

The conservatives now believed that their opportunity had come. The hated Brownlow, who had disfranchised so many of them, in fact all Confederate veterans by means of two franchise laws, and finally brought black suffrage to the state, had stepped down. Their opponents were at odds among themselves, and with Senter's help, particularly by his replacement of radical registrars with conservatives, they might circumvent Brownlow's Franchise Laws to elect a conservative legislature. Consequently, they refrained from nominating a candidate of their own—Johnson himself had been mentioned—and concentrated on the legislature.[6]

The ex-president quickly took advantage of this opportunity. Even before the nominating convention met, he set out on a speaking tour through the state and delivered addresses calculated to appeal to conservatives of all parties.

He started in Knoxville, where he arrived by special train and was welcomed by an enormous crowd of fifty thousand people. As they watched the solemn procession escorting Johnson to the Lamar House, the spectators could not fail to be affected. "That's him. He's the same old Andy yet," they shouted, and Johnson sought to confirm that impression by delivering one of his accustomed speeches. Maintaining that he had stood "as a breakwater at the head of the American people," he took credit for the preservation of the government. He maintained that he was more loyal than Brownlow and was responsible for freeing the slaves in Tennessee. He also attacked bondholders and announced that he would continue to seek vindication.

From Knoxville the former president traveled to Chattanooga, Murfreesboro, and finally Nashville, which he reached on April 7. Wherever he went, there were excited receptions; he would deliver his usual addresses, in which he appealed to the Democrats by advocating the removal of all political disabilities, attacking Grant, and giving himself credit for preserving the Constitution, while pleasing the Republicans and blacks by boasting about his part in bringing about emancipation in Tennessee.[7]

Johnson continued on to Memphis where, in a letter in reply to an address by the Irish Literary Association, he reminded the immigrant population of his anti–Know Nothing stand in years gone by. He was not going to neglect any potential support for his renewed quest for office.[8]

Then disaster struck. Robert, who had been unable to overcome his alcoholism, committed suicide, and the bereaved father had to return to Greeneville. Young Bob had wasted great opportunities; his service in the Tennessee legislature and his escape through the lines had given promise of a splendid career. Yet his affliction proved his undoing.[9]

Robert's death made Johnson more than ever concerned about his sole remaining son, Andrew, Jr., whom everybody still called Frank. Frank was then about to graduate from Georgetown College and sought to console his parents. He wrote his mother promising that he would never "let any kind of intoxicating liquors" pass his lips, and asking her to tell his father that with his two brothers gone, his son would make a man of himself "and be a comfort to both you and him in your old age." Johnson doubtless appreciated the letter. He advised Frank to "study well" and sent him some French stamps for his collection.[10]

After his bereavement, Johnson felt he had to get away. Taking advantage of the occasion of Frank's graduation, he traveled to Washington and stayed at the Metropolitan Hotel. In an interview there with a New York *Herald* reporter, he expressed his dislike of the new president. "The little fellow has nothing in him," he said. "He hasn't a single idea. He has no policy, no conception of what the country requires. . . . He is mendacious, cunning, and treacherous." Gratifying as these remarks were meant to be for the Democrats, Southern conservatives could be even more satisfied when he complained that with a total voting population of 200,000, Tennessee was being governed by 50,000 Negroes and 20,000 whites. On the day after his arrival, July 2, in answer to a serenade at the hotel, Johnson resumed his attacks on Grant and, for good measure, also lashed out against Congress and the increasingly unpopular bondholders.[11]

His declarations were well timed. After holding their convention, because of the rivalry between Stokes and Senter, the Republicans of Tennessee finally did split into two factions. At first Stokes tried to win over a few conservatives, but Senter countered with a promise of universal suffrage and began to replace registrars not favorable to his program. Johnson, who had been conferring confidentially with Senter before the final split of the party, naturally supported him; Senter's conservative policies would facilitate the ex-president's own return to the Senate.[12]

And so Johnson campaigned vigorously, attacking Jefferson Davis to please conservative Republicans and U. S. Grant to win over moderate Democrats. Even though at times hostile mobs threatened to attack him—he was nearly mobbed at Maysville on August 2—he pressed on, and the outcome was favorable. Senter won by a landslide, and the legislature chosen at the same time was solidly conservative, with some of the Senter candidates definitely pledged to vote for Johnson in the forthcoming senatorial election.[13]

This result rendered the former president's election probable; yet there were still some difficulties. Aside from the old antagonism of secessionists and the continuing fallout from his antiradical stance, many Tennesseans, and particularly those in his own part of the state, still cherished their Whig traditions, and those could easily be turned against the man who had ruined the party before the Civil War.[14] As usual, however, Johnson, disregarding all obstacles, kept forging ahead. He continued his public speaking, flattered the Whigs by eulogizing the recently deceased John Bell, and sought to make the most of his peculiar financial opinions.[15] And when the legislature met in October, the outlook was not unfavorable.

But Johnson's enemies had not been idle. The Nashville *Republican Banner* and the Memphis *Avalanche,* representing the former secessionists, to say nothing of the national administration speaking for the radicals, opposed him with every weapon at their disposal. The *Republican Banner* reminded its readers of what it called Johnson's harsh actions as military governor; Grant reputedly said that he would consider his predecessor's return to the Senate a personal insult, and in West Tennessee the conservative Unionst Emerson Etheridge remained his inveterate foe. It was clear that both Republicans and secessionists were out to defeat him.[16]

The legislature started balloting on October 19. By the twenty-first Johnson, with 48 votes to Etheridge's 41 and 24 scattered, was within 4 votes of the necessary majority, but on the next day his opponents, both radicals and secessionists, met in caucus and decided to concentrate on Judge Henry Cooper, the brother of Johnson's former secretary Edmund. Edmund deserted his friend in favor of his relative, and the result was that Johnson lost by a vote of 55–51. It was his first election defeat since 1837.[17]

He was terribly disappointed. Deeply resentful of the Coopers' desertion, he never forgot the injury his opponents, and particularly the Confederates, had inflicted upon him. In spite of his hurt, however, he hosted a sumptuous banquet for five hundred guests at the Stacey House in Nashville—according to the newspapers, a nonpolitical gathering.[18]

After this debacle Johnson returned to Greeneville. Although his neighbors were most deferential to their distinguished fellow citizen, he was not happy about living in the little mountain village—"It is a dull place and likely to continue so," he wrote to his son Frank. But his house was there and his children and grandchildren nearby. The Pattersons were still making their home at the farm some six miles from town, and Mary, who had married again, lived across the street from him, though she was often at the old Stover farm in Carter County. Unfortunately, she was not happy with her new husband, William R. Brown, and much to Johnson's embarrassment, there was talk about an impending divorce. "Squire Brown," he said to his son-in-law, "is there anything in the rumor that you are separating from my daughter, Mrs. Stover? Rather than have anything like that happen in my family, I would sooner have everything I have sunk in the depths of Hell." While Johnson was alive, the Browns stayed together, though they tended to live apart from each other. After his death they finally did obtain a divorce.[19]

Shortly after his return from Nashville, Johnson found a new friend. A young lawyer, a Democrat and former Confederate named E. C. Reeves, opened a law office in town, and within a week of his arrival the ex-president stepped inside, introduced himself, declined the offered chair, and walked back and forth, while young Reeves was, as he put it, standing at attention. Johnson offered Reeves some assistance with his incipient law practice, and their association grew from there. Reeves soon thereafter took over the Greeneville *National Union* and became the older man's amanuensis and secretary. Because the ex-president's right arm had never fully recovered from the old railroad accident, the young lawyer came twice a week to assist him with his writing and to read to him articles Johnson had marked in the many newspapers to which he subscribed. Johnson liked to have material read to him so that he would have an opportunity to discourse on his past. He would discuss the events of his administration, his hatred for Stanton and General Grant, and his reverence for Lincoln. But it was clear that while he admired the Civil War president, Andrew Jackson was his model, and Old Hickory's ideas still guided him.[20]

Politics with Johnson was not merely talk; it was his very life. And he had no intention of remaining inactive. His dislike for his passive life at Greeneville had not abated. "The town is as lifeless as a grave-yard," he wrote to an acquaintance, "and businessmen look like they were all attending funeral obsequies. In fact, all or nearly all our best citizens have gone." He himself wanted to leave, too—for Washington—and in the winter of 1869–70 he negotiated for the purchase of newspapers in Memphis to advance his interests. Nothing came of the deal, but he for one was convinced that his political career was not over.[21]

In fact, circumstances for a reentry into politics seemed favorable. A constitutional convention met in Tennessee in January 1870 to propose a new basic law obliterating the radical franchise legislation while including provisions for a poll tax. This tax would fall most heavily on the freedmen, so that the conservatives would be certain of victory in future elections. Johnson was in full agreement with the repeal of the franchise law—rebels were part of the people, he thought—but he did not like the poll tax because he held that payment for the right to vote merely favored the rich.[22] Nevertheless, when in March the new constitution was adopted, the certainty that the conservatives would dominate the state presented him with a renewed opportunity to vindicate himself by reelection to Congress. If he could succeed in appealing to moderate conservatives as well as to moderate Republicans, he might be able to overcome the opposition of the two extremes, the Confederate brigadiers and the radical Republicans.

The ex-president's real chance lay in the disunity of the conservative party. Consisting of former Whigs, Democrats, secessionists, and moderate Unionists, the party found it difficult to surmount its differences. In 1870, in the first gubernatorial election under the new constitution, former secessionist Whigs favored General John Calvin Brown, the president of the recent constitutional convention, while the former Democrats supported Generals William Brimage Bate and William A. Quarles. Though Bate had been an ardent secessionist, he now sympathized with Johnson, as did Quarles, but eventually both withdrew from the race. Some Democrats were in favor of turning to the Greeneville statesman should Brown obtain the nomination; others wanted Johnson to run for Congress in his home district, but he declined. Apparently, he thought the time was not yet ripe, and in any case, he was more interested in the Senate.

The ensuing election confirmed his fear that the Confederate military ring was now taking over the Democratic party. When the nominating convention rejected resolutions declaring that the war had settled the secession question, nominated Brown, and adopted a plank calling for the immediate "restoration" of all Southern states, Johnson refused to endorse the candidate and in a forceful speech at Gallatin denounced the plank as secessionist and revolutionary. Counseling close cooperation with the Northern Democrats, he supported the independent candidacy of the Memphis industrialist Arthur S. Colyar. In the end Colyar withdrew, and Brown was elected governor, but the Confederates' vindictiveness alienated so many moderates that Johnson could see his chance for the future.[23]

For the time being, he continued to keep his credentials before his fellow citizens. In January 1871 he wrote to the Pittsburgh Young Men's Jacksonian Association, again stressing the importance of amendments to the Constitution for the direct election of presidents and senators and staggered terms for Supreme Court justices. He declared that Old Hickory was still his model, that societies bearing Jackson's name should organize for the purpose of doing away with party conventions, and expressed similar sentiments to former senator Edgar Cowan. In May Johnson took a prominent part in an Industrial Exposition held at Knoxville. Accompanied by dignitaries, he rode in a carriage directly behind the tailors' contingent and delivered a speech once more emphasizing his indentification with mechanics. He thundered against bondholders, cited his own career as an example of the American dream, advocated the sterilization of criminals, and once more proclaimed his allegiance to the Constitution and the Union. "Let the country go on in its mechanism, and its agriculture and its labor," he declared, while reminding his audience of Jefferson's warnings against the dangers of big cities. His old agrarian appeal and his continued solidarity with mechanics was a facile way of uniting former Unionists and secessionists.[24]

To bring these factions together was more essential than ever to Johnson, because his unhappiness at his enforced retirement was becoming ever more pronounced. His sick wife, the lack of activity in the small town, and the absence of friends and relatives made him depressed. He wrote to Martha in June 1871, "Your mother does not seem very well today, continues in bed, yet complaining of nothing unusual with less cough than common. Mary is away and none of the family have been over to see her today. . . . If convenient it would be well enough to come down tomorrow, and perhaps it would have some influence on her mind and spirits. The House seems abandoned by all and I am so solitary as though I were in the wilds of Africa." The restless old statesman had to have some public activity. As he wrote his daughter in December, "There is nothing of interest transpiring in Greeneville[;] all is dull and flat. I long to be set free from this place forever I hope."[25]

What he meant by the last phrase is not quite clear, but he had been reported on his way to Europe for some time.[26] Perhaps he was really thinking of going, although in the last analysis, it was political activity that always provided him with the excitement he craved. And in 1872 Johnson thought he saw a renewed chance for himself. The Grant administration, with its failure to achieve civil service reform, inability to bring Reconstruction to a successful conclusion, and ill-conceived effort to annex the Dominican Republic, had become very unpopular with many reformers. A Liberal Republican party emerged, made up of all sorts of opponents of the president, which finally nominated Horace Greeley as their candidate. The Democrats, attracted by the Liberals' platform calling for an end of radical rule in the South, also endorsed the ticket.

This situation presented Johnson with new options. At first he declined an offer to run for Congress in the First District, but when Tennessee obtained an additional seat entitling it to a congressman at large, he reconsidered. General Benjamin F. Cheatham, with whom he had collaborated before the war, became the Democratic or conservative candidate, but although in the beginning Johnson hesitated to enter the lists against a former associate, he could not forget that Cheatham represented the same Confederate military clique that had defeated him for the Senate in 1869. In addition, if he made the race, he would most probably throw the election to Horace Maynard, the Republican contender, so that the Republican party would become indebted to him. And while he had no hope of winning in 1872, he could still prevent Cheatham from becoming a congressman, advertise his availability, and hope for a future election to the Senate.[27]

To enter the race was not an easy decision. The papers were already charging him with having been intimate with a neighbor's wife, Mrs. Emily Harrell, who subsequently committed suicide. Although even the hostile New York Times pronounced the rumor unfounded, Johnson could expect to hear more about it if he challenged the Democratic candidate; nor was it certain that he could regain the party's support if he frustrated its efforts in 1872. But he needed a forum with which to put his record before the people of Tennessee; the Liberal Republican campaign gave him an opportunity to air his attacks upon Grant, and he was willing to gamble.

Before he finally made up his mind, the ex-president had occasion to revisit the halls of Congress to which he never ceased to aspire. Called to Washington to testify before the Military Affairs Committee of the House of Representatives, which was then investigating the disappearance of some of the records of General Buell's court of inquiry, he declared that his quarrel with the general in 1863 had never been a personal one, but had been a difference of opinion. He denied any knowledge of the whereabouts of the papers, which had disappeared before he took office. In fact, he had never seen them.[28]

After testifying, Johnson returned to Tennessee, where the Democratic Convention was about to meet. To take advantage of the Republican split, he now endorsed the candidacy of Horace Greeley. Not that he liked the Liberals' choice for president, he said in a speech at Knoxville, but Greeley was far better than Grant. He charged his successor with willingness to take bribes, running up the national debt, and causing the country to drift into a system of mobocracy and monarchy, offenses worse than anything with which he had ever been charged. Yet he had been impeached!

A few days later at Nashville Johnson essentially repeated these remarks. In a speech at the Exposition Building, he compared the president's liking for money and gifts with George Washington's unblemished record and repeated his insistence that the nation that had brought him to the bar for merely imagined technical offenses should certainly have stopped Grant. Then he told a reporter of the *Republican Banner* that Tennesseeans were "anxious to break the crust which was forming in this State." Asserting that a people's advocate was needed, he added that he was not afraid of the "snapping . . . at his heels." Then the Democratic Convention formally nominated Cheatham, outraging Johnson's supporters, particularly the immigrant population. Responding to a throng that demanded he make the race, he lashed out at conventions, military rings, and caucuses and replied that if he was needed, he was ready once again to do battle for the people and the Constitution.

After deciding to run for congressman at large, the ex-president pursued his candidacy with great vigor. Barnstorming through the state, he justified his record, blasted his opponents, and renewed acquaintances throughout Tennessee. Strong, fearless, and self-poised, he made a powerful impression on the voters. That Isham G. Harris was in the lists against him made him fight even harder. Was it not Harris who was reputed to have said years earlier that if Johnson were a snake he would lie in the grass and bite the heels of rich men's children? And if, as was likely and eventually would happen, his intervention would bring about a victory for Horace Maynard, at least he would have broken the military ring that had caused his defeat in 1869.[29]

The most interesting parts of the campaign were the debates between Johnson and Cheatham, in which Maynard at times participated.

Charging Cheatham with having labored for years to destroy the government and now wanting office in that same government, he mounted an all-out attack against the general. Except for his assaults on Grant, Johnson tended to concentrate on the Democratic rather than the Republican candidate. To a revival of accusations that he had been responsible for the execution of Mrs. Surratt, an innocent woman, he replied that it had been a military court and not he that had convicted her. Even Republican papers in the North reported that the candidate was much like the Johnson of old. In view of the fact that he was being persecuted by Confederate roughs, they even expressed renewed respect for him.

Typical of these debates was the one at Lebanon. Cheatham led off, followed by Johnson, who spoke so earnestly, quietly, and deliberately that not even the essentially hostile audience could fail to take notice. Maynard closed the proceedings, and many years later General Lillard Thompson, who was present, still recalled how utterly sincere the ex-president had been. After listening to Johnson several times, Thompson judged him the strongest man he ever saw swaying a popular audience. The speaker's blazing eyes seemed particularly unforgettable.

Yet neither the former president's evident dedication nor his impressive demeanor could change the fact that his entry into the campaign was a forlorn cause. Leading Democratic journals that had long supported him and prominent party leaders, particularly Democratic State Committeeman Francis C. Dunnington, turned violently against him—the committee widely distributed Dunnington's slashing campaign speech in pamphlet form—while Confederate sympathizers sought to make the most of his often-quoted statement that treason must be made odious and traitors punished. The result was that Maynard won with 80,250 votes to Cheatham's 66,106, Johnson coming in third with 37,903. He even lost Greene County.[30]

Johnson may have been defeated, but he had laid a foundation for the future. As Sam Milligan, still holding on to the judgeship on the Court of Claims to which his friend had appointed him, put it, the contest had given the people much information they had not had before, a fact that could not fail to produce good results for the state later on. And the campaign did much more, Milligan asserted. "It broke the military ring which dragged the young men of the State into rebellion & ruin" and taught the whole South that treason was not honorable. Young Frank, too, wrote to his father that, hurt and surprised though he was at the defeat, he consoled himself with the thought that the "ring" had been broken and its head, Cheatham, worsted.

Other supporters were also encouraging. C. J. Moody of Shelbyville assured Johnson that his friends would elect the next state legislature and make him U.S. senator in Brownlow's place. His Memphis friend Colonel Arthur S. Colyar likewise thought that if the ex-president refused openly to support the Republicans in the General Assembly and permitted the Cheatham Democrats to organize the legislature, he would be elected to the Senate within two years. In addition, the Republicans knew that they owed their victory to the Greeneville statesman, and even the Democrats in Congress regretted his defeat. There was indeed hope for the next round.[31]

But the following year, 1873, brought only trouble for the former president. To be sure, at first there was some talk of his moving to Nashville or of trying for the Senate because of rumors that Henry Cooper would resign; however, nothing came of it.[32] Then, during the summer, a cholera epidemic struck Tennessee. People fled from the dread disease, yet Johnson, helping where he could, stayed in Greeneville until he himself succumbed. When a doctor who diagnosed the disease persuaded the patient to leave, he was seriously ill.

The ex-president now thought that his time had come. On June 29, before leaving for Martha's farm, he wrote what he believed to be his last statement. "All seems gloom and despair," he confessed.

> I have performed my duty to my God, my country, and my family—I have nothing to fear—approaching death to me is the mere shadow of God's protecting ring—beneath it I feel almost sacred—here I know can no evil come—here I will rest in quiet and peace beyond the reach of calumny's poisoned shaft—the influence of envy and jealous enemies—where treason and traitors in state, backsliders and hypocrites in church can have no place—Here the great fact will be realized that *God is* truth and gratitude, the highest attribute of *men*. Adieu—sic iter ad astra—such is the way to the stars or immortality.

But his farewell message was premature. He was nursed back to health by Martha and the doctors, and by the end of July the newspapers were able to report that although he had been thought beyond help, he had indeed recovered.[33]

Soon after his bout with the cholera, Johnson suffered another setback. He had always been known for his excellent business sense, and even hostile newspapers admitted that his business capacity was "above the average for public men, for in his investments and business relations he manifests considerable shrewdness and tact." In fact, he had succeeded in becoming the wealthiest citizen of Greeneville. When he left the presidency, however, Johnson converted some $60,000 worth of bonds into cash and deposited it with the First National Bank of Washington at 6 percent per annum. At the time, it seemed a good invest-ment, but in September of 1873 the banking house of Jay Cooke failed, a collapse that ushered in a severe depression. The First National Bank went under, and Johnson's deposits, amounting by that time to some $73,000, seemed lost. The newspapers reported that he was ruined, an assertion he was able to refute. After all, he still owned between $35,000 and $40,000 in state bonds, to say nothing of his real estate holdings, including the Lowry block with its large brick storehouse in Greeneville, which he had acquired shortly after his return to the village. But al-though he eventually recovered most of his money in the bank, for the moment the outlook was bleak.[34]

To add to the former president's troubles, the case of Mrs. Surratt again became a matter of public contention. After the revival of the controversy during the 1872 campaign, on August 26, 1873, Judge Advocate General Holt, stung by charges that he had withheld from Johnson the petition for the commutation of the widow's death sen-tence, published in the Washington *Chronicle* a lengthy refutation he called *Vindication of Hon. Joseph Holt* . . . . Asserting that the president had indeed seen the petition, he produced letters from John A. Bing-ham, James Speed, James Harlan, and others to prove his point.

Of these depositions, Bingham's was the most significant. Dated Feb-ruary 17, 1873, it stated that the congressman, who had served as special judge advocate at Mrs. Surratt's trial, had brought the document to the attention of Secretary of War Stanton. Then, after hearing that the president had not seen it, Bingham called upon both Seward and Stan-ton to find out if the report was true. Both assured him that it was not, that the petition had been discussed by members of the cabinet in Johnson's presence, and that the president and his advisers had been unanimous in deciding to deny the petition. When Bingham told Stan-ton that the record ought to be made public, however, the secretary demurred and suggested he rely on the final judgment of the people.

The other letters seemed to support these assertions. Speed freely admitted that he had seen the petition; because he did not feel at liberty to divulge cabinet secrets, however, he refused to say more. Harlan, too, remembered that an informal discussion of the case had taken place in Johnson's presence and that one of his colleagues had vehemently ar-gued that sex was no excuse for crime, a point of view upon which there was general agreement. Two clerks of the Bureau of Military Justice confirmed that the petition had been attached to the record opposite the page Johnson signed. Obviously, these charges required a reply.[35]

Johnson took his time to answer, but in the meantime, he publicized his views whenever possible. In October, accompanied by young Frank, he traveled to Washington to take care of Holt's accusations as well as his own business affairs. Immediately after arriving at the Metropolitan Hotel, where he established his headquarters, he sent for Colonel Moore, presumably to confer about the charges. During his stay at the hotel, great numbers of friends visited him there. On October 23 he responded to a group of serenaders with a few remarks reaffirming his continued devotion to the "preservation of our institutions and the best interests of our country." Unfavorably comparing the days of Washington and Jefferson, when both parties agreed on the maintenance of constitutional safeguards against congressional excesses, with the present, Johnson counseled a firm reliance on a bullion currency and the withdrawal of all national bank notes, though he conceded the government's right to issue greenbacks. He also reiterated his demand for constitutional amendments for the direct election of the president and senators and thundered against monopolies. His well-wishers could hardly have been surprised at these sentiments.[36]

Then, after taking care of his business at the First National Bank by making out an affidavit for his claim to $73,000 to safeguard his interests, Johnson prepared his answer to Holt. As his friends had already pointed out, the judge advocate general's arguments were easy to refute. Why had Holt waited until both Seward and Stanton were dead? (Seward had died in 1872, Stanton in 1869.) And would not Bingham be naturally anxious to clear himself of complicity in Mrs. Surratt's execution? Additional information came from Welles, who reminded Johnson that no cabinet meeting in 1865 had ever dealt with the petition, to say nothing of the fact that the president had been so sick that between June 30 and July 7 his advisers had never formally met. Even Welles, however, admitted that at the time, the entire cabinet, including himself and Johnson, had thought the prisoner guilty.[37]

On November 12 the ex-president finally published his reply. Crisply written, it raised pointed questions that the judge advocate general would find difficult to answer. If Holt wanted to obtain Stanton's and Seward's testimony, why did he wait until both had died? And why, when the charges were first aired against him, did Holt not then ask for a court of inquiry? Emphasizing that the cabinet had not met between July 5 and 7, Johnson admitted that on the day of the execution, two days after the approval of the sentence, an informal discussion had taken place. But he insisted that Holt had discovered only one official who had laid eyes on the petition. That was Attorney General Speed, who, however, had seen it at the War Department and not at the White House. As for himself, he had been made aware of the document only on August 5, 1867, when he sent for the papers.

Then Johnson added a countercharge. If it was a crime to withhold the petition from the chief executive, as Holt admitted, then it was also a crime to withhold it from the public, and it had never been included in Benn Pitman's record of the trial. "If the record in possession of the Judge Advocate General is true," Johnson continued, "then that is false which he has given to the public. If on the other hand, the record published with his official sanction is true, then that in his bureau is false. Judge Holt is at liberty to accept either alternative, and to escape as he may the inevitable conclusion that he did not only fail to submit the petition to the President, but suppressed and withheld it from the official history of the most important trial in the annals of the nation."[38]

The reaction to this refutation was favorable. A "very clear and pungent reply," the Chronicle called it. Holt furiously accused the former president of having slandered him in order to pacify the Roman Catholics, who were angry at the execution of their fellow religionist, but Johnson's friends believed he had the better of the argument.[39] In reality, both parties agreed that a discussion concerning the execution of a woman had taken place and that there had been a general consensus that her sex should no shield any criminal. Therefore, whether the president had seen the recommendation for mercy or not, he would probably have approved of the execution in any case. Because he was not well, as we have seen, it is possible that he overlooked it inadvertently. In 1873 the only question was how the controversy would affect his standing with the members of the legislature of Tennessee, who would have to vote for him if his ambition of returning to the Senate was ever to be fulfilled. Apparently, they believed him.

The entire dispute with Holt was merely an opening gambit for Johnson's final bid for reelection to the Senate in 1875, when Brownlow's term would expire. This final and successful try was his most skillful performance, in which he demonstrated once again that he had never lost his great political finesse, no matter how often he had been thwarted at Washington and Nashville. The odds against him were tremendous: the hatred of the Bourbons—the old conservatives and extreme secessionists—was undiminished; the resentment of the Democrats, whom in 1872 he had deprived of victory, had not been assuaged, and the hostility of the administration was not calculated to make him popular with the Republicans. Yet in the end Johnson succeeded in overcoming all these obstacles.

He began by cultivating the Patrons of Husbandry, or the Grangers, as the dissatisfied farmers organizing all over the country were calling themselves. For the old Jeffersonian-Jacksonian, with his admiration for the tillers of the soil, it was easy to appeal to agrarian protestors, and in January 1874 he made a strong bid for their support. Declaring in a statement to the Patrons' general deputy that the farmers of the country had an undoubted right and imperative duty to combine for their mutual protection, the ex-president launched an attack against monopolies, hated as they were by the Grangers. When asked whether he thought government could be maintained without the intervention of the agricultural and industrial classes, he unhesitatingly repeated the message he had been preaching for fifty years. "I answer, very directly, no. The agricultural and industrial classes constitute, by far, the most numerous and influential of all the classes. They combine, too, more of the elements of integrity. They are more truthful and reliable. Their very occupations lead them in the paths of fair and honorable dealing." After a passage attacking the railroads and regretting the drift of migrants to the cities, he concluded by reaffirming his conviction that the "sturdy yeomanry" of rural districts had always constituted the salvation of the commonwealth and kept it from succumbing to corruption. The Grangers could not have asked for more.

But Johnson had not yet finished. The Grangers, like many other reformers during the widespread depression of the 1870s, favored some form of inflation and a curb on bondholders. Johnson, sympathizing with this view, in May reiterated his conviction that interest payments on state and national bonds should be suspended. Advocating the substitution of greenbacks for national banknotes, he again insisted that specie payments be resumed. In addition, he attacked the state's funding act of 1873; this act had provided for the conversion of the public debt into 6 percent bonds and was resented by farmers disliking the railroads, which had often borrowed these obligations and stood to gain from them. If his financial program did not fit into any easily recognizable economic framework, if its inflationary aspects marked a distinct departure from his old Jacksonian hard money views and his collaboration with McCulloch, it did square with his continued interest in the common people. Moreover, it was designed to appeal to many undecided Tennesseeans badly injured by deflationary trends.[40]

After wooing the Democrats with his refutation of Holt's *Vindication*, Johnson also sought to win over former Whigs, whose influence in Tennessee was probably larger than in any other Southern state. The opportunity to do so offered itself when the Whig ex-president Millard Fillmore died. In a telegram expressing his regrets that he could not attend the funeral in person, Johnson called Fillmore "one of the nation's most distinguished sons." The compliment could not have been overlooked by his former Whig opponents.[41]

Johnson's sentiments in behalf of Fillmore seemed strange, but he was out to make as many friends as possible. His old intimate advisers were passing; Sam Milligan died in April 1874, and the loss was a serious blow.[42] Now his companions were as often Whigs and secessionists as Democrats and Unionists; Colyar had been a Whig and sided with the Confederacy, George W. Jones was a pro-Southern Democrat, and Thomas A. R. Nelson was a Unionist Whig. The ex-president needed them all.

And now more than ever, Johnson was pursuing his goal of vindication. If people called him ambitious, he did not object. Of course he was ambitious, he said at Memphis in May, and he did not think he would be worthy of being called a man unless he was ambitious. Then he went on to appeal to both old Whigs and Democrats. Had he not stood upon the "watchtower" of his country and defended the people's rights? Soon he was informed that he was winning over all but the most extreme members of his old party, and if this was not entirely true, he was nevertheless making progress with Whigs and Democrats alike.[43]

As the time for the meeting of the legislature drew nearer, Johnson became more outspoken. On July 20 he wrote to a Unionist supporter: "In regard to the Senatorial question I have nothing to disguise from you or any other friend. . . . If I could be returned to the U.S. Senate in accordance with popular sentiment reflected by the Legislature, it would be appreciated by me as the greatest compliment of my life, and be a deserved rebuke to treachery and ingratitude." Conservative successes in August increased his chances, and in September, in an address before the Sumner County Agricultural and Mechanical Association at Gallatin, he formally announced his candidacy. Again wooing the Grangers, Johnson insisted that as early as 1865 in his first annual message he had proved his solidarity with the farmers and underscored his point by repeating his financial proposals. He reminded his listeners of his services to the state and the South by recalling his vetoes of radical measures of Congress. Nor had he forgiven his opponents in the 1869 race for the Senate. "Washington had his Arnold," he declared. "Jefferson had his Burr . . . Caesar had his Brutus; our Savior had twelve apostles, one of whom betrayed him while another denied him; and I too had my Edmund and I had my Henry [Cooper]." The audience loved it.

Undeterred by the fact that his enemies called him a repudiator, the former president campaigned in Shelbyville and Chattanooga, where he repeated his financial theories, attacked Governor Brown, one of his main competitors, and again sought to convince conservatives that he had indeed rendered them services during his presidency. Brown had never been a Democrat, he said, while he had always belonged to the party. Moreover, had he not pardoned most of his present opponents, including Governor Brown? He was in admirable trim physically, according to the *New York Times,* and seemed fresher, younger, and stronger than during the last days at the White House, although the paper complained that it was not pleasant "to see the only living ex-President racing around the country after a job he is not likely to get." While Johnson wooed his old supporters in the backcountry, his friends worked indefatigably to line up support among the various delegates to the legislature. His overall plan was to attack Brown and to pit him against the other contenders so that the strongest of his opponents would be fatally weakened.[44]

In the fall 1874 elections the conservatives, helped by resentment of the Republicans' advocacy in Washington of Sumner's Civil Rights Bill, swept both houses of the legislature. Only eight Republicans survived among ninety-two Democrats, although the former were certain to have the decisive voice in choosing the various conservative aspirants for the Senate. Fully aware of this fact, at a victory celebration in Greeneville Johnson publicly complimented the opposition. "We have met an enemy worthy of a good fight," he said, much to the Democrats' annoyance. But he knew exactly what he was doing.[45]

Immediately after the election the main candidates for the Senate began jockeying for position. Chief among these were four Confederate officers, Generals John C. Brown, William B. Bate, and William A. Quarles, Colonel John H. Stephens, and former Democratic congressman John H. Savage, as well as Johnson. The ex-president took rooms in the Maxwell House in Nashville to be on hand to direct the contest, which, in view of the Confederate military ring's opposition, looked most doubtful for him. But he left no stone unturned. His amanuensis, E. C. Reeves, had personally seen every member of the General Assembly; the delegation from Memphis was pledged to him, and Johnson himself persuaded Bedford Forrest, who had come to aid his former colleague General Bate, to go home. According to Oliver P. Temple, Johnson told Forrest that he was a better soldier than either Bate or Brown, and if the Democrats had been serious about the war, they would not have run a "one-horse general." By publicly walking arm in arm with Bishop Holland N. McTyeire, the former president also played up to the Southern Methodist church, to which many former Whig secessionists belonged.[46]

On January 20, 1875, before packed galleries, the balloting began. On the first try Johnson garnered 30 votes to Brown's 15, Stephens' 16, Bate's 13, Savage's 10, and 15 scattered. Amid great excitement and bitterness, the balloting continued for days, with none of the candidates able to win a majority. After the thirty-fifth ballot, on January 23, Brown withdrew, while Bate's strength steadily increased. On the forty-fourth Bate had 48 votes to Johnson's 43, with 4 scattered—in fact, a majority of the Democrats.[47] It was now essential for Johnson to obtain total Republican support, and he apparently conferred with Henry R. Gibson, an East Tennesseean, to whom he made promises about his future behavior. "If elected, I will go to the United States Senate as representative of the Union sentiment of Tennessee, and of an ante-bellum Democracy," he said. "I will advocate no radical measure, but will endeavor to take position on medium ground, as opposed to both extremes. I will not oppose Grant's policy except in very extreme cases. If elected by Republican votes, I will never forget what I owe that party." He also maintained that while he differed on some matters of policy, he would not go to Washington as a Democrat, but as an independent. In any case, against the secessionists, all Unionists must stick together.[48]

Johnson's opponents now became desperate. Meeting in caucus on January 25 to find some candidate upon whom all could agree, they sought to compose their differences. But the ex-president's strategy had worked; they were unable to unite, and the caucus failed to come to any viable conclusion.

That same night Johnson was pacing the floor of his room at the Maxwell House. For half an hour he said nothing; then he stopped at the window, looked out into the darkness, and remarked to his companion, Andrew Kellar, the editor of the Memphis *Avalanche*, "The street is very silent, no one is out, everybody seems to be in bed, but you and I, and we are resting on our arms. The conference held by my opponents is over, or rather their disagreements are adjourned, and I shall on tomorrow get every vote but one from East Tennessee without regard to political dislikes. And the Shelby County delegation being unbroken and carrying the power of Memphis and West Tennessee, I shall be elected after battling 14 days." Johnson insisted that he was not ambitious to gratify political desire. He was seeking "an acquittal by the people of Tennessee, and a triumphal vindication over [his] enemies . . . the Military Secession combination."[49]

His prognosis was correct. On the next day, January 26, after Bate had withdrawn, Johnson received 47 votes on the fifty-fifth ballot, amid great applause. Then for the next half hour, member after member, explaining his actions, switched over to him, until finally, with a total of 52 votes to Stephens' 25 and 21 scattered, the ex-president was elected. Among deafening cheers, the entire assembly rose to its feet, while one member, Alfred E. Taylor, his old Whig opponent's son, ran through the alleys to the Maxwell House to bring him the good news. On finding Johnson walking the floor in his room, Taylor said, "God bless your old soul, on the 53d [sic] ballot you were declared elected Senator." Then Taylor, who weighed but ninety-five pounds, passed out from the excitement, but was revived on the sofa with cold water. Johnson, alternately pale and flushed, remained silent for a while. Finally he exclaimed: "Well, well, well, I'd rather have this information than to learn that I had been elected President of the United States. Thank God for the vindication."[50]

A vindication it truly was. The city went wild. The rotunda of the Maxwell House was soon crowded to overflowing, serenaders appeared in front of the hotel, and congratulations poured in from all over the country. At home, the family had been anxiously awaiting the outcome. Martha had already cautioned her father not to be too disappointed should things turn out badly; Eliza was worse than usual, probably from excitement, but she as well as the others greatly rejoiced at the final result. "Your cup of joy is already full, and ours too great to express . . .," Martha wrote him triumphantly. "I feel it is the greatest victory of your life." And Eliza heard from a well-wisher that in the first speech he had ever heard her husband make, earlier in his career, Johnson attributed his success in life to her influence. Although the victor originally wanted to host a large banquet after his triumph, Reeves talked him out of it—the Bourbons were already downcast enough—and he went home to Greeneville.[51]

The country's newspapers covered the story in detail. "With Andrew Johnson in the Senate, we can dismiss all fears for the safety of the Constitution," commented the Cincinnati *Commercial.* Its radical counterpart, the *Gazette,* queried, "Who, ten years ago, would have thought such a thing possible?" The Chicago *Tribune* and the St. Louis *Globe* expressed satisfaction because the senator-elect had been the only Unionist among the candidates, and the New Haven *Palladium* predicted that Johnson would capture the 1876 presidential nomination at the Democratic Convention. The *New York Times* pledged not to renew its old feud. Johnson was a "man of great natural abilities and force of character," it conceded, and predicted that he would greatly enliven the Senate, an assessment with which the Springfield *Republican* agreed. "Andy is sure to be a positive force in the Senate," it concluded.[52]

After his return to Greeneville, Johnson undertook a trip to Memphis. After continuous ovations along the way, he stopped at the Peabody House, where an immense crowd gathered to wish him well. He responded in his usual way, but he had particular reasons for being grateful to the city's Democrats, who, despite personal friendships with

Bate, had stood by him as instructed. Then he stayed on to enjoy the carnival festivities.[53]

After returning home again, Johnson did not linger long. Executive business, including a reciprocity treaty with Hawaii, had not yet been considered, and Grant called a special session of the Senate to take care of it. Thus the former president returned to Washington in March to be sworn in by the very body that not so long before had tried to convict him and deprive him of the right to hold office. It was a dramatic event, and the whole country was anxiously awaiting the spectacle.

This time he took rooms at the Imperial Hotel on E Street between 13th and 14th streets. Among his visitors was William H. Crook, whom he asked for a scrapbook about Grant. He would need it, for Johnson had made up his mind to speak against the general and punish the Southern brigadiers.[54]

Vice President Henry Wilson, one of the radicals who had voted for Johnson's conviction, called the special session to order on March 5. As luck would have it, not only Johnson but also his predecessor as vice president, Hannibal Hamlin, now returned to the upper house, and the newspapers were full of accounts of the swearing-in ceremony—how crowds flocked to the Capitol to see the ex-president, how his desk was decorated with a bouquet of flowers, how, accompanied by Reverdy Johnson, he entered the chamber to be sworn in by the vice president amid great applause. After the formalities were over, a page handed Johnson another bouquet of flowers, and Lewis V. Bogy, his conservative Democratic friend from Missouri, led him back to his desk on the Democratic side. But he soon redeemed his pledge to the Tennessee Republicans by not joining the Democratic caucus.[55]

Yet the former president was certainly no Republican. His hatred for Grant, as well as his conviction that his Reconstruction policies had been right and Grant's wrong, was unshaken, and within a short time he prepared what was to be his last great public address. The occasion was a debate over Frederick T. Frelinghuysen's resolution approving of Grant's policies in Louisiana, where the army had interfered in disputed elections by ejecting five assemblymen from their seats in the legislature. Considering this action the very embodiment of the Caesarism of which he accused the administration, on March 20 Johnson rose to deliver his philippic.

He began by denying the right of the Senate even to discuss the subject in a special session called to consider other matters and declared the proceeding as illegal as the Senate's censure of Andrew Jackson. And why was Sheridan sent to Louisiana in the first place, to a state where he was not wanted? "I know the determination of that people," he exclaimed. "But what is that to those who are acting behind the curtain and who are aspiring to retain power, and if it cannot be had by popular consent . . . in the midst of the war cry, triumphantly ride into the Presidency for a third Presidential term; and when that is done, farewell to the liberties of the country." It was obvious that Grant's reelection was the purpose of the entire maneuver.

As for the controversy between the Republican government in Louisiana headed by Governor William P. Kellogg and its Democratic rival under John McEnery, Johnson continued, the former had been investigated and found wanting. At any rate, although the president had claimed the authority to guarantee a republican form of government to the state, the Constitution did not confer this power upon him but upon the United States. The country was faced with a statocracy, military rule, and just as he had once alerted the Senate to the danger of secession, so he was now warning it against executive encroachment. Quoting from his beloved Addison's *Cato,* he pleaded with Caesar to "disband his legions" and to "restore the commonwealth to liberty." His speech, which ended with his customary impassioned appeal to uphold the Constitution, was enthusiastically applauded by his colleagues.[56]

The reaction to the speech was predictable. "AVE IMPERATOR: GREAT SPEECH OF ANDREW JOHNSON IN THE SENATE," read the headline in the New York *Herald.* The Nashville *Union and American* called it an "able and timely" address, "a stirring appeal to save the country and the Constitution," while the Chicago *Tribune* considered it intemperate and a fitting companion piece to Johnson's inaugural speech. The New York *Tribune* called the speech disappointing, and Tennessee Republicans charged that Johnson had violated an election pledge not to attack the president, although even Temple found this accusation hard to believe. Obviously, he considered the Louisiana situation one of "the very extreme cases" he had exempted from his promises. At any rate, it was certain that the Greeneville statesman was as combative as ever.[57]

After the special session ended and Johnson took care of some business affairs in connection with his claims against the First National Bank, and whiling away his time by playing with Provost Marshal O'-Beirne's little son at the hotel—he went down on all fours and allowed the child to ride on his back—he made preparations for the return trip to Greeneville.[58] As he saw it, he had true cause to be satisfied. Reelected to the Senate in spite of desperate opposition, he had received the vindication he had sought so long. Popular opinion had finally come to his rescue.

XX

EPILOGUE

WHEN Andrew Johnson came home in the spring of 1875, he had every
reason to take a vacation and relax. He had achieved what he wanted;
he had made a remarkable comeback, and he did not have to plan for
a new election contest in the immediate future. In addition, a holiday
was called for because of the state of his health, which was none too
good—he suffered from heart trouble—to say nothing of the fact that
Eliza was getting worse instead of better.[1]

But he was restless. He continued his real estate operations, lent out
money at interest to acquaintances, and was thinking of new political
activities.[2] By the end of June he decided to go to Ohio, where an
election campaign was in progress. His opponents, particularly Governor Oliver P. Morton, were falsifying history, he thought, and he wanted
to set the record straight. So, on the morning of Wednesday, July 28,
he took a train to Carter's Station on what he thought would be the
first leg of his trip. His daughter Mary lived on the Stover farm near
there, and Eliza, hoping to improve her precarious health, had gone to
visit her.

The train was crowded. Walking up and down the aisle to look for
a seat, Johnson ran into two young acquaintances, W. E. McElwee, a
former Confederate who was traveling on behalf of the American Steel
Association to prospect for iron ore, and his companion, Dave Jenkins,
a Union veteran. McElwee offered Johnson his seat. The ex-president
accepted, and the travelers began to talk. After asking the two men

about their business and discussing the problems of the railroad, which depended on the iron McElwee was seeking, Johnson started to discourse about his years at the White House. Most of the political troubles after the war, he believed, were the fault of Secretary Stanton, whom he called "the Marat of American politics" and a "very bitter, uncompromising, and self-assertive man." He even said he had heard that Stanton was indirectly responsible for Booth's crime, because the secretary had allegedly stopped Lincoln from commuting the death sentence of one of the assassin's friends. After learning that the president had been shot, Johnson said, he walked the floor of his hotel and asked himself more than a hundred times what course he must pursue so that the calm and correct historian would say one hundred years later, "He pursued the right course." He knew right then and there that he would have to contend against inflamed passions and a cry for blood. With the South lying prostrate and helpless, some Northerners would "like to kick the dead lion." Lincoln might have been able to compel obedience to the Constitution and the laws, but Johnson doubted his own ability to do so. Nevertheless, he insisted that he decided that moment to carry out his constitutional obligations and to protect the South against unreasonable hatred. Thus he embarked upon his restoration program and defied the overbearing Congress. As for Mrs. Surratt, he believed her to have been entirely innocent but to have been done in by Stanton.

When the train reached Johnson City, Jenkins got off, but Johnson invited McElwee to go on with him to Carter Station and there to accompany him in the carriage that had been sent for him. The senator continued to reminisce. The death of Lincoln had been a misfortune for the South as well as for the North, he said, because it opened the way for Congress to grasp unconstitutional powers. When the carriage came to a fork in the road, McElwee left to go on to Elizabethton, while Johnson continued on to his daughter's farm.[3]

At Mary's house the old man ate a hearty dinner and talked as effusively as he had on the train. Then he retired to his room upstairs, followed by his granddaughter Lillie. He sat down in an armchair and talked to her, undoubtedly about her forthcoming marriage to Thomas Maloney, a Greeneville attorney. Stepping to the window for a moment because of a distraction outside, she heard a thud, turned around, and found her grandfather lying on the floor, his speech slurred and his left side paralyzed. She summoned help; members of the household rushed in and put Johnson to bed. They wanted to call a doctor, but he insisted he would be better soon and did not need one.

When there was no improvement the next day, two doctors from Elizabethton were summoned to take care of the patient. Their administrations seemed to help the ex-president, who kept talking about domestic matters. But the recovery was short-lived. On Friday night, July 30, Johnson suffered another stroke and lost consciousness. When, accompanied by two family doctors, Martha and Frank arrived shortly afterward, he no longer recognized them, and at 2:30 in the morning, he quietly passed away.[4]

On Saturday after daybreak the body was carried back to Greeneville with great ceremony. Taken in charge by the Masons, it was escorted to the Johnsons' home amid the tolling of bells. As the deceased had requested, his body was wrapped in a large American flag and his head placed upon his copy of the Constitution. The large metal casket lay in the parlor of the house where a steady stream of visitors came to pay their last respects, until shortly after noon on Monday, when the members of the Greeneville Masonic lodge escorted their distinguished member's remains to a catafalque erected in the courthouse. There it lay in state until the next day.

The funeral took place on Tuesday, August 3. Special trains brought guests from near and far, including Governor James P. Porter, state officials, congressmen, members of the judiciary, and other dignitaries. The whole town was draped in mourning; the entire family with the exception of Eliza and Mary, who was taking care of her, had come, and a huge procession of some five thousand people followed the body to its last resting place. The site, selected long ago by Johnson himself, was on Signal Hill just outside of town, where there was a splendid view of the surrounding mountains. The Johnson Guards, the Dickinson Guards, the Knights Templar, and local Masons provided the escort, and in a final Masonic ceremony, Andrew Johnson was laid to rest.[5]

News of the former president's passing took the country by surprise. President Grant issued a proclamation fulfilling his "painful duty" to announce the death of the "last survivor of his honored predecessors." The White House and government departments were draped in black; all business in Washington was suspended on the day of the funeral, and the armed services were ordered to perform the customary ceremonies. Memorial meetings were held in various cities, and newspapers all over the country prominently featured the story.[6]

Even in commemorating the fallen leader, the editorials reflected their owners' prejudices. But whatever their strictures, Northern papers tended to stress Johnson's loyalty during the war, Southern journals, his services to the South afterward. "But for him, after the war, our beloved South would have been ruined beyond redemption," wrote the Little Rock *Arkansas Gazette,* and even Republican papers praised him for his inflexible honesty. Parson Brownlow himself was moved to state that his old opponent had "never betrayed the confidence of his friends by taking that which did not belong to him," while the London *Times* commented that his career, his rise from poverty and ignorance, illustrated both the strengths and weaknesses of the American system. All were agreed that Johnson's course had been extraordinary.[7]

For some unexplained reason, Johnson, whose estate exceeded $100,-000, left no will. He had already deeded the farm near Greeneville to Martha; Andrew, Jr., remained in the homestead, and Eliza was appointed administratrix, but she died six months later. Then Andrew, Jr., took over until, in March 1879, he also died. Although his sisters had turned over their interest in the homestead to him, after his death they had a falling out with his widow, who sued them for much of the property; the case was finally settled by a compromise.[8]

In Greeneville the memory of the town's greatest citizen lived on. The family saw to it that a suitable monument was erected at the gravesite, a large marble shaft adorned with the Constitution and an open Bible, topped by a perched American eagle. It was dedicated in a dignified ceremony on June 5, 1878, when Johnson's friend of long standing, George W. Jones, delivered a lengthy eulogy. Eventually, the homestead, tailor shop, and adjacent properties were taken over by the federal government and operated as a national shrine as a fitting memorial for the seventeenth president of the United States.[9]

So Andrew Johnson had passed into history. For generations after his death, his reputation alternately suffered and flourished. At first, historians tended to concentrate upon his failures as president; then, particularly in the 1920s and 1930s, spurred on by a Supreme Court decision apparently declaring the Tenure of Office Act unconstitutional, they began to rehabilitate Johnson and portray him as a hero, an assessment that was not to change until the civil rights struggle of the 1960s once more pushed racial questions into the foreground. Since then, Johnson's reputation has declined again, with criticism aimed at his lack of sympathy with the aspirations of the freedmen.[10]

After all is said and done, however, it is clear that although the seventeenth president unquestionably undermined the Reconstruction process and left a legacy of racism, he was an able politician. Overcoming all opposition in his own Democratic party, he became a dominant force in it, while at the same time frustrating all efforts of the opposition. His courageous stand for the Union also paid handsome political dividends, enabling him to reach the highest office in the land. What defeated him during his term in the White House was not so much his lack of formal education, nor even his tactlessness, but his failure to outgrow his Jeffersonian-Jacksonian background. Johnson's continued identification with an America of small farmers and "mechanics," his attachment to a strict construction of the Constitution that was no longer in vogue, his refusal to adjust his racial views to the needs of the Republican party, and his persistent belief in the agrarian myth blinded him to the realities of the post–Civil War United States. At a time when the country was being rapidly industrialized, when small villages were giving way to larger towns and cities, when individual family farms were being replaced by impersonal factories, his limited world outlook, so typical of early nineteenth-century America, was no longer adequate. Even Northern farmers were not attuned to his style. Thus, though he was still able to leave his legacy of white supremacy and achieve reelection in a more traditional Tennessee, he failed to impress his contemporaries in the country at large, and his administration was a disaster. Johnson was a child of his time, but he failed to grow with it.

ABBREVIATIONS

AJPP   Andrew Johnson Papers Project, University of Tennessee
AHR   *American Historical Review*
CWH   *Civil War History*
DAB   *Dictionary of American Biography*
ETHSP   *East Tennessee Historical Society Proceedings*
HSP   Historical Society of Pennsylvania
ISH   Illinois State Historical Society
JP   Johnson Papers, Library of Congress
JSH   *Journal of Southern History*
LC   Library of Congress
MHS   Massachusetts Historical Society
MVHR   *Mississippi Valley Historical Review*
NA   National Archives
NCA   North Carolina State Archives
NCHR   *North Carolina Historical Review*
NCAB   *National Cyclopedia of American Biography*
NJHS   New Jersey Historical Society
NYHS   New-York Historical Society
NYPL   New York Public Library

O.R.   *War of the Rebellion: A Compilation of the Official Records of the Union and Confederate Armies* (Washington, D.C., 1880–1901)

PJ   *The Papers of Andrew Johnson*, LeRoy P. Graf and Ralph W. Haskins, eds. (Knoxville, 1967–present)

RG   Record Group (in National Archives)

SHC   Southern Historical Collection, University of North Carolina

SHSW   State Historical Society of Wisconsin

THQ   *Tennessee Historical Quarterly*

TSLA   Tennessee State Library and Archives

UNC   University of North Carolina

UT   University of Tennessee

WRHS   Western Reserve Historical Society

NOTES

I. *RALEIGH POOR WHITE*

1. Richard Banbury Creecy, *Grandfather's Tales of North Carolina History* (Raleigh, 1901), pp. 278–79; Hope Sumerell Chamberlain, *History of Wake County, North Carolina* (Raleigh, 1927), pp. 93ff.; Kemp P. Battle, *The Early History of Raleigh: A Centennial Address Delivered . . . on . . . October 18, 1892* (Raleigh, 1893), p. 46.
2. Moses Amis, *Historical Raleigh from Its Foundation in 1792* (Raleigh, 1902), p. 37; Battle, *Early History of Raleigh*, p. 36; David L. Swain, *Early Times in Raleigh: Addresses Delivered by the Hon. David L. Swan, LL.D., at the Dedication of Tucker Hall and on the Occasion of the Completion of a Monument to Jacob Johnson* (Raleigh, 1867), p. 7 (2d pagination), pp. 6, 12, 13 (1st pagination).
3. Elizabeth Culbertson Waugh, *North Carolina's Capital, Raleigh* (Chapel Hill, 1967), pp. 24–25; Kemp P. Battle, *Sketches of the Early History of the City of Raleigh: Centennial Address, July 4, 1876* (Raleigh, 1877), p. 25.
4. John Savage, *The Life and Public Services of Andrew Johnson* (New York, 1866), p. 16; information furnished to author by George Stevenson, North Carolina State Department of Archives; Waugh, *Raleigh*, p. 26; Hugh Buckner Johnston, Jr., "President Andrew Johnson: A Review of His Early Years in Raleigh," AJPP; W. G. McDonough to North Carolina Historical Society, October 20, 1939, including speech by W. G. McDonough, Johnson Papers, NCA; Raleigh *News and Observer*, June 18, 1967.
5. Abraham Jobe, Autobiography or Memoirs Written by Himself, 1902–1905, TSLA, pp. 235ff.; Savage, *Johnson*, p. 16; cf. [Kenneth Rayner], *Life and Times of Andrew Johnson, 17th President of the the United States, Written from a National Standpoint by a Public Man* (New York, 1866); Swain, *Early Times*.
6. Hugh B. Johnston, Jr., "The 'Missing' Ancestry of President Andrew Johnson" and "Jacob Johnson of Raleigh: A Reappraisal of the Father of Andrew Johnson," Hugh B. Johnston to Patricia Clark, October 11, 1979, AJPP; Lately Thomas, *The First President Johnson: The Three Lives of the Seventeenth President of the United States of America* (New York, 1968), pp. 8–9; Wake County Court Minutes, February Term 1811, with appointment as constable; Swain, *Early Times*, p. 15 (2d pagination); James Sawyer

Jones, *Life of Andrew Johnson, 17th President of the United States* (Greeneville, Tenn., 1901), pp. 12–14.

7. Jones, *Johnson*, pp. 12–14; Wake County Marriage Bonds, September 9, 1801, for marriage application; W. G. McDonough, "Andrew McDonough and His Descendants," AJPP; George Fort Milton, *The Age of Hate: Andrew Johnson and the Radicals* (New York, 1930), p. 60.

8. George Fort Milton to W. E. Dodd, July 11, 1927, Lillard Thompson to Milton, November 15, 1927, George Fort Milton Papers, LC; Henry Watterson, *"Marse Henry": An Autobiography*, 2 vols. (New York, 1919), 1:155ff.; Josephus Daniels to Robert W. Winston, January 21, 1927, Winston Papers, SHC; Ralph W. Haskins, "Internecine Strife in Tennessee: Andrew Johnson vs. Parson Brownlow," *THQ* 24(1965): 321–40, esp. 328–29.

9. Swain, *Early Times*, pp. 13–15 (2d pagination).

10. Raleigh *Star*, January 12, 1812, cited in John H. Wheeler, *Reminiscences and Memoirs of North Carolina and Eminent North Carolinians* (Baltimore, 1966; reprint of 1884 ed.), p. 435.

11. Johnston, "Jacob Johnson," AJPP; Wake County Court Minutes, 1812–15, February 17, 1812 (the entry reads: "Polly Johnson, widow & relict of Jacob Johnson deceased came into Court, and relinquished her right of administration on the Estate of her said late Husband"); Johnston, "President Andrew Johnson," AJPP; William J. Anderson to Johnson, April 8, 1869, JP; Indenture to James J. Selby, February 18, 1822, *PJ* 1:1. The discrepancy between the date of the original indenture and the final recording has caused some confusion. It is possible that Johnson's mother, acting through her second husband, signified her intention in 1818 and carried it out only in 1822. On the other hand, James Litchford, Selby's foreman, believed that Andrew was apprenticed at ten, and the books published during Johnson's lifetime so state; cf. Savage, *Johnson*, pp. 13–15; Rayner, *Johnson*, p. 4. George Stevenson, of the North Carolina Archives, who has made a thorough study of Johnson's youth, believes that it was William who was articled to Selby in 1818. George Stevenson, "Andrew Johnson, the Childhood Years," MS in possession of author.

12. Swain, *Early Times*, pp. 12, 15 (2d pagination); Kemp P. Battle, *Memories of an Old Time Tar Heel*, William J. Battle, ed. (Chapel Hill, 1945), p. 32.

13. Beth Crabtree and James W. Patton, eds., *"Journal of a Secession Lady": The Diary of Amy Devereaux Edmondston* (Raleigh, 1979), pp. 140, 162; Mrs. John M. Winfree to Robert W. Winston, November 13, 1927, Winston Papers, SHC.

14. Battle, *Early History of Raleigh*, p. 36; Swain, *Early Times*, p. 6 (1st pagination), p. 9 (2d pagination).

15. Battle, *Early History of Raleigh*, pp. 36, 47; Swain, *Early Times*, p. 6 (1st pagination).

16. John E. Patterson to Johnson, July 2, 1861, *PJ* 4:537; Clement Eaton, *The Growth of Southern Civilization* (New York, 1961), pp. 167, 172, 174.

17. Milton, *Age of Hate*, p. 14; Notice of Runaway Apprentices, *PJ* 1:1–2; Savage, *Johnson*, pp. 15–16; Crabtree and Patton, *Diary of Amy Devereaux Edmondston*, p. 162; Neal Brown to Johnson, July 15, 1867, June 20, 1868, Francis Johnson Devereaux Miller to Johnson, March 16, 1866, JP; Rayner, *Johnson*, p. 5.

18. Diary of Col. William G. Moore (Large Diary), March 28, 1868, JP; Wheeler, *Reminiscences*, p. 435; J. B. Brownlow to Oliver P. Temple, February 19, 1892, Temple Papers, UT, Knoxville; Felix Alexander Reeve, *East Tennessee in the War of the Rebellion, Military Order of the Loyal Legion of the United States, Commandery of the District of Columbia, War Papers*, no. 44 (Washington, D.C., 1902), pp. 27–28. A parallel story that the reader was an Englishman named Hugh Wolstenholme who later lived as a hermit in the East Tennessee mountains was believed by Wolstenholme's descendants but is unsubstantiated. John Hewitt Memoirs, TSLA; Nashville *Tennessean*, May 1, 16, 23, 1965.

19. Savage, *Johnson*, pp. 14–15, 23. According to another story, an old man who burned charcoal in the vicinity helped Andy to learn reading by pointing out and naming the

letters of the alphabet, while a servant girl taught him to write with pot hooks. Reeve, *East Tennessee*, pp. 27–28. Later the legend that Johnson's wife taught him to read was widely circulated, although it does not seem to be true: Wheeler, *Reminiscences*, p. 435; Greeneville *Intelligencer*, August 6, 1875; Oliver P. Temple, *Notable Men of Tennessee* (New York, 1912), pp. 360–61. It is, however, possible that she improved his skills: cf. Harriet Turner, "Recollections of Andrew Johnson," *Harpers Monthly* 120 (January 1910): 168–76, esp. 170.

20. *Laws of the State of North-Carolina*, 2 vols. (Raleigh, 1821), ch. 69, nos. 18, 19; ch. 35, no. 2; Paul Douglas, *American Apprenticeship* (New York, 1921), pp. 20–21. John R. Commons et al., *History of Labor in the United States*, 4 vols. (New York, 1966, 1:339–47.

21. John Robert Irelan, *History of the Life, Administration, and Time of Andrew Johnson, Seventeenth President of the United States* (Chicago, 1888), pp. 20ff.; Louisville *Courier-Journal*, October 30, 1880.

22. Savage, *Johnson*, pp. 15–16; Temple, *Notable Men*, pp. 357–58; Andrew Forest Muir, "William P. Johnson, Southern Proletarian and Unionist," *THQ* 15 (1956): 330–38.

23. Notice of Runaway Apprentices, *PJ* 1:1–2; James Sefton, *Andrew Johnson and the Uses of Constitutional Power* (Boston, 1980), p. 7. Years later Johnson also accused Selby of failing to carry out his part of the indenture because he failed to teach the lad how to read, write, and cipher to the rule of three. Speech at Knoxville, April 16, 1864, *PJ* 6:675.

24. Blackwell P. Robinson, *A History of Moore County, North Carolina, 1747–1847* (Southern Pines, N.C., 1956), p. 106; Robert Winston, *Andrew Johnson, Plebeian and Patriot* (New York, 1928), p. 11; Fay Warrington Brabson, *Andrew Johnson: A Life in Pursuit of the Right Course, 1808–1875* (Durham, N.C., 1972), p. 6.

25. William Watts Ball, *The State That Forgot: South Carolina's Surrender to Democracy* (Indianapolis, 1932), pp. 17–19; Benjamin F. Perry, *Reminiscences of Public Men with Speeches and Addresses* (Greenville, S.C., 1889), pp. 250–51.

26. Perry, *Reminiscences*, pp. 250–51; Ball, *The State That Forgot*, p. 25; New York *Herald*, April 16, 1865; W. H. Griffin to Johnson, August 20, 1865, JP.

27. Savage, *Johnson*, pp. 15–16; Brabson, *Johnson*, pp. 6–7.

28. Louisville *Courier-Journal*, October 30, 1880.

II. *TENNESSEE TAILOR*

1. Kemp P. Battle, *Memories of an Old Time Tar Heel*, William S. Battle, ed. (Chapel Hill, 1945), pp. 212–13.

2. Nashville *Banner*, December 18, 1927; George Fort Milton to John Brown, May 23, 1929, Milton Papers, LC.

3. Nashville *Banner*, December 18, 1927; Mary E. Mason to Dr. Alexander Whetmore, October 19, 1928, John H. Peebles to Mary Mason, October 9, 1928, Milton Papers.

4. Nashville *Banner*, December 18, 1927; clipping, Archelaus M. Hughes to the Editor, *Daily Herald*, January 8, 1927, in James K. Polk Papers, TSLA; Sims Latta to George Fort Milton, May 22, 1929, Milton Papers; Elizabeth Shelton to Johnson, February 13, 1865, AJPP.

5. Easton Morris, *The Tennessee Gazetteer or Topographical Dictionary* (Nashville, 1834), p. 35; Nashville *Banner*, December 18, 1927; George F. Milton, *The Age of Hate: Andrew Johnson and the Radicals* (New York, 1930), pp. 65–66. It is possible that Johnson's visit to Selby mentioned in the last chapter occurred at the time of this visit to Raleigh rather than at the time of the earlier return.

6. A. D. February to Johnson, October 6, 1868, JP; Felix A. Reeve, *East Tennessee in the War of the Rebellion*, Military Order of the Loyal Legion of the United States, Commandery of the District of Columbia, War Papers, no. 44 (Washington, D.C., 1902), p. 25; Oliver P. Temple, *Notable Men of Tennessee* (New York, 1912), p. 357.

7. Andrew Johnson Patterson to George Fort Milton, January 15, 1926, Milton Papers;

W. G. McDonough, "Address at the Unveiling of a Marker for Andrew McDonough, Sr., October 22, 1939," Andrew Johnson Collection, NCA.

8. A. D. February to Johnson, October 6, 1868, JP; Oliver P. Temple, *East Tennessee and the Civil War* (Cincinnati, 1899), p. 365.

9. Temple, *Notable Men*, pp. 357–60; Greeneville *Intelligencer*, August 6, 1875.

10. Temple, *Notable Men*, pp. 357–60; Richard Harrison Doughty, *Greeneville: One Hundred Year Portrait, 1775–1875* (Greeneville, Tenn., 1975), pp. 57–59.

11. Doughty, *Greeneville*, pp. 57–59; Temple, *Notable Men*, pp. 357–60; Greeneville *Intelligencer*, August 6, 1875. John A. Brown was the source of this account.

12. Henry Watterson, *"Marse Henry": An Autobiography*, 2 vols. (New York, 1919), 1:155–57; Fay W. Brabson, *Andrew Johnson: A Life in Pursuit of the Right Course, 1808–1875* (Durham, N.C., 1972), pp. 7–8; William S. Speer, ed., *Sketches of Prominent Tennesseans* (Nashville, 1888), p. 537; Doughty, *Greeneville*, p. 59; William O. Stoddard, *Abraham Lincoln and Andrew Johnson* (New York, 1888), p. 4; Robert Winston, *Andrew Johnson, Plebian and Patriot* (New York, 1928), p. 20.

13. Greeneville *Intelligencer*, August 6, 1875; Nashville *Banner*, December 18, 1927; Morris, *Tennessee Gazetteer*, p. 144.

14. Greeneville *Intelligencer*, August 6, 1875; Marriage Licence and Certificate, PJ 1:4; Doughty, *Greeneville*, p. 60; Morris, *Tennessee Gazetteer*, p. 167; on Mordecai Lincoln, see Samuel C. Williams, *The Lincolns and Tennessee* (Harrogate, Tenn., 1942), pp. 18–20. Eliza was born on October 4, 1810; thus she was sixteen and a half in May 1827, not seventeen, as has been asserted. The family birth and death dates may be found in AJPP.

15. George W. Jones, *Oration of Hon. George W. Jones, with Other Proceedings at the Unveiling of the Monument to the Memory of Ex-President Andrew Johnson, at Greeneville, Tennessee, June 5th, 1878* (Nashville, 1878), pp. 3–4.

16. William Henry Crook, *Memories of the White House: The Home Life of Our Presidents from Lincoln to Roosevelt*, Henry Rood, ed. (Boston, 1911), pp. 48–59; Margaret Gray Blanton, "Tennessee Johnson's Eliza," ms. in author's possession through the courtesy of Dr. Betty Caroli; John H. Wheeler, *Reminiscences and Memoirs of North Carolina and Eminent North Carolinians* (Baltimore, 1966), p. 435; Harriet Turner, "Recollections of Andrew Johnson," *Harpers Monthly* 120 (January 1910): 170; J. B. Brownlow to Oliver P. Temple, February 19, 1892, Temple Papers, UT, Knoxville; Temple, *Notable Men*, p. 360. William T. M. Riches concludes that Johnson considered Eliza a social liability: "The Commoners: Andrew Johnson and Abraham Lincoln to 1861," Ph.D. diss., UT, 1976, pp. 148ff.

17. Morris, *Tennessee Gazetteer*, p. 62; Doughty, *Greeneville*, pp. 13ff., 154ff.; C. C. Gray to George Fort Milton, January 29, 1929, Milton Papers.

18. Morris, *Tennessee Gazetteer*, p. xviii; Dwight Lowell Dumond, *Antislavery: The Crusade for Freedom in America* (New York, 1966), p. 136; Doughty, *Greeneville*, pp. 32, 46–49; Greeneville *Intelligencer*, August 6, 1875; Temple, *East Tennessee*, p. 365.

19. Greeneville *Intelligencer*, August 6, 1875; Temple, *Notable Men*, p. 361. According to Andrew Johnson Patterson, his grandfather's first shop was on Main Street, near Snapp's Opera House. A. J. Patterson to Mathews, July 31, 1899, AJPP.

20. *New York Times*, May 9, 1870; Excerpt from Account Books, PJ 1:5–13, xxiii.

21. Deed for Wyrick Property, PJ 1:13–14; Greeneville *Intelligencer*, August 6, 1875; Hugh A. Lawing, *Andrew Johnson National Historic Site*, revised reprint from THQ 20 (1960): 4–5. According to his grandson, Johnson bought the shop from George Jones on Main Street and rolled it to the present location. A. J. Patterson to Mathews, July 31, 1899, AJPP.

22. Family Birth and Death Dates, AJPP; James S. Jones, *Life of Andrew Johnson, 17th President of the United States* (Greeneville, Tenn., 1901), pp. 28–31; McDonough, "Address," Andrew Johnson Collection, NCA; Winston, *Johnson*, p. 21.

23. Temple, *Notable Men*, pp. 361–62; St. George L. Sioussat, "Andrew Johnson and the Early Phases of the Homestead Bill," *Tennessee Historical Magazine* 6 (1920): 30;

[Kenneth Rayner], *Life and Times of Andrew Johnson, 17th President of the United States, Written from a National Standpoint by a Public Man* (New York, 1866), pp. 5–6; Greeneville *Intelligencer*, August 6, 1875.

24. Greeneville *Intelligencer*, August 6, 1875; John Savage, *The Life and Public Services of Andrew Johnson* (New York, 1866), p. 20; Doughty, *Greeneville*, pp. 60–61. Alexis de Tocqueville, *Democracy in America*, 2 vols. (New York, 1945), 1:250.

25. Greeneville *Intelligencer*, August 6, 1875; B. Carroll Reece, *The Courageous Commoner: A Biography of Andrew Johnson* (Charleston, W.Va., 1962), pp. 12–13; C. C. Gray to George Fort Milton, January 9, 1929, Milton Papers.

26. Milton, *Age of Hate*, pp. 74–75; Doughty, *Greeneville*, pp. 38–41, 61–62; Winston, *Johnson*, p. 17. If Hawthorne's story is to be credited, the participants were amazingly young, particularly Hawthorne, who would have been only 11! *PJ* 7:250, n. 6.

27. Johnson to Valentine Sevier, June 7, 1832, *PJ* 1:14. It is obvious that Eliza's efforts to improve her husband's spelling met with limited success.

28. Cf. Rayner, *Johnson*, pp. 6ff.; Savage, *Johnson*, p. 19; Greeneville Mayor's Book, AJPP; Doughty, *Greeneville*, pp. 64–65. George Fort Milton did not repeat the usual story that Johnson was elected in 1828, but he, too, mentioned the wrong date for the election for mayor (1831): *Age of Hate*, pp. 74–75.

29. Greeneville Mayor's Book, AJPP; Doughty, *Greeneville*, pp. 61–65. On January 25, 1834, on petition of sundry citizens, it was ordered that the old court and stocks at Cross Street be removed to some suitable place at the new courthouse. The trustees of Greene County were to pay Mayor Johnson $15 for the removal. Greene County Court of Quarter Sessions, Minutes, 1832–34, p. 325.

30. State v. Andw. Johnson, Lawson McGhee Library, Knoxville.

31. Greeneville Mayor's Book, AJPP; Doughty, *Greeneville*, pp. 65–72.

32. Savage, *Johnson*, pp. 20–21.

33. Receipt for Payment of Fine, June 7, 1831, *PJ* 1:8; Johnson to T. H. Herbert, December 11, 1857, item No. 540, American Art Association, Anderson Galleries, First Edition Autographs to Be Dispersed at Public Sale, 1934; Jones, *Oration*, p. 4.

34. Temple, *Notable Men*, pp. 451, 461.

III. GREENEVILLE POLITICIAN

1. Greeneville *Intelligencer*, August 6, 1875; John Savage, *The Life and Public Services of Andrew Johnson* (New York, 1866), p. 26; Nashville *Republican*, March 26, 1835; Paul H. Bergeron, *Antebellum Politics in Tennessee* (Lexington, Ky., 1982), pp. 38–40; Hans L. Trefousse, *Impeachment of a President: Andrew Johnson, the Blacks, and Reconstruction* (Knoxville, 1975), pp. 4–5.

2. *Journal of the House of Representatives of the State of Tennessee at the 21st General Assembly* (Knoxville, 1836), p. 3; Oliver P. Temple, *Notable Men of Tennessee* (New York, 1912), pp. 363–64, 370; James S. Jones, *Life of Andrew Johnson, 17th President of the United States* (Greeneville, Tenn., 1901), p. 21; Greeneville *Intelligencer*, August 6, 1875; *Journal of the Convention of the State of Tennessee Convened for the Purpose of Revising and Amending the Constitution Thereof* (Nashville, 1834), p. 102; Nashville *Republican*, August 13, 1835.

3. Indenture Signed by Andrew Johnson, Alex L. Moorehead, Before M. Lincoln, September 24, 1835, AJPP. Johnson let the shop with its three apprentices for the time of his absence, with himself getting two-thirds of the profits and Moorehead one-third.

4. Morris, *Tennessee Gazetteer*, p. 120.

5. W. W. Clayton, *History of Davidson County, Tennessee* (Philadelphia, 1880), pp. 208–9; Easton Morris, *The Tennessee Gazetteer or Topographical Dictionary* (Nashville, 1834), pp. 108–22. On Johnson's votes to change the site of the capital, see below, p. 46, and *PJ* 1:78–79.

6. Nashville *Republican,* October 6, 1835; J. B. Netherland to Martha Patterson, August 4, 1875, JP.

7. *Tennessee House Journal,* 21st General Assembly, 1st Sess., 14; Thomas Perkins Abernethy, *From Frontier to Plantation in Tennessee* (Chapel Hill, 1932), p. 300.

8. *Tennessee House Journal,* 21st General Assembly, 1st Sess., 81, 136–37, 27, 619. He voted against Joseph C. Guild's motion that the House take up the preamble and resolutions instructing senators to vote for the Expunging Resolutions after having supported them briefly previously. Nashville *Republican,* January 26, 1836.

9. Johnson to Alexander Williams, January 27, 1836, PJ 1:16–17. East, West, and Middle Tennessee constituted the grand divisions of the state.

10. *Tennessee House Journal,* 21st General Assembly, 1st Sess., 103–4, 131–34, 141, 144, 160–61; Temple, *Notable Men,* pp. 364–65; Nashville *Union,* May 8, 1856. Johnson did not, however, oppose all railroad legislation. For example, he supported a bill to incorporate the Cincinnati and Charleston Railroad Company: *Tennessee House Journal,* 21st General Assembly, 1st Sess., 370.

11. *Tennessee House Journal,* 21st General Assembly, 1st Sess., 357, 463–64, 657, 671, 358, 564, 635, 262.

12. Nashville *Union,* February 23, 1836; Benjamin Truman, "Anecdotes of Andrew Johnson," *Century Illustrated Magazine* 63 (1912–13): 435–40, esp. 436.

13. All these men were members of the legislature, though Milligan entered only after 1840. For biographical details, see William S. Speer, ed., *Sketches of Prominent Tennesseans* (Nashville, 1888), esp. pp. 63, 298–302; J. C. Guild, *Old Times in Tennessee* (Nashville, 1878); *Biographical Directory, Tennessee General Assembly, 1796–1969* (Nashville, 1977), esp. pp. 11, 13; and Temple, *Notable Men,* esp. pp. 152ff., 159ff.

14. *Tennessee House Journal,* 21st General Assembly, Called Session, 1, 1, 25, 38–39, 41, 49; Johnson to George W. Jones, December 25, 1836, PJ 1:18–20.

15. Fay W. Brabson, *Andrew Johnson: A Life in Pursuit of the Right Course, 1808–1875* (Durham, N.C., 1972), pp. 15–16; Jones, *Johnson,* pp. 28ff.; Greeneville Mayor's Book, AJPP, p. 258.

16. Temple, *Notable Men,* pp. 367–68; Nashville *Union,* August 12, 17, 1837. The *Union* referred to both candidates as "Republicans." For Campbell's rancor, see L. D. Wood to Johnson, September 22, 1865, JP. Though the writer stated that Campbell resented his later defeat, he was obviously angry at Johnson before.

17. Nashville *Union,* July 18, 1838; Abernethy, *From Frontier to Plantation,* pp. 301–2.

18. Temple, *Notable Men,* pp. 368, 375.

19. *Tennessee House Journal,* 23d General Assembly, 1st Sess., 161, 176, 255, 294, 344, 362, 376–77, 238–39, 445, 475, 514, 262, 246, 494, 50, 73; Nashville *Republican Banner,* October 21, December 23, 1839; Johnson to John Young, March 10, 1840, PJ 1:26–27.

20. *Tennessee House Journal,* 23d General Assembly, 1st Sess., 22; Frank B. Williams, *Tennessee's Presidents* (Knoxville, 1981), p. 76; *Correspondence of James K. Polk,* Herbert Weaver, ed. (vols. 1–4), Wayne Cutler, ed. (vols. 5ff.) (Nashville, 1969-present), 5:247, 301, 420, 573. The votes cited above generally paralleled administration policy. Nevertheless, Polk's and Johnson's banking policies began to diverge at this time. Charles Grier Sellers, *James K. Polk, Jacksonian, 1795–1843* (Princeton, 1957), 386–87.

21. *Tennessee House Journal,* 23d General Assembly, 1st Sess., 8–9, 210, 178; Nashville *Daily Republican Banner,* October 9, 1839. Johnson's antagonist Parson William G. Brownlow liked to accuse him of infidelity for years afterward. *Brownlow's Knoxville Whig,* June 30, December 1, 1855.

22. Temple, *Notable Men,* pp. 271–75.

23. Nashville *Union* (semiweekly), February 11, 1840.

24. *Ibid.,* March 26, June 4, 8, 11, 1840; Temple, *Notable Men,* pp. 375–76; Robert B. Reynolds to Polk, October 22, 1840, Polk to Arthur R. Cozier, April 6, 1840, *Polk Correspondence,* 5:420, 569; DAB 3:546; PJ 1:76 n.

25. Thomas B. Alexander, "Strange Bedfellows: The Interlocking Careers of T. A. R.

Nelson, Andrew Johnson, and William G. (Parson) Brownlow," *ETHSP* 24 (1952): 68–91, esp. 69.

26. E. Merton Coulter, *William G. Brownlow: Fighting Parson of the Southern Highlands* (Chapel Hill, 1937); Steve Humphrey, *"That D . . . d Brownlow . . . "* (Boone, N.C., 1978).

27. Jonesboro *Whig*, October 28, 1840. Brownlow used the term "Toady Johnson" with special relish during the 1844 campaign: see, for example, Jonesboro *Whig*, July 14, 1844.

28. *PJ* 1:27–28. The Democratic majority dropped from 827 in 1839 to 477 in 1840.

29. Brabson, *Johnson*, pp. 16–17; Nashville *Union* (semiweekly), August 16, 1841; L. D. Wood to Johnson, September 22, 1865, JP; Robert B. Reynolds to Polk, March 28, 1841, *Polk Correspondence*, 5:667.

30. Richard M. Woods to Polk, January 6, 1841, *Polk Correspondence*, 5:613; Johnson to Polk, March 4, 1841, *PJ* 1:30–33.

31. Jones, *Johnson*, pp. 28–31; Martha B. Patterson to J. R. Williams, February 7, 1931, AJPP; J. S. Buckingham, *The Slave States of America*, 2 vols. (London, 1842), 2:240; Brabson, *Johnson*, p. 15.

32. Ernie Pyle, *Home Country* (New York, 1947), pp. 98, 467; Jones, *Johnson*, pp. 30–31; Margaret J. Patterson to Mrs. Smiley Brown, April 13, 1944, Margaret G. Blanton Papers, UT; Statement of Andrew J. Patterson, Brabson Papers, UT. William A. Johnson became a cook and employee of a Knoxville hotel; he took great pride in being the only living ex-slave of a president. Disappointed not to have been able to meet Franklin D. Roosevelt when the president came to dedicate the Norris Dam, he was delighted to have Ernie Pyle arrange a meeting with Roosevelt in Washington.

33. Speech at Newport, Ky., September 2, 1861, *PJ* 6:4, 6; Brabson, *Johnson*, p. 17; David Warren Bowen, "Andrew Johnson and the Negro," Ph.D. diss., UT, 1976, pp. 17–18. On Johnson's racist views, see below, pp. 62, 72, 220, 231, 237.

34. Portrait in George F. Milton, *The Age of Hate: Andrew Johnson and the Radicals* (New York, 1930), opposite p. 94.

35. Bergeron, *Antebellum Politics in Tennessee*, pp. 68–70; Joseph Howard Parks, *John Bell of Tennessee* (Baton Rouge, 1956), p. 7.

36. Speech in Defense of the "Immortal Thirteen," October 27–28, 1841, *PJ* 1:36–58.

37. *Tennessee Senate Journal*, 24th General Assembly, 102ff., 135ff., 178ff., 210ff., 228ff., 239ff., 244, 279ff., 285–86, 304–6, 315ff., 410–12, 709; Stanley J. Folmsbee et al., *History of Tennessee*, 4 vols. (New York, 1960), 1:350–53.

38. Powell Moore, "James K. Polk and the 'Immortal Thirteen,' " *ETHSP* 11 (1939): 20–33, esp. 30; Bergeron, *Antebellum Politics in Tennessee*, p. 70.

39. Nashville *Union* (triweekly), November 28, 1841; Polk to Sackfield Maclin, January 17, 1842, James K. Polk Papers, TSLA.

40. Jonesboro *Whig*, November 3, 1841; John R. Nelson to T. A. R. Nelson, November 11, 1841, March 22, 1842, Nelson Papers, Lawson-McGee Library, Knoxville.

41. *Tennessee Senate Journal*, 24th General Assembly, Called Session, 132, 151, 163, 168, 192; Folmsbee et al., *Tennessee*, 1:354.

42. *Tennessee Senate Journal*, 24th General Assembly, 358–61, 655ff., 288, 443, 495, 520, 551, 643; Resolution for the Establishment of Frankland, December 7, 1841, *PJ* 1:6–62.

43. *Tennessee Senate Journal*, 24th General Assembly, 348–49, 459, 465, 582, 608, 615, 581, 617–20, 645ff., 662, 605, 616; To "Citizens of Tennessee," February 9, 1842, *PJ* 1:81–84.

44. Nashville *Union*, May 31, June 28, July 12, 1842. In 1839 some Democrats sought to embarrass the Whigs by demanding that the Whig-directed Bank of Tennessee suspend specie payment. Sellers, *Polk*, pp. 386–87.

45. Speech on Election of Senators, the Veto Power, and Other Matters, October 5, 1842, *PJ* 1:85–97; Speech on Redistricting and Other Matters, October 5, 1842, *PJ* 1:85–99; Nashville *Union*, October 5, 1842.

46. Jonesboro *Whig*, November 16, 1842; *Tennessee Senate Journal*, 24th General Assembly, Called Session, 3, 15; Resolutions on Congressional Districting, October 6, 1842, *PJ* 1:85–86.

47. Jonesboro *Whig*, October 26, 1842.

48. Hans L. Trefousse, "Abraham Lincoln Versus Andrew Johnson: Two Approaches to Reconstruction," in Steven B. and Agnes Hussar Vadar, eds., *Society in Change: Studies in Honor of Bela Kalman Kiraly* (Boulder, Colo., 1983), pp. 251–70, esp. 259ff.

49. *Tennessee Senate Journal*, 24th General Assembly, Called Session, 184–85, 46. Presumably he wanted to increase Democratic strength because in the last few elections the Democrats polled a larger percentage statewide than in a majority of the congressional districts. See Bergeron, *Antebellum Politics in Tennessee*, p. 24.

50. *Tennessee Senate Journal*, 24th General Assembly, Called Session, 58, 83, 119, 135, 173, 181–82; Protest Against Legislative Apportionment Act, November 12, 1842, *PJ* 1:100–5; Temple, *Notable Men*, pp. 216–17, 377–78. Bergeron, *Antebellum Politics in Tennessee*, p. 24, holds that the district was deliberately redrawn by Johnson to create a fiefdom for himself. The Democrats finally allowed the Whig bill to pass because they correctly saw in it some advantages in electing congressmen regardless of Whig legislative districts. Nashville *Union*, November 25, 1842. Brookins Campbell was the chairman of the House committee in charge of redistricting, and Johnson's protest was directed against him, but the House in turn censured Johnson by passing a resolution specifically praising Campbell's actions. *Tennessee House Journal*, 24th General Assembly, Called Session, 199.

IV. FLEDGLING CONGRESSMAN

1. Oliver P. Temple, *Notable Men of Tennessee* (New York, 1912), p. 216.

2. A. Johnson et al. to Aaron V. Brown, December 6, 1842, *PJ* 1:108–10.

3. Johnson to James K. Polk, February 20, 1843, *PJ* 1:113–14.

4. Jonesboro *Whig*, April 19, 1843; Temple, *Notable Men*, pp. 216–17.

5. Jonesboro *Whig*, February 22, March 1, 1843.

6. Jonesboro *Whig*, March 29, 1843. On the charges, see below, p. 56.

7. Jonesboro *Whig*, July 5, April 5, 1843; "Aristides" letter in *PJ* 1:115–18.

8. Nashville *Union*, July 11, August 8, 11, 1843; Jonesboro *Whig*, May 17, 31, June 7, 14, 23, July 12, 19, 1843; James S. Jones, *Life of Andrew Johnson, 17th President of the United States* (Greeneville, Tenn., 1901), p. 40; Humphrey, *"That D . . . d Brownlow . . . "* (Boone, N.C., 1978), pp. 59–60.

9. Kenneth M. Stampp, *The Era of Reconstruction, 1865–1877* (New York, 1965), pp. 50ff.

10. A. Whitney Griswold, *Farming and Democracy* (New Haven, 1948), pp. 21ff., 30, 36–45; Henry Nash Smith, *Virgin Land: The American West as Symbol and Myth* (New York, 1950), pp. 144ff., 151–52, 156; Julian Boyd, ed., *The Papers of Thomas Jefferson*, 21 vols. (Princeton, 1950–83), 2:472. Jefferson later conceded that black backwardness, in which he believed despite his hatred for slavery, might disappear with time. *Ibid.*, 8:186.

11. Temple, *Notable Men*, pp. 367–68, 230–31; John B. Brownlow to Temple, January 31, 1891, April 19, 1892, Temple Papers, UT.

12. To Democratic Committee of Maury County, August 29, 1843, *PJ* 1:118–21.

13. Jonesboro *Whig*, December 13, 1843, also in *PJ* 1:122–30.

14. Margaret G. Blanton, "Tennessee Johnson's Eliza," MS in author's possession through the courtesy of Dr. Betty Caroli, makes no reference to Eliza's accompanying her husband. There is no evidence of her having lived in Washington during Johnson's service in the House, and her reticence was well known. Temple, *Notable Men*, p. 360.

15. Charles Dickens, *American Notes* (London, 1842), pp. 128–35, 155; J. S. Buckingham, *America Historical, Statistic and Descriptive* (London, 1841), 1:282ff., 294, 304ff., 341ff., 360ff.; Sir Charles Lyell, *A Second Visit to the United States of North America* (New York,

1849), pp. 196–204; William M. Morrison, *Morrison's Stranger's Guide to the City of Washington and Its Vicinity* (Washington, D.C., 1844), pp. 12–16, 30–54; Robert Sears, *A New and Popular Pictorial Description of the United States* (New York, 1848), pp. 279–90; Roy Frank Nichols, *The Disruption of the American Democracy* (New York, 1948), pp. 140–42; Margaret Leech, *Reveille in Washington, 1860–1865* (New York, 1941), pp. 6–10.

16. Residences of Andrew Johnson, AJPP; William S. Speer, ed., *Sketches of Prominent Tennesseans* (Nashville, 1888), p. 532.

17. Benjamin Truman, "Anecdotes of Andrew Johnson," *Century Illustrated Magazine*, 63 (1912–13): 436.

18. Temple, *Notable Men*, pp. 452–54; Robert Winston, *Andrew Johnson, Plebeian and Patriot* (New York, 1928), p. 43; Dickens, *American Notes*, pp. 133–34. Between 1847 and 1861 eight separate references to Addison may be found in the *PJ*: 1:352–54, 507; 2:281, 407; 3:232, 241; 4:41; 5:25.

19. *Cong. Globe*, 28th Cong., 1st Sess., 1843–44.

20. Washington *Daily National Intelligencer*, April 18, 19, March 7, June 9, 1844. Johnson did, however, press for the establishment of a mail route for his constituents, from Rogersville to Russelville, Tennessee. *Cong. Globe*, 28th Cong., 1st Sess., 203; for improvements in the Holston River, *ibid.*, 489.

21. *Cong. Globe*, 28th Cong., 1st Sess., 368, 615–16, App. 745; *PJ* 1:166–69.

22. Washington *Daily National Intelligencer*, June 13, 1844.

23. *Cong. Globe*, 28th Cong., 1st Sess., 666–67; *PJ* 1:169–70.

24. Johnson to David D. Patterson, April 13, May 13, 1844, Speech on the Admission of Texas and Other Matters, January 21, 1845, *PJ* 1:160–61, 161–65, 187–207, esp. 205.

25. *Cong. Globe*, 28th Cong., 1st Sess., App. 95–98; *PJ* 1:133–48.

26. New York *Tribune*, January 15, 1844; *Cong. Globe*, 28th Cong., 1st Sess., 139–40; Winston, *Johnson*, p. 46.

27. Pension Office to Johnson, December 27, 1843, Charles A. Wickliffe to Johnson, December 29, 1843, Johnson to William M. Lowry, February 13, 1844, Dicks Alexander to Johnson, February 27, 1844, Blackston McDannel to Johnson, April 1844, Pension Office to Johnson, May 6, 9, 1844, William S. J. Ford to Johnson, May 16, 1844, Johnson to Commissioner of Pensions, July 20, 1844, *PJ* 1:131–32, 152–54, 55–57, 160, 161, 165–66, 171. For Johnson's committee assignment, see *Cong. Globe*, 28th Cong., 1st Sess., 42–43.

28. North Carolina Supreme Court *Reports* (Raleigh, 1916), 33:270–85; Petition of Jury, April 2, 1841, NCA; Hugh B. Johnson, Jr., "Was a First Cousin of President Andrew Johnson Hanged in Raleigh?" *North Carolina Genealogical Society Journal* 4 (1978): 30–34; Jonesboro *Whig*, May 10, 1843, July 14, 1844. For Johnson's eventual admission of the charge, see below, p. 60.

29. Raleigh *Register and North Carolina Gazette* (weekly), June 28, 1844; Raleigh *North Carolina Standard*, June 26, 1844; Jonesboro *Whig*, June 14, 1844; John Savage, *The Life and Public Services of Andrew Johnson* (New York, 1866), p. 17.

30. Johnson to David Patterson, February 27, May 13, 1844, Johnson to William Lowry, March 30, 1844, Johnson to A. O. P. Nicholson, February 12, 1844, *PJ* 1:154–55, 161–64, 157, 148–51.

31. Nashville *Union*, November 25, 1843, September 23, October 8, 1844; Milo M. Quaife, ed., *The Diary of James K. Polk During His Presidency, 1845–1849*, 4 vols. (Chicago, 1910), 2:35–41; Jonesboro *Whig*, July 10, August 14, September 4, October 9, November 16, 1844; Paul H. Bergeron, *Antebellum Politics in Tennessee* (Lexington, Ky., 1982), p. 42; A. O. P. Nicholson to Johnson, July 23, 1844, *PJ* 1:172–73.

32. *Cong. Globe*, 28th Cong., 2d Sess., 170, App. 219–23; *PJ* 1:187–207. In keeping with his Jeffersonian notions, Johnson also refuted Clingman's slurs against the "ignorant yeomanry" of Pennsylvania, charging that there were more illiterate people in North Carolina than in Pennsylvania, where these literate yeomen had voted Democratic. He

also advocated the appointment of federal clerks by districts, a notion to which he
would recur.

33. Washington *Daily National Intelligencer*, January 28, 29, February 4, 28, March 3, 1845;
Cong. Globe, 28th Cong., 2d Sess., 356, 363, 369.

34. Jonesboro *Whig*, December 11, 1844.

35. Washington *Daily National Intelligencer*, February 20, 1845.

36. Nashville *Union* (triweekly), March 27, April 9, 29, May 6, 31, June 17, 1845; Jonesboro
Whig, May 7, 28, 1845; Johnson to [First District Democratic Committee], April 26,
1845, *PJ* 1:216.

37. Jonesboro *Whig*, June 18, 25, July 16, 30, 1845. After attacking Josiah Holloman and
Hudson Bailey in the course of a robbery, Matthew Johnson and a companion were
indicted for manslaughter, found guilty of the death of Holloman, and sentenced to be
branded on the left thumb with the letter "M," to be imprisoned for nine months, and
to pay the costs. Raleigh *Register* (semiweekly), January 17, 1845; Wake County Superior
Court Minutes, Spring Term 1845, State vs. Matthew Johnson, Lewis Dunning, March
31, April 3, April 5, 1845.

38. *To the Freemen of the First Congressional District of Tennessee*, October 15, 1845, *PJ*
1:220–75; Thomas B. Alexander, "Strange Bedfellows: The Interlocking Careers of
T. A. R. Nelson, Andrew Johnson, and W. G. (Parson) Brownlow," *ETHSP* 24 (1952):
68–91, esp. 73–74. Brownlow even printed a scurrilous "obituary" of Johnson.

39. Washington *Daily National Intelligencer*, December 10, 16, 1845, January 14, March 7,
10, April 8, 21, May 12, June 16, 22, July 28, 1846; Nashville *Union* (triweekly), March
17, 1846.

40. *Cong. Globe*, 29th Cong., 1st Sess., 884–87; *PJ* 1:309–14; Washington *Daily National
Intelligencer*, January 27, December 17, 1845, August 10, 1846, February 16, 1847;
Thomas J. Powel to Johnson, May 26, 1846, Johnson to Blackston McDannel, July 22,
1846, *PJ* 1:308–9, 330–33, 314.

41. Jonesboro *Whig*, December 31, 1845; Washington *Daily National Intelligencer*, December
20, 1845, February 19, 1846.

42. *Cong. Globe*, 29th Cong., 1st Sess., 192–93; Washington Curran Whitthorne, MS
Diary, January 15, 1846, TSLA.

43. House of Representatives, 29th Cong., 1st Sess., *Journal*, May 11, 1848, p. 793; *Cong.
Globe*, 29th Cong., 1st Sess., 739, 741, 755, 1011–13, 884–87, 492; *PJ* 1:303–6, 317–24,
309–14, 300–1.

44. St. George L. Sioussat, "Andrew Johnson and the Early Phases of the Homestead Bill,"
Tennessee Historical Magazine 6 (1920): 14–75; James F. Rusling, *Men and Things I Saw
in Civil War Days* (New York, 1899), p. 19.

45. *Cong. Globe*, 29th Cong., 1st Sess., 286–89, 293–94, App. 331–35; *PJ* 1:282–96; Whitthorne, MS Diary, January 31, February 2, 1846; John H. Wheeler, *Reminiscences and
Memoirs of North Carolina and Eminent North Carolinians* (Baltimore, 1966), p. 535; John
J. Craven, *Prison Life of Jefferson Davis* (New York, 1867), p. 299. For Johnson's earlier
views on Oregon, see Nashville *Union* (triweekly), April 16, 1845.

46. *Cong. Globe*, 29th Cong., 1st Sess., 877–78, 884, 885, 887; *PJ* 1:309–14; Dunbar
Rowland, ed., *Jefferson Davis, Constitutionalist: His Letters, Papers, and Speeches*, 10 vols.
(Jackson, Miss., 1923), 1:51, 8:380; Craven, *Prison Life of Jefferson Davis*, p. 299.

47. Johnson to James K. Polk, April 9, 1845, Johnson to Blackston McDannel, July 22, 1846,
PJ 1:213, 331–33; Quaife, *Polk Diary*, 1:328–29 (April 11, 1846). For Martha's school
bill, see *PJ* 1:210.

48. Quaife, *Polk Diary*, 2:35–41 (July 21, 1846); Johnson to an Unidentified [East?] Tennessean, July 21, 1846, *PJ* 1:330–31.

49. Johnson to Blackston McDannel, July 22, 1846, *PJ* 1:331–33.

50. Quaife, *Polk Diary*, 2:35–41 (July 21, 1846); Paul H. Bergeron, *The Presidency of James
K. Polk* (Lawrence, Kansas, 1987), p. 148.

51. Charles Sellers, *James K. Polk, Continentalist, 1843–1846* (Princeton, 1966), p. 10.
52. *Ibid.*; *Cong. Globe*, 29th Cong., 2d Sess., 38–40, App. 89–90; PJ 1:337–47, 350–68.
53. PJ 1:337–47, 350–68; *Cong. Globe*, 29th Cong., 2d Sess., 272, 527, 313; Jonesboro *Whig*, September 16, 1846, March 10, 1847; Washington *Daily National Intelligencer*, February 27, 1847.
54. Johnson to Blackston McDannel, January 10, 1847, PJ 1:368–70.
55. *Cong. Globe*, 29th Cong., 2d Sess., App. 160–63; PJ 1:373–86; Temple, *Notable Men*, p. 217.
56. Temple, *Notable Men*, p. 217; L. C. Haynes to Nicholson, March 21, 1847, Miscellaneous MSS, NYHS.
57. Temple, *Notable Men*, pp. 216–19; Temple to W. G. Brownlow, July 18, 19, 1847, Temple Papers.
58. Temple, *Notable Men*, pp. 219–32; Speer, *Sketches*, p. 541; Jonesboro *Whig*, July 21, 28, August 11, August 18, May 26, 1847; Nashville *Daily Union*, August 13, 1847. The charge about the alleged censure of Taylor was far-fetched; Johnson had merely supported an amendment to a prowar resolution of thanks to General Taylor stating that "nothing herein contained shall be construed into an approbation of the terms of the capitulation of Monterey," but voted for the main question. *Cong. Globe*, 29th Cong., 2d Sess., 295–96.

V. VETERAN CONGRESSMAN

1. *Cong. Globe*, 30th Cong., 1st Sess., 48–49, 179, 181, 105; PJ 1:394–96, 397–99; David Outlaw to Mrs. Outlaw, December 17, 1847, David Outlaw Papers, SHC.
2. *Cong. Globe*, 30th Cong., 1st Sess., 223–24, 312, 457, 786, 800–2, 857, 944–46; PJ 1:400–3, 414, 430–37, 428, 441–44; Washington *National Intelligencer*, March 8, May 27, June 21, July 7, 1848; Nashville *Daily Union*, March 16, 1848.
3. Nashville *Daily Union*, February 1, 1848; *Cong. Globe*, 30th Cong., 1st Sess., App. 853–56; PJ 1:444–61; McDannel to Johnson, January 28, 1848, Johnson to McDannel, March 24, 1848, PJ 1:403–11, 416–17. Johnson complained about Milligan's failure to write but was kept informed about him by McDannel.
4. *Cong. Globe*, 30th Cong., 1st Sess., 637; PJ 1:418–21; Johnson to David T. Patterson, March 23, 1848, PJ 1:416.
5. Nashville *Daily Union*, April 13, 1848; Mary E. Campbell, *The Attitude of Tennesseans Toward the Union, 1847–1861* (New York, 1961), p. 229; Johnson to Blackston McDannel, March 24, 1848, Johnson to A. O. P. Nicholson, May 14, 1848, PJ 1:416–17, 424–27.
6. Jonesboro *Whig*, September 6, October 11, 25, 1848; Thomas B. Alexander, *Thomas A. R. Nelson of East Tennessee* (Nashville, 1956), p. 36; Paul H. Bergeron, *Antebellum Politics in Tennessee* (Lexington, Ky., 1982), p. 22.
7. Johnson to Blackston McDannel and Sam Milligan, October 19, 1847, William L. Marcy to Johnson, December 27, 1847, January 11, March 14, 1848, PJ 1:391–94, 396, 415.
8. Milo M. Quaife, ed., *The Diary of James K. Polk During His Presidency, 1845–1849*, 4 vols. (Chicago, 1910), 4:264.
9. Johnson to Blackston McDannel, November 4, 1848, PJ 1:463–65.
10. Washington *Daily National Intelligencer*, December 20, 1848; Washington *National Intelligencer* (triweekly), January 11, 1849; *Cong. Globe*, 30th Cong., 2d Sess., 38, 55–56, 83–84, 212; Roy P. Basler, ed., *The Collected Works of Abraham Lincoln*, 9 vols. (New Brunswick, 1953–55), 2:218; Nashville *Daily Union*, February 3, 1849; Richard K. Cralle, ed., *The Works of John C. Calhoun*, 6 vols. (New York, 1853–55), 6:311–13.
11. Washington *Daily National Intelligencer*, December 13, 1848; *Cong. Globe*, 30th Cong., 2d Sess., 22–28, 334–36; PJ 1:468–72, 488–90.

12. Alexander Williams to Nelson, April 14, 1849, Nelson Papers, Lawson-McGhee Library, Knoxville; Johnson to "an Intelligent Gentleman in Jonesborough," March 20, 1849, *PJ* 1:677–79.

13. Nashville *Union,* May 21, 1849, *PJ* 1:677–79.

14. Johnson to David T. Patterson, February 28, 1847, Johnson to A. O. P. Nicholson, September 8, 1845, Johnson to David T. Patterson, April 5, 1850, Johnson to Mary Johnson, December 7, 1850, January 18, 1851, *PJ* 1:389, 218–19, 533–34, 591–92, 596–97; William S. Speer, ed., *Sketches of Prominent Tennesseans* (Nashville, 1888), p. 532.

15. Nashville *Daily Union,* May 9, 17, 1849; Johnson to John Stanberry, April 29, 1849, Johnson to David T. Patterson, May 9, 1849, Johnson to Elbridge G. Eastman, May 27, 1849, Johnson to Sam Milligan, June 1849, *PJ* 1:494–97, 509–12.

16. Speech at Evans Crossroads, May 26, 1849, *PJ* 1:498–509.

17. Truman Smith to Thomas A. R. Nelson, July 10, 1849, Nelson Papers; Nashville *Daily Union,* August 10, 1849; Bergeron, *Antebellum Politics in Tennessee,* p. 85.

18. Washington *National Intelligencer* (biweekly), December 4, 11, 13, 15, 18, 20, 22, 25, 1849; Nashville *Daily Union,* January 1, 1850; Knoxville *Register,* January 5, 1850; *Brownlow's Knoxville Whig,* January 12, 1850.

19. *Cong. Globe,* 31st Cong., 1st Sess., 515.

20. *Ibid.,* 1127, App. 669–73; *PJ* 1:539–53.

21. James D. Richardson, ed., *A Compilation of the Messages and Papers of the Presidents, 1789–1897,* 10 vols. (Washington, D.C., 1896–99), 6:2603–9; *Cong. Globe,* 31st Cong., 1st Sess., App. 1049–51; *PJ* 1:573–83; Washington *National Intelligencer* (triweekly), August 31, 1850.

22. Roy M. Robbins, *Our Landed Heritage: The Public Domain, 1776–1936* (Princeton, 1942), p. 113; St. George L. Sioussat, "Andrew Johnson and the Early Phases of the Homestead Bill," *Tennessee Historical Magazine* 6 (1920): 38ff.; *Cong. Globe,* 31st Cong., 1st Sess., 408, 423, 1122, 1449–50, App. 950–52; John Shields to Johnson, June 9, 1850, *PJ* 1:553–54; Homestead speech in *PJ* 1:557–72. The bill was referred to the Committee of the Whole: Nashville *Daily Union,* July 29, 1850.

23. *Cong. Globe,* 31st Cong., 1st Sess., 243, 296–97, 571, 1591; *PJ* 1:524–28, 529–32, 585; Washington *National Intelligencer* (triweekly), April 29, 1850, December 10, 1849; John H. Wheeler, *Reminiscences and Memoirs of North Carolina and Eminent North Carolinians* (Baltimore, 1966), p. 435.

24. *Cong. Globe,* 31st Cong., 2d Sess., 340–41, 759; *PJ* 1:600–2, 611–12.

25. Washington *National Intelligencer,* February 21, 1851; *Brownlow's Knoxville Whig,* February 8, 1851; *Cong. Globe,* 31st Cong., 2d Sess., 225. Despite his vote against rivers and harbors bills, Johnson again appeared to favor improvements in the French Broad and Holston rivers.

26. Johnson to Daniel Webster, January 27, 1851, Webster Papers, Dartmouth College, copy at AJPP; Maurice G. Baxter, *One and Inseparable: Daniel Webster and the Union* (Cambridge, 1984), p. 476.

27. Washington *National Intelligencer* (triweekly), January 11, 23, 25, 30, February 1, March 4, 1851; *Cong. Globe,* 31st Cong., 2d Sess., 22, 94, 120–21, 204, 216, 278, 312–13, 352–53, 752, in part in *PJ* 1:598–600, 608–10.

28. Nashville *Daily Union,* July 13, August 9, 27, December 16, 1850.

29. Nashville *Daily Union,* November 14, 1850; *Cong. Globe,* 31st Cong., 2d Sess., 627; J. B. Brownlow to Oliver P. Temple, January 1, 1896, Temple Papers, UT.

30. John Bell to T. A. R. Nelson, February 25, 1850, Nelson Papers; *Brownlow's Knoxville Whig,* February 16, 1850; Johnson to David T. Patterson, May 30, 1850, Johnson to William M. Lowry, August 12, 1850, *PJ* 1:536–38, 584–85.

31. James W. Bellamy, "The Political Career of Landon Carter Haynes," *ETHSP* 28 (1956): 102–26, esp. 112ff.

32. *Ibid.;* Oliver P. Temple, *Notable Men of Tennessee* (New York, 1912), p. 378; *Brownlow's*

Knoxville Whig, April 26, June 21, 26, July 12, August 11, 16, 1851; Nashville *Daily Union*, August 13, 1851; Johnson to A. O. P. Nicholson, April 16, May 11, 1851, Johnson to Blackston McDannel, July 15, 1851, *PJ* 1:613–14, 615–17, 620–22; John B. Brownlow to Oliver P. Temple, January 31, 1891, April 19, July 16, 1892, Temple Papers; Felix A. Reeve, *East Tennessee in the War of the Rebellion, Military Order of the Loyal Legion of the United States, Commandery of the District of Columbia, War Papers*, no. 44 (Washington, D.C., 1902), p. 29.

33. Martha B. Patterson to J. R. Williams, February 7, 1931, AJPP; Receipt for Payment as Surety Bond, November 11, 1848, Mordecai Wyrick to Johnson, November 17, 1848, Johnson to Mordecai L. Wyrick, November 18, 1848, Deed for Andrew Johnson House, September 10, 1851, *PJ* 1:465–68, 624–25. The price was $950 plus a deed to James Brannon of town lot No. 77, including Johnson's old house.

34. Hugh A. Lawing, *Andrew Johnson National Historic Site*, revised reprint from *THQ* 20 (1960): 7ff.

35. Frank B. Williams, *Tennessee's Presidents* (Knoxville, 1980), pp. 71–72; W. G. McDonough, Speech, NCA; Lawing, *Johnson Historic Site*, p. 17; Memo, Martha J. Patterson, April 9, 1901, AJPP; Ernest Allan Conolly, "The Andrew Johnson Homestead at Greeneville, Tennessee," *ETHSP* 29 (1957): 118–40.

36. Johnson to Mary Johnson, January 18, 1851, Johnson to David T. Patterson, April 5, 1850, Johnson to Mary Johnson Stover, July 16, 1852, *PJ* 1:491n, 596–97, 533–34, 2:66–67; Robert Winston, *Andrew Johnson: Plebeian and Patriot* (New York, 1926), pp. 96–97.

37. Gilbert Patton Brown, "The Unique Personality of Andrew Johnson," *Masonic Review* 23 (December 1931): 16–19; Richard Harrison Doughty, *Greeneville: One Hundred Year Portrait, 1775–1875* (Greeneville, 1975), pp. 31–32. In 1866 President Johnson became a Thirty-third-Degree Mason: Harry J. Seymour to Johnson, October 3, 1866, JP.

38. Johnson to David T. Patterson, March 23, 1848, Johnson to William Lowry, August 12, 1850, In Account with Lyon and Dobson, October 1851, Johnson to David T. Patterson, April 5, 1850, *PJ* 1:533–34, 416, 491n., 584, 627–28.

39. Johnson to Horace Greeley, December 15, 1851, James Elliot to Johnson, March 22, 1852, Johnson to George Henry Evans, May 24, 1852, *PJ* 1:631–33, 2:24–27, 56–57; *Cong. Globe*, 32d Cong., 1st Sess., 120–21, 225, 462, 716, 834, 926, 1019, 1173, 1176, 1275, 1279–80, 1351, App. 529–30; speeches also in *PJ* 2:21–22, 27–29, 33–55; Allan Nevins, *Ordeal of the Union*, 2 vols. (New York, 1947), 2:33; *Brownlow's Knoxville Whig*, January 31, 1852; Walter Prescott Webb, *The Great Plains* (New York, 1931), p. 406; Benjamin Horace Hibbard, *A History of the Public Land Policies* (New York, 1924), pp. 366, 370. Southern opposition contributed to the measure's lack of success in the Senate.

40. Johnson to George Henry Evans et al., May 24, 1852, Speech to the New York Land Reformers, May 27, 1852, *PJ* 2:56–61; New York *Tribune*, May 26, 27, 28, 1852; New York *Herald*, May 28, 1852.

41. *Cong. Globe*, 32d Cong., 1st Sess., 2246, 2250, 2259, 2166, 443, 342–45, 411–12; *PJ* 2:78–83, 76–78, 19, 4–18; Washington *Daily National Intelligencer*, December 16, 25, 1851, January 4, July 15, 1852; Nashville *Daily Union*, January 20, 1852.

42. Johnson to David T. Patterson, April 4, 1852, Johnson to Sam Milligan, July 20, 1852, Speech at Rogersville, September 28, 1852, *PJ* 2:30–32, 67–71, 86–88.

43. Johnson to Blackston McDannel, December 1, 1852, Johnson to David T. Patterson, December 3, 1852, Johnson to Sam Milligan, December 28, 1852, *PJ* 2:90–96, 100–4; cf. Michael F. Holt, *The Political Crisis of the 1850s* (New York, 1978), passim.

44. House Report No. 1, 32d Cong., 2d Sess.; *Cong. Globe*, 32d Cong., 2d Sess., App. 64–67; *PJ* 2:105–19; Cong. Expense Account, 1853, *PJ* 2:136–37. Johnson requested and received payment four years later. The committee met during the recess of Congress.

45. *Cong. Globe*, 32d Cong., 2d Sess., 475–77, 490–91, 1164; *PJ* 2:120–32, 137;

Nevins, *Ordeal of the Union*, 1:166. Dr. Gardiner eventually committed suicide.
46. Nashville *Daily Union*, February 23, 1852, Notes for Speech on Homestead Measure, April, 1852, Johnson to David Patterson, December 3, 1853, *PJ* 2:29, 92–96.

VI. GOVERNOR OF TENNESSEE

1. Johnson to David T. Patterson, December 3, 1852, *PJ* 2:92–96.
2. Mary E. Campbell, *The Attitude of Tennesseans Toward the Union, 1847–1861* (New York, 1961), p. 75; Nashville *Union*, January 10, 13, 15, 19, February 10, 13, 22, April 13, 16, 20, 28, 29, 30, 1853; George W. Jones, *Oration of the Hon. George W. Jones, With Other Proceedings at the Unveiling of the Monument to Ex-President Andrew Johnson, at Greeneville, Tennessee, June 5, 1878* (Nashville, 1878), pp. 9–10; Oliver P. Temple, *Notable Men of Tennessee* (New York, 1912), p. 379; Nashville *Republican Banner*, April 27, 29, 1853; John Brownlow to Temple, April 19, 1892, Temple Papers, UT; Robert G. Russell, "Prelude to the Presidency: The Election of Andrew Johnson to the Senate," *THQ* 26 (1967): 148–77, esp. 160ff.
3. Nicholson to Pierce, April 12, 1853, in Joseph P. Parks, ed., "Some Tennessee Letters, 1844–1864," *THQ* 4 (1945): 234–55, esp. 245; W. H. Sykes to Nicholson, 1854, S. R. Anderson to Nicholson, August 16, 1853, Nicholson Papers, NYHS; Hu Douglas to Johnson, December 30, 1860, *PJ* 4:103–4; Nashville *Republican Banner*, May 4, 1853.
4. Nashville *Union*, April 28, May 25, 1853; Richmond *Enquirer*, *ibid.*; Memphis *Appeal* (weekly), May 11, 1853; *Brownlow's Knoxville Whig*, April 2, 1853; Nashville *Republican Banner*, April 28, 29, May 4, 1853.
5. Temple, *Notable Men*, p. 380; W. M. Caskey, "First Administration of Governor Andrew Johnson," *ETHSP* 1 (1929): 43–59, esp. 45; Herbert Blair Bentley, "Andrew Johnson, Governor of Tennessee, 1853–57," Ph.D. diss., UT, 1972, p. 41.
6. Bentley, "Johnson, Governor of Tennessee," pp. 58–64; Speech at Sparta, June 1, 1853, *PJ* 2:139–44; Henry to J. O. Shackleford, June 3, 1853, Gustavus A. Henry Papers, SHC.
7. Speech at Shelbyville, June 6, 1853, Speech at Memphis, June 20, 1853, Speech at Clinton, July 13, 1853, *PJ* 2:144–64, 166–67; Nashville *Union*, July 1, 1853.
8. Nashville *Republican Banner*, June 9, 10, 11, 1853; Henry to Mrs. Henry, June 6, July 3, 1853, Henry Papers.
9. *Brownlow's Knoxville Whig*, June 2, July 2, 1853.
10. Robert H. Cartmell, Diary, June 15, 1853, Cartmell Papers, TSLA; Fay W. Brabson, *Andrew Johnson: A Life in Pursuit of the Right Course, 1808–1875* (Durham, N.C., 1972), pp. 40–41.
11. Speech at Shelbyville, June 6, 1853, *PJ* 2:155; Memphis *Appeal* (weekly), June 1, 1853.
12. Henry to J. O. Shackleford, June 3, 1853, Henry Papers; Henry Melville Doak Manuscript, p. 149, Henry Melville Doak Papers, TSLA; Announcement *re* Gubernatorial Canvass, July 29, 1853, *PJ* 2:167.
13. Nashville *Union and American*, August 10, 14, 16, October 11, 1853; *Brownlow's Knoxville Whig*, August 27, October 15, 1853; David Campbell to William Campbell, July 15, 1853, Campbell Family Papers, Duke University; S. R. Anderson to Nicholson, August 16, 1853, Nicholson Papers, NYHS. At the same time, a constitutional amendment for the election of judges was ratified: *PJ* 1:509.
14. William B. Campbell to Gen. D. Campbell, July 4, 29, August 10, 1853, Campbell Family Papers; New York *Evening Post*, August 8, 1853; *Brownlow's Knoxville Whig*, August 27, 1853.
15. Johnson to the Democracy of Maury County, September 18, 1853, Johnson to A. O. P. Nicholson, September 8, 1853, *PJ* 2:167–72; Bentley, "Johnson, Governor of Tennessee," p. 106.
16. Memphis *Avalanche* (weekly), June 15, 1853; Temple, *Notable Men*, pp. 378–82; Nashville *Republican Banner*, October 18, 1853. Bentley, "Johnson, Governor of Ten-

nessee," p. 107, casts doubt on the story of Johnson's walking to the inauguration.
17. First Inaugural Address, October 17, 1853, *PJ* 2:172–84.
18. David Campbell to William B. Campbell, October 28, 1853, Campbell Family Papers; Nashville *Union and American*, October 22, 22, 1853, also quoting Nashville *True Whig*; London *Times*, December 3, 1853.
19. W. W. Clayton, *History of Davidson County, Tennessee* (Philadelphia, 1880), pp. 208–9; Nashville *Republican Banner*, November 15, 1853.
20. Bentley, "Johnson, Governor of Tennessee," pp. 13–15, 113, 185–86; W. M. Caskey, "First Administration of Governor Andrew Johnson," ETHP 1 (1929): 48–51.
21. Appointment of Governor's Military Staff, November 16, 1853, *PJ* 2:186–87.
22. William G. Brownlow to Temple, October 26, 1853, Temple Papers; Nashville *Republican Banner*, October 21, 22, 27, 28, 31, 1853.
23. Nashville *Union and American*, December 22, 1853, January 10, 14, 18, 22, February 1, 1854; Nashville *Republican Banner*, January 10, February 10, 1854; H. Blair Bentley, "Andrew Johnson and the Tennessee State Penitentiary," *ETHSP* 47 (1975): 28–45; Bentley, "Johnson, Governor of Tennessee," pp. 109–206; Cave Johnson to Johnson, February 4, 1854, *PJ* 2:217–18. Cave Johnson could not remember whether Johnson used the alleged language.
24. Biennial Legislative Message, December 19, 1853, *PJ* 2:188–208; Nashville *Union and American*, December 13, 20, 30, 1853.
25. Winston, *Johnson*, pp. 85–86; Jones, *Johnson*, p. 391; *PJ* 3:372, n. 8; Henry Watterson, *"Marse Henry": An Autobiography*, 2 vols. (New York, 1919), 1:152.
26. Stanley J. Folmsbee et al., *History of Tennessee*, 4 vols. (New York, 1960), 1:458; A. P. Whitaker, "The Public School System of Tennessee," *Tennessee Historical Magazine* 2 (1916): 1–30, esp. 21; John Heriges to Johnson, August 9, 1854, *PJ* 2:243–46, esp. n. 1, and 341, n. 17. Although the governor gave no overt support to the measure establishing the Agricultural Bureau, he could hardly have opposed it. Cf. Bentley, "Johnson, Governor of Tennessee," pp. 642ff., 132–40, 149–68. The legislature also passed an Omnibus Bill for internal improvements: *ibid.*, pp. 127–29.
27. Bentley, "Johnson, Governor of Tennessee," pp. 219ff., 228, 229ff., 206–12; Nashville *Republican Banner*, January 4, 27, 1854; Nashville *Union and American*, December 31, 1853, January 11, 20, March 15, 1854; Message on Railroad Bonds, January 18, 1854, Message Transmitting Documents from Georgia, February 23, 1854, Samuel Tate to Johnson, October 16, 1854, John C. Farrington to Johnson, October 18, 1854, Samuel Tate to Johnson, November 24, 1854, John L. T. Snead to Johnson, April 25, 1855, *PJ* 2:211–14, 222–24, 246–47, 249–51, 253–54, 268–71. For requests for pardon, see *PJ* 2:209–10, 220–22, 248–49, 252, 257, 265–66, 478–79, 326–27; for extradition requests, 184–85, 224–25, 243, 344, 438; and for various proclamations, 185–86, 224–25, 256.
28. William Pepper to Johnson, January 25, 1854, July 19, 1854, Johnson to Pepper, July 17, 1854, *PJ* 2:215–16, 235–39.
29. Johnson to Robert Johnson, April 16, 1854, Samuel Tate to Johnson, October 16, 1854, *PJ* 2:230–32, 249–50; Bentley, "Johnson, Governor of Tennessee," pp. 229–33; Nashville *Union and American*, November 3, 1853. During his absence from the capital, Johnson missed the visit of ex-president Fillmore, possibly on purpose: Nashville *Republican Banner*, May 5, 1854.
30. Johnson to David T. Patterson, April 2, 1854, Johnson to Robert Johnson, April 16, 1854, Johnson to Patterson, November 2, 1854, *PJ* 2:227–39, 230–32, 254–55.
31. Nashville *Union and American*, January 16, 1855.
32. Johnson to David T. Patterson, February 17, 1855, Johnson to William M. Lowry, February 24, 1855, *PJ* 2:258–60, 261; Herschel Gower and Jack Allen, eds., *Pen and Sword: The Life and Journals of Randal W. McGavock* (Nashville, 1959), p. 311; Nashville *Union and American*, February 7, 1855; Memphis *Appeal* (weekly), January 30, February

9, 1855; Oliver P. Temple, *East Tennessee and the Civil War* (Cincinnati, 1899), p. 237; Bentley, "Johnson, Governor of Tennessee," p. 253.

33. *Brownlow's Knoxville Whig*, March 31, 1855; Nashville *Union and American*, March 28, 29, 1855; Committee of Democratic State Convention to Johnson, March 28, 1855, Johnson to Committee of Democratic State Convention, March 31, 1855, *PJ* 2:263, 264–65; Gower and Allen, *McGavock*, p. 321.

34. State Temperance Convention to Johnson and Gentry, March 29, 1855, Johnson to Committee, April 20, 1855, *PJ* 2:264–65, 266–67; Nashville *Republican Banner*, May 1, 1855; Henry to J. O. Shackelford, June 3, 1853, Henry Papers. *Brownlow's Weekly Whig*, April 18, 1855; Temple, *Notable Men*, pp. 383ff.; William B. Campbell to David Campbell, May 6, 1855, Campbell Family Papers.

35. Speech at Murfreesboro, May 1, 1855, *PJ* 2:271–301; Nashville *Republican Banner*, May 2, 1855; Gower and Allen, *McGavock*, p. 327. Temple's colorful account of the debate during which Johnson allegedly braved the sound of pistols being cocked because of his fierce attacks on the Know Nothings is probably not quite accurate, since the governor expressed his preference for the clan of John A. Murrell, a famous Tennessee outlaw, over the Know Nothings, at Manchester on May 4, and not at Murfreesboro. It was this reference that is supposed to have caused the commotion. Temple, *Notable Men*, p. 386; Johnson on the Know Nothings, *PJ* 2:307–8.

36. Speech at Manchester, May 4, 1855, *PJ* 2:308. For the campaign, see Bentley, "Johnson, Governor of Tennessee," pp. 262ff.

37. *Brownlow's Weekly Whig*, May 5, 1855; Speech at Pulaski, May 11, 1855; Speech at Clarksville, June 5, 1855, *PJ* 2:301–6, 308–15; Nashville *Union and American*, July 3, 12, 13, 1855.

38. Nashville *Union and American*, July 25, 26, 27, 31, August 1, 1855; Johnson to Gentry, July 23, 1855, *PJ* 2:317–18; Thomas B. Alexander, *Thomas A. R. Nelson of East Tennessee* (Nashville, 1956), p. 55.

39. Nashville *Union and American*, August 7, 8, 11, 16, 17, September 25, October 12, 1855; *Brownlow's Weekly Whig*, August 11, 1855; W. M. Caskey, "The Second Administration of Governor Andrew Johnson," *ETHSP* 2 (1929): 34–55, esp. 41–42. By Grand Division, the vote was: West Tenn.: 15,482–15,713; Middle Tenn.: 32,623–27,887; East Tenn.: 19,394–21,714.

40. Speech at Dalton, August 18, 1855, Thomas T. Smiley to Johnson, August 21, 1855, Washington Barrow and Benjamin Cheatham to Johnson, August 28, 29, 1855, Johnson to Washington Barrow and Benjamin Cheatham, August 28, 1855, *PJ* 2:318–22, 324–26; Nashville *Republican Banner*, August 22, 1855; Franklin *Western Weekly Review*, September 7, 1855.

41. Nashville *Union and American*, September 2, 15, October 3, 4, 1855; *Brownlow's Weekly Whig*, August 11, October 27, 1855; James C. Kelley, "William Gannaway Brownlow," *THQ* 43 (Spring 1984): 25–43, esp. 34; Humphrey, *"That D . . . d Brownlow"* (Boone, 1978), pp. 165–66.

42. Philip M. Hamer, ed., *Tennessee: A History, 1673–1932*, 4 vols. (New York, 1933), 1:503; Biennial Legislative Message, October 8, 1855, Second Inaugural Address, October 23, 1855, *PJ* 2:329–43; Nashville *Union and American*, October 24, 1855.

43. Bentley, "Johnson, Governor of Tennessee," pp. 43ff.; Caskey, "The Second Administration of Governor Andrew Johnson," pp. 43–54.

44. Nashville *Union and American*, November 9, 1855, February 8, 19, 21, April 1, June 13, 1856, January 20, 27, 1857; Nashville *Republican Banner*, February 3, 1856; Johnson to Tennessee State Senate, February 2, 8, 9, 1856, Testimony Before Select Committee to Investigate Penitentiary Affairs, February 22, 1856, *PJ* 2:357–58, 359–60, 361–68.

45. *Brownlow's Weekly Whig*, December 1, 8, 1855.

46. Johnson to William M. Lowry, December 22, 1855, *PJ* 2:350–51, 384, n. 1; Genealogical Chart, Appendix I, *PJ* 1:634–35; Johnson to Patterson, October 26, 1855, Bartlett Collection, AJPP; Nashville *Union and American*, January 1, 1856.

47. *PJ* 2:344, 438, 326–27, 474, 479, 358–59, 382, 440, 514–15; Message Transmitting Report on Tennessee-Georgia Railroad Claims Controversy, February 26, 1856, Report of James A. Whiteside, February 25, 1856, *PJ* 2:368–77; Bentley, "Johnson, Governor of Tennessee," pp. 489ff.

48. Johnson to William McLain, February 20, April 11, November 11, 1856, McLain to Johnson, February 26, March 13, October 15, November 15, 1856, Commission to Robert Johnson, November 10, 19, 1856, *PJ* 2:360–61, 380–81, 448–49, 377–78, 380, 445, 450, 447–48, 451.

49. Nashville *Union and American*, April 15, 1856; Gower and Allen, *McGavock*, p. 360; William E. Beard, *Nashville: The Home of History Makers* (Nashville, 1929), p. 90.

50. Brabson, *Johnson*, p. 46; Jones, *Johnson*, pp. 398–99; Johnson to Martha Patterson, June 25, 1856, *PJ* 2:383–84; *Brownlow's Weekly Whig*, May 24, 1856; Nashville *Union and American*, May 22, 1856.

51. Samuel R. Anderson to Nicholson, November 21, 1855, Nicholson Papers; Nashville *Union and American*, January 10, 13, 15, 1856.

52. Bentley, "Johnson, Governor of Tennessee," pp. 525–26; Gower and Allen, *McGavock*, pp. 345–46; Nashville *Union and American*, May 8, 1856; S. R. Anderson to Nicholson, March 15, 1856, Nicholson Papers; Johnson to William M. Lowry, June 26, 1856, Johnson to A. O. P. Nicholson, June 27, 1856, Johnson to Robert Johnson, June 28, July 11, 1856, *PJ* 2:385–94.

53. Johnson to A. O. P. Nicholson, October 28, June 27, 1856, Johnson to Robert Johnson, July 11, 1856, *PJ* 2:445–47, 387–90, 393–94.

54. Speech at Nashville, July 15, 1856, *PJ* 2:395–438; Nashville *Union and American*, July 15, 17, 18, 1856.

55. Gower and Allen, *McGavock*, pp. 378, 380; Nashville *Union and American*, August 15, 23, September 13, 1856; Speech at Huntsville, October 1, 1856, Henry A. Wise to Johnson, September 15, 1856, Johnson to Robert Johnson, September 28, 1856, *PJ* 2:443–44, 441–42, n. 2; Paul H. Bergeron, *Antebellum Politics in Tennessee* (Lexington, Ky., 1982), p. 146.

56. Johnson to Milligan, November 23, 1856, Edward S. Cheatham et al. to Johnson, December 6, 1856, *PJ* 2:452–54, 456–57; Bentley, "Johnson, Governor of Tennessee," p. 549.

57. Bentley, "Johnson, Governor of Tennessee," pp. 551–52; Johnson to Nicholson, October 28, 1856, Johnson to Milligan, November 23, December 10, 1856, Johnson to Lowry, December 14, 1856, *PJ* 2:445–47, 452–54, 457–58; Brabson, *Johnson*, p. 46; William S. Speer, *Sketches of Prominent Tennesseans* (Nashville, 1888), p. 532.

58. Johnson to Milligan, November 23, 1856, James McLaughlin to Johnson, December 20, 1856, Johnson to James McLaughlin, December 20, 1856, *PJ* 2:453, 465–67.

59. Nashville *Union and American*, January 20, February 6, 1857; Johnson to Franklin Pierce, December 18, 1856, Johnson to Elisha Whittlesey, January 27, 1857, *PJ* 2:464–65, 468–69; Samuel R. Anderson to Nicholson, January 6, 1857, in Parks, "Some Tennessee Letters," p. 251; Bentley, "Johnson, Governor of Tennessee," pp. 552ff.; Roy Franklin Nichols, *The Disruption of American Democracy* (New York, 1958), pp. 67, 78.

60. Nashville *Union and American*, February 3, 4, 19, March 13, 1857; Gower and Allen, *McGavock*, pp. 394, 395, 399; Lizinka C. Brown to David Hubbard, n.d., David Hubbard Papers, TSLA; Johnson to Robert Johnson, June 15, 1858, *PJ* 3:191–92.

61. *Brownlow's Weekly Whig*, January 10, 1857; Nashville *Union and American*, February 10, 1857; Nashville *Republican Banner*, March 12, April 14, 18, May 2, 3, 26, 1857; William B. Campbell to David Campbell, May 25, 1857, Campbell Family Papers; Henry Cooper to M. D. Cooper, June 16, 1857, Cooper Family Papers, TSLA.

62. John B. Brownlow to Temple, January 1, 1896, Temple Papers; Nashville *Republican Banner*, July 22, 1857; Johnson to Robert Johnson, July 17, 1857, Johnson to William M. Lowry, July 17, 1857, *PJ* 2:472–76; Russell, "Prelude to the Presidency," pp. 165–66.

63. *Brownlow's Weekly Whig*, July 18, 1857; A. W. Howard to Temple, July 4, 1857, Temple

Papers; Speech at Raleigh, July 24, 1857, *PJ* 2:476–78; Nashville *Union and American*, July 29, 1857.

64. Nashville *Republican Banner*, August 2, 1857; Nashville *Union and American*, July 16, 30, 31, 1857; Campbell, *The Attitude of Tennesseans Toward the Union*, p. 91; Bergeron, *Antebellum Politics in Tennessee*, pp. 122, 130, 133.

65. Johnson to William M. Lowry, August 28, 1857, *PJ* 2:479–80; Nashville *Republican Banner*, September 15, 1857. In December 1860 Johnson's friend Douglas wrote to him from Nashville reminding him that "we did not want you to go to the Senate but *the people would send you.*" Hu Douglas to Johnson, *PJ* 4:103–4.

66. Nashville *Union and American*, October 14, 1857; Final Biennial Message, October 6, 1857, *PJ* 2:483–504.

67. Nashville *Republican Banner*, October 9, 1857. The vote was 57–38, N. S. Brown being the minority candidate.

68. *Brownlow's Weekly Whig*, October 17, 1857; William B. Campbell to David Campbell, October 27, 1857, Campbell Family Papers; Nashville *Union and American*, October 9, 18, 1857; Nashville *Republican Banner*, October 10, 1857; Remarks at Opening of State Fair, October 12, 1857, Valedictory Address, November 3, 1857, *PJ* 2:505–12; Gower and Allen, *McGavock*, pp. 435, 438.

69. Bentley, "Johnson, Governor of Tennessee," pp. 642ff.; Thomas P. Abernethy, *From Frontier to Plantation in Tennessee* (Chapel Hill, 1932) p. 318; Folmsbee et al., *History of Tennessee*, 1:438; A. P. Whitaker, "The Public School System of Tennessee, 1834–1860," *Tennessee Historical Magazine*, 2 (1916): 21.

VII. *UNITED STATES SENATOR*

1. *Cong. Globe*, 35th Cong., 1st Sess., 1; Christian F. Eckloff, *Memoirs of a Senate Page (1855–1859)*, Percival G. Melbourne, ed. (New York, 1909), pp. 4–8.

2. *Philp's Washington Described: A Complete View of the American Capital and the District of Columbia*, William D. Haley, ed. (New York, 1861), pp. 126–36; Paul Herron, *The Story of Capitol Hill* (New York, 1963), pp. 42, 66–69; William M. Morrison, *Description of the Public Buildings and Statues of Washington City* (Washington, D.C., 1860), pp. 7, 8, 12ff., 22.

3. *Biographical Directory of the American Congress, 1774–1971* (Washington, D.C., 1971), pp. 167–74; Hans L. Trefousse, *The Radical Republicans: Lincoln's Vanguard for Racial Justice* (New York, 1969), pp. 91ff., 103ff.

4. J. B. Brownlow to Oliver P. Temple, February 6, 1892, Temple Papers, UT; Charles Johnson to Robert Johnson, June 3, 1860, JP; John J. Craven, *Prison Life of Jefferson Davis* (New York, 1867), pp. 300–2; Albert Iverson to Seward, November 26, 1866, Seward Papers, University of Rochester; Benjamin Truman, "Anecdotes of Andrew Johnson," *Century Illustrated Magazine* 53 (1912–13): 434–36; Milligan to Johnson, January 18, 1860, *PJ* 3:386.

5. *Cong. Globe*, 35th Cong., 1st Sess., 135, 264, 354, 377, 623, 640, 697, 783, 900.

6. George M. Stephenson, *The Political History of the Public Lands from 1840 to 1862* (Boston, 1917), p. 161. For Johnson's opponents, see following pages.

7. *Cong. Globe*, 35th Cong., 1st Sess., 2265–73, 2426, 3042; also in *PJ* 3:132–67.

8. Johnson to Robert Johnson, January 23, 1858, *PJ* 3:6–9, 372, n. 6.

9. *Cong. Globe*, 35th Cong., 1st Sess., 830ff., 834ff., 871, 804, 876–78; Joseph Howard Parks, *John Bell of Tennessee* (Baton Rouge, 1950), pp. 320–26.

10. *Cong. Globe*, 35th Cong., 1st Sess., 737–41, 757–58, 66–68, 1326–27, 1462, 1467–71, 1491–92, 1513–14, App. 372–77, 2588–90, 2399, 2422–24; Washington *Daily National Intelligencer*, February 17, 1858; *Brownlow's Weekly Whig*, June 5, 1858. The speeches are also in *PJ* 3:11–43, 89–107, 115–30, 170–80, 182–84.

11. Johnson to Robert Johnson, June 15, 1858, *PJ* 3:191; Lizinka C. Brown to David Hubbard, n.d., David Hubbard Papers, TSLA.

12. Richard Harrison Doughty, *Greeneville: One Hundred Year Portrait, 1775–1875* (Greeneville, 1975), pp. 89–90; Johnson to Robert Johnson, June 15, 1858, *PJ* 3:191; Genealogical Chart, Appendix I, *PJ*, vol. 1.
13. Isham G. Harris to Johnson, September 7, 1858, Tennessee Democracy on Banks and Currency, September 22, 1858, Johnson to Nicholson, November 22, 1858, *PJ* 3:194–97.
14. Hamlin to Mrs. Hamlin, December 15, 1858, Hannibal Hamlin Papers, Maine Historical Society, Portland.
15. Johnson to Robert Johnson, December 26, 1858, *PJ* 3:203–5.
16. *Cong. Globe*, 35th Cong., 2d Sess., 303, 712, 731, 805, 1074–76, 1143, 1352, 1354; Hans L. Trefousse, *Benjamin Franklin Wade, Radical Republican from Ohio* (New York, 1963), pp. 112–13.
17. *Cong. Globe*, 35th Cong., 2d Sess., 205–6, 208–9, 402–3, 405, also in *PJ* 3:206–14; Washington *Daily National Intelligencer*, January 5, 18, February 9, 14, March 5, 1859; Nashville *Union and American*, January 7, 18, 1859.
18. Dunbar Rowland, ed., *Jefferson Davis, Constitutionalist: His Letters, Papers, and Speeches*, 10 vols. (Jackson, Miss., 1973), 3:501–15; *Cong. Globe*, 35th Cong., 2d Sess., 577–87, 1588, 1590, 1611, also in *PJ* 3:214–50, 260–67; Washington *Daily National Intelligencer*, January 18, February 3, 15, 26, 1859, December 28, 1858; Craven, *Prison Life of Jefferson Davis*, p. 299; Alfred Iverson to Seward, November 26, 1866, William H. Seward Papers, University of Rochester.
19. Johnson to Robert Johnson, February 3, March 8, 1859, Johnson to Charles H. Brainard, April 23, 1859, *PJ* 3:247, 269–70, 271–72.
20. Johnson to Robert Johnson, February 22, 1859, *PJ* 3:256–58; William S. Speer, *Sketches of Prominent Tennesseans* (Nashville, 1888), p. 532; Nashville *Union and American*, February 20, August 7, September 1, 1859.
21. Johnson to Robert Johnson, February 22, 1859, J. R. Anderson et al. to Johnson, April 29, 1859, Speech at Bristol, May 21, 1859, Harris to Johnson, July 7, 1859, *PJ* 3:256–58, 274, 279–80, 285–86; Washington *Constitution*, April 2, 1859, AJPP; Nashville *Union and American*, April 21, 26, August 7, 26, 1859.
22. Charles H. Brainard to Johnson, April 27, 1859, Johnson to Brainard, April 23, June 1, 1859, *PJ* 3:271–73, 280–81, including excerpts from the Boston *Transcript*.
23. Johnson to Robert Johnson, December 21, 23, 1858, Real Estate Bond, August 20, 1859, *PJ* 3:200–4, 293–93. For Johnson's own agrarianism, see above, p. 51.
24. Johnson to Robert Johnson, October 20, 1859, Democrats in Tennessee Legislature to Johnson, November 28, 1859, *PJ* 3:301–4, 310; Nashville *Union and American*, December 3, 1859; Johnson to Harvey T. Phillips, August 15, 1859, Rae Burr Batten to Johnson, November 23, 1859, *PJ* 3:289–92, 307–8; Greeneville *Democrat* in Nashville *Union and American*, October 1, 1859.
25. Allan Nevins, *The Emergence of Lincoln*, 2 vols. (New York, 1950), 2:104; David Potter, *The Impending Crisis, 1848–1861* (New York, 1976), pp. 382ff.; Avery Craven, *The Coming of the Civil War*, 2d ed. (Chicago, 1957), pp. 410–12.
26. *Cong. Globe*, 36th Cong., 1st Sess., 100–7, also in *PJ* 3:318–52; James B. Lamb to Johnson, December 21, 1859, David J. Carr to Johnson, January 7, 1860, *PJ* 3:359–60, 366–67; John M. Carmack to W. T. Avery, February 8, 1860, Gordon-Avery Papers, TSLA.
27. *Cong. Globe*, 36th Cong., 1st Sess., 53, 190, 1118–20, 1219–24, 1293–1304; Johnson's March 22, 1860, speech also in *PJ* 3:418–86; Alvy L. King, *Louis T. Wigfall, Southern Fire-Eater* (Baton Rouge, 1970), pp. 87–91; Nashville *Union and American*, December 29, 1859; James T. DuBois and Gertrude Matthews, *Galusha A. Grow, Father of the Homestead Law* (Boston, 1917), pp. 96–200. The House measure required no payment; the Senate version, 25¢ per acre. Applying to all males over twenty-one instead of merely the heads of families, the House version included all lands subject to preemption instead of only those subject to private entry, and, among other technical differences,

included all aliens who had taken out first citizenship papers instead of merely those already in the United States in 1860. Ray Robbins, *Our Landed Heritage: the Public Domain, 1776–1936* (Princeton, 1942), p. 180; Stephenson, *Public Lands,* p. 197.

28. *Cong. Globe,* 36th Cong., 1st Sess., 1554–55, 1619, 1634, 1649–69; John Dawson to Johnson, March 7, 18, 1860, as well as a partial rendition of congressional debates and Johnson's April 11, 1860, speech, in *PJ* 3:458, 471, 508–12, 524–47; Stephenson, *Public Lands,* pp. 198–203.

29. *Cong. Globe,* 36th Cong., 1st Sess., 1748–54, also in *PJ* 3:556–58; *New York Times,* April 18, 1860.

30. *Cong. Globe,* 36th Cong., 1st Sess., 1796–97, 1991–2011, 2031–44; final remarks on May 10, 1860, in *PJ* 3:593–96; Nevins, *Emergence of Lincoln,* 2:190–91.

31. *Cong. Globe,* 36th Cong., 1st Sess., 2461, 2813, 2862, 2955, 3022, 3159, 3267–70, also in part in *PJ* 3:624–26, 627–42; Washington *Daily National Intelligencer,* June 20, 25, 1860; Stephenson, *Public Lands,* pp. 210–12.

32. Stephenson, *Public Lands,* pp. 213–19; James D. Richardson, *A Compilation of the Messages and Papers of the Presidents, 1789–1897,* 10 vols. (Washington, D.C., 1896–99), 7:3139–45; *Cong. Globe,* 36th Cong., 1st Sess., 3262–72; speech also in *PJ* 3:627–42.

33. Washington *Daily National Intelligencer,* February 21, 25, March 10, 22, May 9, 1860; *Cong. Globe,* 36th Cong., 1st Sess., 1443, 2750.

34. *Cong. Globe,* 36th Cong., 1st Sess., 1266–68, *PJ* 3:490–96.

35. William Flinn to James Buchanan, April 15, 1865, in John Bassett Moore, ed., *The Works of James Buchanan,* 12 vols. (Philadelphia, 1908–11), 11:381; S. R. Anderson to Nicholson, March 15, 1856, Nicholson Papers, NYHS; Johnson to Harvey T. Phillips, August 15, 1859, *PJ* 3:289–92; Chattanooga *Advertiser* in Nashville *Union and American,* September 25, 1859.

36. Greeneville *Democrat,* in Nashville *Union and American,* October 1, 1859; Marguerite Bartlett Hamer, "The Campaign of 1860 in Tennessee," *ETHSP* 3(1931): 3–31, esp. 6–7.

37. Robert Johnson to Johnson, January 10, 22, 1860, Johnson to Robert Johnson, January 12, 15, 1860, William Lowry to Johnson, December 9, 1859, January 27, 1860, Milligan to Johnson, January 18, 1860, Washington C. Whitthorne to Johnson, January 19, 1860, S. R. Anderson to Johnson, January 21, 1860, W. H. Maxwell to Johnson, February 2, 1860, *PJ* 3:376–78, 379–84, 391–92, 316–17, 401–2, 386–90, 410–13; Nashville *Union and American,* January 19, 20, 1860.

38. Johnson to George W. Jones, March 13, 1860, *PJ* 3:466–68. For the resolutions, see Nevins, *Emergence of Lincoln,* 2:179–80.

39. Johnson to George W. Jones, March 13, 1860, Johnson to Blackston McDannel, March 24, 1860, Johnson to Robert Johnson, April 8, 22, 1860, Sam Milligan to Johnson, February 8, March 4, 20, 1860, M. E. Wilcox to Johnson, March 18, 1860, Hu Douglas to Johnson, March 11, 1860, John H. Howard to Johnson, February 5, 1860, *PJ* 3:466–68, 489–90, 517–20, 573–74, 419–20, 452–54, 477–78, 473–74, 460–61, 413–15; papers cited in Nashville *Union and American,* February 18, 19, March 7, 9, 13, 17, April 1, 12, 14, 1860; Ollinger Cranshaw, *The Slave States in the Presidential Election of 1860* (Baltimore, 1945), pp. 177–78.

40. *Official Proceedings of the Democratic National Convention Held in 1860 in Charleston and Baltimore* (Cleveland, 1860), pp. 74–76; Roy Franklin Nichols, *The Disruption of American Democracy* (New York, 1948), pp. 288–312; Johnson to Robert Johnson, April 22, 1860, Washington C. Whitthorne to Johnson, April 29, 1860, Sam Milligan to Johnson, May 7, 1860, William H. Carrol to Johnson, May 2, 1860, *PJ* 3:573–74, 579, 590–93, 586–88, 582; Robert G. Russell, "Andrew Johnson and the Charleston Convention of 1860," *ETHSP* 47 (1975): 46–75.

41. Charles Johnson to Robert Johnson, June 3, 1860, JP.

42. Johnson to Robert Johnson, February 11, 1860, Robert Johnson to Johnson, February 5, 17, May 8, 1860, Charles Johnson to Johnson, March 18, January 29, 1860, Lizinka

Campbell Brown to Johnson, February 2, 1860, *PJ* 3:423–24, 415–16, 432–33, 588–90, 404–5, 472–73, 407–10; Genealogical Chart, Appendix I, *PJ* vol. 1; James S. Jones, *Life of Andrew Johnson 17th President of the United States* (Greeneville, 1901), pp. 398–99.

43. Nashville *Union and American*, May 20, 1860; Sam Milligan to Robert Johnson, May 28, 1860, JP; R. Putin to S. S. Cox, June 12, 1860, S. S. Cox Papers, Brown University; W. S. Crouch to Johnson, May 12, 1860, William E. B. Jones to Johnson, May 15, 1860, Jephtha Fowlkes to Johnson, May 19, 1860, Albert G. Graham to Johnson, May 23, 1860, William M. Lowry to Johnson, May 29, 1860, *PJ* 3:597, 599–600, 601–2, 603–7, 610–11.

44. Murat Halstead, *Three Against Lincoln: Murat Halstead Reports the Caucuses of 1860*, William B. Hesseltine, ed. (Baton Rouge, 1960), pp. 234, 239, 243, 267, 271, 274, 288, 302; Nichols, *The Disruption of American Democracy*, pp. 312–20; Johnson to Sam Milligan, June 18, 1860, *PJ* 3:623.

45. John C. Burch to Johnson, July 12, 1860, Johnson to Abraham L. Gammon, July 31, 1860, Johnson to Nicholson, August 23, 1860, *PJ* 3:645–46, 652–53, 659–60; Mary E. Campbell, *The Attitude of Tennesseans Toward the Union, 1847–1861* (New York, 1961), p. 125; Nashville *Union and American*, July 28, 1860.

46. Speech at Winchester, September 29, 1860, Speech at Fayetteville, October 1, 1860, *PJ* 3:261–67.

47. Hamer, "The Campaign of 1860 in Tennessee," p. 17; Jones to Johnson, August 15, 1860, Johnson to Nashville Democrats, August 28, 1860, Speech at Winchester, September 29, 1860, Speech at Fayetteville, October 1, 1860, Speech at Memphis, October 16, 1860, Theophilus Fiske to Johnson, August 6, 1860, *PJ* 3:656–58, 660–67, 669–71, 653–54; Nashville *Union and American*, September 30, 1860; Herschel Gower and Jack Allen, eds., *Penn and Sword: the Life and Journals of Randal W. McGavock* (Nashville, 1959), pp. 579, 581; *Brownlow's Weekly Whig*, September 29, 1860; Lately Thomas, *The First President Johnson* (New York, 1968), p. 152; Steve Humphrey, "That D . . . d Brownlow" (Boone, 1978), p. 197.

48. Although it has been maintained that Johnson, "by sheer weight of personal influence," carried seven of the counties in East Tennessee that went for Breckinridge, including Greene, Professor Bergeron has shown that the results were very similar to those of previous elections. James Welch Patton, *Unionism and Reconstruction in Tennessee, 1860–1869* (Chapel Hill, 1934), p. 132; Paul H. Bergeron, *Antebellum Politics in Tennessee* (Lexington, Ky., 1982), pp. 162–66.

VIII. UNCONDITIONAL UNIONIST

1. Milton Henry, "Summary of Tennessee Representation in Congress from 1845 to 1861," *THQ* 10 (1951): 140–48; Oliver P. Temple, *Notable Men of Tennessee* (New York, 1912), p. 400; Thomas William Humes, *The Loyal Mountaineers of Tennessee* (Knoxville, 1888), pp. 122–23.

2. Richard Harrison Doughty, *Greeneville: One Hundred Year Portrait, 1775–1875* (Greeneville, 1975), pp. 324–27; Speech at Union Meeting, Greeneville, November 24, 1860, *PJ* 3:673–74; Greeneville *Democrat*, November 20, 1860, scrapbook, Nelson Papers, Lawson McGhee Library, Knoxville. The plank conceding that the election of Lincoln was not a sufficient cause for secession was proposed by General Thomas D. Arnold, Johnson's predecessor in Congress. It was defeated.

3. Washington *Daily National Intelligencer*, December 4, 5, 1860.

4. New York *Herald*, December 10, 1860; *New York Times*, December 10, 1860.

5. Sam Milligan to Johnson, December 13, 1860, Joint Resolution for Amendments, December 13, 1860, Resolution Proposing "Unamendable" Amendments Affecting Slavery, December 13, 1860, *PJ* 3:689–97.

6. *New York Times*, December 14, 15, 17, 1860.

7. *Cong. Globe*, 36th Cong., 2d Sess., 117–19, 134–43, also in *PJ* 4:3–51.

8. *New York Times*, December 20, 1860; Chicago *Tribune*, December 21, 1860; Washington *Daily National Intelligencer*, December 20, 1860; Anthony Ten Eyck to Johnson, December 21, 1860, Warren Bell to Johnson, January 2, 1861, Order for Reprints of Speech, [1861], "A Southerner and Lover of his County" to Johnson, December 19, 1860, Charles R. Cullen to Johnson, December 21, 1860, J. M. Jones to Johnson, December 29, 1860, *PJ* 4:71–72, 115–17, 109–10, 55–56, 65–67, 99–100; Ralph W. Haskins, "Andrew Johnson and the Preservation of the Union," *ETHSP* 33 (1961): 43–60, esp. 53ff.

9. Richmond *Daily Dispatch*, December 22, 1860; Charleston *Daily Courier*, December 20, 1860; John W. Ellis to Robert N. Gourdin, December 24, 1860, Robert N. Gourdin Papers, Duke University; Hiram S. Smith to Johnson, December 26, 1860, "Grand Junction" to Johnson, February 3, 1861, William M. Lowry to Johnson, December 29, 1860, *PJ* 4:92–93, 196, 101–2; Dunbar Rowland, ed., *Jefferson Davis, Constitutionalist: His Letters, Papers and Speeches*, 10 vols. (Jackson, Miss., 1923), 4:561.

10. Absalom A. Kyle to Nelson, January 14, 1861, Nelson Papers; Joseph C. S. McDannel to Johnson, December 29, 1860, William M. Bradford to Johnson, December 31, 1860, Montgomery D. L. Boren to Johnson, January 7, 1861, *PJ* 4:102–3, 107, 130; *Brownlow's Weekly Whig*, January 12, February 16, 1861.

11. Nashville *Union and American*, December 25, 1860, January 2, 9, 11, 1861; Sam Milligan to Johnson, January 8, 1861, Montgomery D. L. Boren to Johnson, January 7, 1861, Hu Douglas to Johnson, December 30, 1860, William H. Carrol to Johnson, January 2, 1861, McDannel to Johnson, February 16, 1861, James W. Harold to Johnson, December 28, 1860, Charles Johnson to Johnson, January 1, 1861, Robert Johnson to Johnson January 13, 15, 17, 1861, *PJ* 4:147–50, 130, 103–4, 117–18, 294–97, 96–97, 110–11, 157–60, 172–73, 178–79. For the failure to instruct Johnson out of the Senate, see R. R. Butler to Nelson, January 17, 1861, Nelson Papers.

12. Verton M. Queener, "East Tennessee Sentiment and the Secession Movement, November 1860 to June 1861," *ETHSP* 20 (1948): 59–83; Robert G. Russell, "Prelude to the Presidency: The Election of Andrew Johnson to the Senate," *THQ* 26 (1967): 162–63; George C. Rable, "Anatomy of a Unionist: Andrew Johnson in the Secession Crisis," *THQ* 32 (1973): 332–54; Hu Douglas to Johnson, December 30, 1860, *PJ* 4:103–4.

13. *Cong. Globe*, 36th Cong., 2d Sess., 304ff., 309; Johnson's reply also in *PJ* 4:150–51; Speech on the Expulsion of Senator Bright, *PJ* 5:127; Johnson to Milligan, January 13, 1861, *PJ* 4:160–62. The issue before the Senate on January 16, 1861, was the Clark Amendment to the Crittenden Compromise, which in effect declared it unnecessary. *Cong. Globe*, 36th Cong., 2d Sess., 409.

14. James Welch Patton, *Unionism and Reconstruction in Tennessee, 1860–1869* (Chapel Hill, 1934), pp. 10–11; Robert Johnson to Johnson, January 13, 15, 17, 1861, *PJ* 4:157–60, 172, 178–79.

15. *Cong. Globe*, 36th Cong., 2d Sess., 720, 744–50, 766–72; Speech on the Seceding States also in *PJ* 4:204–61.

16. *Cong. Globe*, 36th Cong., 2d Sess., 781–91; Thomas Bragg Diary, SHC, February 5, 1861, p. 43; Washington *Daily National Intelligencer*, February 6, 7, 8, 1861; Nashville *Union and American*, February 8, 1861; Richmond *Dispatch*, February 11, 1861. Wigfall charged that Johnson's motive was his desire to be president, because he knew that he could never get any votes in a Southern Confederacy, but if Tennessee remained part of a Northern Union, he had a good chance of being elected, especially if his amendments concerning alternate presidents from North and South were adopted.

17. New York *Tribune*, February 6, 1861; Chicago *Tribune*, February 12, 1861.

18. Patton, *Unionism and Reconstruction in Tennessee*, p. 12; W. C. Kyle to Nelson, February 6, 1861 Nelson Papers; Joseph R. Armstrong to Johnson, February 11, 1861, C. H. Mills to Johnson, February 10, 1861, Richard M. Edwards to Johnson, February 11, 1860, Charles O. Faxon to Johnson, February 11, 1860, *PJ* 4:267–74. Johnson's correspon-

dents warned him not to fight a duel with Wigfall as had been rumored because he was too valuable to the state to risk his life in such an encounter.

19. Blackston McDannel to Johnson, February 16, 1861, J. Warren Bell to Johnson, February 16, 1861, Thomas Shankland to Johnson, February 6, 1861, *PJ* 4:294–97, 291–92, 262–63; A. A. Kyle to Nelson, February 19, 1861, Nelson Papers; New York *Tribune*, February 26, 1861; Washington *Daily National Intelligencer*, January 31, February 21, March 5, 1861.

20. *Cong. Globe*, 36th Cong., 2d Sess., 1342–51, 1354–56; Speech in Reply to Senator Lane also in *PJ* 4:353–64; Washington *Daily National Intelligencer*, March 4, 1861.

21. Hans L. Trefousse, "Abraham Lincoln Versus Andrew Johnson: Two Approaches to Reconstruction," Steven V. and Agnes Hussar, eds., *Society in Change: Studies in Honor of Bela Kalman Kiraly* (Boulder, Colo., 1983); Trefousse, "Lincoln and Johnson," *Topic* 9 (Spring 1965): 63–75.

22. John B. Brownlow to Oliver Temple, September 7, 1891, Temple Papers, UT; J. Milton Henry, "The Revolution in Tennessee, February, 1861, to June, 1861," *THQ* 18 (1959): 97–119, esp. 106–17; Haskins, "Andrew Johnson and the Preservation of the Union," p. 59; Rable, "Anatomy of a Unionist," pp. 348–49, 353–54; Queener, "East Tennessee Sentiment and the Secession Movement," p. 70; LeRoy P. Graf, "Andrew Johnson and the Coming of the War," *THQ* 19 (1960): 208–21, esp. 219–20; James L. Baumgardner, "Abraham Lincoln, Andrew Johnson, and the Federal Patronage: An Attempt to Save Tennessee for the Union?" *ETHSP* 45 (1973): 51–60. For the correspondence, see *PJ*, vol. 4, February and March 1861, esp. Johnson to Edward Bates, March 25, 1861, p. 431.

23. Washington *Daily National Intelligencer*, March 9, 1861; Remarks on Contingent Expenses, March 28, 1861, Response to Washington Serenade, March 7, 1861, *PJ* 4:369–70, 445–48; W. P. Smith to Johnson, March 23, 1861, Ulysses Halls to Johnson, March 26, 1861, JP.

24. William Lellyett to Johnson, February 12, 1861, C. H. Mills to Johnson, February 10, 1861, Benjamin D. Nabers to Johnson, February 13, 1861, Neill S. Brown to Johnson, February 17, 1861, Pitser Miller to Johnson, February 27, 1861, Henry S. French to Johnson, March 11, 1861, Jephtha Fowlkes to Johnson, March 17, 1861, *PJ* 4:281–82, 267–69, 289–90, 300–2, 341–42, 382–83, 401–2. For Johnson's belief in the importance of concessions, see above, pp. 131, 135.

25. Richard N. Current, *Lincoln and the First Shot* (Philadelphia, 1963), pp. 51, 67, 86ff., and passim; Nashville *Union and American*, April 12, 21, 27, 1861; Patton, *Unionism and Reconstruction in Tennessee*, p. 14.

26. Jephtha Fowlkes to Johnson, March 13, 17, 1861, William M. Lowry to Johnson, March 13, 1861, Sullivan County Citizens to Johnson, March 20, 1861, William Henry Maxwell to Johnson, March 29, 1861, William C. Kyle to Johnson, April 3, 1861, T. A. R. Nelson to Johnson, April 5, 1861, Johnson to Ward H. Lamon, April 16, 1861, Johnson to Lincoln, April 16, 1861, Alexander J. T. Thurston to Johnson, April 20, 1861, *PJ* 4:388–89, 401–2, 389, 419–20, 451–52, 456–57, 465–66, 471–73.

27. Lynchburg *Daily Virginian*, April 23, 1861, AJPP; *New York Times*, April 28, 1861; William C. Ballagh to Johnson, October 3, 1864, J. M. Bosang to Johnson, February 3, 1865, E. H. Gill to Johnson, November 22, 1865, JP.

28. Humphrey Marshall to Johnson, April 26, 1866, JP; Nashville *Union and American*, April 24, 1861.

29. William M. Lowry to Johnson, February 27, 1861, Robert Johnson to Johnson, April 29, 1861, Peter H. Grisham to Johnson, July 12, 1861, George Adams to Johnson, July 27, 1861, William P. Johnson to Johnson, December 2, 1860, February 22, 1861, *PJ* 4:339–40, 474–75, 559–60, 602–4, 326–27, 3:681–83.

30. Speech at Knoxville, April 27, 1861, *PJ* 4:473–74; Felix Alexander Reeve, *East Tennessee in the War of the Rebellion, Military Order of the Loyal Legion of the United States, Comman-*

dery of the District of Columbia, War Papers, no. 44 (Washington, D.C., 1902), p. 32; Oliver P. Temple, *East Tennessee and the Civil War* (Cincinnati, 1899), pp. 184–85.

31. Johnson, Nelson, Maynard, Trigg, and Temple to Knox County Representatives, April 28, 1861, *PJ* 4:474.

32. Mary E. Campbell, *The Attitude of Tennesseans Toward the Union, 1847–1861* (New York, 1961), pp. 197–98; Robert Johnson to Johnson, April 29, 1861, *PJ* 4:474–75. As soon as the ordinance of secession passed, they determined to go home while protesting against the procedures of the legislature.

33. Temple, *Notable Men,* pp. 399–402, 172–73; Thomas B. Alexander, *Thomas A. R. Nelson of East Tennessee* (Nashville, 1956), pp. 76–80; Humes, *Loyal Mountaineers,* pp. 110–12; Speech at Elizabethton, May 15, 1861, *PJ* 4:477–78.

34. Jonesborough *Express,* May 10, 17, 1861, Scrapbook, Nelson Papers; Nashville *Union and American,* May 5, 8, 9, 1861; D. Sullins, *Recollections of an Old Man: Seventy Years in Dixie, 1827–1897* (Bristol, 1910), pp. 192–95; Patton, *Unionism and Reconstruction in Tennessee,* p. 53.

35. John B. Brownlow to Oliver P. Temple, August 14, 1893, Temple Papers; Temple, *Notable Men,* pp. 97–98.

36. Temple, *East Tennessee,* pp. 340–43; Humes, *Loyal Mountaineers,* pp. 104–15; O.R., series I, vol. 51, part II, 148–56; Charles F. Bryan, Jr., "A Gathering of Tories: The East Tennessee Convention of 1861," *THQ* 39 (1980): 27–48, esp. 33.

37. Alexander, *Nelson,* p. 83; Temple, *Notable Men,* p. 400. In Middle Tennessee the vote was 58,265–8,198 and in West Tennessee, 29,127–6,117 in favor of secession. Nashville *Union and American,* June 25, 1861.

38. Jephtha Fowlkes to Johnson, May 29, 1861, Amos A. Lawrence to Johnson, May 18, 22, 29, June 14, 22, 25, 1861, Johnson to Lawrence [forgery], June 6, 1861, Johnson to Lawrence, June 25, 1861, *PJ* 4:478–79, 483–84, 485, 404–5, 514, 480–81, 515–17; Barry A. Crouch, "The Merchant and the Senator: An Attempt to Save Tennessee for the Union," *ETHSP* 46 (1974): 53–75; William G. Browning, *Sketches of the Rise, Progress, and Decline of Secession with a Narrative of Personal Adventures Among the Rebels* (Philadelphia, 1867), pp. 121–33. A note from Lawrence in early May offering aid to Johnson was intercepted at the Knoxville Post Office by Postmaster Charles W. Charlton, who apparently thought to obtain the money for the secessionists by writing forged letters to Lawrence. The culprit may also have been the Knoxville lawyer William G. Swan, as asserted by Brownlow.

39. Knoxville *Register,* June 18, 1861, Mary E. Crouch Scrapbook, Confederate Collection, TSLA; Knoxville *Whig,* June 29, 1861, Nelson Papers; John P. Landstreet to M. L. Patterson, August 6, 1891, Temple Papers; A. J. Patterson to R. W. Winston, September 20, 1926, Winston Papers, SHC; Carl N. Hayes, *Neighbor Against Neighbor: Greene County in the Civil War* (Greeneville, Tenn., 1968), p. 29.

40. O.R., series I, vol. 52, part I, 168–79; Humes, *Loyal Mountaineers,* pp. 115–19; Temple, *East Tennessee,* pp. 343–65; for family, see below, pp. 162.

41. Speech at Lexington, June 18, 1861, Impromptu Speech at Cincinnati, June 19, 1861, Speech at Cincinnati, June 19, 1861, *PJ* 4:487–90, 491–98; *Diary of Gideon Welles,* Howard K. Beale, ed., 3 vols. (New York, 1960), 3:62–63 (hereafter cited as Welles, *Diary*).

42. Response to Washington Serenade, June 22, 1861, John Campbell to Johnson, June 24, 1861, William P. Fessenden to Johnson, June 24, 1861, *PJ* 4:505–11.

43. Washington *Daily National Intelligencer,* July 11, 12, 15, 25, 29, 1861; Albert Gallatin Riddle, *Recollections of War Times: Reminiscences of Men and Events in Washington, 1860–1865* (New York, 1895), p. 35; *Cong. Globe,* 37th Cong., 1st Sess., 103, 106, 243, 257ff., 265. LeRoy P. Graf, in his article "Andrew Johnson and the Coming of the War," *THQ* 19 (1960): 208–21, stresses the importance of the resolution to Johnson's thinking.

44. *Cong. Globe,* 37th Cong., 1st Sess., 288–97, also in *PJ* 4:606–49.

45. Cincinnati *Daily Gazette,* August 3, 1861; Daniel F. Heffron to Johnson, July 31, 1861,

William C. Bryant to Johnson, August 2, 1861, Johnson to Henry S. Lane, August 7, 1861, Johnson to Andrew Froment, August 20, 1861, Francis Lieber to Johnson, July 29, 1861, Benjamin A. G. Fuller to Johnson, August 17, 1861, *PJ* 4:653–64, 659, 672–73, 686–87, 650, 682–84; Alexander H. Stephens, *A Constitutional View of the Late War Between the States,* 2 vols. (Philadelphia, 1870), 2:457.

46. O.R., series I, vol. 52, part I, 143–44; Salmon P. Chase to Johnson, June 29, 1861, *PJ* 4:522–23.

47. Jesse Burt, "East Tennessee, Lincoln, and Sherman," *ETHSP* 34 (1962): 3–25, 54–75; Johnson to Simon Cameron, July 6, 1861, Johnson to Lincoln, August 6, 1861, Montgomery Blair to Johnson, August 8, 1861, Johnson to Carlyle Murray, August 14, 1861, *PJ* 4:546, 669–70, 673–74, 677–79; T. Harry Williams, *Lincoln and His Generals* (New York, 1952), pp. 47–49; O.R., series I, vol. 4, p. 365; Abraham Jobe, Autobiography or Memoirs Written by Himself, 1902–1905, TSLA, p. 131.

48. Edward McPherson, *The Political History of the United States of America During the Great Rebellion, 1860–1865* (New York, 1972), pp. 195–96; Nashville *Union and American,* August 25, 1861.

49. Temple, *East Tennessee,* pp. 366ff.; Patton, *Unionism and Reconstruction in Tennessee,* pp. 58ff.; Lately Thomas, *The First President Johnson* (New York, 1968), pp. 215ff. For the invitations, see note 45 above.

50. Cincinnati *Gazette,* August 15, 1861; Temple, *East Tennessee,* pp. 367–68, 391, 385; Temple, *Notable Men,* pp. 308–16; Notice of Sequestration Proceedings, November 27, 1861, Robert L. Stanford to Johnson, December 13, 1861, *PJ* 5:37, 48–50.

51. Lloyd Lewis, *Sherman: Fighting Prophet* (New York, 1932), p. 181; Robert Underwood Johnson and Clarence Clough Buel, eds., *Battles and Leaders of the Civil War,* 4 vols. (New York, 1956), 1:337ff., 382; Speech at Cincinnati, August 31, 1861, *PJ* 4:700–5; Speech at Newport, September 2, 1861, Johnson to Gideon Welles, September 30, 1861, Speech at Columbus, October 4, 1861, *PJ* 5:3–7, 12–29; Cincinnati *Daily Gazette,* September 2, 3, 6, October 5, 1861.

52. F. A. Mitchel, *Ormsby McKnight Mitchel, Astronomer and General* (Boston, 1887), pp. 222–23; Francis F. McKinney, *Education in Violence: The Life of General George H. Thomas and the History of the Army of the Cumberland* (Detroit, 1961), pp. 108ff, 115; Roy P. Basler, ed., *The Collected Works of Abraham Lincoln,* 9 vols. (New Brunswick, 1952–55), 4:544–45; O.R., series I, 4:324–25, 303, 342–43, 347; 7:480, 443–44, series II, 1:891, 897–98; Temple, *East Tennessee,* pp. 377–78. According to Temple, in September Johnson attended a conference with General S. P. Carter, General Thomas, and Maynard, "when the feasibility of burning the bridges [of East Tennessee] was agreed upon." Thomas expected Johnson to furnish government funds for this purpose, but the senator failed to do so (*ibid.,* pp. 375–76). There is some evidence that he was not very pleased with this foolhardy scheme. Montgomery Blair to Johnson, August 8, 1861, *PJ* 4:673.

53. Johnson to James R. Langdon, January 11, 1862, *PJ* 5:94; Nashville *Republican Banner,* November 19, 1861; Washington *Daily National Intelligencer,* December 13, 1861; O.R., Series II, 1:897–98, also in *PJ* 5:43–44.

54. *Cong. Globe,* 37th Cong., 2d Sess., 71; David Donald, ed., *Inside Lincoln's Cabinet: The Civil War Diaries of Salmon P. Chase* (New York, 1954), p. 51; Hans L. Trefousse, "The Joint Committee on the Conduct of the War: A Reassessment," *Civil War History* 10 (1964): 5–19.

55. Harry Williams, "Andrew Johnson as a Member of the Committee on the Conduct of the War," *ETHSP* 12 (1940): 70–81, esp. 74, 77; *Report of the Joint Committee on the Conduct of the War (Sen. Report No. 108),* 37th Cong., 3d Sess., 1:68–71, 113ff., 125–27, 130–60, 75; Rudolf Schleiden, Dispatch No, 1, January 6, 1862, Schleiden Papers, LC (microfilm); Lincoln, *Works,* 5:88; Hans L. Trefousse, *Benjamin Franklin Wade, Radical Republican from Ohio* (New York, 1963), pp. 159–60; George W. Julian, *Political Recollections, 1840–1872* (Chicago, 1884), pp. 201–3.

56. *Report of the Joint Committee on the Conduct of the War*, 2:265ff., 281, 335–36, 370; James G. Blaine, *Twenty Years of Congress*, 2 vols. (Boston, 1884), 1:382ff.

57. *Report of the Joint Committee on the Conduct of the War*, 1:78, 79, 3:161, 173, 182; Hans L. Trefousse, The *Radical Republicans: Lincoln's Vanguard for Racial Justice* (New York, 1968), pp. 175–77, 191.

58. Benjamin F. Wade, *Facts for the People* (Cincinnati, 1864), p. 2; *Report of the Joint Committee on the Conduct of the War*, 1:85.

59. Robert Johnson to Johnson, February 13, 1862, Application to Amend Sequestration Petition, January 18, 1862, Writ of Attachment, January 18, 1862, Michael L. Patterson to Johnson, January 31, 1862, *PJ* 5:143–44, 105–8, 113; *New York Times*, March 2, 1862; H. Leadbetter to Martha Patterson, November 29, 1861, Johnson Papers, Huntington Library; H. Leadbetter to Martha Patterson, November 29, 1861, Homestead File, AJPP.

60. *Cong. Globe*, 37th Cong., 2d Sess., 584–89, also in *PJ* 5:114–35.

61. *Cong. Globe*, 37th Cong., 2d Sess., 273, also in *PJ* 5:141–42. Johnson also introduced a resolution honoring Union soldiers for their brilliant victories at Fort Henry and Donelson: *Cong. Globe*, 37th Cong., 2d Sess., 845–46.

IX. MILITARY GOVERNOR

1. Herman Belz, *Reconstructing the Union: Theory and Policy During the Civil War* (Ithaca, N.Y., 1969), pp. 51ff., 71.

2. *PJ* 5:xxxii–xxxiii.

3. United States Senate, *Executive Journal*, 13:146–48.

4. William Nelson to Chase, February 28, 1862, Salmon P. Chase Papers, HSP.

5. Thomas A. Scott to Stanton, March 4, 1862, Stanton Papers, LC. William H. Seward later took credit for the appointment. John Bigelow, Diaries, September 23, 1868, NYPL.

6. New York *Herald*, March 5, 1862; Philadelphia *Press*, March 5, 1862; New York *World*, March 5, 1862; Chicago *Tribune*, March 6, 1862; *New York Times*, March 4, 1862; William R. Hurley to Johnson, March 4, 1862, William Patton to Johnson, March 4, 1862, Felix Reeve to Johnson, March 4, 1862, Jane H. Campbell to Johnson, March 6, 1862, James D. Johnston to Johnson, March 9, 1862, *PJ* 5:179–81, 187–88, 193–94.

7. Christopher Andrews, *Pioneer in Forestry Conservation in the United States: For Sixty Years a Dominant Influence in the Public Affairs of Minnesota: Lawyer: Editor: Diplomat: General in the Civil War: Recollections, 1829–1922*, Alice E. Andrews, ed. (Cleveland, 1928), p. 153.

8. Appointment as Military Governor, Stanton to Johnson, March 4, 1862, *PJ* 5:177–78, 182; Chicago *Tribune*, March 6, 1862.

9. William R. Plum, *The Military Telegraph During the Civil War in the United States*, 2 vols. (Chicago, 1892), 1:204; *PJ* 5:xxxv, 197, n. 2.

10. Joseph C. Guild, *Old Times in Tennessee* (Nashville, 1878), p. 494; Jane Thomas, *Old Days in Nashville* (Nashville, 1978), p. 129; Henry Villard, *Memoirs of Henry Villard, Journalist and Financier, 1835–1900*, 2 vols. (Boston, 1904), 1:226; Chicago *Tribune*, March 15, April 2, 1862; *New York Times*, March 5, 1862; Don Carlos Buell to Johnson, March 11, 1862, *PJ* 5:195–96.

11. Speech in Nashville, March 13, 1862, *PJ* 5:202–4; New York *World*, March 20, 1862.

12. Johnson to Stanley Matthews, March 17, 1862, Appeal to the People of Tennessee, March 18, 1862, Speech to Davidson County Citizens, March 22, 1862, *PJ* 5:208–12, 222–41.

13. W. G. Brownlow, *Sketches of . . . Secession* (Philadelphia, 1867), pp. 381, 384; Villard, *Memoirs*, 1:233; Johnson to Nashville City Council, March 25, 1862, City Council to Johnson, March 27, 1862, Johnson to Stanley Matthews, March 29, 1862, *PJ* 5:244–45,

247–48, 253–54, 318, n. 3; Clifton R. Hall, *Andrew Johnson, Military Governor* (Princeton, 1916), pp. 42–43.

14. Hall, *Johnson*, pp. 42–44; New York *World*, March 26, 1862; L. Virginia French Diary, p. 49 (April 20, 1862), TSLA; Edwin T. Hardison, "In the Toils of War: Andrew Johnson and the Federal Occupation of Tennessee, 1862–1865," Ph.D. diss., UT, 1981, pp. 79–82, 102–13; Nashville *Dispatch*, April 14, July 4, 1862; Interview with Clergy, PJ 5:487–90; Beth Crabtree and James W. Patton, eds., *Journal of a Southern Lady: The Diary of Ann Devereaux Edmundson* (Raleigh, 1979), p. 217; Herschel Gower and Jack Allen, eds., *Pen and Sword: The Life and Journals of Randal W. McGavock* (Nashville, 1959), pp. 607, 612, 627.

15. Circular Assessing Confederate Sympathizers, August 18, 1862, James S. Negley to Johnson, August 1, 1862, PJ 5:623–25, 583; Proclamation Appointing Nashville City Administration, October 1, 1862, PJ 6:18–19.

16. Randall Milton Ewing to Kinsman, May 18, 1862, Harding-Jackson Papers, TSLA; O.R., series I, vol. 16, part I, p. 816.

17. Gower and Allen, *McGavock*, p. 619; Thomas M. Fox to Johnson, April 5, 1862, Johnson to Stanton, March 28, 1862, Stanton Papers; Johnson to Chase, April 29, 1862, Johnson to Lincoln, May 18, September 1, 1862, PJ 5:268–69, 350, 403, 6:46; Peter Maslowski, *Treason Must Be Made Odious: Military Occupation and Wartime Reconstruction in Nashville, Tennessee, 1862–65* (Millwood, N.Y., 1978), pp. 21–22; LeRoy P. Graf and Ralph W. Haskins, PJ 5:li; Stanley J. Folmsbee et al., *History of Tennessee*, 4 vols. (New York, 1960), 2:83–84.

18. Brownlow, *Secession*, p. 381; Oliver P. Temple, *Notable Men of Tennessee* (New York, 1912), pp. 314–16.

19. Johnson to Stanton, March 29, 1862, PJ 5:254; O.R., series I, vol. 10, part II, p. 79.

20. Johnson to Lincoln, April 12, 1862, Johnson to Buell, April 25, 1862, Johnson to Lincoln, April 26, 1862, PJ 5:301, 333, 336–37. Johnson urged the appointment of the Tennesseean James G. Spears to take command at Cumberland Gap.

21. New York *Herald*, April 24, 1865; Hardison, "In the Toils of War," pp. 207–9.

22. Johnson to Lincoln, July 10, 1862, Lincoln to Johnson, July 11, 1862, PJ 5:549–50, 551–52.

23. O.R., series I, vol. 16, part II, p. 122; Johnson to Halleck, July 13, 1862, PJ 5:556–57.

24. Robert U. Johnson and Clarence C. Buel, eds., *Battles and Leaders of the Civil War*, 4 vols. (New York, 1956), 3:39, 1–25; Johnson to J. Morris Young, August 13, 1862, PJ 5:615–16.

25. Johnson to Lincoln, May 18, 1862, Johnson to G. W. Morgan, May 14, 25, June 2, 1862, Johnson to James S. Negley, June 1, 1862, Johnson to Halleck, June 5, 1862, Johnson to Stanton, June 21, 1862, Johnson to Thomas, August 16, 1862, Thomas to Johnson, August 16, 1862, PJ 5:403, 396–97, 418–19, 432–33, 434–35, 442, 495–96, 617; Freeman Cleaves, *Rock of Chickamauga: The Life of General George H. Thomas* (Norman, Okla., 1948), p. 108.

26. New York *Herald*, April 24, 1865; O.R., series I, vol. 16, part I, pp. 697–98, 59–60; part II, pp. 242, 490; Nashville *Dispatch*, October 4, 1862; Ridley Wills II, "Letters from Nashville, 1862: A Portrait of Belle Meade," THQ 33 (1974): 77.

27. Johnson to Lincoln, September 1, October 29, 1862, Lincoln to Johnson, October 31, 1862, PJ 6:4–6, 44–45. The president wrote that he sincerely hoped Rosecrans might be able to do something for Tennessee.

28. Frank B. Carpenter, *Six Months at the White House with Abraham Lincoln: The Story of a Picture* (New York, 1867), pp. 102–3.

29. New York *Herald*, April 24, 1865; Johnson to Lincoln, January 11, 1863, PJ 6:114.

30. Brownlow to Johnson, May 3, 1862, James A. Moore to Johnson, April 28, 1862, Maynard to Johnson, April 30, 1862, PJ 5:357–58, 341–44, 352–53; O.R., series II, 1:883, 885, 887, 888; series I, vol. 16, part I, p. 710; Fay W. Brabson, *Andrew Johnson:*

A Life in Pursuit of the Right Course, 1808–1875 (Durham, N.C., 1972), p. 87; New York *Herald,* April 24, 1865; *PJ* 6:23, n. 3. In February 1862, after an adventurous flight, Robert had made his way through the Union lines. *PJ* 5:143.

31. Johnson to Lincoln, October 29, November 8, 18, 1862, March 27, August 9, 1863, *PJ* 6:44, 48–49, 64, 197–98, 323–24.

32. Stanton to Johnson, March 4, 1862, Johnson to Stanton, April 23, 1862, Stanton to Johnson, June 21, 1862, Johnson to Lincoln, July 15, 1862, Stanton to Johnson, July 16, August 1, 1862, April 15, 1863, Authorization to Raise Troops, March 28, 1863, *PJ* 5:181, 326–27, 495–96, 461–62, 587, 6:198–99, 211–12; Graf and Haskins, *PJ* 6:xxxvi, xxxix; Hall, *Johnson,* pp. 178–82; James S. Jones, *Life of Andrew Johnson, 17th President of the United States* (Greeneville, 1901), p. 84. By mid-1864 he had raised twenty-five thousand men: Nashville *Dispatch,* June 24, 1864.

33. Maslowski, *Treason Must Be Made Odious,* pp. 37ff.; Johnson to Lincoln, November 8, 18, 24, 1862, *PJ* 5:48–50, 64, 71; Stanton Letterbook, April 2, 1863, p. 110, Stanton Papers; Johnson to Thomas, August 16, 1862, Thomas to Johnson, August 16, 1862, *PJ* 5:617–18; Richard O'Connor, *Thomas, Rock of Chickamauga* (New York, 1948), p. 181.

34. *O.R.,* series I, vol. 10, part II, pp. 126, 128, 129; vol. 16, part II, pp. 36–37, 44, 47, 118–19, 132–33, 135, 148, 175, 228; L. Virginia French Diary, p. 77.

35. T. Harry Williams, *Lincoln and His Generals* (New York, 1952), p. 186; *O.R.,* series I, vol. 23, part II, pp. 174, 195, 207, 208, 220, 380, 526; Rosecrans to Johnson, April 4, 1863, *PJ* 6:206, esp. n. 2 and 3. Johnson was grateful to Rosecrans for taking care of Robert, who had started to drink heavily. Rosecrans to Johnson, April 12, 1863, Johnson to Rosecrans, June 1, 1863, *PJ* 6:211, 235.

36. *DAB* 6:418–20; Johnson to Halleck, June 17, 1862, Johnson to John Sherman, June 18, 1862, *PJ* 5:485–86, 487; *O.R.,* series I, vol. 26, part II, p. 72.

37. *DAB* 7:405; Johnson to Negley, October 20, 1862, Johnson to Lincoln, November 8, 1862, *PJ* 6:32–33, 48–49.

38. Remarks to the Third Minnesota Regiment, April 23, 1862, Johnson to Lincoln, June 14, 1862, Speech at Nashville, July 4, 1862, *PJ* 5:327–28, 477, 534–40; New York *Herald,* June 4, 1862.

39. Hans L. Trefousse, *Ben Butler: The South Called Him Beast* (New York, 1957), pp. 110–11; Benjamin Truman, "Anecdotes of Andrew Johnson," *Century Illustrated Magazine* 63 (1912–13): 436–37; Interview with Rebel Ladies, April 1862, *PJ* 5:261–62, xliv; Hardison, "In the Toils of War," pp. 127ff. Allegedly, Miss Carter actually did put flowers on Johnson's grave.

40. Nashville *Daily Press,* May 25, 1863; Hardison, "In the Toils of War," pp. 116–17, 125, 135; Elizabeth M. Harding to Johnson, September, 1862, Johnson to William L. Utley, October 30, 1863, Johnson to David Tod, March 20, 1862, Johnson to Connally F. Trigg, March 20, 1862, Johnson to Lincoln, June 5, 1862, Lincoln to Johnson, June 4, 1862, Peter Watson to Johnson, August 4, 1862, Johnson to Lincoln, August 17, 19, September 6, 1864, *PJ* 6:3–4, 445–46, 5:218–20, 366, 439, 445–46, 595, 7:99–100, 103–4, 138; Johnson to Lincoln, September 28, October 1, 1864, JP; Wills, "Letters from Nashville," pp. 80–81. On August 9, 1862, Johnson appointed ex-governor William B. Campbell commissioner for Tennessee prisoners: Johnson to Lorenzo Thomas, August 9, 1862, *PJ* 5:603.

41. Nashville *Union,* July 23, 1862; Andrews, *Recollections,* p. 152; Charles A. Dana, *Recollections of the Civil War with the Leaders in Washington and in the Field in the Sixties* (New York, 1898), p. 105.

42. John M. Palmer, *Personal Recollections of John M. Palmer: The Story of an Earnest Life* (Cincinnati, 1901), p. 127; Speech to Davidson County Citizens, March 22, 1862, Speech at Nashville, July 4, 1862, *PJ* 5:231, 536.

43. Johnson to Lincoln, May 22, 1862, Lincoln Papers, LC.

44. James G. Blaine, *Twenty Years of Congress,* 2 vols. (Boston, 1884–86), 1:446; Petition to

the President, December 4, 1862, Johnson to Lincoln, January 11, 1862, *PJ* 6:85–86, 114; John Cimprich, *Slavery's End in Tennessee* (University, Ala., 1985), p. 101.

45. Bowen, "Andrew Johnson and the Negro," Ph.D. diss., UT, 1976, p. 186; Nashville *Union,* February 13, 1863; Nashville *Dispatch,* March 1, 1863; New York *Herald,* March 15, 1863; *Reception of Governor Johnson, of Tennessee, and ex-Governor Wright, of Indiana, at the State Capitol of Pennsylvania* (Harrisburg, 1863); Speech at Indianapolis, February 26, 1863, Speech at Cincinnati, February 27, 1863, Speech to the Ohio Legislature, March 4, 1863, Speech at Harrisburg, Pennsylvania, March 6, 1863, Speech at Philadelphia, March 11, 1863, Speech to the Loyal League, New York City, March 14, 1862, Speech at Baltimore, March 20, 1863, Speech at Washington Union Meeting, March 31, 1863, *PJ* 6:148–62, 165–66, 168–74, 175–93, 200–4; Laura Maynard to Washburn Maynard, March 22, 1863, Horace Maynard Papers, UT.

46. Nashville *Dispatch,* April 21, 22, 1863; Authorization to Raise Troops, March 28, 1863, Stanton to Johnson, April 2, 18, 1863, Johnson to Lincoln, September 17, 1863, Lincoln to Johnson, March 26, 1863, *PJ* 6:198–99, 205, 212–13, 377–78, 194–95, xlviii; O.R., series I, vol. 30, part III, p. 54; *DAB* 4:287; Roy P. Basler, ed., *The Collected Works of Abraham Lincoln,* 9 vols. (New Brunswick, 1953–55), 6:187; Chicago *Tribune,* April 3, 1863; Harry Williams, "Andrew Johnson as a Member of Committee on the Conduct of the War," *ETHSP* 12 (1940): 80; Cimprich, *Slavery's End,* p. 102. While in Washington, Johnson voiced agreement with his friend Washington Snethen's prediction that the war would end with the total extinction of slavery. Snethen to Johnson, January 25, 1865, *PJ* 7:433–34.

47. Hans L. Trefousse, *The Radical Republicans: Lincoln's Vanguard for Racial Justice* (New York, 1968), pp. 203ff. John Cimprich stresses political calculations involving relations with Lincoln, while David W. Bowen emphasizes Johnson's frustrations with Nashville secessionists and believes the governor probably made up his mind in the winter of 1862–63 as a countermove to the influence of the conservative Unionists. Cimprich, *Slavery's End,* pp. 102–3; Bowen, "Andrew Johnson and the Negro," pp. 186, 189.

48. Johnson to Robert Johnson, November 18, 1862, Robert Johnson to Johnson, November 24, December 3, 10, 11, 1862, Johnson to Eliza Johnson, March 27, 1863, *PJ* 6:64, 68, 82, 96, 195–96.

49. Nashville *Union,* April 5, 1863; New York *Herald,* April 3, 1863; Robert Johnson to Johnson, April 7, November 17, 1863, Johnson to Robert Johnson, November 21, 23, 1863, Robert Johnson to Johnson, February, 1864, Johnson to Rosecrans, April 11, October 12, 1863, Rosecrans to Johnson, April 11, 1863, *PJ* 6:207, 480, 599–600, 485, 488, 211, 417–18; O.R., series I, vol. 23, part II, p. 228.

50. O.R., series I, vol. 16, part I, pp. 697–98; *PJ* 6:228, n. 1; Nashville *Dispatch,* May 31, 1863; Nashville *Union,* May 31, 1863; Nashville *Daily Press,* June 1, 1863.

51. Confiscation Proclamation, February 20, 1863, Rosecrans to Johnson, July 7, 1863, Speech at Franklin, August 22, 1863, Speech at Nashville, August 29, 1863, Lincoln to Johnson, September 11, 1863, *PJ* 6:145–46, 285–86, 334–39, 344–45, 362–63.

52. Frank Preston Stearns, *The Life and Public Services of George Luther Stearns* (Philadelphia, 1907), p. 309; Stearns to Secretary of War, September 16, 19, October 24, 1863, Stearns to J. M. Forbes, October 18, 1863, Secretary of War to Stearns, September 18, 25, 1863, War Department, RG 94, 1578, 1592, 1694, 1588, 1600–4, NA; Johnson to Stanton, September 17, 1863, Stanton to Johnson, September 18, 1863, Johnson to Lincoln, September 23, 1863, Testimony *re* Condition of Negroes, November 23, 1863, *PJ* 6:376–77, 378–79, 384, 488–92; Maslowski, *Treason Must Be Made Odious,* pp. 104–7; Cimprich, *Slavery's End,* pp. 82–87.

53. John Wooldridge, *History of Nashville, Tennessee* (Nashville, 1890), pp. 195, 198; Nashville *Dispatch,* May 14, 1862; New York *Herald,* May 17, 28, 1862; Speech at Nashville, May 12, 1862, Maynard to Johnson, May 25, 1862, *PJ* 5:379–87, 418, n. 3; Gower and Allen, *McGavock,* p. 625.

54. Basler, *Works of Abraham Lincoln,* 5:302–3.

55. Lincoln to Grant, Johnson, and others, October 21, 1862, Writ of Election for Congressional Districts, December 8, 1862, Grant to Johnson, January 16, 1863, Pitser Miller to Johnson, March 7, 1863, PJ 6:33–34, 92–93, 121, 166–67. The commissioner was Thomas R. Smith, a native of Maine.

56. Maslowski, Treason Must Be Made Odious, pp. 80ff.; Hall, Johnson, pp. 96–101; Nashville Daily Press, June 25, July 2, 3, 11, 1863; Nashville Dispatch, July 2, 1863; Cimprich, Slavery's End, p. 102.

57. Dana, Recollections of the Civil War, pp. 104–6; Dana to Stanton, September 8, 1863, Stanton Papers; O.R., series III, part III, pp. 789, 819, 823, 825. He had already made the same argument about Article IV when he saw Lincoln in the spring.

58. Johnson to Lincoln, November 2, 1863, PJ 6:448; Nashville Union, November 1, 1863. It was also at this time that Johnson first met General Grant, whom he welcomed to Nashville with a lengthy speech. Johnson and Buel, Battles and Leaders, 3:684.

59. Charles Kortrecht et al. to Johnson, December 26, 1863, Lincoln to Johnson, December 10, 1863, Speech on Slavery and State Suicide, January 8, 1864, PJ 6:528, 514, 548–51; Nashville Dispatch, January 2, 8, 1864.

60. Nashville Dispatch, January 22, 24, 1864; Speech on Restoration of State Government, January 21, 1864, PJ 6:574–90.

61. Nashville Daily Press, January 26, 1864.

62. Proclamation Ordering Elections, January 26, 1864, PJ 6:594–96.

63. Nashville Daily Press, January 28, 30, February 1, 2, 6, 8, 9, 12, 15, 25, March 2, 1864; Edwin H. Ewing to Johnson, February 1, 1864, PJ 6:601–2.

64. Nashville Dispatch, February 16, March 6, 23, 1864; Nashville Daily Press, February 18, March 10, 25, 1864; Basler, Works of Abraham Lincoln, 7:196, 183–84; Hall, Johnson, pp. 23–24.

65. Temple, Notable Men, pp. 407–9; Johnson to Brownlow, April 6, 1864, Johnson to Lincoln, April 11, 1864, Speech at Athens, April 11, 1864, Speech at Knoxville, April 12, 16, 1864, PJ 6:663, 669–79; Nashville Dispatch, May 1, 1864; Wilson D. Miscamble, "Andrew Johnson and the Election of William G. ('Parson') Brownlow as Governor of Tennessee," THQ, 37 (1978): 308–20, esp. 311.

X. VICE PRESIDENT

1. John B. Logan to Johnson, March 14, 1862, A. Clark Denson to Johnson, July 2, 1862, Robert L. Stanford to Johnson, November 24, 1862, Theophilus Fiske to Johnson, June 10, 1863, PJ 5:204–5, 527–28, 6:69, 242; Thomas Champion to Johnson, February 18, 1865, JP; Norman Judd to Lyman Trumbull, May 7, 1865, Trumbull Papers, LC.

2. Nashville Union, November 24, 1863; Chicago Tribune, February 24, 1864; Fairfield, Illinois, War Democrat, February 11, 1864, JP, Series 11.

3. Alexander K. McClure, Abraham Lincoln and the Men of War-Times (Philadelphia, 1892), pp. 425–59, 104–10; McClure to Lamon, July 18, 1891, Ward Hill Lamon Papers, Huntington Library; John G. Nicolay and John Hay, Abraham Lincoln: A History, 10 vols. (New York, 1890), 9:72–73; Tyler Dennett, ed., Lincoln and the Civil War in the Diaries and Letters of John Hay (New York, 1939), p. 18; Charles Eugene Hamlin, The Life and Times of Hannibal Hamlin (Cambridge, Mass., 1899), pp. 468ff.

4. Hans L. Trefousse, Ben Butler: The South Called Him Beast (New York, 1957), pp. 158–60; Roy P. Basler, ed., The Collected Works of Abraham Lincoln, 9 vols. (New Brunswick, 1953–55), 7:203.

5. New York Times, July 10, 1891; Benjamin Truman, "Anecdotes of Andrew Johnson," Century Illustrated Magazine 63 (1912–13): 437; McClure, Lincoln and the Men of War-Times, pp. 110–11, 115–17, 438; Abram Dittenhoefer, How We Elected Lincoln (New York, 1916), p. 83; William O. Stoddard, Jr., ed., Lincoln's Third Secretary: The Memoirs of William O. Stoddard (New York, 1955), pp. 215–16.

6. Hamlin, Hamlin, pp. 461–68; H. Draper Hunt, Hannibal Hamlin of Maine, Lincoln's First

Vice-President (Syracuse, 1969), pp. 180ff.; Alexander H. Rice to Hamlin, June 18, 1864, Hannibal Hamlin Papers, Maine Historical Society, Portland; James F. Glonek, "Lincoln, Johnson, and the Baltimore Ticket," *Abraham Lincoln Quarterly* 6 (March 1951): 255–71. Glonek is one of the few scholars to follow Nicolay and Hay.

7. McClure, *Lincoln and the Men of War-Times*, p. 107; William Frank Zornow, *Lincoln and the Party Divided* (Norman, Okla., 1954), p. 100.

8. Truman, "Anecdotes of Andrew Johnson," p. 437; Clifton R. Hall, *Andrew Johnson, Military Governor* (Princeton, 1916), p. 128; New York *World,* March 26, 1864; Nashville *Daily Press,* March 18, 1864.

9. Glonek, "Lincoln, Johnson, and the Baltimore Ticket," p. 264; Philo S. Shelton to Weed, June 10, 1864, Thurlow Weed Papers, University of Rochester; Martin Ryerson to Seward, April 27, 1865, William H. Seward Papers, University of Rochester; Hamlin, *Hamlin,* pp. 461–67; New York *Herald,* June 9, 1864.

10. *Proceedings of the First Three Republican National Conventions, 1856, 1860, and 1864 . . . As Reported by Horace Greeley* (Minneapolis, 1893), pp. 188–89, 198–99, 227ff., 236–39.

11. Louisville *Press,* June 9, 1864, quoted in Nashville *Dispatch,* June 10, 1864; *New York Times,* June 9, 1864; Noah Brooks, *Washington in Lincoln's Time,* Herbert Mitgang, ed. (New York, 1958), p. 142; S. Newton Pettis to Johnson, June 10, 1864, Charles Watson to Johnson, June 13, 1864, *PJ* 6:730–31, 737; John A. Hiesand to Thaddeus Stevens, June 15, 1864, Stevens Papers, LC. Lincoln evidently knew how to hide his part in the nomination.

12. New York *World,* June 11, 1864; New York *Herald* cited in Nashville *Dispatch,* June 16, 1864; Charles Kerr to George Fort Milton, March 23, 1928, George Fort Milton Papers, LC; Gustave Koerner to Lyman Trumbull, March 10, 1866, Trumbull Papers; McClure, *Lincoln and the Men of War-Times,* pp. 259–60; Hamlin, *Hamlin,* p. 472; Speech on Vice-Presidential Nomination, June 9, 1864, Johnson to Lincoln, July 13, 1864, *PJ* 6:723–28; 7:30; Nashville *Dispatch,* June 10, 1864.

13. Acceptance of Vice-Presidential Nomination, July 2, 1864, *PJ* 7:7–12; Nashville *Daily Press,* August 4, 1864. The letter was drafted by Milligan.

14. Nashville *Daily Press,* February 6, 9, 12, 15, August 20, 1864; *New York Times,* September 13, 1864; Johnson to John W. Wright, August 21, 1864, Daniel Trewhitt to Johnson, August 25, 1864, *PJ* 7:109–13, 118–20; Hall, *Johnson,* pp. 140–47; Edwin T. Hardison, "In the Toils of War: Andrew Johnson and the Federal Occupation of Tennessee, 1862–1865," Ph.D. diss., UNC, 1981, p. 342; Nashville *Dispatch,* September 6, 7, 1864.

15. Nashville *Daily Press,* September 15, 1864.

16. Proclamation Concerning Restoration of Civil Government, September 7, 1864, Proclamation *re* Presidential Election, September 30, 1864, *PJ* 7:141–43, 203–5.

17. Robert V. Remini, *Andrew Jackson and the Course of American Freedom, 1822–1832* (New York, 1981), p. 235, renders this wording, though Jackson consented to the inclusion of the word "Federal," so that the toast was usually reported as "Our Federal Union: It must be preserved."

18. Speech near Gallatin, July 19, 1864, *PJ* 7:30, 41–44.

19. N. P. Sawyer to Frémont, September 13, 1864, JP. Frémont finally did withdraw as a result of Montgomery Blair's resignation from the cabinet. H. L. Trefousse, "Zachariah Chandler and the Withdrawal of Frémont in 1864: New Answers to an Old Riddle," *Lincoln Herald* 70 (Winter 1968): 181–88.

20. Johnson to John W. Wright, August 21, 1864, Speech at Logansport, Indiana, October 4, 1864, Remarks at the Indianapolis Sanitary Fair, October 7, 1864, Speech at Louisville, Kentucky, October 13, 1864, *PJ* 7:109–10, 218–31, 237–38; *New York Times,* October 19, 1864. The Johnson Papers are replete with invitations dating from July through October to speak in various parts of the country.

21. Militia Enrollment Proclamation, September 13, 1864, *PJ* 7:159–60; Hall, *Johnson,* pp. 188–90; Basler, *Works of Lincoln,* 8:60

22. Johnson also had some difficulty explaining away the anti-Semitic remarks he had made about Judah P. Benjamin, whom he had attacked as belonging "to that tribe that parted the garments of our Savior and for his vesture cast lots" and as "a sneaking, Jewish, unconscionable traitor." He sought to reassure the editor of the Cincinnati *Israelite* by reaffirming his belief in complete religious toleration. Herman M. Moos to Johnson, September 16, October 3, 1864, Johnson to Herman M. Moos, September 25, 1864, *PJ* 7:168–69, 208–9, 191–92.

23. Nashville *Daily Press*, April 7, August 20, September 4, 15, October 7, 10, 11, 18, 21, 25, 27, 29, 1864.

24. "The Moses of the Colored Men" Speech, October 24, 1864, *PJ* 7:251–53.

25. Nashville *Dispatch*, October 25, 1864; Nashville *Daily Press*, October 27, 1864; Edward M. Davis to Johnson, November 5, 1864, *PJ* 7:267–68.

26. Basler, *Works of Lincoln*, 8:58–72; New York *Herald*, October 17, 18, 23, 1864; Thomas B. Alexander, *Political Reconstruction in Tennessee* (Nashville, 1950), p. 75.

27. O.R., series I, vol. 39, part I, pp. 488–90, 855; Johnson to Lincoln, August 25, 1864, Johnson to George Ramsey, March 29, 1864, Johnson to Lovell H. Rousseau, May 28, 1864, Johnson to Stanton, July 6, 1864, Brownlow to Johnson, November 14, 1864, Johnson to Jacob Ammen, November 17, 1864, *PJ* 7:120, 6:656, 710–11, 7:17–18, 285–86, 299–300; Ammen to Johnson, November 17, 1864, JP; Richard Harrison Doughty, *Greeneville: One Hundred Year Portrait, 1775–1875* (Greeneville, 1975), pp. 223ff.; Hall, *Johnson*, pp. 187–88.

28. *New York Times*, November 21, 1864; Hall, *Johnson*, p. 156.

29. O.R., series I, vol. 39, part I, pp. 885–86; Brownlow to Johnson, November 18, 21, 30, December 8, 12, 1864, J. P. Bingham to Johnson, November 25, 1864, *PJ* 7:300–1, 307–9, 323–24, 334–35, 336, 314–16; Hall, *Johnson*, pp. 158–60; William C. Davis, *Breckinridge: Statesman, Soldier, Symbol* (Baton Rouge, 1973), pp. 463–68.

30. John Wooldridge, *History of Nashville, Tennessee* (Nashville, 1890), pp. 198–202; Johnson to Brownlow, December 22, 1864, Speech to the Union Convention, January 12, 1865, *PJ* 7:350, 398.

31. George H. Thomas to Johnson, December 30, 1864, Johnson to Thomas, December 31, 1864, *PJ* 7:369, 371.

32. Nashville *Dispatch*, January 9, 10, 11, 15; House of Representatives, 39th Cong., 1st Sess., *Miscellaneous Documents*, No. 55, pp. 1–10; Alexander, *Political Reconstruction in Tennessee*, pp. 18–32; Nashville *Weekly Press*, January 15, 1865.

33. Speech to Union State Convention, January 12, 1865, Johnson to Lincoln, January 13, 1865, Remarks to Union Convention, January 14, 1865, *PJ* 7:392–400, 404, 407–11.

34. Johnson to Lincoln, January 12, 1865, Lincoln to Johnson, January 24, 1865, John W. Forney to Johnson, January 27, 1865, *PJ* 7:420–21, 427, 439. Gideon Welles, years later, maintained that Lincoln believed Johnson's absence from the inauguration ceremonies would "have an unfortunate influence and construction abroad." Welles to Joseph S. Fowler, September 4, 1875, Welles Papers, NYPL.

35. Forney to Johnson, November 15, 1864, *PJ* 7:287–90.

36. Forney to Johnson, January 7, 1865, Francis P. Blair, Sr., to Johnson, November 17, 1864, *PJ* 7:374–76, 293–95; H. C. Page et al. to Lincoln, January 18, 1865, JP.

37. *Impeachment Investigation*, Testimony Taken Before the Judiciary Committee of the House of Representatives in the Investigation of the Charges Against Andrew Johnson, 39th Cong., 2d Sess., and 40th Cong., 1st Sess., No. 7, pp. 780–82; Hardison, "In the Toils of War," pp. 349–50. While Matthews testified about Johnson's alleged statement in 1867, he told the story to others at least as early as March 1866: Warner Bateman to John Sherman, March 28, 1866, John Sherman Papers, LC.

38. Nashville *Daily Press*, March 11, 1865; Proclamation *re* Ratification of State Constitutional Amendments, February 25, 1865, *PJ* 7:487–91.

39. Nashville *Dispatch*, February 9, 25, 26, 1865; Johnson to Henry Wilson, February 16, 1865, American Union Commission to Johnson, February 22, 1865, Johnson to Rich-

ard Sutton, March 9, 1865, Johnson to Stanton, March 3, 1865, Stanton to Johnson, March 3, 1865, Remarks to the Governor's Guard, Louisville, February 26, 1865, Remarks at Cincinnati, February 27, 1865, William S. Mitchell to Johnson, January 28, February 7, 1865, Martha J. Patterson to Johnson, April 16, 1865, PJ 7:474, 482–83, 498, 491–92, 494, 445, 462, 650–61; Forney to Johnson, March 2, 1865, JP, series II; Truman, "Anecdotes of Andrew Johnson," pp. 437–38.

40. New York Herald, March 5, 1865; Hamlin, Hamlin, p. 497.

41. Brooks, Washington in Lincoln's Time, pp. 210–13; Remarks at Vice-Presidential Swearing In, March 4, 1865, PJ 7:506–7; Chicago Tribune, March 6, 1865.

42. Chandler to Mrs. Chandler, March 6, 1865, Zachariah Chandler Papers, LC; L. de Geoffrey to Drouyn de Lhuys, March 7, 1865, Archives des Affaires Etrangères, vol. 1133, p. 125, Ministère des Affaires Etrangères, Paris.

43. Frederick Douglass, Life and Times of Frederick Douglass (Hartford, 1881), p. 364. As Lincoln was busy all morning signing bills at the Capitol, the incident probably happened at a different occasion.

44. New York World, March 6, 7, 1865; New York Herald, March 6, 1865; Richmond Sentinel, March 15, 1865.

45. A. G. Browne, Jr., to John Andrew, March 21, 1865, Andrew Papers, MHS; Richmond Sentinel, March 15, 1865; Francis Lieber to Charles Sumner, March 11, 1864, Lieber Papers, Huntington Library; Johnson to Richard Sutton, March 9, 1865, edited version of Remarks at Vice-Presidential Swearing In, March 4, 1865, PJ 7:514–15, 502–6; Cong. Globe, 38th Cong., 2d Sess., Special Session, 1425, 1427ff.

46. Sumner to Lieber, March 8, 1865, Sumner Papers, Harvard University; Henry Winter Davis to S. P. DuPont, April 22, 1865, DuPont Papers, Eleutherian Mills Library, Greeneville, Del.; Henry Wilson, History of the Rise and Fall of the Slave Power in America, 3 vols. (Boston, 1876), 3:578; Hugh McCulloch, Men and Measures of Half a Century (New York, 1888), p. 373.

47. Truman, "Anecdotes of Andrew Johnson," pp. 437–38; Herbert A. Bentley, "Andrew Johnson, Governor of Tennessee," Ph.D. diss., UT, 1972, pp. 475–76, 671; Charles A. Dana, Recollections of the Civil War, with the Leaders in Washington and in the Field in the Sixties (New York, 1898), pp. 105–6; David Davis to Julius Rockwell, March 20, 1865, David Davis Papers, Chicago Historical Society.

48. Nashville Daily Press, March 20, 1865; Robert Johnson to Johnson, April 3, 1865, A. P. Gorman to Robert Johnson, March 25, 1865, JP; Oliver P. Temple, Notable Men of Tennessee (New York, 1912), pp. 140–41.

49. Remarks on the Fall of Richmond, April 3, 1865, PJ 7:543–46.

50. New York Times, April 10, 1865; Pass to Richmond, April 3, 1865, JP; William H. Crook, Through Five Administrations: Reminiscences of William H. Crook, Body-Guard to President Lincoln, Margarit Spalding, ed. (New York, 1910), p. 44; David Dixon Porter, Incidents and Anecdotes of the Civil War (New York, 1885), p. 287. Both Porter and, less emphatically, Crook maintained that Lincoln refused to see the vice president.

51. Edward D. Neill, Reminiscences of the Last Years of President Lincoln's Life (St. Paul, 1888), p. 47.

XI. UNIONIST PRESIDENT

1. Leonard J. Farwell to James Doolittle, March 12, 1866, Doolittle Papers, State Historical Society of Wisconsin, with copy in JP.

2. Diary of Gideon Welles, Howard K. Beale, ed., 3 vols. (New York, 1960), 2:288–89; Charles Sumner to John Bright, May 1, 1865, in Edgar L. Pierce, Memoir and Letters of Charles Sumner, 4 vols. (Boston, 1894), 4:241. According to Moorfield Storey, Sumner suggested to Stanton that Johnson ought to leave shortly after he had come into the room because Mary Lincoln, who had a strong aversion to him, ought not to see him there should she return. "Dickens, Stanton, Sumner, and Storey," Atlantic Monthly 145

(April 1930): 463–65; John E. Buckingham, *Reminiscences and Souvenirs of the Assassination of Abraham Lincoln* (Washington, D.C., 1894), p. 63.

3. Memorandum, April 15 [sic, probably the next day], 1865, Chase Papers, Historical Society of Cincinnati; Gideon Welles, "Recollection of Events Immediately Preceding and Following the Assassination and Death of Lincoln," Gideon Welles Papers, Huntington Library; James D. Richardson, ed., *A Compilation of the Messages and Papers of the Presidents, 1789–1897*, 10 vols. (Washington, D.C., 1896–99), 8:3503–4; New York *Herald,* April 16, 1865; Cabinet to Johnson, April 15, 1865, Remarks on Assuming the Presidency, April 15, 1865, *PJ* 7:553–54.

4. Welles, *Diary,* 2:289–90; New York *Herald,* April 16, 1865.

5. William M. Stewart, *Reminiscences of Senator William M. Stewart of Nevada,* George Rothwell Brown, ed. (New York, 1908), pp. 193–95, 198.

6. Memorandum, April 15, 1865, Chase Papers, Historical Society of Cincinnati; Welles, *Diary,* 2:289–90; New York *Herald,* April 16, 1865; Ben: Perley Poore, *Perley's Reminiscences of Sixty Years in the National Metropolis* (Philadelphia, 1886), 2:181–82; New York *World,* April 17, 1865.

7. Ben:Perley Poore, ed., *The Conspiracy Trial for the Murder of the President,* 3 vols. (Boston, 1865), 1:62–69, 2:277–79; Buckingham, *Reminiscences,* p. 34; William Hanchett, *The Lincoln Murder Conspiracies* (Urbana, 1983), pp. 83–85, passim. The same conclusion was reached by Thomas Reed Turner: *Beware the People Weeping* (Baton Rouge, 1982), pp. 251–52. It may be that the card Booth left at the hotel was meant for William A. Browning, Johnson's private secretary, in whose box it was found. Cf. Testimony of William A. Browning, AG File, M 599, roll 9, microfilm, NA.

8. David Davis to Julius Rockwell, April 21, 1868, Davis Papers, Chicago Historical Society; T. Harry Williams, *Lincoln and the Radicals* (Madison, 1941), pp. 376ff.; Howard K. Beale, *The Critical Year: A Study of Andrew Johnson and Reconstruction* (New York, 1930), pp. 58–59; David Miller DeWitt, *The Impeachment and Trial of Andrew Johnson* (New York, 1903), pp. 4–5; Robert Watson Winston, *Andrew Johnson, Plebeian and Patriot* (New York, 1926), p. 336.

9. Roy P. Basler, ed., *The Collected Works of Abraham Lincoln,* 9 vols. (New Brunswick, 1953–55), 8:406–8, 399–405.

10. Hans L. Trefousse, "Abraham Lincoln Versus Andrew Johnson: Two Approaches to Reconstruction," Steven B. and Agnes Hussar, eds., *Society in Change: Studies in Honor of Bela Kalman Kiraly* (Boulder, Colo., 1983), pp. 251–70; cf. Carl Schurz, *The Reminiscences of Carl Schurz,* 3 vols. (New York, 1907–8), 3:221; Michael Les Benedict, *A Compromise of Principle: Congressional Republicans and Reconstruction, 1863–1869* (New York, 1974), p. 73; Peyton McCrary, *Abraham Lincoln and Reconstruction: The Louisiana Experiment* (Princeton, 1973), pp. 14–15.

11. Remarks on Assuming the Presidency, April 15, 1865, *PJ* 7:553–54; New York *Herald,* April 16, 1865.

12. George W. Julian, "George W. Julian's Journal—the Assassination of Lincoln," *Indiana Magazine of History* 11 (December 1915): 334–36; James G. Blaine, *Twenty Years of Congress,* 2 vols. (Boston, 1984–86), 2:14. It is certain that the radicals saw Johnson on both April 16 and 17: George W. Julian to Mrs. Julian, April 17, 1865, George W. Julian Papers, Indiana Historical Society, Indianapolis.

13. Sumner to Francis Lieber, May 2, 1865, Charles Sumner Papers Harvard University; David Donald, ed., *Inside Lincoln's Cabinet: The Civil War Diaries of Salmon P. Chase* (New York, 1959), p. 219; *New York Times,* November 8, 1867.

14. Julian, "George W. Julian's Journal," p. 334; Harriet Weed, ed., *Autobiography of Thurlow Weed* (Boston, 1883), p. 474.

15. Washington *National Intelligencer,* April 22, 1865; Remarks to Illinois Delegation, April 18, 1865, Response to John Mercer Langston, April 18, 1865, Response to a Massachusetts Delegation, April 20, 1865, Response to Ohio Delegation, April 21, 1865, Speech to Indiana Delegation, April 21, 1865, Remarks to Pennsylvania Citizens in Washing-

ton, April 28, 1865, *PJ* 7:582–86, 598, 610–15, 654–55; Edward McPherson, *The Political History of the United States of America During the Period of Reconstruction, April 15, 1865–July 15, 1870* (Washington, D.C., 1870), pp. 47–48; *The Diary of George Templeton Strong*, Allan Nevins and Milton Halsey Thomas, eds., 4 vols. (New York, 1952), 3:590–91.

16. Glyndon G. Van Deusen, *William Henry Seward* (New York, 1967), passim.
17. Hugh McCulloch, *Men and Measures of Half a Century* (New York, 1888), passim, esp. pp. 399–412. Johnson was so great an admirer of Andrew Jackson that he forbade his secretary Frank Cowan to remove a desk Old Hickory had once used. "I love the memory of Gen. Jackson," he said. "What was Old Hickory's I revere." Frank Cowan, *Andrew Johnson, President of the United States: Reminiscences of His Private Life and Character* (Greensburgh, Pa., 1894), pp. 10–11.
18. Benjamin P. Thomas and Harold M. Hyman, *Stanton: The Life and Times of Lincoln's Secretary of War* (New York, 1962), pp. 402–613 and passim; Stanton to Johnson, March 3, 1865, *PJ* 7:498–99, xlix.
19. John Niven, *Gideon Welles, Lincoln's Secretary of the Navy* (New York, 1973), pp. 497–64 and passim.
20. J. C. F. Leakes to John Sherman, April 26, 1865, John Sherman Papers; W. G. Moore, Small Diary, p. 3, JP.
21. Moore, Small Diary; p. 3, JP; *DAB*, 8:268–69.
22. *DAB* 3:241–42.
23. W. G. Moore, Small Diary, May 20, 1867, p. 43, JP; Robert T. Lincoln to Johnson, April 25, 1865, *PJ* 7:639. According to Moore, Hooper sent Johnson a bottle of Cayenne pepper in appreciation of his hospitality.
24. Welles, *Diary*, 2:318.
25. William H. Crook, *Through Five Administrations: Reminiscences of William H. Crook, Body-Guard to President Lincoln*, Margarit Spalding, ed. (New York, 1910), p. 85; J. B. Brownlow to William Temple, November 27, 1892, Temple Papers, UT.
26. Martha J. Patterson to Johnson, April 15, 1865, Johnson to David T. Patterson, April 16, 20, 1865, *PJ* 7:560, 567, 597–98; William P. Smith to Reuben Mussey, June 18, 1865, JP; Martha J. Patterson to David T. Patterson, June 19, 1865, JP, series III; Benjamin B. French Diary, July 9, 1865, Benjamin B. French Papers, LC.
27. Milligan to Johnson, April 29, 1865, James W. Scully to Johnson, April 6, 1865, *PJ* 7:664–66, 548–49; Thomas B. Alexander, *Political Reconstruction in Tennessee*, (Nashville, 1950), pp. 71, 76.
28. Noah Brooks, *Washington in Lincoln's Time*, Herbert Mitgang, ed. (New York, 1958), pp. 232–35; Strong, *Diary*, 3:590; *New York Times*, April 19, 20, 1865.
29. Welles, *Diary*, 2:294–96; O.R., series I, vol. 47, part III, pp. 263, 285, 292–93; Sherman to Grant, May 28, 1865, Sherman Papers, Huntington Library; Alexander K. McClure, *Lincoln and the Men of War-Times* (Philadelphia, 1892), p. 22; William T. Sherman, *Memoirs of General William T. Sherman*, 2 vols. (New York, 1886), 2:325ff., 372; Thomas and Hyman, *Stanton*, pp. 410ff. That Sherman was mistaken in thinking his terms were merely those desired by the dead president is shown in Raoul S. Naroll, "Lincoln and the Sherman Peace Fiasco—Another Fable?" *JSH* 20 (1954): 459–83.
30. Sam Milligan to Johnson, April 29, 1865, *PJ* 7:664–66; Chandler to Mrs. Chandler, April 23, 1865, Chandler Papers, LC; Montgomery Blair to S. L. M. Barlow, April 26, 1865, S. L. M. Barlow Papers, Huntington Library; Sherman to Schofield, May 28, 1865, William T. Sherman Papers.
31. Welles, *Diary*, 2:289–99; Richardson, *Messages and Papers of the Presidents*, 8:3505; Turner, *Beware the People Weeping*, pp. 125–26; Varina Davis, *Jefferson Davis . . . a Memoir by His Wife*, 2 vols. (New York, 1890), 2:782; Henry Winter Davis to Samuel DuPont, May 26, 1865, DuPont Papers, Eleutherian Mills Library, Greenville, Del.; New York *World*, May 4, 1865.
32. Jonathan T. Dorris, *Pardon and Amnesty Under Lincoln and Johnson* (Chapel Hill, 1953),

p. 264; Welles, *Diary*, 2:335–38, 366; Joseph Schafer, ed., *Intimate Letters of Carl Schurz, 1841–1869* (Madison, Wis., 1929), p. 336; Benjamin F. Butler, *Butler's Book* (Boston, 1892), pp. 915–16.

33. James Speed to Johnson, April 28, 1865, *PJ* 7:651; Welles, *Diary*, 2:299; Richardson, *Messages and Papers of the Presidents*, 8:3532–33, 3534, 3540–46; *New York Times*, May 10–July 16, 1865; George F. Milton, *The Age of Hate: Andrew Johnson and the Radicals* (New York, 1930), p. 210. Eventually, the conspirators were incarcerated at the Dry Tortugas.

34. Ward Thoron, ed., *The Letters of Mrs. Henry Adams* (Boston, 1936), pp. 6–8, 469; Brooks, *Washington in Lincoln's Time*, pp. 271ff.; Poore, *Perley's Reminiscences*, 2:186–92.

35. F. P. Blair to Johnson, April 18, 1865, with enclosure of R. Sutton to Blair, April 15, 1865, JP; New York *World*, April 17, 18, 19, May 3, 1865; New York *Herald*, April 16, 18, 22, 24, 1865; Chicago *Tribune*, April 17, 1865; New York *Tribune*, May 19, 1865; *New York Times*, April 17, 1865.

36. *New York Times*, May 26, 1865; Chicago *Tribune*, May 25, 1865.

XII. *PRESIDENTIAL RECONSTRUCTIONIST*

1. *Diary of Gideon Welles*, Howard K. Beale, ed., 3 vols. (New York, 1960), 2:280; Gideon Welles, Recollection of Events Immediately Preceding and Following the Assassination and Death of Lincoln, Welles Papers, Huntington Library; Joseph S. Fowler, Johnson MS, p. 7, Fowler Papers, LC.

2. Whitelaw Reid, *After the War: A Tour of the Southern States, 1865–1866*, C. Vann Woodward, ed. (New York, 1965), p. 44.

3. Petition from Colored People of Alexandria, April 29, 1865, From Frederick, Maryland, Citizens, April 24, 1865, Burnham Wardwell to Johnson, April 21, 1865, *PJ* 7:656–58, 626–27, 608–9; Thomas J. Durant to Johnson, May 1, 1865, Carl Schurz Papers, LC.

4. Sumner to Bright, May 1, 1865, Sumner to Lieber, May 2, 1865, in Edward L. Pierce, *Memoir and Letters of Charles Sumner*, 4 vols. (Boston, 1894) 4:242, 247; Chase to Johnson, April 18, 1865, *PJ* 7:578; Chase to Johnson, April 30, 1865, JP; Sumner to Francis Lieber, May 2, 1865, Sumner Papers, Harvard University; Chase to Schofield, May 7, 1865, John M. Schofield Papers, LC.

5. *New York Times*, November 8, 1867; Wade to Campbell, May 6, 1865, L. C. Campbell Papers, Ohio Historical Society. Whether Wade's recollection of the interview, colored as it was by intervening events, is actually correct, is difficult to tell, but the letter to Campbell shows that his attitude was favorable at the time.

6. Chandler to Mrs. Chandler, April 23, 1865, Chandler Papers, LC; L. D. Campbell to Johnson, May 8, 1865; Glyndon G. Van Deusen, *William Henry Seward* (New York, 1967), p. 428; G. W. Childs to F. P. Blair, April 17, 1865, JP; Wade to Butler, May 9, 1865, Butler Papers, LC.

7. Welles, *Diary*, 2:300–1; James D. Richardson, ed., *A Compilation of the Messages and Papers of the Presidents, 1789–1897*, 10 vols. (Washington, D.C., 1896–99), 8:3535–36.

8. Stevens to Sumner, May 10, 1865, Sumner Papers; George W. Julian, *Political Recollections, 1840–1872* (Chicago, 1892), p. 263.

9. Johnson to James Speed, April 21, 1865, *PJ* 7:609–10; Edward McPherson, *The Political History of the United States of America During the Period of Reconstruction, April 15, 1865–July 15, 1870* (Washington, D.C., 1870), pp. 9–12.

10. W. W. Holden, *Memoirs of W. W. Holden*, William K. Boyd, ed. (Durham, N.C., 1911), pp. 44–56; John H. Wheeler, *Reminiscences and Memoirs of North Carolina* (Baltimore, 1966), pp. 59–61; Elizabeth Gregory McPherson, "Letters from North Carolina to Andrew Johnson," *NCHR* 27 (1950): 341–43; Horace W. Raper, *William W. Holden, North Carolina's Political Enigma* (Chapel Hill, 1985), pp. 3–58, 59–61.

11. Edward Bates, *The Diary of Edward Bates*, Howard K. Beale, ed., Annual Report of the

American Historical Association for 1930, vol. 4 (Washington, D.C., 1933), p. 484; Washington *National Intelligencer,* May 30, 1865; New York *Sun,* May 30, 1865.

12. Charles Mason to J. S. Black, June 14, 1865, Jeremiah S. Black Papers, LC; Petersburg, Virginia, *Daily News,* May 30, 1865.

13. Stevens to Sumner, June 3, 14, 1865, Sumner Papers; Sumner to Stevens, June 19, 1865, Stevens Papers, LC.

14. Sumner to Wade, June 9, 1865, Wade Papers, LC; Schurz to Johnson, June 6, 1865, JP; Robert Dale Owen to Johnson, June 21, 1865, JP.

15. Albert Mordell, ed., *Civil War and Reconstruction: Selected Essays by Gideon Welles* (New York, 1959), pp. 214–18; Welles, *Diary,* 2:325; Wade to Sumner, July 29, 1865, Sumner Papers; Stevens to Johnson, July 6, 1865, JP; Stevens to Sumner, August 17, 1865, Sumner Papers. Wade urged Johnson to appoint Butler to a cabinet position. Jesse Ames Marshall, ed., *Private and Official Correspondence of General Benjamin F. Butler During the Period of the Civil War,* 5 vols. (Norwood, Mass., 1917), 5:691.

16. New York *World,* August 28, 1865; M. Blair to J. S. Black, August 30, 1865, Jeremiah S. Black Papers; New York *Herald,* August 20, 1865; Stevens to Sumner, August 26, 1865, Sumner Papers.

17. Welles, *Diary,* 2:315–16; DAB 9:21–22; William C. Harris, *Presidential Reconstruction in Mississippi* (Baton Rouge, 1967), pp. 40–44; *Journal of the Proceedings and Debates in the Constitutional Convention of the State of Mississippi, August 1865* (Jackson, 1865), pp. 144–45.

18. Welles, *Diary,* 2:315–16; NCAB 1:227–28, 9:70; C. Mildred Thompson, *Reconstruction in Georgia: Economic, Social, Political, 1865–1877* (New York, 1915), pp. 144–53; Sarah Woolfolk Wiggins, *The Scalawag in Alabama Politics, 1865–1881* (University, Ala., 1977), p. 10; Olive Hall Shadgett, "James Johnson, Provisional Governor of Georgia," *Georgia Historical Quarterly* 36 (1952): 1–21; Richardson, *Messages and Papers of the Presidents,* 8:3116, 3519.

19. Benjamin F. Perry, *Reminiscences of Public Men with Speeches and Addresses* (Greenville, S.C., 1889), pp. 242–47; *New York Times,* June 25, 1865; DAB 7:483–84; Francis B. Simkins and Robert H. Woody, *South Carolina During Reconstruction* (Chapel Hill, 1932), pp. 32–43.

20. Willam Marvin, "Autobiography of William Marvin," Kevin E. Kearney, ed., *Florida Historical Quarterly* 36 (1958): 177–222, esp. 198ff.; Richardson, *Messages and Papers of the Presidents,* 8:3527; NCAB 11:379; William W. Davis, *The Civil War and Reconstruction in Florida* (New York, 1913), pp. 351ff.

21. Hill to Johnson, June 15, 1865, Duff Green to Johnson, June 25, 1865, Thomas E. Bramlette to Johnson, July 26, 1865, Thomas Cottman to Johnson, June 5, 1865, J. B. Bingham to Johnson, July 13, 1865, JP.

22. Barlow to M. Blair, July 25, 1865, JP; Richard Taylor to Barlow, July 28, 1865, Barlow Papers, Huntington Library.

23. Mrs. John A. Jackson to Johnson, September 2, 1865, Dr. T. J. Rawls to Johnson, September 12, 1865, A. W. Putnam to Johnson, October 30, 1865, E. H. Gill to Johnson, November 22, 1865, Nicholson to Johnson, December 1, 1865, JP: Sidney Andrews, *The South Since the War . . .* (Boston, 1866); p. 92.

24. M. Blair to Barlow, April 18, 1865, Barlow Papers; Joseph A. Wright to Johnson, June 12, 1865, JP; Albert Hamlin to Hannibal Hamlin, June 13, 1865, Hamlin Papers, Maine Historical Society, Portland; Barlow to M. Blair, June 15, 1865, JP; A. J. Glosbrenner to J. S. Black, June 23, 1865, Black Papers; J. S. Black to M. Blair, July 15, 1865, JP.

25. Barlow to M. Blair, September 11, 1865, Barlow to T. G. Pratt, September 11, 1865, Barlow to W. D. Shipman, September 11, 1865, Letterbooks XII, Barlow Papers; Welles, *Diary,* 2:378; Barlow to George B. McClellan, October 12, 1865, Letterbooks XII, Barlow Papers. In other states the Democrats also endorsed Johnson. Eric L. McKitrick, *Andrew Johnson and Reconstruction* (Chicago, 1960), pp. 74–75.

26. F. P. Blair, Sr., to Johnson, August 1, 1865, JP.
27. Hugh McCulloch, *Men and Measures of Half a Century* (New York, 1888), pp. 225–26; Washington *Chronicle,* August 6, 1867, November 12, 1873; New York *Commercial Advertiser,* August 26, 1873; James May to Holt, September 16, 1873, Holt to Speed, April 18, December 19, 1883, Speed to Holt, October 25, December 26, 1883, Joseph Holt Papers, Huntington Library; William Hanchett, *The Lincoln Murder Conspiracies* (Urbana, 1983), pp. 86–88, 94–99, 103–4, 110–14. The recommendation for mercy is in NA, RG, 153, JAG. He also refused clemency for the commander of Andersonville Prison, who was hanged. O.R., series II, 8:792ff.; McKitrick, *Johnson and Reconstruction,* p. 161. On Johnson's illness, see below, p. 223.
28. Johnson to W. L. Sharkey, August 15, 1865, McPherson, *Reconstruction,* pp. 19–20.
29. New York *Tribune,* September 8, 1865; Frank P. Stearns, *The Life and Public Services of George Luther Stearns* (Philadelphia, 1907), pp. 358ff; McPherson, *Reconstruction,* pp. 48–49.
30. McPherson, *Reconstruction,* pp. 49–51; Chicago *Tribune,* October 13, 1865.
31. Johnson to Thomas, September 4, 8, 1865; 39 Cong., 1st Sess., Sen. Ex. Doc. No. 26, *Message from the President of the United States Communicating, in Compliance with resolutions of the Senate of the 5th of January and 27th of February last, information in regard to the provisional governors of States,* March 6, 1866 (hereafter cited as *Provisional Governors*), p. 231. Johnson promised Sharkey to remove the black troops "at the earliest period it is practicable to do so."
32. Hans L. Trefousse, *Carl Schurz: A Biography* (Knoxville, 1982), pp. 145, 153–58; Schurz to Johnson, August 29, 1865, Sharkey to Johnson, August 30, 1865, Johnson to Schurz, August 30, 1865, Schurz to Johnson, September 1, 4, 5, 1865, JP; Schurz to Sumner, October 17, 1865, Schurz Papers.
33. McPherson, *Reconstruction,* pp. 1, 9, 14; Oliver Otis Howard, *Autobiography of Oliver Otis Howard,* 2 vols. (New York, 1907), 2:230–31, 234–35; William S. McFeely, *Yankee Stepfather: General O. O. Howard and the Freedmen* (New Haven, 1968), pp. 103–5, 134.
34. Richardson, *Messages and Papers of the Presidents,* 8:3508ff.
35. Orville Hickman Browning, *The Diary of Orville Hickman Browning,* J. G. Randall, ed., Collections of the Illinois State Historical Library, XX, XXII, 2 vols. (Springfield, Ill., 1933), 2:32.
36. *Impeachment Investigation,* H. R., 40th Cong., 1st Sess., no.7, pp. 825–27; New York *Herald,* October 1, 1865; Jonathan T. Dorris, *Pardon and Amnesty Under Lincoln and Johnson* (Chapel Hill, 1953), p. 140. Senator Joseph S. Fowler denied that Grant's intervention saved Lee: Manuscript about Johnson, Fowler Papers.
37. Welles to Mrs. Welles, August 6, 1865, Welles Papers, LC; Dorris, *Pardon and Amnesty,* pp. 162–66, 177ff.; W. C. Whitthorne to Johnson, September 1, 1865, George W. Jones to Johnson, September 9, 1865; William S. Speer, ed., *Sketches of Prominent Tennesseans* (Nashville, 1888), p. 48; McPherson, *Reconstruction,* pp. 14–15; Welles, *Diary,* 2:382. In certain cases, such as with Lizinka Campbell Brown Ewell's family, Johnson took his time, but the end result was the same.
38. Elizabeth Avery Meriwether, *Recollections of 92 Years* (Nashville, 1958), pp. 183–84; Peter W. Hairston to Fanny, September 28, 1865, Peter W. Hairston Papers, UNC; McKitrick, *Johnson and Reconstruction,* pp. 142ff.
39. Lieber to Sumner, July 28, 1865, Lieber Papers, Huntington Library.
40. L. C. Baker, *History of the Secret Service* (Philadelphia, 1867), pp. 591–604; *Impeachment Investigation,* pp. 5, 8–9, 387–94, 667–68; Arthur Orrmont, *Mr. Lincoln's Master Spy* (New York, 1966), pp. 165–70; Jacob Mogilever, *Death to Traitors: The Story of General Lafayette C. Baker, Lincoln's Forgotten Secret Service Chief* (Garden City, N.Y., 1960), pp. 412–15.
41. McPherson, "Letters from North Carolina to Andrew Johnson," *NCHR* 27 (1950): 485–87, 28 (1951): 66–68. Johnson did send a telegram to deplore the election results,

but this gesture hardly resulted in favorable actions of the legislature. Richard L. Zuber, *Jonathan Worth: A Biography of a Southern Unionist* (Chapel Hill, 1965), p. 208.

42. Mary Clemmer Ames, *Ten Years in Washington: Life and Scenes in the National Capital as a Woman Sees Them* (Hartford, Conn., 1879), pp. 244–45; Benjamin B. French, Diary, July 9, 1865, French Papers, LC.; Ben: Perley Poore, *Perley's Reminiscences of Sixty Years in the National Metropolis,* 2 vols. (Philadelphia, 1886), 2:204–5.

43. French Diary, July 9, 1865, French Papers; New York *Herald,* July 1, 4, August 2, 4, 1865; Welles, *Diary,* 2:324, 329, 340, 341, 352, 354, 355, 366; Poore, *Perley's Reminiscences,* 2:193.

44. Lately Thomas, *The First President Johnson,* (New York, 1968), p. 320; Martha J. Patterson to Johnson, April 15, 1865, *PJ* 7:560; Norman Judd to Trumbull, February 14, 1866, Trumbull Papers, LC; J. W. Scully to Robert Johnson, August 9, 1865, Appointment as Private Secretary, November 5, 1865, JP; Chicago *Tribune,* November 13, 1865; Andrew Forest Muir, "William P. Johnson, Southern Proletarian and Unionist," *THQ* 15(1956) 338; Welles, *Diary,* 2:385–87.

45. *Provisional Governors,* pp. 221, 230, 234, 241, 244, 248, 258–59; Dan T. Carter, *When the War Was Over: The Failure of Self-Reconstruction in the South, 1865–1867* (Baton Rouge, 1985), pp. 30–31, 42.

46. *Provisional Governors,* pp. 200, 201, 249, 254, 226; Perry, *Reminiscences,* p. 284; McPherson, *Reconstruction,* pp. 19, 22–24. South Carolina repealed the secession ordinance instead of nullifying it.

47. Johnson to James B. Steedman, November 24, 1865, JP, series III, B; McKitrick, *Johnson and Reconstruction,* pp. 168–71; McPherson, *Reconstruction,* pp. 29–36; *Provisional Governors,* p. 228.

48. *Provisional Governors,* pp. 198, 179, 249, 254, 233; McPherson, *Reconstruction,* pp. 20, 22–23.

49. Rembert W. Patrick, *The Reconstruction of the Nation* (New York, 1967), pp. 60–61; Carter, *When the War Was Over,* p. 94; *Provisional Governors,* pp. 257, 224, 252–53; Dorris, *Pardon and Amnesty,* p. 200.

50. Medill to Johnson, September 15, 1865, JP; Chicago *Tribune,* October 20, 1865; Wade to Sumner, November 1, 1865, Sumner Papers.

51. Barlow to M. Blair, September 11, October 14, November 8, 1865, Barlow to Russell Houston, October 3, 28, 1865, Barlow to Richard Taylor, October 21, 1865, Barlow Papers; LaWanda and John H. Cox, *Politics, Principle, and Prejudice, 1865–1866: Dilemma of Reconstruction America* (New York, 1963), pp. 68ff.

52. Reid, *After the War,* pp. 219–20; J. T. Trowbridge, *The South: A Tour of Its Battle Fields and Ruined Cities* (Hartford, Conn., 1866), p. 189.

53. 39th Cong., 1st Sess., *Report of the Joint Committee on Reconstruction,* H.R. No. 30 (1866) (hereafter cited as *RJCR*), 2:139–40, 42; 39th Cong., 2d Sess., H.R. No. 16, *New Orleans Riots* (1867), p. 594; J. George Harris to Johnson, May 21, 1865, J. B. Bingham to Johnson, June 6, 1865, JP: *RJCR* 4:72–73; J. W. Sprague to John Sherman, April 4, 1866, John Sherman Papers, LC.

54. Frank R. Levstik, "A View from Within: Reuben D. Massey on Andrew Johnson and Reconstruction," *Historical New Hampshire* 27 (1972): 169; Frederick Bancroft, ed., *Speeches, Correspondence, and Political Papers of Carl Schurz,* 6 vols. (New York, 1913), 1:282; Hans L. Trefousse, "Andrew Johnson and the Failure of Reconstruction," in Hans L. Trefousse, ed., *Toward a New View of America: Essays in Honor of Arthur C. Cole* (New York, 1977), pp. 135–50.

55. Christopher Memminger to Carl Schurz, April 26, 1871, Schurz Papers.

XIII. *PUGNACIOUS PRESIDENT*

1. Cf. Michael Les Benedict, *A Compromise of Principle: Congressional Republicans and Reconstruction, 1863–1869* (New York, 1974), pp. 139ff.; Albert Castel, *The Presidency of*

Andrew Johnson (Lawrence, Kans., 1979), pp. 62ff.; Patrick W. Riddleberger, *1866: The Critical Year Revisited* (Carbondale, Ill., 1979), pp. 23–25; David Donald, *The Politics of Reconstruction, 1863–1867* (Baton Rouge, 1965), pp. 23ff.; Hans L. Trefousse, *Impeachment of a President: Andrew Johnson, the Blacks, and Reconstruction* (Knoxville, 1975), pp. 21ff.

2. Undated MS in Welles Papers, NYPL.

3. *The Diary of Orville Hickman Browning*, J. G. Randall, ed., 2 vols. (Springfield, Ill., 1933), 2:56–57.

4. Harriet Weed, ed., *Autobiography of Thurlow Weed* (Boston, 1883), p. 630; New York *Herald*, August 17, 1865.

5. Thomas G. Pratt to Barlow, August 18, 1865, Barlow to McClellan, October 12, 1865, Barlow Papers and Letterbooks XII, Huntington Library; Henry Watterson to Johnson, December 7, 1865, Montgomery Blair to Johnson, November 21, 1865, JP; New York *Sun*, December 30, 1865.

6. Joseph S. Fowler, Johnson MS, pp. 10, 21, Fowler Papers, LC; Cincinnati *Enquirer*, September 30, 1865, quoted in Eric L. McKitrick, *Andrew Johnson and Reconstruction* (Chicago, 1960), p. 184; Benjamin B. French to Johnson, February 8, 1866, JP.

7. New York *Times*, February 8, 1866. Johnson told a delegation from Montana that if he could restore the states successfully he would not be a candidate, a sentiment he repeated to a London *Times* reporter on April 16 and to a group of supporters on June 11, 1866. London *Times*, May 16, 1866; Browning, *Diary*, 2:79. He included a specific mention of the Johnson-Crittenden Resolutions in his proclamation announcing that the rebellion had ended on April 2, 1866. Edward McPherson, *The Political History of the United States of America During the Period of Reconstruction, April 15, 1865–July 15, 1870* (Washington, D.C., 1870), pp. 15–17.

8. Hans L. Trefousse, The *Radical Republicans: Lincoln's Vanguard for Racial Justice* (New York, 1968), pp. 5–6, 8–9, 30–32, 337–39, 343–44; Fawn Brodie, *Thaddeus Stevens: Scourge of the South* (New York, 1959), passim; David Donald, *Charles Sumner and the Rights of Man* (New York, 1970), passim; Hans L. Trefousse, *Benjamin Franklin Wade: Radical Republican from Ohio* (New York, 1963), passim; Sister Mary Karl George, *Zachariah Chandler: A Political Biography* (Lansing, 1969), passim.

9. Sumner to Lieber, December 3, 1865, Sumner Papers, Harvard University; Lewis Campbell to Johnson, March 9, 1868, Bancroft to Johnson, December 1, 1865, JP. Stevens had come to see the president on the Wednesday preceding the meeting of Congress to tell him to cooperate; Wade, who tried to see Johnson also, was put off by the number of rebels in the antechamber. Benjamin F. Kendrick, *The Journal of the Joint Committee of Fifteen on Reconstruction, 39th Congress, 1865–1867* (New York, 1915), p. 139; New York *Times*, November 8, 1867.

10. Chicago *Tribune*, November 9, 1865; New York *Herald*, December 3–14, 1865; Lloyd Paul Stryker, *Andrew Johnson: A Study in Courage* (New York, 1930), pp. 231–36.

11. Richardson, *A Compilation of the Messages and Papers of the Presidents, 1789–1897*, 10 vols. (Washington, D.C., 1896–99), 8:3551–69; William A. Dunning, "More Light on Andrew Johnson," *AHR* 9 (April 1906): 373–93.

12. Various editorials about the message in JP, series II, XI; *Cong. Globe*, 39th Cong., 1st Sess., 30, 78ff.; McPherson, *Reconstruction*, pp. 66–68.

13. Carl Schurz, *Report on the Condition of the South*, H. Report No. 11, 39th Cong., 1st Sess.; Trefousse, "Carl Schurz's 1865 Southern Tour," *Prospects* 2 (1965): 302–6. Johnson also sought to counteract Schurz's findings by sending Harvey Watterson and Benjamin Truman to the South, and both prepared reports laudatory of his policies. Lately Thomas, *The First President Johnson* (New York, 1968), p. 360; LaWanda Cox and John Cox, *Politics, Principle, and Prejudice, 1865–1866: Dilemma of Reconstruction America* (New York, 1963), pp. 103–4; Brooks D. Simpson, LeRoy P. Graf, John Muldowney, eds., *Advice After Appomattox: Letters to Andrew Johnson, 1865–1866* (Knoxville, 1987), pp. 39–60, 175–98.

14. *Cong. Globe,* 39th Cong., 1st Sess., 72–75, 78ff., 91–95.

15. Mary Clemmer Ames, *Ten Years in Washington: Life and Scenes in the National Capital as a Woman Sees Them* (Hartford, 1879), pp. 245–47; Benjamin B. French, Diary, 10:1, French Papers, LC; Washington *National Intelligencer,* February 5, 1866.

16. Ames, *Ten Years in Washington,* pp. 244, 248; Poore, *Perly's Reminiscences,* 2:215–18; Benjamin B. French, Diary, 10:1, French Papers; Chicago *Tribune,* January 2, 1866; *PJ,* VII, 251. The *Independent* commented favorably on the fact that the president also permitted Negroes to visit him on New Year's Day. *Independent,* January 4, 1866.

17. Washington *National Intelligencer,* January 17, February 13, March 14, 27, 1866; Benjamin B. French Diary, February 11, 14, May 16, 1866; Chicago *Tribune,* April 26, May 15, 1866; Fowler to William A. Croffut, n.d., Fowler Papers, LC; William Henry Crook, *Through Five Administrations . . . ,* Margaret Spalding Gerry, ed. (New York, 1910), p. 80, contrasts the president's appearance with Lincoln's; even the hostile Temple commented on his always having been well dressed: Oliver P. Temple, *Notable Men of Tennessee* (New York, 1912), p. 461.

18. Frank Cowan, *Andrew Johnson, President of the United States . . .* (Greensburgh, Pa., 1894), pp. 6–7; Norman Judd to Lyman Trumbull, February 14, 1866, Trumbull Papers, LC; *Diary of Gideon Welles,* Howard K. Beale, ed., 3 vols. (New York, 1960), 2:468, 472–73, 491, 494; W. H. Seward to diplomats and consuls introducing Robert Johnson, June 18, 1866, JP, series II; Hugh McCulloch, *Men and Measures of Half a Century* (New York, 1888), p. 406; Welles, *Diary,* 2:468, 472, 479, 491, 604–5.

19. Theodore Clark Smith, *The Life and Letters of James Abram Garfield,* 2 vols. (New Haven, 1925), p. 392; A. L. Brewer to John Sherman, June 11, 1865, John Sherman Papers, LC; Horace Rublee to James Doolittle, January 3, 1866, Doolittle Papers, SHSW; Horace Greeley to Schuyler Colfax, December 11, 1865, Greeley Papers, NYPL; D. L. Phillips to Trumbull, December 26, 1865, F. A. Eastman to Trumbull, January 4, 1866, Trumbull Papers, LC.

20. Welles, *Diary,* 2:448–49; Francis Fessenden, *Life and Public Services of William Pitt Fessenden,* 2 vols. (Boston, 1907), 2:18–25; Washington *National Intelligencer,* January 29, 1866; McKitrick, *Johnson and Reconstruction,* pp. 282–83.

21. Horace White, *The Life of Lyman Trumbull* (Boston, 1913), pp. 257ff.; Ralph J. Roske, *His Own Counsel: The Life and Times of Lyman Trumbull* (Reno, 1979), p. 123; McPherson, *Reconstruction,* p. 52; Mark Krug, *Lyman Trumbull: Conservative Radical* (New York, 1965), pp. 238–39.

22. Krug, *Trumbull,* pp. 52–56.

23. Philip Ripley to Manton Marble, February 8, 1866, Marble Papers, LC.

24. Richardson, *Messages and Papers of the Presidents,* 8:3551–69; Browning, *Diary,* 2:56–57; McPherson, *Reconstruction,* pp. 56–58.

25. Welles, *Diary,* 2:434; John H. Cox and LaWanda Cox, "Andrew Johnson and His Ghost Writers: An Analysis of the Freedmen's Bureau and Civil Rights Veto Messages," *MVHR* 48 (December 1961): 460–79.

26. Richardson, *Messages and Papers of the Presidents,* 8:3596–3603.

27. *Cong. Globe,* 39th Cong., 1st Sess., 931–32, 936–43; Fessenden, *Fessenden,* p. 35; Sherman to Bateman, February 10, 1866, Warner Bateman Papers, WRHS. All three voted to override the President's veto of the bill, McPherson, *Reconstruction,* p. 74.

28. Wayne City, Ohio, *Democrat,* clipping, JP, series II, XI; Boston *Advertiser,* February 21, 1866; Chicago *Tribune,* February 21, 1866; *Cong. Globe,* 39th Cong., 1st Sess., 936–43, 950.

29. McCulloch, *Men and Measures,* p. 393.

30. McPherson, *Reconstruction,* pp. 58–63; McKitrick, *Johnson and Reconstruction,* p. 293.

31. John H. Geiger to John Sherman, February 24, 1866, John Sherman Papers. For editorial opinion, including the few favorable comments, see JP, series II, XI.

32. *Cong. Globe,* 39th Cong., 1st Sess., 1307–8.

33. Fessenden, *Fessenden*, 2:35; John Sherman, *John Sherman's Recollections of Forty Years in the House, Senate, and Cabinet*, 2 vols. (Chicago, 1895), 2:365ff.; John Sherman to Warner Bateman, March 1, 1866, Bateman Papers; Thomas Drummond to Trumbull, March 4, 1866, D. L. Phillips to Trumbull, March 5, 1866, Amos Nourse to Trumbull, February 22, 1866, John L. Wilson to Trumbull, March 6, 1866, Trumbull Papers, LC; R. R. Sloan to John Sherman, February 21, 1866, R. P. L. Baber to John Sherman, February 28, 1866, A. Denny to John Sherman, March 23, 1866, John Sherman Papers; Hamilton Fish to Fessenden, March 13, 1866, Fessenden Papers, Duke University; Salmon P. Chase to Nettie, March 14, 1866, Chase Papers, LC; *Harper's Weekly*, March 3, 1866.
34. Beecher to Johnson, March 17, 1866, J. D. Cox to Johnson, March 22, 1866, JP; William Dudley Foulke, *The Life of Oliver P. Morton*, 2 vols. (Indianapolis, 1899), 1:460–67.
35. Welles, *Diary*, 2:460–61.
36. Cox and Cox, "Andrew Johnson and His Ghost Writers," pp. 473–77; Richardson, *Messages and Papers of the Presidents*, 8:3603–11.
37. Washington *Daily Chronicle*, March 28, 1866; New York *Atlas*, March 31, 1866; Chicago *Tribune*, March 28, 1866; Washington *National Intelligencer*, March 31, 1866, JP, series XI. For Johnson's reliance on racism to sustain his veto, see Eric Foner, *Reconstruction: America's Unfinished Revolution, 1863–1877* (New York, 1988), p. 251.
38. W. R. Brock, *An American Crisis: Congress and Reconstruction, 1865–1867* (New York, 1963), pp. 114–15; McPherson, *Reconstruction*, pp. 80–81; *Cong. Globe*, 39th Cong., 1st Sess., 1755–61, 1809.
39. Welles, *Diary*, 2:479–80; Moore, Small Diary, pp. 15–16, JP. Richardson, *Messages and Papers of the Presidents*, 8:2627–30.
40. Donald G. Nieman, *To Set the Law in Motion: The Freedmen's Bureau and the Legal Rights of the Blacks, 1865–1868* (Milwood, N.Y., 1979), pp. 115–17; Benjamin P. Thomas and Harold M. Hyman, *Stanton: The Life and Times of Lincoln's Secretary of War* (New York, 1962), pp. 477–78; George R. Bentley, *A History of the Freedmen's Bureau* (Philadelphia, 1955), pp. 125–28; Oliver Otis Howard, *Autobiography of Oliver Otis Howard*, 2 vols. (New York, 1907), 283–84, 87; William S. McFeely, *Yankee Stepfather: General O. O. Howard and the Freedmen's Bureau* (New York, 1968), pp. 246ff.; Steedman to Johnson, June 26, 1866, Steedman and Fullerton to Johnson, June 14, 1866, JP.
41. London *Times*, May 1, 1866.
42. Welles, *Diary*, 2:452, 454, 456, 457–60, 461–65, 469, 474; Welles to W. A. Croffut, March 13, 1866, Hawley to Welles, February 26, 1866, A. E. Barr to Welles, April 27, 1866, Welles Papers, LC; Eli Thayer to Johnson, March 19, 1866, Johnson to William S. Huntington, March 27, 1866, JP; Cox and Cox, *Politics, Principle, and Prejudice*, pp. 143–50.
43. Cox and Cox, *Politics, Principle, and Prejudice*, pp. 113–27; James L. Baumgardner, "Abraham Lincoln, Andrew Johnson, and the Federal Patronage," *ETHSP* 45 (1973): 80ff.; E. D. Morgan to Weed, December 3, 15, 19, 20, 26, 1865, January 25, March 8, 1866, Thurlow Weed Papers, Rochester University; R. M. Blatchford to Seward, December 17, 1865, Weed to Seward, January 29, March 12, March 14, 1866, Richard M. Blatchford to Seward, March 30, 1866, Seward Papers, University of Rochester; Barlow to J. J. Hughes, December 21, 1865, H. C. Page to Johnson, December 22, 1865, E. Pierrepont to Johnson, March 13, 24, 1866, Henry A. Smythe to Johnson, March 20, 1866, Charles Halpine to Johnson, March 21, 1866, JP; M. Blair to Barlow, January 18, February 12, 1866, Barlow to M. Blair, March 31, 1866, M. Blair to Barlow, April 7, 13, 1866, Barlow to W. D. Shipman, April 10, 1866, Barlow to J. Hughes, April 13, 1866, Barlow to M. Blair, April 14, 1866, Barlow Papers; Thurlow Weed Barnes, *Memoir of Thurlow Weed* (Boston, 1883), p. 451; Cox and Cox, *Politics, Principle, and Prejudice*, pp. 113–28.
44. W. E. Chandler to Johnson, January 14, 1866, Johnson to A. J. Hamilton, February 13, 1866, A. J. Hamilton to Johnson, February 16, March 28, 1866, Thomas Cottman to

Johnson, March 15, 19, 1866, James Madison Wells to Johnson, March 15, 17, 1866, Hugh Kennedy to Johnson, March 17, 1866, JP.

45. G. L. Watson and J. M. Humphreys to Stevens, December 5, 1865, E. K. Pretlow to Stevens, December 27, 1865, William L. Mallet to Stevens, May 28, 1866, Stevens Papers, LC.

46. Chase to Nettie, May 19, 1866, Chase Papers, LC; D. Richards to Trumbull, June 7, 1866, Trumbull Papers, LC.

47. Joshua Hill to John Sherman, January 30, 1866, John Graham to Sherman, February 4, 1866, John Sherman Papers; Elizabeth Van Lew to James R. Doolittle, February 7, 1866, Doolittle Papers; R. J. Powell to Justin Morrill, April 22, 1866, Justin Morrill Papers, LC; Milligan to Johnson, April 15, 1866, JP.

48. Memphis Riots and Massacres, H.R. No. 101, 39th Cong., 1st Sess. (1866).

49. Report of the Joint Committee on Reconstruction, H.R. No. 30, 39th Cong., 1st Sess. (1866).

50. Trefousse, Impeachment of a President, pp. 27–28; Jacobus Ten Broek, The Antislavery Origins of the Fourteenth Amendment (Berkeley, 1951), passim.

51. Trefousse, Radical Republicans, pp. 346–47; McPherson, Reconstruction, pp. 81–82, 83; Browning, Diary, 2:80.

52. Lucius Fairchild to Marcus L. Ward, June 16, 1866, Ward Papers, NJHS; J. D. Cox to Johnson, June 21, 1866, John Binney to Johnson, June 16, 1866, JP; Stephen Field to Chase, June 30, 1866, Chase to Kate [Chase Sprague], June 15, 1866, Chase Papers, LC; W. M. Dickson to Stanton, June 7, 1866, Stanton Papers, LC; Warner Bateman to John Sherman, June 6, 1866, John Sherman Papers; John Sherman to Bateman, June 17, 1866, Bateman Papers; Welles, Diary, 2:521–22; Robert D. Sawrey, " 'Give Him the End of the Poker': Ohio Republicans Reject Johnson's Leadership of Reconstruction," CWH 33 (1987): 155–72.

53. Browning, Diary, 2:79, 80.

54. McPherson, Reconstruction, pp. 83–103; New York Tribune, June 23, 1866.

55. McPherson, Reconstruction, pp. 147–51.

56. Ibid., pp. 103–4; Steve Humphrey, "That D . . . d Brownlow" (Boone, 1978), pp. 312–13; Brownlow to Temple, January 25, 1866; Speech, March 31, 1866, JP, series II. The bill was never passed.

57. Sam Cooper to William D. Campbell, June 22, 1866, Campbell Family Papers Duke University; Brownlow to Chase, July 7, 1866, Brownlow Papers, Duke University; Thomas B. Alexander, Political Reconstruction in Tennessee (Nashville, 1950), pp. 110–11.

58. Doolittle to Johnson, July 23, 1866, JP; McPherson, Reconstruction, pp. 152–54; Cong. Globe, 39th Cong., 1st Sess., 4243; Alexander, Political Reconstruction in Tennessee, pp. 120–21.

XIV. BELEAGUERED PRESIDENT

1. Washington National Intelligencer, February 13, March 28, 1866.

2. L. D. Campbell to Patterson, January 22, 1866, James G. Bennett to Johnson, February 1, 1866, JP.

3. Weed to Seward, March 12, 1866, Seward Papers, University of Rochester; Seward to Bigelow, April 9, 1866, Bigelow Papers NYPL; Diary of Gideon Welles, Howard K. Beale, ed., 3 vols. (New York, 1960), 2:524; Glyndon Van Deusen, William Henry Seward (New York, 1967), pp. 455–56.

4. The Diary of Orville Hickman Browning, J. G. Randall, ed., 2 vols. (Springfield, Ill., 1933), 2:79, 81; Welles, Diary, 2:538–41; "Extracts from the Journal of Henry J. Raymond," Scribner's Monthly Magazine 20 (May–October 1880): 275–80, esp. 276; John A. Dix to F. Blair, June 14, 1866, D. D. Field, July 19, 1866, Blair-Lee Family Papers, Princeton University; Barlow to Montgomery Blair, August 3, 1866, Letterbooks XIII, Barlow Papers, Huntington Library; Doolittle to Mrs. Doolittle, June 20, 1866, Doolittle Papers, Historical Society of Wisconsin.

5. Welles, *Diary*, 2:552–55, 563; Patrick W. Riddleberger, *1866: The Critical Year Revisited* (Carbondale, Ill., 1979), pp. 206–7; James Speed, *James Speed: A Personality* (Louisville, 1914), pp. 93, 96.

6. LaWanda Cox and John H. Cox, *Politics, Principle, and Prejudice, 1865–1866: Dilemma of Reconstruction America* (New York, 1963), pp. 44ff.

7. Herman Watsker to Johnson, June 15, 1865, Arden B. Smith to Johnson, April 5, 1866, William A. Allan to Johnson, April 27, 1866, Rush R. Sloane to Johnson, April, 1866, JP; Benjamin P. Thomas and Herald M. Hyman, *Stanton: The Life and Times of Lincoln's Secretary of War* (New York, 1962), pp. 491ff.; Draft Letter, not sent, July 16, 1866, Stanton Papers, LC; Welles, *Diary*, 2:573–74.

8. Harriet A. Weed, ed., *Autobiography of Thurlow Weed* (Boston, 1883), p. 630; Washington *National Intelligencer*, May 12, August 11, November 21, 1866.

9. Doolittle to Johnson, August 8, 1866, A. W. Randall to Johnson, August 11, 1866, JP; Thurlow Weed Barnes, *Memoir of Thurlow Weed* (Boston, 1884), p. 451; Thomas Wagstaff, "The Arm-in-Arm Convention," *Civil War History* 14 (1968): 101–19, esp. 104–5.

10. 39th Cong., 2d Sess., H.R. No. 16, *New Orleans Riots* (1867); Riddleberger, *1866*, pp. 186ff.; Joe Gray Taylor, *Louisiana Reconstructed, 1863–1877* (Baton Rouge, 1974), pp. 103–11.

11. Voorhees to Johnson, July 27, 1866, Johnson to Voorhees, July 28, 1866, Johnson to Wells, July 28, 1866, Johnson to Herron, July 30, 1866, JP.

12. Browning to Thomas Ewing, November 19, 1866, Ewing Papers, LC; Moore, Small Diary, p. 17, November 10, 1866, JP; James E. Sefton, *The United States Army and Reconstruction, 1865–1877* (Baton Rouge, 1967), p. 86; Sheridan to Grant, August 2, 1866, JP.

13. Chicago *Tribune*, August 2, 25, 1866; New York *Independent*, August 16, 1866; *Harper's Weekly*, August 25, 1866; Thomas Shankland to Holt, August 2, 1866, Holt Papers, LC; James Henderson to Seward, October 8, 1866, Seward Papers.

14. Browning, *Diary*, 2:82; James G. Blaine, *Twenty Years of Congress*, 2 vols. (Boston, 1884–86), 2:185.

15. William Henry Crook, *Memories of the White House*, Henry Rood, ed. (Boston, 1911), p. 61; Frank Cowan, *Andrew Johnson, President of the United States: Reminiscences of His Private Life and Character* (Greensburgh, Pa., 1898), pp. 6–8; Benjamin B. French Diary, July 7, 1866, 10:112, French Papers, LC; Benjamin F. Perry, *Reminiscences of Public Men with Speeches and Addresses* (Greenville, S.C., 1889), p. 298.

16. Richardson, *A Compilation of the Messages and Papers of the Presidents, 1789–1897*, 10 vols. (Washington, D.C., 1896–99), 8:3614–20; Washington *Daily National Intelligencer*, August 27, 1866.

17. Joseph H. Geiger to Doolittle, June 25, 1866, D. D. Field to Doolittle, July 14, 1866, John A. Dix to Doolittle, July 23, 1866, Doolittle Papers; R. P. L. Baber to Johnson, June 28, 1866, W. C. Jewett to Johnson, July 2, 1866, Fernando Wood to Johnson, August 1, 1866, John H. Geiger to Johnson, August 2, 1866, JP; Anthony F. Campbell to Thurlow Weed, July 10, 1866, Weed Papers, University of Rochester; John Fleming to Seward, July 26, 1866, Seward Papers; William Grey to McCulloch, August 9, 1866, McCulloch Papers, LC; "Extracts from the Journal of Henry J. Raymond," *Scribner's Monthly Magazine* 20(May–October 1880): 276; Martin E. Mantell, *Johnson, Grant, and the Politics of Reconstruction* (New York, 1973), pp. 17–18; Albert Castel, *The Presidency of Andrew Johnson* (Lawrence, Kans., 1979), pp. 78–79; Riddleberger, *1866*, pp. 206–8.

18. Hugh McCulloch, *Men and Measures of Half a Century* (New York, 1888), pp. 409–12; *O.R.*, series II, 8:844–45; J. W. Schuckers, *The Life and Public Services of Salmon P. Chase* (New York, 1874), pp. 534ff.; Dunbar Rowland, ed., *Jefferson Davis, Constitutionalist: His Letters, Papers & Speeches*, 10 vols. (Jackson, Miss., 1923), 8:62, 73; Varina Davis to Johnson, May 5, 12, 1866, JP; Varina Davis, *Jefferson Davis . . . a Memoir by His Wife*, 2 vols. (New York, 1890), 2:768ff.; Chase to Flamen Ball, May 12, 1866, Chase Papers, Cincinnati Historical Society; *Cong. Globe*, 39th Cong., 1st Sess., 3089; Browning,

Diary, 2:96–97, 98, 104–5. Varina Davis' sensational account of her interview with the president is evidently based on later events and unreliable.

19. Welles, *Diary*, 2:518–20, 523–24; Elizabeth Blair Lee to F. P. Blair, Sr., September 12, 1866, Blair-Lee Papers; Samuel J. Tilden to Johnson, September 21, 1866, W. P. Phillips to Johnson, August 23, 1866, JP; Brian Jenkins, *Fenians and Anglo-American Relations During Reconstruction* (Ithaca, N.Y., 1969), pp. 146f., 150ff.

20. Thomas D. Schoonover, ed., *Mexican Lobby: Matías Romero in Washington, 1861–1867* (Lexington, Ky., 1986), p. 50; Welles, *Diary*, 2:317, 333; Bigelow, Diary, March 27, 1869, Bigelow Papers, NYPL; Perry, *Reminiscences*, p. 303.

21. Browning, *Diary*, 2:89–90; Raymond, "Journal," pp. 278–80.

22. Edward McPherson, *The Political History of the United States During the Period of Reconstruction, April 15, 1865–July 15, 1870* (Washington, D.C., 1871), pp. 127–29; Chase to Sumner, August 20, 1866, Sumner Papers, Harvard University.

23. James G. Blaine, *Twenty Years of Congress*, 2 vols. (Boston, 1884–86), 2:223–33; New York *Herald*, October 6, 1866. By October 7 the general openly called for impeachment; at Pittsburgh he apparently tried to have an impeachment plank inserted in the resolutions: Hans L. Trefousse, *Ben Butler: The South Called Him Beast* (New York, 1957), p. 305, n. 50.

24. Welles, *Diary*, 2:584–85, 587; Browning, *Diary*, 2:91.

25. Thomas D. Schoonover, ed., *Mexican Lobby: Matías Romero in Washington, 1861–1867* (Lexington, Ky., 1986), pp. 136–38; Gregg Phifer, "Andrew Johnson Argues His Case," *THQ* 11 (1952): 148–70; Phifer, "Andrew Johnson Delivers His Argument," *THQ* 11 (1952): 212–34; McPherson, *Reconstruction*, pp. 129–34 (the New York speech).

26. Welles, *Diary*, 2:588–95; Weed, *Autobiography*, pp. 630–31.

27. Welles, *Diary*, 2:593; McPherson, *Reconstruction*, pp. 134–36.

28. Doolittle to Johnson, August 29, 1866, JP; Henry W. Hurbert to Samuel Tilden, September 2, 1866, Marble Papers, LC.

29. Schoonover, *Mexican Lobby*, p. 139; *New York Times*, September 7, 1866; Mary Lincoln to Sumner, September 10, 1866, Sumner Papers; Daniel Richards to Elihu Washburne, September 11, 1866, Washburne Papers, LC; New York *Tribune*, September 10, 1866.

30. McPherson, *Reconstruction*, pp. 136–41; Chicago *Tribune*, September 11, 1866.

31. Welles, *Diary*, 2:594; Washington *Daily National Intelligencer*, September 11, 12, 1866; *New York Times*, September 13, 14, 17, 1866; New York *Tribune*, September 12, 1866.

32. New York *Independent*, September 13, 1866.

33. Phifer, "Andrew Johnson Delivers His Argument," pp. 213, 214, 227, 232, 234; Doolittle to Browning, October 7, 1866, Browning Papers, Illinois State Library, Springfield.

34. New York *Tribune*, September 26, 1866.

35. Fessenden to McCulloch, September 11, 15, 1866, McCulloch Papers.

36. Burr to Welles, April 27, 1866, Welles Papers, LC; Barlow to W. H. Ludlow, June 20, 1866, Barlow to Hurlbut, September 6, 1866, Barlow to Frank Blair, September 19, 1866, Letterbooks, vol. 13, Barlow Papers; George Craddock et al. to Johnson, July 31, 1866, T. J. Davis to Johnson, October 2, 1866, Samuel Tilden to Johnson, November 2, 1866, Jacob Weaver to Johnson, November 5, 1866, JP; Marble to Joseph Warren, August, 1866, Marble Papers; John Van Buren to Tilden, August 31, 1866, Samuel J. Tilden Papers, NYPL; D. D. Field to Doolittle, July 14, 1866, Doolittle Papers.

37. Weed, *Autobiography*, p. 630; Fessenden to McCulloch, August 15, 17, 1866, McCulloch Papers; Samuel Randall to Welles, October 2, 1866, James E. Jouett to Edgar Welles, August 22, 1866, Welles Papers, Huntington Library; M. Blair to Johnson, August 9, 1866, George Bancroft to Johnson, September 30, 1866, JP; W. S. Sheffield to Ewing, August 15, 1866, Ewing Papers; McCulloch to Weed, September 6, 1866, D. H. Cole to Weed, October 17, 1866, Weed Papers; Hiram Ketchum to Seward, October 10, 1866, Samuel W. Crawford to F. W. Seward, October 5, 1866, Seward Papers; Browning to Doolittle, October 10, 1866, Doolittle Papers; N. B. Milligan et al. to Johnson, November 16, 1866, JP.

38. French Diary, 10:i, January 1, 1866, French Papers; McPherson, *Reconstruction*, p. 63; *New York Times*, July 26, 1866.
39. Washington *Daily National Intelligencer*, August 9, September 5, 1866.
40. McPherson, *Reconstruction*, pp. 194–96; Chicago *Tribune*, August 20, 1866.
41. Charles Eugene Hamlin, *The Life and Times of Hannibal Hamlin* (Cambridge, 1899), p. 506; Wendell Phillips to Hamlin, August 3 [misdated], 1866, Hamlin Papers, Maine Historical Society, Portland; New York *Tribune*, September 28, 1866; John Bigelow, Diary, September 26, 1866; Castel, *The Presidency of Andrew Johnson*, p. 95; I. N. Arnold to Johnson, September 29, 1866, JP; Philadelphia *Ledger*, October 9, 1866; *New York Times*, October 11, 16, 24, 1866; Sumner Stebbins to Seward, October 4, 1866, Seward Papers.
42. Schoonover, *Mexican Lobby*, pp. 55–57, 65–67, 71, 75–77, 98, 136–40.
43. Browning, *Diary*, 2:101; Grant to Johnson, October 21, 1866, JP; Moore, Small Diary, October 24, 1866, JP; Rachel Sherman Thorndike, ed., *The Sherman Letters: Correspondence Between General Sherman and Senator Sherman from 1837 to 1891* (New York, 1894), p. 279.
44. Thomas Ewing, Jr., to Thomas Ewing, Sr., October 19, 1866, Ewing Family Papers; Browning, *Diary*, 2:103, 105, 106; Welles, *Diary*, 2:592; F. M. Cooke to Johnson, November 4, 1866, Johnson to Thomas Swann, November 2, 6, 1866, Moore, Small Diary, November 6, 1866, JP; William S. McFeely, *Grant: A Biography* (New York, 1981), pp. 254–56.
45. Blaine, *Twenty Years of Congress*, 2:240–42, 284–86.
46. Schoonover, *Mexican Lobby*, p. 55; S. S. Cox to Manton Marble, October 3 or 10 (Wednesday), Marble Papers.
47. Howard K. Beale, *The Critical Year* (New York, 1930), pp. 400–3; Van Deusen, *Seward*, pp. 275–76; Welles, *Diary*, 2:628; Richardson, *Messages and Papers of the Presidents*, 8:3643–57.

XV. DEFIANT PRESIDENT

1. Washington *Daily National Intelligencer*, November 24, 1866; Hans L. Trefousse, *Impeachment of a President: Andrew Johnson, the Blacks, and Reconstruction* (Knoxville, 1975), pp. 32–35. Stevens on January 3 introduced a bill declaring the state governments in the South illegal and calling for elections on the basis of universal suffrage. *Cong. Globe*, 39th Cong., 2d Sess., 250.
2. Edward McPherson, *The Political History of the United States During the Period of Reconstruction, April 15, 1865–July 15, 1870* (Washington, D.C., 1870), pp. 154–60; *The Diary of Orville Hickman Browning*, J. G. Randall, ed., 2 vols. (Springfield, Ill., 1983), 2:122.
3. Hans L. Trefousse, *Benjamin F. Wade, Radical Republican from Ohio* (New York, 1963), pp. 270–71, 275–78; McPherson, *Reconstruction*, pp. 160–66.
4. Charles Fairman, *Reconstruction and Reunion, 1864–88*, vol. 6 of *The Oliver Wendell Holmes Devise History of the Supreme Court of the United States* (New York, 1971), pp. 192–237.
5. Charles Warren, *The Supreme Court in United States History*, 2 vols. (Boston, 1922), 2:422–23, 449–50; Cummings v. Missouri and *ex parte* Garland, 4 Wall. 277, 333.
6. New York *Herald*, October 31, 1866; W. P. Phillips to Johnson, November 8, 1866, Hiram Ketcham to Johnson, November 9, 1866, JP; *Diary of Gideon Welles*, Howard K. Beale, ed., 3 vols. (New York, 1960), 3:7–8.
7. *New York Times*, October 24, 1866; Johnson to J. W. Throckmorton, October 30, 1866, JP.
8. *Cong. Globe*, 39th Cong., 2d Sess., 124.
9. Washington *National Republican*, December 28, 1866; Washington *National Intelligencer*, December 29, 1866, JP.
10. McPherson, *Reconstruction*, pp. 352–53, 194.

11. Moore, Small Diary, pp. 20ff., January 30, 1867, JP; *Cong. Globe*, 39th Cong., 2d Sess., 1045; L. Marshall Hall, "William Sharkey and Reconstruction, 1866–1877," *Journal of Mississippi History* 27 (1865): 1–17, esp. 3; *New York Times*, February 5, 1867; James Wickes Taylor to James L. Orr, January 26, 1867, in Taylor to Seward, January 28, 1867, Seward Papers, University of Rochester. Later in February, Johnson was still negotiating with *New York Times* correspondent W. W. Warden and General George P. Este, who vainly tried to reach a compromise with various congressional moderates at a conference at the Metropolitan Club in Washington. RG 233, NA, HR 39A, F 28.1.

12. Wade to B. Storer, December 17, 1866, B. Storer Papers, Ohio Historical and Philosophical Society, Cincinnati.

13. James G. Blaine, *Twenty Years of Congress*, 2 vols. (Boston, 1884–86), 2:281–82; Welles, *Diary*, 3:17–18; McPherson, *Reconstruction*, pp. 183–84. Prior to the passage of the Twentieth Amendment in 1933, Congress met for a short session in December of even years that lasted till the following March. Unless called earlier by the president, it did not meet again until the following December.

14. *Impeachment Investigation*, House Reports, 40th Cong., 1st Sess., No. 7, p. 85; Michael Les Benedict, *The Impeachment and Trial of Andrew Johnson* (New York, 1973), pp. 48–49.

15. Louis J. Weichman to Holt, October 23, 1866, Holt Papers, LC; George W. Blunt to Welles, November 21, 1866, Welles Papers, LC.

16. Blaine, *Twenty Years of Congress*, 2:267–74; Welles, *Diary*, 3:50–51; Browning, *Diary*, 2:132; McPherson, *Reconstruction*, pp. 173–76; Bigelow, Diary, March 2, 1867, Bigelow Papers, NYPL.

17. George S. Boutwell, "Johnson's Plot and Motives," *North American Review* 141 (December 1885): 570–79; George S. Boutwell, *Reminiscences of Sixty Years in Public Affairs*, 2 vols. (New York, 1902), 2:107–8; McPherson, *Reconstruction*, p. 178.

18. Moore, Small Diary, pp. 28–29, March 4, 1867, JP; Browning, *Diary*, 2:134; Richardson, *A Compilation of the Messages and Papers of the Presidents, 1789–1897*, 10 vols. (Washington, D.C., 1896–99), 8:3690–96.

19. McKitrick, *Andrew Johnson and Reconstruction*, pp. 456–85; Blaine, *Twenty Years of Congress*, 2:250–61; Michael Les Benedict, *A Compromise of Principle: Congressional Republicans and Reconstruction, 1863–1869* (New York, 1974), pp. 233ff.

20. Welles, *Diary*, 2:650, 3:10–12; Browning, *Diary*, 2:123.

21. Washington *National Intelligencer* (triweekly), February 14, 1867.

22. Charles Nordhoff to William Cullen Bryant, February 2, 1867, Bryant-Godwin Collection, NYPL.

23. Moore, Small Diary, p. 28, February 18, 1867, JP; F. P. Blair to Johnson, February 24, 1867, Montgomery Blair to Johnson, February 26, 1867, H. A. Smythe to Johnson, February 25, 1867, George P. Este to Johnson, n.d. [February 27, 1867], Fernando Wood to Johnson, February 21, 1867, JP; Weed to Seward, February 21, 1867, Seward Papers.

24. Moore, Small Diary, p. 28, March 2, 1867, JP; Richardson, *Messages and Papers of the Presidents*, 8:3696–3709.

25. McPherson, *Reconstruction*, pp. 172–73; Welles, *Diary*, 3:56; Moore, Small Diary, p. 29, March 10, 1867, JP; Browning, *Diary*, 2:135.

26. Browning, *Diary*, 2:135; Welles, *Diary*, 3:62, 65; Hans L. Trefousse, *The Radical Republicans: Lincoln's Vanguard for Racial Justice* (New York, 1969), pp. 365, 366; Richardson, *Messages and Papers of the Presidents*, 8:3749.

27. J. S. Black to Johnson, March 23, 1867, JP; McPherson, *Reconstruction*, pp. 192–94, 178–81.

28. Trefousse, *Impeachment of a President*, p. 48; Chicago *Tribune*, March 31, 1866.

29. Hans L. Trefousse, *Ben Butler: The South Called Him Beast* (New York, 1957), passim; Trefousse, *Impeachment of a President*, pp. 48–49; Jesse A. Marshall, ed., *Private and Official Correspondence of General Benjamin F. Butler During the Period of the Civil War*,

5 vols. (Norwood, Mass., 1917), 5:594–95; J. W. Shaffer to Butler, May 14, 1865, Butler Papers, LC.

30. Robert F. Horowitz, *The Great Impeacher: A Political Biography of James M. Ashley* (New York, 1979), pp. 102–9, 124–25.

31. Trefousse, *Impeachment of a President*, p. 50; *New York Times*, January 7, 1866.

32. *New York Herald*, January 6, 8, 1867; *Toledo Daily Commercial*, January 7, 10, 1867; *New York Times*, January 6, 7, 1867.

33. *Cong. Globe*, 39th Cong., 2d Sess., 319–20.

34. *New York Herald*, January 9, 1867; for the committee members' politics, see David Donald, *The Politics of Reconstruction, 1863–1867* (Baton Rouge, 1965), pp. 102–5, and Benedict, *A Compromise of Principle*, pp. 368–69; *Toledo Daily Commercial*, January 9, 1867.

35. *Chicago Tribune*, January 9, 1867.

36. George F. Milton, *The Age of Hate: Andrew Johnson and the Radicals* (New York, 1930), p. 411.

37. *Impeachment Investigation*, pp. 1199, 2–15, 29–33, 15–18, 71–78, 78–84, 66–70, 34–50, 50–42, 163–75, 183–94; *Cong. Globe*, 39th Cong., 2d Sess., 1754–55.

38. *Cong. Globe*, 40th Cong., 1st Sess., 12, 18–25; *New York Herald*, March 7, 1867; *Impeachment Investigation*, pp. 271–73, 299–316, 84–99, 111ff., 280–84, 388–84, 398, 406–8ff., 417–49, 544ff., 578–85, 604–18, 644–60, 671–80, 1550–78; *Chicago Tribune*, June 4, 1867.

39. Phineas Watrous to W. C. Moore, May 1, 1867, J. R. Cobb to Johnson, May 11, 1867 (both offering information in return for a position), Moore, Small Diary, p. 33, William Lillen to Randall, March 8, 1867, JP.

40. Bigelow, Diary, March 1, 1867; George Mountford to Seward, April 11, 1867, Seward Papers; French Diary, 10:297, April 1867, French Papers, LC.

41. French Diary, January 2, 1867, 10:236–37, French Papers; Welles, *Diary*, 3:15, 22; *New York Times*, February 5, April 17, 1867; French Diary, 10:261, 272, February 10, 24, 1867, French Papers; Browning, *Diary*, 2:131–32.

42. French Diary, 10:219, 232–33, November 23, December 30, 1866, French Papers; Charles Albert Snodgrass, *The History of Freemasonry in Tennessee, 1789–1943* (Nashville, 1944), p. 398; Welles, *Diary*, 3:144.

43. McPherson, "Letters from North Carolina to Andrew Johnson," *North Carolina Historical Review* 28 (1951): 490–92; *New York Times*, June 3, 4, 5, 8, 1867; Fay Warrington Brabson, *Andrew Johnson: A Life in Pursuit of the Right Course, 1808–1875* (Durham, N.C., 1972), p. 197.

44. *New York Times*, June 22–25, 1867; *New York World*, June 24, 29, 1867; Welles, *Diary*, 3:109, 114, 119–20, 123; Stanbery to Browning, June 30, 1867, Browning Papers, ISH.

45. Trefousse, *Wade*, pp. 281–86; John Bigelow, *Retrospections of an Active Life*, 5 vols. (New York, 1909–13), 4:40; Milton, *Age of Hate*, p. 428; Alexander K. McClure, *Col. A. K. McClure's Recollections of Half a Century* (Salem, Mass., 1902), p. 65.

46. Trefousse, *Butler*, pp. 190–93; Johnson to Stanton, May 9, 1867, Stanton to Johnson, May 14, 1867, Stanton Papers, LC; William Hanchett, *The Lincoln Murder Conspiracies* (Urbana, 1983), pp. 85–86. See Horace White to E. B. Washburne, August 13, 1867, Washburne Papers. Upon Johnson's orders, the diary was published, contrary to Stanton's wishes. Washington *National Intelligencer* (triweekly), May 28, 1867.

47. Varina Davis, *Jefferson Davis . . . a Memoir by His Wife*, 2 vols. (New York, 1890), 2:768ff.; Dunbar Rowland, ed., *Jefferson Davis, Constitutionalist: His Letters, Papers, and Speeches*, 10 vols. (Jackson, Miss., 1923), 6:97; Washington *Daily Chronicle*, May 14, 1867, JP.

48. Victor J. Farrar, *The Annexation of Russian America to the United States* (New York, 1937), p. 35; Ronald J. Jensen, *The Alaska Purchase and Russian-American Relations* (Seattle, 1975), pp. 71ff.; Glyndon Van Deusen, *William Henry Seward* (New York, 1967), pp. 538ff.; Frederick W. Seward, *Reminiscences of a War-Time Statesman and Diplomat* (New

York, 1916), pp. 360–65. The president merely listened during the cabinet meeting to discuss the purchase and took no part in the conversation.

49. T. O. Howe to Grace Howe, April 13, 1867, Howe Papers, Wisconsin Historical Society; Washington *National Intelligencer,* April 15, 1867.

50. Welles, *Diary,* 3:94, 96, 105, 107, 109–14; Philip H. Sheridan, *Personal Memoirs of P. H. Sheridan,* 2 vols. (New York, 1888), 2:253–54, 257, 267–70; Grant to Sheridan, April 5, 1867, May 26, June 7, 1867, Sheridan Papers, LC; Sickles to Adjutant General, June 14, 19, 1867, Stanton Papers; W. A. Swanberg, *Sickles the Incredible* (New York, 1956), pp. 234–35.

51. Welles, *Diary,* 3:77–78; 109–14; Richardson, *Messages and Papers of the Presidents,* 8:3725ff.; Grant to Sheridan, June 24, 1867, Sheridan Papers; Memorandum on Cabinet Meeting of June 20, 1867, Stanton Papers; Benjamin P. Thomas and Harold M. Hyman, *Stanton: The Life and Times of Lincoln's Secretary of War* (New York, 1962), pp. 544–45. For a succinct account of Stanton's collaboration with Grant to counter the president's policies, see Harold M. Hyman, "Johnson, Stanton, and Grant: A Reconsideration of the Army's Role in the Events Leading to the Impeachment," *AHR* 66 (1960): pp. 85–100.

52. Blaine, *Twenty Years of Congress,* 2:294; David Miller DeWitt, *The Impeachment and Trial of Andrew Johnson* (New York, 1903), pp. 221ff.; Fessenden to Edwin D. Morgan, June 26, 1867, Morgan Papers, New York State Library, Albany; Howe to Grace Howe, July 4, 1867, Howe Papers; B. F. Butler to Mrs. Butler, July 4, 1867, Butler Papers.

53. Richardson, *Messages and Papers of the Presidents,* 8:8734–35; McPherson, *Reconstruction,* pp. 335–36; New York *World,* July 22, 1867.

54. Welles, *Diary,* 3:102; Toledo *Daily Commercial,* June 4, 1867; Chicago *Tribune,* June 4, 28, July 23, 1867; *Impeachment Investigation,* pp. 791–813, 815–19, 825–45, 861–78, 778–80.

55. New York *Herald,* July 8, 1867; *Cong. Globe,* 40th Cong., 1st Sess., 515–17, 522; Assassination Conspiracy Material in Butler Papers, July-September, 1867; *New York Times,* October 9, 12, 25, 28, November 1, 8, 11, 1867. Some of the impeachers asserted that the South, despairing of victory, made Johnson president, and he repaid the debt, as Benjamin Loan charged in Congress in January 1867. *Cong. Globe,* 39th Cong., 2d Sess., 443–46.

56. Welles, *Diary,* 3:31, 143–46; Browning, *Diary,* 2:152–54, 56–57; Charles Dunham to Johnson, July 29, 1867, JP.

57. Stanton to Ashley, September 14, 1866, letter in possession of Thomas L. Ashley; Boutwell, *Reminiscences,* 2:107–8; Edward Lewis et al. to Johnson, August 18, 1866, J. R. Doolittle et al. to Johnson, September 18, 1866, F. P. Blair to Johnson, September 20, 1867, Sam Randall to Johnson, October 24, 1866, JP.

58. Browning, *Diary,* 2:74, 142; Moore, Small Diary, pp. 29–31, April 5, May 2, 1867, JP; Welles, *Diary,* 3:110ff.; Thomas and Hyman, *Stanton,* p. 536.

59. McPherson, *Reconstruction,* p. 323; St. George L. Sioussat, ed., "Notes of Colonel W. G. Moore, Private Secretary to President Johnson, 1866–1868," *AHR* 19 (October 1913): 98–132, esp. 107–8.

XVI. FIGHTING PRESIDENT

1. William S. McFeely, *Grant: A Biography* (New York, 1981), p. 262; Samuel Wylie Crawford to Weed, July 21, 1867, Weed Papers, University of Rochester.

2. W. G. Moore, "Notes of Colonel W. G. Moore . . . ," *AHR* 19(1913): 107–8; Grant to Johnson, August 1, 1867, JP.

3. *Diary of Gideon Welles,* Howard K. Beale, ed., 3 vols. (New York, 1960), 3:149–56; Chase to Garfield, August 7, 1867, James A. Garfield Papers, LC.

4. Moore, Small Diary, pp. 37–39, August 6, 9, 1867, JP; "Notes of Colonel W. G. Moore," pp. 108–9; *New York Times,* August 4, 5, 1867; W. Winthrop to Holt, August

12, 1867, Holt Papers, LC; Johnson to Stanton, August 5, 1867, Stanton to Johnson, August 5, 1867, Stanton Papers, LC; Edward McPherson, *The Political History of the United States During the Period of Reconstruction, April 15, 1865–July 15,* 1870 (Washington, D.C., 1870), p. 261.

5. Welles, *Diary,* 3:162–67; *The Diary of Orville Hickman Browning,* J. G. Randall, ed., 2 vols. (Springfield, Ill., 1983), 2:154–56; Moore, Small Diary, pp. 39–40, August 11, 1867, JP; McPherson, *Reconstruction,* p. 261.

6. "Notes of Colonel W. G. Moore," p. 109; James D. Richardson, ed., *A Compilation of the Messages and Papers of the Presidents, 1789–1897,* 10 vols. (Washington, D.C., 1896–99), 8:3754; Moore, Small Diary, August 9, 12, 1867, pp. 38–45, JP.

7. Welles, *Diary,* 3:167–70; Adam Badeau, *Grant in Peace: From Appomattox to Mount McGregor* (Hartford, Conn., 1887), pp. 93–94; Horace White to E. B. Washburne, August 13, 1867, Washburne Papers, LC; J. M. Shankland to Holt, August 13, 1867, Holt Papers; Z. Chandler to Horace Greeley, August 19, 1867, Greeley Papers NYPL.

8. Welles, *Diary,* 3:141–42, 149–52; Philip H. Sheridan, *Personal Memoirs of Philip H. Sheridan,* 2 vols. (New York, 1888), 2:253ff., 269–70; *New York Times,* June 24, 1867.

9. "Notes of Colonel W. G. Moore," pp. 110–12; Moore, Small Diary, pp. 45–58, August 17–29, 1867, JP; Badeau, *Grant in Peace,* pp. 104–5; McPherson, *Reconstruction,* pp. 306–8; R. King Cutler to Johnson, August 23, 1867, JP.

10. Browning, *Diary,* 2:156; Welles, *Diary,* 3:170, 182; McPherson, *Reconstruction,* p. 345; James E. Sefton, *The United States Army and Reconstruction, 1865–1877* (Baton Rouge, 1967), pp. 158–60; Max L. Heyman, Jr., *Prudent Soldier: A Biography of Major General E. R. S. Canby, 1817–1873* (Glendale, Calif., 1959), pp. 303ff.

11. "Notes of Colonel W. G. Moore," pp. 111–12; Badeau, *Grant in Peace,* pp. 107–8; Moore, Small Diary, p. 48, August 24, 1867, JP.

12. Grant to Sheridan, September 8, 1867, Sheridan Papers, LC; Welles, *Diary,* 3:193, 221; Thomas Ewing, Jr., to Thomas Ewing, Sr., September 17, 1867, Ewing Papers, LC.

13. McPherson, *Reconstruction,* pp. 342–44.

14. *Ibid.,* p. 372; *New York Tribune,* October 12, 1867; *New York Times,* October 15, November 14, 1867.

15. Benjamin C. Truman to Johnson, September 7, 1867, C. A. Jordan to Johnson, September 10, 1867, L. D. Campbell to Johnson, October 12, 1867, Matthews Martin to Johnson, October 28, 1867, Robert Matthews to Johnson, November 8, 1867 (for the quotation), JP; M. R. Thayer to Washburne, October 10, 1867, T. B. Shannon to Washburne, October 27, 1867, Washburne Papers; R. C. Parsons to Sumner, October 10, 1867, Sumner Papers, Harvard University; John Binney to Colfax, November 2, 1867, Fessenden Papers, Duke University; W. B. Lynn to J. B. Strong, November 4, 1867, John D. Strong Papers, Illinois State Historical Society; John Bigelow to W. H. Huntington, November 4, 1867, Bigelow Papers NYPL; Richardson, *Messages and Papers of the Presidents,* 8:3756–79.

16. Georges Clemenceau, *American Reconstruction, 1865–1870,* Fernand Baldensperger, ed. (New York, 1969), pp. 133–36; C. A. Page to Washburne, October 12, 1867, Galusha Grow to Washburne, October 13, 1867, John Cochrane to Washburne, October 11, 1867, James G. Blaine to Washburne, October 22, 1867, Washburne Papers; John Bigelow to W. H. Huntington, November 4, 1867, Bigelow Papers. Michael Les Benedict has argued that the elections set the limits on reform in Reconstruction and put nonradicals in charge: "The Rout of Radicalism: Republicans and the Elections of 1867," *CWH* 18 (1972): 334–44.

17. Welles, *Diary,* 3:231–32, 233–34; Albert Castel, *The Presidency of Andrew Johnson* (Lawrence, Kans., 1979), pp. 149–50; T. Ewing, Sr., to Johnson, October 12, 1867, Ewing Papers.

18. William Thorpe to Johnson, September 25, 1867, H. R. Linderman to McCulloch, October 9, 1867, L. D. Evans to Johnson, November 4, 1867, JP; H. H. Jacobs to John Sherman, October 9, 1867, John Sherman Papers, LC; Thomas Ewing, Sr., to Hugh

Ewing, October 16, 1867, Ewing Papers; J. Glancey Jones to Thaddeus Stevens, November 26, 1867, Stevens Papers, LC; Washington *National Intelligencer* (triweekly), October 3, 16, 17, 1867; *Wilkes' Spirit of the Times,* October 26, November 9, 1867; *New York Times,* November 8, 1867; Toledo *Daily Commercial,* November 15, 1867; New York *Independent,* November 14, 1867.

19. Fessenden to McCulloch, September 2, 1867, McCulloch Papers, LC; Carl Schafer, ed., *Intimate Letters of Carl Schurz, 1841–1869* (Madison, Wis., 1928), p. 388; *Garfield-Hinsdale Letters,* Mary L. Hinsdale, ed. (Ann Arbor, 1949), p. 96.

20. Colfax to Garfield, September 11, 1867, Garfield Papers; Welles, *Diary,* 3:239.

21. New York *Herald,* October 21, 1867; Chicago *Tribune* (triweekly), October 31, 1867; *Impeachment Investigation,* House Reports, 40th Cong., 1st Sess., No 7, pp. 1166–1208; *Impeachment of the President,* 40th Cong., 1st Sess., H.R. No. 7, passim; *Garfield-Hinsdale Letters,* pp. 113–14.

22. "Notes of Colonel W. G. Moore," p. 113.

23. Welles, *Diary,* 3:234, 235; George W. Moody to Johnson, April 13, 1866, John Campbell to Johnson, May 21, 1866, A. B. Johnston to Johnson, November 4, 1866, John Pearson to Johnson, February 25, 1867, Ethan Allan to Johnson, March 11, 1867, John Tyler to Johnson, November 26, 1867, Nashville *Daily Press and Times,* September 4, 1867, JP; New York *Herald,* November 19, 1866; Schurz, *Intimate Letters,* p. 392; John Binney to Colfax, September 9, 1867, John A. Andrew Papers, Massachusetts Historical Society; Clemenceau, *American Reconstruction,* pp. 110–11, 120–22; William A. Russ, Jr., "Was There Danger of a Second Civil War During Reconstruction?" *MVHR* 25 (1938): 39–58.

24. Verbatim report, November 30, 1867, Moore, Small Diary, p. 65, November 30, 1867, JP; Browning, *Diary,* 2:167–68.

25. John Sherman, *John Sherman's Recollections of Forty Years in the House, Senate, and Cabinet,* 2 vols. (Chicago, 1895), 1:413; Cong. Globe, 40th Cong., 2d Sess., 61; T. W. Egan to Johnson, October 7, 1867, William Thorpe to Johnson, December 5, 1867, JP; Grimes to Atkinson, October 14, 1867, Edward Atkinson Papers, Massachusetts Historical Society, Boston; Hans L. Trefousse, *Benjamin Franklin Wade, Radical Republican from Ohio* (New York, 1963), p. 365, n. 51. Whether or not impeachment "is limited to solid cases of wilful wrongdoing" is a question that has been argued to this day. For the negative, see John R. Labovitz, *Presidential Impeachment* (New Haven, 1978), pp. 250, 259; for the opposite point of view, see Peter Charles Hoffer and N. E. H. Hall, *Impeachment in America, 1635–1805* (New Haven, 1984), pp. 262–63.

26. Chicago *Tribune,* November 20, December 26, 1867; David Miller DeWitt, *The Impeachment and Trial of Andrew Johnson* (New York, 1903), p. 313; New York *Herald,* July 8, 1867; Horace White to Washburne, August 13, 1867, George G. Fogg to Washburne, November 20, 1867, Washburne Papers.

27. *Cong. Globe,* 40th Cong., 2d Sess., 61ff., 65, 67, App. 54–62; Chicago *Tribune,* December 8, 1867.

28. "Notes of Colonel W. G. Moore," pp. 113–14; Richardson, *Messages and Papers of the Presidents,* 8:3793–94; *Cong. Globe,* 40th Cong., 2d Sess., 402; Washington *Daily Chronicle,* December 21, 1867, JP; Welles, *Diary,* 3:241–42; Clemenceau, *American Reconstruction,* p. 139.

29. Welles, *Diary,* 3:42–43, 247, 249; McPherson, *Reconstruction,* pp. 355–56; John Forsyth to Johnson, December 19, 1867, JP; Sefton, *U.S. Army and Reconstruction,* pp. 160–69; Castel, *The Presidency of Andrew Johnson,* pp. 154–56; L. W. Hall to Garfield, January 4, 1868, Garfield Papers. Early in 1868 Johnson also removed Wager Swayne and Joseph Mower, the radical heads of the Freedmen's Bureau in Alabama and Louisiana: Richard H. Abbott, *The Republican Party and the South, 1855–1877* (Chapel Hill, 1986), p. 104.

30. William B. Uccleston to Thaddeus Stevens, June 28, 1867, Stevens Papers; C. W. Clarke to John Covode, August 31, 1867, Covode Papers, LC; Francis Pierpont to Waitman

Willey, September 11, 1867, Willey Papers, University of West Virginia; W. H. Gibbs to Washburne, September 30, 1867, Washburne Papers; T. W. Duval to Holt, October 24, 1867, Holt Papers, LC; James L. Dunning to Sumner, December 27, 1867, Sumner Papers; Foster Blodgett to Fessenden, December 30, 1867, Fessenden Papers.

31. Welles, *Diary,* 3:187, 190, 204–5, 237, 281; French Diary, 10:354–55, 386, August 13, September 16, 1867, French Papers, LC; Edward Cooper to Matthew D. Cooper, October 28, 1867, Cooper Family Papers, TSLA; B. Dettman to Johnson, August 24, 1867, F. A. Reeve to Johnson, September 2, 1867, JP; Fannie M. Severson to Robert Johnson, October 25, 1867, JP, series II; Ann Judson to Johnson, October 20, 1867, Jennie A. Perry to Johnson, October 30, 1867, May 10, June 9, 1868, J. S. Black to Johnson, November 25, 1867, JP; "Notes of Colonel W. G. Moore," p. 109; William Norwood Brigance, "Jeremiah Black and Andrew Johnson," *MVHR* 19 (1932): 205–18; *New York Times,* September 18, 1867.

32. Welles, *Diary,* 3:156, 183, 190, 237; M. Blair to Barlow, February 14, September 20, 1867, Barlow Papers, Huntington Library; John Tyler to Johnson, August 29, 1867, McCulloch to Johnson, August 19, 1867, Seward to Johnson, August 23, 1867, Moore, Small Diary, pp. 45–46, August 14, 1867, JP; Glyndon Van Deusen, *William Henry Seward* (New York, 1967), p. 474.

33. "Notes of Colonel W. G. Moore," pp. 113–14; Thomas Ewing, Sr., to Johnson, November 28, 1867, JP; Browning, *Diary,* 2:169; Welles, *Diary,* 3:240; Richardson, *Messages and Papers of the Presidents,* 8:3781–92.

34. *Chicago Tribune,* December 18, 22, 1867, January 10, 1868; "Notes of Colonel W. G. Moore," pp. 113–14; McPherson, *Reconstruction,* p. 286.

35. McPherson, *Reconstruction,* pp. 262, 284–86; *Cong. Globe,* 40th Cong., 2d Sess., 433; Badeau, *Grant in Peace,* pp. 110–15, 125–26; "Notes of Colonel W. G. Moore," pp. 114–115; William T. Sherman, *Memoirs,* 2:421–26; Sherman to Grant, January 27, 1868, James G. Blaine Papers, LC.

36. Moore, Small Diary, pp. 69–71, 73–74, January 14, 15, 18, 1868, JP; Browning, *Diary,* 2:174–76; William T. Sherman, *Memoirs,* 2:422–26; Welles, *Diary,* 3:259–63; McPherson, *Reconstruction,* p. 286.

37. McPherson, *Reconstruction,* pp. 283–84; Welles, *Diary,* 3:262; Moore, Small Diary, pp. 74–76, January 28, 1868, JP.

38. Moore, Small Diary, pp. 73, 77–89, January 26, February 3, 17, 19, 1868, Sherman to Johnson, January 27, 29, 31, February 14, 1868, Johnson to Sherman, February 18, 1868, JP; McPherson, *Reconstruction,* pp. 284–92; *Cong. Globe,* 40th Cong., 2d Sess., 977; Richardson, *Messages and Papers of the Presidents,* 8:3800–18; Welles, *Diary,* 3:269–73, 282.

39. Clemenceau, *American Reconstruction,* pp. 139, 143.

40. *Ibid.,* pp. 140–41; *Cong. Globe,* 40th Cong., 2d Sess., 332–33, 384, 476, 517, 664, 722; McPherson, *Reconstruction,* p. 338; *New York Times,* January 14, February 6, 1868; *Cincinnati Daily Gazette,* February 8, 10, 14, 1868; *Chicago Tribune,* November 19, 1867, February 13, 14, 1868; *Richmond Evening Enquirer,* February 17, 1868.

41. Washington *Daily National Intelligencer,* February 15, 1868, JP.

XVII. PRESIDENT IMPEACHED — PRESIDENT ACQUITTED

1. W. G. Moore, "Notes of Colonel W. G. Moore . . . ," *AHR* 19 (1913): 120; Jerome B. Stillson to Barlow, February 12, 1868, Barlow Papers, Huntington Library; J. B. Stillson to Curtis, April 4, 1868, JP.

2. Moore, Small Diary, February 16, 17, 1868, pp. 87–88, JP.

3. *DAB* 8:441–42; E. D. Townsend, *Anecdotes of the Civil War* (New York, 1884), pp. 79–82, 124–25; Benjamin P. Thomas and Harold M. Hyman, *Stanton: The Life and Times of Lincoln's Secretary of War* (New York, 1962); pp. 159, 581–82; *Diary of Gideon Welles,*

Howard K. Beale, ed., 3 vols. (New York, 1960), 3:279; Moore, Small Diary, February 19, 1868, p. 93, JP.

4. Moore, Small Diary, February 21, 1868, p. 94, JP; Welles, *Diary*, 3:234; Stillson to Barlow, February 28, 1868, Barlow Papers. George L. Thomas refused the nomination, and nothing came of McClellan's. Edward McPherson, *The History of the United States During the Period of Reconstruction*, April 15, 1865–July 15, 1870 (Washington, D.C., 1870), p. 346; Albert Castel, *The Presidency of Andrew Johnson* (Lawrence, Kans., 1979), pp. 170, 211.

5. "Notes of Colonel W. G. Moore," pp. 120–21; Thomas and Hyman, *Stanton*, p. 584.

6. Welles, *Diary*, 3:284–85.

7. Richmond *Evening Enquirer*, February 24, 1868; Welles, *Diary*, 3:285; Henry Wilson to Stanton, February 21, 1868, Richard Yates to Stanton, February 21, 1868, John M. Thayer to Stanton, February 21, 1868, Stanton Papers, LC; George F. Milton, *The Age of Hate: Andrew Johnson and the Radicals* (New York, 1930), pp. 503–4.

8. Georges Clemenceau, *American Reconstruction, 1865–1870*, Fernand Baldensperger, ed. (New York, 1928), pp. 153–54; *Cong. Globe*, 40th Cong., 2d Sess., 1329.

9. Bigelow, Diary, February 21, 1868, Bigelow Papers, NYPL; William Bushnell to Johnson, March 12, 1872, JP.; Thomas E. Ewing, Jr., to Hugh Ewing, March 8, 1868, Ewing Family Papers, LC.

10. Moore, Small Diary, February 22, 1868, pp. 95–97, JP; *Trial of Andrew Johnson . . . on Impeachment . . .* , 3 vols. (Washington, D.C., 1968), 1:427–29. For a refutation of Johnson's alleged desire for a Supreme Court test, see Thomas and Hyman, *Stanton*, p. 590. Professor Hyman has also argued that Johnson, like Richard Nixon, decided that as president he unilaterally possessed the power to judge the constitutionality of a law of Congress. Harold M. Hyman and William M. Wiececk, *Equal Justice Under Law: Constitutional Development, 1835–1875* (New York, 1982), p. 455.

11. *Cong. Globe*, 40th Cong., 2d Sess., 1330ff., 1341ff.; Chicago *Tribune*, February 23, 1868; Bigelow, Diary, February 22, 1868.

12. Moore, Small Diary, February 22, 1868, pp. 98–99, JP; Welles, *Diary*, 3:286–88. The Ewing nomination was never considered.

13. *Trial of Andrew Johnson*, 1:233–36.

14. "Notes of Colonel W. G. Moore," p. 122; Moore, Small Diary, February 23, 1868, p. 99, JP; *The Diary of Orville Hickman Browning*, J. G. Randall, ed., 2 vols. (Springfield, Ill., 1933), 2:182.

15. *Cong. Globe*, 40th Cong., 2d Sess., 1360ff., 1382ff., 1391ff., 1400–2; Chicago *Tribune*, February 25, 1868.

16. Moore, Small Diary, February 24, p. 99, JP; Richmond *Evening Enquirer*, February 27, 1868. On the same day, Thomas went to the War Department again, only to be rebuffed by Stanton as before. *Ibid.*, February 26, 1868. Professor Benedict in particular has argued that Johnson considered the whole matter a political question upon which, should the court rule the law unconstitutional, he hoped to win a victory and undermine Reconstruction. Michael Les Benedict, *The Impeachment and Trial of Andrew Johnson* (New York, 1973), pp. 96–97.

17. Welles, *Diary*, 3:294; Milton Lomask, *Andrew Johnson: President on Trial* (New York, 1960), p. 276.

18. *Trial of Andrew Johnson*, 1:1–87; Chicago *Tribune*, February 26, March 13, 4, 5, 8, 14, 24, 1868; Fragment of "Journal of the proceedings of the Honorable Managers of the House of Representatives in the matter of the impeachment of Andrew Johnson, President of the United States," March 3, 1868, Butler Papers, LC. During the swearing in of the senators, the case of B. F. Wade caused some controversy. As Johnson's legal successor, could he administer impartial justice? And was it proper for an interested party to vote on his own elevation? In the end, after some delay, the senator was sworn in, as was David T. Patterson, who also had an interest in the case. In addition, it was held that Ohio was entitled to two votes. Hans L. Trefousse,

Benjamin Franklin Wade: Radical Republican from Ohio (New York 1963), p. 297.

19. For example, cf. the New York *Herald,* New York *Times,* New York *Tribune,* Richmond *Enquirer,* and Washington *National Intelligencer* for the appropriate dates; George S. Boutwell, *Reminiscences of Sixty Years in Public Affairs,* 2 vols. (New York, 1902), 2:119–21; Hans L. Trefousse, *Ben Butler: The South Called Him Beast* (New York, 1957), p. 197.

20. "Notes of Colonel W. G. Moore," p. 123; Moore, Small Diary, February 29, 1868, pp. 104–5, March 3, 1868, p. 105, JP: New York *World,* March 10, 1868; *New York Times,* May 27, 1868; French Diary, 10:528, March 23, 1868, French Papers, LC; Frank Cowan, *Andrew Johnson, President of the United States . . .* (Greensburgh, Pa., 1894), pp. 11–13.

21. S. M. Johnson to Johnson, February 26, 1868, Ewing to Johnson, March 1, 1868, JP; Welles, *Diary,* 3:294, 298, 302; Browning, *Diary,* 2:183–85; Chester L. Barrows, *William M. Evarts, Lawyer, Diplomat, Statesman* (Chapel Hill, 1941), pp. 142, 153; Samuel S. Cox, *Three Decades of Federal Legislation, 1855–1885* (Providence, 1885), p. 187; James G. Blaine, *Twenty Years of Congress,* 2 vols. (Boston, 1884–86), 2:363–65; Thomas B. Alexander, "Strange Bedfellows: The Interlocking Careers of T. A. R. Nelson, Andrew Johnson, and W. G. (Parson) Brownlow," *ETHSP* 22(1952): 86–87; William Norwood Brigance, "Jeremiah Black and Andrew Johnson," *MVHR* 19(1932): 205–18.

22. Welles, *Diary,* 3:311; Chicago *Tribune,* March 14, 1868; Doolittle to Browning, October 7, 1866, Browning Papers, ISH.

23. Moore, Small Diary, March 16, 20, 1868, pp. 115, 122, Large Diary, March 27, 30, April 4, 8, 1868, JP; Fragment of Johnson's Speech, Butler Papers.

24. *Trial of Andrew Johnson,* 1:87–147; Richmond *Evening Enquirer,* March 31, 1868; Boston *Daily Advertiser,* March 31, 1868; *New York Times,* March 31, 1868; Chicago *Tribune,* March 31, 1868.

25. Moore, Large Diary, March 30, 1868, JP; Clemenceau, *Reconstruction,* pp. 174–76; Chicago *Tribune,* April 2, 1868; *Trial of Andrew Johnson,* 1:155–414; Benjamin F. Butler, *Butler's Book* (Boston, 1892), p. 930.

26. *Trial of Andrew Johnson,* 1:461ff., 481ff., 508ff., 517ff., 521–23, 532–37, 663ff., 674ff., 700ff., 707ff.; Moore, Large Diary, April 13, 1868, JP; Chicago *Tribune,* April 13, 1868.

27. *Trial of Andrew Johnson,* 2:1–475, esp. 116–17, 262ff.; Clemenceau, *Reconstruction,* p, 178; Cincinnati *Daily Gazette,* April 28, 1868.

28. Browning, *Diary,* 2:183; Moore, Small Diary, February 26, 1868, p. 100, JP; French Diary, 10:507, March 1, 1868; William Henry Crook, *Memories of the White House,* Henry Rood, ed. (Boston, 1911), p. 125.

29. Moore, Large Diary, March 4, 6, 18, April 22, 1868, JP.

30. *Ibid.,* March 30, April 4, 5, 6, 7, 9, 12, 1868, JP; Browning, *Diary,* 2:189–90.

31. Moore, Large Diary, April 13, 15, 16, 17, 19, 26, May 2, 1868, *National Intelligencer,* April 18, 1868, JP; Welles, *Diary,* 3:352–53.

32. Moore, Small Diary, March 16, 1868, p. 112, Large Diary, March 21, April 24, Smythe to Johnson, April 8, 1868, JP; Welles, *Diary,* 3:332–33, 345.

33. Barrows, *Evarts,* p. 157; New York *Independent,* March 26, 1868; Edwards Pierrepont to Stanton, May 3, 1868, Stanton Papers; George W. Julian to Mrs. Julian, May 5, 1868, Julian Papers, Indiana State Library; Cincinnati *Daily Gazette,* May 12, 1868; S. P. Lee to Mr. and Mrs. Blair, May 12, 1868, Blair-Lee Family Papers, Princeton University. The Boston bar was equally confident of acquittal, Curtis wrote to Evarts. Curtis to Evarts, May 3, 1868, Evarts Papers, LC.

34. Gustavus V. Fox Diary, April 5, 1868, NYHS; Cox, *Three Decades of Federal Legislation,* pp. 392–94; Frank Abial Flower, *Edwin McMasters Stanton: The Autocrat of Rebellion, Emancipation, and Reconstruction* (Akron, Ohio, 1905), p. 342; Welles, *Diary,* 3:338–39.

35. Welles, *Diary,* 3:338–39; Evarts to Schofield, April 21, 1868, Schofield Memorandum, May 1868, Schofield Papers, LC; Moore, Large Diary, April 23, 1868, JP; George P. Brockway, *Political Deals That Saved Andrew Johnson* (New York, 1977), pp. 12ff.

36. Brockway, p. 15; *Political Deals,* Browning, *Diary,* 2:195; Welles, *Diary,* 3:347; Moore,

Small Diary, February 28, 1868, p. 103, JP. For the probable involvement of Fessenden and Trumbull in these negotiations, see Brockway, *Political Deals*, pp. 8–12; Moore, Large Diary, March 27, 1868, JP.

37. McPherson, *Reconstruction*, pp. 336, 351.

38. *New York Times*, May 6, 7, 9, 10, 11, 13, 1868; Chicago *Tribune*, May 7, 10, 12, 13, 1868; Edmund G. Ross, *History of the Impeachment of Andrew Johnson* (Sante Fe, 1896), pp. 129ff.; Browning, *Diary*, 2:196–97; David Miller DeWitt, *The Impeachment and Trial of Andrew Johnson* (New York, 1903), pp. 517–27.

39. Moore, Large Diary, May 10, 1868, Emily Miller to Johnson, May 12, 1868, JP; Browning, *Diary*, 2:197; Welles, *Diary*, 3:352–53, 356.

40. *Trial of Andrew Johnson*, 2:484–89; New York *Tribune*, May 18, 1868, New York *World*, May 17, 1868. Considerable evidence exists that Ross' vote was not as crucial as it would appear from John F. Kennedy's *Profiles in Courage*. Senators Waitman T. Willey, Edwin D. Morgan, and possibly William Sprague were all reported to stand ready to vote for acquittal should their votes be needed. J. B. Henderson, "Emancipation and Impeachment," *Century Illustrated Magazine* 85 (1912–13): 196–209; Benjamin Truman, "Anecdotes of Andrew Johnson," *Century Illustrated Magazine* 63 (1912–13): 438; R. W. Bayless, "Peter G. Van Winkle and Waitman T. Willey in the Impeachment Trial of Andrew Johnson," *West Virginia History* 13 (1952): 75–89; William S. Hawley to Samuel F. Tilden, May 22, 1868, Tilden Papers, NYPL; William A. Dunning, *Reconstruction, Political and Economic, 1865–1877* (New York, 1907), p. 109; Hans L. Trefousse, *Impeachment of a President: Andrew Johnson, the Blacks, and Reconstruction* (New York, 1975), pp. 168–69.

41. Moore, Large Diary, May 16, 1868, JP; Crook, *Through Five Administrations*, p. 133; Crook, *Memories of the White House*, p. 66; Chicago *Tribune*, May 18, 1868.

42. Chicago *Tribune*, May 18, 1868; Moore, Large Diary, May 17, 18, 1868, JP.

43. William Henry Crook, *Through Five Administrations*, Margaret Spalding Gerry, ed. (New York, 1910), p. 133; *Impeachment Investigation*, 40th Cong. 2d Sess., H.R. No. 4; Butler to John Russell Young, May 16, 1868, Young Papers, LC; J. G. Whittier to Greeley, May 16, 1868, Greeley Papers, NYPL; E. B. Washburne to Henry L. Dawes, May 17, 1868, Dawes Papers, LC; *National Anti-Slavery Standard*, May 23, 1868. The Butler Papers for the period contain many of the seized documents.

44. Baltimore *Daily Times*, May 18, 1868, S. J. Anderson to Johnson, March 31, 1868, J. B. Bingham to Johnson, May 23, 1868, JP; Clemenceau, *American Reconstruction*, p. 186; W. H. H. to Marble, n.d., Marble Papers, LC; Welles, *Diary*, 3:319.

45. New York *Herald*, May 22, 1868; Thomas W. Conway to Chase, May 24, 1868, Chase Papers, LC.

46. *Trial of Andrew Johnson*, 2:489–98; *New York Times*, May 27, 1868; Moore, Large Diary, May 26, 1868, JP; Browning, *Diary*, 2:199; Welles, *Diary*, 3:368.

47. Stevens to Butler, February 28, 1868, Butler Papers; Chicago *Tribune*, March 5, 1868; Joseph Medill to John A. Logan, March 5, 1868, Logan Papers, LC; *Harper's Weekly*, March 28, 1868; O. O. Howe to Grace Howe, February 21, 1868, Howe Papers, Historical Society of Wisconsin; William Goddard to Thomas A. Jenckes, March 5, 1868, Jenckes Papers, LC; French Diary, March 8, 1868, 10:512, French Papers; John B. Henderson to Carl Schurz, May 1, 1868, Schurz Papers, LC; Clemenceau, *American Reconstruction*, p. 177; John Sherman, *John Sherman's Recollections of Forty Years in the House, Senate, and Cabinet*, 2 vols. (Chicago, 1895), 1:427; *Trial of Andrew Johnson*, 3:328.

48. Chicago *Tribune*, May 9, 21, 1868; Stillson to Barlow, May 22, 1868, Barlow Papers; Ross, *Impeachment of Andrew Johnson*, pp. 155ff.; Butler, *Butler's Book*, p. 929; C. H. Hill to Garfield, March 17, 1868, Garfield Papers, LC; New York *Herald*, April 15, 1868.

49. Cincinnati *Daily Gazette*, April 14, 1868; Edward Atkinson to Sumner, February 25, 1868, Sumner Papers, Harvard University, Horace White to Washburne, May 1, 1868, Washburne Papers, LC; Clemenceau, *American Reconstruction*, p. 102; E. E. Fogg to

Jenckes, March 23, 1868, Jenckes Papers; Theodore Clark Smith, *The Life and Letters of James Abram Garfield,* 2 vols. (New Haven, 1905), p. 425; Chicago *Tribune,* May 17, 1868; Hans L. Trefousse, "Ben Wade and the Failure of the Impeachment of Johnson," *Historical and Philosophical Society of Ohio Bulletin* 18 (1960): 241–52.

50. Ross, *Impeachment of Andrew Johnson,* p. 169; *Trial of Andrew Johnson,* 3:328. The Democrats in Congress entered a formal protest against the majority's "warring against the other co-ordinate departments, the executive and judicial, endeavoring to subjugate and bring them both under the will and control of Congress," and sent it to the president: Protest, March 2, 1868, JP.

51. *Trial of Andrew Johnson,* 3:328; Charles C. Pomeroy to Stevens, April 14, 1868, Stevens Papers, LC; Chicago *Tribune,* May 11, 1868.

52. Clemenceau, *American Reconstruction,* pp. 139–40; Washington *National Intelligencer* (triweekly), January 14, 1868; Trefousse, *Impeachment of a President,* pp. 139–41, 156–57; Samuel Ward to Barlow, February 25, 1868, Barlow Papers; Thomas Ewing to Hugh Ewing, February 26, 1868, Ewing Family Papers; New York *Herald,* March 11, 23, 1868; David Donald, "Why They Impeached Andrew Johnson," *American Heritage* 8 (1956): 20–26, 102–3.

53. John W. Horner to Mrs. Edmund G. Ross, May 24, 1868, Ross Papers, Kansas State Historical Society, Topeka; H. Holland to Evarts, May 27, 1868, William Evarts Papers, LC; Francis Fellows to Johnson, May 28, 1868, JP; DeWitt, *Impeachment and Trial of Andrew Johnson,* pp. 578–79; Raoul Berger, *Impeachment: The Constitutional Problems* (Cambridge, Mass., 1973), p. 295. Michael Les Benedict, who, like Harold Hyman, believes Johnson deserved conviction, thinks that the outcome proved impeachment a "dull blade" and of no use in attempting to remove presidents. Michael Les Benedict, *Impeachment and Trial of Andrew Johnson,* (New York, 1974) pp. 172ff., 180; Harold M. Hyman, *A More Perfect Union: The Impact of the Civil War and Reconstruction on the Constitution* (New York, 1973), pp. 506ff.

54. Scott and Martin to Johnson, February 18, 1868, Edward A. Pollard to Johnson, February 14, 1868, A. H. Garland to Johnson, March 15, 1868, JP.

55. Washington Morning *Chronicle,* April 18, 22, 1868; A. B. Schuyler to Waitman T. Willey, April 21, 1868, Willey Papers, University of West Virginia; G. Horton to Sumner, April 23, 1868, David D. Durboraw to Sumner, May 2, 1868, Sumner Papers; S. B. Packard to Grant, May 14, 1868, JP; Daniel Richards to Washburne, May 6, 1868, Washburne Papers.

56. Richmond *Whig,* May 28, June 10, 1868; B. F. Perry to Johnson, May 20, 1868, J. B. Bingham to Johnson, May 23, 1868, A. A. Kyle to Johnson, May 29, 1868, JP.

57. Daniel Richards to Washburne, May 18, 1868, George E. Spencer to Washburne, May 23, 1868, James Alcorn to Washburne, June 29, 1868, Washburne Papers; John H. Feriter to Sumner, June 6, 1868, Edwin Belcher to Sumner, June 23, 1868, Sumner Papers.

58. A. K. McClure, *Lincoln and Men of War-Times* (Philadelphia, 1892), pp. 263–64.

XVIII. *PRESIDENT IN LIMBO*

1. Johnson to J. W. Nesmith, June 30, 1868, Johnson to J. W. Davidson, June 8, 1868, series IIIA, JP; *Diary of Gideon Welles,* Howard K. Beale, ed., 3 vols. (New York, 1960), 3:375; James H. Whyte, *The Uncivil War: Washington During the Reconstruction, 1865–1878* (New York, 1958), p. 67.

2. Ross to Johnson, June 6, July 10, 15, 1868, JP; Charles A. Jellison, *Fessenden of Maine, Civil War Senator* (Syracuse, N.Y., 1962), p. 153; Moore, Large Diary, May 27, 29, 30, 1868, JP; Conkling to Seward, May 29, 1868, JP; E. D. Townsend, *Anecdotes of the Civil War in the United States* (New York, 1884), pp. 132–36. While none of the recusants were reelected to the Senate, they did not fare as badly as has been asserted. Several

remained active in the affairs of the Republican party. Ralph J. Roske, "The Seven Martyrs?" *AHR* 64 (1959): 323–30.

3. Welles, *Diary*, 3:375, 390; Moore, Large Diary, June 5, 17, 1868, JP; Johnson to Curtis, June 5, 1868, Seward to Johnson, June 11, 1868, Evarts to Johnson, June 11, 20, 1868, JP. Seward acted as a go-between with Evarts. James G. Blaine, *Twenty Years of Congress*, 2 vols. (Boston, 1884–86), 2:384.

4. *Appleton's Annual Cyclopaedia, 1869* (New York, 1869), p. 592; Johnson to Edmund Cooper, July 8, 1868, Johnson to George H. Parker, July 8, 1868, JP; Welles, *Diary*, 3:383.

5. Thomas Fitzgerald to Johnson, March 24, 1865, JP, series II; Thomas Jefferson Rawls to Johnson, September 12, 1865, A. H. Worthington to R. W. Johnson, January 18, 1868, J. R. Flanagan to Johnson, July 23, 1867, H. R. Lindeman to Johnson, December 28, 1867, JP; New York *Herald*, February 27, 1867; Welles, *Diary*, 3:166, 189.

6. J. W. Bell to Johnson, February 8, 1868, R. W. Williams to Johnson, February 22, 1868, Scott Martin to Johnson, February 18, 1868, H. Fred Liebman to Johnson, February 24, 1868, J. B. Bingham to Johnson, May 23, 1868, R. H. Kerr to Johnson, June 1, 1868, C. H. Mitchner to Johnson, June 10, 1868, R. W. Latham to Johnson, June 12, 1868, Philip Lindsley to Johnson, June 12, 1868, W. O. Kyle to Johnson, June 23, 1868, JP.

7. Moore, Large Diary, July 1, 3, 1868, JP; *The Diary of Orville Hickman Browning*, J. G. Randall, ed., 2 vols. (Springfield, Ill., 1933), 2:203–5; Welles, *Diary*, 3:394–96; James D. Richardson, *A Compilation of the Messages and Papers of the Presidents, 1789–1897*, 10 vols. (Washington, D.C., 1896–99), 8:3853–54; *Harper's Weekly*, July 18, 1868.

8. William Warden to Johnson, June 29, 30, July 1, 5, 1868, Johnson to Edmund Cooper, July 8, 1868, Johnson to George H. Parker, July 8, 1868, Edward Cooper to Johnson, July 2, 1868, S. M. Johnson to Johnson, July 5, 6, 7, 1868, JP; *New York Times*, July 7, 1868.

9. Hugh McCulloch, *Men and Measures of Half a Century* (New York, 1888), pp. 344–45; James Lewis Baumgardner, "Andrew Johnson and the Patronage," Ph.D. diss., UT, 1969, pp. 77ff., 86–92; John Tapley to Doolittle, June 5, 1868, Doolittle Papers, Historical Society of Wisconsin.

10. J. B. Bingham to Johnson, May 23, 1868, JP; Washington McLean to Barlow, October 11, 1867, Barlow Papers, Huntington Library.

11. Blaine, *Twenty Years of Congress*, 2:392ff.; Edward Cooper to Johnson, July 2, 1868, Edward Cooper to Johnson, July 3, 1868, JP; Welles, *Diary*, 3:295, 383–84; Moore, Large Diary, July 3, 1868, JP; Frederick J. Blue, *Salmon P. Chase: A Life in Politics* (Kent, Ohio, 1987), pp. 286ff.

12. *Official Proceedings of the National Democratic Convention Held at New York, July 4–9, 1868* (Boston, 1868), pp. 60, 77–160.

13. Moore, Large Diary, July 9, 1868, Johnson to George H. Parker, July 8, 1868, Johnson to Edmund Cooper, July 8, 1868, JP.

14. Moore, Large Diary, July 10, 1868, J. D. Perryman to Johnson, July 10, 1868, H. F. Lieberman to Johnson, July 13, 1868, J. S. Metcalf to Johnson, July 14, 1868, Jacob Weaver to Johnson, July 14, 1868, M. Mahon to Johnson, July 18, 1868, JP; Ethan Allan to Seward, July 27, 1868, Seward Papers, University of Rochester; Petersburg *Republic*, July 11, 1868, JP, series XI; Charles H. Coleman, *The Election of 1868* (New York, 1933), pp. 278–83.

15. J. W. Leftwich to Johnson, July 27, 1868, John F. Coyle to Johnson, August 20, 1868, JP; Sam Ward to Manton Marble, August 1, 1868, Marble Papers, LC; Sam Ward to Barlow, July 22, 1868, Barlow Papers; Welles, *Diary*, 3:429–30; *New York Times*, October 24, 1868.

16. Fessenden to Grimes, July 12, 1868, Fessenden Papers, Bowdoin College.

17. Richardson, *Messages and Papers of the Presidents*, 8:3846–48; *New York Times*, June 21, 1868; Moore, Large Diary, April 9, 1868, JP; *National Anti-Slavery Standard*, February 8, 1868.

18. Richardson, *Messages and Papers of the Presidents*, 8:3836, 3848–49, 3854–58; *New York Times*, June 26, July 13, 1868.

19. Moore, Large Diary, July 17, 1868, JP; Richardson, *Messages and Papers of the Presidents*, 8:3849–52; Edward McPherson, *The Political History of the United States During the Period of Reconstruction, April 15, 1865–July 15, 1870* (Washington, D.C., 1870), pp. 378–79.

20. Moore, Large Diary, July 17, 1868, JP; Welles, *Diary*, 3:406–8; Browning, *Diary*, 2:207–8; Richardson, *Messages and Papers of the Presidents*, 8:3837–43, 3852; *Cong. Globe*, 40th Cong., 2d Sess., 4450–41.

21. *New York Times*, July 23, 1868; Washington *National Intelligencer*, July 28, 1868; *Cong. Globe*, 40th Cong, 2d Sess., 4334, 4381.

22. *Cong. Globe*, 40th Cong., 2d Sess., 42518, 42520; Thomas Ewing, Jr., to Thomas Ewing, Sr., July 23, 1868, Ewing Family Papers, LC; Fawn Brodie, *Thaddeus Stevens: Scourge of the South* (New York, 1959), p. 366.

23. *New York Times*, August 7, October 6, 24, September 28, November 1, 1868; Moore, Large Diary, November 4, 1868, JP; Welles, *Diary*, 3:450, 453–54, 458, 459, 462.

24. *O.R.*, series I, vol. 48, part II, pp. 669, 895–96, 857; Robert Winston Mardock, *The Reformers and the American Indian* (Columbia, Mo., 1971), pp. 20ff., 24–28, 42ff.; Henry E. Fritz, *The Movement for Indian Assimilation, 1860–1890* (Philadelphia, 1963), pp. 62–70; Robert M. Utley, *Frontier Regulars: The United States Army and the Indian, 1866–1891* (New York, 1973), pp. 111–32ff.

25. Leon B. Richardson, *William E. Chandler, Republican* (New York, 1940), p. 73; Washington *National Intelligencer*, July 1, 1868, August 14, 1868; Moore, Large Diary, June 9, 16, 24, 1868, July 23, 1868, JP: Welles, *Diary*, 3:389–90; Browning, *Diary*, 2:203.

26. *New York Times*, August 1, 7, September 4, 5, 10, October 8, 1868; New York *Herald*, September 8, 11, 23, 24, 25, 28, 1868; Washington *National Intelligencer*, September 3, 1868; J. M. Binckley to McCulloch, September 8, 23, 1868, Binckley to Johnson, September 25, 1868, Charles Yeaton to Johnson, September 28, 1868, Samuel Courtney to Johnson, September 25, 26, October 1, 1868, JP.

27. Charles Yeaton to Johnson, September 28, 1868, JP; New York *Herald*, October 23, 24, 25, 26, November 5, 10, 11, 12, 13, 14, 15, 20, 24, 25, 25, December 25, 1868; Robert Murray to Seward, November 5, 1868, E. D. Webster to Seward, November 5, 1868, Seward Papers.

28. McPherson, *Reconstruction*, pp. 384–91.

29. Welles, *Diary*, 3:475, 477–79, 482, 486; McPherson, *Reconstruction*, pp. 391, 392; Medill to Washburne, December 9, 1868, Washburne Papers, LC; *Harper's Weekly*, December 26, 1868; New York *Tribune*, December 10, 1868; Washington *National Intelligencer*, December 11, 1868; Blair to Johnson, December 18, 1868, Blair-Lee Family Papers, Princeton University.

30. M. F. Pleasants to Moore, February 10, 1869, JP; McPherson, *Reconstruction*, pp. 419–20; William Hanchett, *The Lincoln Murder Conspiracies* (Urbana, Ill., 1983), pp. 88–89; David M. DeWitt, *The Impeachment and Trial of Andrew Johnson* (New York, 1903), p. 281; Jacob Thompson to Johnson, December 26, 1868.

31. New York *Citizen*, August 15, 1868, JP, series XI; San Francisco *Daily Evening Bulletin*, August 1, 1871, Bartlett Collection, AJPP.

32. Washington *Daily National Intelligencer*, December 30, 1868; Welles, *Diary*, 3:494, 496–98; William Henry Crook, *Through Five Administrations*, Margarit Spalding Gerry, ed. (New York, 1910), p. 144; Boston *Daily Advertiser*, January 2, 4, 1869.

33. Crook, *Through Five Administrations*, p. 144; *PJ* 1:635; James F. Duhamel to G. F. Milton, December 3, 1928, Milton Papers, LC; William Henry Crook, *Memories of the White House*, Henry Rood, ed. (Boston, 1911), pp. 57–58.

34. *New York Times*, June 2, 1868; Moore, Large Diary, August 1, 1868, JP.

35. Welles, *Diary*, 3:454; Moore, Small Diary, March 7, 1867, pp. 3–5, JP; Ernest M. Paolino, *William Henry Seward and U.S. Foreign Policy* (Ithaca, N.Y., 1973), p. 204; Glyndon Van Deusen, *William Henry Seward* (New York, 1967), pp. 526–34; Albert

Castel, *The Presidency of Andrew Johnson* (Lawrence, Kans., 1979), pp. 203–4; Charles Callan Tansill, *The Purchase of the Danish West Indies* (Baltimore, 1932), pp. 21, 114, 137, 144; Browning, *Diary*, 2:201; Frederick W. Seward, *Reminiscences of a War-Time Statesman and Diplomat, 1830–1915* (New York, 1916), 375–79; Frederick Welles Williams, *Anson Burlingame and the First Chinese Mission to Foreign Powers* (New York, 1912), pp. 128–30; Frank Cowan, *Andrew Johnson, President of the United States* (Greensburgh, Pa., 1894), pp. 5–6. The administration also scored a success when George Bancroft negotiated a favorable naturalization treaty with Prussia. Bancroft to Seward, March 1, 1868, JP.

36. David Donald, *Charles Sumner and the Rights of Man* (New York, 1970), pp. 364ff., 391–92; Alexander Hamilton to Samuel Randall, December 7, 1868, Randall to Johnson, December 22, 1868, JP; *Papers Relating to Foreign Affairs* (Washington, D.C., 1869), 1:377–83, 400–5; Van Deusen, *Seward*, pp. 508–9.

37. *New York Herald*, February 3, March 3, 1869.

38. Richardson, *Messages and Papers of the Presidents*, 8:3903–4; McPherson, *Reconstruction*, pp. 395–97; *New York Herald*, February 2, 1869; *New York Times*, February 2, 1869; Castel, *The Presidency of Andrew Johnson*, p. 206; James E. Sefton, *The United States Army and Reconstruction, 1865–1877* (Baton Rouge, 1967), p. 187; Joe Gray Taylor, *Louisiana Reconstructed, 1863–1877* (Baton Rouge, 1974), p. 171; C. Mildred Thompson, *Reconstruction in Georgia* (New York, 1915), pp. 184–85; William Clarke Harris, *The Day of the Carpetbagger: Republican Reconstruction in Mississippi* (Baton Rouge, 1979), p. 196. The Copper Bill was passed over Johnson's veto: New York *Evening Post*, February 25, 1869.

39. S. Bentz to Thaddeus Stevens, April 28, 1868, G. W. Atwood to Stevens, June 11, 1868, Stevens Papers, LC; F. J. Meade to E. B. Washburne, January 6, 1868, Arthur Allyn to Washburne, June 15, 1868, Liberty Billings to Washburne, June 7, 1868, G. W. Atwood to Washburne, June 8, 1868, Joshua Hill to Washburne, June 11, 1868, Washburne Papers; G. W. Atwood to Charles Sumner, June 6, 1868, J. Tarbell to Sumner, July 16, 1868, Sumner Papers, Harvard University; A. Mot to Salmon P. Chase, June 17, 1868, Chase Papers, HSP.

40. Welles, *Diary*, 3:497–98, 500, 538; Bigelow, Diary, March 27, 1869, Bigelow Papers, NYPL.

41. *New York Times*, February 11, 1868; Browning, *Diary*, 2:242–43; Welles, *Diary*, 3:516, 536–37, 539–42; *New York Herald*, March 5, 8, 1869.

42. *Appleton's Annual Cyclopaedia, 1869*, pp. 489–93.

43. *New York Times*, March 5, 1869; *New York Herald*, March 4, 1869.

XIX. EX-PRESIDENT

1. New York *Herald*, March 8, 1869; Benjamin Truman, "Anecdotes of Andrew Johnson," *Century Illustrated Magazine* 63(1912–13): 440; Washington *Daily National Intelligencer*, March 12, 1869; *New York Times*, March 12, 1869

2. *New York Times*, March 21, 22, 1869; Nashville *Union and American*, March 19, 21, 25, 26, 1869; Greeneville *National Union*, March 25, 1869, JP, series XI; Felix Alexander Reeve, *East Tennessee in the War of the Rebellion*, Military Order of the Loyal League of the United States Commandary of the District of Columbia, War Papers, no. 44 (Washington, D.C., 1902), pp. 34–36.

3. *New York Times*, March 28, 1869.

4. Nashville *Union and American*, March 26, 1869; Alex Delmar to Johnson, March 26, 1869, Samuel Randall to Robert Johnson, March 26, 1869, Annie Coyle to Johnson, March 27, 1869, S. H. P. Lee to Johnson, March 27, 1869, D. J. F. Finnan to Johnson, March 27, 1869, with Dallas *Weekly Gazette*, March 27, 1869, JP; Fay Warrington Brabson, "The Political Career of Andrew Johnson from His Retirement from the Presidency to His Death," M.A. Thesis, Vanderbilt University, 1912, p. 8; Frank Cowan, *Andrew Johnson, President of the United States* (Greensburgh, Pa., 1894), p. 7.

NOTES

. Johnson to Martha Patterson, May 22, 1869, JP; Oliver Temple, *Notable Men of Tennessee* (New York, 1912), p. 439; Chicago *Tribune*, April 14, 1869.

6. Stanley J. Folmsbee, Robert E. Corlew, and Enoch L. Mitchell, *Tennessee* (Knoxville, 1969), pp. 357–72; James Welch Patton, *Unionism and Reconstruction in Tennessee, 1860–1869* (Chapel Hill, 1934), pp. 200, 226, 241; Williams to Johnson, April 26, 1869, F. H. Gordon to Johnson, February 4, 1869, JP; James C. Parker, "The Gubernatorial Elections: I. 1869—the Victory of the Conservatives," THQ 33 (Spring-Winter 1974): 34–48; Thomas B. Alexander, *Political Reconstruction in Tennessee* (Nashville, 1950), p. 216.

7. Nashville *Union and American*, April 4, 8, 11, 1869; New York *Herald*, April 4, 8, 11, 1869.

8. Memphis *Avalanche*, April 16, 1869, JP, series XI; Nashville *Union and American*, April 23, 1869.

9. Robert Watson Winston, *Andrew Johnson, Plebeian and Patriot* (New York, 1926), p. 494; Milligan to Johnson, April 25, 1869, JP.

10. Nashville *Union and American*, July 1, 1869; Andrew Johnson, Jr., to Eliza Johnson, April 25, 1869, JP; Johnson to Andrew Johnson, Jr., May 11, 1869, Bartlett Collection, AJPP. There is some evidence that in the long run, Frank was unable to keep his promises and became intemperate also. David Rankin Barbee Manuscript, Fay Warrington Brabson Papers, UT.

11. Nashville *Union and American*, July 1, 3, 4, 1869; New York *Herald*, June 28, 1869.

12. Folmsbee et al., *Tennessee*, pp. 368–71; Patton, *Unionism and Reconstruction in Tennessee*, pp. 200, 241; Alexander, *Political Reconstruction in Tennessee*, pp. 216ff., 219, 222.

13. J. S. Golladay to Johnson, July 8, 1869, A. A. Kyle to Johnson, July 12, 1869, A. P. Stewart to Johnson, June 30, 1869, J. C. Murray et al. to Johnson, July 2, 1869, JP; Greeneville *National Union*, July 8, 1869; New York *Herald*, August 7, 1869; Brabson, "Political Career," p. 14; J. A. Sharp, "The Downfall of the Radicals in Tennessee," ETHSP 5 (January 1933): 105–25.

14. A. A. Kyle to Patterson, July 20, 1869, JP; J. B. Brownlow to Temple, April 20, 1892, E. Etheridge to Temple, July 26, 1892, Temple Papers, UT; New York *Herald*, August 2, 1892; John Burch to Johnson, August 2, 1869, JP.

15. New York *Herald*, August 21, 1869; *New York Times*, September 16, 1869; Etheridge to Temple, July 26, 1892, Temple Papers.

16. Nashville *Union and American*, October 8, 9, 1869; M. D. L. Stewart to Johnson, September 12, 1869, Stewart to Willoughby Williams, September 19, 1869, James B. Hambleton to Johnson, October 18, 1869, JP; J. B. Brownlow to Temple, April 20, 1869, Temple Papers; George F. Milton, *The Age of Hate: Andrew Johnson and the Radicals* (New York, 1930), p. 660.

17. Nashville *Union and American*, October 21, 22, 23, 26, 1869; *New York Times*, October 20, 22, 23, 1869; Milton, *Age of Hate*, p. 660; *Journal of the House of Representatives of the State of Tennessee, 36th General Assembly* . . . (Nashville, 1869), pp. 67–69, 74–77, 81–88, 91. Johnson's refusal to accept an offer to buy the necessary votes to win as stated in E. C. Reeves, "The Real Andrew Johnson," Lloyd Stryker, *Andrew Johnson: Profile in Courage* (New York, 1929), pp. 825–37, esp. p. 831, with a wrong date, cannot be substantiated. It is true, however, that Brownlow had a hand in Johnson's defeat. E. Merton Coulter, *William G. Brownlow, Fighting Parson of the Southern Highlands* (Chapel Hill, 1937), pp. 394–95.

18. Nashville *Union and American*, November 6, 1869, September 20, 1874.

19. Reeve, *East Tennessee in the War of the Rebellion*, pp. 33–34; Johnson to Andrew Johnson, Jr., May 11, 1869, Bartlett Collection, AJPP; Lately Thomas, *The First President Johnson* (New York, 1968), p. 622; Statement of Augusta Lincoln Brown, Brabson Papers, UT.

20. E. C. Reeves Memorandum, Andrew Johnson Papers, TSLA; Stryker, *Johnson*, p. 781.

21. Johnson to William Lowry, February 13, 1870, R. S. Saunders to Johnson, December 13, 19, 1869, J. C. Burch to Johnson, December 19, 27, 1869, S. H. Walker et al. to Burch, February 22, March 5, 1869, JP.
22. Folmsbee et al., *Tennessee*, pp. 374–77; Johnson to G. W. Nixon, March 7, 1870, JP.
23. Roger L. Hart, *Redeemers, Bourbons, and Populists: Tennessee, 1870–1896* (Baton Rouge, 1975), pp. 2ff., 10–12; A. S. Colyar to Johnson, May 19, August 30, October 5, 1870, John McGaugey et al. to Johnson, August 22, 1870, JP; Brabson, "Political Career," p. 22; *New York Times*, September 19, October 8, November 9, 1869; Nashville *Union and American*, September 20, 1870; Stanley J. Folmsbee et al., *History of Tennessee*, 4 vols. (New York, 1960), 2:133–34; F. Wayne Binning, "The Tennessee Republicans in Decline, 1869–1876," *THQ* 39 (1980): 471–84; Memphis *Avalanche*, August 28, September 14, 16, 20, 23, 24, October 4, 6, November 8, 1870.
24. Johnson to Malcolm Hay, January 30, 1871, Johnson to Cowan, February 13, 1871, JP; Nashville *Union and American*, May 30, 31, 1871. Cowan had urged him to raise the financial question against international banks. Cowan to Johnson, January 2, 1871, JP.
25. Johnson to Mrs. Patterson, June 13, December 19, 1871, JP.
26. Olbrichs & Co. to Johnson, January 27, 1869, Smythe to Johnson, April 8, 1869, JP; *New York Times*, July 28, 1871.
27. *New York Times*, May 25, June 4, 1872; Nashville *Union and American*, April 21, 1872; Statement of E. C. Reeves, Brabson Papers; Brabson, "Political Career," pp. 26–29.
28. Statement of Horace Baker, Statement of M. P. Reeve, Brabson Papers; *New York Times*, May 25, June 4, 1872; Nashville *Union and American*, June 4, 1872.
29. Nashville *Union and American*, August 11, 18, 23, September 1, 1872; *New York Times*, August 25, 1872; Memphis *Avalanche*, August 18, 21, 22, 23, 25, 1872.
30. Nashville *Union and American*, September 7, 8, 21, 28, October 5, 6, 8, 20, 25, November 1, 16, 20, 1872; *New York Times*, October 22, 1872; T. McNeilly to F. C. Dunnington, September 21, 1872, Edward Ward Carmack Papers, TSLA; J. B. Bingham to Johnson, September 16, 1872, JP; Lillard Thompson to G. F. Milton, November 15, 1927, G. F. Milton Papers, LC. For the Harris story, see Harriet S. Turner, "Recollections of Andrew Johnson," *Harper's Monthly* 120 (January 1910): 168–76.
31. Milligan to Johnson, November 28, 1872, JP; Andrew Johnson, Jr., to Johnson, November 10, 1872, Brabson Papers; C. J. Moody to Johnson, November 19, 1872, Colyar to Johnson, November 16, 1872, JP.
32. Joseph H. Thompson to Johnson, January 17, 1873, A. S. Colyar to Johnson, January 21, 1873, JP.
33. *The Living Age and Outlook*, August 12, 1875, AJPP; Statement of Andrew Johnson Patterson, n.d., JP, series XVIII; Johnson's Statement, June 29, 1873, Johnson Papers, TSLA; Johnson to Dr. Basil Norris, July 12, 1874, JP; *New York Times*, July 24, 1873.
34. Knoxville *Chronicle*, May 6, 1870, quoted in *New York Times*, May 9, 1870; Doughty, *Greenville*, p. 270; 1870 Census, Tennessee, Greene, 10th District, p. 21, AJPP; Ralph W. Haskins, "Internecine Strife in Tennessee: Andrew Johnson vs. Parson Brownlow," *THQ* 24 (Winter 1965): 321–40, esp. 324; Nashville *Union and American*, September 24, 28, October 7, 8, 1873; Columbia *Herald*, October 3, 1873, AJPP; Brabson, "Political Career," p. 33. "I have made it a rule in my life when I have got a dollar to save fifty cents of it," he said. Statement of Andrew Johnson Patterson, Brabson Papers. According to Mr. Richard Doughty, Johnson died the richest man in Greeneville: Interview with Richard Doughty, August 10, 1984. Yet he was not particularly wealthy before the Civil War.
35. Joseph Holt, *Vindication of the Hon. Joseph Holt, Judge Advocate General of the United States* (Washington, D.C., 1873).
36. Nashville *Union and American*, October 14, 18, 24, 1873.
37. *Ibid.*, October 18, 1873; W. J. Moore to Johnson, September 10, 1873, Welles to Johnson, November 5, 1873, JP.

38. Johnson to Editor of *Washington Chronicle*, November 11, 1873, Holt Papers, Huntington Library.

39. Washington *Daily Morning Chronicle*, November 12, 1873, JP, series XI; *New York Times*, December 2, 1873; G. H. Garland to Johnson, December 6, 1873, JP, as an example.

40. Nashville *Union and American*, January 15, May 2, 1874.

41. *New York Times*, March 13, 1874.

42. George Howard to Johnson, April 20, 1874, Johnson to Dr. Basil Norris, April 17, 1874, JP. Johnson had just visited Milligan.

43. *New York Times*, May 22, 1874; L. J. Dupre to Johnson, May 26, 1874, JP.

44. Johnson to Col. R. W. Edwards, July 20, 1874, Johnson Papers, TSLA; Nashville *Union and American*, August 7, September 19, 20, October 7, 10, 11, 1874; *New York Times*, October 17, 1874; W. M. Lowry to Johnson, October 8, 1874, JP; Statement of E. C. Reeves, Johnson Papers, TSLA.

45. Folmsbee et al., *Tennessee*, p. 378; Nashville *Union and American*, November 19, December 6, 1874.

46. Statement of E. C. Reeves, Johnson Papers, TSLA; E. C. Reeves to Brabson, May 23, 1913, E. C. Reeves to E. M. Barbee, July 4, 1928, Brabson Papers; David Rankin Barbee, "When Andy Walked with the Bishop," Interview with Alfred Taylor, March 29, 1929, Brabson Papers; Nashville *Union and American*, December 6, 15, 16, 18, 1874; Temple, *Notable Men*, pp. 440–42.

47. Temple, *Notable Men*, pp. 440–42; Nashville *Union and American*, January 21–27, 1875; *New York Herald*, January 26, 27, 1875; Park Marshall, *A Life of William B. Bate* (Nashville, 1908), pp. 190–93; *Journal of the House of Representatives of the State of Tennessee, 1rst Session, 39th General Assembly . . .* (Nashville, 1875), pp. 106, 115–23, 128–37, 142–58, 162–83; Brabson, "Political Career," pp. 41–44; Nashville *Union and American*, January 24–29, 1875. The Assembly contained ninety-two Democrats and eight Republicans, and Johnson's strength was concentrated in East Tennessee, Memphis, and among Union Democrats.

48. Temple, *Notable Men*, p. 447; *New York Times*, January 27, 1875, Clipping in JP.

49. Statement of Andrew Kellar, Hot Springs, South Dakota, June 1896, Knoxville File, AJPP; *New York Herald*, January 25, 1875.

50. *Journal of the House of Representatives of Tennessee*, 1st Sess., 39th General Assembly, 188–93. 199–201; *New York Herald*, January 27, 1875; Statement of E. C. Reeves, Johnson Papers, TSLA; Interview with Alfred Taylor, December 29, 1929, Brabson Papers.

51. *New York Herald*, January 27, 1875; Nashville *Union and American*, January 27, 1875; Andrew Johnson Patterson to Johnson, January 23, 1875, Bartlett Collection, AJPP; Martha Patterson to Johnson, January 24, 29, 1875, J. W. Dick Bullock to Eliza Johnson, January 27, 1875, JP; E. C. Reeves to D. R. Barbee, July 4, 1928, Brabson Papers; Diary of Archelaus M. Hughes, January 21, 1875, Hughes Papers, TLSA. The Johnson Papers are full of letters of congratulations.

52. Quoted in Nashville *Union and American*, January 28, 29, 31, 1875; *New York Times*, January 27, 1875. Other comments, ranging from dismay to enthusiasm, may be found in the Boston *Morning Journal*, January 27, 1875, the Hartford *Daily Courant*, January 27, 1875, the New Orleans *Daily Picayune*, January 28, 1875, the Philadelphia *Inquirer*, January 27, 1875, the *Daily Arkansas Gazette*, January 30, 1875, and the Baltimore *Sun*, January 27, 1875, among others.

53. Nashville *Union and American*, February 7, 9, 1875; William S. Speer, ed., *Sketches of Prominent Tennesseans* (Nashville, 1888), p. 188, for the debt to Memphis.

54. Nashville *Union and American*, March 20, 1875; William Henry Crook, *Through Five Administrations*, Margaret Spalding Gerry, ed. (New York, 1910), p. 151.

55. *New York Tribune*, March 5, 6, 1875; Nashville *Union and American*, March 6, 7, 1875; *Cong. Record*, 44th Cong., Special Session, 4.

NOTES 445

56. *Cong. Record,* 44th Cong., Special Session, 121–27.
57. New York *Herald,* March 23, 1875; Nashville *Union and American,* March 23, 25, 1875; New York *Tribune,* March 23, 1875; Temple, *Prominent Men,* p. 447. Because Johnson had compared his own dealings with the Brownlow government in Tennessee unfavorably with Grant's interference in Louisiana, the parson wrote a furious letter in reply in which he accused the ex-president of falsehood and called him "the Catiline of the lawless conspiracy." Nashville *Union and American,* April 15, 1875.
58. Johnson to Martha Patterson, April 4, 1875, JP; Interview with Miss O'Beirne, Brabson Papers.

XX. EPILOGUE

1. Greeneville *Intelligencer,* August 6, 1875.
2. James P. Snapp to Johnson, February, 1875, Statement of Loan, July 16, 1875, Fowler to Johnson, May 21, 26, 1875, AJPP; Johnson to William Lowry, May 31, 1875, JP.
3. William Eblin McElwee Memorandum, May 1, 1923, Johnson Papers, TSLA.
4. Greeneville *Intelligencer,* August 4, 6, 1875; Abraham Jobe, Autobiography, p. 146, TSLA; Doughty, *Greeneville,* pp. 254–57.
5. Doughty, *Greeneville,* pp. 257–64; Greeneville *Intelligencer,* August 6, 1875.
6. *New York Times,* August 1, 2, 3, 9, 1875; Joseph Fowler to Andrew Johnson, Jr., August 26, 1875, JP.
7. Philadelphia *Inquirer,* August 2, 1875; New York *World,* August 1, 1875; Chicago *Tribune,* August 1, 1875; Little Rock *Daily Arkansas Gazette,* August 1, 1875; New Orleans *Daily Picayune,* August 1, 1875; Mobile *Daily Register,* August 1, 1875; New York *Tribune,* August 2, 1875; Hartford *Daily Courant,* August 2, 1875; *New York Times,* August 1, 2, 8, 1875.
8. Statement of E. C. Reeves, Johnson Papers, TSLA; State of Tennessee, Greene County, to Thomas Maloney and Andrew Johnson Patterson, May 5, 1879, Brabson Papers; Johnson v. Patterson, Knoxville, September Term, 1884, AJPP; Hugh A. Lawing, "Andrew Johnson National Monument," *THQ* 20 (1960): 103–19, esp. 114.
9. Jones, *Oration; New York Times,* September 30, 1877.
10. Carmen Anthony Notaro, "History of the Biographic Treatment of Andrew Johnson in the Twentieth Century," *THQ* 24 (1965): 143–55; Castel, *The Presidency of Andrew Johnson,* pp. 218–30, 247–55; Eric McKitrick, ed., *Andrew Johnson: A Profile* (New York, 1969), pp. vii–xxii. Myers v. U.S., 272 U.S. 52 (1926), held that a law of July 12, 1876, providing for the removal of a postmaster by the president with the advice and consent of the Senate was unconstitutional, but Humphrey's Executor v. U.S., 295 U.S. 602 (1935) failed to extend this interpretation of presidential power to removal of members of independent commissions. James Ford Rhodes, *History of the United States from the Compromise of 1850,* 8 vols. (New York, 1900), and John W. Burgess, *Reconstruction and the Constitution, 1866–1876* (New York, 1905), are among the first group of works; Dunning, Stryker, Milton, Winston, and Beale, among the second; and McKitrick, Benedict, and Trefousse, among the third. The biographies of Savage, Rayner, and Jones in the earlier period were also laudatory.

INDEX